HISTORY OF PHYSICAL EDUCATION

HARPER'S

SCHOOL AND PUBLIC HEALTH EDUCATION,
PHYSICAL EDUCATION, AND RECREATION SERIES

UNDER THE EDITORSHIP OF DELBERT OBERTEUFFER

History of Physical Education

C. W. Hackensmith

HARPER & ROW, PUBLISHERS
NEW YORK

 For information address Harper & Row, Publishers, Incorporated, 49 East 33rd Street, New York 16, N.Y. 10016.

LIBRARY OF CONGRESS CATALOG CARD NUMBER: 66-10604

B-Q

Dedicated to my wife,

LUCINDA MAE

CONTENTS

PREFACE

As a teacher and professional worker the author has certain objectives in mind. In the first place, a textbook must be useful to both teacher and student. It must be logically and chronologically arranged and packaged in such a manner that the student may easily grasp the concepts as he reads the assignments and uses the bibliography. The same features should encourage profitable discussion between teacher and students within the meager time generally allotted in the classroom.

In the second place, the student of physical education ought not to continue to study the history and development of his calling, divorced from political, social, and educational background. Physical education, like all human endeavors, is unequivocally a part of man's cultural development and cannot exist out of context. As in other professional fields, the physical education student should take a deep pride in the contributions of his own profession to world culture.

In the third place, the world is gradually becoming a community of nations as technological advances conquer time and space. The peoples of the world who yesterday existed as a hazy apparition in our minds, suddenly become sharply focused realities today. Professional workers can no longer remain indifferent to the difficulties and aspirations of these people because their philosophy of physical education evolved in an unfamiliar political and social climate. Physical educators in all lands must overcome provincialism. We are all in desperate need of the respect and understanding of our neighbors. We also need to appreciate that progress in physical education and sports is not confined to one nation but is a characteristic common to many nations. If this book has accomplished these objectives, the years spent in its composition have been worthwhile.

C. W. HACKENSMITH

Lexington, Kentucky
October, 1965

Chapter 1

PRIMITIVE PEOPLES AND ANCIENT CIVILIZATIONS

EARLY MAN AND HIS ENVIRONMENT

In Europe, Asia, and Africa protohumans had diverged from ancestral primate stock by the beginning of the Pleistocene, or glacial epoch, or approximately a million years ago.[1] They managed to live and develop a crude type of culture in an environment subjected to climatic changes of the first magnitude. During the Pleistocene the northern latitudes and mountainous regions experienced four successive advances and retreats of massive ice sheets which carved out valleys, created rivers, and fashioned coast lines. With each glaciation flora was annihilated and fauna retreated in search of a more favorable climate and feeding ground. Protohumans who survived either had to adjust to the polar-like climate or migrate southward in the wake of the fauna.

The last glaciation in North America reached as far south as the Ohio River before the ice mass began its retreat approximately 30,000 years ago and spent itself 20,000 years later. Perhaps 15,000 to 25,000 years ago, hunting parties of peoples predisposed to Mongoloid racial characteristics gradually began pushing into North America. They may have crossed an ice or land bridge which joined Asia with North America at what is now known as the Bering Straits.[2] These primitive Asiatics slowly migrated down the Pacific Coast to the southwestern United States, where the land, arid today, was rich in vegetation and game.

FACTORS IN THE DIFFERENTIATION OF MAN

The eventual emergence of the genus Homo sapiens was an exceedingly slow and gradual process.[3] Java man, unearthed in the drifts of the Solo River in 1891, and twentieth-century archaeological discoveries indicate that his early ancestors more closely resembled the anthropoid ape than man as we know him today. Although these anthropoid-like forms possessed a primitive type of mentality and could communicate, build fires, and chip crude flint and stone tools, anthropologists generally agree that they were variants who were eventually eliminated through natural selection, mutation, isolation, genetic drift, hybridization, and sexual and social selection.[4]

Some of these variants may have perpetuated with little genetic improvement for thousands of years, for example, the Neanderthal man who dominated Central Europe during the latter part of the Pleistocene. However, Cro-Magnon man, Neanderthal man's contemporary, compared favorably with modern man in intellectual and physical features. Cro-Magnon man overshadowed his contemporary in many cultural aspects. He was more skillful at chipping flint and stone, invented the atlatl,* or spear thrower, which antedated the bow and arrow, expressed his artistic skill on the walls of his cave abode, and formulated a concept of immortality as evidenced by his burying his dead with grave offerings of food and tools.[5] But despite his potentialities, Cro-Magnon man attained a cultural level markedly lower than that of the meanest primitive peoples in historic times.

ADVANCES IN PRIMITIVE MAN'S CULTURE

From 8000 to 3000 B.C., a transitional period, the cultures of primitive peoples in various regions of Europe, Africa, and Asia

* "The atlatl is basically a device which adds length to the user's arm and materially aids in increasing the impetus imparted to a thrown projectile. The essential device is little more than a stick with provisions supplied on one end for grasping and a recurved pin or projection on the other to engage a nock or conical depression in the proximal end of the spear. These two elements are held in the thrower's hand with the projectile in the superior position, the long axis of both being approximately parallel. . . . Motion is imparted by an overhand throwing movement." (James H. Keller, "The Atlatl in North America," *Indiana Historical Society Publications,* III:3 [June, 1955], 283).

seemed to be homogeneous. After the last glaciation the climate became more stable and the situation favored the growth of dense forests and the multiplication of game animals. The ready availability of raw materials needed for living in a forest retreat and the abundance of game tended to isolate communal groups; consequently independent though not too varied cultures developed. During this period primitive man fashioned the flint core ax, the grooved or ungrooved stone ax for hafting, an interesting variety of chipped and pressure-flaked flint tools, bone implements, and, toward the end of this area, a crude type of grit-tempered pottery. In the Americas the culture of the Asiatics was transplanted. True, the culture of isolated primitive peoples over the world was neither rich nor progressive, but some communal groups did achieve a way of life that made them receptive to the changes in cultural patterns that were to follow.

Near the close of this period primitive men who lived in fertile river valleys learned, after a fashion, to cultivate wheat, barley, and other cereals. The horse, hitherto slaughtered by the thousands for food, began to be used as a beast of burden and for transportation. Migratory hunters gravitated toward established village sites, where they could still hunt but also enjoy the more dependable food supply derived from tilling the soil and the variety of products furnished by domesticated animals. As the population of the villages increased, a higher level of communal organization was needed to maintain order and protect the people from predators. Gradually, a stratification of social classes was developed: the chieftain or ruler, priests, soldiers, common and skilled workers, and slaves. Since he was no longer occupied solely in the quest for food, man could devote more time to leisure and other aspects of culture. These changes spread at varying rates in all directions and laid the foundation for the development of many ancient civilizations.

THE LIFE OF PRIMITIVE MAN

Basically, primitive man was a hunter, fisher, and food gatherer (mollusk, plant seeds and roots, wild fruits, berries, and nuts). Survival depended upon his capacity for activity, his skill as a hunter and fisher, and the cooperation of nature—or, as a last resort, cannibalism. He lived in caves, rock shelters, and, when the weather was favorable, open areas along river banks and the seashores.

Romantic souls who yearn for the good old days when early man walked hand in hand with nature should examine the graves in cemeteries and in mound burials of prehistoric peoples in North America. What would they find? Many infants and small children, who were dearly loved, as indicated by the generous provisions made for their afterlife; teenagers, young adults in their twenties and thirties, and occasional fortunate ones who lived to see two or three generations come and go. Bone lesions suggest dietary deficiencies, tuberculosis, and the ever-present arthritis. And, we can tell, broken bones often healed imperfectly, causing impairment of motility. Crushed crania and projectile points imbedded in bone and in juxtaposition to the rib cage and pelvic region speak of violent death. Primitive man was also afflicted with supernumerary teeth, malocclusions, caries, pyorrhea, and abscesses. This archaeological evidence hardly confirms the romantic notion of a primitive Golden Age.

PRIMITIVE MAN'S EDUCATION

Primitive man's education was focused primarily on hunting and fishing. The strength, endurance, and skills requisite to the hunt were just as essential to the war campaign. As soon as the male child could effectively handle weapons, he was taught the techniques involved, generally by his father or a close kinsman, and practiced them in games of dexterity and in the hunt. Corporal punishment, which was foreign to the type of personality development primitive people considered ideal, was rarely administered. Slow learners were prodded into action by assigning them humiliating and ridiculous names.[6] Curiously, in a culture in which masculine attributes were highly prized, effeminacy in the male was treated with compassionate tolerance. Exceptional performance, never praised verbally, was recognized by special assignments in the hunt or in battle.

Schmidt notes that it is often difficult to determine where primitive man's productive activity ended and his play began.[7] For example, the ball games of primitive youth resembled miniature battles between enemies rather than friendly games between participants from the same group. But these evidently rugged games taught young men to sustain physical hardships, develop endurance, and appreciate the value of team cooperation. When the elders decided the young man possessed a warrior's qualities, he was declared eligible to participate in the ceremonial rites that marked the transition from adolescence into manhood. In some cultures these rites were merely symbolical and in others sufficiently severe to test the physcial stamina of the best candidate.

Primitive peoples developed a religion by which they explained the creation of man, the concept of immortality, and success and failure in the daily struggle with the forces of nature. This religion, based on belief in spiritual beings, was handed down from generation to generation in folk tales and myths which served as moral lessons and found expression in games, art, song, and dance.

All young males served an apprenticeship in the manufacture of wood, flint, and stone implements. Most, of course, never developed great skill; it was the master craftsmen who produced the objects of art discovered by archaeologists in ceremonial mounds or buried with the chieftain and his family. The primitive maiden's apprenticeship was guided by her mother or the other women. For some girls this tutelage was limited to routine household duties, but the more talented were instructed in basketry, pottery, weaving, and the manufacture of clothing, footgear, and kitchen utensils.

RECREATION THROUGH PHYSICAL ACTIVITIES

Prehistoric peoples failed to develop a written language and hence could not record their cultural attainments in detail. Historians interested in their recreational activities must turn to museum collections of playing equipment, accounts written by early travelers to the Western Hemisphere, and archaeologists' reports. While we may assume that forms of recreation followed a course of evolution from prehistoric to historic times, we must also recognize that there are no sources of information to document the changes during the unrecorded centuries. The Americas nurtured prehistoric populations which developed cultures independently and in free association with one another until European entrepreneurs rediscovered the Western Hemisphere. We can assume that the social customs, games, sports, and dances of the tribal families of the Americas went through an uninterrupted evolutionary process with little adulteration.

During 1902 and 1903 Culin[8] studied exhaustively the games and sports of North American historic peoples, and in 1948 Stewart[9] published an extensive survey of the cultural life of primitive South American peoples. These studies, as well as others less ambitious in scope, contribute much to our knowledge of games, sports, and dances as vital forces in the life of primitive man.

Culin is convinced that the oldest existing games among the primitive peoples of the Americas originated in the southwestern United States. Peoples from this region, he believes, migrated by choice or compulsion to other areas in the Western Hemisphere, carrying with them their games, sports, and dances. His observations are particularly interesting in the light of recent archaeological discoveries in the Southwest: skeletal remains of the horse, camel, bison, and mammoth with a radiocarbon dating of 9000 or more years have been found along with fluted and unfluted flint points.[10] These finds provide some support for Culin's contention that the Southwest was the fountainhead from whence flowed those migratory primitive peoples who formed the nucleus of the racial families of the Americas.

Culin also points out that the games and sports of all primitive peoples in the Western Hemisphere are remarkably similar, regardless of how widely separated these peoples may be.[8] Variations are restricted to differences in design or material used in the construction of playing equipment and are attributable primarily to environmental factors and variations in the skill of the craftsman.

It is interesting to note that another important part of man's social-recreational heritage dates back to prehistoric times. At the close of the transitional period (*ca.* 3000 B.C.) and the establishment of more permanent communal groups, primitive peoples invariably constructed playgrounds. The playground was given special care; its fire-hardened surface was kept free of debris. Here villagers gathered to witness the torture and execution of enemy prisoners, and religious, athletic, and comic dances, as well as games and sports.

RELIGIOUS SIGNIFICANCE OF GAMES, SPORTS, AND DANCES

Religious beliefs played a significant role in every cultural aspect of primitive man's life. His folk tales and myths abound in references to contests and games in which the hero, a friend of man, overcomes the evil one, the antagonist of man, through skill, cunning, and magic. The choreography and costuming of ceremonial dances, as well as of those performed purely for entertainment, had religious significance. Playing equipment, derived from weapons symbolic of those wielded by gods, frequently bore marks or designs associated with special deities. Ceremonial games, sports, and dances, it was hoped, would please or placate the gods, who in return would cause rain, secure fertility, expel demons, or cure sickness. Primitive man's complete acceptance of the will of deities in the fortunes of everyday life extended to his recreational games and sports. He stoically accepted defeat without rancor and victory with humility.

GAMES OF HISTORIC PEOPLES

Historic peoples played three types of games: games of chance, games of dexterity and skill, and children's games.[8] Among the many games of chance were dice and sticks. The dice, which had two faces of distinguishing marks and colors, often were made of split cane, wood or bone staves, beaver or woodchuck teeth, walnut shells, or fragments of pottery. They were tossed into a bowl or basket; score was kept with pebbles, sticks, or flat stones. Ceremonial dice was exclusively a man's game, but men and women played the game, separately, for high stakes. Sticks had many variations and utilized many types of materials. In prehistoric times arrow shafts were probably used, but by the historic period carefully worked sticks and other materials had been substituted. The sticks, which varied in number from ten to one hundred, were divided into two bundles, one of which contained an odd or marked stick. Players wagered on which bundle had the odd stick.

Games of dexterity and skill included archery, snow-snake, hoop and pole, and ring and pin. Archers practiced by shooting at stationary or moving targets. The snow-snake was an implement devised to slide easily over ice or snow when thrown. Some primitive peoples played snow-snake by shooting arrows or casting spears over the ice or snow; the object of the game was to achieve the greatest distance.

Hoop and pole, which appears to have evolved from the prehistoric game of *Chunkee,** was played by all historic peoples north of Mexico. A remarkable variety of implements were used. Hoops were constructed of wooden withes or stone and varied from 3 to 25 inches in diameter. Wooden hoops were not decorated and were quartered by leather thongs or covered with netted materials. Poles, which averaged about 6 feet in length, sometimes were made of two telescoped sections symbolizing the bow. Generally the game was limited to two players armed with poles. The hoop or stone disk was rolled between them; each threw his pole at the moving target in an attempt to spear it or land closest when it came to rest. Scoring varied with the type of hoop; when the stone disk was used, the closest pole won.

Ring and pin resembles very much the European game in which a cup is attached to a ball by a length of cord. The player tosses the ball into the air with one hand and attempts to catch it in the cup held by the other. For the ring, or target, historic peoples used a bone or wooden ring, a bundle of closely wrapped leaves, or a string of perforated deer toe bones marked in ascending values; for the pin, a worked deer, turkey, or seal bone or a sharpened stick.[8]

During prehistoric and historic times children the world over played games of hunting and chase which probably were closely associated with their environment. For example, the children of the Ao Nagas, the headhunters of Assam, India, play *Chuko,* a game in which contestants are divided into tigers and villagers. The tigers attempt to break through the circle of villagers and carry away the

* *Chunkee,* played by all tribes of the Gulf States, consisted of rolling a stone disk (discoidal) on the ground and sliding or throwing forward a stick crooked at the end. The object of the game was to throw the crooked stick in such a manner that the discoidal would lie in the crook when the discoidal came to rest. In his collection the author has *Chunkee* stones made of sandstone, diorite, and quartz that measure 2 to 6 inches in diameter and average ¾ to 2 inches thick. Many *Chunkee* stones can still be found on former Indian village sites.

victim, the "it" of the game.[11] Through his games the primitive child learned much about how to be adult. Diminutive grooved stone axheads, arrowheads, and celts—skinning and chopping tools—found on village sites the world over indicate that children or their elders made toy models of most articles of daily life. In his review of children's games during historic times, Culin lists shuttlecock, tipcat, quoits, stone-throwing, shuffleboard, jackstraws, swings, stilts, tops, bull-roarers, buzz, and cat's cradle.[8]

Sports of Historic Peoples

Competitive sports were important in the religious life of historic peoples, and contests that pitted one village's anthletes against another's were gala occasions for both participants and spectators. The athletes prepared for the scheduled event several weeks ahead by practicing the fundamentals of the game and building endurance through running. During this training period the shaman, or priest, ruled out certain foods and sexual relations as taboo and performed daily rites to counteract any magic spells conjured up by the opposition's shaman. On the day before the contest the shaman administered a purgative concoction of herbal juices, and from that moment until the close of the game no athlete was to defile himself in any way. During the evening before the contest, athletes joined the villagers in ceremonial rites in which they performed as dancers. Win or lose, everyone joined in the feast and the revelry.

Types of Ball Games

Historic peoples east of the Mississippi and in the area adjoining the Great Lakes region played a ball game with rackets; the French *coureurs de bois* called it *"le jeu de la crosse."* It is generally accepted that this game was invented during the prehistoric period, and some authorities suggest that the racket is a direct descendant of the atlatl, or spear thrower. The ball, which could not be touched by hand, consisted of a piece of buckskin stuffed with hair. There was a netted loop at one end of the racket, which was from 24 to 36 inches long and was carried horizontally. Any number could participate, and frequently all the able-bodied men of one village played against all those of another. The length of the playing field generally ranged from 300 to 400 yards; one or two poles at each end served as goals.

Early travelers on the frontier state that some lacrosse fields were as much as a mile or more long. Players were set up on their team's half of the field according to their offensive and defensive ability and the game was started by a toss of the ball in the center of the field. The ball was caught up in the loop by a player, who then started running toward his team's goal. With the throng on the field, this happy situation did not continue long. Defensive players would move in and strike at the handle of the racket to dislodge the ball from the loop. An offensive player could pass the ball to a teammate who was downfield. A point was scored when the ball was thrown at and struck the single post or when it was carried through the two upright poles. Lacrosse was considered a man's game, although records indicate that there were women's as well as mixed teams.

Shinny, orginally designed for women, became so popular among historic people that it was also played by men and by men against women. The playing fields were 200 to 300 yards long, with goals set up at each end. The game started in the middle of the field and players advanced the ball by kicking or batting it with a curved stick. As in lacrosse, it could not be touched by the hand. A score was made when the ball struck the goal post.

Double ball was played only by women among the historic peoples of eastern United States and the Plains; on the Pacific Coast it was exclusively a man's game. Equipment consisted of two soft buckskin balls joined together by a short leather thong and a stick curved or forked at one end. Players kept the double ball in motion by scooping it up from the ground and throwing it forward. Goals consisted of raised mounds of dirt or two upright poles located at each end of a field 300 to 400 yards long.

The ball race, according to Culin, originated in the Southwest and was introduced into the area of what is now California and Mexico by migratory people. Generally the game was a contest between two players who kicked a stone or wooden ball, an inflated bladder, or a flat or round wooden stave over a prescribed course. In the early 1600s William Wood and Roger Williams of Rhode Island fame described another kicking game they witnessed several Algonquin tribes play, which closely resembled the modern game of soccer football.[8]

BALL GAMES OF CENTRAL AND SOUTH AMERICAN INDIANS

The Mayans played a court ball game which, according to Goellner, they may have invented about A.D. 700.[12] He located forty courts, thirty in and about Yucatán, the region inhabited by the Mayans, and the others in Guatemala, Honduras, and southeastern Arizona. The typical ball court is recessed in the ground and the sides, ends, and floor are paved with flat stones. Most courts are shaped like the capital letter "I." Keyed in at the top of one of the side walls and slightly beyond its midpoint is a vertical stone ring. The court at Chichen Itza, Yucatán, one of the largest, is 119 feet wide and 227 feet long; the stone ring on the side wall, which is more than 25 feet above the playing floor, is 4 feet in diameter (outside) and 1 foot thick. The hole in the center of the ring, or the goal, is 9 inches in diameter.

According to Goellner, each team of players (probably three on a side) sought to gain possession of a gum rubber ball and score by rebounding it through the goal. This sport remotely resembled the modern one-goal basketball in objective, though not in playing technique. In the Mayan game the ball could not be touched by hands, feet, or chest, but could be struck with the knees, thighs, hips, or buttocks. Restricted by such rules, players must have required considerable skill to rebound the ball and send it through the vertical goal. That play was fast and furious and the constant impact of ball against flesh painful is indicated by the protective equipment worn—for example, leather hip and loin aprons, helmets, and gloves.

In his *Handbook of South American Indians,* Stewart notes that the Taino people, one of the five ethnological groups of the Arawak of the West Indies, play a game similar in some respects to Mayan court ball.[9] The Taino, however, use a ground-level rectangular court, and the object of the game is to keep the rubber ball within bounds and from crossing a designated line. The ball is struck with the hips, knees, thighs, and buttocks. Men and women play separately or in mixed groups.

RUNNING RACES

In prehistoric and historic times survival undoubtedly was more dependent upon ability to run than in recent centuries. And of course the best runners were especially useful as couriers and advance scouts in peace as well as war. Races of varied distances were routine among all North American Indians and invariably were associated with certain tribal rites. The Shoshone conducted ceremonial races for both men and women. And southwestern tribes, in which relay races were widely popular, even maintained circular running tracks outside their villages.

PRIMITIVE MAN AND THE DANCE

In 1933 commercial diggers excavating the Spiro Mounds in Oklahoma uncovered one of the richest archaeological finds in North America.[13] Among its many treasures were 86 complete marine shells and 94 fragments whose engraved surfaces are a record of village life in A.D. 1300–1400. Ceremonial dance scenes provide clues to the religion of the Spiro people. We know the Spiro danced to propitiate deities. Many of the engravings depict the pageantry of the Busk, Harvest Festival, and Green Corn ceremonies. The eagle, rattlesnake, raccoon, owl, and woodpecker figure prominently in the costumes.

Although the Spiro shells show only select groups of warrior-athlete dancers (women rarely appear in dance scenes, and then probably only as part of the background choral groups), it is probable that these people, like those of other primitive cultures, participated en masse in the ceremonial dances.[14] On these occasions performers lined up opposite one another or formed in a circle with arms resting on each other's shoulders. The participants followed in unison the pattern and tempo of the dance steps set by a skilled leader. Each dancer took pride in his ability to imitate exactly the physical movements and appearance of the creatures associated with the myth or legend portrayed.[13] In primitive society only the war campaign promoted social unification as effectively as the mass ceremonial dance. But as higher levels of civilization were attained, and especially as a result of Western European influence, such rituals lost their significance as a social force.[14]

CHINESE CIVILIZATION

According to tradition, Chinese history reaches back fifty centuries or more, but recorded history dates from the Chow dynasty whose reign began in 1122 B.C. Under the Chow emperors the once nomadic Chinese became an agrarian people, which they are still today. A feudal system developed; landholders acquired fiefs so vast that China became more a confederation of states than a unified empire. Constant warfare among the great feudal states led finally to the overthrow of the Chow dynasty in 249 B.C. The Chin dynasty, from which the country derived its name, then ascended to power.

Chin emperors built the Great Wall to hold back the Tatars and abolished the feudal system. But this dynasty survived only fifty years. For the next 1500 years, dynasty succeeded dynasty. Some did much for the country; others are remembered only for the strife and bloodshed they inflicted on the people. During this period trade commenced with Japan, Persia, and Korea, and paper (second century B.C.) and printing (tenth century A.D.) were invented.[15]

In the thirteenth century Genghis Khan led his Mongol armies to victory over the Chinese. The Great Khan and later his grandson Kublai Khan established a firm rule. But the Mongol dynasty, never popular with the Chinese, was overthrown in 1368 by the Ming dynasty, which reigned for nearly 300 years. In 1644 the Manchus invaded the country and ruled until a republic was proclaimed in 1912.

CHINESE EDUCATION

Until recent times education in China was rigidly monopolized by the gentry and scholars. Peasants, at best poorly educated, worked and paid oppressive rents and taxes. The basis of Chinese education was the teachings of Confucius (551–478 B.C.), whose philosophy guided all thinking in political science and morality. Confucius died practically unknown, but when nobles and scholars discovered his *Five Classics* and the four books written by his disciples, his greatness was finally recognized. While Confucius provided the "textbook" for the privileged classes, his teachings, along with those of Buddha, eventually became the religion of the people. Devotion to one's parents, study, learning, love of the laws of life, and the glorification of the civil service as the greatest of all professions—these were the bases of "textbook" and religion.[15]

The Chinese student had to memorize and reproduce the nine books of Confucius and his disciples. Inevitably this type of education stultified personal initiative and encouraged conformity. Books were written in classical Chinese, which only the upper classes had the opportunity to master. Thus was education of the masses made—and kept—impossible. Finally, in 1917–1919, young scholars revolted, demanding that China be freed of the yoke of the classical language and that the vernacular of daily life be made the language of literature and education.[15]

PHYSICAL AND RECREATIONAL ACTIVITIES OF THE CHINESE

For many centuries whatever records were kept of life in China were concerned primarily with the ruling classes. For example, reliefs on tombs often depict hunting, a sport nobles and gentry found profitable as well as recreational. About 600 B.C. the Chinese developed the art of jujitsu, which they introduced to the Japanese some 400 years later. The most popular sports among the upper classes were boxing and a type of soccer football, both highly valued as military exercises. "Boxing," which dates back many thousands of years, actually included many activities—tumbling, dramatics, imitative movements, several types of wrestling, fencing with various weapons—and was designed primarily as a system of physical training for military service. According to Gardiner, soccer appeared in China well before the birth of Christ, and as early as the fifth century A.D. an air-filled ball formed of eight conical leather strips was used.[16]

While the Chinese valued exercise aimed at developing the warrior's strengths and skills, a stigma was attached to physical activity as a purely recreational pursuit for the adult. Confucianism taught that self-restraint and moderation were the ideal virtues and placed particular emphasis upon the value of meditation and passivity. Active games and sports for recreational purposes, therefore, were considered beneath the dignity of the adult and in conflict with religious ideals. The "rule" was not applied to children; nor was it accepted by other peoples of the Mongolian race.

The cultural pattern established by the primitive Chinese dictated that kinfolk must live in a communal group. Consequently the social unit was not the single family group but rather dozens of such units presided over by the grandmother of them all.[17] Hence the individual enjoyed little privacy or opportunity for the pursuit of personal initiative. Home-centered recreation was of the utmost importance in raising children, and no other peoples have a richer heritage of children's games than the Chinese, Koreans, and Japanese.[18]

INDIA

The original inhabitants of India are lost in antiquity; we know nothing of the first invaders—who they were, when they arrived, whom they found. The most persistent of the invaders, however, were the Aryans who finally occupied India in 1200 B.C. These people brought to India their language, Sanskrit, from which all modern languages sprang, and their religion, Hinduism or Brahmanism, and in succeeding centuries became overlords. In A.D. 1000 the Mohammedan migration brought with it the religion of Islam, or Mohammedanism.

India's indigenous population consists of three groups, the Dravida, the Munda, and the really primitive tribes which live in Central and Southern India.

The caste system is thought to have been introduced between 750 and 500 B.C. The foundation of this social stratification was laid by the Brahmans to distinguish themselves from the non-Brahmans and thus protect their privileged position. The four original castes were: Brahman (priests), Kshatriha (warriors), Vaisya (professionals and tradesmen), and Sudra (laborers). Below these castes and far outnumbering them were the untouchables, or pariahs. The presence of the untouchables is considered a defilement to all castes. Since the early 1900s the untouchables have waged a vigorous fight for social recognition and have gained considerable ground.

Before the British arrived few other than Brahmans received any education. Mohammedans taught their young from the Koran and little else. The British organized hundreds of elementary and secondary schools and did much to deemphasize the demoralizing caste system. Women, kept in seclusion under the old social order, gained more consideration and freedom.

Physical Activities in India

An antiquated Hindu development, Yoga, is still practiced in India and throughout the world. Yoga, a mental discipline, consists of focusing attention exclusively upon an object in order to identify the consciousness with that object. The practice of Yoga is directed along three distinct lines—physical, mental, and spiritual. The physical, however, is considered only a means to the end: mental and spiritual harmony. In the physical the chief aim is to establish a healthy and balanced condition in the body through postures, or Asanas, and by regulating the breathing. Of the eighty-four postures originally practiced, only fifteen are employed today.[19]

Polo may have been introduced to the British by the natives of India, although there is some evidence that the Tatars were long familiar with the game and taught it to the Chinese before A.D. 600. Wrestling and various ball games are known to have been popular in India throughout the centuries.[16]

EGYPT

Egypt flourished long before 3000 B.C. While monuments and inscriptions tell much about the ancient period, its chronology is still in doubt. According to the Egyptian historian Manetho, thirty dynasties of Pharaohs ruled Egypt in succession. The Fourth Dynasty, which reached its zenith about 2800 B.C., left as its memorial the greatest of the pyramids, Gizeh. With the Twentieth Dynasty came a loss of power, and Egypt gradually fell sway to foreign influence and domination. The Assyrians first assumed control in 670 B.C., the Persians in 525 B.C., and the Macedonians in 332 B.C. Until his death Alexander of Macedonia was lord of Egypt. He was succeeded by Ptolemy, one of his generals. The first Ptolemy and most of his descendants brought prosperity to Egypt, and Alexandria became the world's intellectual and literary center. In the second century B.C. the later Ptolemies had to seek aid from Rome, and the last of the sovereigns, Cleopatra, maintained her independence only through her political skill and her personal charm. After Cleopatra's death, Egypt became a province of Rome.

CULTURAL AND SOCIAL ASPECTS OF ANCIENT EGYPT

Egyptian literature dates from the early period of its history. This literature, written in hieroglyphics, defied translation until the discovery of the Rosetta Stone, which provided the key to these ancient writings. The Egyptians were familiar with astronomy—and astrology—and had a considerable knowledge of arithmetic and geometry. They used the bellow, lever, incline plane, and siphon and knew how to secure fiber from flax and spin it into cloth.

Today Egyptian women are subject to restrictive Mohammedan customs, but in ancient Egypt women enjoyed exceptional privileges. A woman's status was equal to that of a man. Women had full power of inheritance and succession and could own property independently of their husbands. Records show that women frequently loaned money to their husbands and charged interest.

PHYSICAL ACTIVITIES OF ANCIENT EGYPT

The Egyptian ruling class relished shows of all kinds. To amuse guests on special occasions, nobles employed professional performers —most of whom were women. Scenes painted on the wall of Beni-Hassan's tomb show acrobats performing backward handsprings, cartwheels, and double stunts and girls carrying one another pick-aback while passing a ball back and forth. This ball play closely resembles the Greek game *ephedrismos*. In the Greek version the player who failed to catch the ball traded places with his mount and became the "donkey." The Egyptians apparently had another ball game, in which teams of three competed in what must have resembled the game "keep away."

In Egypt wrestling developed into a fine art. Beni-Hassan's tomb contains at least 200 illustrations which show the successive steps of going into a hold, representing probably the first attempt to picture in detail the fundamentals of a sport. The Egyptians apparently permitted any type of hold, continued wrestling on the ground after a start from the upright position, and required both shoulders to be pinned to the ground for a fall. As in most ancient civilizations, wrestling was always related to military exercises. Wrestling and such soldierly activities as archery, fighting with the buckler and short stick, and quarterstaff play are invariably depicted in the same painting on a tomb wall. Wrestling, archery, and the other activities mentioned were pursued by the common people and the soldiers, while the nobility found amusement in watching professional performers, in playing chess, and in hunting.

Ancient Egyptians particularly enjoyed bullfights between bulls or between a human and a bull. The bullfighter irritated the bull to make him charge. As he did so, the performer, frequently a young woman, grabbed his horns and with a somersault landed on the bull's back. Also, as in the modern rodeo show, the bullfighter might grab the bull's horns and bulldoze him to the ground.[16]

ANCIENT CIVILIZATIONS OF THE NEAR EAST

The histories of Assyria, Babylonia, Israel, and Persia are so interwoven that an account of Assyria may serve also for the others. During the third millennium Assyria was under Sumerian-Babylonian influence. After Hammurabi the Babylonian kingdom collapsed and Assyria became a free state. While the Assyrians have preserved the names of their reigning monarchs before 2000 B.C., relatively little is known of the history of this nation during the early part of the second millennium B.C. However, about 1100 B.C. the Assyrian king, Tiglath-Pileser I conquered the Mitanni and the Hittites and swept through Mesopotamia and Syria westward to the Mediterranean Sea. His successors, many of whose exploits are recorded in the Old Testament, established an empire in Mesopotamia and Syria, and by military conquests added the North Kingdom of Israel, Babylonia, Elam, Egypt, Palestine, and a large part of Asia Minor to the Assyrian domain. In the reign of the last of the Assyrian kings, Assurbanipal (688–626 B.C.), the state showed definite signs of disintegration, and in 614 B.C. the Babylonians formed an alliance with the Medeans and with them finally succeeded in overthrowing the Assyrian empire. But the Medean hegemony was short-lived and in 549 B.C. the Persians, led by Cyrus the Great, conquered these people and incorporated them into a Medo-Persian Empire.

Physical Activities of the Ancient Peoples of the Near East

Hunting was especially enjoyed by the Assyrian and Persian nobility, who valued it not only for its economic and recreational rewards but also because it kept the warrior in fighting shape. Assurbanipal was as careful to record the number of animals killed as he was the number of enemy slain in battle.

Ancients dreaded above all things a watery grave which would deprive them of a burial tomb. Thus fear as well as military necessity motivated them to practice swimming. We know that the Hebrews practiced swimming because many Biblical passages refer to swimming. Praising God, the prophet Isaiah stated: "And he shall spread forth his hands in the midst of them, as he that swimmeth spreadeth forth his hands to swim" (Isaiah, XXV:11). This passage is often interpreted to imply that the Hebrew was familiar with the breast stroke. An Assyrian bas-relief in the British Museum indicates that other ancient peoples were also familiar with the breast stroke. Assurbanipal is shown crossing a river with his army. Three men, evidently escaping from the Assyrians, are swimming in midstream on inflated bladders and are using the breast stroke as well as a type of side stroke.

Since the peoples of the Near East were constantly engaged in warfare, the use of the horse, javelin, sword, and bow and arrow as regular military exercises was of vital importance. Assyrians and Persians were skillful horsemen and could mount and dismount at full gallop. A hunter armed with javelin and bow and arrow was, in effect, preparing for the next battle. The sling of David and Goliath fame was standard equipment in the Persian army, as was the chariot in the armies of the Near East. Cyrus the Great was the first to improve on the conventional chariot by increasing axle length, providing more protection for the driver, and adding sharp scythes to wheel hubs.

Military education for youths in the ancient countries was concentrated and physically demanding. Xenophon, the celebrated Athenian historian, visited the Persians and in his *Anabasis* gave a detailed description accepted for centuries as an eyewitness account of the rigorous military education of Persian youth. Classical scholars, however, know that Xenophon fervently admired Spartan military education and that in the *Anabasis* he was actually giving a detailed description of the Spartan system to which he subjected his two sons.[16]

The next chapter details further the education and physical development of Greek and Roman youth.

NOTES

1. Mabel Cook and Fay-Cooper Cole. *The Story of Primitive Man.* Chicago: University of Knowledge, Inc., 1940, pp. 13–73; 130–135. William Howells. *Mankind in the Making.* New York: Doubleday & Company, Inc., 1959, pp. 60–135. Gabriel Ward Lasker. *The Evolution of Man.* New York: Rinehart and Winston, Inc., 1961, pp. 79–90.
2. A. Hyatt Verrill. *The American Indian, North, South and Central America.* New York: D. Appleton and Company, 1943, pp. 6–17.
3. W. E. LeCros Clark. *History of Primates.* Chicago: University of Chicago Press, 1957.
4. Ashley Montagu. *Man: His First Million Years.* New York: The American Library of World Literature, Inc., 1957, pp. 72–79.
5. The Marquis de Nadaillac. *Manners and Monuments of Prehistoric Peoples.* (Translated by Nancy Bell [N. D'Anvers]) New York: G. P. Putnam's Sons, 1894, pp. 47; 58.
6. George A. Pettit. "Primitive Education in North America." *Publications in American Archeology and Ethnology,* University of California, 34:1 (1946), 161.
7. Max Schmidt. *The Primitive Races of Mankind.* Boston: Little, Brown and Company, 1926.

8. Stewart Culin. *Games of North American Indians.* Bureau of American Ethnology (Twenty-Fourth Annual Report), Washington, D.C., 1907, pp. 31–35; 36–43; 697–708.
9. *Handbook of South American Indians.* (Julian H. Stewart, editor) Bureau of American Ethnology, Smithsonian Institute, 4:143 (1948), 532–534.
10. H. H. Wormington. *Ancient Man in North America.* Denver: The Denver Museum of Natural History, 1957.
11. Tunis Romein. "Physical Activities of the Ao Naga." (Thesis) University of Kentucky, 1945, p. 37.
12. W. A. Goellner. "Court Ball Game of the Aboriginal Mayas." *Research Quarterly,* 24:2 (May, 1953), 147–167.
13. Henry W. Hamilton. "The Spiro Mound." *The Missouri Archaeologist,* 14 (October, 1952), 62–75.
14. E. Gross. *The Beginning of Art.* New York: D. Appleton and Company, 1897, pp. 209–231
15. Wolfram Eberhard. *A History of China.* London: Routledge and Kegan Paul, 1950, pp. 327–333.
16. E. Norman Gardiner. *Athletics in the Ancient World.* Oxford: The Clarendon Press, 1930, pp. 16; 10–11.
17. Emily I. Case. "Recreation for Woman and Girls." *Mind and Body,* 42:427 (April, 1935), 24–31.
18. Stewart Culin. *Games of the Orient (Korea, China, Japan).* Rutland: Charles E. Tuttle Company, 1958. Stewart Culin. "Korean Games, with Notes on Corresponding Games of China and Japan." (Monograph) University of Pennsylvania, 1895.
19. Paramanda Swami. *Science and Practice of Yoga.* Boston: Ananda-Ashrama Vendante Centre, 1918, p. 3.

Chapter 2

THE ANCIENT GREEKS AND PHYSICAL EDUCATION

For centuries Homer's *Iliad* and *Odyssey* were considered supreme as literature but unreliable as guides to what really happened during and immediately after the Trojan War (1194–1184 B.C.). The poet, historians argued, had celebrated an era two or three hundred years after it had passed, telling of places and events of which no other evidence was known. And, they maintained, it was all the more difficult to distinguish between fact and fancy because Homer had borrowed much from legend.[1]

In the late 1800s the *Iliad* gained new respectability as a historical reference. Heinrich Schliemann, a German merchant and classical scholar, believed, with little encouragement from scholars, that he had gathered enough data to locate Homer's Troy. In 1871 he started excavations at Hissarlik on the Aegean shore of Asia Minor near the Hellespont. After digging through the first layer of an ancient city, Schliemann struck what he called the "second city," unearthing the famous place of Minos.[2] Subsequent excavations on Crete turned up a multitude of cities and evidence of an advanced culture dating from the Neolithic (6000 B.C.) to the Mycenaean (1200 B.C.) Ages.

THE MINOANS

Evans concluded that the dark-skinned and curly black-haired inhabitants of Crete, whom he called Minoans,[2] were neither Greeks nor Romans. We know now that these people were of

Mediterranean stock and that they had lived in the region several millennia before the arrival of the first Indo-Europeans.[3] The Minoans, traders and skillful sailors, carried their manufactured goods and works of art, as well as olive oil, honey, fish, figs and other fruits, and aromatic and medicinal herbs to Aegean and Mediterranean ports in Asia, Africa, and Europe. For example, they imported copper from the island of Phoenicia and Asia Minor and papyrus from Egypt and in return delivered their popular black steatite vases, bronze ware, fabrics, and glazed pottery.

The Minoans provided a limited education for scribes, who kept records on clay tablets and papyrus of business transactions and court activities. Evans tried for more than forty years to decipher the two languages used by the scribes, which he classified as Linear A and B. In 1952 Michael Ventris, an architect and amateur cryptographer, finally solved the Linear B, which he proved to be a forerunner of classical Greek. Linear A, the Minoan language, has not yet been deciphered.[4]

Although the Minoans had no system of public education, males were subject to military training. Cretan archers were respected throughout the ancient world. The Minoans, who began to use the bow and arrow at the close of the Stone Age, must have developed a system of instruction and practice that extended from youth through adulthood.

Evans distinguished two types of spear—the short javelin employed in close-range fighting and the long javelin (6-foot) used in the attack and in hunting. About 2000 B.C. the Minoans developed the short bronze sword for thrusting rather than slashing in hand-to-hand combat. Obviously, swordsmen had to be trained in parries, attacks, counterattacks, and feints. At the same time, horses and chariots were imported from Syria, but they were used to transport men and equipment more than as a weapon.[4]

CULTURAL SIGNIFICANCE OF SPORTS IN RELIGION

According to Evans, the Minoans reveled in their religious processions and rituals, which honored a single goddess, the great Mother Earth, or several goddesses. Music and dancing and boxing and bull-grappling figured in these ceremonies, which usually were conducted in an arena seating about 500 spectators. From Minoan vases we learn that boxers sometimes wore helmets and always wore protective covering for the hands. Men and boys participated. The vases also clearly depict boxing technique.

Minoan artisans embellished vases, murals, frescoes, and jewelry with the figures of bulls and scenes of bull-grappling. The Minoans also gave to posterity the myth of the half-man, half-bull Minotaur. The bull had an important role in religious ceremonies as a sacrificial animal and served as a dangerous prop for acrobats.[3, 4] The acrobat, a man or woman, grasped its horns, and as the bull tossed its head the performer swung high into the air and did a backward somersault to land on the bull's rump. From this insecure seat the acrobat escaped to the waiting arms of a fellow performer. No modern rodeo performer would attempt this feat, but bull-grappling scenes appear too frequently to have existed only in the imagination of the artisan. Their physical development suggests that acrobats and boxers were intensively trained and that only the best of the trainees were permitted to perform in religious ceremonies.

THE MYCENAEAN OR HOMERIC AGE

About 1900 B.C. barbaric Indo-Europeans invaded and settled in the northern region of the Greek Peninsula. Not until 1500 B.C. did they occupy the entire peninsula and attain an identifiable culture. Called Achaeans by Homer, they were the first Greek-speaking people. By 1400 B.C. the powerful Tholos Tomb Dynasty controlled Athens, Thessaly, and Aetolia on the peninsula and the Ionian and Aegean islands.[5] It was these tomb builders who destroyed Knossos and "digested" the Minoan culture.[4]

Mycenae, several miles inland from the seashore and protected by the citadel hill, or acropolis, facing the plain of Argive, became the capital of the Achaean world. To facilitate commerce—their economic welfare was dependent upon trade—the Mycenaeans created a federation which included Corinth, Sicily, Egypt, Palestine, Cyprus, Troy, and Macedonia. Any attempt by members of the federation or free-lance pirates to interfere with trade brought immediate reprisals. Indeed, historians are inclined to believe that it was not the abduction of Helen that "launched a thousand ships," but rather that Agamemnon, King of Mycenae, declared war on Troy because the Trojans had interfered with commerce between Black Sea ports and other members of the confederation.

The Trojan War claimed a grim toll of Achaean leaders, crippled commerce, and exhausted physical resources. And at the same time the Mycenaeans began to be harassed by Dorian tribes, especially the Laconians, or Spartans. Finally, the Mycenaeans succumbed to the Dorian southward thrust.

The centuries that marked the end of the Mycenaean influence and the beginning of the Golden Era of Greek history are designated as the Middle Period. It was during this transitional period that the city-state was developed. Each city and its immediate environs was in effect a separate nation; its citizens owed allegiance to no other power, declared war without consulting their neighbors, and developed forms of government independent of each other. While all were proud of "Greek" traditions, the citizen's first loyalty was to his city-state. Hence a single Greek nation was not forged during the Middle Period.

THE HOMERIC AGE

From Homer we can learn something of Achaean life. He sang of the deeds of a very select aristocracy whose wealth was counted in flocks of sheep and herds of oxen and horses. Without slaves the aristocracy could not have pursued the "good life." Women did not enjoy the same status as men. While a wife had more rights than a concubine, both were considered property; their value was reckoned in terms of so many head of cattle and they could be disposed of in these terms.

Achaean religion reflected many influences, especially that of the Minoans and their early Greek conqueror. And from the Egyptians and other Eastern peoples tomb burials and rituals were adopted.

THE FUNERAL GAMES OF THE "ILIAD"

In the twenty-third book of the *Iliad* Homer describes the funeral games held by Achilles in honor of his friend Patroclus. There was a chariot race, boxing, wrestling, and a foot race. Classical scholars believe that translators interpolated the description of the fight in armor and the archery contest. Prizes for the events—women slaves skilled in handiwork, tripods, horses, mules, caldrons, urns, gold, and silver—were sought because of their utility more than because of the distinction associated with victory. The value of a prize reflected the donor's generosity and symbolized his respect and honor for the deceased.

These games were by-products of Greek military education. Such instruction must have been formally organized even in the Middle Period of Greek history. Instructors, no doubt, were drafted from the ranks of battle-seasoned veterans. Survival in hand-to-hand combat depended on strength and endurance. Hence boxing and wrestling and running were emphasized in the physical-conditioning program of the Homeric Greeks.[8]

THE GOLDEN ERA AND DECLINE

By the close of the sixth century B.C., the Greek city-states were fully developed. Sparta had become a strong military power and Corinth a thriving commercial center, while Athens was beginning to be recognized as the mecca of intellectual and artistic life. Great political advances were also made during this period. Draco drew up a code of law for Athens, and Solon and Clisthenes destroyed the power of the old landholding nobles and established the foundations for the world's first republican government.

It was the war with the Persians that brought the Greeks to the height of their glory. For a half-century after the defeat of Darius and his son Xerxes, the Greeks enjoyed peace. Athens, the paramount sea power, dominated the peninsula and reached a level of culture at which the world still marvels. Her democratic ideas were widely adopted, but Sparta and the city-states she influenced held firmly to an oligarchic form of government.[11]

The old rivalry between Sparta and Athens, still smoldering at the close of the Persian Wars, flamed into a war in 431 B.C. which lasted for twenty-seven years. Despite crushing defeats, the steady erosion of her power, the death of the great Pericles, and a devastating plague, the Athenians fought on. Finally, they were compelled to accept humiliating peace terms. The peninsula bowed now to Sparta, but she proved too hard a taskmaster. Led by Thebes, the city-states rebelled and defeated the Spartans in 371 B.C. Drained by nearly a hundred years of intermittent warfare, the city-states could not repel Philip II's Macedonians, who subdued the Greeks in 338 B.C. The Greeks, united but in chains, were ruled by the Macedonians until the Romans defeated them in 146 B.C. The combined Greek city-states later became a province of the Roman Empire called Achaia.[13]

EDUCATION OF THE SPARTAN YOUTH

At birth the Spartan child was taken before the elders of his family's tribe. The sickly or malformed child was exposed to die on Mount Taygetus. Children were taught not to fear darkness, or being left alone, and they were not addicted to temper tantrums. Easy living was discouraged; houses and food were plain. Spartan mothers, though stern with their children, were keenly interested in their development.

Many of the modern child's amusements delighted the Spartan child. The infant's rattle and rolling hoop, the top—as old as the days of Homer—and the humming top, kites and stilts, wax and clay dolls and toy soldiers, swings and hobby horses—the Spartan child had all these. Older children played organized games which have been popular through the ages—for example, black and white, tug-o'-war, and blindman's buff, which had a variation called brazen fly. Spartan (and Roman) children played several games of skill with nuts which have their counterpart in the modern game of marbles. Nuts were so important in childhood amusements that the phrase "relinquishing the nuts" came to mean putting away childish things on reaching maturity.[12]

PHYSICAL AND MILITARY EDUCATION

The Spartan boy was educated at home until his seventh birthday and thereafter by the state. On his seventh birthday he joined a pack[2] of his same age group. Boys were segregated in packs by age until they were 14 years old. They ate, slept, marched, and exercised together. Twelve-to-fourteen-year-olds were considered to be on the threshold of manhood and Spartan citizenship (preparatory ephebi), and hence their training was intensified. Ephebi (those between 14 and 20) were prepared specifically for military service.[6, 7, 8]

Each pack was led by a capable boy chosen from its members and supervised by a 20-year-old who was responsible for physical and military education and the maintenance of discipline. The Spartan citizens chose an able and respected man to superintend the entire educational system. He could summon the boys to assembly and decide on suitable punishment for laggards; above all he had absolute authority over them.

Organization into packs facilitated physical education. Packs were subdivided into four troops and older boys assisted as squad leaders.[8] The typical physical education program included ball games, wrestling, archery, stone and javelin throwing, boxing, the pankraton (a combination of boxing and wrestling), and hunting. All activities were adjusted to age level and conducted daily. Participation in boxing and the pankraton in the Olympic and the lesser Greek games was discouraged. These contests required the admission of defeat to avoid severe physical injury or death, and Spartans never indulged the habit of admitting defeat.

During the Middle Period and beyond, physical education was conducted in an open area or field (the palaestra or wrestling ground) located near a stream. These exercise grounds often have been called "gymnasiums" by historians, but they were really nothing more than flat open areas. Later, as Sparta devoted more and more of her energies and resources to strengthening her material position, the state-constructed gymnasiums frequently were combined with the older palaestra. The gymnasiums served as training centers for the ephebi and athletes and provided physical conditioning and recreational programs for adults.[1]

Songs and music played an important part in the education of the Spartan youth. He exercised to the rhythm of a flute or oboe and drilled and marched in cadence with martial music. Past victories and dead heroes were honored in hymns and songs and in the dance. Even the Spartan laws were memorized and set to music.[7]

The Festival of Artemis Orthia

Any citizen had the right to beat a boy on any provocation. The acme of this public acceptance of flogging came each year during the religious festival at the altar of Artemis. Boys volunteered to stand before the altar and be lashed. The priestess encouraged the beaters to apply the lash vigorously and even parents among the spectators cried out encouragement. Many a youth died without a whimper; survivors earned the title "altar-conqueror."

Education of the Spartan Girl

Although the Spartan girl ate at home, not in the state communal dining halls as did the boys, she too was organized into packs. Girls were subject to state-supervised physical education from their seventh until their eighteenth birthdays. The object of the program was weight control and physical conditioning in preparation for motherhood. Some continued to exercise until their twentieth year but never beyond this age even if they were not married. The separate gymnasiums for girls and young women were under the jurisdiction of the state superintendent.

The Spartan girl participated in wrestling (sometimes with a boy), throwing the discus and javelin, running events, jumping, dancing, ball games, mountain climbing, and contests of skill and strength. Leg exercises, including special stunts and jumping events, were emphasized. The bronze statue of a Dorian girl dressed for exercise shows her wearing only a cinture, or girdle. Often the girls participated in the nude. In his discussion of physical education costumes for girls in his *Laws,* Plato recommended the Dorian chilton, a short woolen tunic split on both sides for freedom of movement and drawn together in the middle with a belt.

Girls participated with boys in festival processions and at certain festivals danced and sang in the presence of young men, praising the courageous and making fun of the cowards. Regular exercise made the Spartan girl an attractive physical specimen. Her complexion, beauty, and shapeliness were the envy of all women in other Greek city-states. Before marriage, young women wore no veils and mixed freely with young men. After marriage women remained at home and exercises and dances came to an end.[8]

DANCING IN SPARTA

The Spartan was extremely fond of dancing. To him, war resembled a form of dance in which the soldier marched or charged into battle to the sound of the flute, his head crowned and his red cloak flying in the wind. Dancing, accordingly, was not regarded as an end in itself and appreciated for any intrinsic aesthetic value. Rather it was a means to an end or ends; it served Sparta much as today's Russian leaders insist that art should serve the state.

The pyrrhic or war dance was one of the most popular. It was performed by young men, armed from head to foot, who executed all the proper movements to the sound of a flute. The dance was composed of four parts: the *podism,* or footing, which consisted of quick shifting movements of the feet representing the advance and retreat; the *xiphism,* a kind of mock fight in which the dancers imitated all the movements of the combatants such as striking and parrying, throwing the javelin and dodging; the *homos,* which consisted of high leaps and vaulting; and the *tetracomos,* in which the dancers formed a square figure and executed slow and majestic movements.[9]

Plato reduced Greek dances to three classes: (1) military dances, such as the pyrrhic, suitable as exercises of war; (2) domestic dances engaged in for amusement and recreation; and (3) mediatorial dances used in expiations and sacrifices.[10]

AN EVALUATION OF THE SPARTAN EDUCATIONAL SYSTEM

The Spartans have been criticized for overemphasizing physical and military education and not providing intellectual instruction. Aristotle noted that the exercise regime of the Spartan youth made him "beastlike." It did produce formidable warriors, and their athletes dominated the Olympic and lesser games for centuries.

Xenophon stated that it would be difficult to find anywhere men with more serviceable and beautiful bodies than those of Spartans.

His admiration for the body beautiful was a common sentiment among all Greeks. Excess fat was abhorred. In Sparta the state dictated the type and quantity of food served in the communal dining halls to insure a trim figure. Lounging spectators in the gymnasiums were never tolerated; the rule was to strip and exercise or leave the premises. In adult physical education the oldest man in the gymnasium served as leader, and his objective was to see that everyone receive sufficient exercise to keep the body trim and the muscles firm.

Although the Spartans temporarily gained their goal of military preeminence, their educational system did not produce well-rounded, versatile citizens. As Aristotle pointed out in his *Politics:* "Most of these military states are safe only when they are at war, but fall when they acquire their empire; like unused iron they lose their edge in time of peace. And for this the legislator is to blame, because he never taught them how to lead a life of peace." After the defeat of the Spartan armed forces at Leuctra in 371 B.C., the old system of physical and military education fell into decay. And as their bodies deteriorated so did their morals.

THE ATHENIAN GREEK

Athens was organized first as an oligarchy, or government of the nobility, with a chief magistrate known as the archon. Finally, after more than a hundred years of civil strife, the Athenians freed themselves from a system that bred tyrants and in 509 B.C. adopted the constitution proposed by Clisthenes and became a republic.

EDUCATION OF ATHENIAN YOUTH

Primary education for the Athenian boy consisted of grammar, music, and physical education. Drawing and painting were added to the curriculum at the beginning of the fourth century B.C. He studied reading and writing and mastered the seven-stringed lyre with which he accompanied himself in singing the works of the lyric poets. The state did not educate girls; whatever instruction they received was provided in the home by the mother or perhaps a slave. As noted before, women had few rights in republican Athens.

The physical education instructor was called the *paidotribe,* or "boy-rubber." He gave his charges a rubdown with olive oil after each day's lessons. (Later this function was performed by assistants.) The program included boxing, wrestling, the pankration, running, jumping, discus and javelin throwing, and conditioning exercises. As in Sparta, classes were held on the palaestra, an open area of land located near a stream suitable for bathing.

Plato suggested that instruction in physical education begin at age 6, grammar at 10, and music at 13. Aristotle agreed with Plato, who had been his teacher, that physical education should precede grammar and music.[10] Most classical scholars have concluded that all branches of primary education started simultaneously and continued until the youth reached military age.

By approximately 400 B.C., the Athenians had developed a system of secondary education. From his fourteenth until his eighteenth birthday, the Athenian male was instructed in any and all subjects by wandering savants referred to generally as sophists. When he was 18 the Athenian entered the ephebia for two years of compulsory cadet training, the first of which was spent in Athens studying military tactics and physical education and the second in some outlying province on military duty.[7]

The Ephebia of Athens

After their humiliating defeat by the Macedonians at Chaeronea in 338 B.C., the Athenians decided, even though they cherished the ideal of personal liberty, to maintain a citizen army. Three years later the ephebia was established and every able-bodied youth reaching his eighteenth birthday had to enroll for two years. The ephebic college, the Athenian West Point, became the tertiary stage in the educational system. It was administered by a president, or *kosmetes,* whose assistants included at this time ten *sophronestai,* or disciplinary masters. The president was elected annually from the citizenship at large and served only for the honor of the position. The disciplinary masters were elected by the membership of the ten tribes; they received only a nominal fee for their services. Each kept a watchful eye over the morals of the youths in his tribe, checked their meals, provided their clothing, and supervised their physical and military education. In Aristotle's time the ephebic college was staffed by two *paidotribes* and instructors in heavy-armed fighting (*hoplomachos*), archery (*toxotes*), the javelin (*akontistes*), and the use of the catapult (*katapaltaphetes,* or *aphetes* for short).

In the second and first centuries before Christ the ephebia became more and more involved in religious rites and festivals and even assumed responsibility for the ancient torch race. With the addition of literature, rhetoric, and philosophy to the curriculum, the college lost much of its earlier military atmosphere. This deemphasis is clearly evident in the fact that instruction in the use of the catapult was not mentioned after 99 B.C. Archery, never popular among Athenian youth and the lowest-paying teaching position, expired with javelin instruction in 38 B.C. The ephebic college gradually lost its identity as a military school as it merged into the University of Athens.[5]

THE PALAESTRA AND GYMNASIUM

Physical education centered around the palaestra and the gymnasium. The *paidotribes,* according to the laws of Solon, were not to open the palaestrae before sunrise and were to close them at sunset. There were also laws regulating the number and age of boys to be admitted, discipline, and the conduct of the Hermae,* a festival held for boys in the palaestra. Athens had many palaestrae; some were maintained by wealthy individuals for their private use, others were set up by *paidotribes* who charged the boys' parents a nominal fee.

The gymnasium, which appeared about the fourth century B.C., often included a palaestra. For this reason, confusion often arises when classical authors of the fourth century use the terms interchangeably. The Athenian palaestra was located in the city proper for the convenience of the schoolboy. But the gymnasiums, which offered more elaborate accommodations and required spacious fields, had to be built outside the city limits.

* One of the features of the festival of the Hermae was the torch race. Teams of boys from the various palaestrae competed against each other to bring the sacred flame to the altar of Hermes, herald and messenger of the gods and conductor of the dead to Hades.[8]

Famous Gymnasiums

The Academy, the Lyceum, which Socrates knew, and the Cynosarges of Athens and the Platanistas of Sparta were all located in shady areas and close to streams outside the city proper. The Academy was wall enclosed and boasted well-watered groves, trim avenues, and walks. Bastards or those whose parents were not both Athenians had their own gymnasium—the Cynosarges. The Academy and Lyceum were large enough to accommodate riding schools for the wealthier citizen and a parade ground for cavalry. While Athenian gymnasiums were open to patrons of all ages, schoolboys were generally sent to a palaestra.

The principal official associated with public gymnasiums was the gymnasiarch, a citizen of considerable wealth elected to this position by his tribe. As a liturgy, or public duty, other members of the tribe helped him meet the expenses of the gymnasium. His administrative duties are not clearly defined in classical literature, but, as an elected official, he must have been required to conduct the program of the gymnasium and supervise its personnel. As his tribe's representative he had to field a team of runners for the annual torch race. He selected the youths from the tribe, paid for the services of a coach, and met incidental expenses. The gymasiarch also paid for the huge quantities of oil used by the rubbers, or *aleiptes,* employed to massage the gymnasium's patrons.

The public gymnasium also served as an educational and social center in Greek society. Philosophers habitually frequented the gymnasium, where their students and followers gathered about them. Plato became identified with the Academy and Aristotle with the Lyceum. The Cynic philosophers who formed the link between Socrates and the more influential Stoics first met at the Cynasarges. Ultimately these public buildings became centers of learning, or universities.[8]

Activities of the Palaestra and Gymnasium

In addition to the usual exercises—boxing, wrestling, the pankration, running, jumping, discus and javelin throwing, and swimming—the Athenian boy, like the Spartan, did conditioning exercises with or without the halteres (jumping weights). He was taught to sit and arise and move gracefully, and to stand straight. The Athenian boy also practiced gesticulation, which involved a series of movements of the arms and legs in the form of gestures. It served as a preparation for but must have been distinct from dancing because classical authors note that some boys could gesticulate but could not dance. Since the movements resembled those of shadow boxing, gesticulation might have served also as a warm-up activity. The Greeks also practiced isometric contractions and rope climbing, which was widely adopted more than 1500 years later during the Renaissance inspired revival of interest in Greek culture and has carried over to our century.

Ball games, many of them dating from the Middle Period, were popular in Athens and Sparta. The Athenians were so fond of ball play that they bestowed citizenship upon Aristonikos of Karystos because of his skill and ability in handling the ball.

Episkuros, a favorite game among Greek youths, took its name from the line, or *Skuros,* which separated the two groups of players. On either side of the dividing or center line, and parallel to it, were drawn the base lines. The ball was placed on the center line and on signal players of both teams made a dash to gain possession. Whoever secured the ball threw it toward the other team's base line. When the opponent caught the ball, he immediately threw it back. This give and take continued until one of the teams was forced back of its base line.

Harpastum was as popular among the Romans as it was with the Greeks, but information on the game is so scanty that it is impossible to reconstruct it. It seems to have been a game of keep-away and certainly was not a team game because players could drop out when they became tired or disinterested. The Greeks probably had a game that resembled hockey; an ancient mural in Athens shows two players with curved sticks about to execute a bully and four other players with sticks are standing by.[8]

THE "PAIDOTRIBE" AND "GYMNASTES"

In addition to the *paidotribe,* the palaestra's staff included pupil-teachers who gave special attention to the slow learners and the professional flute player. The symbol of the *paidotribe*'s profession was a long forked stick (this trade-mark probably was derived from the Olympic Games; vases show Olympic referees holding such an implement). *Paidotribe* designated the teacher of physical exercises for boys at the palaestra; *gymnastes* designated the coach-trainer of athletes who competed in the games. The *paidotribe* and *gymnastes* are roughly equivalent to our physical education instructor and athletic coach.

From the time of Solon (639–559 B.C.) the education of Athenian youth in Athens was in the hands of the *paidotribe* and the schoolmaster. In most Greek city-states education was voluntary, and the *paidotribes* were private teachers who received a fee of about twenty dollars per pupil during the period of instruction (the city-states hired *paidotribes* to furnish instruction for the cadets of the ephebia).

The type of instruction provided by the *paidotribes* was not adequate for young athletes who wished to compete in the games. This special training was furnished by the *gymnastes,* or coach, who made his appearance about the fifth century B.C. The *gymnastes* usually was a retired athlete who had gained a reputation as a stellar performer in an individual event or the pentathlon. There were many famous coaches, but the names of only a few remain—notably Melesias, who trained and coached thirty wrestling and pankration champions, and Iccus of Tarentum, who himself won the pentathlon at the seventy-sixth Olympic Games and who was considered in his time one of the best *gymnastes.* According to Plato, in his *De virtute,* the successful coach must have some knowledge of the body and the effect of exercise upon it. He should be able to judge the human animal—be able to tell an individual in which form of athletics he would do best and what type of training program was necessary for him to achieve success.[8]

THE DECLINE OF PHYSICAL EDUCATION IN ATHENS

Athenian enthusiasm for physical education was at its peak during the sixth and into the first half of the fifth century B.C. The Persian Wars had engendered a deep respect for the value of the instruction provided in the palaestra.

With the appearance of the Sophists in the last half of the fifth century, physical education had to compete with a new and fascinating interest. The Sophists had a beneficial effect upon literature and oratory and encouraged individualism and independent thought.[12] Their method of reasoning, however, had a damaging effect on social conduct and undermined cherished Greek traditions. Wealthy Athenian youths deserted the palaestra to follow the new philosophy and turned to hunting, horseback riding, and less vigorous pursuits. After 335 B.C. the compulsory cadet training of the ephebia furnished tractically the only systematic instruction in physical education.

The Athenian's interest in physical education was also affected by the introduction of health exercises during the fourth century. Herodicus, a *paidotribe* at Selymbria, testified that he had reached a ripe old age because he had followed a regular health regime throughout his life. He called his system of exercises *gymnastics** from the Greek verb meaning to exercise or to train. Plato, who subscribed to the Spartan idea of the survival of the fittest, stated that instead of extending his life span Herodicus had but prolonged his death. Despite this criticism Herodicus put his ideas into manuscript form for public consumption. Of particular interest to the Athenian was his discussion of the bath. To the average citizen a tranquilizing bath was far more appealing than the physical discomfort offered by the palaestra or the gymnasium. Wealthy Athenians constructed small private gymnasiums in which the bathing facilities were the most distinctive feature. The poorer citizen sought solace in the elaborate baths, which reflected Roman influence, of the public gymnasium.

Professionalism in athletics also undermined interest in physical education in Athens and other city-states. Intellectuals throughout the centuries had warned the Greeks of the danger of the growing public interest in games—in spectator sports. By the fifth century Greek youth, once a good amateur athlete, bowed out of the scene and left the stage to the professionals.[1]

* The Greek word *"gymnos"* means naked, stripped, or lightly clad. The verb form of this root word is *"gymnasein,"* which means to exercise or train. Literally, the verb form means to exercise in the nude.

NOTES

1. Henri I. Marrou. *A History of Education in Antiquity*. (Translated by George Lamb.) New York: Sheed and Ward, 1956, pp. 3–4, 125, 126, 128–130.
2. *The Epic of Man*. (By the Editors of Life.) New York: Time, Inc., 1961, 185–189; Crane Brinton, John B. Christopher, and Robert Lee Wolff, *A History of Civilization*. (Second Edition.) New Jersey: Prentice-Hall, Inc., 1962, pp. 51–53.
3. Charles Alexander Robinson, Jr. *Ancient History from Prehistoric Times to the Death of Justinian*. New York: The Macmillan Co., 1959, pp. 128–133.
4. Arthur Evans. *The Palace of Minos*. (Vols. I–IV.) London: Macmillan and Co., 1921, p. 35.
5. Thomas Woody. *Life and Education in Early Societies*. New York: The Macmillan Co., 1949, pp. 197–198, 206–207.
6. Rachel Sargent Robinson. *Sources for the History of Greek Athletics*. (Lithoprinted by Cushing-Malloy, Inc.) Illini Union Book Store, University of Illinois, Urbana, 1955, pp. 1–31; Andrew Lang, Walter Leaf, and Ernst Meyers. *The Iliad of Homer*. New York: The Macmillan Co., 1928; E. Norman Gardiner. *Athletics of the Ancient World*. Oxford: The Clarendon Press, 1930, pp. 18–27; E. Norman Gardiner. *Greek Athletic Sports and Festivals*. London: Macmillan and Co., 1910, pp. 12–26.
7. Werner Jaeger. *Paidea, The Ideal Greek Culture*. (Translated from the second German edition by Gilbert Highet.) Oxford: Basil Blackwell, 1946, pp. 3–4.
8. Clarence A. Forbes. *Greek Physical Education*. New York: The Century Co., 1929, pp. 12–43, 93–108, 109–178.
9. Kenneth J. Freeman. *Schools of Hellas*. New York: The Macmillan Co., 1908, pp. 124–130.
10. Horatio Smith. *Festivals, Games and Amusements*. London: Henry Colburn and Richard Bentley, 1831, pp. 235–236.
11. Will Durant. *The Story of Philosophy*. New York: Simon and Schuster, 1961, pp. 7–13, 14–40, 44–47.
12. Edward M. Plummer. "Toys and Games for Children Among the Ancient Hellenens," *American Physical Education Review*, **III**, 3 (September, 1898), 157–169.
13. Giorgio de Santillana: "The Birth of Reason," *Life*. 54:6 (February 8, 1963), 62.

Chapter 3

THE PANHELLENIC GAMES

ORIGIN OF THE OLYMPIC GAMES

GREEK games, characteristically informal and spontaneous during the Homeric Age, gradually became more formally organized. Excavations have established that there was a village at the foot of Mount Olympus as early as the twelfth century B.C. Some of the thousands of votive offerings honoring Zeus unearthed at this site date as far back as the ninth century B.C. Since these offerings were associated with festivals that always featured games, it seems logical to assume that the first organized games for those of Greek blood were held at Olympia sometime during the ninth century B.C.

Scholars, however, date the Olympics from 776 B.C., the year of the first recorded games. We know that the Heraeum, the wooden temple in which the discus of Iphitus and the tables of ivory and gold for the victors' crowns were kept, stood then in Olympia. During the early games there was no race course for man or horse—only an open, level stretch of land between two altars which was probably used for boxing and wrestling.

GROWTH AND ORGANIZATION

Within a century competitors from such Greek city-states as Sparta, Athens, and Thebes and from the East met at Olympia: the Olympic Games were firmly established as a nationalistic festival. During the sixth century Greek colonies erected treasuries, or communal houses, on a terrace at the foot of the hill of Cronus at Olympia to which they sent valuable gifts.

The games were held every fourth summer under the supervision of ten judges elected by the people of Elis. Thirty days before the festival contestants presented themselves before the judges for examination. Only those of pure Greek stock who had never committed a crime and had practiced regularly at a gymnasium the previous ten months, the last month at the large gymnasium in Elis under the judges' supervision, were eligible. The names of qualified contestants were placed on a white board which was displayed in a conspicuous spot in Olympia. An athlete who withdrew was disgraced and heavily fined.

Eleven days before the games the judges requested a truce among warring Greek city-states for thirty days (the *Pax Olympica*). Olympia then became a neutral territory. Travelers as well as merchants and their wares were guaranteed safe passage by the power of Zeus—and the proclamations of all Greek heads of state.

During the weeks just before the games thousands descended upon Olympia. Official representatives from the city-states participated in the great procession and in the sacrificial rites to Zeus. Political emissaries took advantage of the festival to form alliances or discuss treaties. Artists exhibited their work, poets recited, scholars and teachers promoted their ideas, and merchants displayed and sold their wares. Only women and girls did not share in the excitement of the Olympic Games; they were not permitted to attend.

The Pageantry of the Olympic Games

The games, which commenced at the second or third full moon after the summer solstice, lasted five days. What proportion of the five days was devoted to athletic competition is not clear, for public and private sacrifices and feasts figured prominently in each day's program.

Most of the first day was devoted to the procession and sacrifices to Zeus. Athletes and trainers stood before the statue of Zeus and swore on the entrails of a pig to use no unfair means to gain victory.

Each day's program opened early in the morning with proclamations or announcements and occasionally an address by some distinguished visitor or one of the judges. A herald announced each event, along with the names of the contestants and their fathers, any Olympic contest they had won, and the city-state they represented. Each contest was begun with a blast from the herald's trumpet. The judges decided ties and supervised the drawing of lots for heats in the races in view of the spectators who crowded the slopes of Cronus. When the herald announced the victor's name, he stepped forward to be crowned by the chief judge. The olive branches that formed the crown were cut from the sacred grove behind the temple of Zeus with a golden sickle by a boy of pure Greek blood whose parents were still living; the crown thus had a religious significance.

After the day's activities contestants and their friends joined in revelry and song. Crowned victors led a procession of friends who lighted the way with torches. The procession ended with a banquet given in honor of the victor by the people of his community.[1]

OTHER CELEBRATED GAMES

Three other games gained prominence during the sixth century B.C. The Pythian Games, held at Delphi in honor of Apollo, were celebrated during the third year of each Olympiad. Prizes included a laurel wreath and palm branch. The Nemean Games were celebrated every other year in the valley of Nemea in Argolis. Victors were crowned with parsley and palm branches. According to legend these games were instituted by Hercules in honor of his father, Jupiter, but later they became a feature of the worship of Hercules. After 582 B.C. the Isthmian Games, which honored Poseidon, were held during the second and fourth years of each Olympiad in the southern part of the Isthmus of Corinth. A wreath of parsley and palm branches was awarded victors; later the Romans substituted wreaths of pine branches.

Many lesser games were held frequently throughout the peninsula. Naturally these were scheduled not to conflict with the four national games.

THE STADIUM

What were the physical facilities of the Greek stadium really like? For a better understanding of these, we must turn to the findings of archaeologists and students of Greek culture.

While Schliemann was excavating at the sites of Troy and

Mycenae, other archaeologists, financed by the German government, were busy at Olympia. In 1893 Charles Diehl published a detailed report on Greek stadiums, gymnasiums, and public buildings.[2] And in 1910 and 1930 Norman E. Gardiner, an English classical scholar and sports enthusiast, contributed valuable interpretations of Greek athletics.[1, 3] Between 1936 and 1940 Oscar Broneer, Acting Director of the American School of Classical Studies at Athens, guided excavations at Corinth. His reports provide a description of Corinthian stadiums.[4]

Every Greek city that sponsored an athletic festival erected a parallelogram-shaped stadium about 200 to 210 yards long and 30 yards wide and enclosed or flanked by either a natural or artificial embankment. Distances of the various foot races were determined by the length of the stadium, or the *stade.* The *stade* race was one of 200 yards or more, and the *diaulos,* the double race, was the equivalent of two *stades,* or approximately 400 yards. The long race, or the *dolichos,* was 7 to 24 *stades.* The Olympic *dolichos* consisted of twenty-four *stades,* or slightly over 2½ miles. Races for boys and girls were fractional parts of a *stade;* boys sometimes ran one-half and girls one-sixth of a *stade.*

In the early days the starting and finishing points were marked by javelins thrust into the ground, but as the number of competitors and the wealth of the Greek city-states increased, the javelin was replaced by a line of stone slabs flush to the ground. Two parallel grooves cut in the stone slabs about 7 inches apart suggest that athletes toed the marks in an upright position, one foot behind the other, waiting for the start of the race.[1]

Broneer reports that chest-high wooden barriers were employed at the start of races during the Isthmian games in Corinth.[4] Arranged in the lanes like a series of narrowed jumping standards in juxtaposition, the wooden crossbars were dropped simultaneously by the starter who manipulated a system of cords. The cords from each barrier were joined together in an underground channel which led to an open pit to the rear of the runners. The starter in the pit gathered all the cords in one hand, as a chariot driver would the reins of his horses, and with a jerk released the runners. This method, which confirms the use of the upright start, certainly had some undesirable features, but it is certainly a tribute to Greek ingenuity.

Without lanes *stade* runners tended to cluster and interfere with one another, while *diaulos* and *dolichos* runners fought for position at the turn. To meet these problems, the Greeks finally devised a system of waist-high stone posts set four feet apart at the start and finish of the *stade*. These posts served as a kind of lane for *stade* runners and a turning post for *diaulos* and *dolichos* runners.

Some stadiums were more elaborate than others. The Panatheniac stadium in Athens—first dedicated in 330 B.C., rebuilt of marble in A.D. 143 to accommodate 50,000, and restored for the Olympic Games in 1896—has 46 rows of marble seats raised on a 6-foot marble base. Stone seats date from about the fifth century B.C.; very few stadiums provided marble seats. About 250 B.C. more elaborate stone seats were built near the center of the race course; they probably were reserved for victors and dignitaries. The curved sphendone, or completed horseshoe, with its rows of seats did not appear until later. Under Roman influence architectural design approached that of the circus, and both ends of the stadium were provided with sphendones.[23]

EVENTS OF THE PANHELLENIC GAMES

RUNNING

The *stade* and *diaulos* attracted many contestants. At the Olympic Stadium places were provided for twenty competitors. The races often were run in heats, with as few contestants for each heat as was compatible with spectator interest. Presumably the judges wanted as many top-flight runners in the final heat as possible to create an exciting race and to make the winner earn his crown. Lots—marine shells upon which were etched the letters of the Greek alphabet—were drawn for heats and positions. It was first place or nothing in the heats; there were no awards for second- or third-place runners.

The athlete ran barefoot and naked. Only contestants in the race in armor started in the kneeling position; in all other races runners started in a standing position, toeing the grooved lines on the stone slab (the crouch start was not introduced until the early 1900s). Undoubtedly, our scientifically trained, spike-shoed runners are far superior to their ancient Greek counterparts.

The Greeks enjoyed comparing the speed of "this" year's runners with the feats of "yesterday's" heroes. Most Greek boys probably knew of the athlete who raced a horse from Coronea to Thebes and beat it. Herodotus tells how Pheidippides ran from Athens to Sparta—150 miles—in two days. And it is Pheidippides' bringing the news of victory from Marathon to Athens, a distance of 26 miles and 285 yards, that is commemorated in the modern marathon.

Toward the close of the sixth century, the race in armor was introduced—probably as an attempt to restore athletic exercises to their former status as military exercises. But the event did not appeal to the specialized athlete. There were many variations of this race. At Olympia and Athens it was a two-*stade* race in length, at Nemea four *stades,* and at Platea (Sparta) fifteen *stades.* Contestants wore tunic, helmet, and greaves, and carried a shield.[1, 5]

JUMPING

The Greeks practiced the running and the standing broad jumps with or without weights (halteres). There is no evidence that they were familiar with the high jump or the pole vault. In the running broad jump they used a threshold, or take-off, made of wood or stone; it served as a point of reference, not a limitation as in the modern broad jump. We know from vases that the take-off point was marked by an upright javelin or stone post. The jumping pit area, called the *skamma,* was dug up with pickaxes or mattocks and the surface leveled. A proverbial expression for the accomplishment of a difficult feat was "to jump beyond the *skamma.*" Phayllus supposedly jumped 55 feet with weights but went 5 feet beyond the *skamma* and broke his leg. In the games individual jumps were marked by pegs at the side of the *skamma;* the best jump was measured by a 6-cubit rod placed end over end (a cubit is the length of the forearm from the elbow to the end of the middle finger, or approximately 18 inches).

The metal or stone halteres used in the running and standing broad jump weighed 3 to 10 pounds. Our dumbbell, although different in shape, probably was derived from the halteres. The modern jumper depends upon his steps and tries to reach his maximum speed at take-off. The jumper with weights depends partly on his run and partly on the forward thrust created by the upward swing of the weights. To explain Phayllus' extraordinary jump, it was erroneously suggested that the Greeks used a form of hop, skip, and jump. On the strength of this explanation, the hop, skip, and jump was introduced in the first modern Olympic Games held at Athens in 1896.[1]

THE DISCUS THROW

The discus appeared between the Homeric Age and 776 B.C., but exactly when and where we do not know. Ancient Greek fishermen used flat stones to secure nets drying in the sun and wind. Since throwing is a natural and satisfying activity, sailing flat stones through the air or skipping them on the water might have been the initial step in the evolution of discus throwing.

The first discuses were made of stone and were roughly circular and thicker at the center than at the circumference. Later, metal discuses were used. Most unearthed discuses measure 6 to 9 inches in diameter and weigh from 3 to 9 pounds; one is 11 inches in diameter and weighs 15 pounds. Lighter discuses were used by the boys in the palaestra, the heavier ones by men in the gymnasium and games.

The area from which the discus was thrown was called the *balbis*. Philostratus provides a detailed description of discus throwing and some information about the *balbis* in a passage in which he recounts how Apollo killed Hyacinthus with a discus:

> The *balbis* is small and sufficient for one man, marked off except for behind, and it supports the right leg, the front part of the body leaning forward, while it takes the weight off the other leg which is to be swung forward and follows through with the right hand. The thrower is to bend his head to the right and stop so as to catch a glimpse of his right side and to throw the diskos with a ropelike pull, putting all the force of the right side into the throw.[1]

The unmarked rear area indicates that the discus thrower could take as many steps as he wished from the rear but could not step on or over the front and side lines.

The Greeks employed a one-step and a three-step delivery. The one-step throw approximated the modern standing practice throw; the athlete stood one stride away from the front line of the *balbis* with both feet together. After several preliminary swings, he stepped forward with the left foot and released the discus without a reverse to maintain balance. Myron's bronze *Discobolus* is stepping toward the *balbis* with his right foot as the right hand is about to release the discus—an unnatural movement. Von Donop attributes Myron's choice of movement to whim or sense of beauty rather than any attempt at accurate portrayal.[6]

The three-step throw compares favorably with our three-step bowling delivery, and the discus even approximated the pattern of movement described by a bowling ball. The thrower started from the rear of the *balbis,* standing with feet together or in stride position, with the discus held high over his head balanced on both hands; he stepped left, right, and left, and released the discus in an almost erect position. Some scholars doubt that this style was used, but it does explain the upright posture of the athlete at the open end of the *balbis* in Costas Dimitiriadis' *Discus Thrower,* which is the copy of a bronze (*ca.* 400 B.C.) found near Rome.

Athletes practiced with their own discuses, and, of course, these varied in size and weight. Contestants in games probably agreed upon one discus. Individual throws were marked with pegs and the best throw was measured with a rod. Since there were such wide variations in the physical specifications of ancient discuses, the attainments of the Greek athlete cannot meaningfully be compared with modern records. Phayllus, considered an outstanding performer in his time, hurled the discus 95 feet.

THE JAVELIN THROW

During the Peloponnesian War the Greeks discovered the value of the javelin for light-armed foot soldiers and cavalry. Consequently, javelin throwing received special attention in the palaestra and gymnasium. At the lesser festivals javelin throwing was a separate event, and in the more important game it was included as one of the events in the pentathlon.

The javelin was a straight wooden shaft about the height of the average Greek male (5 feet, 7 inches) and the thickness of the index finger. In practice long-distance throws the shaft was provided with a blunt ferule for weight and balance. The pointed ferule was employed in target practice.

The javelin used in games was a light weapon thrown with the aid of a 12-to-18-inch leather thong, or *amentum,* firmly bound around the center of the shaft. The thrower inserted his first or first and middle fingers in a loop fashioned at the end of the thong. By shifting the *amentum* back of the center of gravity, greater distance could be secured, but at the expense of accuracy. Much like the rifling in a gun barrel, the *amentum* gave the javelin a rotary motion, which not only helped maintain direction but also increased carrying and penetrating ability.

The *amentum* was widely employed throughout Central Europe. It was used by the Etruscans and Samnites and by the Danes in the early Iron Age. Caesar noted that the Gauls also employed the leather thong.

Two types of javelin throwing were practiced. In one the javelin was held horizontally, as in the Finnish style; in the other the point of the javelin was held upward, as in the American style. The horizontal style was ideal for the warrior or hunter, who walked along with his finger or fingers in the loop of the *amentum* and the shaft of the javelin resting on his shoulder with the point downward. On sighting the enemy or game, he simply raised the javelin to the ready position and let fly. Since speed was not required in games, the athlete carried his javelin with point upward and tail trailing. The Greeks used a throwing line and the reverse to maintain balance after delivery.

WRESTLING

The Greeks practiced upright and ground wrestling. In the upright, the style known during the Homeric period, the wrestlers started from the standing position and attempted to throw one another to the ground. The victor had to remain upright in two out of three throws. Upright wrestling required brute strength and some trickery, such as tripping and sudden shifting of weight. There were two favorite methods of making a throw: one involved turning the opponent's body against the hip and with a snap throwing him to the ground; the other involved lifting the opponent and slamming him to the ground.

In ground wrestling, contestants vied in an area watered until it became muddy. The mud, supposedly beneficial for the skin, made it difficult to secure a hold.

As in a modern tournament wrestlers (and boxers) drew lots for position, and if the number of contestants was greater than a power of two, byes were drawn. The Greek athlete regarded it as a distinction to win a tournament without drawing a bye. Weights were not matched; the Greeks evidently left this problem to the process of natural selection.

THE PENTATHLON

The pentathlon was a combination of the five events—running, jumping, discus and javelin throwing, and wrestling—which constituted the core of military training in the palaestra and gymnasium. A pentathlete developed not only skill as a warrior but also the beautiful body evident in Greek sculpture.

The pentathlon was introduced about 708 B.C., probably to determine the best all-round athlete. Our knowledge of the pentathlon is very sketchy. It is likely that the foot race came first; and after the jump, the discus and javelin throwing; with wrestling, the more tiring event, last.[1] There is no record of how the winner was determined.

BOXING

By Homer's time boxing was highly specialized. Until the fifth century, 10-to-12-foot-long oxhide thongs made supple by being dressed in fat were used as protection for the hands and fingers. From Philostratus we learn that these "soft gloves" were wound several times around the four fingers and the knuckles and passed diagonally across the palm and back of the hand and wound around the wrist and sometimes also up the forearm.

During the fourth century the soft gloves were replaced by the "sharp thongs" (shown on the hands of the *Seated Boxer* in the Terme in Rome), a glove and a hard leather ring which encircled the fingers at the knuckles and extended to the elbow, where it ended in a thick padding of sheep wool to protect the forearm. The sharp thongs were used in the games until the second century B.C.

The cestus, a Roman innovation, was never used by the Greeks in their games. It consisted of a thong beaded with lead and so wrapped over the fingers and knuckles that the smooth thong passed over the palm of the hand. The boxer clenched a hard ball or a cylinder to make the blow even more damaging. His arms and shoulders were protected by a padded fleece sleeve. A variation of the cestus was the iron-spiked glove—a series of metal projections molded with an opening at the base so that they might be strung like beads on a leather thong.

In boxing the Greeks did not have a ring nor did they divide bouts into rounds. There was very little infighting; the main objective was to strike the head. A boxer could continue to strike a fallen opponent; defeat could be admitted by raising the hand. The fight continued until one combatant was unconscious or gave up. Since no weight classifications were employed and competition was open to anyone who wished to accept a challenge, boxing was monopolized by heavyweights. Boys' boxing, no doubt, was more closely regulated than men's.[1]

THE PANKRATION

The pankration has been called a rough-and-tumble fight, a form of jujitsu, and a combination of boxing and wrestling. The object of the pankration was to force the opponent by any means within the rules to admit defeat or to damage him physically so that defeat was obvious. Rules were strictly enforced by an official provided with a rod. If, for example, a contestant was gouging an eye or refused to release a stranglehold on his slowly dying opponent, the official applied the rod until the gouging stopped or the hold was released. A competitor could admit defeat at any time—if he was able—by simply holding up one finger.

In his discussion of the death of Arrhichion, who collapsed at the moment he defeated his opponent in the pankration, Philostratus comments: "Pankratiasts practice a hazardous style of wrestling. They must employ falls backward which are not safe for the wrestler and grips in which victory must be obtained by falling. They must have skill in various methods of strangling; they also wrestle with an opponent's ankle, and twist his arm, besides hitting and jumping on him, for all these practices belong to the pankration, only biting and gouging being prohibited."[1]

There was much preliminary sparring, striking, or kicking in the pankration. The pankratiast used various leg holds, ankle twists (Arrhichion in one bout forced his opponent to yield by twisting his ankle out of the socket), and stomach throws (in which the contestant grabbed his opponent's arms, fell on his back, and in the same motion planted a foot in his stomach to throw him over his head). Another favorite hold was the "ladder trick," in which one contestant jumped on the other's back and wrapped his legs about his opponent's body and his arms about his neck in a stranglehold. Most bouts ended on the ground where striking was ineffective and punishing holds more useful.

CHARIOT AND HORSE RACES

Chariot races in Panhellenic games differed on four major counts from those Homer observed: (1) a turning goal was provided so that races could be run in several laps rather than on a straightaway; (2) a greater number of chariots was entered; (3) barriers were arranged to eliminate confusion at the start; (4) horses were bred selectively for greater speed and endurance. And the two-horse chariot of Homer's period finally was replaced by the four-horse chariot. Because of the great expense involved in breeding horses and maintaining a stable, chariot racing was a wealthy man's sport.[7]

Until the twenty-fifth Olympic Games, races took place in the stadium. Because of the increased number of entrants a course, a *hippodromos,* was built for chariot and horse racing. From Pausanias' detailed description—even to the location of the statues of victors—we learn that the hippodrome was situated southeast of the stadium and extended roughly parallel to it. German excavators estimated that the Olympic hippodrome must have been 2,526 feet—approximately a half mile long. The starting point adjoined one end of the stadium and the turning goal, where charioteers fought for position, was far beyond the stadium proper. Negotiating the turning goal, a dangerous feat, thrilled the often more than 100,000 spectators. Once around the goal, drivers were greeted with a trumpet blast to encourage them onward.

The first horse race, or Olympic Derby, was held at the thirty-third Olympiad (648 B.C.), 22 years after the introductoin of the chariot race. Three hundred years later, Philip of Macedon sent both chariot and race horses to the 108th Olympic Games; his horse won. Philip commemorated this victory on an issue of silver tetradrachmae. In the seventy-first Olympiad a race was introduced for mares in which the riders raced on horseback for the first lap and dismounted and ran on foot beside their mounts for the last lap.

OTHER PANHELLENIC CONTESTS

Contests for trumpeters and heralds date from the first Panhellenic games. Winners played honored roles in the games. The herald announced the names of competitors and the winner of each event, and the trumpeter started all contests and gained the attention of the crowd and contestants when an announcement was to be made. Dramatists, historians, poets, and artists vied for awards at the Olympic and the Pythian games. The Nemean Games featured competition in the cithara, the Greek harp.[1]

PARTICIPATION IN THE OLYMPIC GAMES

While athletes from Corinth, Megara, Sicyon, Hyperesia, Athens, and Thebes appeared frequently among the list of winners during early Olympic games, for more than 140 years (from 720 until 580 B.C.) Spartan athletes were preeminent. Aristotle attributed Spartan success to their efficient system of physical and military education. The Spartans not only added to the prestige of the Olympic Games, but also gave a new impetus to athleticism which eventually led to professionalism.

After the period of Spartan supremacy more of the Greek colonies were drawn into the Olympic Games. These colonies did much to break down Athenian and Spartan domination and to bring about a feeling of nationalism to the Olympic Games.

THE DECLINE OF THE PANHELLENIC GAMES

Even in the sixth century B.C. successful athletes were excessively honored.[1, 8] They were immortalized in statues and glorified in hymns. In the succeeding century rewards became somewhat more substantial. Solon awarded Athenian athletes 500 drachmae (about $100) for a victory in the Olympic Games and smaller amounts for success in the minor festivals. Athenian Olympic victors were given a place of honor at public events, provided with free grain from the state's warehouses, and exempted from taxation.

City-state rivalry accelerated the drift toward professionalism. Croton, famous for its athletes, tried to outdo Sybaris by establishing a festival which was supposed to have dwarfed the Olympic Games in importance. Astylus, a famous Croton runner, performed for anyone who would make an attractive offer. He won the *stade* and *diaulos* races for Croton in 488 and 484 B.C.; in 480 he ran for Syracuse. The Crotons destroyed his statue and turned his home into a prison. Eupolus, a Thessalian boxer, bribed an opponent to let him win. Both athletes were heavily fined when the Olympic officials found out. The fines were cast into six bronze figures of Zeus, called *Zanes,* which, with a warning inscription to all athletes, were placed at the entrance of the Olympic stadium.

The tramp athlete appeared during the fifth century B.C. Since games were staggered to avoid conflicts, the "tramp" could make the rounds, picking up prizes as he went. Theaganes of Thason won more than 1400 prizes traveling the circuit. Under these circumstances athletics became a strenuous and exacting pursuit,[9] and the professional had to specialize in one or two events and secure the services of an expert coach who controlled every detail of his life—particularly his diet. Of no interest to the professional was the "ideal" body. By the time of the Peloponnesian War, "athlete" began to mean a "professional," and the young men, who had once been eager to participate in the games, began to lose interest.[10]

In his play *Autolycus* (only fragments of which survive) Euripides sums up the case against professionalism: "Of all the countless evils throughout Hellas none is worse than the race of athletes. . . . Slaves of their belly and their jaw they know not how to live well.

. . . In youth they strut about in splendor, the idols of the city, but when bitter old age comes upon them they are cast aside like worn out cloaks. I blame the customs of the Hellenes who gather to see such men honoring useless pleasures."[8]

THE EFFECT OF THE MACEDONIAN VICTORY ON THE GAMES

In 338 B.C. the Greeks were conquered by the Macedonians. Philip and his son, Alexander the Great, recognized and admired the Greeks' intellectual superiority, and Philip was familiar and sympathetic with the games. Indeed, Philip instituted the festival of Aegae to honor the marriage of his daughter Cleopatra, and he was regularly represented in Olympic horse and chariot races. Alexander, on the other hand, celebrated his victories at the festivals of Aegae and Dium but eliminated athletic contests and offered prizes instead for tragic poets and musicians and entertained the spectators with wild beast hunts. He regarded athletics with contempt and believed that palaestra exercises had no practical military value. Nevertheless, Alexander considered Olympia the true capital of the Greeks, and he, like his father, financed many improvements in the facilities there.

ROMAN INFLUENCE ON THE GAMES

Even before they defeated the Macedonians and made the Greek peninsula a province, the Romans had fixed attitudes toward the Greeks and their athletics. Exercise, the Roman believed, was beneficial to health, and recreation was necessary for relaxation. But what sensible individual would want to devote all his time to succeeding in competitive sports? Furthermore, it was beneath Roman dignity to submit to months of rigorous exercise under a tyrannical trainer, often a man of low birth, and then to climax it all by making a spectacle of himself in the nude before his friends and fellow citizens. This attitude was reenforced when the Romans discovered the extent and effects of professionalism in Greek athletics. It is no wonder that by the end of the first hundred years of Roman domination the Greek festivals had been nearly abandoned.

The Greeks, however, "Hellenized" the Romans as they had the

Macedonians. In 80 B.C. the dictator Sulla ordered the 175th Olympic Games held in Rome (only the boys' foot race was left to Olympia). Sulla may have planned to keep the Olympic Games permanently in Rome, but he died in 79 B.C. during the Olympiad. His interest in the games, however, was significant because it indicated a more lenient Roman attitude toward the Greek festivals.

As the century before the birth of Christ closed, the Romans revived the old Greek festivals and built new gymnasiums and race courses. Members of wealthy Roman families entered the chariot races at Olympia; inscriptions testify that a Tiberius was victorious in a chariot race and that a few Olympic Games later a Germanicus Caesar won the same event. Generally the Roman influence on Greek athletic competition was brutalizing and degrading. Gladiatorial contests had been introduced to the East by the Romans in the second century B.C. The crowds found the sadistic contests to their taste. Boxing, harsh enough with the Greek sharp thong gloves, became a deadly sport with the introduction of the Roman cestus and spiked glove. The Roman appetite for bloody spectacle spread throughout the colonies. And so was closed one of the greatest epochs in the history of athletics.[10]

THE FINALE

The last recorded victor in the Olympic Games was Valerius Electus of Sinope, who won the herald's contest in the 259th Olympic Games in A.D. 235. By A.D. 325 the once powerful Greek city-states had lost all autonomy and were but components of Constantine's centralized empire. Greek festivals which honored pagan gods were considered sacrilegious by the Christian emperor. Constantine dismantled the Delphi stadium and gymnasium and carried their treasures to Constantinople. Finally Theodosius I, Byzantine emperor and zealous Christian, and relentless persecutor of the heathen, abolished the Olympic Games in A.D. 394.

Theodosius' act was symbolic of both the triumph of Christianity and the final dissolution of the Greek educational system. The last mention of the gymnasium and palaestra appears in the works of St. Basil, Himerius, and Synesius (A.D. 370 to 400). By their time athletic competition with its evils of professionalism had passed into the limbo of history. Although Greek youths continued to play organized games and the traditional ball games for recreational purposes, the educational program focused almost completely on developing the intellect. As Marrou observed: "No one denies that physical education was quite dead in the Christian era and its death was a natural one. . . . It simply died of old age."[11] Henri Marrou could have been kinder. Physical education and all it implied was a temporary victim of social and religious evolution. It simply awaited the day of resurrection, for its principles were clearly defined and its practice was indisputably as ageless as man himself.

The Christian moralists and apologists understandably might have veen critical of Greek physical education on the grounds of its nudity, implied homosexuality,[5] and aggrandizement of the human body. Strangely enough, early Christian polemicists did not develop these arguments. Their brief was not with physical education as an important part of the total education of man—physical, moral, and spiritual—but rather with athletic competition as a spectacle and as a breeding ground for professionalism. Though clouded by other issues, selfish or altruistic, this Christian attitude toward physical education and wholesome amateur athletic competition (as the Greeks knew it in the Golden Era) has persisted through the centuries.

NOTES

1. E. Norman Gardiner. *Athletics in the Ancient World.* Oxford: The Clarendon Press, 1930, pp. 43–44. Edward M. Plummer. "The Olympic Games in Ancient Times." *American Physical Education Review,* 3:1 (March, 1898), 1–18; 3:2 (June, 1898), 93–106.
2. Charles Diehl. *Excursions in Greece.* London: H. Grevel and Company, 1893, pp. 210–293.
3. E. Norman Gardiner. *Greek Athletic Sports and Festivals.* London: Macmillan and Company, 1910.
4. Oscar Broneer. *Ancient Corinth, A Guide to Excavations.* (Fourth Edition.) Athens: American School of Classical Studies at Athens, 1947. (Also, see reports of 1954, American School of Classical Studies at Athens.)
5. Thomas Woody. *Life and Education in Early Societies.* New York: The

Macmillan Company, 1949, 374–395; Henri I. Marrou. *A History of Education in Antiquity*. (Translated by George Lamb.) New York: Sheed and Ward, 1956, pp. 119–122, 131–132.

6. G. von Donop. "Zum Diskobol des Myron!" *Die Leibesübungen,* 17 (1928), 432.
7. Alfred J. Butler. *Sports in Classic Times*. New York: E. P. Dutton and Company, 1930, pp. 39–45.
8. Rachel Sargent Robinson. *Sources for the History of Greek Athletics*. (Lithoprinted by Cushing-Malloy, Inc., Ann Arbor.) Illini Union Book Store, University of Illinois, Urbana, 1955, 115–117, 191–197.
9. "Philostratus: Concerning Gymnastics." (Translated by Thomas Woody.) *Research Quarterly,* **VII,** 2 (May, 1936), 3–26.
10. R. Tait McKenzie. "The Chronicle of the Amateur Spirit." *American Physical Education Review,* 16:2 (February, 1911), 75–94.
11. Henri I. Marrou. *A History of Education in Antiquity*. (Translated by George Lamb.) New York: Sheed and Ward, 1956, 229–249, 265–291.

Chapter 4

THE ROMANS

EARLY HISTORY OF THE ROMANS

FOR approximately one thousand years—from *ca.* 1800 B.C. until *ca.* 700 B.C.—northern European tribes periodically migrated to the Italian peninsula. Somewhere between 1000 and 800 B.C the Etruscans settled about the Tiber and Arno rivers. According to Herodotus these people came from Lydia in Asia Minor; others hypothesize that they were a part of the pre-Italic Mediterranean race which had kindred shoots in Spain, Asia Minor, and the Caucasus. The Etruscans, like the Homeric Greeks, established a closed aristocratic society and reduced the natives to serfdom. Sensuous and cruel, they enjoyed brutal spectacles in the arena. Their religion, unlike the cheerful and imaginative Indo-European creeds, featured the worship of demon gods. The Etruscans undoubtedly traded with the Greeks; they adopted a modified Greek alphabet and Greek weapons and equipment. They also knew something about Greek athletics and even borrowed the Greek funeral celebration, to which they added bizarre variations.[1]

The Etruscan aristocrat's luxurious life, his banqueting, hunting, and love-making, is pictured on tomb walls (the most famous is the Tomba della Bighe of Corneto). Sports, the wall paintings reveal, figured prominently, especially wrestling and chariot racing. But aristocrats were spectators; apparently boxers, wrestlers, and charioteers were drawn only from the lower class and slaves, as were dancers and other entertainers. Famous for their ability to handle and breed horses, the Etruscans probably introduced cavalry drills and chariot races to the peninsula.

Gladiatorial combat may have originated with the Etruscans. Slaves fighting to the death provided an evening's entertainment for an aristocrat's banquet. The practice probably originated with the sacrificial offerings of a human being, usually a prisoner of war, at the funeral of a distinguished chieftain. In time, captives were given a sporting chance for survival—they were armed and loosed on each other at the burial tomb. The "winner," if there was one, lived at least until the next interment.

REPUBLIC AND EMPIRE

The absolute monarchy introduced by the Etruscans gave way to the republic of the Romans, their successors. The senate, or council of fathers whose members were patricians, or nobles, was retained. Officials were chosen by the other legislative division, the assembly, to which all non-noble citizens belonged. In the early years of the republic the plebeians, exploited by the patricians, demanded that all laws be put into written form. Between 452 and 450 B.C., a commission produced the Twelve Tables, the basis of all Roman law including the Justinian Code, the Roman intellect's greatest contribution to Western civilization.[1, 2]

Carthage, the Macedonian Empire (including Athens), Gaul, Britain—all fell before the aggressive republic. But during its last hundred years the republic was racked by civil strife, in part the consequence of conflicting ideals and ambitions. During this period many famous names were written on history's pages—Cicero, Pompey, Caesar, Brutus, Crassus, Lepidus, Anthony, Octavius.

Octavius survived the civil wars and emerged supreme. As Augustus he accepted supreme power from the senate. During his reign (31 B.C.–A.D. 4) Rome reached the height of its glory. He bequeathed to his successors an empire so well organized that, despite many utterly incompetent rulers, it thrived for almost two centuries. And it was only after another 250 years that the last chapter was written. Rome succumbed finally to the barbarian onslaught. In 455 all that remained of the empire was Rome itself, and in that year Rome was completely sacked by the Vandals.[1]

EDUCATION DURING THE REPUBLIC

At first the father (who often depended on a slave-tutor) was responsible for his son's education; formal schools did not exist. For three hundred years the "academic curriculum" consisted chiefly of the Twelve Tables, which had to be memorized. Some use was made of biographical and traditional material relating to early Roman heroes, real and fictitious. Unlike the Greeks, the Romans had not produced a rich literature. Not until the early years of the Empire was the *Aeneid* written. Early republican Romans had no equivalent to the *Iliad* and the *Odyssey*.

The Twelve Tables provided a guide to, if not a complete expression of, Roman ideals. Hence Roman education was very practical, based in large part on the definition of property rights. It was largely from these laws that the Roman derived his concept of individuality and his code of ethics.

In his sixteenth or seventeenth year the Roman youth became a full-fledged citizen (*toga virilis*) and was subject to military training—instruction in the use of weapons and tactics and conditioning exercises.[4, 5]

EDUCATION DURING THE EMPIRE

The Greeks, vanquished in the Macedonian Wars, exerted a profound influence on Roman education. By the middle of the second century B.C. a school system which provided elementary, secondary, and higher education was well established. Most parents sent their sons and daughters to elementary schools, but some citizens preferred the old system of instruction at home.

In the elementary school (*ludus*) reading, writing, and some arithmetic were taught by a slave or a freedman. Seutonius refers to these as the schools of literators or grammatists. There was also a higher type of elementary school in which Latin and Greek (and the *Odyssey* in translation) were taught. By 150 B.C. Latin literature translated from, or written in imitation of, the Greek provided the basis of grammar school work. For secondary education the child attended the school of rhetoricians, where he was trained in oratory and debate. Grammarians also taught in these schools.

Philosophy was emphasized in higher education. Wealthy Romans hired Greek tutors and sent their sons to Greek universities, usually Athens or Rhodes, to complete their education. Cicero was 27 when he studied at Athens and Caesar 25 when he attended Rhodes to study rhetoric.

Considering the times, the University of Athens was large. Theophratus, who had succeeded Aristotle as a professor, drew more than 2000 students, many from other countries, some of them poor. Students who could afford to stay for the year dressed alike and attended the same lectures. Physical and military exercises were required "subjects." Like theology in the Middle Ages, philosophy was the keenest intellectual exercise and the only source of light on the problems of life and destiny.[4, 6]

Education of Roman Women

A plebeian girl was trained in household chores by her mother. The patrician girl was educated at home by a slave or in a coeducational school. Music and dancing (rhythmical movements of the upper part of the body and the arms) were emphasized. She learned to play and sing with the lute or lyre.

Parents sought to assure their daughters a happy and early marriage. For most Roman girls marriage was a sudden release from surveillance and restriction. As a matron she had full authority in her home and was never secluded. She could attend a banquet or the circus, solicit votes for her husband in the streets, make speeches, dress according to her taste, and belong to any religious group. Many Roman women worked as seamstresses, weavers, or fishmongers. Others were physicians, lawyers, managers of estates, and business executives. The story of the influence of women on Roman politics will never be fully known.[7, 8]

ROMAN PHYSICAL AND MILITARY EDUCATION

Campus Martius

Named in honor of the god of war, the Campus Martius was a 300-acre, level plain between the Tiber River and the Capitoline and Quirinal hills that served as an assembly point for men called to arms and a place to conduct military exercises and maneuvers. Here, in the days of the republic, young men ran foot races, boxed, wrestled, threw the discus and javelin, and practiced archery. They played several ball games, including one similar to handball.[5]

The Campus Martius was the site also of festivals and games. One of the oldest Roman festivals was the Equiria, a horse race run over the plain. Seutonius describes the spectacular games held there in honor of Julius Caesar. Noble youths took part in chariot and horse races and cavalry drills. And there was a sham battle between two "armies" of 500 foot soldiers, 30 cavalry, and 20 elephants.

During the last years of the republic the Campus Martius was converted into a suburban pleasure ground for the citizens, with shady walks, baths, and theaters. Eventually Agrippa erected there the old Pantheon, and Augustus built a magnificent tomb for himself.

THE "JUVENES"

During his reign Augustus promoted the *Juvenes,* clubs organized for the purpose of training the sons of patricians for civil and military service. In organization and spirit they resembled to some extent the modern Boy Scouts, except, of course, for the class distinction. Each unit dedicated itself to a deity, a famous general, or a reigning emperor. The Pompeian club, for example, was called *Juvenes Venerii Pompeiani,* or the Young Men's Venus Association. Another took the exclusive title *Nongenti,* or the Nine Hundred. Each club had a president, secretary, and treasurer, and since expenses—maintenance of the club buildings, exhibitions, and prizes—were heavy the boys sought the patronage of a wealthy citizen who would repay the honor by underwriting the costs.

Instruction, focused on physical and military education, resembled the type of training provided the Athenian youth during the first year of his military service. The scope of the *Juvenes'* physical education program was probably similar to that of the Greeks because a gymnasium usually adjoined the clubhouse. At Pompeii the *Juvenes* had their headquarters at the gymnasium near the amphitheater in the older part of the city; they also owned an up-to-date gymnasium with elaborate baths and a clubhouse. Members were taught to use weapons of all types, often by ex-gladiators. Although Augustus forbade the nobility to appear in the arena, some older boys who were club champions did fight in gladiatorial contests.[10]

THE GAME OF TROY

Horseman ship was emphasized in the training of the *Juvenes.* Seutonius notes that Augustus gave frequent performances of the game of Troy, popular among the boys, "thinking it a time-honored and worthy custom for the flower of nobility to become known in this way."[9] In the *Aeneid* Vergil describes the game of Troy as a type of cavalry drill executed by a double company of young and older boys. It contained many elements of the modern cavalry drill, with formations in multiples of two, wheels right and left, circles, and serpentines. An inscription on a wall in Pompeii to a boy named Septimius, who must have been an exceptional performer, reads: "If you have seen the skill with which Septimius performs the serpent ride, whether you are a lover of the shows or of horses, you can hold the scales level [you will be satisfied]."[10]

Performers in the game of Troy occasionally were thrown from their mounts. When a Nonius Asprenas was injured, Augustus presented him with a gold necklace and allowed him and his descendants to bear the surname Torquatus ("adorned with a necklace"). Shortly after this incident, Augustus was forced to discontinue the game because Asinius Pollio, an influential politician, spoke forcibly against it after his grandson had fallen from his horse and broken his leg.[10]

GRECO-ROMAN SHOWS

The gods honored by the Greeks in their dramas and festivals were "related" to the Roman gods. This was another instance of the victor borrowing heavily from the vanquished. In the last days of the republic ambitious generals and politicians, to win popular support, imported Greek dramas and festivals in honor of the gods or in commemoration of some successful undertaking.

Greek tragedies, comedies, and satires were presented in honor of the gods Bacchus, Venus, and Apollo. But the Romans were not as sophisticated theatergoers as the Greeks; to make the plays more palatable, rope dancers, tumblers, and jugglers gave before-and-after performances. As public taste degenerated, the drama was further corrupted.

According to Livy, the Romans had their first opportunity to witness Greek athletic games in 186 B.C. On this particular occasion the athletes were imported from the Greek peninsula, and to assure a good reception for the affair in case the crowd reacted unfavorably, African lions and panthers were also provided. In 80 B.C. Greek athletes were brought to Rome to compete in the 175th Olympic Games.

Augustus was particularly enthusiastic about the Greek games because of their religious significance and their usefulness in perpetuating national traditions. He was responsible for improving the physical plant at Olympia. Augustus also established the Actian Games in honor of his victory over the fleets of Anthony and Cleopatra at Actium (31 B.C.). These games, held every four years, included athletics, musical and equestrian competition, and a regatta. Victors received crowns and bore the title of Actiads.

Greco-Roman games, however, were considered by the masses tame and boring compared to the exciting and spectacular shows of the circus and the amphitheater.[10]

PRIVATE AND PUBLIC GAMES

During the last century of the republic the number and extravagance of private and public games increased rapidly. At first these games, free to the public, were given in honor of the gods at the expense of the state; later they were exploited by politicians until all their religious significance was lost. Games became the chief source of entertainment for the lower classes and the increasing crowds of unemployed. Politicians were criticized or praised according to the amount of money they spent on the games and their degree of novelty.

Private and public games were held in the circus. The word "circus" simply meant a ring, and *ludi circenses* were any kind of amusement staged in the ring. One of the characteristic "acts" was the chariot race, which required a large and level area. The first Roman race course, the Circus Maximus, was established in the valley between the Aventine and Palatine hills. Two thousand feet long and 600 feet wide, it accommodated 60,000 spectators. Augustus had the Circus Maximus enlarged to seat 200,000. After 200 B.C. several other circuses were built in and near Rome. Important among these were the Circus Flaminius (221 B.C.), Circus Caius and Nero (first century A.D.), and the Circus Maxentius (A.D. 309).

The typical Roman circus consisted of a long and comparatively narrow stretch of ground—the race course (arena)—which was almost surrounded by tiers of seats in the shape of a horseshoe. The arena was divided for almost two-thirds of its length by a wide wall called the *spina,* or backbone. The *spina* of the Circus Maxentius, for example, was 950 feet, or one-fifth of a mile, long. At each end of the *spina* were semicircular buttresses called *metae* which marked the inner line of the course at the turns. Once around the *spina* was a *curriculum,* or lap, and a fixed number of laps, usually seven, was called a *missus.* The total distance traveled by the charioteer at the Circus Maxentius (seven laps) was 2.7 miles and at the Circus Maximus 5.2 miles.

Barriers to keep the horses steady at the start and mark the finish line were located at the same open end of the horseshoe-shaped circus. Considering the fact that as many as twelve chariots competed, the sharp turns at the *metae,* and the sandy surface of the arena, speed certainly was not an essential factor. Charioteer and spectator found their excitement in the danger of the race. At first races were open to all who wished to show their horses or their skill in driving, but by the end of the republic teams and drivers were furnished by syndicates. The names of successful drivers (*aurigae*) were inscribed in a place of honor, and they were courted and feted by high and low. Publius Calpurnianus won 1127 races, Caius Diocles in twenty-four years won 4257 and earned $1,800,000, and Flavius Scorpus garnered 2048 by the time he was 27 years old.

PLACES OF EXHIBITION

The first gladiatorial combats took place at the graves of those being honored. These combats were then moved to the circus, but the *spina* blocked the spectators' view. The forum, their next location, also proved impractical because of the demands of public and private business and because seats had to be set up for each contest. The problem was finally resolved by the construction of the amphitheater with its circles of seats from which all could see.

Statilius Taurus built a wood and stone amphitheater in 29 B.C.; it was destroyed in the great fire during the reign of Nero. At the end of the first century B.C., the *amphitheatrum Flavius,* known later as the Coliseum, was constructed. Elliptical in shape, it covered an area of six acres. Underneath the entire building, including the arena, were subterranean chambers–rooms for the regiments of gladiators and props for scenes, dens for wild animals, and space for a large number of water and drainage pipes which could turn the arena into a small lake at a moment's notice, and drain it as quickly. The seating capacity of the Coliseum was 80,000, with standing room for 20,000 spectators.

THE GAMES OF THE AMPHITHEATER

The most important shows were the *venationes,* the hunt for wild beasts. In these, spectators witnessed full-scale hunts by experts; sometimes they were treated to animals hunting and killing their natural prey. Later the game was reversed so that beasts "hunted" men, often unarmed.

Augustus enumerated the games given during his reign: eight gladiatorial shows in which 10,000 gladiators fought and 26 *venationes* of wild beasts from Africa, 3500 of which were killed. On the funeral inscription of A. Clodius, his wife listed all the games he gave to celebrate his elections to office. In one, which lasted two days, he provided the following program: on the first day, a procession of bulls, bullfighters, and common pugilists (boxers who fought in troops like gladiators) in the forum; on the second day, thirty pairs of athletes (wrestlers), forty pairs of gladiators, *venationes,* bulls, bullfighters, bears, boars, and other animals in the amphitheater.[5]

THE GLADIATORS

Gladiatorial exhibitions, which had been popular among the Etruscans, were not revived by the Romans until the middle of the second century B.C. These affairs were financed first by wealthy citizens and later by the state. Augustus provided funds for "extraordinary shows" and set aside the month of December for gladiatorial exhibitions at public expense. All other gladiatorial shows were financed by public officials and private citizens.

During the republic most gladiators were drawn from prisoners of war who preferred death at the sword to slavery. As the demand for this type of entertainment increased, training schools were established during the time of Sulla, in which slaves were prepared for this "profession." Under Augustus and after, criminals (usually noncitizens) were sentenced to the arena or to become the hunted in the *venationes*. Roman citizens, both men and women, who sought a means of expiation or notoriety, volunteered for the arena. They were called *auctorati,* or volunteer gladiators.

Imperial training schools for gladiators were operated at public expense and were supervised by public officials. In addition, many private schools were financed by wealthy citizens to supply their own exhibitions. The schools produced efficient and deadly fighting machines. Gladiators were supervised by a trainer (*lanistae*) who maintained strict discipline, checked diet and sleep, prescribed regular exercise, and provided instruction in the use of weapons by experts (*doctores*).[5]

CLASSIFICATION OF GLADIATORS

Three pairs of gladiators fought at the funeral games of Brutus Pera (264 B.C.); as many as 500 pairs fought at exhibitions in the late empire. Gladiators were classified according to weapons and when they appeared on exhibition. The *Secutores* were armed with a sword (*gladius*) and a type of mace loaded with lead. The *Thraces* carried a scimitar, like those used by the Thracians. The *Myrmilliones* were armed with a shield and a short scythe and wore a distinctive fish ornament on their helmets. The Romans nicknamed these gladiators "Gauls"; the statue *The Dying Gaul* represents a *Myrmillio.* The *Retiarii* carried a trident in one hand, a net in the other. *Retiarii* often were pitted against *Myrmilliones,* and as the former, with his trident and net, pursued the latter, he cried out, "I do not want you, Gaul, but your fish!" The *Hoplomachi,* as the

Greek name implies, were dressed in full armor and carried sword and shield. There were many other classifications—for example, the *Caesariani,* who because of their bravery and skill fought only in exhibitions attended by the emperor, and the *Catervarii,* gladiators chosen from the various classifications to fight as a troop.[7]

By selective matching of these different types, it was possible to enhance the novelty of combat and vary the mode of death. Usually it was the people who decided the fate of the wounded combatant. If he had conducted himself with courage and skill, his pardon was granted. If he had shown cowardice, his death was a foregone conclusion. Spectators indicated "Let him live" by displaying the hand with the thumb doubled under the fingers; they doomed a man by extending the hand with the thumb raised and pointing toward the wounded gladiator.

THE ROMAN BATHS

Rome boasted many public baths, and the ruins of some of the great buildings that housed the baths, or *Thermae,* testify to the love of luxury prevalent during imperial days. Many baths were a combination of library, gymnasium, garden, and lecture room, and some even had handball courts. A bather could progress from a hot to a tepid pool and finally finish with a brisk, cool immersion. Some of the more famous baths were the Titus, Trajan, Caracalla, and Diocletian. The baths of Caracalla, which could accommodate 16,000 people at one time, measured a mile in circumference. Its many apartments, which contained pools of various temperature, were adorned with paintings, stuccowork, and statuary. During the Middle Ages the beautiful baths of the Western Roman Empire were abandoned, but the custom was preserved in the Eastern Empire and adopted by the Mohammedans.

NOTES

1. Charles Alexander Robinson. *Ancient History from Prehistoric Times to the Death of Justinian.* New York: The Macmillan Co., 1959, pp. 440–451, 452–471.

2. Paul Monroe. *Source Book of the History of Education for the Greek and Roman Period.* New York: The Macmillan Co., 1906, p. 337.
3. Crane Brinton, John B. Christopher, and Robert Lee Wolff. *A History of Civilization* (Second Edition). New Jersey: Prentice-Hall, Inc., 1962, pp. 173–189.
4. Henri I. Marrou. *A History of Education in Antiquity* (Translated by George Lamb). New York: Sheed and Ward, 1956, pp. 229–241, 265–291.
5. Thomas Woody. *Life and Education in Early Societies.* New York: The Macmillan Co., 1949, pp. 491–534, 664–668, 737–742.
6. A. S. Wilkins. *Roman Education.* Cambridge: The University Press, 1914, pp. 90–92.
7. Ludwig Friedlander. *Roman Life and Manners Under the Early Empire.* New York: E. P. Dutton and Co., 1908, pp. 228–267.
8. Frank F. Abbott. *Society and Politics in Ancient Rome.* New York: Charles Scribner and Sons, 1909, pp. 41–99.
9. Tranquilis Gaius Seutonius. *The Lives of the Twelve Caesars.* New York: The Modern Library, 1931.
10. Gardiner, E. Norman. *Athletics in the Ancient World.* Oxford: Clarendon Press, 1930, pp. 120, 124–127.
11. Harold W. Johnson. *The Private Life of the Romans.* New York: Scott, Foresman and Co., 903, p. 229.
12. Horatio Smith. *Festivals, Games and Amusements.* London: Henry Colburn and Richard Bentley, 1831, pp. 94–96.

Chapter 5

THE MIDDLE AGES

THE INVASION OF THE WESTERN ROMAN EMPIRE

THE Teutonic tribes that were to humble Rome had once provided her with slaves and contestants in the arena. Caesar's *Gallic War* and Tacitus' *Germania* tell us much about these peoples who inhabited Central European swamp and forest lands. To the urbane Roman they were "barbarians" indeed. Their homes were crude log huts furnished with the barest essentials. They sat and slept on dirt floors; for clothing they had only coarse linen, hides, and furs. A woman's life was not easy: she tilled and harvested grain and tended flocks and herds, in addition to raising children and managing the household. Young women served a kind of apprenticeship under their mothers. Young men, of course, were trained to be hunters and warriors. Caesar respected the fearlessness and skill of the barbarian warrior. The Teutonic cavalryman, who rode bareback on his shaggy and diminutive mount, especially impressed him.

After reaching maturity and demonstrating his mastery of weapons and military tactics, the Teuton youth was presented with a spear and shield in public assembly. This ceremony signified his achieving full status as a responsible member of the communal group. He voluntarily pledged his allegiance to a chieftain. The chieftain, in turn, guaranteed the property rights of the youth and his family and provided his horse, arms, and food.

THE STRUGGLE FOR POWER AMONG THE TEUTONIC TRIBES

After dismembering the Western Roman Empire, the Teutonic tribes turned on each other in a struggle for power. The Vandals, who had firmly established themselves in northern Africa, continued to harass Spain and Italy. They were subdued by a Roman army of citizen conscripts in A.D. 533. The visigoths, long entrenched in Spain, were routed by the Moslems in 711. And in northern Italy the Goths succumbed to the persistent Lombards in 533. The West Goths and the Burgundians, in what is now France, fell before the Franks, who in turn were completely assimilated by the Gallo-Roman "natives."

To the north, the Angles and Saxons, who had subdued the aboriginal British, were plagued by repeated Viking incursions. And to the south, the Moslems, now masters of Spain, crossed the Pyrenees to strike at the heartland of Central Europe. They were repulsed by Charles Martel and his Frankish army at what is now Tours, France.

Charlemagne, promoter and defender of the Christian faith, crushed the Lombards in northern Italy and then subdued and Christianized the Bavarians and the Saxons. In 800 Pope Leo III proclaimed Charlemagne Holy Roman Emperor, successor to Caesar Augustus and Constantine. His domain finally embraced what is now Belgium, France, Germany, Holland, Hungary, most of Italy, Switzerland, and northern Spain.

THE CONTRIBUTION OF CHRISTIANITY TO THE TEUTONS

Unlike the Romans, who had attempted to impress Roman law and customs upon peoples who had neither the ability nor the desire to be assimilated, the Roman Catholics accepted the Germanic sociocultural framework and offered them a religion that gave direction to their robust nature. By one means or another Western Europe was quickly Christianized. As long as it was involved in the political intrigue that busied kings and lesser nobility, the church, governed by the popes, was able to maintain its identity and unity.

FEUDALISTIC SOCIETY

Feudalism had its roots in the system of vassalage devised by Charlemagne's grandfather, Charles Martel, early in the 700s. To secure the loyalty of the ablest warriors, he granted them estates, or fiefs. The vassal administered and derived an income from, but did not own, the fief. He was obligated to render civil and military service to his lord. The vassal, in turn, apportioned his land in small units, or tithes, to peasants who farmed them on a communal basis. For his work, the peasant received food, lodging, and civil and military protection.

By the twelfth century feudalism was the way of life throughout Western Europe.

EDUCATION FOR KNIGHTHOOD

The vassal's son was sent to the lord's castle at an early age to serve as a page, the first step toward knighthood. He waited upon the ladies of the court, ran errands, and learned the basic religious rites and ceremonies. When he had reached an age when he would benefit by training for the hunt and warfare, the boy became a squire. His duties included caring for the lord's horses and armor and accompanying him on his travels and military campaigns. The squire was also tutored in the "gay sciences"—singing, dancing, and group games—designed to make him an interesting and agreeable companion. He was taught venery, the art of skinning and cutting up game, and falconry.[1]

To develop knightly endurance, the squire ran, jumped, wrestled, swam, and climbed ropes and rope ladders. He had to master the spear, bow and arrow and crossbow, battle ax, mace, and broadsword. Equally important was instruction in horsemanship and riding and fighting fully clad in cumbersome armor.

The squire was instructed first in the rudiments of horsemanship and then in the use of lance and shield. When he was sufficiently skilled, the squire, armed with blunt lance and shield, jousted with live opponents. If he failed to parry with his shield and was struck squarely by his opponent's lance, the jouster usually was thrown from his horse. Injuries were more apt to result from striking the ground imprisoned in armor than from being hit by the blunt lance.

After passing all tests (sometimes after special valor in battle), the squire was granted knighthood in an elaborate religious ceremony and thus became a vassal to his lord and defender of the church. The ideal knight was the embodiment of medieval virtue: pure in conduct, champion of those in distress, and defender of Christianity against unbelievers. Motivated by faith as well as by a lust for adventure and profit, knights by the thousands fought in the Crusades.

THE TOURNAMENTS

The medieval tournament originated in France about the tenth century and spread to England and Germany between the eleventh and fifteenth centuries. The early tournaments were little more than military exercises, carefully regulated to protect contestants from injury. Knights wished to demonstrate their prowess; a prince or other nobleman wished to entertain his court and would invite knights within his domain to vie for honors. In time knights and spectators lost sight of the original purpose of the tournaments, and contestants frequently fought to the death on horseback or on foot. Unscrupulous knights would demand a ransom of a defeated opponent as the price for sparing his life.[2] The church finally used its power to outlaw tournaments.

SOCIETY IN THE LATE MIDDLE AGES

The feudalism introduced by Charles Martel was a communal-militaristic system entirely dependent upon an agrarian economy. Trade, essential for the establishment of towns and cities, was practically nonexistent. Had the Teutons been inclined to commerce, Moslem supremacy in the western Mediterranean area would have made trade a hazardous venture. The Franks failed to take advantage of their excellent natural harbors and ideal location for trading; hence they had few towns of any size. The Anglo-Saxons in England were too busy holding the Vikings at bay to think of trade. Thus in the early Middle Ages society was mainly rural. This, naturally, had a marked influence on social, religious, and recreational activity.

The Crusades stimulated East-West trade, exposed Europeans to the advanced Eastern cultures, and awakened a spirit of exploration and discovery which culminated in the epoch-making voyages of the fifteenth and sixteenth centuries. The wide acceptance of money as the medium of exchange in place of barter fostered trade. Craftsmanship was encouraged, leading to the organization of guilds. Towns and cities began to grow, and a middle, or merchant, class began to emerge.

During the thirteenth century the church reached the zenith of its power in secular as well as ecclesiastical affairs. Heretics who challenged its authority were immediately subdued by the military forces it commanded. This and other expressions of its political power sowed the seeds of the Reformation.

ASCETICISM

During the fifth century St. Augustine proposed that in addition to a mind and body man had a spiritual nature of divine origin. Seven centuries later St. Thomas Aquinas related this body-mind-spirit concept to Christian doctrines. Admitting that man was truly an animal, though a rational one, he argued that within man's being was a divine spark which placed him on a higher plane than other animals.[3] His animal qualities were his "lowest" and least desirable. Mind and spirit operated on a higher level and had a closer kinship with the divine than the body, source of the baser appetites and passions. To attain an ideal spiritual existence on this earth and fulfill his divine destiny, man must suppress and mortify his animal nature through fasting, self-flagellation, celibacy, and poverty.

The asceticism introduced into religious and secular orders during the Middle Ages can be traced to Hindu, Buddhist, and Greek sources as well as to the Old Testament.

MONASTICISM

Asceticism found its perfect expression in religious orders. One of the first, the Benedictine order, was founded by St. Benedict in 529.

Each monk spent part of the day in manual labor, study, and prayer. The Benedictines also taught noble-born children and trained brighter peasant boys in the service of the church. The Dominicans, recognized by the church in 1215, were noted for their learning; many served as university professors; original manuscripts were preserved and copied by them. Were it not for the monastic orders, priceless Hebrew, Greek, and Roman works would have been lost to mankind.

MEDIEVAL EDUCATION

During much of the early Middle Ages the only existing schools were those maintained by monastic orders. Later, cathedral schools were founded. Monastic and cathedral schools provided only an elementary education, in such subjects as reading and writing, simple arithmetic, music (singing), religious observances, and rules of conduct. In the twelfth century elementary education was taken over by chantry schools, which were established by grants in wills or by endowments left to priests. Cathedral and monastic schools became grammar schools (grammar was the most important subject taught), which provided a kind of secondary education. The curriculum covered the *trivium* (Latin grammar, rhetoric, and dialectics) or the *quadrivium* (geometry, arithmetic, astronomy, and music), sometimes both.

THE UNIVERSITIES

Many church universities were established as extensions of cathedral and monastic schools. The church competed with kings in granting universities special privileges. The *trivium* and *quadrivium,* or the Seven Liberal Arts, as they were eventually called, constituted the curriculum from the tenth through the twelfth centuries.

By the end of the twelfth century church-dominated schools were beginning to experience an intellectual awakening. Advances were made in mathematics, astronomy, and medicine, and for the first time the church permitted the teaching of Aristotle's philosophy. Christians learned much from Moslems, whose learning was carried from Spain throughout the Western world by the English monk Abelard and others. A spirit of inquiry had at last been stirred and the authority of the church was beginning to be challenged. Scholars sought to unravel the mysteries of and resolve the apparent contradictions in Christianity. This—the twelfth and thirteenth centuries—was the age of scholasticism, the age of Abertus Magnus, Roger Bacon, Duns Scotus, and Thomas Aquinas.

STUDENT LIFE

University students—some as young as 12, others 60 or older—wandered from university to university, sometimes following a popular professor as he moved from school to school, or selecting universities where distinguished scholars taught. They wandered about the countryside in cap and gown; the gown served as a depository for wine, meat, and bread and as a warning to townspeople and peasants, since students often foraged along the way. In 1158 Frederick I, to protect the students, decreed:

> In the future no one shall be so rash as to venture to inflict any injury on scholars, or to occasion any loss to them on account of a debt owed an inhabitant of this province. . . . If any one shall presume to bring suit against them on account of any business, the choice in the matter shall be given to the scholars, who may summon the accusers to appear before the professors, or the bishop of the city.[4]

In 1100 King Philip of France granted similar protection to the students of the University of Paris.

APPRENTICESHIP IN THE CRAFT GUILDS

The medieval craft guild regulated all details of work in a trade and sought to preserve a monopoly for its members. Work was so narrowly specialized that in one town, for example, there might be a dozen guilds engaged in making leather goods. A master was allowed one or more apprentices at a time. The apprentice opened and closed the shop, ran errands, and learned the trade. He could not be asked to perform household chores. If he was treated cruelly, he could appeal to guild officials. At the end of his term, generally about six years, the apprentice could, if he had sufficient capital, become a master craftsman. Each guild had its own patron saint; members went to church in a body. Guilds acted as a mutual aid society for burials and the care of widows and orphans and the sick and poor.

PHYSICAL EDUCATION DURING THE MIDDLE AGES

In the early stages of their evolution societies typically provide instruction in hunting and fighting. This was true during the Middle Ages. As societies become more highly organized, instruction in physical activities is generally made part of the formal educational system, to provide a substitute for the vigorous activities which at one time were an essential part of daily life. In autocratic societies such instruction is apt to be militaristically oriented; in democratic societies such goals as the preservation of health and development of the "ideal" man are also stressed. The structure of medieval society caused other patterns to emerge.

Under the feudal system only the nobleman's son received military education, which was provided at the lord's court, not by the ecclesiastical schools. By the time of the Renaissance court schools, or academies, offered a broader program including academic as well as military subjects. The tradition of preparing only the upper classes for positions of leadership persists in some European countries even today. For example, the twentieth-century English "Establishment" can be traced all the way back to the Middle Ages.

Asceticism markedly influenced the curriculum of ecclesiastical schools. They had no program of physical activity for the development of the body. Medieval art also reflects the influence of asceticism. Christ and His disciples, who led robust physical lives, are portrayed with emaciated bodies and pious, haggard faces.

A general physical degeneration is suggested by the portraits of civil dignitaries and wealthy merchants. Perhaps the slight physiques and gaunt faces merely reflect malnutrition rather than the influence on the artists of a religious ideal.

Unsanitary living conditions and ignorance of disease account for the epidemics and pandemics which plagued Europe throughout the Middle Ages. Sickness and death were thought to be God's will.

This fatalism also contributed to the lack of interest in physical education in the program of ecclesiastical schools.

RECREATION DURING THE MIDDLE AGES

Recreational activities played a vital role during the Middle Ages. Some were, by our standards, crude and brutal and are of only historical interest. Others have persisted to this day.

HUNTING

Kings, nobles, and peasants hunted both for pleasure and for variety in diet. The crossbow, with iron arrowheads for large game and cylindrical lead arrowheads for small game, was the principal weapon. Medieval huntsmen sought out bear, deer, wild boar, hare, and game, sometimes using dogs, hawks, and falcons. During the Crusades more adventuresome knights were introduced to lion hunting.

French hunters placed themselves under the patronage of St. Hubert, who, when Bishop of Liège during the eighth century, was himself a hunter of no small reputation. Four times a year huntsmen gathered to celebrate a feast in his honor. In 1455 Gerand, Duke of Cleves, created the order of the Knights of St. Hubert which was devoted entirely to the huntsman and his interests.[5]

FALCONRY

Falconry, which became a complicated art, was very popular throughout the Middle Ages and the Renaissance. Possession of a hunting bird denoted rank. The nobleman or his lady would appear at public places with a falcon perched on the wrist, and a bishop or abbot would enter church with his hunting bird, which he placed on the altar steps during service. Captured knights freed their birds; the chivalric code forbade their being surrendered. True falcons were imported from Sweden, Turkey, and Morocco, and their training and maintenance were time-consuming and expensive. Medieval huntsmen called all birds of prey "falcons"—for example, the saber hawk, the lanner, the merlin, and the sparrow hawk. Among these smaller "falcons," males were used to hunt patridge and quail and the females were loosed on hare, heron, and crane.

At a medieval court the exhibition of falcons was a great event and the first trial of new birds was discussed for months afterward. The office of Grand Falconer of France, created in 1250, carried as great prestige as any the king could bestow. The Grand Falconer had fifty assistants, 300 birds under his care, and the right to hunt wherever he pleased in the kingdom.

Medieval Entertainers

During the Middle Ages and the early Renaissance, wandering poet-musicians flourished in many European countries. In France they were called *troubadors* or *jongleurs;* in the German states *minnesingers;* and in the Scandinavian countries *skalds.* Some minstrels were attached to royal or noble courts, others wandered from castle to castle, and many entertained village folk. Their songs and stories were often original compositions, but their repertories included ballads and folklore from other times and lands. We are indebted to the minstrels, who sing to us still through such medieval works as *Tristan and Iseult, Parsifal, The Song of Roland,* and the *Niebelungenlied.* From these and other ballads, poems, and legends we have learned much about life in the Middle Ages.

The French term "jongleur" was derived from the fact that minstrels were often accompanied by jugglers, acrobats, sleight-of-hand performers, and trained animals. By the fourteenth century, minstrels, who once had been widely respected, had fallen into disrepute. Men of questionable character filled the ranks of the troubadours. They and their ribald songs were denounced from the pulpit. In 1345 Guillaume de Gourmot, Provost of Paris, prohibited minstrels from singing or telling obscene stories under penalty of fine and imprisonment. However, it was the invention of the printing press that hastened the demise of the minstrel.

"Rope dancers," or tightrope performers, flourished from the fourteenth until the sixteenth century. Their act was much like that we see in circuses today: dancing to music, hanging by feet and teeth, and balancing from death-defying heights.

Dancers and tumblers were also popular. But when they began to ask for money as well as food, they rapidly lost their popularity.

SPORTS AND GAMES

Nobles and peasants enjoyed wrestling, foot races, several ball games, and high and broad jumping. Jousting tournaments, of course, figured prominently in court life. French kings and nobles played tennis and quoits on courts many of which provided for spectators. *Billes et billars,* which resembled our modern game of croquet, was played on level ground with wooden balls which were struck with curved sticks or mallets.

As always, there were many games of chance (dice, for example) and games of *tables* (chess, draughts, and backgammon). The church discouraged dice playing, clerics objecting as much to the obscenities uttered by losers as they did to the impoverishment that players risked.

At festivals and assemblies the young men and ladies played many *Jeux des Valentines,* or games of lovers, and forfeit games. The names of some of these games have survived but not descriptions of how they were played.

DANCING

For centuries the church inveighed against dancing, which it believed corrupted morals. In the Middle Ages the dance took many strange forms. The plague confronted the individual with death in an especially horrible form. Terror-stricken survivors succumbed to a kind of mass hysteria: ecstatic or compulsive dancing at funerals. The church tried but could not restrain the practice. Saint-Saëns's *Danse Macabre* is an attempt to convey the eeriness and madness of such dancing.

Troubadours mention many dances but do not describe them, probably because they were well known to their audiences. There was the *danse au virlet,* evidently a type of round dance during which each dancer sang a verse and all joined in the chorus. Sometimes minstrels sang to the accompaniment of the harp and young ladies danced in couples as they repeated the minstrels' verses. The torch dance was sometimes performed at weddings: each dancer carried a lighted taper and attempted to blow out the light of his neighbor.

NOTES

1. G. P. R. James. *The History of Chivalry and the Crusades.* New York: J. and J. Harper, 1832, pp. 31–53.
2. Sidney Painter. *A History of the Middle Ages (284–1500).* New York: Alfred A. Knopf, 1953, p. 289.
3. Morris Van Cleve. "Physical Education and the Philosophy of Education." *Journal of Health–Physical Education–Recreation,* 27:3 (March, 1956), 22.
4. Dana C. Munro. *The Middle Ages (395–1271).* New York: The Century Co., 1926, pp. 132–133; 366–376.
5. Paul Lacroix. *Manners, Custom and Dress During the Middle Ages and During the Renaissance Period.* London: Chapman and Hall, 1876, pp. 178–237.

Chapter 6

THE RENAISSANCE

THE MIDDLE AGES SET THE STAGE

THE Middle Ages are often spoken of disparagingly as a period of barbarity and ignorance, but this is not entirely true since this era had its own culture. The universities of the period were already laying the foundations of the Renaissance with their increased interest in the Greek and Roman classics. The cathedral and monastic schools also taught Latin grammar and rhetoric, while scholars wrote essays and treatises in Latin. The Crusades had aroused the intellectual curiosity of scholars and students in increasing numbers traveled East to study in universities established long before those of Western Europe. The introduction of more advanced and varied knowledge from the East broadened Western minds, opened new channels of thought, and gave scholarship a more critical and analytical form. By the late Middle Ages men's minds were ready to accept new ideas in all fields of knowledge.

In this transitional period feudal monarchies were gradually being replaced by national monarchies. Whereas the thirteenth century was essentially feudalistic, the fourteenth saw the growing decay of feudal practices. The relationship between ruler and people was undergoing a change. The king was no longer guided solely by the desires of his feudal lords, but was expected to consider the common welfare of all his people. The French people, for example, began to think of themselves not as French but as subjects of the king of France. This change is called by historians the birth of nationalism.

DECLINE IN THE POWER OF THE CHURCH

New heresies challenging the authority of the church were inspired not so much by its political intrigue as by a questioning of its ecclesiastical doctrines. John Wycliffe, the English theologian, preached the doctrine of domain, in which he argued that the "true domain" belonged to God and that man simply acted as his deputy on earth. John Huss, the popular preacher of Prague, aggressively attacked church doctrine and the corrupt life of the clergy. The sincere and scholarly Erasmus criticized the splendor of the papal court and poked fun at its religious ceremonials. All these critics and others prepared the minds of men for the acceptance of the doctrines of Zwingli, Luther, Calvin, and Knox, who ushered in the Reformation.

INVENTIONS AND DISCOVERIES

During the thirteenth and fourteenth centuries Friar Roger Bacon of Oxford and Berthold Schwartz, a German monk, developed a practical explosive which led to the invention of firearms. The adoption of gunpowder as a propellant in small firearms and cannons wrecked the institution of feudalism and changed the military and political history of the West.

The Moslems had been the first to build paper mills in Western Europe, but when the Christians drove them from Spain, they took their paper-making process with them. Around 1250 the Greeks secured the process from the Mohammedans and with their help the first paper mill in Italy was constructed in 1276. Similar mills were set up in Mainz in 1320 and in Nuremberg in 1390. In 1438 Johannes Gutenberg invented a printing press using movable wooden type in Mainz, and in 1450 Johann Fust and Peter Schöffer of the same city cast the first metal type. Henceforth the laborious and expensive process of printing a book by hand was a thing of the past and books now literally poured from the presses in Venice, Paris, Leipzig, and London. The press became a formidable rival of the pulpit and the public speaker and a powerful instrument in the spread of human progress and liberty. Its invention marked the end of medieval scholasticism and the beginning of modern education.

Adventurous sailors discovered the Canary Islands in 1402; the Portuguese reached the island of Madeira in 1419; the Cape Verde Islands were found in 1460; Columbus, in his search for a water route to India, discovered the American continent in 1492; Bartholomew Diaz rounded the Cape of Good Hope in 1497; in the same year Vasco da Gama finally found the sea route to India; and Magellan's ships circumnavigated the globe between 1519 and 1522 and returned to Spain to prove to the geographers that the world was round. In 1507 Waldseemüller published his *Introduction to Geography,* which provided the basis of the modern study of geography.[1]

THE HUMANISTIC EDUCATIONAL METHOD

At the beginning of the Renaissance European scholars knew only two languages which had any perfection of style: Greek and Latin. Since Latin was the universal tongue and Greek was just being introduced, it was Latin that was chiefly cultivated. In the opinion of the humanists, Terence, Ovid, Caesar, Vergil and Cicero provided the best models for the artistic expression of thought on human affairs. While they were concerned primarily with perfection in style, the humanists were also conscious of the humane content of classical literature.

The works of Aristotle, including his *Ethics, Metaphysics, Physics,* and *Psychology,* had been translated into Syriac by the Moslems and then into Latin. His philosophy was taught in universities as early as 1300. Cicero's orations had served as a model of style during the Roman Empire centuries before; now humanist scholars drew attention once more to his classical Latin style. The Italian Petrarch, who is one of the finest exemplars of humanism, became an ardent student of Cicero's style and was said to have matched the master's skill. Petrarch composed all his serious work in classical Latin to preserve it for posterity, and what he considered his less important work, the sensual love sonnets to Laura, whom he adored from afar but to whom he never dared to speak, in the vernacular. Little did he know that future generations would care less for his carefully contrived Latin works, but would prize his more spontaneous love sonnets.

QUINTILIAN. Quintilian, one of the first students of methodology in teaching, was born in Spain about A.D. 40 and moved later with his family to Rome. When he was 26, he was granted the chair of eloquence, the first to be established in the Roman Empire. His most famous work was a series of declamations called the *Institutes of Oratory,* which became a guide in teaching methods during the Renaissance and influenced education for four centuries to come.

In Quintilian's opinion, the teacher cannot have too high an opinion of human nature, nor propose too high a goal. If a child rebels against education, it is not the child's fault, but the method of his teacher. The child's first impressions are the lasting ones: "New vases preserve the taste of the first liquor that is put into them; and wool, once colored, never regains its primitive whiteness." The duties of the teacher should be "to ascertain with all possible thoroughness the mind and character of the child." On the subject of moral discipline, he states, "Fear restrains some and unmans others . . . for my part, I prefer a pupil who is sensitive to praise, whom glory animates and for whom defeat draws tears." He was strongly opposed to corporal punishment for laggards "although custom authorizes it."

In teaching reading and writing Quintilian thought it wrong to make children learn the names of letters and their order in the alphabet before they knew their shapes. He recommended the use of letters cut out of ivory which the children could see, feel, and name. For writing, wooden tablets with the letters cut into the surface should be used. The child could then trace the letters and learn their shape. As soon as he was able to read and write the child should be placed in the hands of a grammarian. As the humanist taught Latin instead of the mother tongue, so, ironically, Quintilian taught Greek to the Roman boy. He divided the instruction of grammar into two parts, the art of speaking and an exegesis of the poets. The rules of grammar were taught through exercises in composition and narrative. He attached much importance to reading aloud to improve enunciation.

GREEK GYMNASTICS

The humanist educators were well aware of the important place given gymnastics in the Greek system of education and, like good copyists, they faithfully included gymnastics in their educational programs for the sons of the nobility and wealthy merchants. They were impressed by Xenophon's admiration for the Spartans' military education and his glowing description of their gymnastic program. They experienced vicariously Philostratus' delight in amateur athletic competition. They noted that Plato, in his *Republic,* placed gymnastics on an equal footing with grammar and music in the curriculum, though he cautioned that exercise must be taken in moderation and not with the fanatic zeal of the athletic contestant. He did not believe that the development of the military athlete was the sole objective of gymnastics: "Moreover, in exercise and toils which he imposes on himself, his object will be rather to stimulate the spiritual element of his nature than to gain strength; and he will not, like the athletes in general, take the prescribed food and exercise merely for the sake of muscular power."

GALEN. Galen's treatise on the *Preservation of Health* must have become pretty hackneyed by the time it made the rounds of Renaissance scholars and pseudo physicians, for many a humanist had drawn on his ideas on exercise, in both education and medical treatment. Galen was born at Pergamum in A.D. 130 and as a young man studied philosophy and medicine at Alexandria, Smyrna, and Corinth. He was appointed physician to gladiators at Alexandria and at 34 he came to Rome as physician to the Emperor Marcus Aurelius, but after a few years returned home. Galen is believed to have written more than 500 treatises on medicine, grammar, logic, and ethics, among which were *Preservation of Health* and *Exercise with the Small Ball.*

In his treatise on health, Galen discussed exercises suitable for youths 14 to 20 years of age. He divides exercises into three categories, those of the arms, trunk, and legs. He further divided them into exercises which promote muscle tone without violent movement, "quick exercises" which promote activity, and those which involve violent activity. Under the first classification, Galen listed digging with the pickax, carrying or lifting heavy weights, rope climbing, and resistive exercises. Under quick exercises, he named running, sparring, punchball, ball play, rolling on the ground, and numerous arm and leg movements, including running in a circle, jump-straddle-hop, kicking the legs alternately backward and forward, and marching on the toes while swinging the arms. He also developed a series of arm exercises employing Greek halteres.

HIERONYMUS MERCURIALIS (1530–1606). This Italian physician drew heavily upon Galen's treatises in his *Six Books on the Art of Gymnastics,* published for the first time by the Guinta Press in Venice in 1569. Running through six editions, it became the standard reference work of physicians and gymnastic instructors for several centuries and was copied wholesale without acknowledgment.

THE RENAISSANCE IN ITALY

It was not surprising that the Renaissance reached its full bloom in Italy. This country had always been a connecting link between the cultures of the West and East. The monuments and buildings of the past served as a reminder of the glories that had once been Rome's. The trade-enriched nobility and merchants of the seaport cities found satisfaction in being patrons of the intelligentsia, rich or poor. The deference with which they treated artists and craftsmen is illustrated by Cosmo de Medici's remark, "One must treat these people of extraordinary genius as if they were celestial spirits, and not like beasts of burden." Through this patronage some of the world's greatest painters and sculptors found full expression of their genius: Leonardo da Vinci, Raphael, Michelangelo, Botticelli, Fra Angelico, Verrocchio, and Cellini.

In the early stages of the Renaissance Italian scholars were concerned mainly with the discovery and reclamation of manuscripts of Greek and Roman classical literature. Poggio Bracciolini discovered the priceless manuscript of Quintilian's *Institutio Oratoria* at the Abbey of St. Gall in 1416. Petrarch spent much time wandering over Italy in search of manuscripts and uncovered several letters and two orations of Cicero, which he translated into the vernacular. Cosmo de Medici, the rich Florentine banker, spent much time and money collecting old Greek manuscripts.

The Italian interest in Greek classical literature dated from the introduction of the first teacher of Greek to the West, Manuel Chrysoloras. From 1397 to 1400 he lectured in the city and the University of Florence, which at that time was the intellectual and artistic center of the world. Demetrius Chalcondyles, another Greek scholar, taught Greek in Perugia in 1450. He transferred to the

University of Padua in 1463 and became the first professor of Greek on a fixed salary in a Western European university.

The Italian scholars stimulated a humanistic approach to education by emphasizing three main ideas: (1) the life of the ancient Greeks and Romans, who possessed a broader range of interests and consequently a wider world of knowledge; (2) the joy of living, satisfaction in this life, and an appreciation of the beautiful; and (3) the realization that nature and everyday life were worth contemplating, a thought that was contrary to the religious teachings of the Middle Ages.

ITALIAN HUMANISTS

The municipality of Florence and its university are often considered the center of the revival of learning, because they were associated with the Medici, Chrysoloras, Boccaccio, Salutati, and Niccoli, but Padua, the second great university of its time, made its own contribution to the Italian Renaissance. Petrarch, who lived in the immediate neighborhood, was closely associated with the university and at his death left his remarkable collection of books to its library. Vittorina da Feltre, who is generally coupled with Petrarch as a true representative of the early Renaissance, received his education and taught there. Guarino da Verona, a student and companion of Chrysoloras and recognized as one of the best Greek scholars of his day, was a close friend of Da Feltre at Padua. Petrus Paulus Vergerius was for many years professor of logic at this institution.[2]

VITTORINO DA FELTRE (1378–1446). Bruto Ramboldoni, Da Feltre's father, was a writer or notary who made a bare existence for his family. From the beginning Da Feltre gave signs of possessing a keen intellect and at 18 he entered the University of Padua to study liberal arts, eventually securing the *Laurea Artium* (doctor of arts). He excelled in grammar, and his poverty compelled him to take the thankless position of master of grammar. He later became proficient in both mathematics and Greek. He remained at Padua as professor of grammar and mathematics until 1415, when he resigned to enter the service of Marquis Gonzaga of Mantua to teach his children. He brought with him a desire to combine the spirit of Christianity with the educational value of classical literature and the Greek passion for bodily development and the dignity of human life.

Marquis Gonzaga presented Da Feltre with a detached villa, or casino, surrounded on three sides by large meadows and bordered by a river. Da Feltre changed its name, La Gioiosa (Pleasure House), to La Giocasa (Pleasant House), and after his school gained fame, he adopted the name Gymnasium Palatinum, or Palace School, in imitation of the Greek gymnasiums, just as the Italian academies took their name from the Academy of Plato at Athens. His first class of three pupils rapidly grew to seventy as his reputation as a master teacher spread throughout Italy, France, Germany, and even to the East. He considered himself the father of his scholars and shared their school life, games, and excursions. Vittorino was particularly given to helping poor but deserving boys secure an education and frequently paid for their entire schooling. At his death a goodly portion of his estate went to clearing indebtedness incurred in this way.

Vittorino employed Quintilian's method of instruction with innovations of his own. He held not only that study should alternate with exercises and games, but that the teacher should provide variations in his teaching method. Although these games were a continuation of the court training of the Middle Ages, Da Feltre regarded exercise as a foundation to health and the first prerequisite of a school program. He carefully graded his pupils' outdoor activities according to age and interest and made participation compulsory. Since he himself was an accomplished gymnast and knew what games children enjoyed, he led and supervised them in riding, running, jumping, fencing, swimming, archery, and various ball games. During the summer he often took the older pupils on hikes into the mountains above Lake di Garda which lasted for several days. Although da Feltre was obligated to include martial exercises as part of court training, he gave a much broader interpretation to the place of gymnastics in education. As a humanist he realized that an individual was truly educated only when mind, body and spirit had each received its proper development.

PETRUS PAULUS VERGERIUS (1370–1444). Vergerius' *Customs and Study of Youth* was written for the use of Ubertinus, the son of Francesco Carrara, the lord of Padua. Vergerius was a keen student of human nature and had definite ideas about the responsibility of the teacher: "The education of children is a matter of more than private interest; it concerns the State, which indeed regards the right training of the young as, in certain aspects, within its proper sphere. I would wish to see their responsibility extended."

In line with court training, Vergerius admonished: "Now war involves physical endurance as well as military skill. So that from his earliest years a boy must be gradually inured to privations and grave exertions, to enable him to bear strain and hardship when he reaches manhood." Taking a page from Plato's *Republic,* he suggested that learning should begin in childhood and that morals should be taught with physical exercises suitable to the youth's age level. His exercises were a recapitulation of those popular among the *Juvenes* in Augustus' reign during the early Roman Empire. He advised the youth to seek recreation from study, "for the string ever stretched will end by breaking." He recommended horseback riding and walks in the country, but had little to say in favor of singing, dancing, and dice playing.

OTHER ITALIAN HUMANISTS. Both Francisco Barbaro (1395–1440) and Da Feltre gave advice to young people in the choice of their mates. To insure healthy offspring, they should be in harmony physically as well as intellectually. To encourage this, Barbaro recommended that young women, like their Spartan sisters, participate in gymnastic exercises as well as young men.

Cardinal Eneas de Piccolomini (1404–1464), later Pope Pius II, dedicated his treatise, *The Education of Children,* to King Ladislaus of Bohemia and Hungary. Having failed to raise a crusade against the Turks, Piccolomini pointed out bitterly that the exercises of court training had fallen into decay. "An effeminate education, called indulgence, breaks the nerve and spirit of the body." He objected to every type of effeminacy, including the use of silk garments. Like most of the humanists he recommended that young people be hardened by country living, with plenty of physical work in the open air and plain food. His recommendations for training for military duty were wrapped in a single package—hunting. This activity, including riding, climbing, swimming, shooting with the bow, and spear throwing, he believed would toughen any youth against changes in weather.

Francesco Philephus, a peripatetic teacher, wrote his *Instruction in Good Living* at the order of Duchess Maria Bonna of Milan, for the education of Duke Philibert of Savoy. He took as his model the training of the feudal squire and recommended that two hours be set aside each day for gymnastics and games. Besides running and ball play, he suggested the Florentine soccer-football game, *Calcio.* The game was played through the months of January to March and supplanted tournaments toward the end of the feudal period. As Count Giovanni Bardi described the game in 1688, it was played with thirty-seven players on a team, fifteen forwards, five wingbacks, five centers, five halfbacks, four three-quarterbacks, and three full-backs. This multitude of players performed on the public square as the crowd looked on from the windows of adjacent buildings and the sidewalks. Moslem-style tents were used for goals and the ball was kicked on the ground. Besides the soccer-type play the contestants could hold and body tackle as in the English game of Rugby.[3]

THE RENAISSANCE IN NORTHERN EUROPE

By the time the Italian Renaissance had reached its zenith, manifestations of the movement began to appear in northern Europe. The merchants of Holland and the free city of Nuremberg, a rich trading center, began to patronize the arts. Many of the Flemish, Dutch, and German painters spent time studying in Italy. The unsuccessful occupation of Rome, Naples, Florence, and Milan during 1494–1512 by the French acquainted them with the spirit of the Renaissance. Their close association with Italy as well as their common religious interests led France to take the leadership of the Renaissance in northern Europe. Guillaume Budé, or Budaeus, (1467–1540) was the most outstanding humanist scholar in France. His belief that Greek was more important than Latin as an instrument of humanist education helped make Paris the center of Greek scholarship for two centuries.

In England and Germany no such close association with Italy existed; as far as they were concerned, the Reformation was the Renaissance. Latin was the language of the church and the literati and the means of international communication, yet these countries held tenanciously to their mother tongues. The Renaissance in Italy was sparked by national pride, while in England and Germany humanist ideas were stimulated by religious zeal.

DESIDERIUS ERASMUS (1467–1536). Erasmus was one of the most influential figures in the Renaissance of northern Europe. Born at Rotterdam, Holland, Erasmus left the church soon after he was ordained as a priest, to enter the University of Paris. In his later life he acted as an adviser on religious and educational matters in Holland, England, France, and Italy. Shortly after the invention of the printing press, he published the Greek Testament and numerous translations of Greek and Roman classics. Erasmus, however, was more than a scholar; he was one of the most devastating critics the church ever had. He criticized the regal splendor of the papal court and contrasted it with the simplicity of Christ and His disciples. He poked fun at the pilgrimages to holy shrines, the adulation of holy relics, and many other religious customs. While Wycliffe and Huss laid the foundations of the Reformation, Erasmus erected its superstructure.[1]

HUMANISTIC SCHOOLS IN NORTHERN EUROPE

The court schools of Italy had their German counterparts in the *Fürstenschulen,* or schools for princes. The most important of these were at Pforta, Meissen, and Grimma. Students were provided with board and room and strict discipline was enforced. Typical of the German schools developed during the Renaissance was the gymnasium, the first of which was founded by John Sturm, a pupil of Wimpfeling, one of the great German educators, at Strassburg in 1537. The academic program of the gymnasium was divided into ten grades, with the work adjusted according to age level and rate of student progress. As in other schools of the humanist period, Latin grammar with selected readings from Cicero and some Greek were taught, but not the native tongue, geography, or mathematics.

The best English example of the humanistic school was founded at Saint Paul's Church in 1510. It was organized along humanist lines by John Colet with the help of Erasmus, who was then a teacher of Greek at Oxford. Colet had attended the University of Florence, 1493–1496, and was deeply impressed by the intellectual spirit of the Italian scholars. He returned to England and introduced the new learning at Oxford, where he remained until he was appointed dean of St. Paul's. Colet's school, which was a copy of the court and municipal schools of Italy, provided the model for Winchester, Eton, Harrow, Charter-House, Rugby, Shrewsbury, and Merchant Taylors, all English public schools financed by tuition and endowments and independent of church or state. The first English humanistic schools were divided into eight classes, which were eventually reduced to six what the English call forms. It has been said that the English schoolboy developed an interest in sports because of his constant exposure to the Greek and Roman classics. This may well be true since English public schools continued the narrow classical curriculum without modification until the Royal Commissioner's report in 1864.

HUMANISTS OF NORTHERN EUROPE

The English humanist believed in the study of classical language and literature partly because they imparted a certain distinctive intellectual polish attainable in no other way. They also considered martial exercises a necessary part of a youth's training, and writers on education generally included a program of suitable physical activities.

The humanist educator of the Reformation, on the other hand, advocated the study of Greek, Latin, and even Hebrew as essential to the study of the Scriptures. As a consequence the humanistic schools of the Reformation had a strong religious bias. A universal understanding of the Scripture as a means of salvation necessarily meant the education of all classes, the goal particularly of the German reformers. The German humanists assigned a place of importance to gymnastics and music—gymnastics because participation served as a deterrent to the pursuit of less desirable pastimes and preserved the health; music because singing was a means of expressing religious faith and a morale builder.

THOMAS ELYOT (1490–1546). One of the first books on humanistic education written in the vernacular was Thomas Elyot's *The Governour*. The fact that he was a lawyer in the service of King Henry VIII and in no way associated with teaching made his achievement all the more remarkable. He was familiar with Quintilian and made free use of his ideas on method. But, unlike the Roman, who taught Greek to his pupils, Elyot suggested that the mother tongue rather than Latin be taught first in the English schools. He did not downgrade the classics, however, because he thought every boy should be familiar with Lucian, Aristophanes, Homer, Ovid, and Vergil by the time he was 14.

Elyot advocated such activities as tennis, dumbbell drills, wrestling, running, swimming, fencing, riding, dancing, and, above all, archery, as part of court training. Painting and drawing should be taught those boys who showed talent, and music was acceptable so long as it was not overdone. He was a genuine believer in the axiom that knowledge is power and one of the finest representatives of humanism in England. His book was widely read and had a profound influence upon Roger Ascham.

ROGER ASCHAM (1515–1568). Ascham was born in Yorkshire County and educated privately. He graduated from St. John's College, Cambridge, where he was later appointed professor of Greek. He left Cambridge to travel in Europe and after his return became Secretary of Latin Letters, or, more plainly, tutor to Queen Elizabeth.

Thomas Fuller, his biographer, described Ascham as "an honest man and a good shooter; Archery (whereof he wrote a Book called Toxophilus) being his only exercise in youth, which in his old age he exchanged for a worse pastime, neither so healthful for his body, nor profitable for his purse, I mean cock-fighting and thereby (being neither greedy to get, nor careful to keep money) he impaired his estate."

Ascham is remembered for his keen interest in archery and for his book, *The Schoolmaster,* written in excellent English. He wrote an elaborate treatise on the teaching of Latin, a classical example of the master teacher trying to reduce method to its simplest form. Of gymnastics he stated that all young scholars should "use and delight in all courtly exercises and gentleman-like pastimes. The best wits to learning must needs have much recreation and ceasing from his books, or they may mar themselves, when base and dumpish wits can never be hurt by continual study."

JACOB WIMPFELING (1450–1528). The early German humanist Wimpfeling authored textbooks and served as an adviser on school organization. His treatise, *A Guide to German Youth,* was of assistance to Luther in formulating his school policies during the Reformation. Wimpfeling advocated a wide familiarity with Greek and Roman literature and urged the study of content as well as form. His treatise also covered the problems of school life, the qualification of teachers, and the relation of education to social welfare.

JUAN LUIS VIVES (1492–1540). The Swiss reformer Zwingli had considerable influence on the educational ideas of Vives, one of the foremost Spanish humanists. In *On Instruction* and *On Christian Education* he contended that religious and classical instruction should constitute the major part of the youth's education. He stressed the importance of exercise in the maintenance of health and recommended long and rapid walks, running, jumping, and throwing the discus. Exercises should be conducted, not in a military manner, but in a fashion appropriate to an educational environment. Since the purpose of exercise was to refresh the young scholar for the continuation of his study, it should not be carried to the point of fatigue.

MARTIN LUTHER (1483–1546). To the basic subjects of Greek and Latin Luther added Hebrew, logic, and mathematics and gave special emphasis to history, science, gymnastics, and music. Luther thus established gymnastics and music as a permanent part of German education. In his *Letter to the Mayors and Aldermen of the Cities of Germany,* he stated: "It was well considered and arranged by the ancients that people should practice gymnastics that they might not fall into reveling, unchastity, gluttony, intemperance and gaming. Therefore, these two exercises and pastimes please me best, namely music and gymnastics, of which the first drives away all care and melancholy from the heart, and the latter produces elasticity of the body and preserves the health."

Luther believed that education should be made available to all regardless of their station in life and, if necessary, should be made compulsory. He argued that since the state required its citizens to render military service for its defense, education was no less important to its welfare. Luther's educational reforms were executed by Philipp Melanchthon, the Preceptor of Germany. Before the latter's death in 1560 there were very few schools in the German states that had not reorganized their educational program along humanistic and Protestant lines.

NOTES

1. Ellwood P. Cubberly. *The History of Education.* New York: Houghton Mifflin Company, 1920, pp. 254–260.
2. William H. Woodward. *Vittorina da Feltre and Humanist Educators.* Cambridge: The University Press, 1921, p. 2.
3. Ludwig H. Joseph. "Gymnastics from the Middle Ages to the 18th Century." *Ciba Symposia,* 10 (1949), 1037–1038.

Chapter 7

REALISM IN EDUCATION

RESULTS OF THE REFORMATION

LEADING Protestants, who condemned the despotism of the Roman Catholic hierarchy, by the sixteenth century had become intolerant of "splinter" Protestant sects. The relationship between Protestants and Catholics continued to be anything but friendly. After Martin Luther's death Charles V, Emperor of Spain, Austria, Burgundia, and the Netherlands, mounted vigorous campaigns against the heretics. This phase of the religious wars came to a close with the Peace of Augsburg (1555), which enunciated the principle "*cuis regio, cuis religio*"—"whose region, his religion," Under it the ruler of a German state could dictate the religion, Lutheran or Roman Catholic, for all his subjects. No such rights were extended to Calvinists, who were hated by Lutherans as well as Catholics. Augsburg proved a truce, not a real peace. Forcing subjects to embrace their ruler's religion only created new tensions. The treaty was ambiguous on many matters, most notably those relating to the disposition of church property. By 1618, mounting hostilities between Protestant and Catholic states erupted into war.

For thirty years the fighting raged. And the German states were so ravaged that the effects of the Thirty Years' War were felt by many for two hundred years.

The bloody struggle ended with the Peace of Westphalia (1648), which granted Roman Catholics, Lutherans, and Calvinists equal rights.[1] The ruler of each German state still could decree the religion of his subjects, but dissenters were given five years in which to leave. Religious strife divided other countries. In France the

Huguenots were hounded mercilessly. Few escaped death or enforced exile. Persecuted in their homelands, Huguenots, Calvinists, Puritans, Scots and Scotch-Irish Presbyterians, and English Catholics sought refuge, many of them in the New World.

Europe was not again to suffer a religious war. Catholics and Protestants each accepted at least the necessity of tolerating the existence of the other. Religious controversy persisted, but the struggle was waged through education and other means, some harsh but none so extreme as the sword.

DEVELOPMENT OF THE SCIENTIFIC ATTITUDE

For a thousand years or more Europe was intellectually stagnant. In large part this reflected the attitude of the church. Natural phenomena were given supernatural explanations. Whatever afflicted man was believed to be a manifestation of God's will. Thus it was to God, through prayers and good works, that man was advised to turn. For the sick, prayers were prescribed by priests, or "magical" potions by superstition-ridden laymen. Plagues were believed the work of the devil. Christians wanted to annihilate the Moslem infidel, from whom they could have learned so much of physics, chemistry, medicine, and astronomy.

Glimmers of "light," of intellectual curiosity, can be detected as early as the eleventh and twelfth centuries. The cloud of ignorance began markedly to recede in the fifteenth and sixteenth centuries.

In A.D. 138 the Egyptian astronomer Ptolemy declared that the earth was the center of the universe. For nearly 1500 years this theory was accepted throughout the Christian world. To challenge this belief was to commit heresy. The Polish Nicolaus Copernicus (1473–1543) in the year of his death permitted his friends to publish his *De Revolutionibus Orbium Celestium,* which proposed the theory that the sun was the center of the solar system and that the planets, including the earth, revolved about it. In 1609 a German, Johan Kepler (1571–1630), proved the Copernican theory. Galileo Galilei (1564–1642) developed the telescope and discovered Jupiter's satellites and Saturn's ring, and Isaac Newton (1642–1727) determined mathematically the distance of the moon from the earth.

Paracelsus (1493–1541), a professor of medicine at the University of Basel, was the first to question the medical theories of Hippocrates and Galen. Vesalius (1514–1564), a Belgian, was the first to dissect a human body and for this sacrilegious act was forced to do penance by going on a pilgrimage to Jerusalem. William Harvey (1578–1657) discovered the circulation of the blood years before he mustered the fortitude to publish his findings. Francis Bacon (1561–1626), an English philosopher and statesman, broke with Aristotelian deductive logic; in his *Novum Organum* Bacon formulated the principles of inductive reasoning, which he declared the only road to success in scientific investigation.[2]

CRITICISM OF EDUCATION

Critical thinkers of the sixteenth century questioned the value of humanistic education. Most "educators" sought to impart only a mastery of Ciceronian speaking and writing. Obsessed by style, they were little concerned with or aware of content. Students spent long hours on Latin, but little time preparing for life. Scholarship, generally, was of poor quality: methods of instruction were inefficient, and most students were just not interested. They spoke and thought in their native tongue.

The critics of the humanistic approach to education fall into three groups: the humanist realists, the social realists, and the sense realists, or innovators. The humanist realists accepted Latin and Greek and classical literature as the foundation of education, but they objected to emphasizing mastery of Ciceronian style to the exclusion of all else. They agreed, however, that the classics provided a good practical basis for planning a career and for life in general.

The social realists accepted the classical languages and literature with certain modifications. However, they faulted the traditional approach because it neglected instruction in social attainments and ignored the affairs of the world.

The sense realists were so called because they advocated the use of illustrative materials in instruction. They believed the curriculum should not rely solely on classical languages and literature and argued that even Greek and Latin grammar should be taught in the vernacular. Students, they maintained, should be instructed in useful arts and sciences, while educational methods should be based on scientifically sound principles.

HUMANIST REALISTS

FRANÇOIS RABELAIS (1483–1553)

Rabelais was born near Chinon, France, the son of a lawyer and gentleman farmer. He was in turn a priest, monk, physician, and writer of humor and satire. In 1530 he received his degree in medicine from Montpellier and was appointed head physician at the great charity hospital at Lyons. Rabelais' contribution to education came not from his satirical dissection of traditional approaches, but rather from his influence upon Montaigne, Locke, and Rousseau. An incessant critic of a narrow humanistic orientation, he deplored the system of "word-teaching" and argued for instruction in the realities of life. Education, he insisted, should encompass the social, moral, spiritual, and physical aspects of life. He believed that books were the source of all education and that mastery of the content and ideas in books alone prepared the student for life.

More pointedly than any of his contemporaries Rabelais called attention to the importance of gymnastics and games in education. He valued them because they developed sound bodies and fostered a sense of joy in participation; manual work he recommended as a source of recreation; and military exercise he recognized as vital for the training of future man-at-arms. Rabelais' gymnastics and games were those of the court schools, supervised by tutors.[4]

JOHN MILTON (1608–1674)

Milton was born in London; his father, a composer, was a man of considerable learning. The younger Milton studied the classics at Saint Paul's school and was graduated from Christ's College, Cambridge. Literature, religion, politics—Milton's was a varied career until blindness caused him to devote himself to writing, with the assistance of a secretary.

Milton, the towering poet, is remembered also for his *Tractate on Education,* one of the most cogent statements of the humanist-realist approach to education. Milton complained that time was squandered on instruction in ancient languages. The traditional eight-year course could, he argued, be taught in one year. The other seven years, he believed, should be devoted to agriculture, physiology, geography, ethics, economics, politics, history, theology, and church history. About gymnastics hc commented:

> . . . Boys should divide their day's work into three parts as it lies orderly: —their Studies, their Exercises and their Diet. . . . Therefore, about an hour and a half, ere they eat at noon, should be allowed for exercise and due rest afterwards. . . . The exercise which I commend first is the exact use of their weapons, to guard and to strike safely with edge or point. . . . They must also be practiced in all locks and grips of wrestling, wherein Englishmen were wont to excel, as need may often be in fight, to tug or grapple, and to close.

SOCIAL REALISTS

MICHEL DE MONTAIGNE (1533–1592)

The son of a land proprietor, Montaigne was born in Périgord, France. He studied law at the Collège de Guyenne at Bordeaux and from 1557 until 1570 was councilor of the Bordeaux Parliament. When his father died, Montaigne retired from law to live a life of leisure on the family estate. An ardent student of the classics and well versed in philosophy, theology, and politics, Montaigne was a brilliant essayist and probably the finest example of the cultivated gentleman of his era. As Bode states:

> The controlling purpose of the true aristocrat was to raise himself to the highest level of perfection. His business in life was not with the trades and handicrafts, but with himself. Intellectual and artistic interests, social graces and manners, must be cultivated in order that he might become a "gentleman and a scholar," a living work of art.[5]

This concept of the ideal life had its roots in earlier civilizations. The sons of Roman and Greek aristocrats studied in foreign lands, to broaden their outlook and to acquire the *savoire faire* of gentlemen. Foreign travel was no less important in Montaigne's scheme of education.

MONTAIGNE'S THEORY OF EDUCATION

In the essays "Of Pedantry," "Of the Education of Children,"[6] and "Of the Affections of Fathers to Their Children" Montaigne developed most of his ideas about education. Criticizing the humanistic school, he stated: "If the mind be not better disposed by education, if the judgement be not better settled, I had much rather my scholar spent his time at tennis." He believed that time spent on formal drills and exercises in classical language and literature was wasted.

Montaigne advocated that the aristocratic youth be educated by a tutor, who should make studying pleasant. Travel he encouraged:

> That he may sharpen his wits by rubbing them upon those of others, I would have a boy sent abroad very young. . . . [From this experience he shall learn] what secret springs move us, and the reasons of our various resolutions; for, I think, the first doctrines with which one seasons his understanding ought to be those that rule his manners and direct his sense; that teach him to know himself, how to live and how to die. Among the liberal studies let us begin with those which makes us free.

MONTAIGNE'S VIEWS ON EXERCISE

Montaigne believed that the young aristocrat's education should stress physical well-being as well as cultural attainment. He regretted that nobles and gentry coddled their sons: "It grieves men to see their children come home from manly exercise, sweaty and dusty, to drink cold water when they are hot, to mount an unruly horse, or to take a foil in hand against a skillful fencer." The ideal aristocrat, according to the essayist, was a strong, healthy individual, a dignified man-at-arms, a man of action who immediately demanded the respect of his peers and those beneath his station.

Since all roads in his theory of education led to one end, the cultivated gentleman of leisure, Montaigne developed a concept of the purpose of education much ahead of his time:

> It is not enough to fortify his soul; you must also make his muscles strong. The mind will be oppressed if not assisted by the body. . . . Our very exercises and recreations, running, wrestling, dancing, hunting, riding, and

fencing, will be part of his study. I would have his manners, behavior and bearing cultivated at the same time with his mind. It is not the mind, it is not the body we are training; it is the man and we must not divide him into two parts.[6]

JOHN LOCKE (1632–1704)

Sometimes styled the intellectual ruler of the eighteenth century, John Locke was born in Somersetshire, England. He studied at Oxford, graduating with a degree in medicine. In 1666 Locke became physician to his patron, the Earl of Shaftesbury. He also was appointed King's Commissioner for the poor. His responsibilities included overseeing the education of the children of the poor who studied in workhouse schools and as apprentices.

In his treatise *Some Thought Concerning Education*[6] Locke, like Montaigne, considered the education of only the sons of the nobility and gentry. He, too, recognized that court children were coddled and pampered; the treatise set forth health rules Locke hoped would serve as a guide to aristocratic parents. A comparison of his views with those of Montaigne shows agreement on the essential points. Both stressed the importance of selecting a properly qualified tutor. Locke commented: "One fit to educate and form the Mind of a young Gentleman is not everywhere to be found."

Like all realists of his time Locke condemned the humanistic education: "Latin and Learning make all the Noise; and the main Stress is laid upon Proficiency in Things a great Part Whereof belong not to Gentleman's Calling; which is to have Knowledge of a Man of Business, a Carriage suitable to his Rank and to be eminent and useful to his Country, according to his Station." Locke, like Montaigne, maintained that foreign travel should climax the young gentleman's education.

Locke recognized the necessity of court exercises, but managed to fit them into his disciplinary theory of education. He advocated the discipline of the body by means of diet, exercise, and exposure to hardships. He considered "a sound mind in a sound body . . . a short but full description of a happy state in this world" and basic to moral and intellectual training. A youth should be trained to deny and subordinate all his desires and apply reason to his acts. To encourage the formation of proper habits in health and exercise, he suggested a system of rewards and punishment.

SCHOOLS OF THE COURTIERS

During Locke's lifetime continental courtier schools reached their zenith in France during the reign of Louis XIV. Whatever was French—court etiquette, language, literature, education—was emulated throughout Europe. The ideal was the man of affairs "who could speak French, had traveled, knew history and politics, law and geography, heraldry and genealogy, some mathematics and physics with their applications, could use the sword and ride, was adept in games and dancing, and was skilled in the practical affairs of life."[7]

The French, like the Italians, called the courtier schools academies; in 1649 there were twelve academies in Paris alone. Young English gentlemen studied first with a tutor at home and then were sent to a continental academy for instruction in military science, mathematics, modern language, fencing, dancing, and singing. French fencing masters were employed by the nobility and gentry throughout Europe. In German states *Ritterakademieen* (knightly academies) were patterned after the French model.

SENSE REALISTS

RICHARD MULCASTER (1531–1611)

This famous English schoolmaster taught at Merchant Taylors and Saint Paul's for fifty years. He was an aggressive advocate of the use of the vernacular. To promote his ideas on education he wrote the treatise *The Elementaire, which entreateth chiefly of the right writing of the English tung.* He maintained that learning should not seek to repress the child but that "the end of education and training is to help nature to perfection." Mulcaster stated that boys and girls should participate together in exercises and games, arguing that the child's natural abilities were best developed in this way. He also maintained that education in a school was preferable to education by a tutor, and that universities should provide professional training for teachers as they did for law, medicine, and the ministry.

In 1581 Mulcaster published his *Positions,* his fundamental principles of education which were much influenced by the work of Vives, the Spanish educator.[8] His discussion of exercise dwelled at length on the work of Galen, Hippocrates, and other Greek physicians and Hieronymus Mercurialis' *The Art of Gymnastics,* which he said had just come off the press. He included, of course, comments based on his own teaching experience.

In his verbose manner Mulcaster explained his choice of exercises as follows:

> I will not here runne through all the kindes of exercises that be named by Galene or any other writer, whereof many be discontinued, many be yet in use, but out of the whole heape I have pickt out these for within dores, lowd speaking, singing, lowd reading, talking, laughing, weaping, holding the breath, daunsing, wrastling, fensing, and scouring the top. And there for without dores, walking, running, leaping, swimming, riding, hunting, shooting, and playing ball.[9]

Mulcaster thought the football played by his boys was a little rough but did "much good to the body. . . . It helpeth weake hammes, by such moving, beginning at a meane, and simple shankes by thickening of the flesh no lesse then riding doth. Yet rash running and to much force oftentimes breaketh some inward conduit, and bringeth ruptures." He considered exercise important to the health of the pupil and a method of relaxation from study.

Historians of education generally agreed that Mulcaster would have received early recognition of his theories had his literary style not been so difficult. This would have shocked Mulcaster, who believed that the best in English style was exemplified in his writing: "I need no example in any of these, whereof mine own penning is a general pattern." He was a contemporary of Shakespeare and a competitor in the presentation of plays at Queen Elizabeth's court. Mulcaster directed plays written by his most talented schoolboys. Shakespeare immortalized him as the schoolmaster in *Love's Labour Lost,* of whom Armado exclaims: "I protest the schoolmaster is exceeding fantastical, too, too vain, too, too vain."

WOLFGANG RATKE (1571–1635)

While a student in England the German Ratke read *Advancement of Learning,* in which Bacon suggested that the new scientific knowledge should be employed in the method of instruction in schools. Ratke immediately got in touch with Bacon and discussed the matter with him. How much help Bacon gave him will never be known, but the younger man developed a plan. He returned to his homeland and offered to sell his secret method to the princes of the German court, guaranteeing that its employment of the German language would promote unity of government and religion, offer instruction in the useful arts and sciences, and reduce the time and effort necessary to learn Latin, Greek, and Hebrew. The princes accepted his offer and set up an experimental school in Anhalt. However, he turned out to be a poor manager, the school failed, and he ended his career in prison as an impostor.

In his *New Method,* published in 1617, Ratke outlined his fundamental rules of teaching, which later revolutionized the approach to methods of instruction: (1) the order of nature must be sought and followed; (2) one thing must be taught at a time and this thoroughly mastered; (3) the retention of the thing learned must be insured by constant repetition; (4) the vernacular must be used in all instruction, including languages; (5) the instruction must be given with order and discipline in the classroom; (6) the procedure of instruction must be by questions and answers and free of memorization; (7) the method of instruction and all books must conform; (8) the knowledge of things must precede words about things; and (9) the individual experience, contact, and inquiry of the learner must supplant authority.

JOHN AMOS COMENIUS (1592–1670)

John Comenius was born in Austria and received his higher education from the universities of Amsterdam and Heidelberg. Comenius began teaching school at 22 and at the same time began preparing to be a preacher in the Moravian Church. While teaching at Lissa in Poland, he formulated his principles of school instruction for his *Great Didactics,* which was published in 1657, 25 years after he completed it. In 1658 he published the *Orbis Sensualium Pictus* (*World of Sense Objects Pictured*), a primer and the first illustrated textbook for children.

In the *Great Didactics* Comenius argued that every human being has a right to an education simply because he is a human being and not because he has a soul to save or has too much leisure on his hands; that instruction should be in the vernacular; that education should be started in infant school if encyclopedic knowledge is to be attained; that teaching should proceed from the particular to the general; and that girls as well as boys should be educated.

COMENIUS AND PLAY

In his *School of Infancy* Comenius offered suggestions on how a mother should help in the preparation of the child for what he called his pansophic, or encyclopedic, education. On the value of play he stated:

> The more the child is thus employed, runs and plays . . . the more quickly does it grow and flourish, both in body and mind. . . . Therefore, a place should be found in which children may run about and exercise themselves with safety. . . . In the second, third and fourth years, let their spirits be stirred up by means of agreeable plays with them, or their playing among themselves, by running about, by chasing each one another, by music and any agreeable spectacle, as pictures, etc.[10]

Comenius had definite ideas about the type of play suitable for children. He forbade the boys at the Gymnasium in Lissa to play in the streets and encouraged them to play outside of town, choosing one of their group as a leader. As a consequence of his religious background he looked with disfavor upon dancing: "The dance is a circle whose centre is the devil." In the organization of his school program he encouraged boys to run, jump, and play ball games "since it is necessary to put the body in motion and allow the mind to rest." He prohibited games played with dice, wrestling, boxing, and swimming because in his opinion these activities were useless and dangerous. In the *Outline of the Pansophic School* he warned that care should be taken not to overstrain the minds of pupils and recommended that they play for half an hour after each hour's work and rest for an hour after dinner and supper.

EDUCATION OF GIRLS

Most realists were concerned with the education of girls. Mulcaster believed that "young maidens" should attend the public grammar schools as well as the universities, but he hastened to add that the custom of society was against him. He also recommended that for girls, "some exercise of the bodie ought to be used." Comenius maintained that public schools should be opened to both boys and girls; most girls, he believed, would go no further than the vernacular public schools.

Most girls, however, were educated in the home by their mothers. Woman was considered inferior—a lower-class drudge or an upper-class ornament. Intellectual attainments were thought impractical for women. An exception to the exclusion of women were the French convent schools which François Fenelon (1651–1715) had in mind when he wrote *The Education of Girls*. These schools provided instruction of a practical and devotional nature for orphaned girls and young ladies. The convent at Saint-Cyr, which was under the strict disciplinarian Madame Françoise de Maintenon (1635–1719), the second wife of Louis XIV, taught girls reading, writing, a little arithmetic, catechism, and the practical art of household duties. As a rule, however, most convents of this period educated young women exclusively for a life of devotion and made no provision for study of a scholastic nature.

NOTES

1. Vivian H. H. Green. *Renaissance and Reformation—A Survey of European History Between 1450 and 1660*. London: Edward Arnold & Co., 1952, pp. 307–328.
2. Crane Brinton, John B. Christopher, and Robert Wolff. *A History of Civilization* (Second Edition). New Jersey: Prentice-Hall, Inc., 1962, pp. 561–594.

3. H. G. Good. *A History of Western Education.* New York: The Macmillan Co., 1949, pp. 170–198.
4. François Rabelais. *Gargantua and Pantagruel.* New York: The Modern Library, 1928, pp. 48–53.
5. Boyd Henry Bode. *How We Learn.* New York: D. C. Heath and Co., 1940, p. 56.
6. *The Essayes of Michael Lord of Montaigne* (Volumes I and II). (Translated by John Florio.) New York: E. P. Dutton & Co., 1927.
7. Robert H. Quick. *Some Thoughts on Education by John Locke.* Cambridge: The University Press, 1880.
8. William H. Woodward. *Vittorina de Feltre and Humanist Educators.* Cambridge: The University Press, 1921.
9. Richard Mulcaster. *Positions* (With an Appendix Containing Some Account of His Life and Writings by Robert H. Quick). New York: Longmans, Green & Co., 1888.
10. Will S. Monroe. *Comenius' School of Infancy.* New York: D. C. Heath and Co., 1893.

Chapter 8

THE ERA OF ENLIGHTENMENT

A PERIOD OF TRANSITION

THE eighteenth century was marked by two trends, the recognition of the inalienable rights and dignity of man and his attempt to master his environment through critical analysis and scientific investigation.

At the start of the century England was the only European country with a democratic form of government which the people had won step by step from autocratic rulers. Government based on the consent of the people had its origin in the Magna Charta (1215), through which the English barons took the first steps to limit the power of future kings. For the next five centuries the English people tenaciously fought despotic monarchs for their constitutional rights and liberty, a struggle which culminated in 1689 with the passage of the Bill of Rights. On continental Europe the divine right of the kings still operated, though some monarchs had caught the spirit of humanitarianism and practiced the policy of Frederick the Great, "Everything for the people but nothing by the people." The French monarchs, Louis XIII and Louix XIV, did not practice benevolence, but instead curbed the power of the nobles and parliament and suppressed the liberties of the common people. Church and state, represented by a handful of clergy and nobles, controlled the destiny of 25 million people who were ignorant, hard-working, taxed beyond reason, yet intensely patriotic.[1]

EDUCATION IN THE EIGHTEENTH CENTURY

At best the elementary schools of the eighteenth century left much to be desired. The hours were long and boring, and the faculties were drawn from all walks of life, from gravediggers to clergymen. Whipping posts were common and the typical schoolteacher was pictured carrying a rod or with a bundle of switches nearby. One Teutonic schoolmaster recorded that in his 51 years of teaching he had administered 911,527 blows with the cane, 124,010 blows with the rod, and a mere 20,989 blows with the ruler. Children attended school for years to receive only a smattering of reading, writing, numbers, and a limited amount of catechism and Bible selections which they learned over and over again.[2]

In secondary education the tutorial system still prevailed and public and Latin grammar schools as well as church schools continued to provide a narrow curriculum along humanistic lines. A new type of secondary school, however, made its appearance which offered a more practical type of education to satisfy the demands of industry, agriculture, and commerce.

In the universities, still enslaved to medieval theology and seventeenth-century humanism, various scientific and mathematical studies, as well as a reformed type of philosophy influenced by French sources, found their way into the curriculum. Another innovation was the appearance of teacher-training institutions in France and the German states.

EDUCATIONAL REFORM IN FRANCE

By the middle of the eighteenth century the ideas of the French philosophers that education should be extended to all citizens of the state without class distinction and that education is a civil rather than a clerical responsibility had borne fruit in the New England colonies of North America and under the benevolent kings and progressive Lutheran educators of the German states. The French philosophers' theories, however, did not improve the situation at home, though beginning in 1750 a reform movement began which attacked the narrow and useless humanistic curriculum of the secondary schools and colleges of the Jesuit Order. Among other grievances, critics complained that the schools neglected instruction in the French language, ignored the history and geography of France, and wasted time in the learning of nonessentials. One of its most effective and provocative of critics was Rousseau.

JEAN JACQUES ROUSSEAU (1712–1778)

Rousseau was born in Geneva, Switzerland, of French Huguenot parents. As a youth he served as an apprentice to an engraver and at 16 ran away to the Duchy of Savoy, where he made the acquaintance of Madame de Warens. For the next ten years he lived in her home, where he came into contact with some of Europe's most brilliant intellectuals. Rousseau later became secretary to the French minister at Venice, but his vanity and sensitivity to criticism forced him to give up the position. He brought suit against the minister for breach of contract but soon learned that the common man had little hope of securing redress from an aristocrat. This incident was the turning point of his career, and henceforth he devoted himself to a study of the philosophy of government and social conditions. A keen student of Montaigne, Hobbes, and Locke, he developed many revolutionary ideas of his own in social, political, and educational theory.

THE "DISCOURSE ON INEQUALITY"

In 1753 Rousseau won the prize offered by the Academy of Dijon for an essay on the subject, "What Is the Origin of Inequality Among Men and Is It Authorized by Natural Law?" In this work, called the *Discourse on Inequality,* he gave an imaginary description of a man in a state of nature, having no particular need of his fellow creatures and concerned with little beyond the necessities of the moment, until the intrusion of human society corrupted his life:

> As long as men remained satisfied with their rustic cabins; as long as they confined themselves to the use of clothes made of the skins of other animals, and the use of thorns and fish bones in putting the skins together . . . as long as they undertook such works only as a single person could finish,

and stuck to such arts as did not require the joint endeavors of several hands, they lived free, healthy, honest and happy as much as their nature would admit . . . but from the moment one man began to stand in need of another's assistance; from the moment it appeared an advantage for one man to possess the quantity of provisions requisite for two; all equality vanished, property started up; labour became necessary; and boundless forests became smiling fields, which it was found necessary to water with human sweat, and in which slavery and misery was soon seen to sprout and grow with the fruits of the earth.

Men, accustomed from their infancy to the inclemency of the weather, and to the rigour of the different seasons; inured to fatigue, and obliged to defend, naked and without arms, their life and their prey against the other wild inhabitants of the forest, or at least to avoid their fury by flight, acquired a robust and almost unalterable habit of body; the children, bringing with them into the world the excellent constitution of their parents, and strengthening it by the same exercises that first produced it. . . . The body being the only instrument that savage man is acquainted with, he employs it to different uses, of which ours, for want of practice, are incapable; and we may thank our industry for the loss of that strength and agility, which necessity obliges him to acquire.[3]

"ÉMILE"

In 1762 Rousseau published his influential book, *Émile,* in which he attacked the religious, social, and educational conditions not only of France but of all Western Europe. In *Émile* he described the education of an imaginary boy and his wife-to-be, Sophia, according to the naturalistic method. Rousseau contended that a child's three teachers were nature, man, and experience (sense perceptions). Since he felt that the last two could destroy the benefits of the first, he removed his fictitious youth from the society of men to the seclusion of a woodland where he could romp and play at will in a recapitulation of the physical activities of the primitive past. Émile ran about bareheaded and barefooted, slept upon a rough bed, and ate nourishing but plain food. Émile's actual study began at the age of 12 and ended at 15 and was obtained not from books but through sense perceptions, observation, experimentation, and the association of ideas. Its materials were the wonders of nature, its motivation curiosity and interest.[4]

Rousseau's most influential contribution to educational theory was his notion that the natural impulses of the child should be freed from the restriction and discipline of formalized education in favor of learning through play, games, manual arts, and direct acquaintance with nature. He also attacked the contemporary view that human nature was innately sinful, insisting that man was inherently good and that this goodness should be allowed to express itself. Although Rousseau's natural education was more theoretical than practical, it undermined the type of religious education which held that man was born in sin, and laid the foundation for future advances in child education.

EXERCISE AND PLAY

Rabelais and Locke endorsed physical education in the court training schools for military and health reasons. Rousseau, on the other hand, saw it as part of the total development of the individual from childhood to adulthood:

> Since everything that comes into the human mind enters through the gates of sense, man's first reason is a reason of sense experience. It is this that serves as a foundation for the reason of intelligence; our first teachers in the natural Philosophy are our feet, hands, and eyes. . . . To learn to think we must therefore exercise our limbs, our senses, and our bodily organs, which are the tools of our intellect; and to get the best use out of these tools, the body which supplies us with them must be strong and healthy. Not only is it quite a mistake that true reason is developed apart from the body, but it is a good bodily constitution which makes the workings of the mind easy and correct.[5]

Giving this notion practical application, Rousseau noted that flying a kite improved the coordination of hand and eye, but contributed very little to the child's physical and social development. He did not object to such physical activities as afforded amusement to the child, but he preferred the social benefits to be derived from games. He wondered why children were not permitted to engage in the same sports as men, such as tennis, billiards, archery, and football. To those who argued that such games were beyond the strength and ability of the child and much too complex for his age level, Rousseau answered that adjustments could easily be made in playing facilities and size of equipment to suit the needs of children. To those who considered football too rough and hazardous game for youngsters, he said that children must learn to take pain and physical discomfort as preparation for the vicissitudes of adult life: "To dash from one end of the room to another, to judge the rebound of a ball before it touches the ground, to return it with strength and accuracy, such games are not so much sports fit for a man, as sports fit to make a man of him."[5]

Rousseau's emphasis on the child's natural inclination to play and the value of such activity in the learning process had an important influence upon the education of the preschool child and led to the establishment of kindergartens in Europe and America during the first quarter of the nineteenth century. He states that to the child, "Work or Play are all one . . . . his games are his work; he knows no difference. He brings to everything the cheerfulness of interest, the charm of freedom, and he shows the bent of his own mind and the extent of his knowledge."[5] Play developed the child's body and helped him to see the relationship between his own and other bodies, and the use of his "natural tools."

Rousseau, however, advised against compulsory play, which would diminish the natural charm inherent in activities that are self-motivated:

> Besides, we must never forget that all this should be play, the easy and voluntary control of the movements which nature demands of them, the art of varying their games to make them pleasanter, without the least restraint to transform them to work; for what games do they play in which I could not do so, so long as they are amusing themselves harmlessly and passing the time pleasantly, their progress in learning is not yet of such great importance. But if one must be teaching them this or that at every opportunity, it cannot be done without constraint, vexation, or tedium.[5]

ROUSSEAU AND THE NATURALISTIC SCHOOLS

Many experimental schools based on Rousseau's naturalistic method came into existence, and were called philanthropinums, from the Greek meaning "brother of man." These schools not only provided a broader curriculum for both sexes and all classes, but also included physical education, excursions into the countryside, vocational training, and gardening. The teachers of physical education were guided by practices formulated in the court training schools of the Renaissance, modified by their individual interpretations of Rousseau. These two factors combined dominated European education during the nineteenth century and paved the way for modern concepts of physical education.

BASEDOW AND THE PHILANTHROPINUM

Johann Basedow (1724–1790) was born in Hamburg and educated in theology at the University of Leipzig. Later becoming a tutor, he developed his famous method of teaching through conversation and play associated with objects in the classroom. In 1774 he published a book on method (*Methodenbuch*) which contained many of Rousseau's ideas on the natural education of children. Later in collaboration with other German educators he produced a series of books adapted to the needs and interest of children of various age levels.

On the strength of his reputation as a successful educator Basedow secured the help of Prince Leopold Franz in the establishment of a naturalistic school, or Philanthropinum, in the Duchy of Anhalt in 1774. Prince Franz provided Basedow with two buildings, a garden, and 12,000 thalers. Language was taught by the conversational method, instruction was provided in the manual arts and gardening, and both physical education and supervised play were featured in the school program. Like most of the philanthropinums of the time this school was open to all classes.

Basedow turned out to be quarrelsome, vulgar, and inclined to be boastful. His inability to get along with the people with whom he worked led to his dismissal. The Philanthropinum eventually closed in 1793, three years after its director's death.

PHYSICAL EDUCATION IN THE PHILANTHROPINUM

The school's prospectus of 1774 stated that five hours a day were to be devoted to study, three hours to fencing, riding, dancing, gymnastics, music, and other activities, and two hours to manual arts. Johann Friedrich Simon was appointed physical education instructor and served from 1776 to 1777. Simon gave weekly lessons in dancing, fencing, and riding. When he found that the young children did not perform too well in these activities, he instituted what he called the Greek pentathlon, which consisted of running, jumping, climbing, balancing, and the carrying of heavy weights. He also taught his pupils shuttlecock, tennis, skittles, and several ball games. His successor, Johann du Toit, a military man, provided a program of singing, reading aloud, swimming, skating, musket practice, archery, marching and playing soldier, extensive hikes over the countryside, woodworking, and gardening.

OTHER PHILANTHROPINUMS

An immediate boom of similar schools followed, many of which bloomed by day and perished overnight. One of the most successful of these was the Schnepfenthal Educational Institute founded by Christian Salzmann (1744–1811) and sponsored by Duke Ernst II of Saxe-Gotha. The first physical education teacher employed at the Institute was Christian Carl André, who remained for one year. His program included gymnastics, throwing at a target, running, jumping, and a type of calisthenic drill. Sunday afternoons were spent in hikes and excursions. André left in 1786 and was succeeded by Johann Friedrich Guts Muths (1759–1839).

CONTRIBUTIONS OF GUTS MUTHS

Guts Muths served the Schnepfenthal Institute for fifty years and was called the "Father of the *Deutsch Turnverein.*" He was a contemporary of Freidrich Ludwig Jahn (1778–1852), who adopted his ideas and developed the German Turner Society into an influential international organization during the nineteenth century. Guts Muths was a graduate of the University of Halle, where he studied mathematics, physics, theology, modern languages, and pedagogy. In addition to being an accomplished gymnast, he was skilled in woodworking, sketching and painting.

Guts Muths set the pattern for the German system which was adopted by many Central European countries and introduced to America as early as 1825. As in the case of all philanthropinums,

Guts Muths conducted his program out of doors on a level open place surrounded by trees. Guts Muth's program included exercises on the climbing mast, horizontal bar, vaulting apparatus, balance beam, and rope ladders, and stunts in tumbling. It is certain that he derived many of his ideas for his program from Mercurialis' *The Art of Gymnastics* and Saint Archange Tuccaro's *Three Decalogues on the Art of Jumping and Tumbling in the Air* (Paris, 1589). Guts Muths's contemporary, Gerhard Ulrich Anton Vieth* (1763–1836), probably not only furnished him with ideas for activities and apparatus design but also influenced his program planning. Guts Muths was an efficient teacher of gymnastic skills, graded his exercises according to difficulty and age level, and kept a record of his pupils' progress.

Joseph Rockl, who spent nine days as a visitor at the Institute, commented on the frugal diet of the pupils, their light and simple clothing, the airy rooms for sleeping and study, their personal cleanliness and active outdoor life which included hiking, work in the garden, and gymnastics. He was impressed by the riding school, the grounds for jumping and vaulting, and the swimming area.

Guts Muths's first publication was his *Gymnastics for the Young* (1793). This book was published in England in 1800 and in Philadelphia in 1802 and 1803. The English and American editions erroneously credit C. G. Salzmann, Director of the Schnepfenthal Institute, as the author. In it Guts Muths classified his exercises as follows: (1) walking and running; (2) jumping, free and with apparatus; (3) lifting and carrying exercises of the back muscles, pulling, pushing, thrusting, and wrestling; (4) fencing; (5) climbing; (6) exercises to maintain equilibrium, or balancing with the aid of apparatus; (7) throwing and archery; (8) bathing and swimming; (9) exercises of suppleness, to train the aesthetic sense, will

* In 1794 Vieth completed the first volume of his *Encyklopaedie der Leibesübungen* (*Encyclopedia of Bodily Exercise*), in which he described activities closely resembling those sponsored by physical education teachers of the philanthropinums. Vieth classified his exercises as passive and active. Under passive exercises he included lying, sitting, swinging, bathing, massage, and others. Among active exercises he listed walking, jumping, and vaulting (long, front, rear, squat, and straddle). Vieth's apparatus included the balance beam, jumping ropes, climbing ropes and poles, horse, buck, table, and horizontal bars at various heights which were probably the forerunner of the horizontal and parallel bars used by both Guts Muths and Jahn.

power, and organs of speech; (10) dancing; and (11) exercises to train the senses. His other publications include *Games* (1796), *Manual on the Art of Swimming* (1798), *Book of Gymnastics for Sons of the Fatherland* (1817), and *Catechism of Gymnastics, a Manual for Teachers and Pupils* (1818).

JOHANN HEINRICH PESTALOZZI (1746–1827)

One of the great educators of all time, Johann Pestalozzi was born in Zurich, Switzerland. His family were Italian Protestant refugees who settled in Switzerland about the middle of the sixteenth century. He received his higher education at the University of Zurich where he studied theology and law and became interested in Rousseau's *Social Contract* and *Émile.* Pestalozzi, familiar with the poor living conditions of the Swiss peasants, decided that he would lead a movement for social reform. After he left the university, however, he found out that he first had to make a living and tried his hand at farming. He failed miserably at this and turned to writing. In 1781 he attained sudden success with a book called *Leonard and Gertrude,* a story of Swiss peasant life sympathetically and understandingly written.

Through necessity Pestalozzi accepted teaching assignments at Neuhof and Stantz, where he taught the orphaned and destitute children of Swiss parents who had been killed resisting the French. He discovered that his love of children was a great asset in teaching, and through observation and experimentation he began to formulate his educational principles. When the Neuhof and Stantz schools were closed because of his own shortcomings and through government intervention, in 1799 he accepted teaching assignment at Burgdorf, where he continued to experiment.

In 1800 the authorities decided to establish a teacher-training institute at Burgdorf and Pestalozzi added his pupils to those of Herman Krüsi. The new arrangement left Pestalozzi virtually head of the institute, and he seized the opportunity to put into practice the principles he had been evolving. During the next three and a half years Pestalozzi established an international reputation as the discoverer and practitioner of a more scientific methodology in elementary education. In 1804 the Swiss government appointed Pestalozzi director of the newly established Institute of Teacher Training at Yverdun, where he remained for twenty years.

PESTALOZZI'S EDUCATIONAL THEORIES

The best two sources of Pestalozzi's ideas on educational theories and methods are his *Report of the Method* (1800) and *How Gertrude Teachers Her Children* (1801).[6] The Swiss educator, like his predecessors, drew upon past and contemporary thought and was particularly indebted to Comenius, Locke, and Rousseau. Pestalozzi accepted Rousseau's natural method but believed that the educational process must go on in the society of men. Nature had placed obstacles in the path of the learner and it was the responsibility of the teacher to help the child overcome these obstacles. The aim of elementary education was to continue the mother's role of teacher in the home in the same spirit of Christian love. As an administrator at Yverdun Pestalozzi had to sacrifice personal contact with the children, and thus lost much of the vitality which characterized his early activities as a teacher and experimenter.

From both Locke and Rousseau the Swiss educator adopted the principle of sense impressions as the starting point for his experimentation with elementary school children:

> You are, as a physical living being, nothing but your five senses; consequently the clearness or mistiness of your ideas must absolutely and essentially rest upon the nearness or distance with which all external objects touch those five senses, that is, yourself, the centre, because your ideas converge in you. . . . All that you feel of yourself is in itself a definite sense-impression; only that which is without can be confused sense-impression to you. . . . We must follow exactly the same course nature followed herein with the human race. We dare not do otherwise. And she unquestionably began with sense-impression.[6]

The teacher had the children regard every object presented to them as a unit apart from its background, note its form including size and proportion, and finally describe it in words. This method of instruction rapidly became known all over the world as "object teaching." Pestalozzi quickly discovered that picture books were valuable teaching aids and that the material in these books had to be organized at the level of the child's ability to comprehend. In designating sense impressions as the basis of the learning process, Pestalozzi antedated the era of systematic psychology.

In his discussion of method, Pestalozzi constantly referred to the principle of *Anschauung*. Locke defined this as the internal perception of the mind, but the more modern Pollard provided a better rendering of this German term.[2] He suggested that Pestalozzi, like many teachers from time immemorial, experienced *Anschauung* when he reached complete union with the mind of the child. At this moment, he suddenly became conscious of the difficulties he must surmount to solve a particular problem in presentation. *Anschauung* made it clear to Pestalozzi that "All branches of instruction demand essentially psychological analysis of their methods, and age should be exactly fixed at which each may, and ought to be, given the child."[6] As a teacher Pestalozzi abided by the principle that the learner must be stimulated to self-activity rather than goaded to action by harsh disciplinary measures. He demonstrated to all who visited his schools that teaching was a sympathetic form of guidance, a process that need not sacrifice the needs of the individual child. Pestalozzi's greatest contribution to education was the freeing of countless thousands of children from the monotonous treadmill of formal training inherited from the past.

PESTALOZZI AND PHYSICAL EDUCATION

Pestalozzi believed that physical education should receive just as serious consideration in the school program as traditional subjects. The principle of *Anschauung* should work just as effectively, and the instructional material, activities (*Fertigkeiten*), should be arranged in progressive steps according to age level. It was his belief, at the time that he wrote *How Gertrude Teaches Her Children*, that these activities contained the basic movemants that man would be called upon to perform throughout life. Pestalozzi listed as natural activities those which involved striking, carrying, thrusting, throwing, drawing, turning, circling, swinging, running, jumping, and climbing. In his opinion civilization had become negligent in failing to train the child in these movements, and was far behind primitive society, where they were practiced out of necessity.[6]

In a report on his school at Burgdorf, Pestalozzi stated that physical education activities were conducted under the supervision of a teacher of his staff. He encouraged the joint participation of teachers and pupils, but burdened with administrative responsibilities and a constant conflict of interest among staff members, he himself was obliged to employ physical educators who had been trained in the German system of gymnastics. Thus more and more time was devoted to formal exercises on apparatus and less and less to natural activities. At both Burgdorf and Yverdun an hourly period five afternoons per week was devoted to gymnastics.

At one point of his career at Yverdun, Pestalozzi became interested in a system of gymnastics popularized by the Germans called *Gelenkenbüngen* (exercises to develop flexibility in the joints). He experimented with artificially devised movements of the limbs and trunk to improve grace of movement. Somewhere along the line Pestalozzi had allowed his broader view of physical education to be submerged by the popular European movement of gymnastics as an exclusive activity in the physical education program.

PESTALOZZI'S EUROPEAN DISCIPLES

Pestalozzi's Institute received international acclaim and became a mecca for those who wished to study his educational methods. Many of these visitors remained at the Institute for a short while to observe; others secured positions as teachers for a year or two, then moved on. Many wrote of their observations and experiences at the Institute. Some were sent by their governments to study Pestalozzi's methods in order to establish similar schools in their homelands. Among those who visited or taught at Pestalozzi's schools were Froebel, Herbart, and von Fellenberg.

FRIEDRICH FROEBEL (1782–1852)

This German educator was born in Thuringia, the son of a rural clergyman. Froebel's mother died when he was very young, and under the domination of a stepmother who was a typical fairy tale stepmother, he developed into a retiring and introspective child. Following a two-year apprenticeship as a forester in the great Thuringian forests, where he learned to love nature, he spent two years under Pestalozzi at Yverdun (1808–1810) as a pupil and teacher.

At the close of the Napolconic Wars, in which he served, Froebel founded at Griesheim the Universal German Educational Institute, which he conducted for twenty years along Pestalozzian principles. During these years he published his book, *The Education of Man* (1826), and formulated his belief that the most needed reform in education was in that of young children.[8] After returning to Switzerland to serve as a teacher in the Infant School, he went back to Germany and opened a school for young children. This school, which he called the *Kindergarten,* featured play, games, songs, and small projects in which self-activity was paramount.

Froebel believed that the education of the child should begin at birth and be developed through the natural method. Since the child learned by doing and through self-activity, the materials of instruction should be selected from life itself.

FROEBEL ON PLAY

Though the *Education of the Man* was published in 1826, the modern physical educator and recreation worker can still find inspiration in his discussion of the growth and development of the child's play. No one had had a deeper understanding of this phase of child life. "The plays of childhood are the germinal leaves of all later life; for the whole man is developed and shown in these, in his tenderest dispositions, in his innermost tendencies. The whole later life of man, even to the moment when he shall leave it again, has its source in the period of childhood."[8] Froebel discovered the true nature and function of play and how to so guide it as to lead gradually and naturally into work. He saw play not as an end in itself, but as a transitory phase through which the child could be led into productive adult activity which would yield the same satisfaction, freedom, and serenity.

THE SOCIAL VALUE OF GAMES

Froebel delineated the social value of games with an understanding unusual for an educator of the early nineteenth century. While the play of the child consisted of activities for their own sake, the games of the adolescent took on a definite and conscious purpose. This could be observed in all his activities, such as boxing, wrestling, ball games, and games of hunting and war. Froebel's grasp of the value of games to social development is expressed in his *Education of the Man:*

It is the sense of sure and reliable power, the sense of its increase, both as an individual and as a member of the group, that fills the boy with all-pervading, jubilant joy during these games. It is by no means, however, only the physical power that is fed and strengthened in these games; intellectual and moral power, too, is definitely and steadily gained and brought under control. Indeed, a comparison of the relative gains of mental and of physical phases would scarcely yield the palm to the body. Justice, moderation, self-control, truthfulness, loyalty, brotherly love, and, again strict impartiality . . . who, when he approaches a group of boys engaged in such games, could fail to catch the fragrance of these delicious blossomings of the heart and mind, and of a firm will; not to mention the beautiful, though perhaps less fragrant, blossoms of courage, perseverance, resolution, prudence, together with the severe elimination of indolent indulgence? Whoever would inhale a fresh quickening breath of life should visit the playgrounds of such boys. . . . Would that all who, in the education of boys, barely tolerate playgrounds, might consider these things! There are, indeed, many harsh words and many rude deeds, but the sense of power must needs precede its cultivation. Keen, clear, and penetrating are the boy's eye and sense in the recognition of inner meaning; keen and decided, therefore, even harsh and severe, is his judgement of those who are his equals, or who claim equality with him in judgement and power.[8]

JOHANN FRIEDRICH HERBART (1776–1841)

The German philosopher Johann Herbart was born at Oldenburg. He studied at the University of Jena and was a pupil of Johann Fichte, who taught that each individual formed his own ideas of the external world and that the chief aim of education should be to develop character. Herbart taught at the Universities of Göttingen and conducted a practice school at Königsberg. At first, he followed Fichte's teachings, but later rejected some of his ideas, such as the Aristotelian faculty psychology, which classified mental phenomena into separate compartments of knowledge such as feeling and will and their subcapacities. Advocates of faculty psychology held that the school should train each mental faculty through some distinct and appropriate discipline. Herbart based education on the concept that mind and body functioned as a unit and that the mind was not endowed with inborn faculties as Pestalozzi had postulated. The mind, according to Herbart, was a blank at birth and possessed only the power of relating to its environment through the senses. The mind acquired moral concepts through experience; good and evil were not inherent, but depended upon what one was taught.

Herbart maintained that interest was the most important element in successful instruction and that it was the duty of the teacher to provide the learner with new and real experience. He advocated five formal steps of instruction: preparation, presentation, apperception, generalization, and application.

Philipp Emanuel von Fellenberg (1771–1844)

The fellow countryman of Pestalozzi, von Fellenberg, was a real-life counterpart of Rousseau's *Émile*. As a boy he roamed the woodland and countryside adjoining his father's castle at Wildenstein near the river Aar. Like Émile he had a tutor, Albert Rengger, who was a close friend of Pestalozzi and who devoted his entire time to the education of the young aristocrat. By the time von Fellenberg was 15 he had read Pestalozzi's *Leonard and Gertrude* with a marked sympathy for the lot of the underpriviledged and uneducated Swiss peasant. As a youth he resolved to champion the cause of the poor peasants and later prepared himself by living and working among them.

After his father's death von Fellenberg purchased an estate at Hofwyl near Berne and established one of the first vocational schools in Europe for the education of the children of peasant farmers. He made every practical phase of agriculture a part of his instruction, including soil experimentation, farm mechanics, crop production, tillage, and fertilization. Five years later, in 1809, von Fellenberg took inventory and announced to the world that he had not only provided a practical education for hundreds of Swiss farm boys but also increased the value of his estate fivefold by following scientific agricultural practices. Public interest in the educational program was immediate, and a steady flow of visitors from both Europe and America made their appearance at Hofwyl.

Since his own sons had arrived at school age, von Fellenberg decided in 1811 to open a boarding school for young gentlemen on the same estate as his thriving vocational school. Within two years this institution became one of the most famous academies in Europe and in time was attended by the sons of many wealthy merchants and nobility from the German monarchies, Russia, Scotland, and America. Enrollment was limited to one hundred boys and the tuition approximated $1500 per school year. The instructional staff numbered thirty-five masters, each of whom was a recognized specialist in his field.

PHYSICAL EDUCATION

In von Fellenberg's opinion the physical development of his pupils was adequately covered by their work in the fields and shops at Hofwyl. This opinion was shared by other educators, particularly those who organized schools for the children of the poor. In von Fellenberg's academy, however, although the boys were occupied by their studies five hours in the morning and four hours in the afternoon, they were permitted to engage in the activity of their choice during free periods. Qualified instructors were provided in the playing of musical instruments, gymnastics, horseback riding, fencing, dancing, and swimming. In addition, facilities had been constructed on the estate for many of these activities. So firmly did von Fellenberg believe that life in the open was conducive to health that he provided every boy in his academy with a garden plot for which he was personally responsible from planting to harvesting.

During holidays many of the boys were too far from home to travel and spent these days of freedom in the company of their fellows hiking to points of interest in Switzerland or adjoining countries.

AN EVALUATION OF VON FELLENBERG

Many historians consider von Fellenberg an educational thinker of little consequence. When his contributions to educational theory are compared with those of his brilliant contemporaries, this evaluation may be true. It must be remembered, however, that von Fellenberg was a practical man and an organizer. His strength lay in his ability to put the theories of others to practical use.

This pragmatic approach led him to miss the broader objectives of physical education expounded by Rousseau and Pestalozzi. As a substitute for an organized physical education program, where could one find more natural and utilitariar activities than those involved in the cultivation and harvesting of crops, or in the repair of farm machinery and tools? In his academy von Fellenberg had to satisfy the interests of a discriminating clientele whose social background demanded a different treatment than the peasant boys in the vocational school. With the acumen of a businessman von Fellenberg selected the activities most suitable for the young gentleman and conducted them in the best traditions of the Renaissance court schools. He was never confused in his objectives, and his approach to physical education must be evaluated with this in mind.

NOTES

1. R. R. Palmer. *A History of the Modern World.* New York: Alfred A. Knopf, 1950, pp. 310–321.
2. Hugh M. Pollard. *Pioneers of Popular Education, 1760–1850.* London: John Murray, 1956, pp. 3–11; 41–42; 49–50.
3. *French and English Philosophers.* (The Harvard Classics, edited by Charles W. Eliott) New York: P. F. Collier & Son Company, 1910, pp. 210; 172–173.
4. I. N. Thut. *The Story of Education.* New York: McGraw-Hill Book

Company, Inc., 1957, pp. 229–246; H. G. Good. *A History of Western Education*. New York: The Macmillan Company, 1949, pp. 201–222.

5. Jean Jacques Rousseau. *Émile, or Education*. (Translated by Barbara Foxley, M.A.) New York: E. P. Dutton and Company, 1914, pp. 90; 111; 126; 112; 104.
6. Johann Heinrich Pestalozzi. *How Gertrude Teaches Her Children*. (Translated by Lucy E. Holland and Francis C. Turner) Syracuse: C. W. Bardeen, 1915, pp. 86, 199; 149–150; 126; 177–178.
7. *The School of Infancy*. (Edited with an Introduction by Ernest M. Eller) Chapel Hill: University of North Carolina Press, 1956.
8. Freidrich Froebel. *The Education of Man*. (Translated from the German and Annotated by W. N. Hailman, A. M.) International Education Series. New York: D. Appleton and Company, 1887, pp. 55; 113.

Chapter 9

PHYSICAL EDUCATION IN NINETEENTH-CENTURY CONTINENTAL EUROPE

EUROPEAN POLITICS, 1800–1850

FOLLOWING the Congress of Vienna at the close of the Napoleonic Wars in 1815, Austria became a leading European nation, and Prince Metternich, one of Europe's major political personalities. Both Metternich and Frederick William III of Prussia established policies which kept their central governments all-powerful and permitted the people only such constitutional liberties as were compatible with the interest of the state. In both states the clergy and military joined forces to produce intelligent, patriotic citizens, but, above all, obedient and well-disciplined soldiers.

In spite of their progressive monarchs, the peoples of Europe manifested a persistent desire for constitutional reforms. The years between 1815 and 1850 were marked by an incessant struggle between autocratic and liberal factions. Nicholas of Russia followed his predecessor, Alexander, in restricting the constitutional liberties of the people. In France Charles X was deposed in the Revolution of 1830 when he sought to limit the rights of the people, as was his successor, Louis Philippe, following the Revolution of 1848.

King Frederick William III was unusually tolerant of Prussian liberals, although the state was honeycombed by secret societies which advocated the unification of Germany and the extension of constitutional rights to the people. Each university had its group of professor and student organizations (*Burschenschaften*) who enunciated or published liberal views. The Germany gymnastic societies (*Deutsch Turnvereins*) contained members bold enough to preach their democratic views to those who would listen.

The Prussian monarch's tolerance, however, came to an abrupt end in 1819 when Karl Ludwig Sand, a member of the student organization at the University of Jena led by Charles Follen, assassinated August von Kotzebue, a German dramatist and alleged Russian spy. Following this incident Metternich called a conference of the German princes which adopted the Carlsbad Decree. This decree outlawed secret societies, censored the press, provided police supervision of universities, and delegated to a committee of seven the responsibility of tracking down revolutionary conspiracies and demagogic associations.

The work of Metternich and political conditions in the German states made impossible any unified movement such as the Revolution of 1830 in France. The death of Francis I of Austria in 1835 weakened Matternich's influence in the German confederation, and with the accession of King Frederick William IV to the Prussian throne liberals hoped that this German state would take the leadership in moving toward constitutional reform and national unification. This hope proved vain, and outbreaks sparked by the Paris Revolution of 1848 were quickly suppressed by the armed forces of the imperial government.

NATIONALISTIC TRENDS, 1850–1900

The emergence of France as a military power in the Crimean War and the steady progress of Italy toward national unity had a strong influence upon the German states. In the Crimean War against Russia (1853–1856) Great Britain and France formed an alliance with each other for the first time in two centuries. Anxious not to go to war against Russia, Frederick William of Prussia made an alliance with Austria ostensibly to keep the Russians out of the lower Danube but actually to discourage Austria from joining England and France in Turkey. In 1859 Austria became involved in a war with France and Sardinia over her possessions in northern

Italy and appealed to Prussia for military support without success. King William I succeeded to the Prussian throne in 1861 and as his minister of state chose Otto, Count von Bismarck. Throughout his diplomatic career Bismarck dedicated himself to establishing Germany as a world power and to its final unification. Seeking to end German dependence upon Austria, he manipulated the Austrians into the war of 1866 with a show of German military strength. He maneuvered the French into the Franco-German War of 1870. During the war he pushed negotiations for a conference of Prussia, Bavaria, and Württemberg at Munich to complete formalities for the unification of the German states.

He guaranteed the survival of Austria-Hungary as a first-rate power by concluding an alliance with that state against Russia, but made it clear that he did not approve of Austria-Hungary's ambitions in the Balkans. Bismarck also disapproved of the Reich's colonial expansion, which might conflict with the imperial interests of Great Britain and France. The ascension of Emperor William II to the throne in 1888 represented the emergence of a new Germany, an arrogant, self-confident Germany which recognized no limits to its power. The conservative Bismarck did not fit into the new regime, and he resigned in 1890.[1]

EDUCATION IN NINETEENTH-CENTURY EUROPE

Napoleon left the responsibility for elementary education to the local community, which he required to furnish schools and teachers and pay for them out of local tax funds. His own interest was in the technical and scientific training of the secondary school pupil. The Law of 1802 established two types of secondary schools in France: the communal colleges, which were established and supported by private and religious interests, and the *lycées,* which were inaugurated and financed by the government. The Law of 1833 made the maintenance of elementary schools mandatory in every community, and the Law of 1850 required elementary schools to provide instruction in agriculture, trades, hygiene, history, geography, singing, and gymnastics in addition to the conventional subjects.

The Prussians showed a keen interest in the Pestalozzian method of instruction and in 1809 commissioned Carl August Zeller, a former pupil of Pestalozzi at Yverdun, to establish a teachers' seminary at Württemberg. In addition, the Prussian government sent seventeen teachers to Switzerland to study the Pestalozzian system in order to found similar seminaries. This practice was adopted by the other German states. Although the Germans recognized the effectiveness of the Pestalozzian method, they considered the purpose of education to be the perpetuation of the state. Geography, history, and language were taught as much for their patriotic as for their educational value. Singing patriotic songs was also encouraged outside of the school in singing societies, on hiking excursions, and at festivals. The gymnastics practiced in Pestalozzi's school were adopted from the German system, but in the Prussian schools they were more highly organized and prized for their hygienic and military value. In the teaching of religion emphasis was on self-sacrifice, humility, and obedience to authority.

During the first two decades of the nineteenth century the Prussian government laid the foundation for mass education by establishing elementary schools (*Volksschule*) and providing teacher-training institutions to underwrite the system. In 1816 a uniform course of instruction in secondary schools was adopted by the government. The curriculum included Latin, Greek, German, mathematics, history, geography, religion, and science. By 1810 teachers were required to take qualifying examinations in secondary school subjects.

THE DEVELOPMENT OF GYMNASTICS IN CENTRAL EUROPE

During the Napoleonic campaigns many European states suffered the humiliation of defeat. The Prussians had felt confident in the military heritage established by Frederick the Great, and Napoleon's easy victory at Jena in 1806 came as a blow to German pride. As an ally of Napoleon the Danes waged war on land and sea at a terrific loss of manpower as well as material resources. Denmark finally had to cede Norway to Sweden. The Swedes fought the Russians and lost Finland, which had been in their possession for many centuries. These defeats stirred the nations to rebuild their armies in order to redeem themselves should the opportunity present itself. Thus the era of the Napoleonic Wars was an opportune moment for expert gymnasts who had the ability to organize and lead. Governments established army training schools where these men could teach potential instructors in the armed service.

GYMNASTICS IN SCHOOL AND SOCIETY

As the military pressure for physically trained men abated and the training of gymnastic leaders for the armed service became routinized, gymnastic leaders turned their attention to the field of education. In some cases the shift from the military to the school was made without much modification. Other leaders soon discovered that a program suitable for army personnel was beyond the capacity and foreign to the interests of children in school. Although many instructors recognized the fact that children like to play, they were guided in their choice of school programs by the mechanistic theory of bodily exercise inherited from the past. And they found such programs well suited to peoples accustomed to regimentation by the state.

GYMNASTICS IN OTHER AREAS

Gymnastic leaders also applied the mechanistic theory to the ill effects of occupations upon the body and to the area of physical rehabilitation. They recognized, for example, that certain occupations led to the shortening of the flexor muscles of the upper body, thus limiting the normal range of movement of the joints, shoulder girdle, and spinal column. This shortening of the flexors destroyed flexibility and body balance. To counterbalance this, gymnastic leaders of the nineteenth century devised exercises and apparatus to lengthen the flexors and tone up the extensors.

Closely related was the entrance of gymnastic leaders into the field of physical rehabilitation. These early pioneers in muscular reeducation applied all available knowledge in anatomy and physiology in their use of exercises and apparatus.

THE GERMAN SYSTEM

FRIEDRICH LUDWIG JAHN (1778–1852)

The "Father of Gymnastics" was born in Linz, Prussia. He received his education in the higher classical school at Salzwedel and entered the University of Halle to study theology. He never completed his university education, but left school to wander on foot through the German confederation. After several positions as tutor to the sons of noblemen, he applied for employment in a school but was not accepted because he lacked the qualifications. Determined to teach, Jahn enrolled in one of the many Pestalozzian seminaries in Berlin and, when he had completed his courses, became a teacher of mathematics and history at Graue Kloster. In 1811 Jahn affiliated himself with Plamann's famous Pestalozzian school for boys in Berlin.

As customary in Prussian schools of this era, Jahn spent Wednesdays and Saturday afternoons in outdoor activities with his boys. In the spring of 1810 Jahn made a practice of meeting his boys at Graue Kloster in an open area enclosed by trees near the school which he called the *Turnplatz.** There he assembled the material necessary to construct apparatus recommended by Guts Muths and other contemporaries and laid out a figure-eight running track. In the circles of the figure eight Jahn provided a palaestra, or wrestling area, and a jumping pit with standards for high jumping and pole vaulting.

On this open-air gymnasium he led his boys in simple exercises, stunts, and games. When by the spring of 1811 Jahn united the boys from Graue Kloster with those of Plamann's school, he was obliged to adopt some plan of organization. By summer of the same year he had formally initiated the program which later was to serve as a guide in the development of the German Turner Societies. Jahn appointed *vorturners,* or squad leaders, graded and classified activi-

* *Turnen* in German means to exercise. A *Turnplatz* is a place to exercise and the equivalent to the playground area with apparatus. *Turnkunst* is the art of exercise and *Turnhalle,* a more modern innovation, an exercise hall or gymnasium.

ties according to age and difficulty, and varied them to insure a balanced and interesting program. He soon found that street clothes were impractical and added nothing to the *esprit de corps* of his boys, so he adopted long trousers and a gray unbleached linen jacket as a uniform. This gymnastic costume became a trade-mark not only in the German states but in other parts of the world where Turners migrated.

AN EVALUATION OF JAHN

Jahn is sometimes condemned for introducing the world to a formalized and artificial type of exercise. Criticism of this kind often results from a failure to understand the philosophy and objectives of a foreign way of life. Jahn recognized the inclination of youth to run, jump, climb, and throw, and his personally planned program gave important consideration to these natural activities.[2] His apparatus work was conducted as stunts, and boys were encouraged to invent new patterns of movement to challenge one another. In his book, *German Gymnastics* (1816), he expressed a dislike for artificial exercises and was himself critical of Pestalozzi, who promoted exercises in his school at Yverdun designed to improve the flexibility of the joints.

After the Sand-Kotzebue incident in 1819, Jahn, suspected of spreading liberal views, was imprisoned and not released until six years later. From the day of his release until his pardon in 1840 by King Frederick William IV, Jahn was kept under constant police surveillance and was forbidden to live within a ten-mile radius of Berlin or any city in which a higher school or university was located. Recognized and revered by the Germans as the originator of the Turner movement, which eventually became world-wide, Jahn made his contribution in the space of eight years. The final character of his program was determined by his successors and not by him.

ADOLPH SPIESS (1810–1858)

Spiess was born in Lauterbach, the son of a Thuringian father. He entered the University of Giessen in 1828 to study theology and there became proficient in fencing and gymnastics. He left Giessen in 1829 with a group of fellow classmates and hiked to Schnepfenthal, where he visited Guts Muths's classes. The following year he enrolled in the University of Halle to continue his study of theology. In 1833 Spiess applied for the position of teacher of gymnastics, singing, writing, and drawing at Pestalozzi's school at Burgdorf, Switzerland, and was accepted.

At this time Friedrich Froebel, the founder of the kindergarten movement, was also associated with the Burgdorf school, and Spiess was considerably influenced by his philosophy of play and exercise as an educational method. Spiess's program provided gymnastics for two successive hours three afternoons a week. He also devised special exercises for girls and took the children on frequent hikes. In the fall Spiess held a gymnastic exhibition (*Turnfest*) at which the children demonstrated what they had accomplished during the school year.

SPIESS'S FREE EXERCISES

Through his experiences in teaching the German system at Burgdorf Spiess became convinced that this type of gymnastic exercise was unsuitable for the school situation. He therefore devised a series of exercises that could be performed in the classroom. Based on the mechanistic theory, these later became known as "free exercises," which could be performed with or without apparatus in the hands.

In his free exercises Spiess combined the six parts of the body (two arms, two legs, head, and trunk), six directions (up, down, forward, backward, right, and left), and the different forms of locomotion.[3] He soon realized that the mathematical possibilities of the various combination of these were practically unlimited.

Spiess separated muscular work from the vital physiological functions of respiration and circulation and, because of his scanty knowledge of body mechanics, failed to consider the physical principle of levers. Physiological facts were of little significance to Spiess because he knew that he had a system of free exercises which was simple to teach, easy to perform, and economical in its space requirement. To move his pupils into position to perform the free exercises, he arranged marching formations (*Class Exercises in*

Marching, 1846). Since he had a gift for music he devised rhythmical accompaniment for his free exercises and marching drills, and this feature added much to their popularity in the schools.

SPIESS'S PROMOTION WORK

The ascension of King Frederick William IV presaged a more liberal attitude toward the *Turnverein.* Sensing the change of attitude, Spiess returned to Prussia in 1842 and approached the influential leaders of the Turner Society with the hope that they might adopt his system of free exercise. The leaders, however, were too satisfied with German gymnastics to consider a system which had not been tried and proven.

In 1848 Spiess received an appointment to introduce gymnastics in the schools of the state of Hesse. At Darmstadt he introduced his free exercises in two secondary schools for boys (*Gymnasium* and *Realschule*) and in a higher school for girls (*Mädchenschule*). A public gymnasium (*Turnhaus*) was built in Darmstadt in 1852 for the use of both boys and girls. This gymnasium, one of the first of its kind to be constructed for the use of the public schools, featured movable partitions which made it possible to separate the 100-by-60-foot room into two gymnasium areas.[4]

By 1849 Spiess found it necessary to establish a four weeks' course for teachers of his free exercises in the schools of the Grand Duchy of Hesse, and between 1852 and 1854 his classes at Darmstadt attracted many official visitors from the German states and foreign countries. Spiess had succeeded in making free exercises a part of the school program and in so doing had introduced the gymnasium as an important part of the school's facilities. In the ensuing years his free exercises also became an accepted part of the activity program of the German Turner Society.

THE EXPANSION OF THE GERMAN SYSTEM

From its modest start on the *Turnplatz* near Plamann's school in 1811, Jahn's system of gymnastics gradually attracted the enthusiastic support of the German people. For the first time they had an opportunity to participate in a popular movement through which they could gather to exercise, sing, and march. The Turner Society was strictly a German institution, compatible with the political climate and social traditions of its people.

Although the Prussian government suppressed the Turner movement from 1819 until 1840, the members of the various societies met in secret and continued to practice gymnastics as well as spread propaganda for a united Germany. The perpetuation of the German system was not dependent upon a single leader or teacher but was a way of life and the common property of all Germans. Government restrictions only served to nurture the growing interest in the movement, and by 1850 the membership had increased to huge proportions. Though Jahn had become a marked man during the troublesome years, his work was ably carried on and expanded upon by Eiselen, Friesen, Massman, Passow, Arndt, Harnisch, von Raumer, Bernardi, Strauss, and Goethe, among others. Until 1847 no other book on a secular subject was so widely read as Jahn's *German Gymnastics,* and in that year Eiselen, one of Jahn's close companions, made the first revision.

The first Turner festival (*Turnfest*) was held in Coburg, Saxony, in 1860 and was attended by thousands of members of the organization from 139 cities and villages. In 1868 delegates from the various Turner Societies in the German states and Austria met at Weimar and organzed the German Gymnastic Association (*Deutsche Turnerschaft*). The Franco-German War of 1870 only halted temporarily the activities of the societies. The final unification of German, an objective of the Turners for more than fifty years, helped to increase the number of societies and augment the membership of the established ones. In addition, the physical stamina of the Turners as soldiers was fully recognized, and the Reich looked with favor upon the German Gymnastic Association, which was to exert an important influence upon future educational and national affairs.

THE RECREATION MOVEMENT IN GERMANY

Toward the end of the century many factors contributed to a change of attitude toward organized recreation and sports participation and stimulated their promotion. Herbert Spencer, widely read in continental Europe, not only influenced nations to revise secondary schools curriculums, placing more emphasis upon mathematics and science, but also made it quite clear that gymnastics could not compare with sports participation, competitive or recreational, in the development of desirable social characteristics. In 1878 Wilhelm Max Wundt, a physiologist and experimental psychologist, aroused considerable interest in play and recreation as expressions of animal and human behavior. Under the influence of Wundt's work, Karl Groos, a professor of biology of the University of Basel, Switzerland, produced his exhaustive studies, *The Play of Animals* (1896) and *The Play of Man* (1899). In the closing years of the nineteenth century interest in play and games contributed to the child-study movement in America and the play movement in Europe as counteragents to the harmful physical effects of modern sedentary life.

EARLY CONTRIBUTORS

Through Konrad Koch, a teacher of history and classical languages, and August Hermann, a gymnastic instructor, at Martino-Katharineum Gymnasium (secondary school) in Brunswick, German boys were introduced to the English games of Rugby and cricket and the American game of baseball between 1874 and 1876. By 1878 these games became so popular that they were made a regular part of the school's physical education program two afternoons a week. Koch and Hermann were appointed supervisors of the play period, and a modest budget was provided to purchase playing equipment. By 1879 the school authorities made participation in these and other games a requirement for the lower and middle grades, and by 1882 for the upper grades.

At the convention of the German Gymnastic Teachers Association at Brunswick in 1876, Hermann said that the German people must, like the English, make gymnastics and participation in games a national habit if they were to combat the deteriorating effects of modern life. Other speakers, who had visited England, pointed out that enthusiasm for games was not restricted to the schoolboy but was to be found among Englishmen in every walk of life. The English found in this participation certain values which the Germans might well consider.[4]

EMIL HARTWICK

In 1881 Emil Hartwick, a Prussian judge and an expert gymnast in his student days at the universities of Heidelberg and Berlin, led a movement to promote games and outdoor sports in Germany. Under his influence the Central Association of Bodily Education in the Nation and School was organized in 1882. Its aim was the promotion of bodily exercise through gymnastics, skating, swimming, bathing, rowing, games, and festivals. This organization was one of the first to appoint a medical section to observe the physical effects of exercise on the individual, which has since become standard practice in European countries.

Local branches of the Central Association were quickly formed in the larger German cities, and Jahn's *Turnplatz,* which had moved indoors to accommodate the Turners and schoolchildren, once more returned to its former function as an outdoor playground. By 1882 playgrounds were established and equipped in Düsseldorf, Bonn, Witten, and Berlin, and by 1884 in Bremen and Chemoritz. Other German municipalities provided leadership for public participation in games and other recreational activities.

Hartwick was pleased with the general response but disappointed in the small membership in the subsidiary associations and the financial support given the playground movement. Hartwick's greatest stumbling block was the German Association, whose leaders assumed an indifferent attitude. At the height of his career, in 1886 Hartwick was shot and killed in a duel, and the playground movement in Germany had for the time being lost its momentum and one of history's pioneer recreational leaders.

OTHER PLAYGROUND LEADERS

Hartwick had convinced Gustav von Gossler, Prussian Minister of Education and Public Worship, of the worthiness of his cause. In his student days the Prussian minister had been an expert all-round athlete. At the ninth national convention of the German Gymnastic Association in Berlin in 1881 he told gymnastic leaders that games and outdoor activities should share the program with formal gymnastics. In 1882 von Gossler passed an edict which required the provision of outdoor playgrounds for gymnastics and active games.

Emil von Schenckendorff, a proponent of the manual arts idea, which paralleled the playground movement in Germany in the 1880s, got in touch with Hartwick in 1882 to request some form of activity to counteract the effect of school routine on his boys at the Görlitz Manual Training School. At Hartwick's suggestion and with the able assistance of Gustav Ernst Eitner, a gymnastic instructor in the secondary school, von Schenckendorff succeeded in introducing a games program not only into his school but also into the elementary and secondary schools of Görlitz.

At the national convention of language teachers at Görlitz in 1889 Eitner provided a program of games as a feature of the meeting. The visitors received the exhibition with enthusiasm, and several teachers suggested that since few were familiar with games instruction a normal course should be established to teach them. Von Schenckendorff accepted the suggestion and with the support of von Gossler organized such a normal course in 1890 with Eitner at its head. In his first playground course Eitner lectured on the theory of play and games, discussed the mechanics of some sixty games and provided demonstrations and actual practice in thirty-four. Eitner published a games manual, *Die Jugenspiele,* which had six printings in the year 1890.

With the continued favorable acceptance of the playground movement, von Schenckendorff invited a group of influential public figures to meet in Berlin in 1891 to consider a large-scale national promotional scheme. This meeting resulted in the formation of the Central Committee for the Promotion of Games, designed to assist individuals or local organizations in the introduction of games and other recreational activities to the public. The Central Committee not only accelerated the playground movement in Germany but also laid the foundation for the establishment of sports clubs in every village and city in Germany and later in practically every foreign country on the Continent.[4]

TEACHER PREPARATION IN GERMANY

As gymnastics and Spiess's free exercises were introduced into the schools of the German confederation, the problem of teacher preparation became acute. To meet the demand for qualified gymnastic instructors in the elementary and higher schools, the Prussian government founded the Royal Central Gymnastic Institute in Berlin under the joint control of the Ministers of War and Education. Captain H. Rothstein of the Prussian Army was appointed director.

General Ernst von Pfüel (1779–1866) as chief of staff had organized the first military swimming school (*Schwimmanstalt*) at the Berlin Institute some time after 1815. Swimming pools were rare even in teacher-training institutions financed by the government, but prospective teachers attending the Royal Central Gymnastic Institute received swimming instruction. General Pfüel introduced the "fishing pole" technique, in which the learner was suspended in the water by means of a staff and rope attached to a wide belt encircling his midriff. This method of instruction was used in the military and naval schools of other countries and to some extent in school systems.

A Conflict of Gymnastic Philosophies

As a government official Captain Rothstein had become familiar with the Swedish system of gymnastics and when he organized the Institute at Berlin was inclined to favor this "scientific" system as opposed to the Jahn-Eiselen system of German gymnastics. When Captain Rothstein banished the horizontal and parallel bars from the program of the Institute, he provoked violent reactions, which precipitated a debate on the respective merits of the two systems. In 1862 a commission of medical men of such caliber as Rudolph Virchow and Emil Du Bois Reymond was appointed to study the problem and make a recommendation. The commission recommended that the two pieces of apparatus in question should be retained, and Captain Rothstein resigned. In the same year Prussia made German gymnastics obligatory in elementary schools and the future of the Jahn-Eiselen system was assured.

GYMNASTIC LEADERS IN SWEDEN

A. O. Lindfors (1781–1841)

Lindfors graduated from the University of Lund in 1802 and returned the following year to get his Ph.D. He wrote his dissertation on the subject of gymnastics (*Arte Gymnastica*), the first of its kind presented as partial fulfillment of the doctorate degree in any university. In this study Lindfors made a distinction between "*gymnastica naturalis*" and "*gymnastica artificiosa*." In his opinion artificially devised exercises had educational value and were an improvement over spontaneous natural activities.[5]

Lindfors placed artificial exercises in three categories: (1) military gymnastics, (2) pedagogical or athletic gymnastics, and (3) medical gymnastics for the prevention and correction of physical defects. In his treatment of the second category Lindfors recommended the Greek pentathlon of running, jumping, javelin and discus throwing, and wrestling and Plato's *orkäsis,* which consisted of games, acrobatics, and dancing. He cited the educational value of games directed by a well-prepared teacher and antedated Froebel's appreciation of the importance of play and games in the development of self-expression and personality in children.

Lindfors was appointed lecturer in education at the University of Lund, where he controlled the qualifications of tutors, who he insisted should be as well prepared to teach gymnastics as they were other subjects. He eventually gave up his active interest in gymnastics.

PEHR HENRIK LING (1776–1839)

Ling's father was a clergyman and his mother a close relative of the famous Swedish author, Olof Rudek. Ling and Lindfors grew up in the same parsonage in southern Sweden, attended the same classical school and the University of Lund. Ling crystallized his thinking on Swedish gymnastics in his book, *General Principles of Gymnastics* (*Gymnastikens Almanna Grunder*).

Between 1794 and 1799 Ling served as a tutor and a city clerk in Stockholm. At an early date he showed literary talent of great promise. In 1799 he left Sweden for Denmark, where he met men who stimulated his literary efforts, which later earned him the title of Poet Laureate of Sweden. Ling also developed an interest in gymnastics and became a master performer in the art of fencing.

In 1804 Ling returned to Sweden and secured an assignment as substitute teacher for an aging fencing master at the University of Lund. After the latter's death Ling was given a full-time appointment as instructor of gymnastics, fencing, and horseback riding. He studied anatomy and physiology and applied his knowledge, rudimentary as it was in his time, to gymnastics.

Ling's Contribution to Swedish Gymnastics

Ling not only accepted Lindfors' three categories of gymnastics but made practical contributions to all three areas. As a consequence of the Napoleonic Wars Sweden realized the importance of conditioning men for military service and asked Ling to prepare men to give army personnel physical training. At the Royal Central Institute of Gymnastics, established in 1814, Director Ling provided a course in gymnastics and fencing and published army manuals on gymnastics and bayonet fighting. He also experimented with physical rehabilitation in a special room where he accepted persons of all ages and degrees of physical handicaps.

Ling's aim was to develop the body by maintaining a balance between antagonistic pairs of muscles and by teaching the pupil to subjugate his will to the command of the teacher. He believed that body movements should not be determined by apparatus, as in the German system, but that the apparatus should be designed so as to secure the desired results, whether they were military, educational, or rehabilitational.

Ling originated the stall bars (*ribbstol*) Swedish boom (*bom*), saddle (*saddlebom*), window ladder (*stege*), low combination benches (*bank, balansribba,* and *lutplan*), and vaulting box (*plint*). To these he later added the horse (*hast*) and the horizontal, vertical, and oblique climbing ropes.[6] These pieces of apparatus were efficiently arranged in the gymnasium or exercise hall, and class members exercised upon them according to their individual needs and at the command of the teacher.

Ling's Successors

Upon his death in 1839 Ling was succeeded by Lars Gabriel Branting as director of the Institute. Branting continued Ling's policies and spent considerable time in the promotion and development of medical gymnastics. During Branting's administration the scientific Swedish method of gymnastics attracted the attention of military and educational authorities in other lands. The Prussian government sent Lieutenants Rothstein and Techow to the Institute in 1845 and 1846, and Eulenberg and Neumann of Prussia, Melchior of Austria, and Roth of England also came to visit and observe.

Branting was succeeded by Gustaf Nyblaeus, a former army officer and a keen student of Spiess's free exercises. Under Nyblaeus the course at the Institute was extended from one to two years and a separate course for women teachers was established. Nyblaeus gave each of the three areas in gymnastics the status of a separate department. He appointed Hjalmur Ling, Ling's eldest son, head of the educational gymnastic department, Truls Johann Hartelius head of the medical gymnastic department, and himself head of the military gymnastic department.

Hjalmur Ling, who succeeded Nyblaeus, completed Spiess's work by assigning each exercise to its proper category according to the way it affected parts of the body and the organism as a whole. He then arranged the exercises in an orderly progression from the least demanding. This approach to the free exercises of Spiess became known the world over as the "Day's Order." In 1886 Ling was followed by Lars Mauritz Törngren, under whose administration medical gymnastics were given as a third-year course and the length of the courses in all areas was increased.

GYMNASTICS IN DENMARK

FRANZ NACHTEGALL (1777–1847)

The son of a Copenhagen tailor, Franz Nachtegall received his early education in a private school. He enrolled in the University of Copenhagen to study theology but discontinued his education upon the death of his father. Taking employment as a tutor, he sought relief from his long teaching hours in gymnastics and fencing. He enjoyed fencing so much that he gave private lessons in his free time. Convinced that he had found his true vocation, in 1799 he opened a private outdoor gymnasium, which attracted 150 university students and townspeople.

Early in the Napoleonic Wars Denmark was forced by her geographical location to ally herself with the French Emperor. She faced all Napoleon's aggressors, and the drain on her manpower and material resources was disastrous. When the government established the Institute of Military Gymnastics in 1804, Nacthegall was made its director.

Military Versus Educational Objectives

In the ensuing years the Institute was hard-pressed to meet the demand for personnel qualified to condition soldiers for military service. Before the close of the Napoleonic Wars the government sought to meet its military needs by extending gymnastics to the schools. In 1809 an ordinance was passed requiring the teaching of gymnastics to potential soldiers in the secondary schools, and in 1814 a similar ordinance was passed affecting elementary schools. Historians hail these ordinances as landmarks in the history of physical education, but viewed in terms of their *modus operandi* they lose much of their glory. The schools' teaching personnel was drawn from noncommissioned officers who had been trained at the Institute of Military Gymnastics and their warlike objective was clear. The dominant position of the military in the preparation of teachers of gymnastics in the schools lasted until the turn of the century.

The Playground Movement

As in other countries, the emphasis on games became more pronounced in Denmark when the authorities realized that English games helped develop desirable social traits not encouraged by individualized gymnastics. The Copenhagen Playground Association was founded in 1891, and a promotional organization similar to the German Central Committee was organized in 1897. In 1896 the Copenhagen Playground Association proposed to Wilhelm Pardenfleth, Minister of Education, that the government provide grants-in-aid to assist local school authorities establish and equip playgrounds. The proposal was approved and appropriations made for a three-year period. As a sequel a Committee for Promoting Group Games Among School Children was appointed, part of whose responsibility was the administration of state funds for recreation.

Teacher Preparation

Denmark was one of the first nations to establish an institute to train military personnel to serve as gymnastic instructors in the armed services. Nachtegall's teaching procedures probably served as a guide for both military schools and teacher institutes established in other countries after 1804. Although Nachtegall had drawn heavily upon Guts Muths's *Gymnastics for the Young,* his program, at the Institute was attractive enough to hold a position of respect for more than a quarter of a century.

Toward the close of the nineteenth century, Denmark, like other European countries, became interested in the Swedish system for schools. Guts Muths–Nachtegall gymnastics were gradually replaced under teachers trained in the Swedish system or imported from Sweden. In 1898 the Danish government established a one-year course for the training of gymnastic teachers. This course was organized by K. A. Knudsen, who was well versed in the Swedish system.

PHYSICAL EDUCATION IN SWITZERLAND

Because of its central location and liberal attitude, Switzerland had through the centuries become a haven for the oppressed. In the 1820s many Turners who were under police surveillance skipped across the border, to return later to their homeland, move on to other countries which desired their service, or remain in Switzerland as citizens. Because of this situation and the receptive nature of the Swiss the German system of gymnastics became well entrenched in Switzerland. At one time membership in the Swiss

Gymnastic Society in proportion to population was the highest in Europe.

PHOKION CLIAS (1782–1854)

In 1770 Clias' father emigrated from Switzerland to the English colonies in America, and it was here that Clias was born. After the elder Clias' wife died he returned to Europe by way of Holland, where he placed Phokion and his brother in a school. The restless Phokion ran away from school and wandered through Holland and the northern German states. His wanderlust satisfied he returned to his father's homeland and entered the Swiss Army. In 1814 Clias became an officer in the light cavalry and in order to keep his men in condition introduced such activities as gymnastics, swimming, and wrestling. This experience helped Clias decide that gymnastics would be his life's vocation, and he offered his services free to an orphan asylum at Berne. Clias accepted other students in his classes and was finally asked to establish a normal course in gymnastics for Swiss teachers. In 1816 Clias published a teachers' manual, which clearly indicates that, like his contemporaries, he was heavily indebted to the publications of Guts Muths.[7]

In 1817 and 1819 Clias attempted without success to introduce his gymnastic system in France. In the 1820s he was given an opportunity to teach gymnastics to three companies of light infantrymen, and he must have been most successful because he attracted the attention of several visiting British officers. They recommended him to the proper authorities and he was invited to England, where he was given the rank of captain and placed in charge of the gymnastic program of the royal military and naval schools. He also taught at the Charterhouse Public School and gave private lessons in gymnastics and swimming. He was injured during classwork in 1825 and returned to Switzerland. In 1841 he emerged from retirement to practice medical gymnastics at Besançon, France, where he eventually taught in the city and normal schools and the military garrison. In 1844 at 62 Clias was appointed superintendent of gymnastics of the elementary schools of Paris, a position he held until the Revolution of 1848.

The Diversity of Clias' Interest

Clias was a dedicated teacher. Some time between his entrance into the Swiss Army in 1814 and 1819 he must have attended the military swimming school of General von Pfüel in Berlin. His *Gymnastic Exercises* (1825) Clias shows that he was familiar with the Prussian method of swimming instruction. While teaching at the orphan school at Berne, he invented what he called the "giant step," an apparatus more commonly known today as the giant stride.[8] His injury in 1825 turned his attention to medical gymnastics. In the years between 1825 and 1841, of which we know little, Clias must have studied Swedish medical gymnastics and might very well have attended the Institute at Stockholm. It is certain that he practiced this art in Berne before he went to Besançon. Clias was a remarkable man who could with equal right be claimed as a gymnastic leader by three countries.

GYMNASTIC LEADERS IN FRANCE

France, unlike other countries, had no native son who promoted gymnastics in the early part of the nineteenth century. The Napoleonic Wars, which stimulated interest in gymnastics in other countries, did not have this effect in France. Napoleon levied most of his troops from other countries to placate the French people, who after his early campaigns resented the conscription of their sons to serve on foreign soil. It was not until the last campaigns of 1813–1815 that Napoleon began to draw heavily upon French manpower by conscription. French military schools, however, like those in other European countries, provided conditioning such activities for their officers as gymnastics, fencing, swimming, and horseback riding.

Francis Amoros (1770–1848)

Born in Valencia, Spain, Amoros was the son of the Marquis of Sotelo. As a young man he served with distinction in the Spanish Army against the French in Algeria. He rose to the rank of colonel and held positions of importance in the war ministry. In 1808 as a result of his Spanish campaign, Napoleon replaced King Ferdinand with his brother Joseph Bonaparte. As a soldier Amoros' loyalty was committed to the Spanish crown, but he seemed to have had the ability to get along with the new king and was given positions of responsibility. When Napoleon was exiled to Elba in 1814, and King Ferdinand was returned to the throne, Amoros, now viewed as a traitor, joined the French Army as it retreated across the Pyrenees.

Amoros quickly adjusted to his adopted country and became a French citizen in 1816. In 1806 King Ferdinand had appointed Amoros as gymnastic director of the new Pestalozzian school at Madrid established by Voitel. In need of some means of livelihood in France, Amoros established an open-air gymnasium in association with a private school in Paris and resumed his old vocation as a gymnastic instructor.

Amoros' Contributions

Amoros' most important publication was his *Manuel D'Education Physique, Gymnastique et Gmorale* (1830), which contained an atlas of fifty pages and some 300 illustrations. Like Ling in Sweden and Sargent at Harvard University, Amoros was addicted to apparatus of every description. He was probably one of the first to use the trapeze, still and flying rings, knotted climbing ropes, inclined board, and strength-testing apparatus in his physical education program.[6] Throughout his professional career he had a great interest in the acrobatics of the theater, and discussed acrobatic gymnastics in his manual.

Although Phokion Clias had failed to interest French authorities in a civil or military gymnastic institute, he paved the way for Amoros. In 1819 Amoros was requested to supervise the layout of an open-air gymnasium and organize a training program for schoolteachers and military personnel. He served as a director of this institute until it closed in 1834. He then founded his own private school near the Champs-Élysées on rue Jean-Goujon, which he conducted until his death in 1848.

In 1852 an institute was established in association with the Military School at Joinville-le-Pont near Paris. This institute, known later as the High School of Physical Education, provided a four-month course for commissioned, and a three-month course for noncommissioned, officers. After the Franco-German War the French authorities placed its graduates along with unqualified army personnel in schools as gymnastic instructors. This situation was condoned until increased public interest in the scientific Swedish system created a demand for better-trained gymnastic teachers. In 1891 Georges Demany was requested to establish a normal school that trained teachers more scientifically. This school was eventually placed under the jurisdiction of the Minister of Education and the Medical College of the University of Lyon.

THE CONFLICT OF SYSTEMS IN BELGIUM

Since the middle of the seventeenth century Belgium has been exploited by every nation which gained temporary possession of it through treaty or annexation. Napoleon's *coup d'état* in 1799 marked the beginning of a new era for this nation. During the consulate and the empire Belgium was divided into nine political divisions, each with its own administrative head (prefect), and the French system of courts, code of laws, and currency were adopted. French rule was never popular, and the Belgians welcomed the occupation of their country by the Allies in 1814. To protect Belgium from future encroachment, the English succeeded in including it in the old republic of the United Provinces, which by the Treaty of Vienna in 1815 became part of the Kingdom of the Netherlands. The rule of King William I did not prove as politically stabilizing as the Congress of Vienna had hoped. With the support of opponents of the old regime and an influential segment of Belgian society which feared the power of the Catholic Church, the new king attempted to make his position secure. He placed the three universities, Ghent, Louvain, and Liège, under state control; created the Athénées, or state secondary schools; and adopted the Dutch language in place of the popular Franch. Political unrest and internal dissatisfaction and the French Revolution of 1830 helped combine the liberal forces and Catholics in a successful bid for independence.

Gymnastic Leadership in Belgium

Under Dutch rule (1814–1830) there was no organized system of gymnastics in Belgium, and it was not until after the country secured its independence that advocates of gymnastics made their appearance. The Frenchman Triat opened the first gymnasium at Brussels in 1840, where he taught the Amoros system of gymnastics. In 1846 Joseph Isenbaert (1822–1905) directed a program of gymnastic exercises for the secondary schools of Antwerp. In 1854 Isenbaert offered a course of gymnastics for girls which he taught free of charge. From the time of independence until 1860 Isenbaert laid a strong foundation for future gymnastic leaders.

A contemporary of Isenbaert was Jacob Happel, who founded the Antwerp Society of Gymnastics in 1857 and eight years later the Belgian Federation of Gymnastics (1865). In 1860 he introduced what he called the Belgian system of gymnastics and established an institute to prepare teachers in this system. The next year A. S. Ulrich inaugurated the Swedish system, precipitating a battle of systems which lasted approximately fifty years. The position of the Swedish advocates was strengthened by the work of Alexis Sluys at the Brussels normal school, Charles-Buls, and the Chilean, J. Cabezas, who offered the first course in the Ling system there in 1893.

In the middle of the 1890s the proponents of the conventional system of gymnastics and those of the Swedish system entered into a struggle for the right to organize physical education in the schools of Brussels. In 1898 a commission composed of representatives from the professions of medicine and gymnastics was appointed to consider the merits of the two systems. It recommended that the schools adopt the more scientific Swedish system, give regular instruction in swimming, make showers available, construct gymnasiums according to the Swedish plan, and require periodical physical examinations and anthropometric measurements.[9] These recommendations influenced other Belgian municipalities at the turn of the century.

THE GYMNASTIC MOVEMENT IN CZECHOSLOVAKIA

Ever since the Thirty Years' War Bohemia, the basis of the future Czechoslovakia, had been held in subjugation by Austria-Hungary. The Czechs never accepted this loss of identity and waged a constant underground campaign for their freedom. Since they were unable to initiate an open military offensive, they organized a gymnastic union with a military structure which became known as the Falcons or Sokols.

The driving force behind the Sokols was Miroslav Tyre (1832–1884), who was born in Decin. He received his early education in the town of his birth and his higher education at Charles University, Prague. When he requested permission to attend lectures at the University of Vienna, he was refused. The idea that Czechs were considered a second-rate people by their oppressors aroused his racial pride and he joined forces with the patriot Henry Fugner to the Sokols.

Although the gymnastic clubs of the Sokols were often in trouble because of their political activities, they were never severely molested. Patriotically motivated, these clubs grew rapidly in villages and towns where the Slavic population was concentrated. By 1882 the Sokols had grown to sufficient size to warrant the celebration of their first Jubilee Festival at Prague. Their gymnastic program featured exercises with or without apparatus, following the German system, and emphasized sports of the combative type. The Sokols became known internationally for their mass demonstrations, called Slets, in which thousands of individuals performed exercises in perfect unison.

PHYSICAL EDUCATION IN OTHER EUROPEAN COUNTRIES

During the nineteenth century the Jahn-Eiselen system of gymnastics was introduced into the Austrian elementary and secondary schools through individual initiative. In the reorganization of Austrian education in the middle of the century physical education was required for two periods per week in both the secondary (1849) and elementary (1869) schools. The brothers Albert and Rodolphe Stephani vigorously promoted Jahn-Eiselen gymnastics and Spiess's free exercises.

Both Finland and Norway followed the trends of their neighbor, Sweden. To prepare teachers in gymnastics, Finland in 1894 established courses in association with the University of Helsinki, and Norway offered a two-year course at the Central Gymnastic School, founded in affiliation with the University of Christiana.

For many centuries prior to the eighteenth century Poland had been one of the great nations of Europe. After the partitions of 1772, 1793, and 1795, the Poles lost their identity under the cultural and political influence of the Austrians, Prussians, and Russians. In that part of Poland influenced by the Prussians the German system of gymnastics naturally played an important role in the school program. In Austrian Poland a gymnastic institute was established in 1895 at Cracow under the leadership of H. Jordans, and a similar institute was founded at Warsaw in Russian Poland through the initiative of Helen Kuczalska.

Portugal began to appreciate the importance of physical education toward the close of the eighteenth century. During the reign of King Joseph I, the Minister of State, Marquis of Pombal, secured a legislative act which required instruction in fencing, horsemanship, and dancing in the Royal College of the Nobles. The government military and naval schools adopted physical education as part of their program in 1863 and 1866, respectively. Organized physical education programs existed in private academies as early as 1866.

In Spain the gymnastics of Colonel Amoros formed the basis of early programs in academies and military and naval schools. When physical education became a required subject in 1879, it was the Amoros system that was adopted. Before the close of the century, however, Ling's Swedish system gained favor, and in 1892 it became the official method of instruction in the Central School of Gymnastics, which prepared physical education instructors for the schools and gymnastic societies of Spain.

NOTES

1. H. G. Wells. *The Outline of History*. New York: Garden City Books, 1961, pp. 735–797.
2. John Dambach. "Physical Education in Germany." *Contribution to Education,* No. 731, Teachers College, Columbia University, 1937, pp. 12–14.
3. Jean Chryssafis. "Aristotle on Kinesiology." *Journal of Health and Physical Education,* 1:6 (June, 1930), 14–15.
4. Fred Eugene Leonard and George B. Affleck. *A Guide to the History of Physical Education*. Philadelphia: Lea and Febiger, 1947, pp. 113–119; 133–135; 140–144.
5. Signe Prytz. "A. O. Lindfors." *Journal of Health and Physical Education,* 8:1 (January, 1937), 3–5.
6. Leopold F. Zwarg. "A Study of the History, Uses and Values of Apparatus in Physical Education." *Mind and Body,* 38 (1931–1932), 556–565.
7. Fred E. Leonard. *Pioneers of Modern Physical Training*. New York: Association Press, 1915, pp. 43–47, 49–51.
8. P. H. Clias. *An Elementary Course of Gymnastic Exercises*. London: Sherwood, Gilbert and Piper, 1825, pp. 140; 145–184.
9. Pierre Seurin. *L'Éducation Physique dans le Monde,* Bordeaux: Editions Bière, 1961, pp. 42–43.

Chapter 10

GYMNASTICS, SPORTS, AND RECREATION IN THE UNITED KINGDOM IN THE NINETEENTH CENTURY

ENGLISH INTEREST IN GAMES, SPORTS, AND RECREATION

WHILE continental Europe was adopting gymnastics systems during the nineteenth century, England favored games, sports, and recreation. This contrast of interest has been the source of much speculation. Some attribute English disinterest in gymnastics to the excellent defensive position of the British Isles. Instead of a large body of infantrymen the English developed naval forces whose men were conditioned naturally in the course of their shipboard life.

Others point out that since the Magna Carta in 1215 the English people had won gradual concessions from tyrannical monarchs until they had achieved constitutional liberty. A free people have the right to determine not only their political destiny but also the conduct of their lives. To such a people regimentation is distasteful and gymnastics as they were practiced on the Continent were a form of regimentation. In addition, the English viewed gymnastics as artificial and devoid of the social values, they believed were associated with games and sports. This attitude dominated the English scene for more than a hundred years and made the introduction of gymnastics difficult for even the most astute promter.

Other factors which encouraged the English proclivity for games, sports, and recreation include the country's temperate climate and the shorter work day made possible by the Industrial Revolution. The British Isles are warmed by the Gulf Stream, producing a climate which encourages out-of-doors recreation. For some centuries England had developed a predominantly manufacturing economy which utilized raw materials furnished by her colonial possessions, and growing technological advances shortened work hours and made more free time available for leisurely pursuits.

INTRODUCTION OF THE SWEDISH SYSTEM

It is apparent that to be accepted in England any system of gymnastics would have to possess sufficient utilitarian value to survive the competition of sports and recreation. By 1830 the Swedish system had gained considerable status as a scientific approach to bodily exercise. Medical gymnastics were also gaining international support from those who recognized their therapeutic potential.

In 1838 John Govart In De Betou, a graduate of the Swedish Central Institute of Gymnastics, arrived in England to practice medical gymnastics. During 1840 and 1850 he was followed by C. Ehrenoff and Carl August Georgii, who built a practice with the cooperation of physicians. More important to the success of the Swedish system in England, however, were three local enthusiasts, J. W. F. Blundell, M. J. Chapman, and Mathias D. Roth. Both Chapman and Roth had attended the Swedish Institute and all three had published innumerable pamphlets on the merits of the Swedish system which aroused public interest.[1]

In 1853 Roth founded a private institution of medical gymnastics and published a book on Ling's free exercises. At the same time Roth decided to promote educational gymnastics for schools. He launched an aggressive but unsuccessful campaign with the government to introduce Swedish gymnastics into English elementary schools. After 1860, however, government interest in army reform led to the extension of military gymnastics to the elementary and public schools. This reform included the introduction of military drill into the public schools, the erection of a gymnasium for the army, and the establishment of a Normal School of Gymnastic Training for the military at Aldershot. When Parliament discussed the possibility of compulsary gymnastics in the elementary schools, Roth intensified his campaign.

In 1870 the House of Commons received the Education Bill. Armed with data on the rejection of army and navy recruits for physical reasons and the prevalence of physical defects among railway workers and children in the workhouses, Roth approached influential members of the House of Commons. He argued that sports and games were inadequate exercise for elementary school children and that only gymnastics would prepare them properly for industrial work and as army and navy candidates. In spite of his lobbying the Education Bill was passed without including compulsory gymnastics for elementary school children.

In 1878 the London School Board, at the request of one of its members who was a close friend of Roth, secured the services of Miss C. Löfving, a graduate of the Swedish Institute, to give a normal course to prepare teachers of gymnastics. In its first year the course had more than 600 applicants. In 1881 she was succeeded by Bergman Österberg, also from Sweden, who in 1885 resigned to found the Bergman Österberg Physical Training College, the first to train physical education teachers in England. Now that gymnastics had been adopted for London girls, an unsuccessful attempt was made in 1882 to extend the program to boys.

Archibald MacLaren ("ca." 1820–1884)

MacLaren was born at Alloa, Scotland, and at 16 went to Paris where he became interested in gymnastics and fencing. Some time later he went to England and opened a fencing school at Oxford, and in 1858 established a gymnasium offering public instruction in gymnastics and fencing. He was then asked to formulate a plan for the training of army instructors in gymnastics at Aldershot. MacLaren spent most of his remaining professional life in association with the British Army.

MacLaren is generally considered a gymnastic leader without a system, on the basis of an article in *Macmillan's Magazine* of February, 1863, entitled "National Systems of Bodily Exercise." In it

MacLaren stated that he was not satisfied with any programs of bodily exercise that had been developed from the time of the ancient Greeks to the contemporary Germans, Swedes, and French. In his opinion the goal of physical exercises should not be bodily strength but the development of health. With this statement he furnished his antagonists, who considered him a confused thinker, with additional ammunition.

In his book, *A System of Physical Education,* MacLaren stated, "All exercises may be classed under two distinct heads, Recreative and Educational."[2] Like the gymnastic leaders on the Continent, he felt that recreation consisting of school games, sports, and other leisure-time pursuits encouraged one-sided development, while systematic exercise developed the whole body. Like his contemporaries, MacLaren pointed to the physical development of the ancient Greeks as the ideal product a well-balanced program, none of them seeming to realize that the Greek program had consisted of track and field events and wrestling rather than artificially devised movements. During his sojourn in Paris, MacLaren had been fascinated by the use of anthropometric measurement to evaluate a systematized program of bodily exercise. At Aldershot he used such measurements and kept extensive records. He also pioneered in the use of photography to record the physical improvement of his military trainees.

HERBERT SPENCER (1820–1893)

As one of the great intellectuals of his time, Spencer attempted to apply Darwin's theory of evolution to all forms of organic life as well as to social and political institutions. Spencer's stress upon scientific education helped revolutionize the curriculum in the higher schools of Germany, which in turn laid the foundation for the great scientific advances made in that country.

In 1859 Spencer appraised the growth of gymnastic systems on the Continent and the increasing English interest in the Swedish system. In *Education, Intellectual, Moral and Physical* he stressed the importance of diet and exercise to the well-being of the youth of his time. Spencer applauded the English schoolboy's enthusiasm for games and sports, but lamented the fact that girls were neglected because the public looked with disfavor upon a "robust physique" in females. Unlike his contemporaries, Mathias Roth and Archibald MacLaren, Spencer saw little value in artificial exercises, claiming they produced fatigue in particular areas of the body disproportionate to their developmental value and were in addition monotonous and uninteresting to perform. He believed that gymnastic exercises were inferior to games and sports in respect to both quantity and quality of muscular exertion. Spencer did call attention to the need for a program of exercise for girls in school, though his attitude toward sports is typical of the English in general.

DEVELOPMENT OF AMATEUR SPORTS

Certain national characteristics can be noted in British amateur sports. Many games and sports originated at a rural, grass-roots level and are what the Germans call *Volkspiele,* or peoples' games. These had been played in their original form for many generations. Any change in the method of play was purely accidental, but if the innovation was accepted by the people, it was passed along as a permanent addition to the playing rules.

Through the centuries the English have ignored all suggestions from outsiders which might improve play from the standpoint of participant or spectator. Soccer, for instance, failed to win the recognition of the Football Association for thirty years after its formation in 1863 because suggestions for changes in the game were persistently rejected. Many appeals have been made to leading English cricket clubs to make changes that would enliven the game and add to spectator interest, but the typical English response has been, "But then it wouldn't be cricket!" From their view, any change was a threat to the integrity of a sport which was part of the cultural life of the people.

The people of the United Kingdom have also shown a predilection for adopting the sports of other people and making them a part of their own culture. Likewise, as immigrants, they have introduced and promoted sports in their colonial possessions and in foreign countries with a zeal bordering on that of the missionary.

Another characteristic peculiar to the Englishman is his maintenance of an interest in sports after leaving school and his continued participation throughout life. After completing his education, the Englishman identifies himself with an amateur club composed of his fellow alumni. He may play Rugby, association football, or cricket until he is 35 or 40, switch to tennis in middle age, and in the twilight of his life turn to golf, bowling, or hiking. The Englishman takes pride in being physically fit, and when he cannot achieve this through sports, he will, as a last resort, take gymnastic exercises. The fact that amateur sports clubs in the nineteenth century were made up of the graduates of public schools and universities led to the provision of sports facilities in both metropolitan and remote rural areas. The Englishman took his sports for granted, and accepted them as an integral part of his life. Because of this, he became a staunch supporter of local or national movements that sponsored physical fitness through sports, or what he called physical recreation.[3]

Democratization of Sports and the Amateur Ideal

Membership in amateur sports clubs in the last quarter of the nineteenth century included not only professional and business men but also tradesmen, workmen, and individuals from all walks of life. However, their domination by public school and university graduates led to accusations of snobbishness and brought into sharp relief a class distinction in sports. The eventual democratization of sports through the establishment of national associations provided the answer to this situation.

Another characteristic of British sports is the idealistic attitude toward amateurism fostered by the public schools and universities. Some view this belief in "sports for sports' sake" rather than for monetary gain as a kind of snobbishness perpetuated by those of social rank and wealth. Others point out that such an ideal was untenable in a society geared to the worship of materialistic values and that the line between amateurism and professionalism was sometimes very thin. In any case, the English and Scots kept a constant vigil over their amateur sports and weeded out the professional as soon as he was discovered. During the nineteenth century the world inherited from the English the image of the amateur sportsman as a gentleman with all the noble virtues of a knight of King Arthur's Round Table and a paragon of fair play. As Howard

J. Savage stated it, "It is still one of the fortunate aspects of the persistence of the sport tradition of the English public school that it strengthened and seasoned the British amateur tradition."[3]

ARCHERY

Through the centuries the English were famous for their military prowess with the short bow and crossbow. The long bow, introduced in South Wales around the twelfth century, proved an even more formidable military weapon. At one time over one-half the foot soldiers of the English Army were long bowmen, and they proved their worth during the Hundred Years' War, particularly in the Battle of Agincourt (1415) when 15,000 English archers of Henry V destroyed 60,000 heavily armed French troops. Because English royalty was so thoroughly impressed by the military effectiveness of the long bow, archery practice was instituted on Sundays and holidays, and any game or sport which interfered with this practice was prohibited. In the fifteenth century archery practice was encouraged in Ireland by statute, and Scottish monarchs promoted it by every means short of royal command. Firearms, introduced at Pont de l'Arche in 1418, gradually displaced both the long bow and crossbow. The long bow, however, remained a recreational implement and a hunting weapon for those who preferred it to the gun.

As the Prince of Wales, King George IV became the patron of the Royal Toxophilite Society in 1787 and introduced the York Round at 100, 80, and 60 yards, with the values of 9, 7, 5, 3, and 1 given to the target rings. Early archery contests were held by this society at Lords' cricket ground in London, among them competition for the Crunder Cup and Bugle, in which 144 arrows were shot at 100 yards. Another important archery society was the Woodsmen of Arden (1785), which had its headquarters at Meriden in Warwickshire. This society featured clout shooting at long ranges and frequently entered into competition with the Royal Company of Scottish Archers.

In 1844 a few influential archers suggested that a national meet should be held at York in addition to the many local competitions. A series of such meets led to the establishment of the Grand National Archery Society in 1861. This organization became the legislative body for archery in England. In matches the York or the St. George Rounds were adopted for men, requiring the shooting of 144 arrows, 72 at 100 yards, 48 at 80 yards, and 24 at 60 yards. For women competitors, the National Round required 48 arrows at 60 yards and 24 at 50 yards. The society provided prizes for both gross and point scores and devised several methods for handicapping expert competitors.[4]

BADMINTON

The game of badminton was discovered in India during the period of colonization and introduced into England in the 1870s. Its name was taken from the Duke of Beaufort's county estate near the village of Badminton in the County of Gloucestershire, where the game attained considerable popularity. The rules formulated in Poona, India, in 1876 were followed until the Bath Badminton Club revised them in 1887. In 1895, when the Badminton Association was formed, the rules were revised once more, and adopted throughout the world. The All-English Championships for men's and women's doubles and mixed doubles were first held in 1899 and for men's and women's singles in 1900. The first international badminton matches were played between England and Ireland.

BOWLS

The game of bowls is almost as old as archery, and was one of those which interfered with archery practice during the reigns of Edward III and Richard II. Many bowls clubs existed in England during the eighteenth century, but there was no national body to regulate the game. The Willowbank Bowls Club, one of the oldest in Scotland, failed to secure support for a national association in the mid-nineteenth century, but did succeed in establishing a code of rules which were accepted by local clubs. Scottish immigrants took the game of bowls with them to Australia, Canada, New Zealand, South Africa, and the United States. In Australia the Bowling Association of Victoria and New South Wales was founded in 1880, and Scotland finally succeeded in nationalizing the sport when the Scottish Bowling Association was established in 1892.

As played by English-speaking people, bowls utilizes the level and crown greens, or lawns. Historically, the level green was used first and is the more common type. The crown green (the sportier of the two) has a slope of 18 inches and is popular in the North and Midland counties. The rules do not prescribe the size of the green, but the fixed minimum distance of 25 yards at which a bowl may be bowled at a jack (earthenware ball), dictated that an ideal green should be at least 24 yards square. In the old days the bowl was weighted on one side to secure a bias, but artisans soon found that they could turn out bowls with a convexity that satisfied the rules of a minimum bias of 6 feet on a jack 30 yards distant.

A match consists of four rinks of four players, or a total of sixteen individuals. A rink's four players are designated the leader, second player, third player, and skip or captain. The positions of the players remain fixed during the game, and each player of a rink bowls alternately in the required order standing on a mat with one or both feet to protect the lawn. The skip is responsible for picking the players of his rink, each of which should have a particular skill or ability necessary to the strategy of the game. The skip is the last man to play, and he attempts to correct poor bowls by his teammates or lays a block in front of the jack to obstruct the opponent's bowl. The English award a point for the bowl closest to the jack. It is a function of the third player to measure the distance of the bowls from the jack. In the Scottish game 3 points are given for a bowl within 1 foot of the jack, 2 points for one within 2 feet and 1 point for one within 3 feet. To assist in the determination of the distance, the Scotch draw concentric circles about the jack.[4]

CRICKET

Matches in cricket were held in England as early as the seventeenth century. In the following century many cricket clubs were organized, one of the most famous being the Marylebone Cricket Club (1788), which had its home at Lord's cricket ground in London. The MCC revised the earlier rules and from 1800 to 1850 served as matchmaker in Great Britain. During these years clubs were organized for the first time in metropolitan areas, the counties, and educational institutions. Although English immigrants successfully introduced cricket into the commonwealth nations and colonial possessions in the nineteenth century, the sport never met wide acceptance in Ireland, Scotland, or Wales. This failure was due in part to the lack of suitable grounds—level and excellent turf—adverse climatic conditions, and the absence of a supply of seasoned players such as those furnished by the English public schools and universities. In Canada cricket had to meet the competition of baseball, which the average Canadian finds more exciting. On the other hand, cricket was made to order for Australia, where excellent climate and grounds permit year-round play.

To most foreign observers cricket is a baffling and somewhat mystifying game. A team consists of eleven players. At the center of the playing field, upon which the turf has been grown with painstaking care, are two wickets 22 yards apart. These wickets, 27 inches in height, consist of three stumps placed close enough together to stop the ball. On top of each is placed a bail, which is displaced when the ball strikes the stumps. The team that has the bat places a batsman at each wicket, and the team in the field places its players in the best positions to stop or field the ball. The bat is 36 inches in length, with a blade 22 inches below the handle and 4½ inches wide.

Two umpires are appointed and each takes his position at one of the wickets where the batsmen are stationed. The umpire renders decisions only when an appeal is made.

The bowler takes his position at the wicket opposite the batsmen and, with an underhanded delivery, bowls the ball within the bounds of a white line, or crease, toward the batter's wicket. The batter stands in front of his wicket and is limited in his movement by the batter's box, which is marked off by white lines (popping crease). The bowler's objective is to strike the stumps of the wicket; the batsman defends the wicket by stopping the ball or driving it out in the field to earn a run.

When the batsman hits the ball into the field, he runs to the opposite wicket and exchanges places with the other batsman. If the batsman reaches the "base" before the ball is fielded, he earns a run. When the bowler has delivered six balls at one wicket to the batsman, the umpire calls "over"; then the bowler at the other wicket takes over and the game continues as before. A batsman is out if the bowler strikes the bat and/or the wicket and dislodges the bail, if he hits a fly ball which is caught, if the ball is thrown at the wicket and dislodges the bail while he is running between the wickets, and if he steps out of the batter's box while the bowler is in the act of delivery. The game continues until all batters but the odd one have been out, since the play has left him without a partner to be stationed at the other wicket.

Match games consist of two innings, and the management usually allows three days to complete a game. Since matches are so long-drawn-out and usually accompanied by social activities, more informal matches are limited to one inning, which, if started early in the morning, can be completed in one day.[5]

Hockey

As early as 1875 a game resembling field hockey was played in England, but it was in 1883 that the Wimbleton Club took the game under its wing and began to establish the rules now in use. Clubs were soon organized around London and in the North, West, and Midland counties of England. In 1866 the Hockey Association was established, and before the close of the century England, Ireland, Scotland, and Wales formed the International Hockey Board. English women as well as men were enthusiastic about the game and even before 1900 were engaged in international matches. The promotional work of Constance M. K. Applebee, a staff member of the British College of Physical Education, did much to interest girls and women in field hockey in the United Kingdom and other countries.[6]

Rowing

Boat races for stakes were held on the Thames River during the eighteenth century, and as early as 1775 a regatta was held on the Thames off Ranelagh Gardens. Amateur rowing between gentlemen started about 1800, and amateur rowing clubs combined forces in 1818 to form the world-famous Leander Club. The Oxford and Cambridge races started in 1815, and the first race between eight-oared crews took place at Henley-on-Thames in 1829. Since 1856 the boat race between Oxford and Cambridge, with the exception of the war years, has been an annual affair.

In 1839 the town council of Henley-on-Thames, to stimulate business, established the Henley Royal Regatta and as prizes offered the Grand Challenge Cup for the winner of eight-oared boat races and the Town Challenge Cup for the four-oared boat race. The program of the regatta was gradually extended to include other prizes such as the Steward Challenge Cup for four-oared boats, the Silver Goblets for paired oars and the Ladies Challenge Plate for eight-oared boats (1845), the Diamond Sculls for single scullers (1844), the Visitors Challenge Cup for crews from schools and colleges in the United Kingdom (1847), and the Wyfold Challenge Cup for four-oared boats (1855). In 1895 a crew from Cornell University entered competition for the Grand Challenge Cup and defeated the famous Leander Club. It was, however, an empty victory since the Leander crew failed to receive the starting signal and remained behind while Cornell rowed to the finish line unopposed.

In 1882 the Amateur Rowing Association was founded to select crews to represent England in international rowing matches. The distinction between an amateur and professional competitor arrived at by the ARA at this time is of historical interest since it was later adopted by other athletic associations, including the International Olympic Committee. An amateur does not enter a race for a stake, money, or entrance fee, compete for a prize with or against professionals, pursue or assist in the practice of athletic exercise of any kind for profit, work in or about boats for money or wages, or compete in a boat race when he has been disqualified as an amateur in any other branch of sport. The duties of the Amateur Rowing Association later included the maintenance of standards among amateur oarsmen, promotion of interest in boat racing, and management of the many regattas scheduled during the summer months.[6]

RUGBY

According to the original laws of the Ruby Union established in 1871, the playing field (pitch) was 140 yards long and 70 yards wide and teams were permitted to have twenty players on a side. In 1876–1877 the number of players was reduced to fifteen to a side, and in 1886 a point system for scoring goals and trys was adopted and the playing field fixed at 110 yards long by 75 yards wide with end zones (in-goal areas) 25 yards long. The player positions were designated as eight forwards, one scrum half, four three-quarter backs, and one fullback.

The game is started by a place kick, during which the opponents must remain behind a restraining line. On receiving the ball, a player can propel it in any direction with any part of his body except the hands and arms. If, because of impetus given to it by the offense, the ball is first touched by the defense in the end zone, the defense brings the ball out to the 25-yard line and starts the play with a drop kick. If the defense sends the ball into the end zone and it is first touched by the defense, play is again resumed by a scrum 5 yards from the defender's goal line. In the scrum the forwards of both teams are lined up in two or three rows and the half scrum rolls the ball without English and with moderate speed along the ground between the forward walls. The first three forwards of each team are restricted from playing the ball; only the center player, called a "hooker" because of his skill with the foot in gaining control of the ball, can first play the ball in a scrum. The English call this type of play a tight scrum as opposed to the loose scrum, where several players try to gain control of a loose ball on the ground during play.

A player of the offense carrying the ball over the goal line of the defense scores .3 for a try. When a try is scored any player of the offense can bring the ball out any distance in the field of play at a right angle to the goal line from the spot where the ball was in touch and attempt to place kick for a field goal. The defense must remain behind the goal line, which is the restraining line, until the kick is made. If the place kick is successful, the try is converted into a field goal with a value of 5 points. A player kicking a field goal in the run of play scores 3 points. A player who makes a fair catch during the run of play from an opponent's kick or loose ball in flight can dig his heel in the turf at this point and call out, "Mark!" He is then allowed the privilege of a free kick, which may be either a place kick or a drop kick at the spot, with the usual restraining line for the defense. If the player succeeds in his try for a field goal, he scores 3 points. For certain rule infractions teams are awarded penalty kicks and should the kick score a field goal, the team is awarded 3 points. In deciding the winner of a game goals always have precedence over tries regardless of the number accumulated.

The organization of the Rugby Union in 1871 and the revision of the older playing rules did much to promote the game in the United Kingdom and other countries influenced by the English. The parent organization was followed by the Scottish Union (1873), Irish Football Union (1874), North of Ireland Rugby Union (1874), North of Ireland Rugby Union (1875), Welch Rugby Union (1880), and Combined Irish Rugby Union (1881). Other Rugby Unions were founded during the 1870s in Australia, Canada, France, South Africa, and the United States. In 1888 New Zealand organized a Rugby team composed mainly of Maori tribesmen, who later visited England and defeated many of the better Rugby clubs. In 1890 an international board was established to handle matches and to serve as a clearinghouse for disputes. The game of Rugby football formed the basis of American and Canadian football in the nineteenth century.[4]

SOCCER

The British Football Association, which represented soccer clubs in England, was established in 1863. At this date the game was played in a much cruder form than its modern counterpart. A side consisted of a goalkeeper, one back, one halfback and eight forwards. During play the forwards roamed the field dribbling the ball without much thought of team strategy or play-making. The goalkeeper was considered an obstruction to be removed by charging regardless of whether or not he was playing the ball.

It was not until 1883 that the Association adopted rule changes which helped to modernize the game. Player positions now included a goalkeeper, two backs, three halfbacks and five forwards. Crossbars replaced the tapes which once marked the goal. The two-hand overhead throw-in was substituted for the one-hand throw-in. In the 1890s the goalkeeper received protection from charging except when he was playing the ball or obstructing the play of another player. The penalty kick was introduced for minor infractions. Before this time, each team had its own umpire and the referee was used only to settle disputes. The umpires were dropped and referee became the sole arbiter. This change resulted in the formation of the

Referees Association in 1893, which started a similar movement in other countries of the world.

The British Football Association promoted the first international competitions in 1871 and 1872, and for more than a decade the Scottish Queen's Park team dominated international soccer competition. In 1883 the BFA cup was won by England, and the cup rarely left the North and Midland counties during the remainder of the century.[4]

SWIMMING

Before 1800 England, like the nations of the Continent, favored the breast stroke in recreation and in training the armed forces. About 1809, Phokion Clias, the Swiss physical educator, introduced the English to the side stroke, combined with the frog kick of the breast stroke. Clias recommended this new style as a more rapid method of propelling the body through the water than the conventional breast stroke. Experimentation led to the discovery of the overarm side stroke, in which the top arm was lifted out of the water in preparation for the thrust. Again using the frog kick, this stroke was decidedly speedier than Clias' underwater side stroke.

With the introduction of the English swimming championships in 1871, the search for a still better racing stroke was intensified. Experimentation led to the discovery of a leg kick which combined more naturally with the overarm side stroke. Authors of this era describe this leg kick as the equivalent of running under water, the forerunner of the scissors kick. The English swimming champion, Joey Nuttall, was one of the foremost exponents of this new style.

In the *Swimming Record* of August, 1873, the editor described a race won by J. Trudgeon. Trudgeon raised each arm out of the water preparatory to the thrust, and the editor likened the action to one peculiar to the Indians. Trudgeon, who gave his name to the new style, combined the arm stroke with the scissors kick.[7]

Near the end of the century Richard Cavill of Sydney, New South Wales, proposed that Trudgeon's arm stroke be combined with a straight-leg flutter kick which he had seen used by the natives of Colombo, Ceylon. Using this new style Cavill was able to swim 100 yards in 58 seconds flat, which, in his time, was the equivalent of breaking the four-minute barrier in the mile. Cavill's performance as a racing champion gave swimming a tremendous impetus and laid the foundation for future experimentation in racing strokes.

During the last quarter of the nineteenth century fresh- and salt-water records were established by England and Scottish swimmers in such events as the 100-, 220-, 440-, and 500-yard speed races; the half-mile, mile, and long-distance swims; and the plunge for distance. Many books and articles in magazines and newspapers appeared on the subject of swimming. Swimming instruction was introduced in schools and universities, most of which depended upon natural facilities. Swimming clubs arranged competitions and provided instruction in lifesaving techniques and methods of resuscitation. This enthusiasm for swimming permeated continental Europe and found its way to the United States.

Swimming clubs in England were first represented by independent metropolitan associations, in 1869, and these organizations were integrated into the Swimming Association of Great Britain in 1874. This regulatory body was concerned mainly with the problem of amateurism and professionalism and the management of racing meets. In 1885 the SAGB appointed a committee to establish a standard set of playing rules for water polo. Disputes over the question of professionalism led to a schism between the parent body and several independent clubs. Both factions gradually realized the importance of a united front if professionalism was to be controlled and in 1886 joined to organize the Amateur Swimming Association. The new organization patterned its constitution and by-laws after the well-established Amateur Athletic Association and National Cyclist Union, both of which had been successful in the control of professionalism.[7]

TENNIS

Games of the tennis type have been traced to Egypt, Persia, and Arabia, where they existed as early as A.D. 800. From its beginning tennis was a game of royalty or the wealthy, who could afford the construction of the elaborate courts. The French knew the game as *jeu de paume,* and in England there is evidence that it was played as early as the time of Chaucer. During the sixteenth and seventeenth centuries it reached its greatest popularity in both England and France. Samuel Pepys, the British government official and diarist, stated that in the seventeenth century Oxford has two courts and Cambridge five.

Tennis was played in a roofed building with provision for light through the walls and roof. In England this building was called a penthouse. The walls and floors were of cement, and the size of the court varied with the size of the penthouse. A string stretched across the court above the net limited the height that the ball could be volleyed. The details of the construction of the side walls and their openings as well as the end walls are complicated. The game lost considerable ground during the latter nineteenth century when building demands in metropolitan areas resulted in the destruction of many courts. Tennis was relegated to those private clubs whose membership could afford the construction and maintenance of courts.[4]

The game of lawn tennis is relatively modern and its invention is attributed to an Englishman, Major Walter Wingfield. In 1874 Major Wingfield devised and patented a new and improved portable court which was shaped like an hourglass. At the time, the All-England Croquet Club of Wimbleton was about to close its doors because of financial difficulties. The idea that tennis might be a game for commoners gave the club new hope and it announced that, in addition to croquet, it intended to sponsor lawn tennis. Under its wing lawn tennis grew in popularity, and in 1877 the first lawn tennis championships were held at Wimbleton.

The court at this time measured 78 by 27 feet with the net 3 feet 3 inches high at the center. The court dimensions have remained fixed, but the height of the net varied up and down through the years from 3 feet 3 inches to 4 feet 9 inches, until finally in 1884 it was set at 3 feet 6 inches. From Wimbleton lawn tennis has spread to every corner of the world. The Lawn Tennis Association was founded in England in 1886 and the International Tennis Federation in 1912.

Track and Field Athletics

In the early years of the 1800s professional running and walking races attracted wide public interest. These contests were conducted over prescribed courses announced in the local newspapers and were bet on by promoters and public. At first amateurs emulating professional pedestrians ran or walked under fictitious names, but by 1838 they had gained sufficient public following to come out in the open and compete under their own names. From that period on, amateur competition in track events made progress in England, and athletic clubs were formed to represent athletes and arrange meets.

It was not until 1850 that any kind of amateur competition was held in English universities. In that year Exeter College, Oxford, held a track meet which consisted of the 100-, 330-, 440-yard, and mile run straightaway and a 140-yard hurdle race over ten flights arranged 10 yards apart. Hurdle races were then performed by jumping each flight with both feet at the same time. In a summer meet held in 1851 by Exeter College the high jump and long (broad) jump were added to the events. Lincoln College held the next track and field meet, followed by St. John's, Emmanuel College, Balliol, Pembroke, Wadham, and Worchester in 1856. Cambridge, while less active in the promotion of athletic meets, initiated university sports in 1857 and Oxford opened university sports to all undergraduates in 1860. In England there is no official university athletic board which controls athletic policies, and sports competition is conducted by the student body and coached by student-players.

The first athletic meet between Oxford and Cambridge was held in 1864 on the Christ Church cricket ground at Oxford, and the program included the 100-yard, 440-yard, and mile run, 100- and 200-yard hurdle races, 2-mile steeplechase, and high and long (broad) jumps. The Mincing Lane Athletic Club held its first meet the same year, and by 1866 many athletic clubs had been organized, "to supply the want of an established ground upon which competition in amateur athletic sport might take place, and to afford as completely as possible to all classes of gentlemen amateurs the means of practicing and competing against one another, without being compelled to mix with professional runners."[8]

The Amateur Athletic Club, consisting of university alumni, and the London Athletic Club directed the destiny of amateur athletics in England for more than a decade. Both clubs were responsible for the English Open Championship and the first English Championship meet held in 1866. By 1870 the Amateur Athletic Club lost its influence to the London Athletic Club, which also sponsored the

Public Schools Challenge Cup Meeting, Public School Cross-Country Races, Ranelagh Harriers and Public School Relay Meet.

Until the early 1870s approximately two-thirds of the athletes who participated in the English Championship meet came for the universities. To avoid conflict with their summer program of cricket and boating as well as university examinations, the AAC and LAC scheduled the meet in the early spring months, March or April. Meanwhile the provincial and metropolitan athletic clubs had grown in sufficient number and strength to demand consideration. Their athletes were drawn from the laborering, merchants, and business classes. They claimed that the meet as scheduled interfered with a workday and was held too early in the season to permit adequate training. In 1879 many of the independent clubs threatened to withdraw from competition if the AAC and LAC did not change the meet to the summer months. Since a deadlock was inevitable, Oxford athletes invited all clubs to a conference to reach an agreement. As a result, the Amateur Athletic Association was formed in 1880, and representatives agreed to hold the English Championship meets in the summer months at London, the Midland, and North counties in rotation.[8]

ATHLETICS IN THE ENGLISH PUBLIC SCHOOLS

At the close of the eighteenth and beginning of the nineteenth century games and sports played an important part in the life of the English schoolboy. The favorite sports were cricket, boating, and poaching. Cricket matches were played by Winchester and Eaton as early as 1746 and by Eaton and Harrow in 1805 and 1818. The first recorded boat race was held in 1818 by Winchester. Hunting was a sport of the English aristocrat, and since attendance at boarding schools curbed this recreation, schoolboys would annoy nearby landowners by poaching their game. Frequent complaints to head schoolmasters often led to stern disciplinary measures. Shrewsbury Public School, to replace the poaching habit, organized a hunt with an entire entourage of huntsmen, whips, gentlemen, and hounds, with two boys carrying the scent.

Football appeared in public schools early in the nineteenth century and was generally played according to local tastes and rules.

The fact that William Webb Ellis ran with the ball when custom dictated kicking it was not a startling innovation in view of the many forms of Rugby in vogue. Cricket was looked upon as the gentleman's game, while Rugby football was looked upon as a game for the rougher element in the public schools.

ATTEMPTS TO CONTROL ATHLETIC INTEREST

As a general rule headmasters at the beginning of the century were not in sympathy with the athletic interests of the English schoolboy since interschool competition was accompanied by unfavorable publicity and beer drinking. But they tolerated school athletics rather than face the student revolt which generally resulted from attempts to prohibit them. Matthew Arnold, headmaster of Rubgy from 1828 to 1842, cleverly side-stepped the problem when he permitted the boys to adopt legalized self-government. This helped promote athleticism in the English public schools. The schoolboy took charge of his athletics, taxed the school members for its support, served as his own coaching staff, and established his own rules of conduct. Thomas Hughes, who attended Rugby during Arnold's administration, describes in *Tom Brown's Schooldays* (1857) the efficacy of student self-government and the vital part played by athletics in the public schools. Occasionally headmasters joined forces to check athleticism, but these moves were generally thwarted or ended in a compromise.

DEDICATION TO ATHLETICISM (1860–1880)

In 1861 Parliament appointed the Clarendon Commission to investigate the revenue and management of certain schools, including Eaton, Winchester, Westminster, Charterhouse, St. Paul's, Merchant Taylors, Harrow, Rugby, and Shrewsbury. The Commission recognized the tendency of public school athletics to place a high premium upon courage and stamina and suggested that while these qualities were desirable more time should be devoted to the fundamental skills of sports. This body thought gymnastics of little value and stated that cricket and football provided more worthwhile social benefits. The Commission also had very little to say in favor of military drill, which many public schools had recently inaugurated. The Commission's judgment on the higher social value of cricket and football was based on the belief that team sports promoted team spirit and group loyalty. It was on this basis that the Englishman distinguished major from minor sports and held gymnastics in low esteem.

During the next twenty years athleticism in the public schools made even greater gains. Peter MacIntosh of Birmingham University, a capable historian of physical education in England, has suggested several reasons for this.

Although not generally discussed in English literature, boarding school life encouraged a certain amount of immorality. It was thought that the physical fatigue brought on by athletic participation would discourage such behavior. Headmasters also believed athletic competition helped reduce disciplinary problems. Another factor which seemed to perpetuate athleticism was the house system of intramural competition. School boarding houses made natural units of competition in spite of the fact that equality among them was frequently lacking. Eaton adopted intramural competition in 1860, and it was not long until other public schools followed suit. Each master in the school identified himself with a particular house and served as its adviser and frequently its coach.

PUBLIC REACTION TO ATHLETICISM

In 1880 Edward Lyttelton published an article in the *Nineteenth Century Magazine* critical of the lengths to which the athletic fever in the public schools had gone. He cited the fact that German and French officials were more impressed by the cult of athleticism than by intellectual achievement in the English public schools. German admiration for English sports stimulated the recreation movement in that country. At the turn of the century Baron de Coubertin reported that 200 *lycées* and colleges had adopted the English system of interschool athletic competition.

The emphasis on athletics reached its zenith in 1884 when Edmund Warre was elected headmaster of Eaton. Warre had been a rowing coach and a military man, and his goal was to have every boy in his school engage in a sport. He once confided to a friend that he was deeply concerned because 300 boys had escaped his athletic dragnet. In 1889 an Eatonian started a long series of articles in the *Times* which deplored the overemphasis upon athletics in public schools. The writer complained that the older boys made the younger ones practice cricket fourteen times and football five times per week. Though this statement was probably an exaggeration, the point was well made.

But in spite of the forays against athleticism the Englishman remained totally dedicated to the traditions and spirit of athletics in the public schools.

SPORTS IN SCOTLAND

One of Scotland's most popular games with all age groups is curling. Curling is a winter sport using stones shaped like old-fashioned flatirons and weighing up to 44 pounds. The game is played on an ice rink 144 by 28 feet by four players each of whom uses two stones, playing each stone alternately. The players shoot for a tee and the stone nearest to the tee counts. This game seems to have had its origin during the sixteenth century, and many crude curling stones have been retrieved from the bottoms of lakes to become museum pieces. The first Caledonian Curling Club was organized in 1833, and ten years later Queen Victoria granted it the title of Royal Caledonian Curling Club. It has established branches in Canada, New Zealand, Norway, Sweden, Switzerland, and the United States.

The Caledonian Games

Another sporting event indigenous to Scotland is the Caledonian Games, which reached an organized form early in the nineteenth century. They included contests in throwing the hammer (12–22 pounds), running broad and high jump, pole vaulting, running hitch-kick, tossing the cawber, 200-to-300-yard dashes for men and boys, one-half and mile runs, high hurdles (8 hurdles, 5 feet in height, over 600 yards), hop, step and jump, sack, three-legged, wheelbarrow and egg races, wrestling, and various dances such as the broadsword, Highland fling, and Scottish reels. The Scots brought the Caledonian Games with them to America, and the first recorded contests were held in Boston in 1853. Caledonian Societies were organized in many states of the Union and found their way into New England universities. The Caledonian Games had an important influence upon the early development of amateur track and field competition in the United States as well as in the country of their origin.[9]

Golf

The Dutch, with whom the Scots had commercial relations, played a game with clubs and a ball called *kolven*. The earliest known reference to golf in Scotland is in a degree issued by Parliament in 1457 which warned the people against the playing of golf when they should be practicing archery. Many famous golf clubs were organized in Scotland during the eighteenth century, and in England during the following century. The game was a favorite of royalty, and monarchs frequently became patrons of the exclusive clubs. During the eighteenth and most of the nineteenth century golf clubs were fashioned by craftsmen associated with a club, and a leather ball stuffed with feathers was employed. Between 1880 and 1885 commercial manufacturers entered the field and replaced the leather ball with a hard-core rubber one. By the turn of the century golf had become a pastime within the reach of all classes.

The Royal and Ancient Golf Club of St. Andrews became the premier club in the world and the supreme authority in golf. This club frames and revises rules, and, except in the United States, its decisions in golf are accepted without question throughout the world. The British Open and Amateur Championships and the Walker Cup Matches when played in Great Britain are conducted under its jurisdiction.[4]

SPORTS IN IRELAND

Ireland is the only European nation which can claim the distinction of holding games similar to those of the ancient Olympics. These festivals were held about 2000 years ago in honor of Queen Tailte and featured athletic contests, dancing, and singing.

Handball is believed to have originated in Ireland about 1000 years ago and has developed into a national game in that country. In the eighteenth century courts were constructed with a hard clay floor and a front wall of brick or stone. Most courts were located near or adjoining a tavern and the early rules permitted time-out for refreshment. The old handball resembled a miniature baseball, with a cork center around which thread or yarn was wound, the whole encased with a tight horsehide cover. Under the old rules a game consisted of 15 points, the server took his position anywhere behind the short line, a series of three shorts constituted a handout, a player could kick the ball, and points were called aces. During the last quarter of the nineteenth century the game underwent some changes, including the adoption of a hard or soft rubber ball. One addition which was discarded, to be applied later to squash, was the tell-board. The tell-board was 4–6 inches wide, extended the width of the court, and was inserted flush with floor. A ball striking it was a dead ball and this eliminated the opportunity for a kill or ace.

William Bragg of Tipperary was considered one of the most scientific players in the 1850s and promoted the game through exhibition tours of Ireland. Phil Casey was a recognized champion in both Ireland and the United States, where he emigrated in the 1870s. Casey is considered the father of handball in the United States and constructed the first one-wall handball court in Brooklyn. After 1895 many international matches were played for high stakes between the champions of Ireland and the United States. In the twentieth century the Gaelic Athletic Association took handball under its wing and returned it to the status of an amateur sport.[10]

Hurling, another national game of the Irish, in many respects resembles field hockey. The stick is called a hurley, and according to Irish legend the ancient heroes were all skillful hurlers. Like handball hurling was played for big stakes between parishes with an unlimited number of players on a side. When the Gaelic Athletic Association was founded in 1884, the game was revised and given amateur status. The Association arranged provincial, county, and All-Ireland championship meets.

NOTES

1. Peter C. McIntosh. *Physical Education in England Since 1800*. London: G. Bell and Sons, Ltd., 1952, pp. 97; 13–31; 56–59.
2. Archibald MacLaren. *A System of Physical Education*. Oxford: The Clarendon Press, 1895, XLVI.

3. Howard J. Savage. *Games and Sports in British Schools and Universities.* Bulletin No. 18, The Carnegie Foundation, New York, 1928, pp. 5; 198.
4. *Encyclopaedia Britannica.* Chicago: Encyclopaedia Britannica, Inc., 1958, 2: 265–266; 3: 979–980; 11: 471; 11: 485–486; 13: 783–784; 10: 499.
5. *The World Book Encyclopedia.* Chicago: The Quarrie Corporation, 1940, 3: 109–110.
6. *The Encyclopaedia Britannica.* New York: Encyclopaedia Britannica, Inc., 1910–1911, 13–14: 555; 23–24: 784–785.
7. Archibald Sinclair and William Henry. *Swimming,* London: Longmans, Green and Company, 1895, pp. 78–89; 307–316.
8. F. A. M. Webster. *Athletics of Today—History, Development and Training.* London: Frederick Warne, Ltd., 1929, pp. 13; 14–18.
9. Robert Korsgaard. "A History of the Amateur Athletic Union of the United States." (Dissertation) Teachers College, Columbia University, 1952, p. 25.
10. Bernath E. Phillips. "Bringing Handball up to Date." *Journal of Health and Physical Education,* 9:4 (April, 1938), 222.

Chapter 11

PHYSICAL EDUCATION IN CONTINENTAL EUROPE IN THE TWENTIETH CENTURY (I)

THE PRELUDE TO WORLD WAR I

TROUBLE had been brewing in continental Europe ever since the close of the Franco-German War. The war left the French humiliated and embittered at the loss of Alsace-Lorraine. Under Emperor William I, Germany entered a prolonged period of progress and prosperity, but the leadership became increasingly aware that Germany needed commercial outlets if economic stability was to be maintained. Great Britain's growing commercial supremacy, therefore, was viewed with concern and envy by the German monarchy. At the same time the Germans were experiencing difficulties in the extension of their sphere of influence to Eastern Europe, where complex racial and territorial factors thwarted their ambitions.

The treaties closing the Balkan Wars in 1913 left Serbia richer in expanded territory, but Bulgaria and Turkey gained little and remained unreconciled. To make matters worse, the treaty left Serbia as a barrier in the way of Austro-Hungarian dreams of a commercial corrider to Asia Minor. In the foreground of the situation in East Europe was the Austro-Serbian conflict and in the background the German-Austrian alliance counterbalanced by the Russian-Serbian friendship. This attempt to preserve the balance of power in Eastern Europe only served to add complications to an already precarious situation. All that was needed to start a chain reaction and lead to World War I was a serious diplomatic incident, which was furnished on June 28, 1914, when the Serbian Gavrilo Prinzip assassinated the Austrian Crown Prince Archduke Ferdinand and his wife, Sophia, at Sarajevo, capital of the Austrian province of Bosnia.

POLITICAL CHANGES AFTER WORLD WAR I

The war was followed by the failure of the Allies to cooperate in the establishment of a durable peace. Though the Versailles Treaty left Germany intact, the Allies imposed such heavy reparations upon the Germans that the new republic was unable to stabilize its economy. Later attempts to lighten reparation payments came too late, and the German people lost faith in their republican leaders. As a consequence, the people turned to the National Socalist (Nazi) Party, which promised them a new Germany. Austria formed a cooperative Christian-German federal state with an authoritarian government, until 1938 when the country was seized by the Nazis and made a federal division of Germany called Östmark. At the close of World War I Hungary assumed the status of a minor kingdom, with a population consisting largely of Magyars (Hungarians) and minority groups of Germans, Slovaks, Rumanians Croats, Serbs, and others.

The kingdom of Bulgaria was beset by conflicts over territory ceded to Greece and Yugoslavia by the Treaty of Nevilly but managed to survive until World War II. Czechoslovakia became a republic and enjoyed democratic government until 1938, when the Nazis moved in to completely destroy the nation. The kingdom of Rumania experienced continual political unrest until 1930, when King Carol II ascended the throne. The Serbs, Croats, and Slovenes by mutual assent created the kingdom of Yugoslavia in 1929, but constant conflicts between these races led to a military dictatorship. During World War I Spain assumed the role of a neutral nation, but in an attempt to put down the insurrection of Riffian tribes in Spanish Morocco during 1921 suffered a humiliating defeat. Internal dissatisfaction led to civil war, with Germany and Italy supporting the Rebels and Russia the Loyalists. The Rebels were victorious in 1939, and the war hero, General Francisco Franco, became dictator.

After the Russians made a separate peace with the Germans and withdrew from World War I, the country experienced a difficult period marked by famine and revolution. Following Lenin's death, by clever statesmanship and intrigue, Stalin outstripped his competitors and assumed the dictatorship. In 1928 he inaugurated the first of his Five-Year Plans to strengthen the economy of the nation. A second Five-Year Plan was invoked in 1933 with a little more success than the first. The armaments race of 1938 and 1939 stimulated Russian heavy industry, and with an improvement in economic conditions, the Soviet leadership reaffirmed its revolutionary aims. As the world community became conscious of Russian objectives, a sharp cleavage developed between Communist and democratic nations.

WORLD WAR II AND ITS AFTERMATH

Adolf Hitler, leader of the Nazi Party, used the harsh terms of the Versailles Treaty, so-called discriminatory action against Germans in minority nations, and the need for expansion of a revitalized Germany as reasons to plunge the world into a second great conflict. Fifty-seven Allied and Axis nations were eventually involved in a struggle which led Hitler and his cobelligerents to defeat. The four Allied powers divided Germany into Eastern and Western sectors, one occupied by the Soviet Union, the others by the Allies. Berlin was jointly occupied by the military forces of all four.

During the period of readjustment following World War II Great Britain lost her predominant position in world affairs to nations which had been strengthened as a result of the conflict. Backward peoples in the Far East, Southeast Asia, and Africa demanded the right of self-determination, and colonialism gave way to the drive for nationalism. In Eastern Europe political unrest led to the eventual acceptance of Communism by Bulgaria, Czechoslovakia, East Germany, Hungary, Poland, Rumania, and Yugoslavia. Of the seven Russian satellites, Yugoslavia was the only one in which the country's Communists and not emissaries from Moscow created the army and bureaucracy. Austria escaped the political manipulations of the Communists, and was established by the four powers as a sovereign, independent, and democratic state with its pre-1938 frontiers intact.

EDUCATION IN EUROPEAN COUNTRIES

Progressive European nations in the twentieth century conceived of education as the basis of their social, political, and industrial progress, and their national welfare and prosperity. As a part of the political philosophy developed in the nineteenth century, education was accepted as a function and responsibility of the state. State constitutions, whether or not fully implemented and enforced, provided for a comprehensive school system from the kindergarten through the higher technical schools or universities. In European states education is administered by the department of education in each district or province into which the country is divided. Each of these subdivisions has a chief administrative officer who is responsible to the national minister. The minister of education is in turn responsible to the legislature. Numerous subdivisions within the minister's department are responsible for special areas of the national program, each of which is headed by a director who works with the local administrators. The district or provincial subdivisions may or may not have considerable autonomy, depending on the country, but they are responsible for the general administration in their area, including teacher training, schools for the blind and deaf, registration of private and parochial schools, trade and technical schools, public and traveling libraries, and teacher certification.

Through the centuries European countries developed a two-ladder system of education. The first ladder represents the education of the common people or masses. This includes the primary grades, from which students may enroll in agricultural, technical, vocational, commercial, and continuation schools. Elementary education in the majority of countries has been free and compulsory since the first half of the nineteenth century. Many nations enforced the law, while others failed because of political and religious strife, economic conditions, or indifference on the part of those in authority.

The second educational ladder is designed for those who can

afford the tuition and other expenses and who have the intellectual capacity to pursue a rather rigorous educational regimen. The primary grades for this group are considered preparatory to the secondary schools, which in some European countries are among the best in the world. From the secondary schools, students progress to the higher technical schools (civil, mechanical, electrical, chemical, architectural, and metallurgical engineering among others) or the university, where they prepare for the professions. It is among this last group that the state hopes to find its future leaders.

In those countries which have embraced the political philosophy of Communism, education has become technical rather than humanistic. All education in the Soviet Union is permeated by the ideology and directed toward the needs of the Communist Party. The purpose of education according to the *Great Soviet Encyclopaedia* (1948) is:

> To develop in children's mind the Communist morality, ideology and Soviet patriotism; to insure unshakable love toward the Soviet fatherland, the Communist Party and its leaders; to propagate Bolshevik vigilance; to put an emphasis on atheist and international education; to strengthen Bolshevik will-power and character, as well as courage, capacity for resisting adversity and conquering obstacles; to develop self-discipline; and to encourage physical and aesthetic culture.

Compared with the state of education in the Soviet Union and its satellite nations before World War II, when illiteracy reached as high as 48 percent in several countries, the centralized control of education in Communist states has worked miracles since the war.

PHYSICAL EDUCATION AND SPORTS

The control and regulation of physical education and sports in the schools of continental Europe is usually the function of a subdivision within the ministry of education. This subdivision is headed by the state director of physical education and sports, who is usually assisted by a board, council, or committee. The latter group may be composed of leading physical educators, physicians, public health officials, government representatives in finance, school facilities, etc., and executive officers of the national youth organization, sports federation, and Olympic Committee. The board, council, or committee not only acts in an advisory capacity to the state director, but also controls and regulates physical education in public schools and higher institutions, establishes standards and approves training programs for physical educators and sports leaders, approves plans for and collects data on facilities, grants funds for the construction of facilities and the subsidization of physical education and sports projects, promotes voluntary sports organizations outside the school, manages regional, national and international competition in amateur sports, and makes provisions for the athletes who have been selected for Olympic competition.

In the following discussion the organization and administration of physical education and sports in only two representative Communist satellites will be given.

AUSTRIA

In 1912 the office of state supervisor of physical education was established within the department of the Minister of Education. The school program continued to be strongly influenced by the German system of gymnastics and free exercises. Prior to World War II natural gymnastics were introduced into the schools as the result of the work of Karl Gaulhofer, Margaret Streicher, and A. Slama. During the Nazi occupation greater emphasis was placed on activities which were of military value. After the cessation of hostilities interest was revived in gymnastics, natural gymnastics, amateur sports, and dancing. Concerned by the plight of unemployed youth during the period of readjustment, Austria gave special attention to sports participation and organized recreation for this group.

TEACHER PREPARATION

In 1913 the normal school of gymnastics affiliated with the University of Vienna offered a two-year teacher preparation course for men and a one-year course for women. In 1924 this was extended to four years for both sexes. At the present time Austria has three professional schools for the training of physical education teachers, affiliated with the universities of Vienna, Graz and Innsbruck.[1] The four-year curriculums include courses in sport techniques, body mechanics, anatomy and physiology, history, philosophy, principles, and tests and measurements. Sport instruction emphasizes both theoretical basis and performance. Men and women professional students are taught together in track and field, fencing, rhythmical activities, and basketball. European girls and women play court basketball under the same International Basketball Federation rules as boys and men.

BELGIUM

In the postwar years Belgium adopted a broader program of participation in games and sports. The main core of the school physical education program, however, continued to be Swedish gymnastics. According to a report in 1960 by Maurice Van Der Stock, Supervisor of Physical Education, City Schools of Brussels, the time allocated to physical education in the schools of Belgium is generally insufficient, though varying considerably from province to province.[2] As a rule secondary schools provide two periods a week for gymnastics, one for instruction in swimming, and an afternoon a week for games and sports. Variations from this practice range from daily periods of gymnastics to only one period per week. Attempts to legislate physical education as a required subject have failed. Fortunately the favorable attitude of faculties in higher institutions toward physical exercise has encouraged voluntary student participation in gymnastics and sports.

Larger cities and towns provide gymnasiums for school and public use, in addition to many private gymnasiums. Belgium has also established for the combined use of school and public 575 playing fields and courts for such sports as soccer, football, hockey, and tennis, as well as 199 indoor and 157 outdoor swimming pools.

TEACHER PREPARATION

The state established a teacher-training institution at Brussels in 1905 to prepare gymnastic leaders in the Ling system. Three years later the College of Physical Education was founded at the University of Ghent, one of the first institutions to grant a doctorate in physical education. Among the early candidates to be granted the advanced degree were Lucien Dehoux, a native son, and A. Leal d'Oliveira, President of the FIEP and editor of the *Bulletin de la Fédération Internationale d'éducation Physique* (see Appendix 1). The leadership of the College of Physical Education has contributed importantly to the philosophy and practice of gymnastics in France, Portugal, Spain, the Netherlands, and South America. In association with the university's medical faculty, the staff members have contributed outstanding research in the areas of body mechanics and the physiology of exercise. The most recent addition to the facilities for teacher training in Belgium was the creation by the state in 1956 of the National Institute of Physical Education.

CZECHOSLOVAKIA

In the 1920s amateur sports were controlled and regulated by the National Sports Committee, composed of delegates from the various sports associations. The strongest of these was the association of soccer football, which had members from Czech, German, Hungarian, Polish, and Jewish teams. In addition to sports clubs, every village and town had hiking clubs, which belonged to the National Hikers Club. In the early thirties this national association had 80,000 members and owned 100 huts and inns distributed throughout the countryside.[3]

During the Nazi occupation the gymnastic and sports organizations were wiped out, and hundreds of Czech and Slavic gymnastic leaders perished in Nazi concentration camps. After the defeat of Germany in 1945 interest in gymnastics and sports revived. Effective reorganization, however, did not take place until 1948, when the gymnastic societies of the labor unions and Catholics joined with more than thirty sport associations to form the Sokol Federation. In 1949 the National Assembly placed gymnastics and sports under the supervision and control of the government, where they developed into a national movement of significant political and social importance. Their general plan of organization was adopted by the Roman Catholic Orels (Eagles), Jewish Makabees, German Turner Society, German Workers Union, and Workingmen's Union.

When Czechoslovakia gained its freedom at the close of the war the Sokols, under the leadership of Joseph Schreiner, made several important changes in program. One of these was the inclusion of rhythmical gymnastics and the dance in the women's program, and another was the establishment of a training center at Prague called Tyrs House. This center offered short courses to selected gymnasts sent there by local Sokol societies. Gymnasts so trained were not eligible, however, to teach in the Czechoslovakian school system. To be certified as a teacher, a Sokol had to enroll in the University of Prague, Bratislava, or Brno and while securing his academic degree complete the requirements in physical education.[3]

In the postwar period interest in games and sports was stimulated by the work of YMCA physical directors, who also introduced camping, swimming, and lifesaving, which in turn were made part of the school program. Another contribution of the YMCA was the promotion of the playground movement according to American plan of organization. This movement received considerable impetus from citizens of German and Hungarian extraction and particularly the Sokol societies, which furnished their gymnasiums and playing areas for recreational use.

Under Communist domination the Czechs have not lost their enthusiasm for massive demonstrations. At the second National Spartakiade in 1960 some 720,000 participants took part, and the major feature of the event was a gymnastic exhibition in which 30,000 performed in unison.

FRANCE

By 1900 the elementary schools of France had become secular, free, and compulsory. The gradual replacement of teachers with a religious bias by those without ascetic views had a salutary effect upon the promotion of physical education in the schools. In addition, the government had accepted responsibility for the support of the schools, which made possible the standardization of curriculums. After World War I education was placed under the absolute jurisdiction of the minister of education, with the result that local education lost its autonomy and school programs became inflexible. The academic program received the major attention, and vocational as well as technical training fell into neglect. In recent years the French people have indicated a desire for a broader curriculum in keeping with the modern needs of the student population.

Between 1900 and 1920 physical education in France was influenced by three systems: the so-called French system, which was in reality the gymnastics developed by Amorós; the Swedish system; and the natural exercises devised by Georges Hébert.* The gymnastics of Amoros were favored by the government and represented by the strong French Gymnastics Association with the aggressive Charles Cazal at its head. The Swedish system had the endorsement of the medical profession, and its staunchest supporter was Dr. Philippe Tessler. Hébert was backed by his experience as director of physical training at the military school of Lorient, the influential Marquis de Polignac, and the press, which publicized his natural method both locally and internationally. These three systems fought for position in the educational system of France for two decades.

During World War I, however, their backers cooperated to provide physical training programs for the French Army. Hébert directed physical training for the Fourth Army, and Dr. Bellin du Couteau directed the physical training program of officer candidates at Saint-Cyr, Saint Maixent, and Issoudun. After the arrival of YMCA physical directors with the American Expeditionary Forces toward the close of the war, the complexion of the army physical training program changed considerably. French Army personnel who had observed the balanced program of conditioning exercises and games conducted by the YMCA leaders, and their effect upon morale of the soldiers, eagerly sought their assistance. Eight regional centers were established to train selected army personnel to lead and organize sport programs, with a YMCA physical director assigned to each. As a result, thousands of French soldiers were introduced to volleyball, basketball, track and field athletics, swimming, boxing, and wrestling.

YMCA physical directors also introduced mass play and games to schoolchildren in many French cities and towns. Games were also

* These included: (1) marching, (2) running, (3) jumping, (4) climbing, (5) quadrupedism, (6) balancing, (7) lifting and transporting, (8) throwing, (9) exercises of defense and attack, and (10) swimming.

organized in summer camps for underprivileged children under the direction of the Société des Foyers de l'Union Franco-Américaine, an organization financed by the YMCA.

THE POSTWAR PERIOD

After demobilization the government favored the officers trained in the YMCA regional centers as instructors of physical education in the schools. Trained as leaders in the armed forces, these men lacked the necessary qualifications and experience to teach in the schools. Under the 1928 Physical Education Law a state secretary of physical education and an assistant were appointed to supervise physical education in the schools, regulate amateur sports, and cooperate with the French Olympic Committee. One of the first moves of the secretariat was to improve the physical education leadership in the state-supported schools.

Ray-Gollier, Inspector General of Physical Education in the schools of Paris, had organized monitor schools to train physical educators, and these schools produced a teacher with much better qualifications than those currently in service in France. The secretary of physical education established similar monitor schools at the old YMCA Regional Institutes at Rennes, Nancy, Marseille, Montpellier, and Lille, among others. The monitor course required one year to complete and granted the graduate the *Diplome Supérieur d'Éducation Physique*. Holders of his diploma were eligible to teach in secondary schools and higher institutions. These Regional Institutes formed the basis of the broader teacher preparation programs of modern times.[4]

MODERN TRENDS

In 1952 four million elementary school children between the ages of 6 and 14 in state-supported schools received a total of 4½ hours of physical education per week. Physical education is taught by the classroom teacher, who received instruction during her teacher-training program. In addition, the elementary school teacher must attend a three-weeks' course in physical education at one of the regional centers. Secondary school pupils receive two one-hour periods of physical education per week plus three hours of participation in sports and recreational activities outside the school. Physical education in universities is still optional, although the trend since World War II seems to be toward a required program.[4]

GERMANY

Up to World War I German elementary and secondary schools required physical education two hours a week consisting of free exercise, apparatus work graduated according to age and sex, marching tactics, and tumbling. In 1910 a ministerial degree increased instruction from the fourth grade up to three hours per week with a compulsory play period two afternoons a week.

Ministerial decrees of the 1920s introduced rhythmical activities of native or foreign origin, games, and sports. A 1924 decree required students in the upper elementary grades and secondary schools to attend a daily period of physical education and recommended that swimming be provided where possible. Annual interschool athletic competitions (*Reichsjugendwelkämpfe*) were inaugurated similar to those established by the New York City Public School Athletic League. In addition, German boys enrolled in the preparatory classes of the German Turner Society.

In the early years of Nationalist Socialism every social club and educational institution which fostered a physical education and sports program came under the control of a government bureau which prescribed activities, methodology, and membership. Activities were divided into twenty-one classifications, each of which was administered by a sports leader who coordinated programming, use of facilities, and the conduct of competitions. In the early days of Hitler the scientific aspects of physical education were emphasized, and physicians, physiologists, therapists, and sports authorities combined their efforts to discover the best pedagogical and training methods to meet the physical needs of the individual. Toward the close of the war years scientific research became incidental to the struggle for survival.

THE SPORTS MOVEMENT IN GERMANY

Many factors contributed to the change in the European cultural tradition which viewed gymnastics as a *sine qua non* in educational and military programs. The revival of the Olympic Games in 1896 focused the attention of continental Europe for the first time upon sports competition as an expression of national pride. Nations which had devoted their energy solely to gymnastics and considered sports purely recreational were hard-pressed to find athletes of Olympic caliber. Germany, impressed by the performance of American athletes at the Stockholm Olympic Games in 1912, appointed a commission to visit the United States the following year to study the athletic and physical education programs and facilities of selected higher institutions. This commission, led by Dr. Carl Diem, formulated plans to establish a College of Physical Education to train educators an dsports leaders, which was interrupted by World War I.

The sports movement in Germany prior to World War I was distinctly a private enterprise. Sports enthusiasts organized their own clubs, associations, and a central body to regulate amateur sports and process candidates for the Olympic Games. In the postwar era this movement became centralized in the *Deutscher Reichausschub für Leibesübungen,* which campaigned for the construction of sports facilities in school and community, stimulated interest in sports in the school, and arranged achievement tests to encourage all-round athletic competence. In the 1920s the *Reichausschub* became the driving power behind the promotion of games and sports in Germany, and by 1927 there was hardly a German city of any consequence that had not assigned large tracts of land for playing fields, courts, and general play areas. Hamburg, with the largest number of sports facilities, utilized many city blocks on the outskirts of the city. Frankfurt constructed 142 playing fields, sports grounds, gymnasiums, and swimming pools. Leipzig sacrificed some of its beautiful community gardens to make room for sports grounds and constructed one of the largest and best equipped stadiums in Europe. By 1929 the *Reichausschub* reported 20,000 sports clubs sponsoring gymnastics, 15,000 track-field athletics, 2000 aquatics, and 8000 miscellaneous sports, representing a total membership of several million.[5]

When the National Socialists came into absolute power in 1933, they found a vigorous and growing national federation of sports in operation. The *Reichausschub* was a prosperous federation of 38 affiliate associations composed of 25,000 sports clubs with a total membership of 6½ million. In addition to the *Reichausschub,* there were many minor sport organizations, such as the Socialist Workers

Sport Movement with 1700 clubs and the old university student social and dueling clubs represented by the Burschenschaften, with 110 fraternities and a membership of 36,000. The Socialist Workers were disbanded by Hitler and its clubs were absorbed by the associations. The *Burschenschaften* was formally dissolved at Wartburg Castle near Eisenbach in 1935 and its student members absorbed by Hitler's youth bunds. The *Reichausschub* suffered a severe blow when Hitler discontinued the youth section of all sports clubs and drafted their members into youth bunds.

In the postwar era Germans in both West and East Germany reorganized the old sports clubs disbanded by Hitler and entered once again into competition. In 1946 a German gymnastic competition was held at Frankfurt and the following year at Cologne. The enthusiasm for sports participation continues unabated in both West and East Germany in spite of occupation restrictions on the organization of central controlling bodies.

SPORTS MEDICINE IN GERMANY

Before the 1900s physicians and physiologists had been interested in the medical and physiological aspects of exercise. Physicians conducted studies in connection with high-altitude mountain climbing, and the medical technicians of the German Imperial Army directed studies on the expenditure of energy and fatigue in military exercises. In 1911 German physicians meeting to consider the physiology of exercise formally established a research laboratory at the Dresden Hygiene Museum.

In 1923 Dr. Carl Diem, director of the newly organized Berlin College of Physical Education, invited physicians interested in the medical aspects of exercise and sports to meet at this institution, where they organized the medical Association for the Promotion of Physical Education. The same year staff members of the College of Physical Education cooperated with Dr. A. Bier of the Medical School of the University of Berlin to organize a course in the theory and practice of physical education for medical students. This course, the first of its kind in Europe, consisted of four hours of lecture and three hours of practical work a week.

INTERNATIONAL CONGRESS ON SPORTS MEDICINE

The first International Congress on Physical Education and Sports was held in conjunction with the Olympic Games in Amsterdam in 1928. As an outgrowth of the interest stimulated by this conference, the first International Congress on Sports Medicine was held in 1933 in Rome, Italy. Subsequent meetings were held at Paris in 1934 and at the time of the Olympic Games in Berlin in 1936. The Berlin Congress was attended by 1500 physicians and research physiologists from forty nations, and it was decided to hold all future congresses in conjunction with the Olympic Games.

THE GROWTH OF RECREATION

The commission which visited the United States in 1913 also observed some of the more extensive American recreation systems. One of these was the Chicago system, where the commissioners were impressed not only by the organization and vast facilities, but by the fact that they had been made possible through legislation. On its return to Germany the commission suggested legislation requiring municipalities to lay out three square meters of playground area per capita. The outbreak of war frustrated the commission's recommendation. German recreation leaders, however, did not forget, and in the postwar years many municipalities achieved or surpassed the proposed minimum of three square meters of playground space per capita.

The Nazi *Reichausschub* in 1935 reported 861 large sports areas which measured more than an acre in size, 50,000 school playgrounds, and 28,000 playgrounds used exclusively by city recreation systems. Shortly before World War II the German government completed at Cologne a recreation park which became a showpiece for the German Reich with its beautifully landscaped grounds, shelters, nurseries, kitchens, wading and swimming pools, playing fields, courts, and bridle paths.

THE YOUTH HOSTEL MOVEMENT

The industrialization of Germany before World War I stimulated the rapid growth of towns and cities, new prosperity, and economic progress, which challenged the older values and traditions. Reacting to this transition with a feeling of insecurity, the German youth escaped to the world of nature, where he sought temporary solace in more peaceful surroundings. On foot and by bicycle and boat thousands of young people explored the countryside, traversed fields and mountains, rivers and streams, discovering the old Germany. They went on excursions lasting days and weeks, alone and with friends, living in tents, ruins of old castles, or rooms rented from country folk. As the youth movement grew, the German government gave it support by establishing *Jugendherbergen* (Youth Shelters). These shelters included clubhouses, country homes, barns, ancient towers, castles, and monasteries. Supervision and maintenance were provided and a small fee charged for their use. The smaller shelters usually consisted of two sleeping rooms with minimum essentials. The larger ones in popular areas contained many small sleeping rooms with bedclothing, social room, library, fully equipped kitchen, bathing facilities, and outdoor areas for dancing, games, and sports. By the start of World War I a network of youth shelters was spread across Germany and the youth hostel movement had grown beyond the pioneer stage.[6]

After the war the youth hostel movement lost much of its drive, but by the time the National Socialists came to power, the movement had started to grow once more. Hitler featured hosteling as well as camping as part of his youth bund program.[7]

TEACHER PREPARATION

The German government for many years supported and regulated institutes for the training of gymnastic teachers at Berlin, Spandau, Dresden, Munich, Karlsruhe, and Würtemberg. In the first decade of the twentieth century one-third of their courses consisted of instruction in the basic sciences, history, first aid, and types and construction of apparatus. The remainder of the curriculum included practice in free exercises, marching tactics, apparatus work, tumbling, and organized games.

As a result of the report of the 1913 Commission under Dr. Carl Diem professional training courses in the institutes were extended to three years. Many of these institutes sought affiliation with state universities to strengthen the professional curriculum and established research laboratories in association with the medical staffs.

Among the contributions of the Reichausschub was the establishment of the College of Physical Education (*Deutsche Hohescschule für Leibesübungen*) in 1920 as an affiliate of the University of Berlin. During the era before World War II the college made valuable contribution to research in the physiology of exercise, athletic training, and sports medicine.[8]

After World War II the college, which had been abandoned by the Nazis, was reopened. Since Berlin was separated from West Germany by a hundred-mile corridor which left it standing like an island in East Germany, the College of Physical Education was moved to Cologne with Dr. Diem still at its head. Specialists in physical education and sports in West Germany use the college as their center of operation. The College of Physical Education in Leipzig, East Germany, has attained considerable professional stature under the leadership of Günter Erbach and the favorable attitude of the Communists toward physical education and sports.

GREECE

The reluctance of the Greek government to accept Athens as the site of the first modern Olympic Games in 1896 was not entirely financial. Deeply proud of its ancient athletic history, Greece had lost touch with her past. Gymnastics, required by law in 1834, were emphasized in the schools, but sports played an insignificant role. During the post World War I era school boys and girls were excluded from membership in sports clubs, and athletic participation was restricted to such organizations as the YMCA, YWCA, Boy Scouts, and recreational groups. The dominant promoters of gymnastics in Greece include George Pagon, Jean Fokianos, Jean Chryssafiss, Sotirios Peppas, Phillipe Karvelas, and Evangelos Pavlinis.

After World War I the Greek government invited the International YMCA Committee to send physical education leaders to metropolitan areas. They introduced Greek youths to games and sports, and the enthusiasm for these activities infiltrated the schools. In 1930 the government established a Division of Physical Education in the Ministry of Education and provided funds for the construction of facilities for sports and recreation. During the following years Jean Chryssafis, State Director of Physical Education, reported a total of 280 teachers of gymnastics in schools and universities and the construction of some 150 stadiums in towns and villages. World War II left Greece in a depressed economic condition, and the installation of facilities for gymnastics and sports was severely curtailed.

Greek sports are controlled by the Secretariat of General Athletics, under the President of the government. Sports clubs are formed into regional unions and these in turn are assembled into federations. Since World War II the Greeks have shown an increased interest in games and sports, particularly basketball. Soccer and volleyball are also popular.

Physical education is taught on all academic levels and teacher qualifications vary for each gradient. Instruction in the elementary school is the responsibility of the classroom teacher, who has received preparation during his normal school course. To teach on the secondary level the physical educator must have earned the certificate of gymnasium and passed a special examination after two years at a normal school. Professors of physical education in the middle schools, colleges, and universities must complete a three-year course at the Academy of Physical Culture at Athens. Admission to this institution requires the certificate of gymnasium and an entrance examination.[2]

HUNGARY

Physical education in Hungary has been dominated in turn by the German and Swedish systems. At the close of World War I Hungary showed a keen interest in sports and recreation. In 1921 a plan to organize his interest was presented to the National Assembly, but on account of the economic and political situation action was postponed until 1924. The plan called for the establishment of two regulatory and supervisory bodies, the Department of Physical Education and the Natioal Board of Physical Education, under the Minister of Education.

The Department of Physical Education supervised physical education programs in all schools, established standards and supervised teacher-training institutions, and controlled and regulated school athletics. This last responsibility was divided between the National Federation of School Sports and the Intercollegiate Sports Association. These organizations promoted and supervised intramural and interschool sports competition in secondary schools and universities.

The National Board of Physical Education was divided into four sections represented by commissions. The first of these established policies and standards for physical education in the schools and for sports competition out of school. The second section, known as the Commission of Sports Federation, controlled the activities of sports clubs in twenty-one sports associations. The third section, called the Commission on International Sports, had the responsibility of arranging international athletic competition, including Olympic Games try-outs.[9]

The final section of the National Board was known as the Commission of Levente Association. The Levente (Young Hero) was the idea of Dr. E. Karofiath and resembled the German Turner Society or Sokol in organization. Boys 12 to 21 years of age could join their community Levente clubs, which were limited to a membership of fifteen. Industrial, commercial, and agricultural establishments which employed 1000 individuals of whom 100 were qualified by age and sex were required by law to organize Levente clubs. Boy Scouts had the privilege of organizing Leventes within the troop. The members of these Leventes were required to attend a prescribed program of activities twice a week led by former army personnel and teachers. Local communities with the assistance of the state provided funds for the construction of sports facilities. The commission made no provisions for girls or women.

TEACHER PREPARATION

Before World War I the government supported and controlled institutes for the training of gymnastic teachers, which, in general, conducted two-year courses. In 1925 the government established the (Royal) College of Physical Education at Budapest, and Imre Szukovathy was appointed director. Currently this institution has the responsibility for the preparation of teachers of higher institutions, athletic trainers, and sports leaders at the Superior Normal School or the Institute for Athletic Trainers and Sports Leaders.

Scientific research in physical education and sports is conducted by specialists through several professional organizations. Among these are the Institute of Scientific Research in Physical Education and the National Institute of Physical Education and Hygiene of Sport and College of Physical Education. The work of these organizations is coordinated by the Scientific Council of Physical Education, which has an appointive membership of about one hundred physical education specialists. In 1959 Hungary established the Institute of Scientific Research in Physical Education and Sport to conduct experimental studies in pedagogy and methodology.[1]

ITALY

Between 1900 and World War I the academic program received most of the attention in Italian schools. Where a physical education program existed, its quality depended upon the attitude of the school administrator and the training of the gymnastic instructor, who had attended short courses offered by private and municipal institutes. In the postwar period interest in physical education and sports increased and physical education became a required subject in the schools.[10]

Currently physical education is required in both elementary and secondary schools. In the lower grades the program consists of free exercises, games, sports, and rhythmics. Emphasis is placed upon fundamental movements, which are integrated with lead-up games and rhythmic activities. The Italian Minister of Education prescribes a minimum of thirty minutes per day for instruction in physical education and an hour daily for outdoor activities. In the upper grades the program consists of individual and team sports, rhythmic activities, and gymnastics. The colleges and universities promote sports on a larger scale then they do in the United States. The most popular are tennis and fencing, but soccer, volleyball, track and field athletics, basketball, and in the Alpine regions winter sports have a considerable following. Each public school and higher institution in Italy has its sports club, which receives financial assistance from the Italian National Olympic Committee.

In Italy physical education and sports are the responsibility of the Central Committee for Physical and Sports Education, attached to the Ministry of Education. The Italian National Olympic Committee promotes sports among the general public and serves as an intermediary for the Federation of Sports. The government allows the Olympic Committee a certain percentage of the funds derived from *Totocalcio,* a state-controlled professional soccer lottery in which the public spends some two million dollars weekly trying to pick the winners of thirteen games. With this income the committee provides schools and sports clubs with funds for gymnasiums, swimming pools, equipment, and instructional staff. Through its assistance in the construction of pools swimming is rapidly becoming a recreational activity of major significance. A survey in 1957 indicated that ninety-six swimming pools were under construction throughout Italy. The state soccer lottery also furnished the money to construct the stadium and other facilities for the 1960 Olympic Games in Rome.[11]

Teacher Preparation

The preparation of gymnastic teachers in Italy before World War I was dependent upon privately owned institutes. In the postwar years the University of Bologna established a training course in physical education for teachers in the secondary schools and higher institutions. This was later extended from two to four years. Like the College of Physical Education in Berlin, the University of Bologna also provided a course in the theory and practice of sports for medical students who wished to qualify as sports physicians.

In the early 1930s at the height of Fascist rule physical education in the schools was placed under the control of the *Opera Nazionale Balilla.* Under its regime instruction was made uniform and regular teachers replaced by specially trained instructors who were under the supervision of the *Balilla* and military officers. To meet the increased demand for physical training instructors, the Fascists established an institute at Rome in the early 1930s. This institution eventually became the College of Physical Education, admission to which was limited to candidates with a baccalaureate degree. Its curriculum provides a two-year course leading to a diploma and a four-year course granting a doctor of science degree in physical education.

THE NETHERLANDS

Physical education in the Netherlands (Holland) has been influenced by the gymnastic systems of the Danes, Swedes, French, Belgian, and Austrians. The schools in 1910 adopted the rhythmical gymnastics of Dalcroze and Bode and in 1922 the locomotion drills of the Austrians, Gaulhofer and Streicher. This mixture of theories and practices hardly encouraged uniformity in school programs. Recognizing this fact the Society of Professors of Physical Education (1862) established a teacher-training program to assure some uniformity of instruction in the schools.

A law of 1920 stipulated the procedure by which physical education might be introduced in the school program of municipalities. Directors of public, Catholic, and Protestant schools were requested to submit a plan of study to the state supervisor of instruction. When the school representative and the state supervisor were in accord, the proposed plan became obligatory.

Physical education is currently required in elementary schools two periods a week and in upper schools three periods a week. The indoor program generally consists of locomotion drills, which involve the fundamental movements of running, jumping, skipping, hopping and others; freely moving exercises with Indian clubs, wands, hoops, and balls done to the rhythm of percussion instruments; and progressive apparatus work. The outdoor program includes low organized games, volleyball, field ball, hockey, basketball, and softball. As is customary in most European countries, boys and girls participate in the same games, and basketball, field hockey, and volleyball are popular coeducational activities. Folk and social dancing are learned in the home or through social clubs, but modern dance is popular in the physical education program because its fundamental movements are a regular part of instruction.[12]

Before 1940 participation in physical education and sports in higher institutions was left to the individual student. Between 1940 and 1950 higher institutions began to assume more responsibility for the organization of physical education and sports programs. Instruction, however, is given after school on a voluntary basis, and this practice does not encourage student participation. Currently about 50 percent of the students enroll in classes, which are staffed by sixty physical education teachers. The government pays for the construction of facilities and teacher salaries, but the students pay about one-half the cost of equipment.

Sports are enthusiastically accepted by the youth of the Netherlands, and approximately 40 percent of the young people belong to sports clubs. The remainder are neglected because of the lack of promotional work and the absence of sports instruction in some of the narrower programs of physical education in the schools. The city of Amsterdam has taken steps to rectify this situation through a voluntary corps of sports instructors who, with the cooperation of sports associations, teach youngsters the fundamentals of basketball, handball, soccer, and volleyball. Since World War II sports participation by the general public has grown. M. E. Kupers, Director of the Department of Physical Education and Sports, Amsterdam, reported that membership in sports clubs increased from 900,000 in 1950 to 1,400,000 in 1959.

TEACHER PREPARATION

Before 1912 teachers of physical education got their training in other countries and submitted to examinations to qualify for teaching positions. In 1912 the professional leadership in the Netherlands provided a course in teacher preparation which extended over a period of three years. Professors of physical education organized a series of short courses in theory the first year and supervised the training of the candidate the second and third years. Under this system only 30 percent of the students passed the examination and secured their diplomas. In 1945 five private institutes were established to prepare teachers in physical education. These institutes offer a four-year course leading to a diploma and though private receive financial support from the government.[12] In the elementary schools the regular classroom teacher provides instruction in physical education. The government has been encouraging qualified teachers to secure the diploma in physical education by paying 50 percent of the expenses and a bonus after the successful completion of the examination, but response to these incentives has been poor.

NOTES

1. Josef Recla. "Physical Education in Austria." *Journal of Health, Physical Education and Recreation,* 20:5 (May, 1949), 310. John E. Nixon. "The Vienna Physical Education Institute." *Journal of Health–Physical Education–Recreation,* 29:4 (April, 1958), 68.
2. Pierre Seurin. *L'Éducation Physique dans le Monde.* Bordeaux: Edition Bière, 1961, pp. 33; 46–47; 187; 205–206.
3. Lewis W. Reiss. "Physical Education in Czechoslovakia." *Journal of Health and Physical Education,* 3:8 (October, 1932), 6–13. Thomas Woody. "Sokols, 1948." *Journal of Health and Physical Education,* 19:6 (June, 1948), 393.
4. Ballin Au Couteau. "The Development of Physical Education in France." *Journal of Health and Physical Education,* 3:9 (November, 1932), 52–53. Christian Lazard. "Organization of Physical Education in France." *Journal of Health and Physical Education,* 51:1 (January, 1934), 8–11. A. P. Leger. "Physical Education in France." *Bulletin of Physical Education,* 2 (March, 1952), 21–25.
5. Seward C. Staley. "Physical Training and Sports in Pre-Nazi Germany." *The Athletic Journal,* 21:5 (January, 1941), 22.
6. Frederick H. Wohler. "The New Physical Education in Germany." *Journal of Health and Physical Education,* 1:8 (October, 1930), 3.
7. Adelaide H. Miller. "The German Youth Movement." *Journal of Health and Physical Education,* 8:6 (June, 1937), 352.
8. Carl Diem. "Development and Aim of Physical Education in Germany." *Journal of Health and Physical Education,* 19:6 (June, 1948), 390.
9. Seward C. Staley. "Hungary Develops a New Program of Physical Education." *Journal of Health and Physical Education,* 1:2 (February, 1931), 7–11.
10. Seward C. Staley. "Physical Education in Fascist Italy." *Journal of Health and Physical Education,* 1:4 (April, 1930), 3. Seward C. Staley. "Sports in Europe." *Journal of Health and Physical Education,* 2:8 (October, 1931), 3–8.
11. Arthur Weston. "Physical Education in Italy." *Proceedings,* The College Physical Education Association, 1957, 173–183. Arthur Weston.

"Physical Education in Italy." *Journal of Health–Physical Education–Recreation,* 29:3 (March, 1958), 68.

12. C. Graamans. "Physical Education in the Netherlands." *The Physical Education,* 13:1 (March, 1956), 28–31; Bonnie McPherson. "Teaching Physical Education in the Netherlands." *Journal of Health, Physical Education and Recreation,* 25:3 (March, 1954), 52.

Chapter 12

PHYSICAL EDUCATION IN CONTINENTAL EUROPE IN THE TWENTIETH CENTURY (II)

POLAND

In 1919 the Commission of National Education in Poland recommended that physical education be required in the public schools and this recommendation was followed by favorable legislation. Elementary schools required physical education for a ten-minute period daily, consisting of gymnastics and games. Secondary schools required two hours' weekly instruction in gymnastics and two afternoons a week for games and sports. Both elementary and secondary schools encouraged the formation of sports clubs and scouting.

In 1927 the government established the Board of Physical Education and Military Preparation within the Ministry of Education, to finance school camping, activities preparatory to military duty, and sports. The Board utilized the Union of Polish Scouts to promote sports clubs and outdoor activities and formed brigades within the schools to provide military training for boys and girls. About three years later the government appointed a Scientific Council on Physical Education to act in an advisory capacity to the Board. This Council was composed of outstanding leaders in physical education, government representatives, and members of the Federal Sports Union. It included a Medical Committee, Committee on Standards, and Women's Committee.

The Board approved plans for the construction of facilities in schools and communities and granted state funds for their cost. The Board organized training centers for sports leaders in metropolitan areas and graduates were obligated to establish similar centers in rural areas. Under the supervision of the Medical Committee these centers provided physical examinations and medical consultation for sports participants. With the assistance of the Women's Committee the Board supervised sports competition for women and organized national achievement tests for young and old of both sexes.[1]

SPORTS DEVELOPMENT IN POLAND

Prior to World War II sports received a real boost through the work of the YMCA. In 1930 Walter Sikorski, a Springfield College graduate, introduced volleyball, basketball, and swimming into the program of the Association at Cracow. Volleyball has since become one of the most popular activities in schools and youth organizations. The popularity of basketball also continues to grow even under the Communists. Polish enthusiasm for sports has been reflected in the formation of the Federated Academies of Sports. In addition to clubs in educational institutions, Poland has many industrial sports clubs. The growth of public interest in swimming has been phenomenal. Even before the invasion of Hitler Poland had excellent swimming pools at Poznań, Billsko, Katowice, Zakopane, Lwów, Andrychow, Visla, and Grudziadz.[2]

TEACHER PREPARATION

In 1895 under the leadership of H. Jordans a two-year course for gymnastic teachers was organized at the University of Cracow, and in 1906 through the initiative of Helen Kuczalska a similar course was established at the University of Warsaw. From 1909 to 1919 Eugene Piasecki gave lectures on the theory of physical education at the Medical College of the University of Lwów.

Some months after the restoration of Poland in 1919 Piasecki was appointed director of the Institute of Physical Education at the University of Poznań, where he organized a three-year curriculum. The Institute was first established as a part of the College of Arts and Sciences and later affiliated with the Medical College at the university. A similar institute was founded at the University of Cracow in 1927. Diplomas from these institutes permitted the holder to teach physical education in secondary schools and higher institutions. Research laboratories were conducted at both institutes in association with the medical staffs at the universities of Cracow, Lwöw, Poznań, and Warsaw.

In 1921 the Polish government established the Central Military School of Physical Education in Poznań to train gymnastic leaders. At about the same time the government also organized temporary one-year courses to prepare civilian gymnastic leaders and in 1925 established a State Institute of Physical Education at Warsaw which provided a two-year course. In 1929 the Central Military School of Physical Education and the State Institute of Physical Education were combined as the Central Institute of Physical Education and transferred to Bielany near Warsaw. Teacher preparation at this school included courses in the theory and practice of physical education, sports, scouting, and camping.[3]

As a result of World War II Poland lost the universities of Lwów and Wilno with her eastern territories. In 1945 four new universities were established at Wroclaw, Toruń, Lódź, and Lublin. At present the Academy of Physical Education at Warsaw is one of the leading professional schools in Poland. Equally important are the schools at Poznań, Cracow, and Wroclaw. All these institutions provide a four-year curriculum leading to a master's degree in physical education. In 1960 the Academy of Physical Education was granted the right to confer the doctor of science degree in physical education. The other three institutions will have the same privilege as soon as their complements of scientific personnel meet the required standards. Students follow a general curriculum for the first two years and specialize the last two years. To be certified, sports leaders must attend the professional schools two years, or they may enroll in the many sports clinics sponsored by the sports federations.[4]

PORTUGAL

In 1908 the newly established *lycée* of Lisbon included a gymnasium in its physical plant, and in the same year boarding schools dependent upon public assistance and military schools under the jurisdiction of the Minister of War included instruction in educative gymnastics. The first teachers of physical education in Portugal were graduates of the Amoros school of gymnastics in France. By the turn of the century, however, the Swedish system had become fairly well entrenched, and the first gymnastics instruction manual was published by the government in 1900. Among those who promoted the Swedish system the Portuguese recognize particularly Lois Monteiro, Antonio Martins, and Pedro José Ferreira.

STATE ORGANIZATIONS

In Portugal health, physical education, and sports come under the Director General of Physical Education, Sports, and School Health in the National Office of Education. The Director General is assisted by an advisory board drawn from the national youth organizations, Olympic Committee, National Institute of Physical Education, administrative staff of the National Stadium, sports federations, sports medicine, and others.

The physical education and sports activities of children of school age are regulated and conducted by the National Foundation for Joy in Work. Two commissioners, one for boys and one for girls, supervise the general program of the fourteen major areas into which Portugal and its overseas provinces are divided. Each subdivision possesses many regional centers, staffed by instructors who teach gymnastics, games, and the fundamentals of sports, and conduct sports clinics, excursions, outings, and moral and cultural conferences, as well as furnish health instruction.

In the *lycées* and private schools instruction is generally required two periods per week, and Saturday is devoted to games and sports. Although instruction in physical education was introduced in the higher institutions of Portugal at an early date, the present tendency is to place emphasis on sports participation and competition. Higher technical schools, however, require students to take regular instruction in physical education the first two years. As a rule higher institutions have excellent facilities in the way of large gymnasiums, swimming pools, numerous playing fields, and the usual cinder track.[4]

Portugal, like other European countries, experienced a steady growth of interest in sports in the postwar period. Individual sports have their own associations and federations, and hold regular local, regional, and national competitions. Portuguese law requires that sports clubs employ qualified physical educators. Each club must also retain a sports physician who prescribes the kind and amount of exercise patrons may take and conducts a periodical check of their fitness. The clubs promote competition in track and field athletics, boxing, wrestling, basketball, field hockey, volleyball, soccer football, handball, tennis, mountain climbing, swimming and diving, and nautical sports. In addition, centers of sports medicine in Lisbon, Porto, Graga, Coimbra, and Faro are equipped to conduct extensive research in the medical and physiological aspects of exercise and sports competition.

Teacher Preparation

The first normal course for physical education teachers was established in 1921. Similar courses were instituted for the training of military and naval instructors in 1925 and 1933, respectively. In 1930 Portugal created the College of Physical Education, which was discontinued in 1940 when the government founded the National Institute of Physical Education next to the National Stadium in Lisbon. The same legislation provided for the establishment of additional institutes at Coimbra and Porto. The current national preparatory school at Lisbon offers programs leading to instructorships and professorships in physical education. The latter require a bachelor's degree for admission, the former a certificate from a *lycée*.[4]

SCANDINAVIA

The Scandinavian countries have developed systems of gymnastics which satisfy the environmental and cultural needs of a homogeneous people. Gymnastic leaders, in general, share the same philosophy, principles, and methods, but each country has contributed professional leadership, particularly in gymnastics, and such names as Nachtegal, Lindhard, Knudsen, and Bukh of Denmark, Pikhala, Collan, Heikel, Björksten, and Karvonen of Finland, and Ling and his Swedish successors are known internationally to workers in physical education.

Physical education is compulsory in the public schools of Scandinavia. The period varies from two to three hours a week in both elementary and secondary schools. Gymnastics is the core of the program, supplemented by an extensive after-school program of games, sports, and recreation.

The average gymnasium measures 56 by 28 by 25 feet and has been designed to accommodate gymnastics rather than sports. In rural sections barns, old warehouses, and residential buildings are employed. World War II halted construction of any kind, and in the postwar period only a few modern gymnasiums have been built. As a rule, in Scandinavian countries school gymnasiums are available to the general public during free hours as community centers or continuation schools for adults.

Both urban and rural schools promote achievement tests, which except for the addition of apparatus work resemble the old Athletic Badge Tests of the National Recreation Association. A few schools conduct interschool competition in soccer, basketball, handball, and track and field athletics, but these highly organized sports are left largely to sports clubs, which manage their own competitions.

Rural schools, which are separated by considerable distances, rely upon intramural athletic competition. Children are encouraged to participate in outdoor games and sports during the long winter months. Among the favorites are skating, tobogganing, and skiing.

Promotion of Sports

Each country has a central body which promotes and controls sports under the Ministry of Education. This official body also provides financial assistance to amateur sports associations.

In Denmark these are organized under the Danish Sport Federation (*Dansk Idraets-Forbund*); they number thirty with a membership of 500,000. The Danish Rifle, Gymnastic, and Sports Association and the Danish Gymnastic Association have a smaller membership since they draw their members mostly from the rural sections.

In Finland the State Athletic Board promotes and regulates

amateur sports through the Physical Education Association of Public Schools and the Athletic Association of High Schools. In addition, the State Athletic Board controls all amateur sports outside the school. The largest of these outside sports organizations is the Finnish Gymnastic and Athletic Union with sixteen associations representing that many different sports. Twenty-seven other associations include the Laborers' Athletic League, Finnish Ball Association, Sport Medicine Association, and Yatching Association. Their total membership comprises one-sixth of the population of Finland. Another division of the Ministry of Education is the Outing Board, which is responsible for the promotion of outdoor education and travel.[5]

In Norway amateur sports are controlled by the Norwegian Sports Confederation (*Norges Indrettsforbund*), which represents twenty-eight sports associations with a total membership of 250,000. For convenience of administration the country is divided into districts called *Indrettskrets.* The area about the city of Oslo, for example, is an *Indrettskret,* and has a population of 215,000. This district supports 114 sports clubs representing every one of the twenty-eight sports under the Confederation's jurisdiction. Its most popular sports are skiing, soccer, and handball. The Confederation requires each district to maintain a medical council and a health committee to provide medical service, consultation, and health supervision. The district personnel cooperate in nationwide studies on the incidence of sports injuries, geriatrics as related to sports participation, and other vital statistics, studies, and surveys.[6]

At the time that Germany was actively promoting games and sports in the early 1900s Sweden was already engaged in an extensive sports program. The Swedish games and sports movement, however, did not crystallize until about 1910, and five years later the Swedish Commission for the Promotion of Games and Sports was established to improve the vigor of Swedish schoolchildren. The Commission adopted the Athletic Badge Test as an incentive for physical improvement among schoolchildren and sponsored the Swedish Schoolboys Athletic Week held annually at Stockholm. In 1919 the Commission reorganized the achievement tests to include gymnastics, skiing or cross-country running, and swimming events. At the same time it took steps to establish uniform sports rules and to provide state aid for the construction of sports facilities in schools and communities.

Financial cooperation between the government and municipalities has done much to make this country sports-minded. The Swedish Sports Federation (*Svenska Idrottsförbundet*), which controls amateur sports in and out of schools, receives a percentage of the state income derived from the national soccer football pool. In addition, the separate municipalities allocate tax funds for the construction of facilities for sports and recreation and the purchase of sports equipment. On a per capita basis Sweden has more sports facilities than any other nation in the world. In 1954 the country reported 800 well-constructed cinder tracks, all municipally owned, 64 indoor tennis courts, 500 outdoor swimming pools, 160 ski jumps, 110 slalom runs, and 400 grounds for winter hockey. The tremendous interest in sports is also reflected in the hundreds of sports clinics conducted annually under the auspices of the Swedish Sports Federation.[7]

The Federation controls thirty-four sports associations with a membership just short of a million. The soccer-football association, which represents the most popular amateur sport in Sweden, is composed of 2866 clubs, while skiing, in second position, has 2832 clubs. This country with a population approximating that of New York City has 20,000 sports clubs and 2000 gymnastic societies with more than 40 percent of the population represented.

In spite of the large membership in sports clubs, gymnastics are still held in high regard by the Swedes. The founder of the Swedish system, Pehr Henrik Ling, is revered, and the 100th anniversary of his death was memorialized by the Swedish Gymnastic Association in 1939 by what is called the Lingiad. This is celebrated by a festival every decade at Stockholm, attended by representatives from many parts of the world.

Teacher Preparation

Denmark possesses one of the world's oldest professional schools, the Military Gymnastic Institute established by the government at Copenhagen in 1804. This institution offers a two-year course for instructors of physical training in the Danish Army. Prior to 1900 the government established a one-year course for gymnastic teachers in elementary schools. This course was planned and organized by K. A. Knudsen, an advocate of the Swedish system, who was transferred to the newly organized State Gymnastic Institute in 1923.[8]

In 1909 the University of Copenhagen appointed Dr. J. Lindhard as special lecturer in the theory of physical education, and shortly thereafter he was made full professor. Later the theoretical courses were taught by the university staff, while the practical work was taken over by the State Gymnastic Institute. This cooperative enterprise made it possible for candidates who held the diploma to teach in secondary schools. Through financial assistance from the Rockefeller Foundation, a research laboratory was constructed opposite the State Gymnastic Institute. Here Lindhard, Krogh, Hansen, and their associates conducted their classical studies in the physiology of exercise.

The Gymnastic Institute of Finland was founded in 1908 as an affiliate of the University of Helsinki. Three professors conducted a three-year course. Graduates were eligible to teach in secondary and normal schools. The institute became well known for its system of women's gymnastics, developed along Swedish lines by Elli Björksten.

After Ling became the first director of the Royal Central Institute of Gymnastics in 1813, Norway sent its military officers and noncommissioned officers there to be trained. From time to time Norway felt the need of a teacher-training institution, but it was not until 1870 that the Central School of Gymnastics was founded at Oslo. In 1915 the school's name was changed to the State College of Physical Education. Today the State College prepares teaching personnel for both civilian and military agencies and provides short courses for the training of sports leaders.

To meet social and educational changes in Sweden the state appointed a Committee on Reorganization to study the professional program of the Royal Central Institute of Gymnastics at Stockholm. The committee recommended that the educational gymnastic department be reorganized as the Central Institute of Gymnastics with university rank. The medical gymnastic department was to become the School of Medical Gymnastics and to be operated under the supervision of the universities of Uppsala and Lund. The Caroline Medical Institute of Gymnastics covered two years and led to a diploma. The program included the theory and practice of gymnastics, fencing, games, and sports. After 133 years in a rehabilitated cannon factory, the Central Institute of Gymnastics was moved to modern quarters in 1944 adjoining the Olympic Stadium at Stockholm.

SPAIN

Gymnastics dominated the physical education program of Spanish elementary and secondary schools until after World War I, when thc country was caught up in the wave of sports enthusiasm. In 1926 an interministerial commission was appointed to study the reorganization of physical education, but was abandoned upon the formation of the Second Republic. During the civil war in 1938 the Minister of Education created the National Council of Sports, and shortly after the Franco government assumed power, many physical education and sports organizations were established in response to youth movement and labor union interest. In 1956 the old National Council of Sports was absorbed into the new National Delegation of Physical Education and Sports (DNEFD in Spanish).[4]

Organization of Physical Education and Sports

The organization responsible for the conduct of physical education and sports in Spain includes the Spanish Olympic Committee, Secretariat of National Movement, the Minister of National Education, the Minister of Interior, the Minister of Labor, and the corps of firemen and policemen in municipalities. The Secretariat of National Movement is responsible for integrating the activities of the various national organizations. Organizations that can be called upon to provide personnel to teach physical education and furnish sports leaders include the National Delegation of Physical Education and Sports, which represents forty-three federations with a membership of a half-million; the Women's Section of the National Council of Physical Education; the Spanish Union of Universities of the National Direction of Physcial Education; the Spanish Youth Organization of the National Association of Physical Education; and Direction of the Labor Union for Education and Recreation of the National Association of Physical Education and Sports.

According to legislation enacted in 1940, instruction in physical education and sports is the exclusive responsibility of the organizations enumerated above, which provide personnel on call and as approved by the Secretariat of Movement. The Minister of Education makes the assignments according to qualifications and experience. Physical education was made obligatory by the same legislation in elementary, secondary, and technical schools and the first three years in higher institutions.

DEVELOPMENT OF SPORTS

The sports federation in Spain is represented by 42 associations with a membership of 255,000. Soccer football is by far the most popular sport and is represented by 2668 sports clubs; basketball, 695; track and field athletics, 208; swimming, 142; and boxing, 27. Soccer football draws 3500 professional and 42,500 amateur participants, while gymnastics is represented by some 31 clubs with a membership of 215 men and women gymnasts. Spain has constructed many attractive sports facilities, such as the Sport City of Burgos, the Sport Palace at Madrid, and the Sport City of Real Madrid completed in 1962. Professional preparation was established at the Central School of Gymnastics in Madrid in 1883 and the Central School of Physical Education in Toledo in 1919. Currently, students in these schools take their foundation courses in biological science under the faculty of medicine of the universities of Madrid and Toledo. Theoretical and practical work at the two schools is conducted by the faculty of the gymnasium, who employ the facilities available on the university campus. Successful completion of the course and the state examination entitles the graduate to the title of Professor of Physical Education. The National Federation of Sports Medicine has also organized courses within the medical programs of these institutions for students who wish to qualify as physicians to sports clubs and associations.

TEACHER PREPARATION

In 1898 at the time of the reorganization of the normal schools it was decided that the elementary school teacher should have some knowledge of the practice of gymnastics to assist him in the classroom. In 1901 a course in gymnastic instruction suitable for the lower schools was introduced into the preparatory programs of normal schools.

SWITZERLAND

At the turn of the century the Swedish system had gained a considerable following in Switzerland, and by 1914 the school programs in the various Swiss cantons offered a combination of the German and Swedish systems or favored one system over the other. As a general rule physical education was required three periods a week, with one of these periods devoted to free play and sports. Separate gymnasiums were maintained for boys and girls in the public schools. These gymnasiums were well equipped with apparatus of the system in vogue; one of the distinguishing features of this era was the use of the cork carpet as a safety measure. Each school had modern shower baths, and swimming instruction was provided in municipal pools. Schools in metropolitan areas provided for six or seven half-day hiking excursions (*Schulewanderung*) to nearby points of interest which had academic as well as recreational value.

Participation in sports within the secondary school is the responsibility of the physical education teacher, who conducts practice periods two to three afternoons a week in the sports clubs. In addition to attending these clubs within the school the Swiss schoolboy belongs to gymnastic and sports clubs in the community. Students in higher institutions belong to Turner Societies and their own sports clubs. In the upper grades of elementary school boys belong to riflery and archery clubs.

Since World War II the Swiss government has supported a program to improve the physical fitness of the youth and adult, and the national slogan is "Strong Youths, a Free People." The youth movement touches everyone between the ages if 15 and 20. Every year some 100,000 youths are instructed by means of special courses in track and field athletics, riflery, games and such recreational activities as skiing, swimming, mountain climbing, hiking, bicycling and other outdoor activities. The leadership for this vast movement is trained through six-day courses at the State Institute of Gymnastic and Sports located at Macolin. An annual government appropriation of 1,500,000 Swiss francs finances the special courses in leadership and the special classes and examinations of youths in gymnastics and sports.

For the adults there are 70 athletic associations with a total membership of approximately 1,500,000. Fifty-two of these are affiliated with the National Association of Physical Education. The government allows these associations considerable freedom in the management of their affairs yet subsidizes them with an annual grant of 100,000 Swiss francs. The associations conduct clinics and exhibitions and train leaders.

TEACHER PREPARATION

In the early 1900s the Swiss government made no attempt to control physical education in the schools. As a result, teacher qualifications varied widely, school programs lacked uniformity, and professional promotion became a struggle for position. In the postwar era the government organized the Gymnastic Teachers Association to establish some semblance of uniformity in program planning and objective.

In spite of the intelligent and aggressive leadership of this organization and the full cooperation of state authorities, physical education teachers in the schools of the cantons continued to pursue their own particular interests. Since they received their training in other countries, it was obvious that the most important step toward the improvement of the situation was the establishment of teacher-training courses in Switzerland. In 1922 a one-year teacher-training course was organized at the University of Basel and shortly thereafter at the universities of Arosa, Bern, and Zurich. In 1927 the International YMCA Committee helped considerably by organizing the YMCA College at Geneva as a training center for physical education leaders of European origin.

In 1944 the Swiss government established the State Institute of Gymnastic and Sport under the administration of the Federal Military Department at Macolin. This institution organizes and conducts the leadership courses so vital to the success of youth movement and offers professional courses to candidates for the diploma of Master of Gymnastics and Sport. Candidates in the state professional program also attend this institution for special courses.

The facilities of the State Institute of Gymnastic and Sport are available to gymnastic and sports organizations who wish to conduct their own courses and clinics. A research division has been established which conducts experimental studies in exercise and sports, supervises and collects data on the construction of physical plants for gymnastics and sports, and produces documentary and instructional films which are made available to educational institutions and sports clubs. In recent years the State Institute has sponsored courses and symposiums which attract professional leaders from many countries.

Swiss normal schools now offer preparatory courses in gymnastics for elementary teachers and those who wish may take additional course work to qualify themselves for the Diploma of Gymnastics as special teachers on the elementary level.

Teachers in Swiss secondary schools must now receive special preparation at the universities of Basel, Lausanne, and Geneva and the State Polytechnic Institute of Zurich. Admission is based upon former teaching experience, or the *brevet d'instituteur* secured from the normal school. Successful completion of this four-institution program earns the candidate the diploma of Master of Gymnastics and Sport.[4]

UNION OF SOVIET SOCIALISTS REPUBLICS

Shortly after the close of World War I the Soviet Union established the National Soviet on Physical Education as an exploratory and promotional agency. This body was instrumental in the establishment of courses in the theory and practice of physical education for medical students and short courses for physical education leaders who conducted programs for workers in industrial plants. It was also influential in calling together representatives of the Soviet republics in the first Congress on Physical Education held in 1924 at Moscow.

The 285 delegates to the Congress formulated a plan for united action in the development of physical education in the U.S.S.R.

One of their first tasks was to establish standards in physical education according to age, sex, and occupation. They also drew up plans for an Institute of Physical Education at Moscow to train physical education leaders. The Congress recommended that hygiene instruction be provided the general public, physical education be required in all medical schools, higher institutions (two years), and industrial plants, and that a three-month course in child hygiene be required of physicians. At a similar meeting in Warsaw in 1929 the Congress recommended that a definite sum of money be provided all organizations which promoted physical education, including Turner Societies, sports clubs, and winter sports organizations. The Congress further recommended that special grants be given for the establishment of youth camps throughout the Soviet Union.[9]

Following this Congress the U.S.S.R. created a Supreme Council of Physical Culture, which consisted of sixty-five representatives from the Soviet republics and various branches of the government. The Council's first official act was to make physical education compulsory for all children, youths, peasants, and workers. To implement this vast program the Supreme Council requested the Supreme Economic Council to provide all the apparatus and other equipment needed. Already established Institutes of Physical Education were alerted and plans for similar training schools in Soviet republics were formulated. The aim of the program was to develop among the Russian people a high level of physical fitness, a variety of motor skills which had utilitarian and military value, and a deep conviction in the mind of every man, woman, and child that in the maintenance of their health and physical fitness they were contributing to the future success of the Soviet Union.

PHYSICAL EDUCATION IN THE SCHOOLS

Depending on the individual Soviet republic, physical education is required two to three hours per week in public and higher schools. As a general rule, elementary and secondary schools open the school day with ten to fifteen minutes of gymnastic exercises which show the influence of the Danish, German, and Swedish systems. Games, sports, and rhythmics are scheduled for the recess periods. Boys and girls of the upper grades are encouraged to seek membership in the sports clubs, which, as in most European countries, are active in the afternoons and on weekends. These clubs compete in gymnastics, basketball, track and field athletics, soccer, volleyball, skiing, boxing, wrestling, and table tennis. Nicholai Ozolin, Director of the Central Scientific Research Institute of Physical Education at Moscow, stated that in 1956 more than eleven million pupils competed in eleven All-Union Spartakiades.

Compulsory physical examinations are required of all pupils at the beginning of the school year, and those participating in sports clubs must have a physical examination at the opening of each sport in season. The majority of the schools in the Soviet republics employ a physician, most of whom are women, and a school nurse. The physician provides physical examinations, medical supervision of sports clubs, health instruction and first aid, and exercise prescriptions for children who are physically below par. They also supervise the physical education program in summer camps (Young Pioneer Camps), which are attended by all children who have reached the age of 15.[10]

SPORTS DEVELOPMENT IN SOVIET RUSSIA

After World War I the Soviet Union became one of the most sports-minded nations in history. In order to implement a "sports for all" program the government since 1921 has appropriated as much as $100 million annually for the construction of facilities and purchase of equipment. The Russians drew from both English and American sources. They were particularly interested in the all-round sports programs of Springfield College in America and the YMCA College, Geneva, and made a thorough study of the philosophy and programs of both institutions.

The Russian exploratory period ended with the adoption of the ideology of pure amateur sports participation and competition. Adulation for athletic victors was suppressed since the Russians viewed this practice of bourgeois countries as encouraging personal aggrandizement. Amateur awards and professional monetary rewards were to be eliminated. Under this premise Soviet athletes were forbidden to participate in the Olympic Games. Through persistent propaganda the Supreme Council of Physical Culture broadcast this concept of pure amateurism and achieved it through the strict control and regulation of all sports conducted by school sports clubs, trade unions, army units, villages, and other social units.

Soccer, basketball, and volleyball were popular in this era of sports for all. Other activities included track and field athletics (light and heavy), gymnastics, apparatus work, water sports, sharpshooting, and various winter sports. Rough and hazardous sports were eliminated or controlled in such a manner that the danger of physical injury was minimized. In this category boxing and wrestling were the least popular activities. Women participated in sports with the same enthusiasm as men, although they did not pursue the same program.[11]

In 1934 the Moscow *Daily News,* a paper for English-speaking readers, reported a parade in Moscow's Red Square in which 125,000 physical education and sports enthusiasts passed in review. The Soviet Union stated at this time that 61 million athletes were registered with the Supreme Council on Physical Culture. The U.S.S.R. Handbook for 1936 indicated that general participation in sports was 2,100,000, with skiing, soccer, swimming and volleyball, one million each; *Gorlutke,** 600,000; and ice hockey, tennis, basketball, boxing, and wrestling represented by a total of 650,000.

The Intourist Guide of 1937 listed twelve stadiums in Moscow alone, one of which had seating accommodations for 120,000 spectators. It is in stadiums like those in Moscow and other Soviet republics that the Spartakiades for school youths who are members of sports clubs are held, as well as Spartakiades to which the athletes of the various republics and satellite countries are invited. A unique stadium is that located at Tiflis, in the Soviet Republic of Georgia, which, although it seats only 17,000 spectators, has some unusual architectural features. In the back of each tier of seats are shelters to which spectators can escape during inclement weather. Inside the superstructure which supports the seats, areas have been provided for the quarters of the Institute of Physical Education,

* *Gorlutke,* or *Gorokea,* is a native Russian game in which pegs 6 inches in length are arranged in a flat design on a hard dirt or cement base about the size of a card table top. The players take a position about 30 feet away and throw at the pegs a club about the size of a softball bat. The club is thrown horizontally in an effort to strike the base in a flat manner and thus derange the pegs.

restaurants, light and heavy gymnastics facilities, a motion picture and photography plant, first aid and medical sections, and a swimming pool.

THE POSTWAR ERA

An inventory of sports facilities available to the peoples in the Soviet republics in 1945 showed that there were 650 stadiums, 3500 gymnasiums, and 10,000 playing fields. A new approach, however, was in evidence in sports promotion. In his political and economic cold war with the Western democracies, Premier Stalin saw propaganda value in sport excellence and mobilized all the Soviet Union's untried potential in this new area to demonstrate Communist superiority.

In 1946 Soviet teams played those from Albania, Bulgaria, England, Finland, France, Norway, and Yugoslavia. The Russian teams showed considerable superiority in soccer, but the French and Norwegian teams were more successful in track and field athletics and skating events. It was in these contests that Russian athletes gave the first hint of their cultural immaturity in international sports competition by their unsportsmanlike conduct. These incidents, which were to be projected later to the Olympic Games, were also an indication of the pressure being exerted on them to glorify the U.S.S.R. in the eyes of the bourgeois countries. Athletes were usually confined to their quarters and moved as a body from place to place lest they be contaminated by the athletes of the Western democracies. This Soviet attitude toward the intermingling of Russian and non-Communist athletes was later altered, but the pressure to win remained the same.

RUSSIA'S PARTICIPATION IN THE OLYMPIC GAMES

In 1948 Russia sent observers to the London Olympic Games but did not send individual representatives or a team to compete. In the Helsinki Olympic Games of 1952 the Soviet Union sent a full team and according to unofficial team scores was defeated by the United States Olympic team by 614 to 503½ points. The Russian athletes swept the field in gymnastics. Women athletes of the Soviet Union came in first in the broad jump, 8-pound shot, and discus throw. The men athletes won first place in three classifications of weight-lifting, rifle shooting, single sculling, and 8-man rowing. At the Melbourne Olympic Games in 1956 the Western democracies held their position in the track and field events, but the Russians gained in the special events. The Soviet athletes, for instance, won 23 of a possible 96 medals in gymnastics, and it was the boast of the Russians that there were 77,000 gymnasts in the Soviet republics who were just as well qualified to make the Olympic team.

In the 1960 Winter Olympic Games at Squaw Valley, California, the victories as signified by gold, silver, and bronze medals were Soviet Union, 7–5–59; Germany, 4–3–1; United States, 3–4–3; Norway, 3–3–0; Sweden, 3–2–2; Finalnd, 2–3–3; and Canada, 2–1–1. In the Rome Olympic Games the Western democracies won the greater percentage of track and field and swimming events. The Japanese won the team competition in gymnastics as well as many of the individual events. The Russian women athletes made a practically clean sweep of the team and individual events in gymnastics. In terms of individual performance as measured by gold, silver, and bronze medals the U.S.S.R. won 43–29–31; U.S.A., 34–21–16; Germany, 12–19–11; Italy, 13–10–13; Australia, 8–8–6; Hungary, 6–8–7; Poland, 4–6–11; Great Britain, 2–6–12; and Japan, 4–7–7. The Soviet Union had on the basis of unofficial point scoring defeated the United States in the Winter Olympic Games and the Rome Olympic Games in 1960.

EUROPEAN SPECULATION ON THE OLYMPIC GAMES

In Europe the general feeling exists that the Soviet Union will take over the traditional superiority of the United States in the Olympic Games. Those who express this opinion suggest that the Russian state system of scientific coaching will eventually produce athletes vastly superior to anything the Western democracies can offer. In the Soviet Union the old method of selecting gifted students for the ballet schools at Leningrad and Moscow has been applied by the government to the production of athletes. In 1955 the Soviet Union established 820 special sports schools for athletically talented boys and girls 10–16 years of age, with an enrollment of 190,000 children. Five years later the number of the schools reached 1000, with 2,500,000 children enrolled and a staff of 7000 coaches.

Other Europeans feel that while Russia may be making progress at the present time, a gradual improvement in athletic performance everywhere may eventually reduce the Olympic track and field victories not only of the Soviet Union but also of the United States. The improvement in the standard of living among minority nations should favor the production of higher-caliber Olympic athletes.[12] The Rome Olympic Games in 1960 showed a greater spread of points among such countries as India, Iran, Italy, Morocco, the Netherlands, Pakistan, Switzerland, and Turkey. Latin-American and Russian satellite countries will also field Olympic athletes in the future who will share in the points for track and field events. This shift to a more balanced competition is already in evidence in the Winter Olympic Games, and it is interesting to contemplate what may happen to total point scores should Chile and Japan seriously enter the field of winter Olympic sports.

NOTES

1. Stanislaw Rouppert. "Some Physical Education Problems in Poland." *Journal of Health and Physical Education,* 3:9 (November, 1932), 49–51.
2. Howard Stepp. "Physical Education in Poland." *Journal of Health and Physical Education,* 10:8 (October, 1939), 448–451.
3. Eugene Piasecki. "Physical Education in European Universities." *Journal of Health and Physical Education,* 1:5 (May, 1930), 3–5.
4. Pierre Seurin. *L'Éducation Physique dans le Monde.* Bordeaux: Editions Bière, 1961, pp. 131–132; 315–316; 320–321; 323–324; 376–377.
5. Lewis Pikhala. "Physical Education in Finland." *Journal of Health and Physical Education,* 3:9 (November, 1932), 47–48; John W. Masley. "H.P.E.R. in Finland." *Journal of Health, Physical Education and Recreation,* 22:6 (June, 1951), 14–15.
6. L. K. Anderson. *Health Work in a District Organization of the Norwegian Sport Federation.* International Conference of Sport and Health, Oslo, Norway, 1952, pp. 195–198.

7. R. R. Ylanan. "Sweden the Land of Sports." *Physical Recreation,* 6 (January–March, 1954), 13–17.
8. Howard G. Knuttgen. "Physical Education in Denmark." *The Physical Educator,* 18:2 (May, 1961), 70–74.
9. Sam Harby. "The Physical Education Movement in Soviet Russia." *Journal of Health and Physical Education,* 1:6 (June, 1930), 7–11.
10. Arthur A. Esslinger. "Health, Physical Education and Recreation Programs, in the U.S.S.R." *Journal of Health–Physical Education–Recreation,* 29:6 (September, 1958), 33–35; 68. John B. McLendon, Jr. "The Soviet Union's Program of Physical Culture and Sports." *Journal of Health–Physical Education–Recreation,* 33:4 (April, 1962), 28.
11. Percy M. Dawson. "Sports in the U.S.S.R." *Journal of Health and Physical Education,* 8:10 (December, 1937), 585–587.
12. Ernst Jokl *et al. Sports in the Cultural Pattern of the World.* (A study of the 1952 Olympic Games at Helsinki) Institute of Occupational Health, Helsinki, Finland, 1956.

Chapter 13

PHYSICAL EDUCATION IN THE BRITISH COMMONWEALTH IN THE TWENTIETH CENTURY

THE BRITISH COMMONWEALTH

In the Statute of Westminster in 1931 these political subdivisions of the British Commonwealth were enumerated: the United Kingdom of Great Britain and Northern Ireland, the Dominion of Canada, the Commonwealth of Australia, the Dominion of New Zealand, the Union of South Africa, the Irish Free State, and Newfoundland. This enumeration, of course, is far from up to date and will probably suffer changes in the future. Since World War II this list must now include the Indian Union and Pakistan (1947), the Union of Burma (1948), and Ceylon (1948). In 1949 Newfoundland requested and was granted the right to become the tenth province of the Dominion of Canada. In the same year the Irish Free State, which organized a constitution and adopted the name of Erin in 1937, seceded from the Commonwealth.

Under the British Empire it was the practice of the government to establish law and order in its dependencies and to adopt a policy of *laissez faire* toward economic and social development. The promotion of education, therefore, became a function of the Christian missionaries, philanthropic groups, or public-spirited individuals. The changing social philosophy of the more enlightened and prosperous peoples of the world toward the less-developed nations has outmoded this policy.

In interpretating its educational responsibilities to its dependencies the British Commonwealth was vitally influenced by the reports of two commissions sent to West Africa (1920–1921) and East and Central Africa (1924). As a consequence of these reports the government undertook to expand its educational services and facilities in the primary and secondary levels in the dependencies. In 1946 the Inter-University Council for Higher Education in the Colonies was established as an organ of the United Kingdom and colonial universities. By 1953 substantial sums had been granted the development of colonial university education under the Colonial Development and Welfare Acts. In recent years funds granted by the United Kingdom and supplemented locally have been allocated to establishing technical colleges in the Gold Coast, Nigeria, Kenya, and Fiji.

THE UNITED KINGDOM

The Boer War which engaged Great Britain in conflict with the Transvaal and Orange Free State at the turn of the century vitally affected future military training in the British Army and physical education in the United Kingdom. The early humiliating reverses of the British forces in South Africa and the large number of medical rejections raised a question in the minds of many as to whether the physical vigor of the Englishman had not degenerated. The Scottish Royal Commission on Physical Training (1903) and the English Interdepartmental Committee on Physical Deterioration (1904) presented reports which helped shape future trends of physical education in the United Kingdom.[1]

The 1904 school syllabus adopted by the Board of Education devoted the lion's share of the elementary school physical education program to the Swedish system. This was understandable in view of the system's influential backers and the ready supply of women teachers being turned out by Swedish institutes in the United Kingdom. But in spite of its many positive values, a program devoted exclusively to gymnastics was not really congenial to the English. In its ensuing annual reports the Board of Education admitted that its members felt the Swedish system was dull and monotonous and that the absence of games and rhythmical activities was a serious deficiency. The Board's subsequent syllabuses, however, indicate little effort to improve the situation.

The Fisher Education Act of 1918 recommended that elementary and secondary schools require physical education and that schools provide additional facilities for holiday and school camping. Militarists reasoned that state-subsidized school camps would allow for the introduction of military drill into their programs. They also reasoned that since the war had created a serious shortage of trained personnel these camps might be supplied with military personnel from the Army Physical Training Staff. Their enthusiasm was dampened when Sir George Newman of the medical department of the Board of Education suggested that the school camp program should emphasize therapeutic exercises, games, and rhythms rather than military drill. Since under the Fisher Act school camps were purely permissive, the school authorities followed the line of least resistance.

THE POSTWAR ERA

The war left the United Kingdom in an economic depression. The critical social problem of the moment was the plight of the unemployed young. Unable to find work they wandered the streets and engaged in questionable pursuits. Influential public figures called attention to the need for positive action in the rehabilitation of this lost generation of youth who were victims of social changes beyond their control. One solution was the extension of recreational opportunities. Speaking to this point with considerable conviction were Lord Dawson of Penn, a physician with a reputation for worthwhile civic projects, and Dr. L. P. Jacks,* a recreation leader known on both sides of the Atlantic.

In 1925 the National Playing Fields Association was organized and financed by public subscription. This voluntary agency purchased and constructed several hundred new playing fields in the first year of its existence. In 1927 the Carnegie United Kingdom Trust granted the Association more than a million dollars, with

* Dr. Jacks published the *Education of the Whole Man* (1932). He is particularly famous for his catchy phrases, such as "Man is a skill-hungry animal" and the term "physically illiterate."

which it acquired 6000 acres and converted them into 870 playing fields and playgrounds.

In 1934 the British Medical Association, becoming interested in the general problem of physical exercise and recreation, appointed a Physical Education Committee, which two years later made a survey report. The survey indicated that 84 percent of the girls in secondary schools had access to a gymnasium, 750 amateur athletes belonged to Rugby and soccer football associations which played each Saturday, 72 percent of the boys between the ages of 14 and 18 received no form of physical exercise, and 40 percent of the population between 14 and 40 received inadequate physical exercise and recreation. The report closed with the opinion that the schools had contributed little to the leisure-time activities of the nation's youth and that provisions for physical exercise and recreation left much to be desired.

In February, 1937, the British government issued a White Paper on Physical Training and Recreation, accompanied by plans for establishing a National Advisory Council on Physical Training and Recreation with more than thirty subcommittees. The following July the Physical Training and Recreation Act became law. The Act provided eight million dollars to be spent over a three-year period for the development of physical education and recreation in the United Kingdom. By 1939 a total of 789 grants had been made, amounting to approximately six million dollars. World War II brought a halt to the program.

The national promotion of physical education and recreation had a salutary effect upon the development of physical education in British higher institutions. The National Union of Students in their report, *Student Health* (1937), stated that only four universities offered regular physical education classes and that, with the exception of Oxford and Cambridge, only 25 percent of any student body had an opportunity to participate in games and sports. The report recommended the appointment in all universities of a director of thysical education responsible for the organization of a program beneficial to all students. In 1938 the National Fitness Council and the University Grants Committee appropriated a substantial sum for the construction of physical education facilities in universities. Before the onset of World War II directors of physical education had been appointed at the universities of Liverpool, Leeds, Manchester, and Birmingham, which was something new in the annals of British universities.[1]

WORLD WAR II AND THE POSTWAR PERIOD

The war engaged the attention and energy of all citizens of the United Kingdom and affirmed everyone's conviction of the value of physical exercise and recreation. All activity to prepare youth and adults for military service and defense industries was centered in the Central Council for Recreative Training. The Central Council conducted physical fitness classes for men, women, and children on a nationwide basis in public parks, playgrounds, and factory buildings. Physical education leaders in elementary schools emphasized remedial and corrective exercises. Older children participated in the harvest camps and probably had more camping experience than any generation before their time. The County Badge Test was introduced by the German refugee Kurt Hahn and made part of the physical fitness program.

Near the close of the war Parliament enacted the Education Act of 1944, which made mandatory the optimal provisions of the Fisher Education Act of 1918. Section 53 of the 1944 Act required local authorities to provide facilities for physical education and recreation in the school. The law also transferred to the Ministry of Education the function of the National Fitness Council established during World War II and the Grants Committee set up by the Physical Training and Recreation Act of 1937.

TEACHER PREPARATION

In 1905 women teachers of Swedish gymnastics were being trained in twenty-seven institutes in the United Kingdom, and the majority of these were channeled into the elementary schools. Male teachers got their training at private schools and institutes on the Continent and were certified for teaching through examinations given by such professional organizations as the British College of Physical Education (1891), Gymnastic Teachers Institute (1897), and National Society of Physical Education (1897). Instructors trained by the

Army Physical Training Staff were also available, but schools were reluctant to employ teachers with an army background. To meet the growing teacher demand, the Board of Education established a one-year course at University College, Reading, for women and a similar school at Sheffield Training College for men. Both of these courses were discontinued in 1923.

The Ling Association had maintained high professional standards in gymnastics institutes for both men and women through the years. After World War I Dr. Janet Campbell of the Board of Education started a move to convince the administrators of these institutes that the University of London should be made the center for the examination and the granting of certification for their graduates. The directors agreed, and in 1932 the university granted the first diploma.

The intense interest in the recreation movement in the 1930s prompted the Carnegie Trustees to grant a sum of $125,000 for the establishment of a teacher-training institution for men. In 1933 the Carnegie Training College was founded at Leeds with a one-year course, open only to men who had already secured a teacher's certificate or who had a university degree.

The Physical Training and Recreation Act of 1937 anticipated the establishment of a National College of Physical Training, but subsequent implementation of the law ignored this part of the act. In 1944 the McNair Committee on the Training of Teachers and Youth Leaders recommended that colleges for the training of physical education specialists be established throughout the United Kingdom, wherever possible in association with existing universities. The University of Birmingham was one of the first to offer a professional curriculum for both men and women majors leading to the baccalaureate degree, in 1946.

AUSTRALIA

The smallest continent on the globe, Australia covers a land area about the size of the United States. The Commonwealth includes the political subdivisions of Queensland, New South Wales, Victoria, Northern Territory, South Australia, and Western Australia. The English, Scots, Irish, and Welsh who emigrated to Australia gravitated to the more desirable coastal plains and valleys of the eastern part of the continent. The aboriginal tribes are located in the Northern Territory, South Australia, Western Australia, and the northern section of Queensland.

Education in Australia was in the hands of church representatives and private individuals until 1848, when New South Wales established the first system of state education. It was not, however, until 1880 that elementary education in the Commonwealth became secular and supported by the state. The cost of education beyond elementary school in Australia is too expensive for many. In 1948 the state accepted compulsory education to age 15, but were not able to implement the law because of social and political conflicts. One of Australia's serious educational problems is reaching children in the remote rural areas. Several experiments have been attempted to teach them by correspondence courses, area schools, and school broadcasting.

Each state capital has its university, those of Sydney and Melbourne having the highest prestige. Canberra and Armidale, New South Wales, have university colleges. The proportion of university graduates from private and denominational universities has far exceeded the number from state institutions. Since 1950, however, the commonwealth government has provided liberal scholarships to all students who can benefit from higher education.

THE DEVELOPMENT OF PHYSICAL EDUCATION

Physical education programs at the turn of the century were strongly influenced by the cultural patterns developed in the mother country. Swedish gymnastics dominated the elementary school program, and private and denominational secondary schools emulated the athletic programs of the English public schools. Following World War I, Australia felt the influence of the international sports movement and provided facilities for greater participation in sports and recreation in the schools and among the general public.

As a national defense measure Australia appointed a National Fitness Council as a division of the Commonwealth's Board of Education in 1938. Within the Council a Grants Committee was set up to allocate funds for physical education and recreation. The committee worked with the various State Fitness Councils to organize courses for the training of physical education leaders in the universities. The fitness program covered not only the youth in school but both youths and adults outside school. The Council helped promote camping, youth hostels, youth work in rural areas, and amateur sports.

The Australians are intensely interested in sports. Facilities for tennis are supplied through municipal and privately owned courts. Public and private golf courses and bowling greens are located in practically every city and town of the more populated areas. The national game is cricket, and, in addition to local matches, games are played against English teams. Soccer is almost as popular with both amateurs and professionals. Every country has an activity in which it takes special pride, and in Australia this is represented by the Royal Australian Surf Lifesaving Association. This organization was founded around 1900, and the membership pays for the privilege of belonging.

BURMA

The British annexed Burma in slow stages through the Burmese wars of 1824, 1852, and 1885. In 1937 Burma was separated from India and given self-government. In 1940 a group of thirty young patriots who belonged to the semisecret Thakin Society left Burma to receive military training under the Japanese. These Thirty Comrades, as they were called, returned to their homeland to lead 4000 Burmese as an auxiliary force in the Japanese campaign to conquer Burma in 1942. After the Japanese occupied Burma, a military government was formed under Major General Aung San. In 1944 Aung San made secret overtures to the British, an Anglo-Burmese treaty was signed in London in 1947, and the Union of Burma was founded in 1948.

The majority of the Burmese are Buddhists, and their religion plays an important part in their lives. The spiritual head of the village is a yellow-robed monk, and the monastery in which he lives serves as the village school. Since these schools provide an elementary education, the number of illiterate men and women is small, although the women are less well educated than the men. In addition to the monastic schools, the Burmese government supports 5138 elementary and 416 secondary schools with over a half-million pupils in attendance. The University of Rangoon was founded in 1920 as a federal institution and, with the University college of Mandalay, acquired degree status after World War II.

PHYSICAL EDUCATION AND SPORTS

The physical education program has been strongly influenced by India's physical education movements, since Burma was a province of that country. It consists of gymnastics, marching, games, and relays, and the teacher is still called the drillmaster. Toward the close of the school year the program is slanted toward preparation for the annual gymnastic exhibition. These mass demonstrations are a delight to the people of the East, who like huge spectacles of any kind. Voluntary sports participation is encouraged through sports clubs and interscholastic meets. The elementary and secondary school programs are under the control of the Minister of Education and supervised by two inspectors of physical education, U Ba Than and U Than Win, the latter of Nbomis, a graduate of the University of California. These educators have formulated plans to modernize the physical education program within the cultural pattern of the people.

At the University of Rangoon compulsory physical education is taught by the staff of the College of Education and, as in the public schools, is of a formal nature. The sports program reaches about one-fourth of the 9000 students through clubs representing fifteen different sports. These clubs conduct intramural competitions, and intercollegiate meets are held in tennis, badminton, and rowing with universities in Thailand and India.

DEVELOPMENTS IN SPORTS

The favorite Western game is soccer football. Because of his short stature the Burmese finds volleyball and basketball played according to the International Federation Rules difficult to negotiate. But in sports like soccer and field hockey he makes up for his loss of height by his dexterity, speed, and endurance. The native game of *Chinlon* is often shown in travelogues. In this game five or six players form a circle facing one another and with their knees, feet, and heels keep a woven cane or gutta percha ball airborne without changing their basic positions.

The National Fitness Council, a division of the Ministry of Health, is the promotional agency for sports in Burma. The Council works in close cooperation with the National Sports Federation in the supervision of all voluntary sports organization and provides financial assistance in obtaining facilities, equipment, and personnel. The National Council delegates its authority to forty district councils, which handle much of the local administrative work. The national body employs ninety men and forty women in the district councils, in addition to a considerable staff of organizers who train and supervise sports leaders. Local and national championships are arranged in tennis, swimming, gymnastics, badminton, boxing, weight-lifting, track and field athletics, and the national game of *Chinlon*. In 1958 the Soviet Union, in exchange for rice, built an Olympic sports area in Rangoon consisting of a stadium, sports hall, velodrome for cycling, tennis stadium, swimming pool, and boat club.[2]

TEACHER PREPARATION

In 1958 Burma had 424 men and 193 women teachers of physical education in some 700 schools, most of whom were poorly qualified. Teachers in the elementary schools have only a Middle School education (grades 1–7), while those in the secondary schools have had several years in high school or one year of normal school. Six-week summer courses are offered at the University of Rangoon for in-service training, and teachers are encouraged to attend through allowances for traveling, board, and room. The normal schools at Rangoon and Mandalay provide a specialized course in physical education which is attended by students selected by the Community Boards within the districts. These courses offer instruction in the activities listed in the syllabus for the middle and secondary schools, and the University of Rangoon offers, in addition, courses in classical dance, free exercises, drills with Indian clubs and wands, and deep breathing exercises. Graduates of the University of Rangoon are also prepared in another subject matter area than physical education.

CANADA

By the British North American Act of 1867 the entire control of education in Canada was left up to the individual provinces. The Constitution makes only the single condition that the privileges of denominational and separate schools in Ontario and Quebec shall not be denied. In the ten English-speaking provinces English-Canadian schools predominate, and Roman Catholics maintain separate schools. In Quebec Roman Catholic schools are predominant, but English schools are represented. Boys and girls are taught separately in both elementary and secondary schools. In the Northwest Territories and the Yukon the federal government and religious bodies provide education for the Eskimos and Indians. Approximately one-fourth of Canada's fourteen million inhabitants are in school. Canada supports more than 150 colleges and universities, about 50 teacher preparation institutions, 30,000 day schools under public control, 1000 private elementary, secondary, and business schools, and approximately 300 Indian schools.

Physical Education in Canada

Physical education in the English-speaking provinces has been molded by the legislative bodies and local authorities, the contributions of immigrants, and the country's natural resources. Although the Swedish system was practiced to some extent in the less remote provinces, the traditional English devotion to games, sports, and outdoor recreation worked against the acceptance of any gymnastic system. Scottish immigrants brought the Caledonian Games and added curling to the long list of winter sports in the Dominion. The Germans arrived in sufficient numbers at the turn of the century to organize the first German *Turnverein* in 1906. But the secondary schools and higher institutions with few exceptions have pursued a typically English athletic program. Canada's forests, mountains, lakes, and endless water passages provide ample opportunity for such outdoor activities as camping, canoeing, boating, swimming, hunting, and fishing.

MODERN TRENDS

In October, 1943, Canada's Parliament passed the National Physical Fitness Act, and a National Council on Physical Fitness was appointed, consisting of a director and representatives from the then nine provinces. The Council urged all communities to establish their own physical fitness programs in cooperation with the provincial councils. Universities were encouraged to organize programs and provide trained teachers and recreation leaders. The Council also recommended that physical education and recreation personnel then engaged in the war be given postwar positions in local physical fitness programs. Lastly, a one month's camping experience every year was recommended for all Canadian children from ages 5 to 14. Parliament voted a matching fund of $250,000 to each province which enlisted in the program, and the National Council announced that it stood ready to accept grants, bequests, and other contributions to increase this amount.

The reaction to the National Physical Fitness Act was immediate and beneficial. By 1947 British Columbia, Alberta, Saskatchewan, and Manitoba had enlisted in the program. The Canadian Camping Association incorporated under a revised constitution and bylaws and held its first conference in Ottawa to consider the future of camping. The Canadian Physical Education Association (see Appendix) through its school personnel supported local physical fitness programs and provided leadership in many other ways. Surveys of existing programs indicated that much needed to be done to raise standards in both urban and rural areas.

In 1954 the National Physical Fitness Act was repealed, and the National Council of Health and Safety took over the responsibilities of the National Council on Physical Fitness. In 1961 a decree provided the sum of five million dollars to assist in the promotion of physical education, leisure-time activities, and amateur sports.

SPORTS DEVELOPMENT

Cooperation in sports between Canada and the United States has been close and friendly for many years. The first YMCA in North America was established in Canada, followed shortly by one in the United States. As the sports programs of both countries grew, the Associations arranged international contests in basketball. By the turn of the century competition had progressed sufficiently to encourage Dr. Luther H. Gulick, YMCA College, Springfield, Massachusetts, to organize the Athletic League of North America. This body regulated athletic contests between the Associations of the two countries.

Between 1890 and 1905 intercollegiate athletics in the United States were the object of much criticism because of the high incidence of fatal injuries in football and unethical practices in the recruitment and subsidizing of athletes. When early in 1906 faculty representatives met the problem by organizing the Intercollegiate Athletic Association of the United States (National Collegiate Athletic Association, 1910), the Dominion followed suit and organized the Canadian Intercollegiate Athletic Association.

CANADIAN FOOTBALL

Modern Canadian football evolved from the English game of Rugby, which was first played in the maritime provinces and moved gradually westward. Matches with schools in the Untied States did much to alter the playing rules. The American names were adopted for player positions, the snap substituted for the heeled ball, and the forward pass was introduced in 1931.

Canadian football is played on a field 110 by 65 yards, with end zones (in-goal areas) of 25 yards. Twelve players constitute a team, and the extra man, called a flying wing, is used in the backfield on offense and as a linebacker on defense. Since the offense is allowed only three downs to make 10 yards, it must try for big gains, which encourages a more open game than is prevalent in the United States. The wide field encourages lateral passing and the deep end zones forward passing for touchdowns. The backfield can be in motion toward the opponent's goal when the ball is snapped, and the punt receiver is protected within a radius of 5 yards whether he catches the ball on the run or standing still. In the Canadian game a touchback is not allowed and the ball is played as though it were in the field of play. The equivalent of an American safety is called a "rouge" and scores one point. Another unusual feature of the Canadian game is that a point can be scored if the team in possession of the ball kicks it over the defending team's deadline, 25 yards behind the goal line.[3]

Intercollegiate games with schools in the United States are growing in popularity, and American players are gradually developing a taste for the Canadian version of football. At present it is customary for collegiate teams playing in the Dominion to play one half by Canadian and the other half by American rules. Canadian secondary schools playing football south of the border use American interscholastic rules during the entire game.

Probably one of the oldest intercollegiate relationships between Canada and the United States is represented by the game of lacrosse. Intercollegiate competition in this sport started as early as 1885, and prior to World War II the U.S. Intercollegiate Lacrosse Association played a series of games with both the champions of Canada and England.

Other Canadian Sports

Amateur sports in Canada present a cross-section of the Old and New Worlds. From the Old Canada adopted cricket, curling, bowls, field hockey, Rugby, and association football. From the New World the Canadians adopted baseball, basketball, and volleyball. The national game of Canada, however, is ice hockey. It has been suggested that ice hockey was adapted from field hockey, the Irish game of hurling, or the European game of bandy, popular in the Netherlands and other countries as early as the sixteenth century. Regardless of its origin, the Canadians deserve credit for the promotion of modern ice hockey. The Amateur Hockey Association of Canada was organized and a code of rules drawn up in 1887. Through exhibition tours by the Ottawa, Quebec and Montreal Hockey Clubs the game was introduced into the United States, where it became a popular addition to the athletic programs of Northern states.

Canadian intercollegiate coaches have adopted many of the training techniques of their American counterparts. The highly organized intramural athletic systems in United States colleges and universities appealed especially to Canadian athletic administrators since they were conducted on a strictly amateur, "sports for all" basis and provided incentives for the competitors. Canadian universities have even adopted the American idea of summer school coaching clinics and have drawn upon United States coaching talent.

An important outcome of the postwar Olympic Games was the inauguration in 1920 of athletic meets between English-speaking nations. These meets were generally held immediately following the Olympic Games when all nations had their athletic talent mobilized. The good fellowship engendered by the internationl competition between the British Empire and the United States resulted in the formation of the British Empire Sports League and the establishment of the British Empire Games. These games are held every fourth year of the Olympiad in either Great Britain or one of the dominions. The first was held 1930 in Hamilton, Ontario.

RECREATIONAL DEVELOPMENT

In 1946 recreational leaders from Ottawa, Montreal, Hamilton, and Brantford attended the National Recreation Congress at Atlantic City, New Jersey. A recreation commission was organized in Calgary, Alberta, and a growing number of towns, cities, and communities in Manitoba and Saskatchewan established recreation programs. Saskatoon and Regina, Saskatchewan, established youth centers and the province sponsored juvenile hockey leagues for schoolboys. Manitoba promoted Rugby football, and the province's Junior Curling Bonspiel had a record entry of 185 high school rinks for the annual spiel at Winnipeg. In 1948 the city of Toronto reported that her recreation facilities included 123 playgrounds, 67 playing fields, 37 bowling greens, 18 wading pools, 273 tennis courts, 30 community centers, 67 indoor school playgrounds, 90 hockey rinks, and 100 pleasure skating rinks.

When the National Physical Fitness Act was abrogated in 1954, the Department of Labor stepped in, paying half the cost of community swimming pools, playing fields, bowling greens, community centers, hockey rinks, and other facilities.

TEACHER PREPARATION

One of the first professional curriculums in Canada was established at McGill University in 1912. Dr. R. Tait McKenzie, Canadian born and later one of the great professional leaders in the United States, was a special lecturer in anatomy and physical education at McGill at the time. In 1945 McGill established a four-year course in professional training leading to an academic degree. The course was open to both men and women and affiliated with the College of Medicine, of which Dr. McKenzie was once a staff member. The following year the University of Alberta established a similar curriculum, and in 1947 the University of British Columbia inaugurated a School of Physical Education with an enrollement of ninety students, of whom two-thirds were men. In 1952 the University of British Columbia offered a one-year program leading to a diploma in physical education, sponsored by the National Council on Physical Fitness. This trend in the establishment of professional schools should improve the quality of the physical education and recreation programs in public schools and higher institutions.

INDIA

In the first half of the twentieth century the major problem in Indian constitutional reform was that of reconciling the claims of the powerful Moslem community and the large Hindu majority. By 1913 the attitude of the Moslem League, formed in 1906, became so hostile to British authority that Aga Khan resigned the presidency. Both factions desired self-government, and before the provincial elections of 1937 the Moslem League under Mohammed Ali Jinnah favored cooperation with the Indian National Congress representing the Hindu segment, of which Mohandas Gandhi was leader.

At the close of World War II the Labour government returned to power in England and announced that as soon as possible a constitution-making body would convene in India. When the cabinet mission in 1946 found it could not secure agreement among the main Indian political parties, it came up with ideas of its own. It rejected the Moslem request that Pakistan be organized as a separate state on the grounds that a separate dominion was incompatible with the requirements of India's defense. An interim government was organized with Jawaharlal Nehru as vice president until some of the stumbling blocks to negotiation could be removed.

In 1947 Britain announced that it would turn over governmental control into Indian hands by June, 1948. For the sake of immediate peace and independence, Mohandas Gandhi and the other political leaders of the Indian National Congress agreed to accept the partition of India.

EDUCATIONAL PROGRESS

Until the third decade of the nineteenth century the British made no attempt to impose European culture on India. With the growth of the English humanitarian and evangelical movements in the 1830s, missionaries were allowed to operate in India without license. English became the language of instruction and Western literature and science the chief studies. Thus British domination brought the Indian into close association with the liberal and democratic ideas of the West.

In 1854 the British established a network of schools and colleges, financed by public funds, local authorities, and private management, assisted by government grants-in-aid. Unfortunately, the majority were staffed by public officials, who focused the attention of students on the values common to public office-seekers and developed a class of half-educated, unemployable youth who fomented political unrest and ignored the indigenous values of Indian culture. The British government recognized the defects in this educational system, and early in the twentieth century established a Ministry of Education in India.

PHYSICAL EDUCATION

Physical training of the warrior class dominated the early period of education, while the general populace was left to find its recreation in songs and dances associated with festivals and marriage ceremonies. Occasionally, it was treated to exhibitions in the use of military weapons and tournaments in archery and wrestling. The people of India worship personal power and body control, which play an important part in both their secular and religious exercises. Among these is Yoga-Asana, which was designed to avoid disease and maintain a balance between the body, mind, and spirit. Although the Asanas feature breath control, the Hindus have a special cult, Surya-Namaakras, which is devoted exclusively to breathing exercises. The Hindus worship Hanuman, the presiding diety of *vyayam,* or exercise.

India also has many cults of physical culture, such as Ramamurthi and Krishna Rao which feature feats of strength and resemble the cult of the strong man in Occidental nations. Wrestling has always had its share of devotees in India, and divergent schools of wrestling have been a part of the cultural pattern for centuries. As part of their training Indians wrestle in small pits dug in the ground and use a wrestling pole, the *mallakhamb,* to practice wrestling holds and as conditioning exercises.[4]

The Indians also have many native games whose origins are lost in antiquity. *Kabaddi* is played with seven players to the side, divided into raiders and catchers, and is probably a distant relative of the Assamese game of *Chuko,* in which the raiders simulate tigers, the dreaded enemy of all Indians. Other games include *Lathi,* single stick fighting; *Lezim,* a rhythmical dance starting with a slow beat and building to a crescendo; *Karla,* which requires the skillful manipulation of long, heavy Indian clubs; and *Kho-kho,* a game especially popular with girls, which employs nine players to the side and poles as the home base, and in play resembles tag.[5]

In the 1850s the public officials who were utilized as teachers introduced the English games of field hockey, Rugby football, cricket, and soccer into the upper grades of the elementary and secondary schools. Indian pupils readily took to these sports, and it was not long before the pressure of winning tournaments and cups placed the emphasis on sports participation for the few to the neglect of the many. From 1880 to World War I gymnastics and military drill were included in the school program. In many cases the gymnastic and drillmasters' only qualification was their military experience, which had taught them to use force and punishment to maintain discipline. As a consequence, the reaction of Indian pupils to their exercise periods was one of contempt.

THE YMCA AND PHYSICAL EDUCATION IN INDIA

In 1908 Dr. J. Henry Gray established the first YMCA in India at Calcutta, Bengal. Many other associations were to follow in India, Burma, and Ceylon. With the advent of the YMCA, the Indian physical education program changed to one of individual and team sports and recreation activities. In addition to English sports, the YMCA introduced volleyball, basketball, track and field athletics, and playground ball. The YMCA approach to calisthenics and drills was quite different from that of the instructors of the previous thirty years. The playground movement was initiated, and recreation systems were established in the larger metropolitan areas.

In 1920 H. C. Buck founded the National YMCA School of Physical Education (YMCA College of Physical Education, 1931) at Madras for the training of physical directors.

In 1930 J. Buchanan, physical director of the YMCA at Calcutta, called for the organization of Youth Welfare Councils on a provincial basis composed of influential and interested citizens. The Councils were to work with existing military organizations, improve the health of India's youth through the extension of health service and instruction in the schools, and provide qualified leadership by establishing a college of physical education in each province and additional training for selected leaders abroad. The Buchanan Plan proved to be of major significance in the development of physical education both before and after the partition of India.[4]

CURRENT TRENDS

In 1956 the Indian government created the Central Committee of Physical Education and Recreation. A secretary within the cabinet of the Minister of Education was appointed President of the Central Committee, responsible for all matters relating to physical education and recreation in India. Physical education in the schools is a state responsibility, and each political unit has a state director of physical education, who in turn is assisted by the local supervisors of physical education in the schools.

The Central Committee has recommended that physical education be required in the elementary and secondary schools and that instruction consist of three or four periods a week. As matters stand now, the majority of the states require physical education in the public schools, but a few still persist in leaving it optional. The Central Committee has been also instrumental in providing financial assistance to the states in the construction of facilities to help implement the school programs. Another contribution of the Central Committee has been the upgrading of the qualifications of teachers in the elementary and secondary schools. In spite of this good work, the state of physical education in India still hinges upon the debate as to whether or not it should be included among the subjects in which students are examined at the close of their elementary and secondary years. This uncertainty has had a significant influence upon the attitude of the general public toward physical education as well as upon the professional workers in the field. Currently, the state of Bombay is the only political unit in India which has made any attempt to solve the problem.[6]

Elementary and secondary schools do not include interscholastic athletics in the physical education program. Communities, however, conduct competition in games and sports for children of elementary school age. Physical educators occasionally coach boys and encourage them to enter regional and interregional competition. In 1955 a championship meet was sponsored by the Indian Federation of National Student Games. In colleges and universities the Committee of Inter-University Sports manages and conducts competitions and tournaments.

SPORTS IN INDIA

The Indians have made cricket and field hockey national games. Cricket was introduced at the close of the eighteenth century, and provincial competitions were followed by international matches with European countries. In 1912 the Moslems developed an interest in cricket and entered into the competition. Parsee teams visited England in 1886 and 1888 to play informal matches, but it was not until 1932 that an Indian team was granted a test match. In combination with the Moslems the Indians fielded many excellent cricket teams through the years, but after the partition in 1947 their teams were weakened by the loss of the Moslems. As a dominion India sent its cricket team to England for the first time in 1952. Pakistan was admitted to the Imperial Cricket Conference the same year and made history in 1954 when it became the first team to win its test match on its first visit.

In field hocky India ranks with Germany, the Netherlands, and Pakistan, and for some thirty years has dominated international competition in this sport. At the Amsterdam Olympic Games in 1928 India became world champion in field hockey, and four years later at Los Angeles its team was voted by sports writers the most skillful in any sport on the program. The Indians feature short passes instead of the long ones common in European play. Both the Indians and Pakistani use a short-toe hockey stick and employ a left-hand grip well behind the stick. This enables the players to reverse the stick without changing hands and gives them remarkable control of the ball.

After World War I sports were promoted vigorously in the provinces of Bengal, Madras, and Punjab. In 1920 the Indian Olympic Association was founded to process the athletes representing India at the Paris Olympic Games in 1924. Sports associations which have Olympic representation, such as hockey, soccer, wrestling, and track and field athletics, are affiliates of the Indian Olympic Association. Other sports associations, such as badminton, cricket, and tennis, have their own independent organizations and conduct regional, national, and international competitions and tournaments.

In Western Asian, Asian, and Olympic games, India has participated in free-style wrestling, field hockey, soccer, water polo, cycling, and track and field events. However, their unofficial team score at the Olympic Games has never been impressive. This has been a matter of national concern since the formation of the dominion, and the government has invested substantial sums in the Pajkumari Sports Coaching project to improve the quantity and quality of Indian athletes.

TEACHER PREPARATION

In addition to the YMCA College of Physical Education founded by H. C. Buck in Madras in 1920, the British government opened preparatory schools in physical education at Calcutta, Lahore, Hyderabad, Bombay, and other cities. These schools provided instruction in gymnastics, games, scouting, and native activities. The school at Bombay, called the Kandivali Institute of Physical Education, combines the best features of Western methods with indigenous ones. In 1947 several other professional schools were organized, bringing the total of such institutions in India to forty-one. These schools granted the diploma of master of physical education and certificates of qualification for teachers of physical education in secondary schools.

In 1957 the Central Committee of Physical Education and Recreation established a professional training course at Gwalior in north-central India called the Lakshmibai College of Physical Education. The professional course leads to an academic degree and is under the direction of P. M. Joseph, a former graduate of Springfield College, U.S.A. In 1960 the government of Punjab established at Chandernagor another college which grants the license of physical education instructor.

SOUTH AFRICA

For more than a century the Dutch and British were engaged in sharp competition to gain possession of South Africa. This rivalry finally exploded in the Boer War of 1899–1902. It was a bitter struggle and left a legacy of hate and suspicion which the Afrikaans (Boers) and British have not entirely lost. The Union of South Africa became a reality in 1910 when the two British colonies Cape and Natal were combined with the Boer republics, Orange Free State and Transvaal.

At the close of the Boer War there were no definite safeguards for the rights of the millions of Negroes except that the British had promised them that no political change would be made until the Boer states had achieved self-government. When this became a reality the radical element of the government was in control and the opportunity for an equitable settlement was lost. In 1912 a small progressive group of Negroes formed the African National Congress, but this political body never became effective in a social climate in which three million whites dominated eleven million Negroes. The Negroes feel that their greater number gives them the democratic right to govern the country, but the whites refuse to yield this right to a people hundreds of years behind them in development. The steady infiltration of Communists into the African National Congress and South African Indian Congress in recent years is an ominous sign.

The South African population is represented by four racial groups: Europeans, natives, Asiatics, and colored people. The two main languages are English and Afrikaans. The latter is a language created by the early Dutch, German, and French settlers, based on seventeenth-century dialects in Holland.

South Africa is a highly exploited country, with citrus fruit, pineapple and banana ranches, sugar plantations, and ostrich, stock, and grain forms. In addition, it has many mineral industries, including gold, diamonds, coal, copper, asbestos, and manganese. The European women have much leisure time since servants are inexpensive and plentiful. The homemaker plays golf and tennis, and since grass is difficult to grow, many homes have tennis courts in place of front lawns. On the other hand, the lot of the Negro is far less fortunate. A third of the Negro population lives in traditional kraals in the reserves, a third on the farms of the whites, and the rest in shabby quarters which cling to the outskirts of towns and cities.

Education for white children in South Africa is compulsory between the ages of 7 and 16, but children may leave after grade six if they can secure employment. The school system is not coeducational and is segregated. School buildings are generally one-story structures surrounded by ample play space. Education is not compulsory for Negro and colored children. The Union of South Africa has nine universities, headed by the University of South Africa, the federal institution which conducts courses and gives examinations.

PHYSICAL EDUCATION

Programs in white schools consist of gymnastics, apparatus work, games, and rhythmical activities. The physical education period opens with ten to twenty minutes of instruction in gymnastics, balance beam exercises, and apparatus work, followed by lead-up games and rhythmical gymnastics or dancing. Rhythmical gymnastics are based on the work of Dalcroze, Bode, or Medan, and dances include native, American folk and square, and occasionally creative dance after Laban.

Although gymnastics are an important part of the program in both elementary and secondary schools, sports are well represented in the latter. Baseball is particularly popular in Durban and Johannesburg. Other sports are Rugby, cricket, basketball, tennis, and track and field athletics. In South African secondary schools the coach of the Rugby football team also serves as athletic director of the various sports clubs. Like the secondary schools the universities have voluntary sports clubs, which engage in intercollegiate competition. The South African Gymnastic Union and the South African Sports Federation have both been active in the promotion of gymnastics and sports in schools and among the general public.

The first department of physical education was organized at the University of Stellenbosch in 1936 and Ernst Jokl, M.D.,* formerly of the College of Physical Education, Berlin, appointed director. This department assumed leadership in the promotion of physical education programs in the European and native schools of South Africa and the word "Joklize," meaning to exercise, was added to the vocabulary of the Afrikaans, British, and native population.[7]

The interest of the United Kingdom in the National Physical Fitness and Recreation Act of 1937 was reflected among the leadership of South Africa. The Minister of Education appointed a committee to consider the current status of physical education in the commonwealth and make recommendations for improvement. As a result, the government appointed a National Advisory Council on Physical Education under the chairmanship of M. C. Botha, Secretary of Education. A substantial appropriation was provided to deal with technical and scientific problems association with physical education and sports.

TEACHER PREPARATION

In 1938 the Witwatersrand Technical College at Johannesburg considered the feasibility of a standard professional teachers' train-

* At present Director of the Physical Education Research Laboratory, Department of Physical Education, University of Kentucky.

ing course to accelerate the progress of physical education in the schools. Subsequent studies, however, indicated that few of the county districts could support a full-time physical education specialist. As a substitute measure it was decided to utilize the teacher on the job and provide additional training with a one-year course at Witwatersrand. For the academic teacher who could not afford to spare one year for professional course, preparatory courses were arranged on a summer school basis.

Since 1938 South Africa has made great strides in the area of teacher preparation. The normal schools offer a three-year course which leads to the certificate of specialist and makes the holder eligible to teach on the elementary level. Five higher institutions have established departments of physical education, and the pioneer institution, the University of Stellenbosch, has organized a four-year professional curriculum. Physical education majors are encouraged to select their second teaching areas in chemistry, physics, biology, and botany to make them more desirable teaching candidates. The undergraduate professional curriculum grants the bachelor degree, while advanced graduate courses lead to the master's or doctoral degree in physical education (D.Ed.Ph.). The South African Sports Federation, which comprises twenty-nine associations, provides short courses, clinics, and a camp to prepare sports leaders and athletic trainees to serve the various sports clubs.*

NOTES

1. Peter C. McIntosh. *Physical Education in England Since 1800*. G. Bell and Sons, Ltd., 1952, pp. 142–143; 241–243.
2. Ralph A. Piper. "Physical Education in the Far East." *Journal of Health–Physical Education–Recreation,* 29:6 (September, 1958), 77. Ralph A. Piper. "Physical Education and Sports in Burma." *Proceedings,* The College Physical Education Association, 1958, pp. 202–207.
3. *Canadian Intercollegiate Football Rule Book, 1962*. Canadian Association for Health, Physical Education and Recreation, 515 Jarvis Street, Toronto 5, Canada.
4. A. D. F. Thomason. "Physical Education in India." *Mind and Body,*

* Personnel interview with Jan F. Botha, Chief, Division of Adult Education, Department of Education, Arts and Sciences, Pretoria, South Africa, 1962.

35:375 (February, 1929), 407–416. George F. Andrews. "Physical Education in India." *Journal of Health and Physical Education,* 4:2 (February, 1933), 10–12.

5. Hartley Price. "Physical Education in India." *Proceedings,* The College Physical Education Association, 1956, p. 326.
6. Pierre Seurin. *L'Éducation Physical dans le Monde.* Bordeaux: Editions Bière, 1961, pp. 217–222.
7. Fred Eugene Leonard and George Affleck. *A Guide to the History of Physical Education.* Philadelphia: Lea and Febiger, 1947, pp. 423–427.

Chapter 14

PHYSICAL EDUCATION IN ASIATIC COUNTRIES

THE NEAR EAST

THE Near East, or Southwest Asia, includes Turkey, Syria, Lebanon, Israel, Jordan, Iran, Iraq, Afghanistan, Saudi Arabia, Yemen, and the Aden protectorate.

In ancient times Syria was a fertile strip of land between the eastern coast of the Mediterranean and the Arabian Desert from the Gulf of Alexandretta to Sinai. At the close of World War I Syria was placed under the mandate of the French, and in 1944 the independent states of Syria and Lebanon were formed.

In 1945 the British and United States governments set up a joint committee to make recommendations concerning the future of Palestine. Two years later at a special assembly of the United Nations it was recommended that Palestine be made a single federal state shared by the Jews and Arabs, with Jerusalem as a common capital. This arrangement resulted in a jurisdictional dispute and led to armed conflict. A United Nations commission brought a temporary halt to hostilities. In a surprise move in 1948 the Jewish National Council and General Zionist Council announced the formation of an independent state, Israel. The announcement reopened hostilities between the newly established nation and its Arabian neighbors. Ralph Bunche, representing the United Nations as mediator, secured separate armistices between Israel and the Arabian states and the new state became a reality.

During World War I Turkey became a belligerent on the side of the Axis and suffered severe reverses. As the Turks faced the possibility of involvement in World War II through Nazi influence, the country decided to remain neutral. In 1944, however, she yielded to the pressure of the United Nations and declared war on Germany.

During World War I Persia (Iran) had been overrun by the armies of Turkey, Russia, and Great Britain and like Turkey wanted to avoid another such disaster during World War II. The status of neutrality was difficult to maintain in the face of well-organized Nazi propaganda, but, becoming apprehensive when the efficient Nazi war machine advanced toward the Caucasus, the Persians declared war on the Axis powers in 1943. During the war the Allies occupied Persia as a corridor for transporting military supplies and because of its valuable oil resources. After the war the British and United States armed forces withdrew, but the Soviet Union dallied in the northern sector. External and internal political pressure finally forced the Soviet Union to withdraw its troops, but the Communists managed to persuade the province of Azerbaijan to secede from Persia.

Iraq became a British protectorate after World War I. Composed of three Turkish provinces, Basra, Baghdad, and Monsuland, its boundaries were settled between 1922 and 1937. As the Germans gained momentum on the Eastern front in World War II, the country saw an opportunity to rid itself of the last vestige of British control. The British, however, were not about to lose Iraq's vital oil reserves, and their air force and mobile desert army soon brought Iraq back into the Allied fold.

Until 1919 Afghanistan was an unlimited monarchy. At this time King Amanullah introduced a system of democratic government, but public acceptance was slow in this backward country. During World War I Afghanistan sided with Turkey, the chief Islamic power, and fought short engagements with the British, by whom they were defeated. Although it was economically dependent upon Germany, Afghanistan held a position of neutrality during World War II.

THE CULTURE OF THE NEAR EAST

The traveler in the Near East can observe primitive medical methods and faulty health practices rooted in the traditions and superstitions of past centuries. The old feudal system which was practiced until recently still influences land tenure, and it required the occupation of foreign armies to break down class distinctions among the people. In this ancient land old traditions live side by side with modern social customs and technology. In Jerusalem the chants and responses of the monks, priests, and nuns can be heard above the hum of tractor engines as the farmer works the land on the outskirts of the Holy City. Through the windows of the synagogue the cries of the Hassidic Jews and the rhythmical beat of their feet in the ritual dance are clearly audible above the din in the street. The aged and bearded Talmudic scholar pores long hours over the ancient lawbooks, and in his long coat and broad-brimmed hat, he makes a ludicrous figure dodging taxis in the street The most spectacular change in customs has transpired in Turkey, where the fez and veil, Mohammedan traditions of long standing, succumbed to modern dress after World War I. The older population in the Near East clings tenaciously to the traditions and customs of the past, but the younger generations look forward to the new order of things.

The peoples of the Near East need health education in the areas of food preservation, drinking water inspection, sanitary sewage disposal, insect control, first aid, and other measures important to community welfare. Some governments have cooperated with the Near East Foundation in the elimination of disease by such methods as the use of airplane spraying to control malaria. Nutritional deficiencies are common, and adequacy of diet is closely associated with educational progress.

In the past only a few active sports were considered dignified in the Near East, and these were centered around the skill of horsemanship. Polo has been a favorite sport for centuries, and a polo field is still in existence which belonged to Shah Abbas the Great (1600). Games on horseback involving the use of guns and swords and demonstrations of skillful riding are also popular among the Arabs.

Less active social games, however, are more characteristic of the Near Eastern countries. Tricktrack is a board game similar to backgammon, familiar to young and old. *Barchiz,* a game of Hindustanian origin, is a forerunner of parchesi, played with conch shells and elaborate carved pieces instead of dice and cardboard disks.

Shataranj, or chess, is another of the many board games of the East. Casual mingling of the sexes is still taboo, and the men sit for hours in coffee shops drinking Turkish coffee, smoking narghiles and playing tricktrack, while the women gather weekly at the cemetery to pray for the dead and linger to chat afterward. All join in the celebration of weddings and feast days, which are occasions for group singing, games, and dancing.[1]

EDUCATIONAL PROGRESS IN THE NEAR EAST

Education in the Near East has made its greatest progress since World War II. Previous to this time education was provided by foreign interests through private schools and by native religious schools in towns and villages. With education in the hands of the few the masses were neglected, and with the exception of a few countries illiteracy was very high.

When Syria and Lebanon secured their independence, their governments took over the foreign schools and reduced their number. Besides elementary and secondary schools Syria supports the University of Damascus (1923), which in 1952–1953 had a student enrollment of 2500 and a faculty of 107 teachers. Lebanon has an expanding system of public schools in addition to many private schools of foreign origin. It has three principal universities: the Catholic Jesuit University of St. Joseph (1881) at Beirut, the American University of Beirut founded as a Protestant College in 1866 and given university status in 1920, and the Lebanese State University established in 1951.

In Israel free elementary education is provided all children by the state. Secondary school education is supported by the municipalities and voluntary groups. Hebrew is the language employed in all lower and higher schools. Israel has several universities, among which are the Hebrew University of Jerusalem, Bar-Ilan University near Tel Aviv, and Tel Aviv University. In addition to these Israel has thirty two- and three-year teacher-training institutes which prepare teachers for the elementary schools. The army is an important educational agency and assists in the orientation and assimilation of new immigrants as they arrive.

In Turkey elementary education is compulsory in theory until the age of 12. Although opportunities for elementary education have improved, many children in the remote provinces are neglected. Among the problems facing the Turkish government are the lack of adequately trained teachers and a reluctance to shift from the Arabic to the Latin alphabet, which makes impossible uniformity of instruction. The secondary schools provide a three-year college preparatory coursc. Boys may attend vocational and technical schools and girls institutes which furnish training in domestic science. The government has established agricultural institutes in rural sections. Higher institutions include the University of Istanbul, University of Ankara, University of the Aegean at Izmir (1955), and the Istanbul Technical University reorganized in 1941.

The Persian constitution of 1906 recognized the need for state-supported compulsory education, and by 1911 the state Council of Education reported the establishment of 128 elementary, 2 secondary schools, and 3 colleges. After 1950 the United States government assisted in the extension of education to the rural areas. In 1949 the Persian government introduced a plan establishing minimum four-year elementary school and a five-to-six-year secondary school. Persian universities place emphasis on native literature and poetry, and the University of Tabriz has faculties in only literature and medicine. The University of Teheran, established in 1934, has a much more general curriculum.

The first primary schools were established in Iraq in 1913 and secondary schools in 1930. The Iraqui government has a compulsory school law which requires children to attend school for the first six grades, but there is such a shortage of teachers that the law has little meaning. In 1947 Iraq reported an illiteracy figure of 91.5 percent. Since then the country has used the income from her oil resources to improve her educational facilities. In 1953 Iraq reported that the state supported 1451 elementary schools, with an enrollment of 250,000 pupils. Iraq also has eleven teacher-training institutions and twelve universities.

In Afghanistan elementary education became compulsory in 1931, and about 300 schools were established. Every province has private secondary schools, staffed with English-, French-, and German-speaking teachers. In addition, there are military, tribal, and religious schools. Only recently a start has been made on education for girls, in Kabul and the larger cities. Afghanistan has one university, founded at Kabul in 1946.

PHYSICAL EDUCATION IN THE NEAR EAST

TURKEY

The Physical education program in Turkish schools has been influenced by the German and Swedish systems. In the postwar era the YMCA established its first association at Constantinople, and the games of volleyball, basketball, and playground ball were received with enthusiasm by the Turks. The sports movement before World War II encouraged the formation of sports associations and a national sports federation. In 1926 Turkey established an Institute of Physical Education in affiliation with the University of Ankara. Selim Sirry Bery, who had been trained in the Swedish system, was appointed director.

IRAQ

The government of Iraq has organized a directorate of physical education under the Ministry of Education to promote and establish programs of physical education in the schools. The director, Akram Fahmi, received his professional training in the Swedish system. Those programs which have been established in the elementary school consist of gymnastics and rhythmics, while the private secondary schools are strongly dominated by the English tradition of sports. Basketball, soccer, and volleyball are familiar to the boys, and girls play excellent volleyball. With the increased royalties derived from oil Iraq is rapidly building more schools and such facilities as stadiums and swimming pools. In 1952 the government established an Institute of Physical Education at Baghdad, and later a course in methods of physical education was added to the curriculum of the Girls' Elementary Teacher Training College at Baghdad.[2]

LEBANON

The center of the physical education and sports movement in Lebanon has been the American University at Beirut. In 1897 a Swedish instructor of gymnastics was appointed to provide the students with a regular program of exercise. Soccer football was introduced informally in 1896 by one of the staff members, and other sports followed such as track and field athletics, volleyball, and basketball. In 1934 Abd-es-Sittal Trabulsi was appointed athletic director. A soccer football association now has a membership of more than twenty sports clubs. An Omnisport Federation, consisting of fifteen sports clubs, includes basketball, skiing, volleyball, weight-lifting, ping-pong, and other activities.

AFGHANISTAN

In 1956 at the request of the Afghanistan government, Theodore Harder, of the University of California, was assigned by the Asian Foundation to assist the Minister of Education, Dr. Ali Ahmed Papol, in the organization of a national physical education and sports program for the schools. His first move was to conduct a survey of the status of physical education in the nation's school. He found that there were few qualified teachers and just as few programs and facilities. He also discovered that the people were opposed to an athletic program because, they contended, children and youth were too physically weak to endure it. A subsequent study by Harder of college-age youths revealed that the average weight was 112 pounds, and that these youths lacked shoulder girdle strength and body balance but had exceptional endurance when it came to such running games as soccer and field hockey.

Harder outlined a program of physical education for the schools of Kabul and the provinces and then proceeded to organize a professional training course for physical education leaders. In 1959 he inaugurated a three-year professional teachers course in affiliation with the University of Kabul. His staff consisted of two German instructors, a former Japanese Olympic athlete, a German Boy Scout organizer, and himself. For the science courses Harder secured the cooperation of the medical staff of the University of Kabul. The first class entered the school in the winter of 1959–1960.[3]

ISRAEL

At the beginning of the century schools in Palestine were influenced by the German and French systems of gymnastics. Rishon le

Zion, the first sports organization, was formed in Jaffa in 1906 and shortly thereafter was followed by the Bare Giore in Jerusalem. In 1912 the secondary schools of Jaffa introduced gymnastics in the school program under the leadership of Zoi Nishry, who published the first manual of gymnastics for teachers in the language of the Bible. In the same year the various sports associations formed the National Maccabi* Organization at Nes Tsiyona. At the close of World War I the British Army of Occupation introduced soccer football, which became one of the most popular sports. The English were also responsible for initiating the Boy Scout movement in Palestine in 1919 and other Near Eastern countries. In the postwar era Palestine witnessed a steady growth of interest in sports on the part of both the schools and the general public.

As an independent state Israel made physical education compulsory in all state-supported schools. In grades one to eight physical education instruction is required two hours, or four half-hour periods, a week, and the program consists of gymnastics, games, and rhythmics. In addition, upper grades in the elementary school participate in track and field athletics and swimming when facilities are available. Secondary schools require two hours a week of gymnastics and games and encourage membership in sports clubs as an extracurricular activity. High school youths are also required to devote two hours a week to the Gadna program, which provides premilitary training for boys 14–17 years of age. The boys are formed into military battalions and subjected to instruction in tactics, riflery, first aid, and experiences in camping and scouting. There is no counterpart of this kind of training for girls, but all girls physically fit are subject to two years of military service when they reach the age of 18.**

The General Council of the Ministry of Education in Palestine established the first department of physical education at Tel Aviv University in 1939. Sports participation and informal competition

* A Jewish dynasty of heroes who were credited with being the deliverers of Judea and Judaism from the persecutions of the Syrian King, Epiphanes. The name of Maccabeus belonged to Judas the son of Mattathias. According to Scripture Maccabeus, through his heroism and loyalty to the faith of his fathers, was responsible for an illustrious period of Jewish history.

** Information secured through conversations with Dr. Emanuel Simon, Medical Adviser to the Minister of Education, Tel Aviv, Israel.

had been an extracurricular activity in Jewish universities ever since the close of World War I, and in 1953 the Academic Sports Union was established as an intercollegiate athletic association to control and regulate competition. Members of Asa, as it is called in Israel, have competed in the International Student Olympic Games at Budapest in 1954 and at San Sebastian in 1956.

Before 1945 the majority of the teachers of physical education in the schools of Palestine received their training in Denmark and the remainder in Sweden, Germany, England, Poland, Austria, and the United States. In 1945 the General Council established the Physical Culture Teachers College at Tel Aviv, and this institution graduated seventy-nine physical education teachers before the formation of the state of Israel. As a tribute to General Orde Wingate, who served Palestine in the days of British occupation, the General Council formulated plans for the establishment of the Wingate Institute of Physical Culture. With the help of the Kallenbach legacy and the American Fund for Israel Institutions, the Wingate Institute for Physical Culture was completed in 1957 and the older Physical Culture Teachers College moved to the new location near Tel Aviv. The Wingate Institute emphasizes four areas: athletic coaching and the training of sports leaders for youth organizations, teacher preparation in physical education, recreation leadership, and research in physical and sports education. The Hebrew and Tel Aviv universities also provide teacher-training courses in physical education.

THE SPORTS MOVEMENT IN ISRAEL

After World War I many gymnastic and sports leaders returned to Palestine from Central and Eastern Europe. In 1920 Joseph Aloof (Wolpianski) organized the sports activities for the Maccabis at Tel Aviv. In 1925 they sent a soccer football and track and field team to the Zionist Congress at Vienna. In 1934 two Maccabean teams were sent to meets in foreign countries, one to the Asian Games in India and the other to the Women's International Sport Meeting in London. In 1944 the Maccabis introduced for the first time the torch race at Modiin, the birthplace of the organization.

The first Maccabean Games were held at Tel Aviv in 1932 in a newly constructed stadium. The Maccabean Games extend over an eight-day period, and include all sports popular in the Maccabi sports clubs.

The Young Maccabi Youth Federation is an affiliate of the older organization, devoted to scouting as well as sports. In the year 1924, during the Revisionist Movement in Palestine, the Beitar, a youth group, was founded as a branch of the Joseph Trempledor Youth Organization. This group has fielded several championship soccer teams and is well represented in boxing. The Elitzur, a religious sports union, was formed in 1938 and is at present affiliated with the Israel Sports Federation. This organization refrains from sports competition on the Sabbath, which is a popular day for sports meets in European and Asiatic countries. In spite of this problem the members of the Elitzur have sports clubs in gymnastics, light athletics, and soccer, and compete in rowing and sailing races.

The Federation of Amateur Sports was founded in 1931, and two years later the Palestine Olympic Committee was organized. The committee refused the invitation to attend the Olympic Games at Berlin in 1936, and it was not until the Mediterranean Countries Games held at Athens in 1947 that the Federation sent athletes to represent Palestine. The first Olympic Games in which athletes from Israel competed was that held at Helsinki in 1952.

The first branch of the Hapoel, an industrial sports organization, was established by the General Federation of Jewish Workers at Haifa in 1924, and with other branches formed a national association in 1926. The aim of the Hapoel was to promote physical fitness among industrial workers for labor and defense. In 1927 the national association joined the International Labor Sports Federation* and sent representatives to the first international sports meet in 1928. A large contingent participated in the Workers Olympic Games in Vienna in 1931. In addition to their interest in sports, the Hapoel organization sponsors a nautical section which trains seamen for service in the Israeli fleet.

* The 1930 report of the International Labor Sports Federation showed 21,212 sports organizations representing a membership of 360,000 in 18 countries. The majority were located in Germany, Austria, Czechoslovakia, Finland, Switzerland, Poland, Denmark, France, and Belgium.

The Israel Maritime League was established in 1937 to develop Jewish seamanship and provide instruction in swimming. It founded nautical schools at Haifa and Tel Aviv in 1938, and has sponsored swimming classes in twenty-six centers catering to some 10,000 children each year since Israel has become an independent state. The oldest sea-scouting troop in Israel which has the support of the Maritime League was organized in 1920 at Tel Aviv and was followed closely thereafter by a second troop at Haifa.[4]

SOUTHEAST ASIA

Geographically Southeast Asia includes Burma, former Indochina (Cambodia, Laos, and North and South Vietnam), Indonesia, the Federation of Malaya, and the Republic of the Philippines. Indonesia includes the Netherland Indies (with the exception of Netherlands New Guinea), Sumatra, Java, Bali, parts of Borneo, the Celebes, and hundreds of medium- and small-size islands in the world's largest archipelago. New Guinea is the second largest island next to Greenland and is an extension of the continent of Australia from which it is separated by one hundred miles at its closest point. Political control of New Guinea is shared by the British Commonwealth and the Netherlands. When Indonesia started forming its republic after 1945 the government felt that Netherlands New Guinea (Irian) should be included, and a committee established in 1950 has yet to solve the dispute. Eastern New Guinea, the other half of the island, consists of Papua with its capital Port Moresby and the Territory of New Guinea, both of which are administered by Australia. The Federation of Malaya is composed of nine Malay states (Johore, Pahang, Negri Sembilan, Selangor, Kedah, Perlis, Kelantan, Trengganu and Perak) and two British settlements (Penang and Malacca).

CAMBODIA, LAOS, AND VIETNAM (FRENCH INDOCHINA)

The French unified Cambodia, Laos, and Vietnam into French Indochina in 1887. During World War II the Japanese occupied Indochina and used it as a base of operation. After their withdrawal the Vietminh, a nationalist party, led by the veteran Communist

Ho Chi Minh, seized power and declared Vietnam an independent state. After some dispute the Allies at Potsdam decided the Chinese Communists should occupy North Vietnam and the British South Vietnam. The British were soon superseded by the French, against whom the Vietnamese rebelled in the Indochinese War of 1946–1954. The war ended with the heroic stand of the French against the Vietminh forces at Dienbienphu and French withdrawal into the Hanói and Haïphong zones. The International Conference at Geneva left French Indochina divided into four states: North Vietnam, called the Democratic Republic of Vietnam, was organized under Communist ideology. South Vietnam remained in a state of flux, with Bao Dai in tentative authority but the political power really in the hands of powerful religious sects. Cambodia remained a kingdom, but in 1947 received a constitution which called for a prime minister to be designated by the king and responsible to a national assembly elected by universal suffrage. In 1953 the king dissolved the assembly and assumed full power himself. Laos also received a constitution in 1947 with practically the same political format as that of Cambodia. According to agreement, these four independent states were to remain members of the French Union. French troops were stationed provisionally in all states, whose independence was guaranteed in 1954 by the Southeast Asia Treaty Organization.

The Vietnamese are related to the Mongoloid races, with the exception of those in the southern region, who have a strong admixture of Indonesian races. The Chinese have had a strong influence on the culture of the people, and the religion is mainly ancestor worship represented by Confucianism, Chinese Buddhism, and Taoism. Because of French occupation many Vietnamese are Roman Catholic. The Cambodians appear to be the product of Hindu migrations from the north. Their religion is predominantly Buddhism, and worship of local genii or spirits is common. While Buddhism is the religion of the people, Brahmanism is the religion of the court. The Laotians are related to the Siamese or Thai and the Shan of Burma, and the people are dedicated Buddhists. In all these states the Buddhist monks live by alms and in return teach the young to read and officiate at marriages, funerals, and religious celebrations.

When the French government set up a protectorate over the ancient kingdom of Cambodia it established the Royal Corps de Ballet at the capital, Pnom-Penh, which performs during the Water Festivals, the Buddhists' observances of religious holidays.

INDONESIA

The Arab and Indian Moslem traders who operated in the islands at an early date brought with them the Islamic religion. In 1602 the Dutch East India Company arrived and from then into the twentieth century commercially exploited the Indonesian islands. Their compulsory cultivation of valuable crops necessitated strict political control and curtailed the freedom of the people. Early in the twentieth century the Dutch sensed the growing dissatisfaction of the people and hastened to make amends, but it was too late. With the desire for free enterprise came the eventual demand for self-government.

When the Japanese attacked Indonesia in 1942 the people, never before involved in the defense of their islands, felt disassociated from the conflict between the Dutch and the Japanese. The administration of the Japanese occupation was harsh, but early in 1945 they permitted the Indonesians to make plans for independence. The announcement of their independence was met with military action by the Allies, and it was not until 1950 that the Republic of Indonesia was recognized.

Under Dutch rule school attendance was not compulsory and the illiteracy rate amounted to 98.6 percent. The population of Indonesia is heterogeneous and as many as 110 Malayan dialects are spoken throughout the islands. This fact has been an educational deterrent, and for the past decade a language of basic Malayan content has been developed called "Indonesian." Education in the republic is under the Ministry of Culture and Education, administered by seven specialized departments. Only 86,000 teachers were available in 1953, 25 percent of the teaching force necessary. Indonesia has five higher institutions, including the University of Indonesia at Djakarta and Bandung, the University of Gadja Nada, Djokja; the University of Padjadjaran, Bandung; and normal schools at Tondano, Celebes, and Medan, Sumatra.

PHYSICAL EDUCATION IN INDONESIA

Prior to World War II physical education had been introduced into the fourteen secondary schools, but in the elementary schools it was a matter of chance. Under the republic physical education became a specialized department of the Ministry of Education. Now required two hours a week in the elementary and secondary schools is a program of gymnastics, free exercises, games and sports, national dances, and *"pentjak,"* a self-defense skill. Physical education has not yet been extended to the higher institutions. Oen Bing Tiat, Director of Physical Education at the University of Padjadjaran, was influential in the organization of the National Council of Physical Education in 1957 to promote physical education and sports in Indonesia. As in all Asiatic countries, the development of physical education in Indonesia is linked with complex social, economic, and political problems.

All higher institutions offer teacher-training courses, with a three-year program leading to a bachelor degree. Eligibility for admission is a junior high school education or its equivalent. Teachers who wish to qualify for positions in the junior high schools must complete a three-year course in one of the normal schools. Teachers in senior high schools must take an additional two years. In addition, nine schools of physical education (*Sekola Guru Pendidikan Djasmani*) located throughout the islands specialize in training teachers for the elementary schools.[5]

THE FEDERATION OF MALAYA

The Portuguese were the first to exploit the commercial possibilities of the Malayan peninsula, with Malacca as their center of operation. The Dutch seized Malacca and as much of the Malayan peninsula as suited them. Unable, in turn, to stop the aggressive British East India Company, in 1824 they agreed to cede all rights in Malaya in exchange for exclusive commercial privileges to Sumatra. The British established settlements at Singapore, Penang, Malacca, and the Province of Wellesley as part of the jurisdiction of British India, and in 1867 Malaya came under the direct control of the colonial office. During World War II the Japanese took Singapore and occupied the Malayan Peninsula. Their withdrawal did not lead to immediate peace since the Chinese Communists were already there. After ten years of political unrest an agreement was finally reached which in 1957 admitted the Malayan Federation into the British Commonwealth as an independent state.

Malaya is basically a Moslem country, with Christians, Buddhists, and Hindus in the minority. Their educational problems are those of a multiracial community. A 1952 ordinance provided free, compulsory elementary education and established multiracial schools in which either Malay or English was available as the language of instruction and Chinese and Tamil as subsidiary languages. Secondary education is only available in schools which use the English language. The University of Malaya (1949) at Singapore serves as a higher institution for advanced study.

The Malayan Federation shows the influence of English occupation. From the YMCAs in the English settlements interest in sports has extended to the provinces. Gymnastics, games, and rhythmics make up the elementary school programs, while the English secondary schools promote a program similar to those of other Asiatic countries which belong to the British Commonwealth. Soccer, basketball, swimming, and tennis are popular, but it is badminton which has gained the biggest following, and every householder with the space has a badminton court in his back yard.

THE PHILIPPINES

The Philippines form an irregular archipelago with eleven islands—Luzon, Mindanao, Samar, Negros, Palawan, Panay, Mindoro, Leyte, Cebu, Bohol, and Masbate—more than 1,000 square miles in area, and some 462 one square mile or more in area. The Spanish under Miguel de Legazpi made the first permanent settlement on the island of Cebu in 1564. Spanish interest in the Philippines was purely commercial, and by 1842 there were some forty Spanish shipping concerns and some dozen commercial firms located in Manila. Legazpi brought with him representatives of the Augustinian, Franciscan, Jesuit, and Dominican orders, who immediately took possession of the more desirable agricultural land. This land monopoly by the religious orders remained a constant source of irritation to the native population. In 1890 the Filipinos in protest against their exploitation formed the Young Filipino Party, and in 1896 insurrection broke out under the leadership of Emilio Aquinaldo. At the close of the Spanish-American War the Filipinos declared their independence and made Aquinaldo president of the provisional republic.

After the treaty with Spain relationships between the United States and the republican leadership in the Philippines grew progressively worse. In 1899 Aquinaldo declared war on the United States, and after several years of guerrilla warfare the Filipinos surrendered at Samar. Governor General William Howard Taft of the United States purchased the 400,000 acres of agricultural land from the religious orders for $7,200,000. These lands were sold to the Filipinos at a reasonable price and on easy terms to bolster the country's economy. Under a distinguished series of governor generals the Philippines prospered, and in 1929 the people started a campaign to secure their independence. In 1934 the Tyding-McDuffie Act provided for that independence as of July 4, 1946. With the invasion of the Japanese the commonwealth cabinet left the country and conducted the government from Washington, returning when U.S. forces made their first landing on Leyte in 1944. The commonwealth ended on July 4, 1946, and the Republic of the Philippines began with Manuel Roxas y Acuña as president.

During the Spanish regime elementary education was provided by the curates. In 1863 compulsory education under civil control was established by a decree that was never implemented. The United States organized a system of mass education in 1901, American soldiers serving as teachers for two years until sufficient teachers could be secured from the States. Eagerly adopting the American system, the Filipinos developed one of the most extensive programs of education in the Orient. By 1948 the Filipino literacy rate reached 60 percent, the highest in Asia, and in 1954 the republic allocated 29 percent of the national budget to education.

PHYSICAL EDUCATION IN THE PHILIPPINES

The Director of Public Schools as head of the Bureau of Education has complete jurisdiction over physical education. The program consists of gymnastics, marching, and formal drills, the whole being slanted toward the mass demonstration given annually during the National Interscholastic Athletic Meet. Physical education is a required subject in the elementary schools, and secondary school pupils are required to play in games and sports. To stimulate interest in athletic participation the Athletic Badge Test was introduced. Intramural athletic competition provides material for the interscholastic teams. All sports activities culminate in a series of athletic meets which are conducted on a district, provincial, regional, and national basis. They feature track and field athletics for boys and girls, volleyball for girls, and gymnastics, basketball, and softball for the boys.

The University Council of the University of Philippines passed a resolution in 1920 that all university students should take one hour of physical education a week during the four years of school and the next year made swimming a requirement for men and optional for women. Since many students postponed physical education until the last year because of the lack of enforcement, in 1941 the Council changed the requirement to two periods a week to be completed in the first two years of school.

The increased demand for teachers after World War I prompted the university to sponsor summer schools in physical education and athletic coaching in 1925. In 1928 it offered a two-year professional course in the College of Education. In 1933 a four-year professional curriculum leading to a Bachelor of Physical Education proved less popular because it included courses in botany, zoology, and chemistry. In 1951 the curriculum was revised to attract more candidates and the double-major feature was incorporated in the new curriculum. The year previous the Board of Regents approved a Certificate in Physical Education which could be earned by attending four summer sessions.[7]

THE DEVELOPMENT OF SPORTS IN THE PHILIPPINES

Although the Filipinos had their native games and dances prior to the arrival of the Spaniards, the religious orders during the years of occupation did little to encourage these indigenous activities. In 1900 the American soldier-teachers encouraged the revival of native activities and added popular American games. They also introduced interscholastic competition in baseball and track and field athletics, and the first national interscholastic athletic meet was held at Manila in 1910 under the auspices of the Philippines Carnival Association. After 1933 the national meets were held in some fifteen different cities. Each host city constructed grandstands and playing fields, which gradually added to the sports and recreation facilities in the islands. In addition to athletic events, these meets featured mass gymnastics by public school children, native games and dances from different regions of the islands, and demonstrations of foreign games, gymnastics, and dances.

Through the influence of United States government officials and YMCA physical directors, the Philippine Amateur Athletic Federation was chartered in 1912. E. L. Brown, general secretary of the YMCA, in 1913 organized the first Far Eastern Olympic Games, and the first meet held in Manila in the same year, with the Philippines, China, and Japan as charter members.[7]

THAILAND (SIAM)

For centuries Siam was engaged in territorial warfare with the Cambodians, Peguans, and Burmese. The incorporation of lower Cochin China, Annam, and Tonkin by the French and the gradual annexation of Burma by the British in the nineteenth century eliminated the danger of territorial encroachment from Siam's old rivals. In its place, however, Siam was faced with the threat of French aggressiveness and British territorial ambitions. Conspiracies in Siam in 1912 and 1917 foreshadowed a conflict between the civilian population and the monarchy. In 1932 a small but determined group of civilians and military personnel engineered a revolution and Siam became a constitutional monarchy. In the late 1930s Siam moved into the Japanese orbit and in 1941 permitted Japanese troops to move through the country to attack British Malaya. In 1950 Thailand joined the United Nations in the defense of South Korea, and in 1954 became one of the signatories of the Southeast Asia Treaty.

Up to 1900 education in Siam was mainly in the hands of Buddhist monks and missionary schools, and as late as the 1950s many of Thailand's elementary schools were still conducted within Buddhist temple precincts. In 1921 four years of elementary education were made compulsory. In 1950 three years of compulsory secondary education were considered, but qualified teachers were difficult to secure and, more important, too few pupils had completed the four-year elementary school within the age limit of 7 to 15. The first teacher-training school was established in 1892 and the University of Chulalongkorn at Bangkok in 1917.

Physical education, under the control of the Minister of Education, is a required subject in the elementary and secondary schools and for the first two years of college. The program includes gymnastics, games, and sports, and tests are employed for classification and determination of motor fitness. Scouting is a required activity in the elementary schools. Teachers in physical education are prepared at the College of Physical Education at Bangkok, which is open to both men and women. In Thailand the classical dance is taught and preserved, but as in so many Asiatic countries, no effort is made to preserve dances of tribal groups.

THE FAR EAST

China encompasses an area of approximately four million square miles and supports a population of perhaps 600 million. The Chinese are a Mongoloid people and through invasions and settlements have had a genetic influence upon the inhabitants of Korea, Japan, and other Asiatic countries. More significantly, however, they have been a wellspring of cultural development for thier neighbors and in this role have developed a sense of superiority which has been felt by other Asiatic countries through the centuries. From the Chinese the Japanese received the Confucian code of ethics and Buddhism. To the Koreans and Indochinese they contributed their concept of family relationships and the niceties of court manners. Even the style of clothing and hairdress of modern Korea and Japan had their origin in the seventeenth-century T'ang Era, and Chinese dialects and written script provided the basis of the Korean and Japanese language as early as the fifth century A.D.

Japan consists mainly of four islands: Hokkaido, Honshu, Kyushu, and Shikoku. The Japanese have been called the "dwarf people" by the Chinese. In 1900 the average height of the male was

5 feet, 1 inch and the female about 2 inches less. By World War II the average height of the male had increased to 5 feet, 4 inches. The U.S. occupation during and after World War II was a revelation to the Japanese people because among the soldiers were many of Japanese ancestry (Nisei), who were as tall and husky as their fellow Americans. The Japanese were simply victims of dietary deficiencies in protein, vitamins, bone-building substances, and trace minerals. The Chinese, Japanese, and Koreans have for centuries lived in communal family groups housed in small, space-saving, fragile structures. These houses were characterized by rice-straw matting on the floor, sliding wall panels, rice-paper-covered windows, and a minimum of furniture. In these cramped living quarters the Orientals developed a code of human behavior which assured peace among the members of the household and favored a repertoire of quiet parlor games. In his classic study of games, Stewart Culin in 1895 found in the Far East approximately one hundred card, board, guessing, and manipulative games.

CHINA

After centuries of seclusion, between 1860 and 1894 the Chinese permitted foreign commercial interests to establish treaty ports for colonies and accepted Roman Catholic religious orders and Protestant missionaries. These missionaries were responsible for China's first contacts with Western education and medical science. A rapid change in Chinese cultural patterns began with the Sino-Japanese War over territorial rights in Korea. By 1895 the Japanese had successfully invaded Shantung and Manchuria and occupied the seaports that commanded the entrance to Peking. With the assistance of students educated in Japan, Chinese radicals overthrew the Manchu dynasty and established a provisional republic in 1912 with Yuan Shih-k'ai as head. By the time China declared war on Germany in 1917 China was on its way to political disintegration.

At the close of the war the political scene was dominated by the rise of the Nationalist Party under the leadership of Chiang Kai-shek and Communist sympathizers. During the postwar era these two forces engaged in a constant political and military struggle. At the conclusion of World War II in spite of General Marshall's attempt to negotiate peace between the two factions their hostility led to open civil war. By 1948 the Communists had driven the Nationalists out of provisional capitals at Nanking, Canton, and Chungking. In 1949 the Nationalists and their leader, Chiang Kai-shek, fled to Taipei in Formosa and left the Communists in control of China proper. In 1954 the Communists adopted the Constitution of the People's Republic of China.

SOCIAL AND EDUCATIONAL DEVELOPMENTS IN RED AND NATIONALIST CHINA

As soon as the Communists gained control of the Chinese mainland they introduced sweeping reforms in every segment of Chinese life. Among these were the redistribution of land to peasants, laborers, and tenants, the marketing and distribution of produce under the cooperatives, and the establishment of banking institutions and trade companies to stabilize the economic structure of the republic.

Education was brought under state control, and schools and colleges formerly operated under missionaries and foreign interests were confiscated. Education was made compulsory. Particular emphasis was placed upon technical training to meet the demands of industrialization, and secondary and higher education became increasingly directed toward the turning out of engineers, agronomists, and medical personnel.

Women were given social and political equality with men, child marriages were made illegal, and women were given the right to select their marriage partners. The right of women to property ownership, employment, and health insurance was also recognized. In Formosa the Nationalists, with the financial and military assistance of the United States, stabilized their economy and built up an effective fighting force. The educational system established by the Japanese before they occupied the island was reorganized. By 1952 approximately 80 percent of the children attended elementary school, and facilities for secondary and high education were extended.

PHYSICAL EDUCATION IN CHINA AND RED CHINA

The change of policy toward foreign intrusion during the Manchu dynasty favored the development of physical education in the schools. Foreign interests introduced the German and Swedish systems, which were eventually adopted in the training program of the police and armed forces. Students who attended universities in Europe and the United States returned with an enlarged knowledge of sports. Even more important were the contributions of the missionary schools and the YMCA to the acceptance of physical education and sports within the school program.

In reorganizing the educational system in 1902 the government introduced many Western subjects into the curriculums of the elementary and secondary schools. In 1905 physical education became a required part of the school program. To provide leadership, institutes were established and students were sent abroad for training. During the republic a Chinese Education Commission visited the United States and among its recommendations suggested that better professional training courses than those current in China be offered. Shortly thereafter a course of better quality was organized at Nanking Teachers College and at Soochow University under the joint sponsorship of the university officials and Dr. Willard Lyon, a pioneer YMCA worker in China. Through the efforts of Abby Shaw Mayhew, of the University of Wisconsin, who went to China in 1912 to help organize the program of the YWCA, the Physical Training School for Chinese Women in Shanghai was established. Additional professional courses were organized at the Gingling Girls College and Central China University. In 1929 the government enacted the Physical Education Law, establishing a directorate of physical education in the Ministry of Education. Supervisors of physical education were appointed and school programs were organized systematically throughout the nation.[8]

Under the republican regime programs in the elementary schools consisted of gymnastics, marching, and games. Programs in the secondary schools and colleges featured Swedish gymnastics and sports, including track and field athletics, soccer, basketball, baseball, and swimming. A 1921 report from Mukden indicated that all city schools had playing areas and were staffed by physical educators. A survey of facilities and equipment in 1930 showed a general improvement over former years.

Since the establishment of the People's Republic of China the government has followed the lead of the Soviet Union, and physical education is a requirement not only in the schools but also among industrial workers and peasants. Red China supports six institutes for the training of physical educators and athletic coaches, among them the Central Institute of Physical Culture in Peking.

SPORTS PROMOTION

Besides the contributions of the YMCA and foreign sports enthusiasts the greatest impetus to the sports movement in China was provided by the Far Eastern Olympic Games, organized in 1913. China sent forty athletes to the first meet at Manila and 200 to the games held in Shanghai in 1915. In the postwar years the first All-China National Meet was held at Wuchang, and hundreds of athletes representing schools, colleges, clubs, merchants, clerks, and laborers competed in track and field athletics, soccer, baseball, and tennis. In 1926 China's soccer team defeated the United States and Great Britain in their first international meet. In 1930 facilities were constructed at Mukden, Hangchow, Hankow, Nanking, and Shanghai. In the same year the government supported the All-China National Meet at Hangchow. More than 1000 athletes competed, and for the first time 200 were women.

The government of the People's Republic of China today promotes sports the length and breadth of the country. All educational institutions, industrial plants, and rural communities have their sports organizers and facilities. Red China has continued to conduct the All-China National Meet under the direction of the All-China Athletic Federation. In addition, there are gymnastic and track and field competitions among the secondary schools and colleges in the thirteen cities of the Port Arthur–Darien area, national athletic meets, championship contests for the National Student Sport Association, and international athletic meets with the Soviet Union and her satellite nations.[9]

Physical Education in Free China and Hong Kong

In the Republic of China a state director of physical education is appointed by the Ministry of Education to coordinate school programs throughout the republic. A National Physical Education Committee of specialists serves as an advisory body.

The program in the elementary schools consists of fifteen minutes of free exercises at the opening of school in the morning and thirty minutes' daily instruction through grades 1 to 6. Secondary schools and colleges follow the practice of morning exercise, plus fifty-minute instructional periods twice a week. An hour's sports activity a day is required of secondary school pupils; for college students it is elective. Intramural championship contests in ball games, cycling, cross-country runs, mountain climbing, and swimming are held spring and fall. All-city teams compete annually in a variety of sports. A department of physical education in the army plans the program for military personnel.

A department of physical education in the Taiwan Teachers College offers a course for the preparation of teachers in the secondary school and colleges. Normal schools offer training courses for elementary school teachers.

Professional sports do not exist on Formosa. The China National Amateur Athletic Federation governs all sports competitions, including the Olympic Games, Far Eastern Olympic Games, and the Asian Games. The Taiwan Provincial Athletic Association includes all voluntary sports organizations. It has seventeen member associations representing thirteen different sports. The more popular associations are basketball, baseball, regulation American football, and swimming. Every city in Taiwan has a stadium with a 400-meter running track, outdoor basketball courts, baseball diamonds, and a swimming pool.[10]

The fact that Hong Kong is a British crown colony has encouraged the development of sports in the government schools, but physical education as a required program has not fared so well. In 1948 the report of the director of education of Hong Kong stated that in twenty schools there were only one gymnasium and three playgrounds. The facilities in seventeen grants-in-aid schools were somewhat better: one had a gymnasium, fourteen had playgrounds, and two a swimming pool. Qualified physical education personnel are scarce since there is no professional training center and few teachers are imported. In 1950 the military authorities promised to provide teaching personnel and better facilities. Through the efforts of the South China Athletic Association and the Chinese YMCA interschool athletic competition has been organized in soccer football and basketball. The athletic event of the year in which all schools participate is the competition for the governor's shield. Interschool athletic competition is also held for girls.

JAPAN

During the reign of the Tokugawa family the Shogun Iyeyasu gave the Dutch permission in 1609 to establish a factory for trade in Hirado. This breech in the seclusion maintained by Japan for centuries was followed by the appearance of Portuguese Jesuits and Spanish Franciscan and Dominican friars on the islands close to Japan proper. The shoguns who followed Iyeyasu became suspicious of the Roman Catholic missionaries and pursued a methodical policy of annihilating them and their Christian converts. Out of fear of foreign aggression and the desire to stabilize their own government the shoguns became more and more antiforeign. In 1636 the Tokugawa government decreed that henceforth no Japanese vessel or citizen on penalty of death should leave Japan, all Spaniards and descendants of Spaniards should be expelled, and finally that no vessel of the seaworthy type should be built in the empire. The only exception was the Dutch, who had ingratiated themselves with the shoguns in various ways.

For more than 200 years the Japanese remained in seclusion. In 1853 Commodore Matthew Perry steamed into Uraga Harbor with four battleships, presented a request from the President of the United States for a commercial treaty, and after distributing mechanical toys and musical instruments left. The Japanese were thrown into a panic such as they had not known since the days of the Mongol invasion. They decided they had no choice but to accede to the request of the United States. When Commodore Perry returned in 1854 he was informed that Japan would open the ports of Shimoda in Izu and Hakodate, provide refuge for shipwrecked sailors, and permit ships to refuel and secure provisions in Japanese territory. Although sentiment in Japan remained against foreign intercourse the U.S. agreement paved the way for similar treaties with Russia, Holland, England, and other foreign countries.

When the 15-year-old Mutsuhito succeeded his father, Komei, as shogun in 1867, he decided that any further attempt to keep Japan in seclusion was useless. Without bloodshed the other shogunates forfeited their feudal rights and placed their hereditary lands at the disposal of the young emperor who became known as the honorable Meiji (Enlightened Government). Under the guidance of Meiji Japan was quickly transformed into a modern nation.

Toward the close of the century Japan secured control of Formosa, a free hand in Korea, and concessions from Russia in Manchuria. World War I ended disastrously for Japan, but during the 1920s she made many friendly overtures to foreign countries. The ensuing years, however, were marked by internal political struggles, and in the 1930s Japan emerged as a totalitarian state dedicated to aggressive imperialism. After World War II the most striking changes in Japan have been toward democratization and decentralization of governmental administration.

EDUCATION IN JAPAN

During the Meiji regime Japan accepted Western science and technology without altering her own cultural standards, for she had witnessed the loss of traditional values by other Asiatic countries that had been westernized. Since the Japanese adopted many of the educational and technological advances of Occidental nations they were unjustly called imitators.

In the modern era the Japanese have believed that elementary education should be compulsory but that secondary and higher education should be the privilege of the selected few. This approach is an exception to the general rule in Asiatic countries, which have created countless colleges of inferior quality, while neglecting elementary education. During the political unrest of the 1930s military instruction by regular army officers was introduced into the secondary schools.

In 1946 the United States Education Mission to Japan recommended that the power of the Ministry of Education should be restricted, that the operation of higher institutions should be independent of the central government, and that control of elementary and secondary schools should be placed in the hands of elected local school boards. Compulsory school attendance was raised from 6 to 9 years, secondary education extended to more children, coeducation encouraged, and the number of universities increased.

DEVELOPMENT OF PHYSICAL EDUCATION IN JAPAN

Before 1871 Japanese physical education and military training were one and the same: swordsmanship, fencing, archery, swim-wrestling, jujitsu, *kemari* (a kind of football), and hand-to-hand fighting. When the national school system was organized in 1871 the Swedish system was introduced into the elementary schools and the Dutch were invited to organize physical education in the secondary schools. By the close of the century the program was largely of the formal type, with emphasis on gymnastic and military drills. By 1910 the Swedish system had been adopted in both elementary and secondary schools, and in 1913 a department of physical education was organized in the Ministry of Education which prescribed a program consisting of gymnastics, games, and sports such as judo and fencing. After 1912, when Japan sent her first Olympic team to Stockholm, interest in sports increased rapidly, reaching a peak in 1932 when the Japanese swimming team returned victorious from the Los Angeles Olympic Games. For a short period the physical education program benefited from the sports fever and the emphasis shifted from gymnastics to games and sports.

In 1935 an imperial directive placed army personnel in charge of military training in the schools and the physical education program again changed character. Physical education became physical training with a military objective. Between 1935 and 1945 military training was an integral part of school life, and boys were instructed in squad drill, military maneuvers, rifle practice, bayonet fighting, and use of the hand grenade. In 1941 the department of physical education was changed to the Bureau of Physical Education, which was given the responsibility for a physical fitness program for defense and labor. One of the its unique innovations was the daily broadcast between 7:50 and 8:30 A.M. of physical exercises for elementary school children led by the classroom teacher.

MODERN TRENDS IN PHYSICAL EDUCATION

In 1945 the Allied powers in Japan reorganized the physical education program to eliminate any residual military emphasis. The Bureau of Physical Education was reorganized to include subdivisions in physical education, athletics, student welfare, and school hygiene. Physical education was made a required subject from elementary through secondary schools. Physical educators convened from every part of Japan to share in the formulation of a new program. In 1949 physical education was required in both old and newly created universities.[11]

The physical education program for girls and women in schools and universities continues to emphasize Danish and Swedish gymnastics. Considerable interest is shown in rhythmical gymnastics and dance in general. Simple folk games and square dancing are very popular. Women's sports include basketball, volleyball, and tennis. Swimming would be a favorite if facilities were available. Japanese girls particularly like field or play days (*Undaki*), featuring sports competition and various kinds of relays.

SPORTS DEVELOPMENT IN JAPAN

In 1873 the members of the American colony in Tokyo played baseball on their time off. The watching Japanese youngsters were fascinated by the game. By 1890 Japanese schools began to organize teams of their own, and as early as 1905 Waseda University sent a baseball team on a tour of the United States. Today Japanese travel thousands of miles to see the All-Japan High School Baseball Championship, and the annual game between Keio and Waseda universities draws 50,000 fans. Japan has thirteen major league clubs and any schoolboy knows the line-ups.[12]

In 1876 William Clark, an English teacher and former athlete at Cambridge University, introduced Japanese students at Sapparo Agriculture College to rowing and track and field athletics. In the

1900s Franklin H. Brown, YMCA director at Tokyo, acquainted Japanese youth with volleyball, basketball, and mass games. It was Brown's influence that sent the first Japanese team to the Stockholm Olympic Games in 1912. The Japanese also participated in the first Far Eastern Olympic Games and Asian Games.

Popular sports in Japan include Rugby and soccer football, which are winter sports played by high schools, colleges, and industrial teams. Basketball is gradually growing in popularity, particularly in the state of Nigata, where severe winters have encouraged the building of excellent indoor facilities. Ice hockey and figure and recreational skating are supported by six rinks in Tokyo, which are booked months ahead. Bowling is a new recreational activity, which the Japanese like but still find too expensive. Regulation American football is restricted to a few colleges, and an annual Rice Bowl is held. Badminton and softball are popular among girls and women. Other sports which promise to be favorites in the future include table tennis, sailing, golf, mountain climbing, and skiing.[12]

Many native sports have an ancient and military background. *Sumo* is a form of Japanese wrestling that dates back to the first century B.C. Like professional wrestling in the United States, *Sumo* televises well. *Sumo* wrestlers are very corpulent and go through an elaborate ceremony lasting fifteen minutes before they rush at one another like two steam locomotives. Jujitsu originated about 1500, and in its early form did not differ much from Occidental wrestling. Through the centuries schools of jujitsu were established which had their own rules for securing and breaking holds. In 1882 Dr. Jigoro Kano combined the best features of the various schools to create what he called judo. He made judo a defensive sport which used many Graeco-Roman techniques, such as throws over the buttocks and leg trips. The judo expert attempts to conclude the bout as soon as possible by securing a stranglehold or by placing a joint of the limb at a mechanical disadvantage. Karate came to Japan by way of the Ryukyu Islands and is probably, like jujitsu, of Chinese origin. The specialist in karate toughens the fingers, knuckles, and soles of the feet by pounding them against a rough surface. A karatist can split a layer of nine cedar boards with one blow and easily kill a man. When General MacArthur commanded the U.S. Army of Occupation he outlawed the Butokukai, the national association of karate specialists.[13]

SUMMARY

For centuries the racial families of Asia developed their particular cultures in comparative isolation until the arrival of Portuguese, Dutch, Spanish, French, and English traders in the sixteenth and seventeenth centuries. These foreign powers subjugated the native population in order to gain control of the rich mineral and agricultural resources of the East. In some instances foreign occupation proved beneficial to the native population, but in most cases it was little more than selfish exploitation. During World Wars I and II Asiatic countries became pawns in the balance-of-power struggle among European nations, and the war years stirred deep feelings of resentment against colonialism and a growing desire for self-determination. At the close of World War II many Asiatic countries took advantage of the period of reconstruction to set up independent states under the protection of the Western democracies, or adopted the Communist ideology.

In the vast populated areas of Asia life has become a matter of survival in a rugged environment. Primitive farming methods, superstition and ignorance, lack of medical services, hospitals, public health measures, and adequate diets have created many complex social problems. Vital statistics gathered in 1940 indicated that the average daily caloric intake of food ranged from a high of 2500 in the countries of the Near East to between 1800 and 2000 in the countries of India, Southeast Asia, and the Far East. The annual income in Israel, Japan, and Turkey averaged $115, while in Indonesia, India, Burma, Vietnam, Korea, and the Philippines it was $53. Infant mortality per thousand live births is probably one of the best single indexes of the material welfare of a people. In Sweden this mortality rate was .39 per thousand in 1940, while in Burma it was 208, in India 160, and in Japan 88. In facing the future Asiatic countries must resolve their social and economic problems if progress is to be made in their general education, physical education, and recreation.

Asiatic countries have centuries-old heritages of games, sports, and dances. These developed to meet the social, religious, and military needs of the people, and have survived the march of civilization. The adoption of Western educational methods brought in foreign programs of physical education with emphasis on gymnastics and drills. The YMCA and YWCA and individual enthusiasts aroused an interest in new games and sports and restored many ancient games and dances. However, the progress of physical education in the schools has been impeded by social taboos, the absence of a philosophy of physical education, the low status of its instructors, poorly trained and too few teachers, and inadequate facilities and equipment. School programs often ignore the rich heritage of local games and dances and concentrate on gymnastics and drills which will contribute to the annual exhibitions, in keeping with the Oriental love of pageantry and show. Since World War II Asiatic countries have shown an increased interest in more informal programs of physical education and in sports promotion. This modern trend has been assisted in nations under the influence of Western democracies by foreign financial aid and consultant services. In Communist-dominated countries it has been motivated by a desire to prepare the people for labor and defense and to gain world recognition through athletic supremacy.

OLYMPIC-TYPE COMPETITION IN ASIATIC COUNTRIES

Asiatic countries, inspired by the role of the Olympic Games in developing better international understanding, have organized athletic meets of a similar nature, even to the duplication of the ceremonies and general atmosphere. The Far Eastern Olympic Games held in Manila in 1913 started the movement of Asiatic Games organized along the lines of the Olympics. That the initial pioneer stage has passed and the games have reached maturity is indicated by the conduct of the Third Asian Games held in Tokyo. At these games the Emperor and Empress of Japan and the Shah of Iran were present in the stand of the forty-million-dollar stadium to review the parade of 1400 athletes representing twenty Asiatic countries. Michio Oda, Japan's first Olympic gold medal winner, completed the last lap of the 1000 runners assigned to carry the lighted torch from southern Japan to the stadium in Tokyo. So significant did the Asian Games Committee consider this reenactment of the Olympic Games ceremony that at the Second Asian Game in 1954 the torch was transported to southern Japan by a Japanese naval plane.

The spirit of the Olympic Games has set the pattern for other Asiatic countries. In the early 1930s the Asiatic countries located east of Suez and west of Singapore formed the Western Asiatic Games Federation and held the first Western Asiatic Games at New Delhi, India, in 1934. Countries in the South Pacific area are engaged in the promotion of an Inter-Pacific Sports Tournament, which may take on the stature of the South Pacific Games if Dr. Sahu Kahn of the Fiji Islands can secure the cooperation of the neighboring islands.

NOTES

1. Tedfor P. Lewis. "Health, Physical Education and Recreation." *Journal of Health, Physical Education and Recreation,* 20:3 (March, 1949), 159–161; 210–213.
2. Mabel Lee. "Physical Education in Iraq." *The Physical Educator,* 13:3 (October, 1956), 112–113.
3. Theodore Harder. "Physical Education and Athletics in Afghanistan." *Proceedings,* The College Physical Education Association, 1959, pp. 63–68.
4. *Physical Culture and Sport in Israel.* Government YearBook, Ministry of Education and Culture, Jerusalem, 5718, 1957.
5. Richard C. Havel. "Physical Education in Indonesia." *Proceedings,* The College of Physical Education Association, 1959, pp. 58–63.
6. Aquino Serafino. "The Physical Education Program in the Philippines." *Journal of Health, Physical Education and Recreation,* 20:7 (September, 1949), 450. Pedro Ablan. "Athletics in the Philippine Public Schools," *Proceedings,* First Asian Physical Education, Health and Recreation Congress, Manila, 1954, pp. 15–19.
7. Candido Bartolome. "Teacher-Training in Physical Education in the University of Philippines." *Proceedings,* First Asian Physical Education, Health and Recreation Congress, Manila, 1954, pp. 81–88.
8. Snowpine Lui. "The Physical Education Movement in China." *Journal of Health and Physical Education,* 3:4 (April, 1932), 17–21.
9. *Sports Flourishes in New China.* All-China Athletic Federation, Peking, 1955. *A General View on Physical Culture and Sports of New China.* (Edited by the Federation of Trade Unions of China) Peking, 1956.
10. Shitze P. Wu. "Physical Education in China." *Proceedings,* First Asian Physical Education, Health and Recreation Congress, Manila, 1954, pp. 39–49.

11. *Education in New Japan.* General Headquarters, Supreme Commander for Allied Powers, Civil Information and Education Section, Education Division, Tokyo (May, 1948) pp. 118–120; 324.
12. Herbert Warren Wind. "The Bouncing Ball." *Sports Illustrated,* 8:7 (February, 1958), 57; 59; Herbert Warren Wind. "Around the Mulberry Bush," *Sports Illustrated,* 8:8 (March, 1958) 61–62; 57–58.

Chapter 15

PHYSICAL EDUCATION IN LATIN AMERICA

POLITICAL EVOLUTION OF LATIN AMERICA

THROUGH the centuries political unrest and violence have played a major part in Latin-American history. After 300 years of Portuguese and Spanish domination, Simón Bolívar, the South American champion of liberty, freed Venezuela, José de San Martín overthrew the Spaniards in Argentina, and Chilean and Brazilian patriots won their freedom from Portugal in 1822. Freedom from European control was followed by internal conflicts between rival political groups, and revolutions became a trade-mark of Latin-American governments during the nineteenth and twentieth centuries. In spite of democratically written constitutions, Latin-American countries have been largely ruled by military dictatorships.

Economic and social progress has been retarded by the failure of nations to work together for the common good. Their histories are marked by border disputes and diplomatic intrigue. The first international congress was convened in 1826 by Bolívar, who dreamed of South American solidarity. In spite of many similar meetings since, social and educational progress has been exceedingly slow. The arrival of political freedom and higher standards of living in Latin America will not be accomplished painlessly, as is evidenced by recent revolutionary movements in Argentina, Bolivia, Cuba, El Salvador, and the Dominican Republic.

The United States grew concerned about foreign intervention in Latin America shortly after it became a nation, and in 1823 the Monroe Doctrine warned the countries of Europe not to interfere in the affairs of these nations. As a result of the Spanish-American War the United States helped Cuba gain her independence. President Theodore Roosevelt used armed force to protect American interests in Latin-American countries, and in 1899 the Pan-American Conference was organized to protect mutual interests and create goodwill. President Franklin D. Roosevelt inaugurated the Good Neighbor policy in the hope of improving relations, and in 1948 the Organization of American States was formed to strengthen inter-American relationships.

Unfortunately, many Latin-American countries still resent the United States, as shown by recent events in Cuba and other republics. This resentment, created by early United States exploitation, has been exacerbated by recent Communist infiltration. In an economic conference at Bogatá, Colombia, the United States proposed a new plan of social and economic aid similar to the Marshall Plan which played such an important part in the revival of European countries at the close of World War II. The U.S. has also furnished aid through the Inter-American Development Bank, Development Loan Fund, and numerous technical assistance programs.

SOCIAL AND ECONOMIC CONDITIONS

After the Spaniards had stripped the Indians of their treasures of gold and silver they were driven to mining operations for further exploitation and to agriculture for subsistence. At first they used native labor, but finding it unsatisfactory, they imported Negroes from Africa. The maintenance of a vast labor force in the mines and on the farms necessitated the importation of soldiers. These Spanish soldiers rarely brought their families with them and intermingled with Indian women to create a large population known as mestizos. The present population also includes full-blooded descendants of Spanish, Dutch, and French ancestry, plus mixtures of white, Indian, and Negro blood.

Spanish monarchs were zealous churchmen and never sent an

expeditionary force to the new country without a contingent of Catholic priests to convert the heathens. Their efficiency is attested to by the fact that approximately 90 percent of the Latin-American population is Roman Catholic. Fiestas, or religious holidays, are observed with religious rites, singing, dancing, and feasting. During their occupation the Spaniards left a taste for horse racing, bullfights, and a deep personal pride in titles.

More than half the population of working age in Latin America are employed on small farms or plantations (haciendas). In Central America and the islands of the Caribbean, bananas, cacao, rubber, coconuts, and chicle are raised. The main crop in Brazil, Guatemala, El Salvador, Haiti, and Colombia is coffee. Cuba, Jamaica, Puerto Rico, and the Dominican Republic raise sugar cane. Argentina and Uruguay are leading cattle- and wool-producing countries. Venezuela has rich oil fields; Colombia, Venezuela, the Guianas, and Brazil, gold and silver mines; Colombia, coal, iron, and emerald mines; and Surinam, beauxite ore. The economic welfare of these countries depends entirely upon the export of these raw materials, which are at the mercy of fluctuating prices. Authorities agree that the Latin-American countries should move toward greater industrialization, to create jobs and to raise standards of living.

Latin-American countries have a crucial shortage in housing, not only for the low-income population in the rural areas but also to accommodate the rural migration to the cities. The Peruvian and Brazilian governments have initiated ambitious housing projects, including schools and playground areas. These projects, however, are located in cities along the coast lines. Few towns in the interior have electricity or public transportation, and the people live in houses with thatched roofs and wood or mud walls.

HEALTH AND EDUCATION

The health problems of Latin-American countries are now the concern of the United States and the United Nations. Some countries have assumed the initiative themselves, as is evidenced by the aggressive movement in this century to establish national ministries of health. The chief health problems are the reduction of the infant mortality rate, the provision of medical service through hospitals and clinics, and the control of communicable diseases. Nutritional deficiencies continue to plague the poorer classes, who depend upon a diet heavy in sugars and starches, with a general absence of meat, milk, eggs, and vegetables. People located on the highlands and plains where cattle are raised fare somewhat better.

Education in Latin America is beset by the problems common to countries with low-income populations. In some countries half of the children do not attend school although compulsory education laws are on the books, and illiteracy in places runs as high as 70 percent. Responsibility for public schools and higher education generally rests with a Ministry of Education. The Ministry, in turn, delegates its responsibility to bureaus which implement the laws.

PHYSICAL EDUCATION IN SOUTH AMERICA

Early programs of physical education were influenced by various European systems of gymnastics. The theory and practice of these and other European philosophies of physical education still have a strong influence. In Brazil physical education was exposed successively to the German and French systems and eventually the theory and practice of YMCA physical directors.[1] Programs in Venezuela were closely associated with the military and then the Swedish system. A Belgian pedagogical mission represented by Henry De Genst and Julien Ficher introduced the Swedish system to Bolivia in the early 1900s. Chile became interested in the Swedish system through the influence of Scandinavians employed to survey the Trans-Andean railway route. The government sent Joaquin Cabezas García to Sweden in 1890 to make a study of *sloyd* (manual arts) and Swedish gymnastics and on his return appointed him national director of physical education.[2]

The French-Amorsian system of gymnastics was introduced into the Peruvian schools in 1905. In 1906 physical education became a required subject. In 1919 the Peruvian program consisted of a combination of games and sports and the French system of natural gymnastics devised by Georges Hébert.[3] Colombia favored the Swedish system. In Argentina physical education was started in the secondary schools in 1898 and in the elementary schools in 1905; the programs were mainly Swedish gymnastics and games.

As a result of the promotional work of the YMCA and the widespread interest in amateur sports, games and sports have been added to the school programs, though South American physical educators are still committed to the European philosophy that instruction in gymnastics is essential for the all-round development of the child. Popular sports include soccer, baseball, basketball, volleyball, and track and field athletics. There is also some emphasis on native folk and other forms of dancing. Since higher institutions generally have fairly well-developed programs, the tendency has been to leave the physical education requirements to the discretion of the individual institution. In 1951 the Pan American Institute of Physical Education, however, recommended that higher institutions provide organized physical education programs.

South American countries in general follow the pattern of European countries in state organization, supervision of physical education in the schools, and the control of voluntary sports organizations. In Argentina the Bureau of Physical Education supervises physical education and controls sports in the public schools. In Chile sports competition is conducted in the elementary and secondary schools under the supervision of the Primary School Sports Federation and School Sports Association. These associations are administered by the Chief Inspector of Physical Education, responsible to the Minister of Education. Paraguay has established a National Council of Physical Education which consists of three sections, Physical Education, Sports, and Scouts, each with its administrative head.

TEACHER PREPARATION

Teacher preparation as a general rule is controlled by the Ministry of Education. Again Europe has set the pattern, and professional schools are called Institutes of Physical Education. The Chilean government established an institute for teachers in gymnastics at Valparaiso in 1906 and appointed Joaquin Cabeza García as director. This institute later became part of the Institute of Physical and Technical Education. About the same time the government of Argentina directed Dr. Enrique Romero Brest to organize the National Institute of Physical Education, which later became an affiliate of the National University. The Institute of

General Belgrano at Buenos Aires also provides professional preparation and is open to both men and women. In Brazil the National School of Physical Education and Sports is a branch of the National University at Rio de Janeiro, and it also offers a one-year course in the theory and practice of physical education for medical students. Brazil also has a professional school for women, the Institute of Physical Education for Girls at Rio de Janeiro.

In 1932 Peru established the Instituto Nacional de Educación Física, which in 1946 was absorbed by the College of Education of the San Marcos National University of Lima. In the late 1930s Ecuador founded the Institute of Physical Education, which offered a three-year course for physical educators and two-year courses for athletic coaches and teachers of rhythmics and the dance. In 1945 Paraguay abandoned the older Institute of Physical Education for the new National School of Physical Education built on a sixteen-acre tract at Asunción. In Bolivia a professional curriculum was organized in 1926–1927 in affiliation with the University of La Paz, which was later recognized as the Institute of Physical Education.

All these institutes furnish the teaching and supervisory personnel for the public schools and higher institutions of the entire nation. The number of graduates annually ranges from twenty in Colombia to much larger numbers in countries like Argentina and Brazil. Regardless of the number of leaders produced, they would be inadequate to meet the demand if the many national programs now on paper were to be put into actual operation. South American countries have in general placed little emphasis on graduate education. This again is a result of the European attitude that candidates for advanced degrees should be qualified to do productive research in human mechanics and the physiology of exercise.

PROFESSIONAL GROWTH IN PHYSICAL EDUCATION

The foundations of the South American Conference of Physical Education Teachers Association were laid in the period prior to World War I, in what was known then as the Continental Convention of South American Associations. The charter members of the Conference held a second meeting in Buenos Aires in 1919, where they decided to establish an Amateur Athletic Union to regulate sports competition, publish sports rules and technical books, and promote national interest in the folk dances of each country.

The first Pan-American Congress of Physical Education was held in 1943 at Rio de Janeiro, its stated purpose being the general improvement and scientific orientation of physical education. A second conference was held in Mexico City in 1946, at which the members declared that physical education was a vital force for social justice and liberty, and discussed ways and means whereby the friendship could be strengthened among the nations of the Western Hemisphere.

The Third Pan-American Congress was sponsored in 1950 by the Physical Education Commission of Uruguay, and the meeting was held at Montevideo. The professional leaders represented included Paul A. Previtalli and Carlos M. Barragan of Uruguay; Dr. Luis Bisquert, University of Chile; Major Jão Barbosa Leite, Brazil; and Dr. E. R. Brest of Argentina and President of the South American Conference of Physical Education Teachers Association. Dorothy Ainsworth, Hiawatha Crosslin, Norma Young, and C. H. McCloy represented the United States and the AAHPER, and Felicio M. Torregrosa, University of Puerto Rico, the West Indies.

At the Montevideo meeting the representatives interested in sports medicine organized their own group. The leaders in this field included Julio A. Mondria, Argentina; Guillerme de Souza Gomez, Luis H. Maluf and Waldemar Areño, Brazil; Luis Bisquert, Chile; and José Faravelli Musante and Francisco Devincenzi, Uruguay. The main business of the conference was the program of physical education in the elementary school and the relationship of health and physical education. The next Pan-American Congress of Physical Education was held at Bogotá, Colombia, in 1953.[4]

SPORTS INTERESTS IN SOUTH AMERICA

The more popular sports associations in South American countries are combined in national sports federations while those with a limited following have separate federations. The Brazilian Sports Confederation, as an example, controls soccer, swimming, tennis, rowing, and track and field athletics, and other sports have their own bodies who regulate participation and conduct meets. Sports competition in Peru is under the jurisdiction of the National Committee of Sports, which represents the various amateur athletic associations as well as the National Commission on Recreation. In Argentina sports are conducted by the municipalities. In Chile the National Sports Council was organized in 1938 to regulate sports associations and federations. A report in 1948 indicated that Chile had 12 federations, 296 sport associations, and 1900 athletic clubs, with a total membership of 350,000. These figures, however, do not include the many athletic clubs which were not members of the National Sports Council. These free-lance clubs do not receive financial assistance from the government and represent informal teams organized in towns, rural sections, and among workers. The city of Santiago, for instance, listed 400 nonaffiliated athletic clubs in 1939. Clubs of this nature sometimes form the basis of more permanent organizations which eventually join sports associations.[2]

The popularity of sports varies from nation to nation, but soccer holds first place for participants and spectators alike. The Maracana Stadium in Rio de Janeiro seats 150,000 spectators, and police protection is needed to keep the fans away from the players, who are idolized as national heroes. The government of Brazil built a horseshoe stadium in São Paulo in the early 1940's which seats 80,000 spectators of soccer, swimming, and track and field events. In Brazil soccer, basketball, and volleyball are the most popular amateur sports, while horse racing and riding, polo matches, and alligator hunting have their share of devotees.

In Argentina as many as 300,000 spectators turn out on a Saturday or Sunday afternoon for a single soccer match. Baseball and boxing are also popular. In Argentina golf, enjoyed by people in every walk in life, is favored by excellent climate and a diversity of topography that lends itself to the construction of challenging courses. Although bullfighting has been banned by most South American countries, it remains a favorite entertainment in Colombia and Peru.

Chileans are very sports-minded, and the 3000 miles of mountain ranges and 4000 miles of coast line provide excellent skiing, mountain climbing, boating, sailing, and deep-sea and fresh water fishing. Skiing, like physical education, was introduced to the Chileans by the Scandinavian engineers who surveyed the route of the Trans-Andean railroad in 1880. In the 1930s a Swiss ski instructor, Wendell Hilty, who appreciated the great potentialities for skiing on the slopes of the Andes, did considerable promotional work in the country. In 1935 A. R. Edwards built the first ski cabin in the Farcelones, and thereafter the sport gained rapidly in popularity. The Chileans are recognized internationally for their superb horsemanship and thoroughbred racing stock.

Bolivia is noted for its excellent hunting, and both the Indian with his bow and arrow and the modern Nimrod can stalk wild pigs, deer, and turkey. In the 1940s the Bolivian and Peruvian governments stocked Lake Titicaca with trout from the Great Lakes, which present a challenge to any fisherman. In addition, Bolivia has excellent deep-sea fishing, which furnishes food for the natives and sport for the fisherman.

SPORTS INDIGENOUS TO SOUTH AMERICA

A game called *El Pato*,[5] or the duck, is played in Argentina. It is said to have been developed by the gaucho herders and Calchaqui Indians in the seventeenth century. The original game was played on horseback and the ball (duck) was made of rawhide furnished with four leather loops to serve as handles. Inside the ball was a roasted duck. The object of the game was to deliver *El Pato* to a designated ranch while opposing horsemen attempted to intercept the rider assigned the task. Since the horsemen had to gain possession of *El Pato* while in the saddle, the scuffling that ensued often resulted in falls that led to serious injury or death beneath the thrashing hooves of the horses.

In 1840 the dictator of Argentina placed a ban on the sport, and it was not until 1937 that Alberto del Castillo Posse revived it. Posse drew up new rules, and in 1938 presented an exhibition game before government officials. The modern game is played on a field 100 by 200 yards with basket goals at each end. Four horsemen constitute a team, and although body contact is prohibited the game is vigorous and exciting. In 1941 Argentina formed the Pato Federation, with a membership of twenty-four clubs.

The Brazilians play a court ball game called pelota, which was played in the Basque provinces of Spain centuries ago. The word "pelota" means ball, and in Madrid, Barcelona, Buenos Aires, Havana, Mexico City, and Miami the game is called *jai alai* or *pelota vasca,* one of the fastest games in the world. In Cuba pelota means baseball, which has the same popularity it has in the United States and Japan. Pelota can be played with bare hands against a front wall (*frontón*) very much like modern one-wall handball. However, it becomes a much faster game when long, leather or wooden, glove-like protectors (*cesta*) are worn or sickleshaped, wickerwork implements (*chistera*) are employed in returning the ball. Several players can participate, but in championship matches three players, two forwards and a back, make up a side. On the serve the ball must be returned by the opposing players to the *frontón* above a line 3 feet from the floor. Some courts resemble a one-wall handball court, and others are enclosed on three sides with a wall 30 feet in height bounding a playing area 55 by 100 feet. The ball is a little smaller than a baseball and resembles it in construction. Players have been known to bounce the pelota 3 feet from the *frontón* and strike it with such force with the *chistera* that it rebounds 80 feet. At the National University of Mexico City the students play an adaptation of pelota called frontennis on courts walled on three sides and 100 feet in length. The ball employed is the official one-wall handball, and the striking implement is a regulation tennis racket with the gut strung to a 45-pound tension.[6] In Colombia the people play a game called *tejo* (tay-ho) which they inherited from the Chicha Indians. The modern version employs metal rings weighing about 2 pounds which the players throw at a circle of metal imbedded in the earth 60 feet away. The closest ring scores, and the equivalent of a ringer in horseshoes is signaled when a ring strikes one of the four containers of gunpowder placed equidistant on the imbedded circle. *Tejo* courts, like the handball courts in old Ireland, are standard equipment in the taverns of Colombia. The Colombians have a saying that love without kisses is like *tejo* without beer.

CONTINENTAL AND PAN-AMERICAN GAMES

The first all-South American athletic meet was held in Buenos Aires in 1910, and the participating nations were Argentina, Brazil,

Chile, and Uruguay. Subsequent meets were held in Montevideo and Santiago. At these meets South American countries ran into difficulties with the English terms used in track and field athletics. In many cases no equivalents existed in Spanish or Portuguese; thus the broad jump became "The long leap without impulse," which would make poor copy for the printed program and other communication media.

In 1942 the American Olympic Association changed its title to the United States of America Sports Federation, with two major subcommittees assigned to the International Olympic Games and the Pan-American Games. Plans had been initiated under the leadership of Avery Brundage, President of the Sports Committee, to hold the Pan-American Games at Buenos Aires in 1942, but World War II forced cancellation of the games. The Pan-American Sports Congress, representing twenty-nine nations, successfully launched the Pan-American Games at Buenos Aires in 1951. These games were patterned after the Olympic Games and had as their purpose the strengthening of inter-American relationships. On the basis of total-point score Argentina was victor, trailed by the United States, Chile, and Brazil. Twenty-two nations competed in the second Pan-American Games held in the rarefied atmosphere of Mexico City 7400 feet above sea level. The United States dominated the track and field events, while Mexico swept the boards in equestrian events. The Third Pan-American Games, held in 1959 at Soldier Field, Chicago, was underwritten by the United States, which provided five million dollars (Public Law 833) to be used at the discretion of the Pan-American Committee. For the first time the Pan-American Winter Games were held at Lake Placid, New York.

RECREATION IN SOUTH AMERICA

At the close of World War I considerable interest was manifested in recreational programs in municipalities and schools. In Ecuador the Division of Physical Education and Sports developed recreation centers, playgrounds, and public baths. Rio de Janeiro provided organized recreation as early as 1930 and began constructing a system of parks, playgrounds, and swimming pools. During the depression era Buenos Aires expanded her summer recreation program into a year-round program. Brazil calls her playground areas

Plazas ejercicion Fisicos, or literally, "places for physical exercise." The Buenos Aires' program includes physical education, games and sports, vacation day camps for children, arts and crafts, music and singing, social activities, library services, and participation in fiestas. Parks are generous in expanse and equipped with buildings that house kitchen facilities, dining halls, and storage rooms. South American children gain camping experience through scouting and public camps established for undernourished children. The Buenos Aires day camps resemble the type so popular in the United States where the campers arrive in the morning and return home in the afternoon.[7]

South Americans participate in many forms of recreation associated with their workday lives and religious celebrations. From the Spanish they inherited a love of pomp and pageantry, and the people of every country enjoy military parades, fiestas, carnivals, and religious ceremonies. Work comes to a halt and merchants close their stores as all join in preparation to celebrate. A parade may take a day, while a fiesta or carnival may last several days. In Colombia folk dance festivals are popular, with early native dances and colorful costumes. At San José de Sucro near Lima, Peru, a Grape and Wine Festival is held annually which includes prayers of thanksgiving, parades of floats, games, and dancing. South Americans are also fervent theater goers and during the spring months attend outdoor performances of plays and musicals.

MEXICO

The Aztecs, a native Indian tribe known as Mexica, inhabited the present region of Mexico as nomadic hunters. These people emerged into Mexican history about the year 1000, when they took possession of the country. In 1325 the Aztecs established a permanent settlement on the marshy island near the Lake of Tezcoco which they named Tenochtitlán (Mexico City). The tribal family at this time numbered several thousand, but within the space of two centuries, or at the close of the reign of Montezuma II, they had reached 200,000. In this short span of time the Aztecs built their impressive pyramid-like temples, accumulated fabulous treasures in gold and silver, developed their knowledge of mathematics, astronomy, and medicine, and constructed an amazing number of causeways, aqueducts, and public buildings.

When Hernando Cortes landed in Vera Cruz in 1519 the people held in subjugation by the Aztecs gave aid to the invaders and the Aztec military force fell before Cortes' superior generalship, armament, and tactics. With Mexico City as a base of operation, the Spaniard accumulated a domain that extended from St. Augustine, Florida, to New Orleans, thence north to St. Louis and west via Sante Fe to San Francisco.

The spirit of liberalism that manifested itself in other parts of the world in the early 1800s sparked a movement toward independence in the Spanish colony. In 1821 Augustín de Iturbide, a creole ex-officer in the Spanish Army, made a successful diplomatic and military coup and established independence.

In his victory negotiations Iturbide insisted that the Catholic Church be assigned exclusive control of the education of some six million people, of whom about 30,000 were literate. The Church in this era was more concerned with the preparation of upper-class youth for the priesthood and law than with general education, and had founded the Royal and Pontifical University of Mexico in 1553. During the first hundred years of its independence Mexico experienced many political revolutions.

In the twentieth century Mexico has enjoyed industrial and agricultural development, increased trade and commerce, reorganization of the educational system, and internal improvements. In 1953 Mexican women were granted universal suffrage, and in 1954 Presidents Ruiz Cortines and Dwight D. Eisenhower pledged continued cooperation between Mexico and the United States.

Social and Educational Developments

The modern Mexican is the end product of an ethnic blending of various Indian tribes, Negroid elements, mestizos, and European stock. These ingredients have been so mixed in the crucible of time that the government census no longer bothers to designate degrees of blood relationship or ethnic heritage. The term "Indian" is applied to about one-half of the population, who live mainly in the rural districts. These people go barefoot or wear sandals, dress in native costume, and exist on maize and beans. The other half of the population wear European-or American-made clothes, sleep in beds rather than hammocks or on the ground, eat a varied diet accompanied by wheat bread, and feel that they are modern. Thus in Mexico, as in the South American countries, the great middle class is missing, and the social structure is divided into the ignorant and underprivileged "Indian" on the one hand and the intellectuals and business class on the other.

Mexico expends a great deal of public money on the expansion of elementary education, and in 1952 elementary schools numbered 26,000, with 55,000 teachers and 4,000,000 pupils. In 1926 the government authorized federal support of secondary schools, and by 1951 such schools represented more than half of the 550 secondary schools supported by the state and other agencies in Mexico. Thanks to the zealous efforts of former presidents to improve education in rural areas the Mexican government makes a distinction between its promotion of urban and rural schools. The success of its "action" rural schools in extending educational opportunities to children in the rural sections has been phenomenal. The census figures of 1922 showed 309 action schools and in 1950, 16,868. Since the need of rural education is so urgent, not only in Mexico but in other Latin-American countries, the Organization of American States and the Educational and Social Council of the United Nations have jointly sponsored a regional center for elementary education at Pátzcuaro, Michoacán. Fellowships are granted Latin-American teachers to encourage attendance at this regional center. All universities in Mexico are either federally or state supported with the exception of the fabulous, autonomous National University at Mexico City, which was a municipal dream brought to reality in 1952.

PHYSICAL EDUCATION IN MEXICO

According to Oscar Castillon, beyond the activities of a few athletic clubs and two YMCA associations very little interest was manifested in physical education in Mexico before 1910.[8] The Military College of Mexico provided a program of physical training for its cadets which consisted of Swedish gymnastics and apparatus work after the German system. During the administration of President Venustiano Carranza (1914–1920) the government began to encourage physical education and sports. A program of physical education was introduced at the University of Mexico in 1918, and the Federación Atlética Mexicana was organized in 1920. Interest in physical education and sports continued to grow, and each succeeding government head not only sponsored physical education in city schools but sent missions to remote rural areas to promote and teach games and sports.

In 1933 the Mexican government appointed a National Physical Education Committee to promote physical education, sports, and recreation. This body assisted communities throughout Mexico in appointing councils to survey local needs for physical education and recreation. The results of the surveys motivated the government to seek the assistance of leaders from Europe and the United States in the organization of programs. To satisfy the demand for trained personnel the National Institute of Physical Education was established at Mexico City in 1936, under the supervision of the Bureau of Physical Education in the Ministry of Education. This institute offered a three-year professional course, and by 1941 had graduated 600 physical education and sports leaders.

Progress in Sports in Mexico

The Mexicans had been introduced to sports prior to World War I through the efforts of sports-minded individuals, YMCA leadership, and relations with the United States and South America. The sports movement received considerable encouragement from President Carranza, and after the war from Presidents Plutarcho Calles and Pascual Ortiz Rubio. In 1923 the Mexican Olympic Committee was organized, and since 1924 Mexico has sent a team to every Olympic Games. Mexican athletes have been outstanding in equestrian events, pistol and trap shooting, basketball, and boxing.

The Mexican government served as the first host to the Central American Games in 1926, with Cuba and Guatemala in attendance. By 1930 Mexico reported 2000 athletic clubs, with a membership of 150,000, of whom 20,000 were women. During this period Mexico City developed one of the largest recreation centers in the world, the Centro Social Deportivo Venustiano Carranza. Public recreation centers, private athletic fields, gymnasiums, swimming pools, tennis courts, and baseball diamonds made their appearance in great numbers. Stadiums were constructed in Mexico City, Jalpa, Guadalajara, and Torreón, and Monterrey built one of the finest physical education plants in the country.[8]

In 1933 President A. L. Rodriguez established the Confederation of Mexican Sports, which in organization and function resembled the Amateur Athletic Union of the United States, and had jurisdiction over seventeen amateur sports. In 1933 Mexico participated in the Pan-American Athletic Games held at Los Angeles and was a regular participant in subsequent games in Mexico City (1934) and Panama City (1938).

Mexico organized the Pan-American Junior Pentathlon in 1933 to encourage international athletic competition among the youths of the Western Hemisphere. This meet was open to all youths 17 years of age and under and provided participation for more than a half-million youngsters in Central and South America and the Caribbean countries.

In 1940 the Mexican government sent the naval gunboat *Durango* on a goodwill tour to Chile, Peru, Ecuador, Colombia, and Panama with an entourage of athletes who competed with their neighbors in equitation, track and field events, basketball, fencing, swimming, tennis, and pistol and trap shooting. In addition to these inter-American athletic contests, the University of Mexico competes with colleges and universities of the United States on a home-to-home basis in regulation American football and basketball. Baseball is an already well-established sport, and basketball and football are rapidly gaining popularity.

Construction of Sport Facilities

The support of President Cárdenas and the promotional work of the Confederation of Mexican Sports had a stimulating effect upon the construction of sports and recreation facilities in the 1940s. Many stadiums, swimming pools, and playing fields were built in communities throughout Mexico. The federal government financed the construction of five large recreation centers in Mexico City, Central Mexico; Irapuato, Guanajuato; and Mérida, Yucatán.

More than 3,000 basketball courts were built, many in high-altitude areas which required the blasting of mountain ridges to level the surface. Facilities for sports in Mexico for the year 1942 included 750 soccer fields, 1500 volleyball courts, 350 baseball and 150 softball diamonds, 250 tennis courts, 88 *jai alai, frontennis,* and handball courts, 50 regulation Olympic swimming pools, 32 rodeo rings, and 18 gymnasiums.[9] These are a good index of the relative popularity of specific sports in Mexico.

As the Aztecs had built the great temple of Teocalli at Tenochtitlán in 1486, President Ruiz Cortines, as one of his last public benefactions in 1959, built a sports temple on 500 acres of a former slum area which he called Sports City. This sports center, one of the finest in the Western Hemisphere, includes 53 soccer fields, 16 regulation American football fields, 26 basketball courts, 3 track and field stadiums, 4 Olympic swimming pools, stadiums for cycling and automobile racing, auditoriums, bullfighting rings, theaters, children's playgrounds, parks, fountains, and landscaped gardens. Sports City also has generous dressing rooms, shower facilities, and lounges.

THE REPUBLICS OF CENTRAL AMERICA

Central America is the isthmus which separates North and South America and includes, besides several Mexican states and the territory of Quintana Roo, the republics of Guatemala, Honduras, El Salvador, Nicaragua, Costa Rica, and Panama. In prehistoric times the region represented by Guatemala and Honduras and the Mexican states of Yucatán, Campeche, and Chiapas was inhabited by one of the most elaborate Indian civilizations of the Western Hemisphere. The Mayan tribes who lived here had exceptional ability in mathematics, astronomy, and architectural design and domesticated a large variety of maize and beans, some of which found their way to North America via Mexico and the tributaries of the Mississippi River.

The Mayan racial family probably came from the southwestern part of the United States. By voluntary migration or compulsion the Mayans moved to the safety of Central America, taking with them the games, sports, and dances of their ancestors.

In 1519 when Hernando Cortes began the conquest of the Aztecs in Mexico, his lieutenant, Pedrarias, established the city of Panama. The city eventually became the seat of the Spanish government, and Negroes were imported for pearl diving and as merchandise in one of the greatest slave markets in Spanish America. Pedro de Alvarado, another lieutenant of Cortes, advanced from Mexico to subjugate the Indian civilizations in Guatemala and El Salvador. Pedrarias and Cortes joined forces to conquer Nicaragua. Honduras was added to the Spanish domain by Cristóbal de Olid, who, when he discovered gold, forgot his obligations to the crown. Cortes, after one of the most spectacular marches in history through the jungles of Central America, righted the wrong. Costa Rica, which had been ignored by the Spaniards, was settled by other European countries about the middle of the sixteenth century.

THE PEOPLE AND EDUCATION OF CENTRAL AMERICA

Over one-half the population of Central America lives on the narrow slopes of the Pacific coast line. This area is much higher and drier than the interior and therefore more habitable. In the Caribbean lowlands extending through British Honduras the population is extensively Negro, and these people intermarried with the scattered Indian tribes of the Mosquito, Paya, and Carib. The products of this cross-fertilization are called zambos, or sambos. The remainder of the population includes white descendants of the Spanish colonists and a mixture of Spanish and other European stock with native Indians and Negroes. Costa Rica has a large population of pure Spanish stock mixed with English and German blood lines. El Salvador is predominantly populated by mestizos, while Guatemala has the largest Indian population in Central America.

The highland Indians of Guatemala and Chiapas are the most unusual and colorful primitive people in the world. They speak a Mayan dialect and in their dress, primitive living habits, and religious ceremonies are equally distinctive. The Chiapas Indians have developed arts and crafts to a high technical perfection which for sheer beauty and originality are difficult to duplicate. Religious ceremonies combine a veneer of Catholicism with pagan rites, and their festive celebrations provide a pageantry of color and dance which are unequaled in the world.

State education in the republics of Central America strongly resembles that of other Latin-American countries. The responsibility for control and distribution of funds is lodged in a Ministry of Education with its subdivisions. All republics have compulsory school laws which require children to attend until they reach working age, but rural areas tend to ignore the law. Elementary education is sorely handicapped by lack of qualified teachers, school facilities, and supplies. Although elementary schools are financed to a lesser or greater degree by the republics, secondary school education is supported by fees and tuition.

PHYSICAL EDUCATION IN CENTRAL AMERICA

Because of their proximity to Mexico and South American countries the physical education programs of Central American schools have a strong similarity. Programs in urban schools, therefore, consist of gymnastics, games, sports, and rhythmics. Sports are conducted after school hours, and there is interschool competition in such sports as track and field athletics, soccer, basketball, baseball, swimming, and tennis. Where urban areas are too small to support interscholastic competition, intramural competition is popular.

In poorer districts organized physical education programs in the schools are practically nonexistent. The school buildings themselves are poorly constructed, and often reclaimed buildings and warehouses serve as substitutes for urgently needed schoolhouses. Under these circumstances schools depend upon open areas near the school building for playgrounds, and the children with or without supervision play the games and perform the dances which have been handed down through generations. Many of the republics have indicated a desire to improve these conditions, and have appointed committees to consider reorganizing physical education programs. Guatemala, for example, in 1955 appointed such a committee and invited consultants from other countries, among them Dorothy Ainsworth from the United States.

Central American countries formerly imported physical educators from Europe and other Latin-American countries. In the past decade some of these countries have gradually established courses in normal schools and universities to train their own teaching personnel. In the Canal Zone, which is under U.S. jurisdiction, physical education teachers are brought from the States. Panama at one time sought to entice physical education teachers trained in the United States by offering travelling expenses and attractive salaries. Experience showed that these tourist-teachers proved, in general, a poor investment because of their short tenure, but three-to-five-year contracts improved the situation.

SPORTS DEVELOPMENT IN CENTRAL AMERICA

Between 1910 and 1920 many sports associations and clubs were founded in the urban areas of the more progressive countries. Sports competition among individual clubs and national teams from Central and South American and Caribbean countries were common in this era. Early in the spring of 1923 Count Henri Baillet Latour, associated with the International Olympic Committee, made visits to Cuba, Panama, Mexico, and several South American countries. Count Latour was impressed by Latin-American interest in sports, and through his influence and the organizing ability of E. Aquirie, a Springfield College graduate, a Congress of Central American Games was formed. As members of this Congress, Mexico, Costa Rica, Panama, El Salvador, and Guatemala were invited to send representatives to Paris in 1924 under the auspices of the International Committee.

The Congress adopted a *"Carta Fundamental"* for the conduct of the Central American Games. Mexico was designated as the first host in 1926, with Cuba to follow in 1930. The International Olympic Committee pledged that it would patronize the games if the Central American countries carried out the Congress' agreement. It was decided that the events should include track and field events, fencing, baseball, pistol and trap shooting, basketball, swimming, and tennis. The winner of the Central American Games at Mexico City was the host country, followed by Cuba and Guatemala. In 1930 Cuba lived up to her role as host country by sending battleships to collect the athletes from the nine participating Central American countries.

Since the first Pan-American Athletic Games held in Los Angeles in 1933, Central American countries have been regular participants. In the reorganization of these games under the title of Pan-American Games, Guatemala, Panama, Costa Rica, Nicaragua, and El Salvador have sent athletes to represent their countries in the 1951, 1955, and 1959 Pan-American Games. Several Central American countries also send athletes to the Olympic Games, and one of these, Guatemala, has been particularly successful in pistol and trap shooting, fencing, wrestling, gymnastics (women), weight-lifting, swimming, track and field athletics, and cycling.

THE WEST INDIES (GREATER ANTILLES)

Cuba, Santo Domingo, and Puerto Rico are three large islands arranged in a slanting line about 1200 miles in length. A fourth island, Jamaica, lies south of these three. The four make up what is called the Greater Antilles to distinguish them from the Antipodes, Andes, Antibes, and smaller islands of the archipelago classed as the Lesser Antilles. Cuba is the largest island in the group, with a land area greater than Santo Domingo, Puerto Rico, and Jamaica combined.

CUBA

Columbus discovered Cuba on his first voyage, and later this country became one of the links in the Spanish chain for operations against Mexico and explorations in Florida. Cuba remained almost continuously in the possession of Spain until the Spanish-American War, after which the United States assumed a protectorate role until 1902. In this year Cuba formed a republic and took over the government from military authorities. The United States was probably a little hasty in granting Cuba independence since its political climate through the years has been characterized by strife leading to a rapid succession of presidents and eventually a dictator with Communist support.

The Spaniards so completely dominated the aboriginal Indians in Cuba that no mestizo population of consequence emerged. Instead, Cuba has a large mulatto population, the result of the miscegenation of Negro slaves and whites until slavery was abolished in 1886. The number of pure Spaniards in Cuba is large compared with other Latin-American countries.

Elementary education in Cuba is compulsory and supported by

the state. In 1945, 570,000 children of school age attended school and an equal number did not. Vocational schools in the municipalities and agricultural schools in the provinces are an important part of the government's educational program. Teachers in the elementary and secondary schools attend normal schools, or receive their training at the University of Havana (1728) or Oriente, Santiago de Cuba (1947).

SANTO DOMINGO (DOMINICAN REPUBLIC AND HAITI)

The island of Santo Domingo was held by the Spaniards as a colony until the Treaty of Ryswick in 1697, when the Haitian portion was ceded to France and the remainder stayed in Spanish possession. Through the years both the French and Spanish tried through military force to unite the island under one flag. In 1844 the Dominican Republic was formed from the old Spanish colony, while Haiti continued to remain under the French protectorate. Under self-government the Dominican Republic experienced constant political conflict, and in 1869 the republic requested annexation by the United States. Unfortunately, political sentiment in the United States at that time was against such a move. Since then the U. S. has stepped in several times to assist the Dominican Republic in the stabilization of its economy. There are no natural boundaries between Haiti and the Dominican Republic, and border skirmishes are frequent between the armed forces of the two countries.

Both the French and the Spanich utilized Negro slaves on the sugar plantations, and as a consequence the population is a mixture of white and Negro blood. The French, however, made an attempt to educate their mulattoes, while the Spanish left education to chance in the Dominican Republic. The language, culture, and cuisine of Haiti are basically French with Negro modifications. The Dominican Republic, on the other hand, stresses Aryan superiority and uniformity of customs, language, and political ideology. The Haitians, with the exception of the European diplomatic corps, are plagued with problems of nutrition and child and maternal health. The peoples who live in the fishing villages along the coast lines of both countries are better nourished than those who live in the mountainous regions.

The French not only provided Haiti with a system of elementary education but made it compulsory and free in 1910. In rural areas, however, the system works very imperfectly. Although education has made considerable progress in recent years, general ignorance prevails among the adult population. Roman Catholicism has been the state religion since 1869, but superstition prevails and the mystic rites of voodoo are still practiced. The University of Haiti was founded in 1921 and a normal school for women teachers in 1924. In the Dominican Republic elementary education is supported by the local community with grants-in-aid from the government. Secondary schools and the National University are supported by the government.

PUERTO RICO

Of all the countries of the Greater Antilles Puerto Rico is the most European. After the Spanish-American War the United States established a military government in Puerto Rico from 1898 until 1900, when Congress provided a civil government. In 1917 Puerto Rico became a territory of the United States "organized but unincorporated," and citizenship was conferred collectively, with the right of the natives to retain the old status if so desired.

In their serach for profitable territory in the Greater Antilles the Spaniards considered Puerto Rico to have the least potential, and as a consequence the island has fewer people of Negro extraction. The standard of living is the highest in the Caribbean, and education and public health are the best in Latin America. A certain social problem has been created between Puerto Rico and metropolitan areas in the United States by the air shuttle between the two countries. In spite of the social conflicts thus caused, this easy access to the United States has done much to Americanize the Puerto Rican. Yet however much he likes his baseball, boxing, American clothes, hot dogs, soft drinks, and asserts his bubbling enthusiasm at presidential nomination conventions, he is still bound to his past.

In 50 years of educational effort Puerto Rico has achieved 70 percent literacy. The educational system is headed by a commissioner of education who is appointed by the governor. Public schools follow the 6-3-3 plan of organization popular in the United States and attendance is compulsory. Since Puerto Rico receives many of the privileges of the mainland state governments, in 1949–1950 free lunches were made available in 1500 schools. The University of Puerto Rico was established at San Juan in 1903, and when the country became a territory in 1917 the university was reorganized and conducted as an American state university. Besides normal schools for teachers, other higher institutions include the University of Santa Maria and the Polytechnic Institute.

PHYSICAL EDUCATION AND SPORTS IN THE WEST INDIES

During the military occupation of Cuba between 1899 and 1902 much was done for public works, sanitation, civil service, public health, and education. As in the Philippines, American soldiers introduced the Cubans to baseball, track and field athletics, and other sports which they added to their own. As in other Latin-American countries, Cuban schools have also been influenced by European systems of gymnastics, particularly in the private and public secondary schools of the urban areas. The junior and senior high schools conduct athletic competitions in baseball, football, basketball, swimming, track and field athletics, fencing, and golf. Before Cuba passed under Communist influence, picked secondary school athletic teams competed against those of the seaboard states. In 1949 Dr. Thomas McDonough, Emory University, Georgia, arranged a one-day dual swimming meet between the junior and senior high schools of the capital cities of Atlanta and Havana. The international meet proved successful and eventually developed with the assistance of civic organizations in both cities into what became known as the Havalanta Games. In addition to swimming, the program of athletic events included competition in baseball, basketball, bowling, golf, fencing, pistol and trap shooting, and track and field athletics. Universities in Cuba also field sports teams which compete with one another.

Cuba has a national sports federation which controls and supervises amateur athletic competition and also has an active Olympic Committee. Ever since 1910 Cuba has been a charter member of every sports federation organized by Latin-American countries and a regular participant in the Central American, Pan-American, and Olympic Games. In every instance Cuban athletes have done creditably in competition, which speaks well for the strength of the sports movement in that country. Cuban athletes show ability in gymnastics, basketball, pistol and trap shooting, yachting, fencing, weight-lifting, boxing, and swimming. Although baseball and *jai lai* attract many amateur competitors, these sports are also highly professionalized and have a considerable following. Like cockfighting and horse racing, baseball and *jai lai* lend themselves to heavy public wagering.

As a commonwealth of the United States Puerto Rico has been strongly influenced by American educational methods and organization, and this is also true of physical education programs in the school. Before military occupation by the United States Puerto Rican schools had adopted gymnastics, which in addition to games, sports and rhythmics is still included in physical education programs. The Department of Physical Education of the University of Puerto Rico at Rio Piedras, under the directorship of David C. Furman, has served as a center for the promotion of physical education on the island. In 1954 the Puerto Rican Association of Health, Physical Education and Recreation held its first meeting with approximately a hundred professional workers and interested individuals in attendance.

NOTES

1. Inezil Penna Marinho. "Historical Synthesis of Brazilian Physical Education." *The Physical Educator,* 11:1 (March, 1954), 24.
2. R. Salas and J. Bravo. "Physical Education in Chile." (Translated by E. Foster and H. Pierce) *Journal of Health and Physical Education,* 19:7 (September, 1948), 478–479; 482; 507.
3. César Belevan-Barcia. "Physical Education in Peru." *The Physical Educator,* 10:2 (May, 1953), 54; 55.
4. Felicio M. Torregrosa. "The Third Pan-American Physical Education Conference." *The Physical Educator,* 8:1 (March, 1951), 16.
5. M. Crawford. "Pato a Rough Rider's Game." *American,* VII (December, 1955), 17–18. R. T. Turner. "Gaucho Ball Game." *InterAmerican,* IV (June, 1945), 15–17.

6. David C. Furman. "Physical Education and Athletics in Mexico." *Proceedings,* The College Physical Education Association, 1958, p. 201.
7. Eduardo G. Ursini. "Recreation in Argentina." *Mind and Body,* 41:421 (May–June, 1934), 58–60. A. Pangburn. "The Argentinians at Play." *Recreation,* XXV (November, 1931), 461–462.
8. Oscar F. Castillon. "Physical Education in Mexico." *Journal of Health and Physical Education,* 5:5 (May, 1934), 11–15.
9. Lamberto A. Gayou. "A National Sports Program." *Journal of Health and Physical Education,* 14:1 (January, 1943), 8–10.

Chapter 16

THE ENGLISH COLONIES IN AMERICA, 1607–1775

THE COLONIAL PERIOD

DURING the seventeenth century general political, economic, and religious unrest in England encouraged emigration to the colonies in North America and the West Indies. In 1540 King Henry VIII had succeeded in separating the English Catholic Church from Rome, and in 1588, during the reign of Queen Elizabeth, England became Protestant. The effect of this transference of religious loyalty was still being felt when the Thirty Years' War (1618–1648) erupted on the Continent. Englishmen lived in constant dread that the Catholic party in Europe might attempt an invasion of the island. To aggravate matters, Charles I became involved in constant quarrels with Parliament over its rights and privileges as opposed to his insistence on the divine right of the king. His dissolution of Parliament in 1629 led to political conflict and eventually to the Great Rebellion of 1640. Englishmen who did not relish the possibility of being drawn into an international struggle with Catholic forces and a civil war in their own land looked to the colonies as a refuge from the political turmoil.

In the same era colonial expansion had become an economic necessity to England. In her transition from an agrarian to a manufacturing and trading nation during the fifteenth and sixteenth centuries, England found herself in urgent need of raw materials and greater commercial outlets. Exploitation of the natural resources of the colonies and the establishment of a closed system of agrarian-industrial barter with them offered at least a partial solution to the problem. The changeover from an agrarian to an industrial economy also caused a gradual shift of the rural population to metropolitan areas. During the reign of Queen Elizabeth half the population was unemployed and in need of the necessities of life. The poor begged in the streets, while their children were inadequately clothed and fed. If colonization of this segment of the population could be achieved, England would be relieved of a pressing social problem.

RELIGION AND COLONIZATION

Although Savelle[1] and Wright[2] state that relatively few Englishmen emigrated to the colonies for religious reasons alone, the harassment and persecution of nonconformists combined with other factors furnished the incentive for many to leave home. Many were dissatisfied with the English Reformation because the Anglican episcopate still retained the papal church organization and many of the Catholic rituals. Among these dissenters from the Church of England were the Puritans led by John Wycliffe and the Quakers, or Society of Friends, founded by George Fox.

The Puritans felt that the Church of England had not gone far enough in the adoption of the doctrine and church discipline advocated by the Protestant reformer, John Calvin. The Puritans accepted the Bible as the word of God and as a code of conduct. Their version of the consecrated life had little patience with idleness in any form, an attitude fortified by the envy of these poor, hard-working Englishmen and Scots of the leisure class in their countries. For this reason, the Puritans objected to Anglican participation in games, sports, and dancing at the conclusion of church services on the Sabbath.[3]

The Quakers, on the other hand, felt that obeying the letter of the Scriptures was secondary to following the Spirit of God. Unlike the Anglicans and Puritans, the Quakers believed that the Light of Christ could be found in the spiritual makeup of every human being. Every personality was sacred; hence Quakers did not accept social distinctions between superior and inferior classes. Many of their difficulties stemmed from their refusal to bear arms against their fellow men or take oaths of allegiance to any authority. The Puritan was vindictive and oppressive in his religious beliefs while the Quaker was righteous and democratic.

Stock companies and representatives of the crown enticed immigrants to the American colonies with the promise of religious freedom, inexpensive and fertile land, and riches through trade with the Indians for furs and deerskins.[4] Those immigrants who could afford to pay their own passage and those who could not hired themselves out as indentured servants for from three to seven years to ships' captains, who in turn sold the agreements to farm and plantation owners when the ship docked. So effectively were the colonies promoted that within twenty years after the first permanent settlement at Jamestown in 1607, 70,000 Englishmen had left their native land to seek colonial homes.

COLONIAL GOVERNMENT

The executive and administrative head of the colonial government, whether a royal province, proprietorship, or corporate type, was the royal governor, who served as an agent of the crown. He was assisted by an executive council, appointed or approved by the crown. In his civil responsibilities the governor was assisted by the colonial legislature, composed of an upper and lower house. The upper house, except in Pennsylvania, represented virtually all the members of the executive council. The lower house, or representative assembly, consisted of colonists elected by their peers. To hold office in the assembly or to be able to vote, a colonist had to meet certain property, monetary, and religious qualifications, which differed from colony to colony.

From the beginning, the lower houses insisted upon the right to introduce all legislation having to do with the expenditure of funds. The colonial legislatures also took control of legislation for education and claimed the exclusive right to establish and regulate schools and colleges. After the Revolution they continued to reserve this right. In spite of the efforts of the royal governors to check the power of the colonial legislatures, they continued to extend their rights and privileges in civil affairs. In most cases, governors found it more expedient to tolerate the increasing independence of the colonial legislatures than to court open conflicts between the executive and legislative branches. Even before the Revolutionary War, the colonial legislatures had so successfully usurped the civil authority of the governors that the latter were rendered practically ineffectual as agents of the crown.[1]

EDUCATION IN THE ENGLISH COLONIES

Education in the early colonies was given by parents in the home, but as villages and towns developed, the traditional practices of the mother country were adopted. Wealthier colonists provided their children with tutors or sent them to the town elementary school taught by a schoolmaster or clergyman. Children of the poor received instruction in the rudiments of reading, writing, and occasionally ciphering from the dame schools, which were as popular in the colonies as they were in England. These English charity schools were fixed institutions in Delaware, Maryland, New Jersey, and Pennsylvania. Because of the effectiveness of the English Poor Laws (1601) in providing apprenticeship training for poor children, the colonists accepted this vocational schooling as fundamental.[5] They did not, however, accept the compulsory stipulation of the English law, but encouraged instead voluntary arrangements between apprentices and master craftsmen.

The Massachusetts Bay Colony was the first to give thought to secondary school and higher education. The leadership of the colony included sixty former graduates of Cambridge University in England, who appreciated the need for a higher institution to prepare ministers of the Gospel. In 1636 the Massachusetts General Court established a college at Newton (Cambridge), and in 1638 its name was changed to Harvard in honor of John Harvard, who willed the college half his property and his personal library. A Latin grammar school was established at Boston in 1635, followed by others at Charlestown and Ipswich (1636), Salem (1637), Dorchester and Newberry (1639). Like their English counterparts, these schools offered a program of humanistic studies centered around Latin and Greek. In Massachusetts they were supported by tuition fees, tax levies, and income derived from town lands and fisheries.[2]

THE CHARACTER OF EDUCATION IN THE COLONIES

In New England the Massachusetts Bay Colony was the Zion of the Calvinist dream of a religious state of which education was to be the cornerstone. As the servant of the church, the state was to provide its children with an educational opportunity to "learn and labor, read and understand the Bible and to respect the capital laws of the land."

For the first twenty years of colonization the Puritan fathers accepted the current plan of education, but suspicion was growing that all parents were not cooperating as they should. In 1643 the Massachusetts General Court passed a law which required selectmen of the various towns to check the educational progress of all children and to find parents and guardians who were negligent in their duties to the religious state.

This check system was in operation only five years when the General Court passed the first compulsory school law in the English colonies. This law required all townships with fifty householders to provide an elementary school and pay for a schoolmaster. Each township with one hundred householders was required to provide a Latin grammar school. The Connecticut and New Haven colonies enacted similar laws in 1650 and 1655. When New Hampshire separated from the Massachusetts Bay Colony in 1880, its legislature adopted the same law. Maine and Vermont were too sparsely settled during the eighteenth century to be concerned. Rhode Island and the Providence Plantation of Roger Williams, settled by refugees from religious persecution in Massachusetts and elsewhere, were less interested in setting up states subservient to a single religious faith.

The middle colonies of Delaware, Pennsylvania, and West New Jersey were settled by Quakers, who invited immigrants to settle without religious discrimination. As a consequence, the Quaker colonies made no attempt to unite elementary education and religious training. With the exception of the Dutch colony, New York was officially Anglican, and the educational practices of the mother country prevailed. Although sympathetic to Calvinistic doctrine, the Dutch and Walloons came to New Netherlands in the service of the Dutch West Indies Company rather than for political or religious reasons. They therefore adopted the elementary school system of their homeland, where education was a function of the church. Children of the wealthy merchants, landed gentry, and Dutch patroons in the middle colonies attended private tuition schools or parochial schools under the bishop of the diocese or the Dutch synod. Children of less well-to-do colonists reccived elementary instruction in charity schools or served apprenticeships in the various trades.

In the southern colonies the official religion of Virginia was Anglican, while Maryland was settled predominantly by Roman Catholics. Both colonies, as well as South Carolina, accepted colonists of other religious faiths, among them French Huguenots, Scotch Presbyterians, and German Pietists. Because of this diversity of faiths, the idea of the state providing learning as a servant of the church had little appeal to these colonies. Among the religious sects the responsibility for elementary and religious instruction was assigned to the clergy. Wealthy planters employed English and French tutors and frequently sent their sons to England to attend Latin grammar schools and universities. Children of the poor attended endowed private elementary schools and received apprenticeship training.

RECREATION IN THE EARLY COLONIES

The early colonist was too occupied with the serious business of establishing himself and his family in an alien and inhospitable country to find time for the recreations he once enjoyed in the mother country. The cooperation of every settler was essential to survival, and both the liberal Anglicans and the strict Puritans adopted regulations against what were considered nonessential and frivolous pastimes. In the Virginia colony the Anglicans passed ordinances which forbade gambling, drinking, and dancing and ordered strict observance of the Sabbath. The Puritans of Massachusetts, Connecticut, and East New Jersey legislated against card and dice games, quoits, bowls, ninepins, and "shovelboard." From the pulpit ministers denounced dancing as "lascivious," and only the popular Boston clergyman, John Cotton, dared to approve of mixed dancing on the condition that a precedent could be found in the Old Testament. Even theatrical plays and interludes, once a favorite entertainment in the mother country, failed to escape censorship, and any colonist caught drafting amateur performers for this purpose was subjected to fifteen lashes or sentenced to the pillory.

In New Amsterdam only those restrictions were enforced which were considered necessary to the safety and welfare of the inhabitants. The Dutch Reform Church pursued a liberal policy toward recreational activities, and members of the congregation were permitted to engage in games, sports, and dancing at the close of church services on the Sabbath and religious holidays. The Dutch also followed their European custom of celebrating New Year's Day, May Day, and Christmas. The game of ninepins was as popular as in Europe, but instead of a hard clay alley or board planks, a green or lawn was used as the bowling surface. Besides ninepins, which was later changed to tenpins to avoid gambling restrictions, the colonists of New Netherland participated in hunting and fishing, card games, backgammon, bowls, ice skating, bandy on ice, sleighing, sledding, winter carnivals, and agricultural fairs.

Between 1630 and 1640 the colonies experienced a great influx of immigrants, the majority of whom were Englishmen and the remainder a wide cross-section of other European nationals. The Puritan "blue laws" were a source of irritation to the new arrivals, who openly defied ordinances which denied them the freedom to participate in recreational diversions of their choice. Many of the nonconformists formed wagon trains and moved to the western frontier; others sought refuge in the more liberal colonies. For those newcomers who pretended to conform, the local tavern became the recreation center. Here they could visit with friends and exchange news, play card and dice games, enjoy mixed dancing, and seek solace in rum. In spite of many ordinances against these "dens of iniquity" and frequent revocations of licenses, the New England town tavern, like the town hall, became a permanent feature of community life in the colonial and early national periods.

THE ENGLISH COLONIES DURING THE EIGHTEENTH CENTURY

New England

In New England the political life of the colonist centered about the town hall and meeting house; it was here that grievances were heard and discussed, representatives of the people elected, and the laws of the community formulated. Church pews were assigned according to social rank, and this same deference to caste operated in the everyday associations of the colonists. Yet it was recognized that no colonist had to remain in the social class in which circumstances had placed him. By the avoidance of indolence and extravagances and the application of good business acumen, a colonist could easily rise above his station.

Instead of depending upon a single staple for livelihood, as in the southern colonies, New England used the commodities from her farms, forests, and fisheries as a supplement to trade and commerce, which were concentrated on rum and Negro slaves. Beginning in the seventeenth and extending into the eighteenth century, Puritan shippers secured molasses from the West Indies, distilled it into rum in the colonies, and exchanged it for slaves in North Africa. The first slave trade was carried on with West Indian sugar plantation owners, but as soon as the indenture system expired in the southern colonies, New England shippers found a ready market for slaves in Virginia, Maryland and the Carolinas. The traffic in human beings was not exactly in character for the self-righteous Puritan, and as a salve to his conscience, he created the fiction that he was an instrument of God delegated to lead the ignorant heathens to their salvation.

By the close of the seventeenth century, the steady stream of immigrants diluted the effect of Puritan restrictions in New England. The colonists revived many of the English diversions of card and dice games, bowls, billiards, ninepins (skittles), shuffleboard, and Maypole and Morris dances. The town tavern found it good business to furnish such entertainments as cockfighting, bearbaiting, boxing and wrestling matches, contests in marksmanship, exhibitions of animals strange to the colonists, mechanical gadgets, and theatrical plays and interludes. The town gallows was generally located near the tavern, and the more morbid of the town's population were treated to the drama and excitement of an occasional public hanging.[6]

As a pleasant escape from the daily routine of life, the New England colonist looked forward to certain red-letter days on the calendar. Thanksgiving was a popular feast day, and election day furnished an opportunity to visit with neighbors and catch up on the news. The royal governor had the authority to raise a militia* and designate the number of times eligible males should meet for the purpose of military training. As a general rule, the militia met eight times during the year and was composed of men 16 to 60 years of age. Militia days were occasions for drills, parades, athletic contests in jumping, foot races and wrestling, and practice in marksmanship. The day was concluded in the convivial atmosphere of the town tavern.

THE MIDDLE COLONIES

The colony of New Netherlands was absorbed by the English in 1664, and East and West New Jersey combined with the royal province of New York and were provided with a crown governor in 1702. The succession of governors who followed presented their political friends with millions of acres of land in the area between the Mohawk, Hudson and Connecticut rivers as far south as the Catskills. These new landowners, like the Dutch patroons, established feudal estates and employed tenant farmers, indentured servants, and slaves to work the land. Farther south, the Quakers retained political control of Pennsylvania until the Revolutionary War and of all the English colonies had the most autonomous provincial government. Delaware remained predominantly Quaker and with Pennsylvania provided refuge for the persecuted German

* The Assembly of the Pennsylvania colony, controlled by the pacifist Quakers and sympathetic Germans, refused to maintain a militia. The Scotch-Irish and Germans on the frontier, who were barely holding their own against marauding Indians, became disgusted and, to secure protection, were about to petition the crown to make Pennsylvania a royal province shortly before the Revolutionary War.

sects and Scotch-Irish Presbyterians during the first half of the eighteenth century. The Germans (Pennsylvania Dutch) augmented the farm labor force, while the Scotch-Irish tended to move westward toward the frontier in search of cheaper land.

The middle colonies developed an economy based mainly upon the export of agricultural produce and livestock which the estates of the New York aristocrats and the farms of the Quakers and Germans raised in surplus quantities. In addition, the middle colonies derived considerable income from the export of furs, rum, flour, iron pigs and bars (Pennsylvania), and from shipbuilding (Delaware). Philadelphia became the mecca of colonial and European intelligentsia and the wealthiest city in the colonies.

Social life was gayest in New York, where the aristocrats lavishly entertained friends on their estates and ladies, dressed in the latest London fashions, took excursions by chaise or chair to country taverns and picnic areas on the East River. The winter months provided gay sleighing and skating parties, ice carnivals, balls, concerts, and assemblies arranged to celebrate special occasions. Fashionable crowds gathered twice a year at the Hempstead and Salisbury race tracks to wager on their favorite thoroughbreds and especially to be seen and recognized. During the off-season, aristocrats found time for shooting matches, hunting, riding to the hounds, boating, cricket, golf, battledore, shuttlecock, tennis, and fives (handball). Both the aristocrat and the commoner had a failing for cockfighting, bearbaiting, and plays. Theatrical troupes appeared in the royal province as early as the first decade of the eighteenth century, but did not become regular public entertainment until the 1750s. The plays were Elizabethan in style and spirit. Stage hands removed props in view of the audience, and actors frequently assisted in changing scenes. The wealthy were accorded special seating and the commoners were relegated to the gallery.[3]

In spite of the disapproval of the Quakers, in Philadelphia the upper class enjoyed assemblies, of which dancing was an important part, sumptuous banquets, horse racing, and fish fries. The common people spent their leisure hours playing cards, hunting and fishing, sleighing, skating, and dancing.

THE SOUTHERN COLONIES

In Maryland, South Carolina, and Virginia, when indentured servants completed the terms of their argeement, planters found it more practical and efficient to use slave labor. In 1650 the total population of Virginia was 15,000, with 300 Negro slaves; a half-century later the population had increased to 70,000, with one-third of that number slaves. With its emphasis upon a one-crop economy, tobacco or rice, the social structure of the southern colonies consisted of aristocrats at the top, far below them the laborers and servants, and at the very bottom the poor whites and Negro slaves.

The tobacco plantations of the Tidewater section of Virginia and Maryland and the rice plantations of South Carolina were widely separated, but in their communal organization they resembled the manors of English feudal lords. The colonial mansion was generally of Greek revival style, attractively furnished with accessories from England and France, and surrounded by beautifully landscaped grounds. Apart from the mansion, and sometimes cleverly hidden from view as at Thomas Jefferson's Monticello, were the slave cabins, blacksmith shop, smokehouses, root cellars, barns and stables with tack rooms attached. Nearby stood the mill, for which horses or oxen furnished the power to grind corn for meal and the mash of the whiskey distillery. The colonial mansion radiated an atmosphere of elegance and comfortable living and became a symbol of affluence in the Southern colonies.

The Piedmont section of Maryland and Virginia was settled by English yeomen, Scots, Irish, and Germans who came from the Tidewater section or Pennsylvania looking for cheaper land. This section was characterized by small landholdings on which the farmer following a diversified agriculture program supplemented by income from fur trading. Unlike the Tidewater plantation owners, who had easy access to shipping ports on the Atlantic and on navigable rivers, the landowners of the Piedmont and South Carolina used towns as collection points for farm produce, furs, and deerskins, from which they were carried by wagon to shipping ports on the coast.

Since many planters of the southern colonies were members of the liberal Anglican Church or other tolerant sects, they accepted dancing as an indispensable social activity, worthy of special instruction. Ministers of the parish rarely voiced objections to southern minuets, "giggs," reels, and country dances. Since the circuit-riding clergy were lucky to hold church services more than once a month since plantations were so far distant from the parish house, they left the responsibility for education to the individual planter. Parents employed English and French dancing masters to teach the latest dances and social manners and utilized their services in running plantation balls and dancing parties. So popular was dancing that William and Mary College (1693) permitted dance teachers to organize classes on the campus as early as 1716, "where all Gentlemen's sons may be taught Dancing, according to the newest French manner."[7]

Picnics and barbecues were regular social events on the plantation during the summer months. Evenings at the mansion found the members of the family and guests engaged in carding wool, spinning, sewing, and quilting, as well as in card and table games, musicales, interludes, and storytelling. Southern gentlemen enjoyed cockfights, horse races, fox hunts, hunting and fowling, boxing matches, and fencing bouts.[8]

Servants and Negro slaves shared in the conduct of many of the southern gentlemen's leisure activities and frequently provided the music for the balls and dancing parties, which sometimes continued for several nights. The joys and sorrows of the plantation slave furnished the incentive for many of his nostalgic songs and spirituals and the inspiration for many of his imaginative stories, which were passed along by word of mouth for more than a century before they were recorded.

The English, Scots, Irish, and Germans of the Piedmont amused themselves by dancing running sets, three- and four-handed reels, and the Irish trot to the rhythmical cadence of the fiddle and by singing folk tunes and ballads to the melodious tone of the dulcimer. So much were these entertainments a part of their lives that the colonists retained them in their western exodus to the highlands beyond the Alleghenies. The Piedmont farmer raised and trained beagles and coon dogs for his hunting pleasure and foxhounds and game cocks to supply the planters. Fox hounds furnished many hours of recreation for farmers who, warmed by a fire and corn "likker" on a cool and moonlit autumn night, released the hounds to follow the scent of the fox. The hounds' distant bays as they pursued the quarry over hills and down creek beds sometimes lasted until the break of dawn.

THE FRONTIER

The frontier started when the first English colonists stepped onto the shore of the Atlantic coast. After the first settlements had been carved out of the virgin forests and villages and towns arose in their stead, the more desirable land, once so inexpensive and plentiful, became limited in quantity and much more costly. Since the heart's desire of new arrivals was the ownership of land and all the advantages it entailed, the movement was constantly westward toward the frontier where the land was undeveloped and cheap. The Scotch-Irish Presbyterians, German pietists, and French Huguenots moved westward toward the undetermined boundaries of Pennsylvania, Maryland, and Virginia, until the Appalachians impeded their progress. Colonists in the royal province of New York followed the trails blazed by Dutch and English fur traders to the borders of French-held territory. In the South the colonists moved into the areas opened by the fur traders in North and South Carolina, Georgia, and as far as Spanish Florida. This pattern of western movement was maintained with slight variations until the middle of the eighteenth century.

The factors which forestalled a mass movement toward the land beyond the Alleghenies, described by explorers and fur traders as fertile beyond belief and abounding with wildlife, included: (1) the need of a passageway through the mountains, (2) the French claim to the land drained by the Ohio and its tributaries, and (3) conflict between the Indians and the settlers, the one dependent upon the woodland and its natural resources for a livelihood and the other upon plowed fields and pastures. The first of these impediments was removed when Dr. Thomas Walker, a land agent of the Loyal Company, discovered the Cumberland Gap through the Alleghenies in 1750. The second deterrent** was eliminated by the success of the English over the French and Indians (1754–1760) as a part of the Seven Years' War. The final obstacle was removed when the colonists and the British regulars defeated the Indian tribes led by the Ottawa chieftain Pontiac in a series of frontier encounters extending through 1762 and 1763. The way west was now open to the land-hungry colonists and ever-present land speculators.[9]

THE COLONIST ON THE FRONTIER

In many respects the colonists who settled the virgin land west of the Alleghenies were a different breed from those who had first landed on the Atlantic shore a century and a half earlier. Many of the first colonists were graduates of English universities or came from middle-class families who had a high regard for intellectual attainments. As each succeeding generation of colonists advanced toward the receding frontier, the arduous physical labor demanded to establish a home in the wilderness left little leisure for the acquisition of knowledge and the appreciation of culture. The colonist who joined the western movement, therefore, had received his education from the school of experience, divorced from the rich cultural inheritance of the past and tempered by the materialistic colonial way of life. As ably described by Moore, "He was his own man, a free agent in the state of nature, but necessarily a man, culturally speaking, without a home."[10]

The first settlers quickly dispensed with the superficialities which marked their former social environment. As in the first settlements on the seacoast, colonists in the West soon learned that the co-operation of everyone was necessary to survival against the forces of nature and their enemies. Whether in the wilderness or in the safer confines of the frontier fort, colonists learned to depend upon one another to soften the blows of adversity and share in the multi-

** Based upon fear of the effect of western expansion upon the agrarian-industrial barter system and the growing independence of the English colonies, the crown issued the Royal Proclamation of 1763, which recognized the rights of Indians west of the mountains and "all lands and territories lying westward of the source of the rivers which fall into the sea from the west and northwest aforesaid." But nothing short of military force could have stopped the momentum of the westward movement.

plicity of necessary chores. This sharing of oneself and one's worldly goods to help those in need became a trait that persisted beyond the colonial period.

The struggle to tame the forests and wrest a living from the soil required a considerable expenditure of physical energy. Muscles were needed to girdle and cut down virgin trees, roll logs to be used in raising cabins and outbuildings, and plant, harvest, and market crops. Women and older children worked alongside the men, and yet women found time to care for the home, do the household duties, teach the children, and raise the big families essential to the labor force on the farms. As Clark has pointed out,

> What early travelers saw was sweaty human beings wrestling with tasks which exhausted one generation before they were finished. To fail to comprehend the place of grinding, sweaty, devitalizing labor is to fail to understand the most important source of economic success on the frontier. Work became a habit of the settlers and throughout American history it has remained a national virtue. . . . To this extent the frontier adopted the old Puritan trait of glorifying labor.

RECREATION ON THE FRONTIER

Without an opportunity to relax and break the monotony of daily labor, the colonist would have found life unendurable. Leisure-time activities were adjusted to life on the frontier. Hunting and fishing served both as a relaxation and as a source of food supply. Buffaloes, bears, deer, beaver, otter, muskrats, raccoons, and squirrels were present in abundance, and wild turkey, quail, geese, and wild pigeons were "beyond number and imagination." Streams and lakes teemed with fish of all description, and the frontiersman used the Indian weir, which they had perfected beyond the skill of its originator, trolls, nets, seines, and angling to catch them. Log-rolling, cabin raising, corn husking bees, weddings, and other communal activities called for feasts, dancing, and drinking.[11]

The frontiersman's participation in sports was purely individualistic, and he matched his skill in contests of marksmanship, in squirrel and turkey shoots, foot races, wrestling matches, and rough-and-tumble fights. An English visitor to the Ohio Valley recorded his impression of these fights as follows:

It may not be improper to mention, that the backwoodsmen, as the first emigrants from the eastward of the Allegheny mountains are called, are very similar in their habits and manners to the aborigines. . . . They depend more on hunting than agriculture . . . and their cabins are not better than Indian wigwams. They have frequent meetings for the purpose of gambling, fighting and drinking. . . . They fight for the most trifling provocations, or even sometimes without any, but merely to try each other's prowess, which they are fond of vaunting of. Their hands, teeth, knees, head and feet are their weapons, not only boxing with their fists . . . but also tearing, kicking, scratching, biting, gouging each other's eyes out by a dexterous use of the thumb and finger, and doing their utmost to kill each other, even when rolling over one another on the ground.[12]

NOTES

1. Max Savelle. *The Foundations of American Civilization. A History of Colonial America.* New York: Henry Holt and Company, 1942, pp. 59–71; 66; 349–360.
2. Louis B. Wright. *The Atlantic Frontier. Colonial American Civilization (1607–1763).* Ithaca: Cornell University Press, 1959, pp. 43; 147–152.
3. Foster Rhea Dulles. *America Learns to Play. A History of Popular Recreation.* New York: D. Appleton-Century Company, 1940, pp. 8–13; 50–57.
4. John Richard Alden. *John Stewart of the Southern Colonial Frontier.* Ann Arbor: University of Michigan Press, 1944; Newton D. Mereness. *Travels in the American Colonies.* (Edited under the auspices of the National Society of the Colonial Dames of America) New York: The Macmillan Company, 1916, pp. 95–172; 175–212.
5. R. Freeman Butts and Lawrence A. Cremin. *A History of Education in American Culture.* New York: Henry Holt and Company, 1953, pp. 102–107. Elwood P. Cubberly. *The History of Education.* New York: Houghton Mifflin Company, 1920, pp. 325–326.
6. Edward Field. *The Colonial Tavern. A Glimpse of New England Town Life in the Seventeenth and Eighteenth Centuries.* Providence: Preston and Rounds, 1897. Mary Caroline Crawford. *Social Life in Old New England.* Boston: Little, Brown and Company, 1914, pp. 417; 435.
7. Joseph E. Marks, III. *America Learns to Dance. A Historical Study of Dance Education in America Before 1900.* New York: Exposition Press, 1957, pp. 62–65. Samuel Foster Damon. *The History of Square Dancing.* Barre: Barre Gazette, 1927.

8. Ruth White Fink. "Recreational Pursuits in the Old South." *The Research Quarterly,* 23:1 (March, 1952), 28–37.
9. Thomas D. Clark. *Frontier America. The Story of the Westward Movement.* New York: Charles Scribner's Sons, 1959, pp. 4–24; 15.
10. Arthur K. Moore. *The Frontier Mind. A Cultural Analysis of The Kentucky Frontiersman.* Lexington: University of Kentucky Press, 1957, p. 239.
11. Thomas D. Clark. *A History of Kentucky.* Lexington: The John Bradford Press, 1950, pp. 66–78.
12. Thomas Ashe. *Travels in America Performed in 1806.* First printing in London, 1806. Reprinted for W. Sawyer and Company by E. M. Blunt, Newburyport, Massachusetts, 1808, p. 171.

Chapter 17

THE EARLY NATIONAL PERIOD OF THE UNITED STATES, 1776–1860

By the late eighteenth century America was predominately agrarian and nine out of ten able-bodied men were engaged directly or indirectly in agriculture. Shortly before the turn of the century, the discoveries and inventions of Englishmen and Americans laid the foundation of the industrial and agricultural revolutions.

The industrial revolution developed two new social groups, the capitalists and the factory workers. The capitalists were the enterprising men who financed and promoted industries or who sold their production. The factory workers soon composed the largest segment of the population and were drawn mainly from the farms. As large-scale farming systems took over in what is sometimes called the agricultural revolution, the subsistence farm began to decline.

Factory work demanded fourteen to fifteen hours of labor a day from men, women, and children working under conditions deleterious to health and spirit in towns characterized by crowded and unsanitary living. A demand inevitably arose for the improvement of working conditions, the removal of children from labor's ranks, and the formation of unions to protect the workers' rights. The large labor group was to become a force in shaping legislation for education on the state level.[1]

From the Revolutionary War to 1830, immigration to the United States reached a low level and on the basis of the census was at the rate of 4000 a year. By 1860 more than four million people had emigrated to the United States. Of these, 1.5 million were Germans, a like number were Irish, and the remainder were English, Welsh, and other nationalities. These immigrants swelled the labor forces of factories, railroads, and road-building.

EDUCATION

In education a fairly definite line of demarcation separates the period of 1776–1830, when the social climate favored aristocratic tendencies, and that of 1830–1860, when American political and social structures became essentially democratic. During the first phase, the old Latin grammar school with its humanistic curriculum remained unaltered, supported by tuition fees and endowed funds. The private tutor was still in evidence in wealthier homes, and young gentlemen traveled to the New England universities for their higher education.

In the Land Ordinance of the Northwest Territory of 1785, the federal government earmarked land for the establishment of public schools, and the liberalized policy of 1800 set aside certain lands in every state for educational purposes, but because of the scattered population of the frontier, little beyond the setting up of district schools was accomplished. President Washington's proposal for a national university stimulated much discussion, but no action, and Thomas Jefferson advocated a plan of popular education which evoked little response from southern leaders.

The second phase, 1830–1860, was distinguished by: (1) public demand for a more useful type of education than that provided by the Latin grammar school, answered by the English school and the academy; (2) the rise of the working class, or "common" man, who found a champion in President Andrew Jackson, and who by right of suffrage became more influential in determining educational policies; (3) the cultivation of a favorable public attitude toward universal education by such leaders as Horace Mann, Henry Barnard, Samuel Lewis, and Catherine Beecher; (4) the gradual acceptance of state-supported and -supervised elementary and secondary schools, colleges, and universities; and (5) the resolution of the question of public support for denominational schools through tax funds.[2]

Elementary Schools

The scope of the elementary school curriculum expanded rapidly after 1800. For example, the number of textbooks listed for sale during the years 1804–1832 increased from 93 to 407. The number of books on spelling, reading, and arithmetic increased fourfold; grammars, threefold; geographies, sixfold; and histories, eightfold. Elementary schools in Massachusetts offered instruction in bookkeeping and the Boston elementary schools taught music. In the southern states spelling, reading, writing, and arithmetic were considered basic for the common schools, while geography, history, and grammar were considered more advanced studies for the academies or high schools.

Secondary Schools

In 1751 Benjamin Franklin wrote his *Idea of the English School,* in which he pleaded for the use of the English tongue in school and a more useful curriculum than that of the Latin grammar school. His views had the full support of the merchant group and other critics of the humanistic schools, traditionally committed to the preparation of youths for college and university. In reaction private English schools were organized to meet the commercial interests of the middle class and to provide a practical vocational education. These schools furnished instruction in algebra, geometry, trigonometry, and astronomy; civil and military engineering (surveying, gauging, navigation, fortification, and gunnery), geography, history, modern foreign languages, music, fencing, and arts and crafts. Their most important feature, however, was instruction in the English language. Advertisements in the 1780s indicate that classes were conducted at hours to suit the patrons, and that girls were eligible to attend.

In the early nineteenth century the English schools were gradually replaced by the academies, which because they furnished terminal education for many were called "the people's college." By 1830 there were approximately 1000 academies in America serving pupils of a wide range of age and interest. Like the English schools, they were coeducational, but as the academy movement gained momentum separate schools called female seminaries were established. Between 1830 and 1850 female seminaries became the vogue in the South, and many of them eventually became colleges for women.

The fact that the academies charged tuition created a dual system of secondary education and placed the stigma of pauperism upon the common school. Eventually a move was started to democratize the academies and to incorporate them into a state-supported and -controlled school system. By 1860 more than one hundred public-supported high schools were founded in Illinois, Maine, Michigan, New York, Ohio, Pennsylvania, and South Carolina.

COLLEGE AND UNIVERSITIES

The higher institutions of the colonial period were founded out of religious motives with the exception of Benjamin Franklin's academy, chartered as the College and Academy of Philadelphia (1775) and incorporated as the University of Pennsylvania in 1791. The humanistic curriculum prevailed, but the intellectual and scientific trends of the latter part of the eighteenth century led to significant changes. The traditional plan of one tutor for all subjects was changed to a small staff of specialists in several disciplines.

The period following the Revolution witnessed the extension of higher education to the western frontier and to the South. Transylvania University (1787), the first university west of the Allegheny Mountains, was originally organized as a Presbyterian seminary. The University of Michigan (1817) and Indiana University (1820) were established from federal land grants and endowments. In the South the University of Virginia (1825) was founded by Thomas Jefferson, and the University of Alabama (1831) was established through federal land grants. Altogether, twenty-one publicly supported higher institutions were created prior to 1860, to form the greatest system of free public education in the world.

FOREIGN INFLUENCE ON PHYSICAL EDUCATION

Progressive educational leaders early recognized the value of recreation and systematic exercise as a respite from academic work and as a means of preserving students' health. A few initiated exercise programs which showed foreign influence. In spite of it's nationalistic spirit, education looked to Europe for guidance in methods and materials of instruction.

THE PESTALOZZIAN MOVEMENT IN AMERICA

William McClure, a scholar and philanthropist of Scottish descent, was the first to sponsor the Pestalozzian movement in America. On one of his business trips to Switzerland, he visited Pestalozzi's school at Yverdun and Fellenberg's vocational school at Hofwyl. He attempted to inveigle the master himself to come to the new country to set up an experimental school, but Pestalozzi's advancing age and the language barrier made him refuse. Instead, he recommended Joseph Neef (1770–1853), whom McClure engaged to organize a Pestalozzian school near Philadelphia in 1809.

Neef was born in Alsace in 1770 and as a young man studied for the priesthood. At 21 he discontinued his studies to join Napoleon's army. Receiving a head wound during the Italian campaign in 1796, he retired to teach music, French, and gymnastics in Pestalozzi's school at Burgdorf. Neef was an excellent disciple of the Pestalozzian method, and his schools in Pennsylvania and Kentucky received favorable comment from visitors and educators. His first school, located near the Falls of the Schuylkill some four miles from Philadelphia, enrolled more than one hundred pupils.[3]

In his *Sketch of a Plan and Method of Education* (1808), the first pedagogical book in English published in the New World, Neef discussed the importance of gymnastics and recreation:

> The most superficial observer of children must be forcibly struck with their untamable activity, with their great predilection for bodily exercise, with their untiring fondness for running, jumping, climbing, bathing and swimming, and they always prefer the fresh open air, however cold or hot, to the inclosed air of a house. . . . My pupils shall run, jump, climb,

slide, skate, bathe, swim and exert their adroitness, display their dexterity and exercise their bodily force, just as much as they please, or at least as it is rational to allow them.[4]

A pupil at the Philadelphia school, C. D. Gardette, stated that Neef supported a variety of activities. The pupils swam in the Schuylkill River, skated, hiked, and performed gymnastic stunts. As a military man, he encouraged fighting and wrestling, for which he incurred the criticism of parents. Neef was also fond of military tactics and drilled the boys like an army sergeant, and on occasions the woods rang with the sounds of mock military skirmishes.

OTHER PESTALOZZIAN SCHOOLS. Amos Bronson Alcott (1799-1888), who in 1805 accepted a teaching position at the Cheshire School, Connecticut, was a very progressive educator and a student of Pestalozzi's philosophy. In the *American Journal of Education* for January and February, 1827, Alcott gave a full account of his teaching methods at Cheshire. His attitude was that gymnastics should train the physical powers in preparation for practical use, and in proportion to their respective capacities, with special exercises for the eye, ear, hand, and voice, and emphasis on "play-games" such as balancing, jumping, hopping, swinging, and running. Alcott was a firm believer in social recreation, and his pupils spent their evenings in the instructor's room, where they engaged in storytelling and quiet games and play. Alcott organized similar programs in schools in Philadelphia and Boston.

Henry Bernard, the pioneer educator who organized the first American teachers' institute in Connecticut (1839), was an active Pestalozzian propagandist.

THE LANCASTRIAN MOVEMENT

In 1798 Joseph Lancaster, an English schoolmaster, discovered the advantage of using monitors, or pupil assistants, to reduce the cost of instruction. In 1803 he outlined his monitorial system in the publication *Improvements in Education as it Respects the Industrial Classes of the Community*. Lancaster suggested that the instructor teach the older and brighter boys the daily lessons with the help of printed cards. These monitors would then take a group of ten or more boys to a designated teaching station and teach them in turn what they had learned. The monitorial system was utilized first to teach reading and catechism, and later writing, arithmetic, spelling, and other subjects. The Lancastrian method was popular in English and American charitable schools between 1810 and 1830 but in the United States succumbed to the free public school system.

Lancaster was aware of value of playground activities as a diversion from study, in keeping pupils off the streets, and in developing desirable moral qualities. He advocated regular fifteen-minute play periods during the school day and a noon-hour recreational period. A manual printed by the Philadelphia Society for the Establishment and Support of Charity Schools (1820) served as a guide for the organization of Lancastrian schools in New England. It recommended that each school should have a playground adjacent to the school building, that its surface be covered with sand, and that it be enclosed with a board fence. To conserve time, the children should be marched to and from the playground.

According to Billet the Boston Monitorial School for Girls in 1823 provided a program which included calisthenics, jumping, running, and exercises such as hanging and swinging from high bars and raising and lowering weights.[5] The New York High School, a private school for boys conducted according to the monitorial method, introduced a gymnastic program about 1827.

THE GERMAN SYSTEM IN AMERICA

The success of the American and French Revolutions left many European states in a condition of political unrest. This was particularly true in the German states, where radical groups demanded a united nation and the right to popular sovereignty. Among these were the student associations (*Burschenschaften*) of the universities and the Turner Societies, whose members were a source of irritation to autocratic interests. Many fled to other countries to avoid surveillance and possible imprisonment.

The development of the academy and high school movement in the United States between 1825 and 1830 and the interest of educational leaders in some form of regular exercise for pupils made this country an attractive haven for many of these German refugees. How many of these Turners found teaching positions in American educational institutions will probably never be known. Fred E. Leonard, in an examination of the first three volumes of the *American Journal of Education* (1826–1828) and in a study of catalogues and other published materials of higher institutions in New England, found many indications of gymnastic programs bearing the German trade-mark.[6]

Leonard compiled a biography of three of these German Turners who, though unsuccessful in their effort to introduce the German system in New England, went on to make important contributions to their adopted country.[7]

Charles Beck, through George Ticknor, professor of French and Spanish at Harvard University, secured a position as instructor in Latin and gymnastics at Round Hill School, Northampton, Massachusetts, in 1825. Disappointed by the reception given gymnastics by the students, he resigned his position in 1830 to become instructor of Latin at Harvard.

Charles Follen was assisted by Ticknor in getting the position of instructor in German at Harvard University, where he organized voluntary classes in gymnastics. He resigned in 1825 to accept the directorship of the Boston outdoor gymnasium and swimming program initiated through public subscription by John C. Warren, professor of anatomy and physiology, Harvard University. Lack of public interest caused Follen to return to Harvard as instructor of ethics and ecclesiastical history.[6]

The resignation of Follen in 1827 left Warren without a director. He immediately wrote Friedrich Jahn, who in 1825 had been released from prison, and offered him the position. Jahn declined the offer and recommended Francis Lieber, an expert gymnast and swimming instructor. Under Lieber, the swimming program conducted in the nearby Charles River was successful, but public apathy over the gymnastic program continued. By 1829, class attendance had fallen to four students and Warren closed the outdoor gymnasium. Lieber later served as professor of history at the University of South Carolina (1835) and Columbia University (1857) and as a consultant on international law to President Abraham Lincoln.[7]

GYMNASTICS IN THE MILITARY ACADEMIES

In 1818 Captain Alden Partridge resigned as superintendent of the West Point Military Academy and began to agitate for reform of the higher educational institutions in America. His main contention was that college and university students lacked a regular and systematic course of exercise for the preservation of health. He pointed out that many students were forced to discontinue their studies because of ill health. Partridge organized six military academies in New England. He evidently built his program exclusively around military tactics and gymnastics because the Connecticut legislature refused to grant him a charter for a military academy at Middleton due to the scarcity of academic courses. The military academy movement was far more successful in the South.

THE MANUAL LABOR MOVEMENT IN AMERICA

Fellenberg's manual labor program in connection with agriculture and mechanics at Hofwyl in Switzerland had been brought to the attention of American educators through reports by A. D. Bache, president of Gerard College, Henry Barnard, William McClure, and others. Fellenberg's school efficiently combined the academic with the manual labor program, and some educators reasoned that the physical activity involved in the latter might well serve as a substitute for a formally organized program of exercise to promote the student's health.

The Society for Promoting Manual Labor in Literary Institutions was organized in 1831 and Theodore Weld appointed general agent. Weld spent considerable time traveling throughout the country. The manual labor plan appealed particularly to small denominational schools as a "work your way through college" feature. The state of Indiana offers good examples. The Presbyterians established the Wabash Manual Labor College in 1832, and similar schools included Hanover, Franklin, Depauw, and Earlham. By the Civil War this type of organization had lost its popularity, to appear later in a more constructive form in the manual training movement.

EDUCATION OF GIRLS AND WOMEN

Benjamin Rush (1745–1813) was the earliest advocate of female education in the United States. This physician and signer of the Declaration of Independence had a great interest in all reform and philanthropic movements. He was influential in founding the Young Ladies' Academy in Philadelphia in 1787, and his ideas on female education were widely read and quoted in the early nineteenth century.

During the late eighteenth and early nineteenth centuries a novel type of secondary school for girls developed called the "female seminary," which extended from Maine to Georgia and as far west as the frontier. Noah Webster in 1806 mentions "two distinguished schools for young ladies" in Connecticut, the Union School at New Haven and the Academy in Litchfield. These academies, he stated, provided instruction in the primary branches, geography, grammar, languages, and the higher branches of mathematics.

It must be kept in mind, however, that the academies were usually not free, but depended on tuition to defray their expenses. Girls from poorer families were dependent upon parochial and charity schools or did without an education. Several attempts had been made to provide public education for girls through high schools supported by public funds, but these failed because of their great popularity. A public high school for girls was established in Boston in 1826, and the enrollment was so large that it closed within eighteen months because the public was unwilling to meet the expense of such a large student body. The New York Girls' High School was founded in the same year with an outlay of $20,300 for facilities, staff, and equipment, but failed for the same reason.

FEMALE SEMINARIES AND PIONEER LEADERS

As the academy movement gained momentum, a rash of private seminaries sprang into being. These were in the main poorly financed, staffed, and equipped. At their worst, however, they were an improvement over the eighteenth-century private day and boarding schools known as finishing schools. Several of America's greatest women educators started to fame in these female seminaries.[9]

Emma Willard (1787–1870) was born in Berlin, Connecticut, of good New England stock and received her education from the town academy.[10] Her first teaching position was in a district school at Kensington, followed by a similar job in Troy, New York. She several times approached the New York legislature at Albany with a request that it establish a female seminary. Although she failed, the city of Troy financed an academy for girls and placed her in charge.

Mary Lyon (1797–1849) was the fifth of seven children born to a humble farmer in Buckland, Massachusetts.[10] She was a devout Puritan who, through the influence of Rev. Joseph Emerson, dedicated herself to the advancement of education for women. During a succession of teaching assignments Mary Lyon formulated plans for a female seminary for the daughters of poor farmers and laborers. With the help of Dr. Edward Hitchcock, later president of Amherst College, she finally secured a charter to establish the Mount Holyoke Seminary at South Hadley.

Although Emma Willard and Mary Lyon included domestic duties in the school program, as was the custom among female seminaries, both saw value in exercise and dancing to preserve health and improve poise. At the Middlebury Female Seminary Emma Willard included dancing to develop graceful carriage, but felt that domestic chores associated with living at the school provided sufficient exercise. Mary Lyon, on the other hand, believed that calisthenics and dance-like steps (double springs, skipping steps, and the five positions of ballet) belonged on the exercise program.

Born in East Hampton, Long Island, Catherine Beecher (1800–1878) came from a distinguished New England family. After her fiancé, Alexander M. Fisher, a professor of mathematics at Yale University, lost his life at sea in 1822, she devoted the remaining fifty-six years of her life to the furtherance of education for women.[12]

Like Emma Willard and Mary Lyon, Catherine Beecher accepted several teaching positions and established seminaries at Hartford, Connecticut (1821) and Cincinnati, Ohio (1832). She became active in the Women's Educational Association of Boston, which was important in the seminary movement in the West during the 1850s.

She wrote her *Physiology and Calisthenics for Schools and Families* in 1856 as a guide for teachers and for home consumption.

In her seminaries, Catherine Beecher introduced calisthenics related to the Swedish system. At Cincinnati she stated:

> I invented a course in calisthenic exercises accompanied by music which was an improvement over the one I adopted at Hartford. The aim was to secure all the advantages supposed to be gained in dancing schools, with the additional advantages for securing graceful movements to the sound of music.[13]

In her book physiology was treated from the structural rather than functional approach common in her day. Always a critic of the absurd fashions in women's dress, she found space for adverse comments on tight-fitting corsets and the practice of wearing voluminous dresses over countless petticoats.

GERMAN-AMERICAN GYMNASTIC SOCIETIES

The agitation for reform in the German Confederation of States between 1848 and 1849 led to the emigration of many Germans to the United States. Naturally they sought out their compatriots in such metropolitan areas as Chicago, Cincinnati, Columbus, Louisville, Milwaukee, and St. Louis. With amazing speed they established their own schools, churches, newspapers, singing societies, and Turner organizations. The first Turner Society was founded by Frederich Hecker in Cincinnati, in 1848, and in the same year Hecker assisted in the establishment of a society in New York. In 1850 steps were taken to form a national *Turnerbund* and the first *Turnfest,* a competitive gymnastic meet, was held in Philadelphia in 1851. Between 1851 and 1860 fourteen national *Turnfests* were held in the United States.

But all did not go well for the *Turnerbund.* A conflict between the eastern and western contingent in 1858 split the organization. The younger generation of German-Americans organized societies on their own after the German model but with American innovations, in Cincinnati, Indianapolis, Louisville, and New Orleans. The new societies held their first *Turnfest* at Oxford, Ohio, in 1858.[14]

MOVEMENTS OF RELIGIOUS ORIGIN

One of the early educational movements in America was the Sunday school plan of instruction. Robert Raikes, a Gloucester printer, originated the idea in England during the 1780s as a means of keeping factory children off the streets on Sunday and at the same time provide them with some kind of education.

The Sunday school movement started in the United States in Hanover County, Virginia, in 1786, and subsequent schools were founded in Charleston, South Carolina (for Negro children in 1787), Philadelphia (1791), New York (1793), and Pawtucket, Rhode Island (1797). Churches eventually recognized the value of the Sunday school and between 1808 and 1824 organized agencies to encourage Sunday school attendance for all classes, rich and poor. The churches, however, began to object to the use of Sunday school for secular instruction and changed the original plan to an hour or so of religious teaching. The Sunday school movement was contemporaneous with the struggle to establish public-supported schools and because of its democratic approach was helpful in molding favorable public opinion.

THE YOUNG MEN'S CHRISTIAN ASSOCIATION

In 1841 George Williams, a London dry-goods clerk, conceived the idea of assisting young men to lead a moral and upright life through prayer meetings. The response to his idea was excellent, and in 1844 he founded a club which he called the Young Men's Christian Association.

George M. Van Derlip, a New York University student, actually started the chain of events leading to the organization of the first association in Boston in 1851. Van Derlip, who was visiting abroad, was commissioned to write an account of his experiences at the London World's Fair for the *Christian Watchman and the Reflector,* a Baptist weekly published in Boston. His account of the YMCA exhibit attracted the attention of Thomas V. Sullivan, a retired sea captain, who for years had been working to establish a "home away from home" for seamen. He was a member of a committee of seven who met on December 29, 1851, to draw up a constitution, and the YMCA movement was launched in the United States. A few weeks earlier, unknown to Sullivan and his fellow committee members, a similar association had been organized in Montreal, the first in North America.

The Boston constitution stated that the association had "a strong desire for the promotion of evangelical religion among young men of this city." To accomplish this, the association rented several rooms. A library of several hundred books and newspapers from a number of New England towns was made available. Services included prayer meetings, Bible classes, lectures, an employment bureau, a boarding house register, and a social program.

The Boston YMCA was quickly followed, in 1852, by associations in New York, Worcester, Springfield, Buffalo, Portsmouth (New Hampshire), Washington, D.C., Concord (New Hampshire), New London, Hartford, Detroit, Baltimore, and New Orleans. By January, 1856, fifty-six associations had been organized in the United States and Canada, and by 1860 there were 205 YMCAs with 25,000 members.[15]

THE LADIES' CHRISTIAN ASSOCIATION

The first Ladies' Christian Association was organized at a meeting in the chapel of New York University in 1858 and Mrs. Marshall O. Roberts was elected director. The Association's 1860 report mentioned religious services for 100 women employed at the Tract House and for 500 engaged in work at a hoop skirt factory. At the suggestion of Rev. Herman Dyer that it should provide a comfortable and safe boarding place for young women away from home, the organization opened its first house on June 1. 1860. It was so successful that houses in other localities in the city were purchased for similar use.[16]

THE YOUNG MEN'S HEBREW ASSOCIATION

In the early 1840s a Jewish youth movement arose which resulted in the formation of literary societies. These organizations took the name of Young Men's Hebrew Literary Associations and promoted a program of religious services, lectures, debates, dramatics, and social activities. The first was founded in Philadelphia in 1850 under the sponsorship of the noted Rabbi Isaac Lester. Cities that soon had similar organizations included New York (1851), Baltimore (1854), New Orleans (1855), and Richmond (1856). Toward the end of the 1850s, a related though independent movement was that of the Young Men's Hebrew Association. Its purpose was the cultivation of a better knowledge of the history, literature, and doctrines of Judaism, the elevation of moral character, and the defense by honorable and peaceful means of the faith of the Jewish people. The older literary societies were rapidly assimilated into the YMHA, and organizations were formed in Augusta, Georgia (1857), Cleveland (1858), and other urban centers. The YMHA dates its origin to the conversion of the Baltimore Literary Association (1854) to the new organization.[17]

SPORTS INTERESTS, 1776–1860

Many sports were introduced by the English and other European immigrants before the Civil War. These were often of a recreational nature, but many provided an opportunity for wagering, and the sums that changed hands would be considered substantial even in modern times. Sports interest was gaining momentum just before the conflict and, after some hesitation in the postwar years, continued its forward trend in the 1870s.

EARLY ROWING CONTESTS

The earliest record of a rowing race involved sixteen whaleboats with crews of six men each in the Cape Cod area in 1765. The next recorded races were held in 1807, 1811, and 1824 by members of the merchant marines on the East and Hudson rivers and between the Robbins Reef Light and Castle Garden, New York. The first boat race of an international nature was held in 1824 between a picked crew of the English frigate *Hussar* and the American sailing vessel *Whitehall* off Hoboken Point. Between 1824 and 1833 rowing races became more frequent at Newburg in the Hudson Valley and at Poughkeepsie. These races were conducted with six-oar crews over courses of four and four and one-half miles. Racing enthusiasts organized the Castle Garden Amateur Boat Club Association in 1834, the Detroit Club in 1839, and the rowing clubs of Philadelphia joined together in 1858 in what they called the Schuylkill River Navy. Rowing reached Boston between 1842 and 1843, and in 1851 Charleston, South Carolina, sent entries to a regatta held in New York. The City of Chicago held a regatta on Lake Michigan in 1857 over a four-mile course for fours and sixes.[18]

In 1852 Harvard and Yale held the first intercollegiate rowing contest on Lake Winnipesaukee, New Hampshire, as part of a publicity stunt to promote summer resorts in the area. The race consisted of crews of eights and coxswains who were chosen for their knowledge rather than their avoirdupois. The reaction of the college authorities to this stunt was mixed since it was unprecedented. The contest also gave the students a chance to leave the campuses of their respective schools and cavort in town and tavern. The next race was postponed until 1855, and four years later Harvard and Yale were joined by Brown in a college regatta. By this time Bowdoin and Wesleyan organized crews and prepared to enter the competition, but the Civil War halted rowing activities, which were resumed in the postwar years.

THE CALEDONIAN GAMES AND TRACK AND FIELD ATHLETICS

The first recorded Caledonian Games were held in Boston in 1853. Caledonian Societies were organized first in the New England States, then in the frontier states. Events included track and field events in addition to specialty races, wrestling, and native dances such as the Highland fling and broadsword dance. In addition to the Caledonian Games, the Scots introduced the game of curling.

Contributing to the development of interest in track and field athletics was the English sport of pedestrianism. This involved matched races, running or walking, over a prescribed distance, between athletes of established reputation. The prowess of performers was advertised through handbills, newspapers, and by word-of-mouth, and challenges were issued through the same channels. The contests invariably involved high stakes, which were furnished by individuals or groups who believed in their favorites' capabilities. Although pedestrianism existed before the Civil War, it did not reach its peak until after the war.

BASEBALL

A ball game which employed bases and a variety of bat and ball games were played by English children during the eighteenth century and brought by them to the colonies. English rounders and the games of four-o'-cat and town ball were popular in New England, and the games of trap and buff ball were played in the South.[19] Although A. G. Spaulding and his researchers came to the conclusion that baseball, like basketball and volleyball, was a game of purely American origin, it is certain that early versions of the game played during the colonial and national periods contributed to its final form.[20]

According to Robert W. Henderson[21] and other reliable scholars,[22] the popular belief that Abner Doubleday adopted the diamond in place of square baselines in 1839 and created the first set of workable rules is entirely erroneous. It is known, for instance, that in their baseball games children anticipated adults by many years in the use of diamond-shaped baselines. As for the first set of rules, the credit goes to Alexander J. Cartwright, who in 1842 organized a baseball club composed of business and professional men in Hoboken, which later became known as the Knickerbocker Club and in 1845 printed the first set of rules. By the close of the 1850s baseball had spread to practically every section of the country. In 1858 the National Association of Base Ball Players was organized with delegates from twenty-five clubs, mainly from New York and New Jersey.

In intercollegiate circles Amherst, Princeton, and Williams were among the first to field a baseball team. Princeton organized a team in 1858 called the Nassaus and played their first intercollegiate match in 1860. The earliest intercollegiate match, however, took place between Amherst and Williams on July 1, 1859. It was not until 1879, however, that the first intercollegiate league was organized.

OTHER SPORTS INTERESTS

The people of the British Isles developed a strong interest in wrestling during the eighteenth and nineteenth centuries. Many who emigrated to the New World favored particular wrestling styles. The Lancashire style, which suited American taste, resembled the modern "free style."[23] According to the records, George Washington used the Cornish style while Abraham Lincoln used a combination of the Cumberland and Westmoreland styles.

Under the influence of French faculty members, foil fencing was introduced at an early date in New England universities and colleges for women. The New York Turner Society sponsored fencing in 1851 under the leadership of Frank Seigal, who later became a general in the Civil War. The Society conducted national championship matches as early as 1853.

Cricket is mentioned in the literature of early America.[19] William Byrd, who kept a diary from 1709 to 1712, mentions playing cricket at Westover, Virginia, and Ebenezer Davis stated that he witnessed a game of cricket in the city square in New Orleans in 1849. Like Rugby, cricket was no doubt introduced to the American schoolboy by his English cousin, but with less lasting success. The professional team that toured the United States and Canada in 1859 acquainted many Americans with the game, but left no permanent impact.

Interest in swimming was well developed in the colonies. So prevalent was it in England that Benjamin Franklin, a strong and skillful swimmer, was tempted at one time to remain in that country and devote his time to swimming instruction. The German refugee Francis Lieber found his swimming classes far more popular with the Bostonians than the gymnastic exercises of his open-air gymnasium. In this era little interest was shown in speed swimming, and the breast stroke was considered the most practical style for both recreation and lifesaving.

NOTES

1. R. Freeman Butts and Lawrence A. Cremin. *A History of Education in American Culture.* New York: Henry Holt and Company, 1953, pp. 145–152; 196–227. *The Life History of the United States. The Growing Years,* Volume 3: 1789–1829. (Margaret L. Coit and the Editors of *Life*) 1963, pp. 49–53.
2. Edgar W. Knight. *Education in the United States.* Columbus: Ginn and Company, 1951 pp. 135–306.

3. Will S. Monroe. *History of the Pestalozzian Movement in the United States.* Syracuse: C. W. Bardeen, Publisher, 1907.
4. Joseph Neef. *Sketch of a Plan and Method of Education Founded on an Analysis of Human Faculties and Natural Reason Suitable for the Offspring of a Free People, and All Rational Beings.* Philadelphia (No publisher listed), 1808. (Philadelphia Public Library)
5. Ralph E. Billet. "Evidence of Play and Exercise in Early Pestalozzian and Lancasterian Elementary Schools in the United States." *The Research Quarterly,* 23:2 (May, 1952), 127–135.
6. Fred Eugene Leonard and George B. Affleck. *A Guide to the History of Physical Education.* Philadelphia: Lea and Febiger, 1947, pp. 249–252.
7. Fred E. Leonard. *Pioneers of Modern Physical Training.* New York: Association Press, 1915, pp. 71; 63; 77.
8. J. C. Warren. *Importance of Physical Education.* Convention of Teachers, American Institute of Instruction. Boston: Hilliard, Gray, Little and Wilkins, 1831, pp. 27–51.
9. Thomas Woody. *A History of Women's Education in the United States.* (Volume I) New York: The Science Press, 1939, pp. 329–342.
10. Willystine Goodsell. *Pioneers of Women's Education in the United States.* New York: McGraw-Hill Book Company, Inc., 1931.
11. Emma Willard. *A Plan for Improving Female Education.* (A reprint of the second edition, 1819) Middlebury College, Vermont, 1918.
12. Martha Bacon. "Miss Beecher in Hell." *American Heritage,* 14:1 (December, 1962), 28–29; 102–105.
13. "Catherine Beecher." *Bernard's American Journal of Education,* 28 (1878), 83.
14. Fred E. Leonard. "German-American Gymnastic Societies and the North American Turnerbund." *American Physical Education Review,* 15:9 (December, 1910), 617–628.
15. Charles Howard Hopkins. *History of the YMCA in North America.* New York: Association Press, 1951.
16. Elizabeth Wilson. *Fifty Years of Association Work Among Young Women (1866–1916).* New York: National Board of Young Women's Christian Association of the United States, 1916.
17. Benjamin Rabinowitz. *The Young Men's Hebrew Association (1854–1913).* New York: National Jewish Welfare Board, 1948, pp. 2–11.
18. Robert F. Kelley. *American Rowing, Its Background and Traditions.* New York: G. P. Putnam's Sons, 1932, pp. 16–24; 101.
19. Ruth White Fink. "Recreational Pursuits in the Old South." *The Research Quarterly,* 23:1 (March, 1952), 35.

20. Paul Stagg. "The Development of the National Collegiate Athletic Association in Relationship to Intercollegiate Athletics in the United States." (Dissertation) New York University, 1946.
21. Robert W. Henderson. *Early American Sports.* (Revised edition) New York: A. S. Barnes and Company, 1953.
22. Foster Rhea Dulles. *America Learns to Play*. New York: D. Appleton-Century Company, Inc., 1940, pp. 185–191.
23. Keith Edward Bowen. "A History of Intercollegiate Wrestling in the United States of America." (Dissertation) Indiana University, 1952, pp. 68–72. Henry A. Stone. *Wrestling: Intercollegiate and Olympic.* (Second edition) New Jersey: Prentice-Hall, Inc., 1950.

Chapter 18

PHYSICAL EDUCATION IN THE UNITED STATES, 1861–1900

INDUSTRIAL GROWTH

THE demand created by the Civil War for rifles, guns, ammunition, and other military supplies provided a running start for an industrial expansion that dwarfed the gains of previous years. Many factors were favorable to the industrial and agricultural growth of the North and West. America possessed a wealth of natural resources which had never been tapped. Virgin timber lands furnished lumber for the manufacture of wooden products and building materials. Vast supplies of iron ore, copper, zinc, and lead were available to the steel mills and nonferrous fabricators. Seemingly unlimited sources of coal, gas, oil, and water supplied the motive power for factories, which increased from 140,000 in 1860 to 500,000 by 1900.

Favorable action by Congress enhanced the growth of both industry and agriculture in the form of protective tariffs, the establishment of a national banking system, and the generous land grants of the Homestead Law. Networks of railroad tracks, steamship lines, and telegraph systems fostered the spirit of nationalism by making manufactured goods and sectional produce as well as the speedier exchange of news available to all. Inexpensive electrical energy added material comfort to many homes and gave the manufacturer a source of cheap power for the production of new consumer goods.

Large corporations, monopolies, unfair trade practices, and an increased demand for factory workers went hand in hand with industrial expansion. The growth of cities was phenomenal, and the slum districts of immigrants crowded the modest homes of the middle class and the ornate mansions of the *nouveau riche.* Worsened living conditions in the cities encouraged crime and juvenile delinquency, the spread of communicable diseases, and an increase in problems of sanitation. These in turn spurred the development of recreation, social agencies, and public and school health services. The demand for factory workers and laborers of all kind favored lenient immigration policies, and new citizens-to-be arrived in a seemingly unending stream after 1870. Agriculture, particularly in the West, became mechanized, and through the application of scientific knowledge farmers increased yields and production.

DEVELOPMENT OF EDUCATIONAL PHILOSOPHIES

Before the Civil War, drawing its inspiration from the philosophical idealism of the German Kant, Schelling, and Fitche, and the English Carlyle and Coleridge, a nonsectarian religious movement developed called transcendentalism. Ralph Waldo Emerson was its most celebrated exponent. Transcendentalism held that perception took place within the mind itself, as opposed to perception through the experience or things. Knowledge of all things beyond the boundaries of experience, including religion, was revealed to the individual through his consciousness. The transcendentalists looked with disapproval upon materialism, industrialism, and the exploitation of man by man and were therefore associated with many social and political reform movements, including anti-slavery, women's rights, temperance, prison reform, child labor, and vegetarianism. The transcendentalists emphasized the dignity and worth of the individual man and stressed the unique character of his spiritual nature, his self-reliance, and his self-cultivation.

IDEALISM

After the war transcendentalism lost ground to an idealistic philosophy, influenced by German sources, but characteristically American. This philosophy made an important contribution to

American colleges in the last half of the nineteenth century by replacing sectarian doctrines with nonsectarian beliefs. Darwin's theory of evolution, which drew the heavy fire of Christian faiths during this period, was easily resolved by the idealists, who contended that the universe was going through a constant process of growth in accordance with God's will.

Since the educational theories of Pestalozzi and Froebel stressed respect for the child's personality and its development, the idealist accepted their theories, particularly at the elementary school level. The idealist's greatest contribution to American education was his stress upon the development of the individual's personality as an end in itself.

CLASSICAL HUMANISM

Classical humanism of the late nineteenth and early twentieth centuries was a dualistic educational philosophy which combined idealism with traditional faculty psychology. The classical humanists held that man had certain distinctive qualities or reason, moral precepts, and religious beliefs which set him apart from the animal and physical world. Truths, values, and knowledge were unchangeable and existed in a sphere above nature. Education was a matter, not of sense perceptions, but of disciplining the mental faculties and developing the moral, spiritual, and aesthetic faculties. This type of education was best obtained from the classical languages and literature, mathematics, philosophy, religion, and fine arts.

Thus the humanities were far superior as an educational discipline than the sciences, social sciences, and technical and vocational subjects. The humanist claimed that the study of the humanities would discipline the student's mind, cultivative his moral and ethical character, develop an aesthetic appreciation of the finer things in life, and provide a broad liberal education regardless of his eventual career. The classical humanists formed a line of defense against the new psychology of the early twentieth century, the social and physical sciences, the elective system proposed by Charles W. Eliot, and deplored the attention given to the needs, interests, and freedom of students.[1]

APPLICATION OF EDUCATIONAL THEORIES

Before the Civil War education had begun to meet the demands of a progressively industrialized society through a broader and more practical curriculum, and to be extended to both sexes and all classes on a free basis. In the postwar period the early followers of Pestalozzi reached maturity and the trend was toward the child-centered school. In the more progressive elementary institutions the schoolroom became a miniature society in which individual development was the objective, motor expression the method, and social cooperation the means. Experimentation with the educational principles of Froebel and Herbart completely revitalized the elementary school during the last half of the nineteenth century and provided the basis for later progress under John Dewey and others.

DEVITALIZED SECONDARY AND HIGHER EDUCATION

Attempts to liberalize the secondary school and college and university curriculum were resisted by the traditionalists, who clung tenaciously to the mental discipline that was supposed to accrue from the study of foreign language, mathematics, and other subjects. The Committee of Ten on Secondary School Studies reported to the National Education Association in 1893 that the high school courses required for college entrance also prepared the pupil for participation in life.[2]

The Committee of Thirteen, which was appointed as a result of the report of the Committee of Ten, to consider college entrance requirements, recommended four units in foreign language, two in mathematics, two in English, one in history, and one in science.[3] The attitude and standards upheld by these two committees influenced the pattern of the American secondary school for the next twenty-five years.

GYMNASTICS IN EDUCATION

The strenuously active days of frontier life had drawn to a close, and Americans were pursuing of the easier way of life which advances in technology had made possible. In 1800 the 14-16-hour workday was common. A 13-hour day was the rule in 1840, followed by a 10-12-hour day in 1880, and an 8-hour day appeared a possibility before the turn of the century. Many medical and educational leaders deplored the fact that man had succumbed to a sedentary and easy way of life. The medical examiners' reports of men between the ages of 18 and 45 drafted during the Civil War showed that 50 percent in the professional class, 46 percent in the mercantile class, and 43 percent in the semiskilled and skilled laboring class had been rejected because of physical disability. The remedy for this situation, in the opinion of physicians as well as advocates of exercise, was a regime of systematic exercise in the school and home.

American schools had already been introduced to foreign systems of gymnastics in the first half of the nineteenth century. Advocates of the various systems quickly and ably defended gymnastics as a sure means to bodily and mental discipline.[4] Gymnastics held other attractions, such as a ready supply of teachers from gymnastic societies and short-term training schools; systematic instruction with a minimum of interference with the school program; economy of space since gymnastics could be taught in halls, corridors, basements, abandoned buildings, and even barns; and good public relations through annual gymnasium exhibits or festivals.

Since gymnastics had gained such an acceptable status in education, it might be well to consider some of the gymnastic leaders of the period and their systems.

DIO LEWIS' SYSTEM

A farm boy, Dio Lewis (1823–1886) was born in Cayuga County, New York. He left school when he was 12, and after six months of work in a cotton factory and two years in a farm implement factory decided to try his luck at teaching school. At 18 he left New York and organized a school at Fremont, Ohio, but left shortly because of ill health. After serving as a physician's apprentice for several years, he entered Harvard Medical School in 1845, but did not complete his degree. In 1852 Lewis joined the Sons of Temperance movement and gained a reputation as a temperance and health lecturer in the United States and Canada. On tour he devoted his spare time to the "invention of a new system of gymnastics" and in 1860 he settled in Boston, where he introduced the Lewis system and made plans to open a normal school for gymnastics.

In August, 1860, Lewis accepted a thirty-minute lecture spot at the American Institute of Instruction. His subject was his new system of gymnastics and his presentation was so enthralling that the thirty minutes stretched to two hours and the audience wanted still more. As a consequence he received immediate support in establishing the Normal Institute for teacher preparation the following year. This institute was the first training school for gymnastic instructors in the United States. When it closed its doors in 1868, Lewis had graduated more than 250 teachers, most of whom were women.

Lewis published ten editions of his book *The New Gymnastics for Men, Women and Children* between 1862 and 1868.[4] The work leaned heavily on foreign sources. Lewis' contributions included the suggestions that gymnastics exercises be done to music, that the bean bag replace dumbbells for women and children, and that gymnastic crowns be made of lead. These crowns weighed from 3 to 100 pounds and were worn from five to fifteen minutes to improve posture.

Through his ability as a lecturer, writer,[5] and promoter, Lewis focused public attention on the crying need for organized exercise for men, women, and children. When he arrived on the American scene, the gymnasium was associated in the public mind with prize fighters, weight-lifters, and rowdies, and he helped educate the public to the fact that it could serve the welfare of all. Though his Institute had a short career, his graduates carried his ideas to the public schools and women's colleges and prepared the way for the acceptance of other systems and eventually sports in colleges for women. His Normal Institute, primitive and deficient as it was, focused the attention of other gymnastic leaders on the need for teacher-training schools.

THE GERMAN SYSTEM

Since many of its members volunteered for military service in the Union forces, the *Turnerbund* practically ceased operations during the Civil War. At the close of the war representatives of the *Tur-*

nerbund met in Washington, D.C., and changed their organization's name to the North American Gymnastic Union.* They agreed that all active members should participate in a program based on the Jahn-Eiselen system of apparatus work and Speiss's free exercise until the age of 30. They also agreed to organize classes for boys and girls.

Local and national *Turnfests,* or gymnastic festivals, had been held yearly from 1851 to 1860. After the war these festivals were held irregularly, sometimes as much as eight years apart. The *Turnfests* acted as a cohesive force in perpetuating the Turner spirit in America. No other organization so actively opposed late nineteenth-century proposals to substitute military drill for gymnastics in the school, and the Turners contributed much to the cause of the playground movement in the United States. Many of their performers in the twentieth century have represented their country in the Olympic Games.

In 1886 the Turners initiated an active campaign to acquaint the American public and educators with the merits of the German system and to attract American-born members of all age groups. They sent delegates to the annual meetings of the American Association for the Advancement of Physical Education, prepared a demonstration and exhibit at the World's Fair in Chicago, 1893, and began their monthly publication *Mind and Body* in 1894. William A. Stecher prepared a textbook on the German-American system of gymnastics for teachers and pupils in private and public schools.[6]

The Normal School of the North American Gymnastic Union (1866) at Milwaukee was under the direction of George Brosius between 1875 and 1888. His graduates became directors of gymnastics in many public schools of the Middle West. Henry Suder was appointed director in Chicago, 1886; William Reuter, Davenport, 1887; Karl Zapp, Cleveland, 1887; George Wittich, St. Louis, 1890; Hans Ballin, Sandusky, 1890; Anton Liebold, Columbus, 1892; Carl Zeigler, Cincinnati, 1892; Hans Rasmussen, Milwaukee, 1892; and Robert Nohr, Dayton, 1892. Ballin, Liebold, and Ras-

* This was subsequently changed to the American Gymnastic Union (1919) and the American Turners (1939).

mussen published schoolroom manuals on gymnastics, and Nohr and Wittich were regular contributors to *Mind and Body*.

THE SWEDISH SYSTEM

The seminaries for young women in the United States showed an early interest in the Swedish system. It was not, however, until the 1880s that active promoters of the system arrived in this country. Hartwig Nissen (1855–1924), one of the first, organized the Swedish Health Institute in Washington, D.C., and taught Swedish gymnastics at the Franklin School and at Johns Hopkins University. Nissen's Institute attracted national attention when he improved the health of several government officials.

Baron Nils Posse (1862–1895), a graduate of the Royal Central Institute of Gymnastics, arrived in Boston in 1885. His special interest, like Nissen's, was medical gymnastics, and he immediately contacted the city's physicians in the hope of selling his services. Meanwhile, Mrs. Mary Hemenway, one of Boston's wealthiest women, and Miss Amy Morris Homans, who made a formidable team in working for civic improvements, had become conscious of the need for exercise in the Boston public schools. On the recommendation of friends, Mrs. Hemenway employed Baron Posse to teach twenty-five women instructors the Swedish system of educational gymnastics.* This move led to the adoption of the Swedish system by the public schools and the establishment of the Boston Normal School of Gymnastics, which Mrs. Hemenway endowed and of which she made Baron Posse the first director in 1889.

Other leaders of the Swedish system in the United States included Claese J. Enebuske, who succeeded Baron Posse as director of the Boston Normal School in 1890; Jakob Bolin, instructor of gymnastics at the Anderson Normal School; William Skarstrom, instructor at Columbia University and Wellesley College; Alice Tripp Hall, a graduate of Wellesley College and instructor at Goucher College;

* As a result of her experience as a nurse during the Civil War, Mrs. Hemenway believed that the one thing American youth needed most was physical education. She sent representatives to Europe to study the various systems, and they concluded that the Swedish system was not only the best but the most scientific.

and Dr. Kate Campbell Hurd, first medical director of the Bryn Mawr School for Girls.

Mrs. Hemenway and Miss Homans sponsored a conference for all those interested in gymnastics in Boston in 1889.[7] It included four sessions and attracted more than 2000 persons. A large portion of the program was devoted to a discussion of the Swedish system by Baron Posse, but representatives from Amherst and Harvard universities discussed the merits of the German system currently being followed at these institutions. The conference emphasized the importance of teacher training, dedicated the profession to the continuation of formal gymnastics, encouraged the physical examination of pupils as a prerequisite to taking gymnastics, and recommended the scientific approach to physical education.

THE DELSARTEAN SYSTEM

François Delsarte (1811–1871) was born in Solesmes, France. Showing remarkable musical talent at an early age, he was granted a scholarship to the Conservatory of Music in Paris. Turning from music to the theater, he studied the stylized acting technique of the time, noting the natural reaction of bodily posture to emotional stresses, and for many years conducted classes for stage and operatic performers.

Delsarte did not put his theories into written form, and most of the available information was taken from the lecture notes and reminiscences of his students.* This fact permitted a wide latitude in the interpretation of Delsarte's methods.

Among his students was Steele Mackaye, an American who in 1871 was the first to lecture on Delsarte in this country. Mackaye, like his teacher, left no record, and it remained for Genevieve Stebbins and Emily Bishop to provide the first printed description of the Delsartean system of physical culture, as it was called.[8]

The system, which consisted of a series of expressive exercises, was adopted by many private schools of elocution and oratory in the late nineteenth century.[9] Although Delsarte had no intentions of creating a gymnastic system, his interpreters introduced the public

* The best library collection on Delsarte in the United States belongs to the Speech Department of the Louisiana State University, Baton Rouge.

and particularly women to the pleasure to be derived from a light form of exercise. The true interpretation of Delsarte's theories as embodied in art forms had to wait until the twentieth century.[10]

GYMNASTICS AND THE YMCA

The interest in health and gymnastics following the Civil War encouraged the Young Men's Christian Association to expand its original objective to include physical improvement. As the New York City Association stated in its revised constitution of 1866: "The object of this association shall be the improvement of the spiritual, mental, social and physical condition of young men."[11] Gymnasiums with baths were constructed in such metropolitan areas as San Francisco, New York, and Washington, D.C.

With the new gymnasiums, the problem of finding leaders arose. According to the ideals of the Association, a director of gymnastics had to be a natural leader, a good organizer, and a "Christian gymnast." Circus performers and prize fighters who were considered were openly contemptuous of these ideals. The Boston Association finally secured Robert J. Roberts (1849–1920), a Sunday school teacher and disciple of George Winship, who had popularized weight-lifting in America. Failing to arouse interest among his young men in his weight-lifting program, Roberts conceived a program which was a compromise between Winship's heavy exercises and Dio Lewis' light gymnastics.

In 1885 the Association founded the International Training School at Springfield, Massachusetts. Roberts, appointed the first director of the gymnasium department, guided the program away from heavy exercise and made gymnastic exercises attractive to all. He resigned in 1890 and was succeeded by Luther Halsey Gulick, who became one of Springfield College's most progressive leaders and one of the most distinguished men in modern physical education.

LUTHER H. GULICK. (1865–1918). Born in Honolulu of a missionary family, Dr. Gulick's education was constantly interrupted by travel and foreign residence. At Oberlin College he became interested in William Blaikie's *How to Get Strong and How to Stay*

So, which was to inspire many future leaders, and he decided that gymnastics was his field. He left Oberlin to enroll in the Sargent School of Physical Training at Cambridge and after a six months' course secured a position as director of physical training at the YMCA in Jackson, Michigan, in 1886. In the fall of the same year he enrolled in the medical school of New York University and completed his medical degree in 1899.

When Gulick succeeded Roberts, the Association considered the gymnastic work merely a means to attract young men to its religious program. Dr. Gulick convinced the International Committee that physical development was as necessary as mental and spiritual education to the development of the whole man. He devised the red triangle to represent the unity of purpose of the Association: the education of body, mind, and spirit. Gulick raised the professional status of the director of physical training and developed a curriculum for training teachers which gained international recognition.

DR. GULICK'S INTEREST IN SPORTS. As Hopkins so ably put it, Dr. Gulick "found the YMCA doing calisthenics and left it on the basketball court and playing field."[11] He also valued body-building activities and attempted to keep sports in balance with these.

During Gulick's early years at Springfield College, James Naismith invented basketball (1891) as an indoor game suitable for the winter months.[12] It became immediately popular in YMCA programs throughout the country and eventually found its way into public schools, colleges and universities. G. W. Morgan, a graduate of Springfield, found basketball too strenuous for the businessmen in his classes and in 1895 conceived a game which he called "mintonette." When Morgan told Dr. Gulick about his new indoor game, Gulick invited him to bring two teams to Springfield for an exhibition game, and eventually volleyball, like basketball, made the circuit of the YMCAs in the United States and later abroad.

Dr. Gulick became concerned over the excessive popularity of basketball, and as an antidote he devised the pentathlon, which consisted of track and field events. Basketball, however, continued to gain in popularity. In 1896 the Association organized the Athletic League of North America to coordinate its expanding athletic interests and keep competition on a high plane. The *Era* became its official publication.

THE FIRST YWCAs IN AMERICA

Young women were continually arriving in Boston to seek employment from all parts of New England, and no agency was available to offer them protection or care for them when they were unemployed or ill. Lucretia Boyd, a missionary, discussed this situation with the Boston City Missionary Society and outlined a plan for a Young Women's Christian Association in 1859, but the membership, though they approved her plan, felt that they could not carry it out alone. In 1866 thirty ladies met at the home of Mrs. Henry F. Durant and organized the Boston Young Women's Christian Association. Two rooms were secured in the Congregational Building and placed in charge of a general secretary, Mary Foster, a woman of attractive personality and a wise counselor. The venture was so successful that two houses were purchased in 1868, which provided lodgings for eighty young ladies. The YWCA was firmly established, and Associations grew with rapidity throughout the country.

In 1884 a new building in Boston was purchased for the purpose of training leaders and also to house an employment bureau, assembly hall, administrative offices, and reading room. It also contained a large dining hall and sleeping rooms for 156 young women, and the entire fifth floor was devoted to the Durant Gymasium, one of the first in a YWCA building. The board of managers employed Anna Wood of Wellesley College as the first gymnastic teacher. The early programs featured drills with Indian clubs, dumbbells, wands and hoops, and calisthenics. The program was influenced by the Dio Lewis, Delsartean, and Swedish systems and had a phase in which Dudley A. Sargent's mechanical devices were used.[13]

PUBLIC INTEREST IN SPORTS

In the postwar years pedestrianism became an anachronism as other track activities made a stronger bid for attention. The Caledonian Societies, once confined to the New England states, spread westward and in 1870 were numerous enough in this country and Canada to form the North American Caledonian Association. The younger members withdrew in 1875 to found the Scottish American Club, which became one of the major athletic clubs in the East. Baseball emerged from the Civil War as a popular amateur game and as a professional sport. Professional baseball teams organized the National League (1875), American Association (1882), and American League (1900). Although metropolitan athletic clubs had been organized as early as the 1860s, their real growth took place between 1870 and 1890. Extending across the nation, they became a strong force in regulating track competition and promoting a surprising variety of sports. These clubs held dozens of track meets weekly, beginning with Washington's Birthday and ending on Thanksgiving Day. On one occasion two athletic clubs in the same location sponsored a track meet on the same day and together drew 800 participants representing 150 athletic clubs. In the last decade of the nineteenth century New York City and its environs alone boasted more than one hundred athletic clubs. The contribution of these clubs to the development of sports interest in the United States deserves more study than it has received.

The number of golf courses and enthusiasts was great enough to warrant the formation of the United States Golf Association in 1894 to conduct amateur and professional competitions. In the next ten years the United States became a formidable rival of Great Britain in international matches. The National Bowling League was founded in 1875 and became the American Bowling Congress in 1895. Through the efforts of the Boston Athletic Club and the New York Racquet and Tennis Club, tennis gradually attained popular status and like golf was considered a socially acceptable sport for women. The eventual demand for local and national competition led to the establishment of the United States Lawn Tennis Association in 1881. Other activities popular in this period were archery, canoeing, cricket, croquet, curling, cycling, equestrianism, hiking, ice skating, quoits, roque, swimming, and yachting.

THE REVIVAL OF THE OLYMPIC GAMES

When the Frenchman, Baron Pierre de Coubertin, proposed that the ancient Olympic Games be reinstated, the United States had no official team to send to Athens in 1896. The country was represented by a volunteer group headed by William M. Sloane, a professor of history at Princeton University, and supported by students of Princeton and the Boston Athletic Association. Some of the wealthier members of the first U.S. Olympic Team paid their own expenses, and those who could not finance the trip were assisted with funds raised by Oliver Ames, former Governor of Massachusetts.

The Boston Athletic Association sent H. Blake, a distance runner; E. H. Clarke, all-round athlete; W. W. Hoyt, pole vaulter; T. P. Curtis, sprinter; and T. E. Burke, amateur quarter-mile champion. This group was accompanied by John Graham, instructor in the Boston Athletic Association, and J. B. Connolly of the Suffolk Athletic Club. Professor Sloane's group consisted of R. Garrett, field events; H. B. Jamison, quarter-miler; F. A. Lane, sprinter; and A. C. Taylor, pole vaulter. In addition to the United States, England, France, Germany, Denmark, Hungary, Switzerland, and, of course, Greece, were represented at Athens. The athletes of the BAA scored heavily, and Jim Connolly, who paid his own way, won the hop, step, and jump, while Bob Garrett was an easy victor in the discus throw and shot put. The United States won first place in nine of the twelve track and field events.[14]

GYMNASTICS IN THE PUBLIC SCHOOLS

John Philbrick, superintendent of the Boston City Schools, visited the New York City schools in 1858 and noted that "some of the school buildings are furnished with excellent gymnastic apparatus and in some schools calisthenic exercises were practiced."[15] For the next two years Philbrick was an aggressive proponent of exercise and more play space for children in the Boston city schools. When the war fever hit Boston in the 1860s military drill was temporarily introduced into the public schools, and it was not until 1865 that Lewis B. Munroe was appointed director of physical and vocal gymnastics.[16] Munroe taught his system to 130 elementary school teachers. Since Boston was the locale of Dio Lewis gymnastics, the Swedish system under Posse, and the best misinterpreters of the Delsartean system, the public schools were subjected to each successive system as it was introduced.

In 1890 a special committee was appointed by the Boston Board of Education to conduct a survey of gymnastics in the public schools of the Midwest.[17] As might have been expected, it found that the boys' program was under the influence of the German system. The girls had adopted successively phases of Dio Lewis' light gymnastics and the Delsartean system.

In 1860 the Cincinnati Board of Eudcation finally succumbed to overtures by the local Turner Society and decided to permit two special teachers to teach for a daily quarter-hour period on an experimental basis in six selected schools. The experiment was so successful that the program was extended to all elementary schools in the city. Under Carl Betz Kansas City in 1885 probably had one of the most complete and carefully planned gymnastics programs in the country. Betz published six manuals on free gymnastics, light gymnastics, marching tactics, and games which were used extensively by cities in the Midwest. In Chicago, in 1864, a system of calisthenics was in use for girls in high schools. In 1884 a trial program by the Turners was introduced into the elementary schools and gradually extended to the secondary schools under Henry Suder and his assistants in 1892. In Cleveland Karl Zapp employed Betz's method to train elementary school teachers to teach gymnastics.

LEGISLATION FOR PHYSICAL EDUCATION

John Swett, Superintendent of Public Instruction of the State of California, was instrumental in securing the first state legislation for physical education in the public schools in the United States. A mandatory clause in the California School Laws of 1866 provided that regular instruction and attention be given to "such physical exercise for the pupil as may be conducive to health and vigor of the body, as well as the mind."[18] This general law was implemented by the rules and regulations of the same year: "In all primary schools exercises in free gymnastics . . . shall be given at least twice a day and for a time not less than five minutes for each exercise."

Agitation by the Turner Society and professional and educational associations in the 1890s led to legislation for physical education in several states. Ohio passed a law in 1892 which required that instruction be given in "physical culture" in public schools of cities of first and second classes and in all educational institutions financially supported wholly or in part by the state. North Dakota passed legislation in 1899, and Pennsylvania attempted to enact laws in 1890 and 1895, but failed.

GYMNASTICS IN MEN'S COLLEGES AND UNIVERSITIES

During the 1850s there were many indications of interest in gymnastics for men in American colleges and universities. The catalogue of the University of Virginia for 1851–1952 stated that a certain J. E. D'Alfonse provided instruction in gymnastics on the campus. Dartmouth in 1852 seems to have had a follower of the German system who gave students instruction on the horizontal bar. *The Princeton Book,* published by the graduates of Princeton University in 1879, related how the Class of 1859 decided to provide a gymnasium for the students. It was a barnlike structure painted red in which an instructor of the German system led the students through exercises on the parallel bars, springboard, trapeze, ladder, and flying rings. Miami University students under the leadership of F. H. Roemler, a Turner from Cincinnati, organized the Miami Gymnastic Association in 1857. Harvard constructed a gymnasium in 1858 and employed Abram Molineaux Hewlett, a gymnast and ex-boxer, to provide instruction. In 1859 Yale University built a gymnasium 50 by 100 feet, with a ceiling clearance of 25 feet. The basement area had a ceiling height of 10 feet and contained bathing facilities and bowling alleys. Gymnasium privileges and instruction cost the student four dollars a year.

GYMNASTIC LEADERS

The health of college and university students had always been a matter of concern to physicians and administrative heads. The deleterious effect of study upon the health of students was freely discussed throughout the nineteenth century. As ironic as it may seem to the modern scholar, the nervous strain induced by college study forced many young men and women to leave school in ill health during the 1800s. This situation, in addition to other health problems common to an educational community, emphasized the need for some kind of health service for the student body.

As a general rule administrators had accepted the concept of the preservation of health through exercise and a knowledge of the laws of hygiene, but they were beset by another pressing problem. Exuberant students who had informally organized sports on the campus had become a source of irritation to faculty members and townspeople. Something had to be done which would curb the more active students, yet stimulate the more studious ones who were not inclined to engage in physical activities.

President William A. Stearns of Amherst College solved the problems when he announced, in 1854, the establishment of a department of hygiene and physical education and the future appointment of a director with full academic status. The professor would give lectures in hygiene, instruction in gymnastics, and supervise student health, and therefore must have both a medical degree and training in gymnastics. President Stearns thus gave hygiene and physical education academic status in the hierarchy of university disciplines and set a precedent for other higher institutions. Heretofore, universities had employed gymnasts of recognized ability or distinguished athletes, but had never fully accepted them into the university family. In the future experts in gymnastics who had obtained medical degrees could become professors of hygiene and physical education. Many capable men satisfied these requirements and through their position of leadership in higher institutions made important contributions to the fields of health and physical education.

EDWARD HITCHCOCK (1828–1911). Edward Hitchcock succeeded John Hooker, the first director of the department of hygiene and physical education at Amherst College, in 1861. Dr. Hitchcock was the son of a professor of chemistry and natural history at Amherst College who later became that institution's third president. He graduated from Amherst in 1849 during his father's administration and, after several years' teaching in a seminary, entered the Harvard Medical School, from which he was graduated in 1853.

During Dr. Hitchcock's early administration students attended a program of light gymnastics, marching, and dumbbell drills four days a week. He also took anthropometric measurements and determined arm strength by means of chin-ups. Dr. Hitchcock has also been credited with sponsoring one of the first organized intramural athletic programs in American colleges and universities. He served as chairman at the time the American Association for the Advancement of Physical Education was organized in Brooklyn in 1885 (see Appendix).[19]

DUDLEY A. SARGENT (1849–1924). The son of a ship's carpenter and spar-maker in Belfast, Maine, the young Sargent joined a group of high school boys who had formed a gymnastic club. By constant practice the club members became proficient enough to give exhibitions in the town hall in Belfast and surrounding communities.

In the fall of 1869 Dr. Sargent accepted the position of gymnastic instructor at Bowdoin College and two years later entered the school as a freshman. During his sophomore year he also accepted the position of director of gymnastics at Yale. On his graduation from Bowdoin in 1875 he enrolled in the Yale Medical School, from which he graduated in 1878.

Upon receiving his medical degree, Dr. Sargent established a private gymnasium in New York, where he elaborated upon a system of bodily measurements he had started at Bowdoin and Yale. He developed a number of appliances such as chest weights, chest-expanders, and machines which measured the strength of individual or groups of muscles. He used his strength-testing apparatus to discover the weaker muscles, which he proceeded to strengthen through his many mechanical devices.

Upon completion of the Hemenway Gymnasium at Harvard in 1880, Dr. Sargent was appointed director and given the rank of assistant professor. He made attendance at his gymnastic classes voluntary and gave the individualized exercises which he had originated in New York. Upon entrance all Harvard freshmen were given an examination which included anthropometric measurements, strength tests, and personal history. During his career Sargent accumulated more than 50,000 individual anthropometric records, and on the basis of these lifelike statues were constructed of the typical American youth and exhibited at the World's Fair in 1893. Dr. Sargent was a pioneer in strength tests and used them to determine the membership of athletic squads at Harvard. In 1881 he founded a gymnastic training institution for young women attending the Harvard Annex, which later became Radcliffe College. Many of his women graduates received positions in public schools and colleges for women.

EDWARD M. HARTWELL (1850– 922). Dr. Hartwell was born at Exeter, New Hampshire. His father was a graduate of Harvard Law School and his mother the daughter of Dr. Ruben Mussey, who held a medical professorship at Dartmouth College for twenty-five years and later became professor of surgery at the Medical College of Ohio, Cincinnati. Dr. Hartwell received his B.A. and M.A. degrees from Amherst College and was recognized as an expert gymnast and accomplished athlete. After several years' teaching he got his Ph.D. at Johns Hopkins University. He climaxed his educational career with an M.D. degree from the Medical College of Ohio in 1882.

In 1883 Johns Hopkins constructed a $10,000 gymnasium, supplying it with many of Dr. Sargent's appliances. Hartwell was familiar with Sargent's theories, and when the position of director of the gymnasium was offered to him he accepted. At Hopkins he introduced Dr. Sargent's physical examination, prescribed individual work instead of conducting class exercises, and lectured on hygiene. He remained at Johns Hopkins until 1890.

Dr. Hartwell contributed to the history of physical education through his study and evaluation of the American and European systems of gymnastics and particularly through his surveys of gymnastics in the United States in 1897–1898 and 1903.[20] In later life he became keenly interested in Swedish medical gymnastics.

WILLIAM G. ANDERSON (1860–1947). Born at St. Joseph, Michigan, Dr. Anderson was the son of a Congregational clergyman. When his father was pastor at Quincy, Illinois, he associated with the circus men who wintered in that town and became a skilled gymnast. During 1877–1878 while a student at the Roxbury Latin School in Boston, he became a pupil of Robert J. Roberts at the Young Men's Christian Association. In 1878 he enrolled at the University of Wisconsin and left after his sophomore year to accept a directorship in physical education at the Cleveland Medical College, where he attended medical school and graduated with an M.D. degree in 1883. After several years in Columbus and Toledo, he accepted a position in 1885 as director of the Adelphi Academy

(College) in Brooklyn and later organized the Brooklyn Normal School for Physical Education (1886). In 1892 Anderson became associate director of the Yale University gymnasium and took his Brooklyn school along with him under the name of Anderson's Normal School of Gymnastics, which was later changed to the New Haven Normal School of Gymnastics (1901). Dr. Anderson was active in the promotion of teacher education, the placement of teachers in the South and Far West, and in the organization of early state associations of physical education.

While at the Adelphi Academy in Brooklyn, Dr. Anderson conceived the plan of a national organization to promote the profession and facilitate the exchange of ideas among teachers of physical education. In 1885 he invited his colleagues and friends to meet at Adelphi Academy. The outcome was the formation of the Association for the Advancement of Physical Education, of which Hitchcock was elected the first president.

EXPANSION OF FACILITIES, 1870–1900

Between 1870 and 1900 gymnasiums appeared in increasing numbers in colleges and universities. Facilities were expanded to include offices for personnel, rooms for physical examinations and special activities, indoor running tracks, bowling alleys, billiard rooms, baths and showers. Intercollegiate and intramural athletics increased the demand for playing fields, outdoor running tracks, and spectator stands. In addition to the Hemenway Gymnasium at Harvard (1880) and the gymnasium constructed at Johns Hopkins (1883), Dr. Hartwell in 1885 reported gymnasiums at the following institutions: Lehigh, (1882); Cornell, Tufts, and Wooster (1882–1883); Amherst (1883–1884); and Dickinson, Lafayette, and Minnesota (1884).[20]

The men's programs in eastern schools were first influenced by the German system. Welch used the Dio Lewis system at Yale, Dartmouth, and Wesleyan, and Nissen introduced the Swedish system at Johns Hopkins. The Morrill Act of 1862 encouraged the founding of agricultural and mechanical colleges, and those in the Midwest strongly favored the German system.

INTERCOLLEGIATE SPORTS

The Rowing Association of American Colleges was formed in 1871 by delegates from Harvard, Brown, Amherst, and Bowdoin. In the regatta held that year, Massachusetts State College defeated Brown and Harvard over a three-mile course on the Connecticut River. The success of a smaller college in this first race over a straight course encouraged other schools to join the Association. By 1873 the membership had grown to eleven schools. Races featured six-oared boats steered by the bow oar. In 1880 the crew was changed to eight oars, and it was such a crew from Yale that competed in the Henley-on-Thames Royal Regatta for the English Challenge Cup in 1896.

In 1867 a Princeton College team defeated the Princeton Seminary in an American version of Rugby. In 1869 Princeton lost to Rutgers in what is considered the first intercollegiate football game. In the ensuing years Columbia, Yale, Harvard, Cornell, McGill, Union, and Pennsylvania fielded football teams. Princeton compiled the first set of rules in 1871, which resembled those of soccer football more than they did modern football. In 1874 McGill University played two games with Harvard, one by Harvard rules and the other by All-Canadian rules. The first set of rules of the modern American game was drawn up in 1876 by representatives from Columbia, Harvard, Princeton, and Yale. At this same meeting these institutions formed the first intercollegiate football association. The new rules did not lead to harmony, and in 1894 the New York Athletic Club invited representatives of Harvard, Pennsylvania, Princeton, and Yale to meet for a rules discussion. Differences in opinion split the representatives into two camps. The insistent demand of midwestern colleges and smaller schools that they be represented caused even more confusion. The two factions finally agreed to set up common rules. A committee of five college representatives assisted by Paul Dashiell of Johns Hopkins and Alonzo A. Stagg of the University of Chicago, as the court of last resort, kept the peace for the time being.[21]

Cricket was introduced at Haverford College, Pennsylvania, in the early 1830s but was not formally organized until 1861. In that year matches were played with independent cricket clubs, and in 1876 Haverford played the first intercollegiate match with the University of Pennsylvania. The following year Haverford, Pennsylvania, and Harvard formed the Intercollegiate Cricket Association. In 1896 a picked team from Haverford toured England in a series of fifteen matches with public schools and universities. The strength of the American team is indicated by the fact that it won four matches, lost four, and tied seven.

Between 1870 and 1880 larger schools were too occupied playing football and English soccer to be interested in lacrosse. Smaller colleges like Lehigh, Stevens, Swarthmore, and Johns Hopkins started intercollegiate competition in lacrosse by the late 1870s. By 1881 Harvard, Princeton, New York, and Columbia fielded teams and formed the Intercollegiate Lacrosse Association in 1882. Lacrosse gained intercollegiate prestige and interest when West Point and the Naval Academy entered the competition in 1900.

Harvard and Columbia were among the first universities to organize fencing clubs and conducted competitions in the 1880s. They were instrumental in the establishment of the Intercollegiate Fencing Association in 1894. The foil remained the only weapon in intercollegiate competition until the saber was added in 1914 and the dueling sword in 1920.

The first ice hockey rules were drawn up by R. F. Smith of McGill University, and he adapted them to field hockey. Johns Hopkins organized a college team in 1894 and in that year played a local Baltimore club. In 1895 and 1896 Harvard sponsored the creation of the Ice Hockey Association, and Harvard and Brown played the first intercollegiate match in the United States.

In the 1870s a modified game of soccer was played by Columbia, Yale, Harvard, McGill, Pennsylvania, Cornell, and Union. During 1876 English Rugby was adopted by New England schools and soccer was dropped. By the 1880s the football played in New England schools fell into three distinct classifications: Rugby, association, and Gaelic. Rugby permitted the ball to be carried, association football prohibited the use of hands and the ball had to be played with the feet, and Gaelic football allowed the use of both hands and feet. Both Gaelic and association football were played during 1880–1890. The Intercollegiate Association Football League was formed in 1905 with Columbia, Cornell, Harvard, Haverford, Pennsylvania, and Princeton as members.

From the first championship meet held in 1897 at Ardsley Casino near Dobbs Ferry, New York, intercollegiate golf competition has been conducted through the years by the USGA. It was not until 1939 that the NCAA sponsored the first championship meet at Wakonda Country Club, Des Moines, Iowa.

The National Collegiate Tennis Association was founded in 1883 when representatives from Yale, Amherst, and Trinity met at the latter institution. The Association conducted tournaments until 1927, when the management of intercollegiate meets became the joint responsibility of the NCAA and USLTA.

Intercollegiate swimming was started at the University of Pennsylvania in 1897 under George Kistler, who conducted dual meets with nearby colleges. By 1899 Yale and Columbia had also developed teams, and with the entrance of Chicago and Wisconsin into the field of competition the Intercollegiate Swimming Association was created in 1905.

Wesleyan, Trinity, and Yale were members of the first Intercollegiate Basketball League, founded in 1895. The YMCA publication *Triangle* in 1892 furnished players with the first set of rules, and two years later Luther H. Gulick edited the YMCA basketball guide. In 1898 the Amateur Athletic Union collaborated with Dr. Gulick to publish a revised guide.

The first intercollegiate competition in gymnastics was held at New York University in 1889, and the Intercollegiate Association of Amateur Gymnasts of America was organized in 1900.

THE ESTABLISHMENT OF ATHLETIC ORGANIZATIONS

In 1873 representatives from Brooklyn and New York formed the National Amateur Gymnastic and Athletic Tournament Association, which was short-lived. In 1878 Ed Plummer, editor of the *Sportsman,* secured the cooperation of enough athletic clubs to organize the American Association of Amateur Athletes, which after a few months also expired.

The following year the athletic clubs in and around New York City established the National Association of Amateur Athletics of

America to regulate and promote amateur competition in the United States. In 1885 the Pacific Coast Amateur Athletic Association was formed and operated independently of the NAAA. Because of a dispute over the amateur status of a boxer the New York Athletic Club withdrew in 1888 and organized the Amateur Athletic Union of the United States. That same year the AAU conducted the first annual championship contests in boxing, wrestling, and fencing, and a track and field meet on the grounds of the Detroit Athletic Club. During the summer of 1888 officials of the NAAA and AAU arranged to join forces, and the AAU became the first national body to represent amateur sports in the United States.[22]

In 1875 the Intercollegiate Association of Amateur Athletes of America (ICAAAA) was formed to conduct track and field competition in colleges and universities. The charter members were twelve New England colleges and universities, and by 1900 fifteen institutions had at one time or another been members. The AAU claimed jurisdiction over track and field athletics in this era and at their meets required the registration and certification of participants as evidence of amateur standing. This proved irksome to intercollegiate representatives, who preferred to be responsible for the determination of the amateur status of their athletes.

In addition to the ICAAAA and AAU, the Athletic League of North America of the YMCA played an important role in promoting track and field athletics in the United States and Canada. For a time the Athletic League was allied with the AAU, until its entrance into remote communities and changes in its services made the alliance with the AAU untenable, and the relationship was discontinued in 1911.

GYMNASTICS IN WOMEN'S COLLEGES

In general, exercises in colleges for women during 1860–70 followed the pattern set by Mary Lyon at Mount Holyoke Seminary in 1837, namely, calisthenics, dancing, and domestic duties. The catalogue of Elmira Female College, founded in 1856, stated, "Careful attention will be paid to health and physical culture." Exercises were taken in the open air and "a modest amount of domestic occupation will be apportioned each pupil." The Vassar Female College catalogue of 1865 announced that in addition to calisthenics there would be instruction in riding, boating, swimming, skating, and gardening. Wells College in 1868 offered instruction in calisthenics and vocal music.

The light gymnastics of Dio Lewis found favor in many colleges for women between 1865 and 1880. The catalogues of Rockford, Vassar, Elmira, Smith, Mills, and Mount Holyoke indicate that Lewis gymnastics had replaced the calisthenics of earlier years. Lucy B. Hunt, a gymnastic instructor at Smith, wrote a book on the subject in 1882, and if it can be trusted as a guide, young women there were tossing bean bags, marching, executing wand drills to the schottische, and doing Dio Lewis' ring exercises to the strains of Strauss waltzes.

In the 1880s Radcliffe, Bryn Mawr, Wellesley, Vassar, Rockford, and Mount Holyoke introduced the Sargent type of program. At Radcliffe women tudents were encouraged to use Sargent's private gymnasium. Women were given anthropometric measurements, weaker muscles discovered by strength tests, and appropriate exercises prescribed. In 1888 Goucher College initiated the Swedish system, and other colleges for women followed suit. The Delsartean system had a temporary influence in the 1890s at Elmira and Rockford colleges. The only women's colleges following the German system by the turn of the century were Mills and Elmira.[23]

GYMNASTICS IN COEDUCATIONAL INSTITUTIONS

Oberlin College, founded in 1833 as a coeducational institution, introduced calisthenic drills for women as early as 1847. From 1850 to 1900 the Lewis, Delsartean, Swedish, and German systems all exerted their influence, and Sargent's anthropometric measurements and strength tests were inaugurated. Toward the close of the century women were permitted to elect sports over and above the gymnastic requirement. Oberlin offered croquet in 1860 and tennis in the 1880s. The University of Wisconsin provided a varied program in 1889 which included coeducational tennis and bicycle riding, bowling, ice hockey, croquet, and walking.

One of the most progressive and influential women physical

educators in the Midwest during this era was Delphine Hanna (1854–1941), who administered the program at Oberlin from 1885 to 1920. Early in her career she studied under Sargent and later attended Cornell, Oberlin, and Michigan, where she received the medical degree. She established the first coeducational teacher-training course in the Midwest in 1886, and in her first class were Thomas D. Wood, Fred E. Leonard, and Luther H. Gulick. Another illustrious student, Jesse F. Williams, graduated with the class of 1909. Dr. Hanna contributed much to the development of physical education in the Midwest, through her active leadership and professional enthusiasm.[24]

As in the case of the men's early program, women conducted their activities out of doors, in small rooms, or halls and wings of campus buildings. Vassar was the first to construct a gymnasium, the Calisthenium, in 1865, which also included an indoor riding ring. Smith College built a wooden structure in 1879, and Bryn Mawr included a gymnasium when it opened in 1885. Goucher College built the first swimming pool in 1888 and was followed a year later by Vassar. In the Midwest seven new gymnasiums were completed between 1890 and 1900. The first gymnasium at Michigan State Normal College was constructed in 1894 and the Barbour Gymnasium at the University of Michigan in 1896. With few exceptions most midwestern gymnasiums were shared by both men and women.

TEACHER PREPARATION, 1860–1900

Dio Lewis opened his Normal Institute on July 4, 1861, and following the European format, he employed four medical men from the Harvard Medical School to teach courses in anatomy, physiology, and hygiene and several prominent educators to lecture on the philosophy and methodology of pedagogy. Dr. Lewis gave instruction in his new gymnastics as well as the Swedish system. Class members were divided into small units to provide experience in teaching. The course lasted for ten weeks and was offered twice a year, with classes beginning in July and January.

In the years following many normal schools were established by organizations and individuals. The normal school of the American Gymnastic Union was founded in 1866; the International Training

School of the YMCA (Springfield College) in 1886; and the School of Physical Education, YMCA College, Chicago (George Williams College) in 1890. Privately organized normal schools included the Sargent School of Physical Education (1881), the New Haven Normal School of Gymnastics (1886), the Chautauqua School of Physical Education (1888), the Boston Normal School (1889), the Posse-Nissen School of Physical Education (1890), and the Savage School of Physical Education (1898).[25]

In her study of teacher education in this era, Barbara Hall pointed out certain similarities in the conduct of these schools.[26] All required a high school education or its equivalent for admission, character and family background references, and a physical examination. Faculty members who taught the theory courses were of high caliber and professionally recognized. Since the biological sciences were taught by medical men the normal schools had to have ready access to hospitals and clinics. This gave weight to such courses as corrective physical education, physical diagnosis, and principles of movement (kinesiology). All teacher institutions provided music to accompany exercises, instruction in exercise progressions, voice training, marching tactics, apparatus work, aesthetic dancing for women, corrective gymnastics, a variety of sports, and teaching experience within the school and in public schools.

All normal schools required written examinations, recitations, and set standards of skill performance. As a general rule, the passing grade ranged between 60 and 70, and students who did substandard work were dropped. The staff members pooled their personal libraries for student use, and every normal school subscribed to the current periodicals in education, physical education, and voice training. These schools granted a certificate for the successful completion of one year's work and the diploma at the close of two years' work. Most of them also offered postgraduate work and special courses for those who wished to learn new techniques and innovations in physical education.

Private normal schools also gave courses during the summer months. William G. Anderson gave physical education courses at Chautauqua* as early as 1886, and he followed the Chautauqua

* This unique system of popular education in the United States was inaugurated at Chautauqua Lake, New York, in 1874 by the Sunday-School Assemblies

circuit as far south as Albany, Georgia.[27] Dudley A. Sargent organized a summer school course for both men and women at Harvard University in 1887, at which he introduced many innovations to the field of physical education.[28] Baron Nils Posse used the Chautauqua circuit to present the Swedish system, taught a short course at Martha's Vineyard Summer Institute, and gave summer courses at his Boston School for many years.

PROFESSIONAL PREPARATION IN STATE AND PRIVATELY ENDOWED INSTITUTIONS

Teacher-training programs were organized in state and privately endowed institutions in the last decade of the nineteenth century. One of the early professional programs was that set up in 1890 by Clyde E. Ehinger and his wife at the State Normal School at West Chester, Pennsylvania. Both were graduates of the Brooklyn Normal School, and they followed many of the practices of this institution. Foundation courses were included among the regular schedule of classes in the normal schools, practical work was elective, and practice teaching was conducted in the senior year in the high schools of the area.

Wilbur P. Bowen presented a course at Michigan State during the school year 1893–1894. Both Dr. Bowen and his assistant, Mrs. Fannie Burton, were graduates of Michigan Normal, and he had done course work at Sargent's Summer School and the Chautauqua School of Physical Education, while Mrs. Burton had attended the Emerson School of Oratory at Boston. Dr. Bowen offered theory courses in anatomy, physiology, body mechanics, corrective exercises, and the history of physical education and systems. Practical work included the use of Sargent's machines, marching tactics, exercises combined with marching, and heavy apparatus work. During the school year 1895–1896 instruction in sports was added to the program. Dr. Bowen was probably one of the first to provide extension materials for the in-service teacher. He also organized units

---

for the instruction for Sunday school teachers. By 1879 the program was extended to include instruction in language, general education, and subjects of current interest.

composed of his students to give public demonstrations of teaching methods in physical education.[29]

Among state universities the University of Washington listed professional courses in physical education in the catalogue of the academic year 1896–1897 but these courses appear to have been discontinued in 1898. The Universities of California, Indiana (women), and Nebraska offered professional courses during the school year 1897–1898. The University of Illinois organized a professional program for men in 1898, and the University of Wisconsin provided courses on a coeducational basis during the school year 1899–1900. But in general it was not until legislation made physical education mandatory in state-supported schools that these institutions gave much attention to the training of physical education teachers. It was not until the early 1900s that the department of education was divorced from the college of liberal arts to become a separate college or school. Physical education training benefited from this transition since both the undergraduate and graduate program in many cases became a part of the department of education and later, the college or school of education.

The teacher-training program at Oberlin College was organized by Delphine Hanna in 1892 and open to men and women. The two-year program included courses in chemistry, physics (mechanics), physiology, anatomy, osteology, myology, zoology, histology, comparative anatomy, psychology, drawing, history of physical education, orthopedics, elocution, first aid, and hygiene. She prescribed exercises for individual improvement and held class drills five times a week throughout the school year.[30] By 1895 both theoretical and practical work were included in the regular college schedule, and in 1899 the professional program was reorganized and extended to four years.

NOTES

1. R. Freeman Butts and Lawrence A. Cremin. *A History of Education in American Culture.* New York: Henry Holt and Company, 1953, pp. 164–187.
2. "Report of the Committee on Secondary School Studies Appointed at

the Meeting of the National Education Association, July 9, 1892." *Proceedings,* National Education Association, Washington, D.C., 1893, p. 53.

3. "Report of the Committee on College Entrance Requirements." *Proceedings* National Education Association, Washington, D.C., 1899.
4. Dio Lewis. *The New Gymnastics for Men, Women and Children.* (Sixth edition) Boston: Ticknor and Fields, 1864, pp. 9–12; J. Madison Watson. *Hand-Book of Calisthenics and Gymnastics.* Chicago: George Sherwood and Company, 1864, pp. 11–12.
5. Dio Lewis. "New Gymnastics." *American Journal of Education,* XI (1862), 531-556; XII (1863), 665–700.
6. William A. Stecher. *Gymnastics–A Textbook of the German-American System of Gymnastics.* Boston: Lee and Shepard Publishers, 1896.
7. *Physical Training. A Full Report of the Papers and Discussions of the Conference Held in Boston in November, 1889.* (Reported and edited by Isabel C. Barrows) Boston: Press of George H. Ellis, 1899.
8. Genevieve Stebbins. *Delsarte System of Expression.* Boston: Edgar S. Werner and Company, 1885.
9. Emily M. Bishop. *Americanized Delsarte Culture.* New York: The Chautauqua-Century Press, 1892, pp. 11–24.
10. Ted Shawn. *Every Little Movement.* Pittsfield: The Eagle Printing and Binding Company, 1954.
11. Charles Edward Hopkins. *History of the YMCA in North America.* New York: Association Press, 1951, p. 246.
12. James Naismith. *Basketball, Its Origin and Development.* New York: Association Press, 1914.
13. Elizabeth Wilson. *Fifty Years of Association Work Among Young Women (1866–1916).* New York: National Board of the YWCA, pp. 43; 98–101; 308.
14. "The New Olympic Games." (Editorial) *Outing,* XXVIII (April–September, 1896), 21–23. Pierre de Coubertin. "The Olympic Games of 1896." *The Century* Magazine, LIII (New Series XXXI) (November, 1896, to April, 1897), 39–53.
15. Edward M. Hartwell. *Report of the Director of Physical Training.* Boston: School Document No. 22, 1891.
16. Lewis B. Munroe. *Manual of Physical and Voice Training.* Philadelphia: Cowperthwait and Company, 1869.
17. William A. Mowry. *Report of the Committee on Physical Training.* Boston: School Document No. 15, 1890.
18. Dudley S. DeGroat. "Physical Education in California, 1854–1900." *Journal of Health and Physical Education,* 10:2 (February, 1939), 67–68.

19. Joseph Edmund Welch. "Edward Hitchcock, M.D. Founder of Physical Education in the College Curriculum." (Dissertation) George Peabody College for Teachers, 1962.
20. Edward Mussey Hartwell. *Physical Training in American Colleges and Universities*. Washington: Bureau of Education, Circular of Information No. 5, 1885, pp. 59; 68; 92.
21. Paul Stagg. "The Development of the National Collegiate Athletic Association in Relationship to Intercollegiate Athletics in the United States." (Dissertation) New York University, 1946, pp. 13–17.
22. Robert Korsgaard. "A History of the Amateur Athletic Union of the United States." (Dissertation) Teachers College, Columbia University, 1952, pp. 40–67.
23. Dorothy S. Ainsworth. *The History of Physical Education in Colleges for Women*. New York: A. S. Barnes and Company, 1930, pp. 13–20; 24–27; 36–41.
24. Miriam Gray. *A Century of Growth. The Historical Development of Physical Education for Women in Selected Colleges of Six Midwestern States*. Ann Arbor: Edward Brothers, Inc., 1951.
25. Earl F. Ziegler. "History of Professional Preparation for Physical Education in the United States, 1861–1948." (Dissertation) Yale University, 1950.
26. Barbara C. Hall. "An Historical Study of the Early Development of Teacher Education for Women in Physical Education." (Dissertation) Teachers College, Columbia University, 1952, pp. 165–167.
27. Harold L. Ray. "Chautauqua. Early Showcase for Physical Education." *Journal of Health–Physical Education–Recreation,* 33:8 (November, 1962), 37–41; 69.
28. Bruce L. Bennett. "Life of Dudley A. Sargent, M.D. and His Contributions to Physical Education." (Dissertation) University of Michigan, 1947, pp. 83.
29. Ruth Elliott. "The Organization of Professional Training in Physical Education in State Universities." (Dissertation) Teachers College, Columbia University, 1927, pp. 16–23.
30. "Normal Physical Training." (Editorial by Luther H. Gulick) *Physical Education,* 1:9 (November, 1892), 165–166.

Chapter 19

PHYSICAL EDUCATION IN THE UNITED STATES, 1900–1917

SIGNS OF SOCIAL PROGRESS

THE demand for skilled and semiskilled workers in metropolitan and manufacturing centers in the early twentieth century added momentum to the shift of rural population to urban areas and greatly increased sociological problems. Reformers and humanitarians intensified their efforts to improve the lot of city-dwellers crowded into tenement houses, factory districts, and slum areas. With the increase in juvenile delinquency the public's puritan prejudice against play gradually vanished, and tax-supported recreational systems made their appearance in both large and small communities. The gradual emancipation of woman in the home, the improved attitude toward her enfranchisement, and the increase in the number of women employed in industry gave her a more independent social position, which was reflected in her choice of clothes, entrance into sports, and demand for equal educational opportunities.

Growing scientific knowledge not only furnished new products for industry but also improved medical service and encouraged more effective school and public health education and service. Early in 1900 strong public sentiment was generated for the improvement of the health and physical welfare of children. This led to the enactment of child labor laws, the organization of official and voluntary health agencies on local, state, and national levels, the supervision of and instruction in health in the schools, and increased concern for the handicapped child.

EDUCATIONAL DEVELOPMENT

During 1900–1917 school terms were lengthened and compulsory school attendance laws strengthened. The increase in wealth encouraged parents to keep their children longer in school and made college attendance possible for many. The average rural and urban elementary school still followed the traditional method of rote and book learning. Although experimentation went on in metropolitan areas, most teachers were satisfied with the older methods of teaching. The secondary schools continued to have two distinct objectives: terminal education for the many and college preparation for the few. In the early 1900s terminal education persisted in name only, and the high school curriculum included English, science, social studies, foreign language, commercial subjects, fine arts, and physical education. By 1917 the terminal pupil was receiving more consideration, and subjects like typing, stenography, bookkeeping, commercial law, domestic science, industrial arts, and manual training were well established in the high school curriculum.

As far back as 1888 Charles W. Eliot suggested to the Department of Superintendents of the National Education Association that something would have to be done eventually about the crowded high school curriculum and the needlessly prolonged elementary school education under the 8-4 plan, but nothing was done about the problem for two decades. Concomitant with the extensive school surveys after 1910, new plans of organization made their appearance. The most frequently recommended solution was the 6-3-3 plan, which created a new rung in the educational ladder, the junior high school.

Advances in Higher Education

In colleges and universities the elective system proposed by George Ticknor of Harvard finally triumphed, but administrations still retained the right to prescribe what were called foundation subjects during the freshman and sophomore years. In professional schools standards appeared for the evaluation of the quality and quantity of instruction.

Clark University in 1889 devoted considerable attention to psychology and education. Columbia University organized a Teachers College in 1898, which was given equal status with other professional schools in that institution. At the turn of the century the University of Chicago established a School of Education, and Harvard University a Graduate School of Education. As the scientific approach to education gained momentum, departments of education appeared in public and private colleges.

In 1902 the first junior college was founded in Joliet, Illinois, as an extension of secondary education in that city. The junior college movement, however, reached its greatest development in California under the leadership of A. F. Lange of the University of California and David Starr Jordan of Stanford. The movement was accelerated by legislation in 1907 which permitted district boards of education to prescribe postgraduate courses for superior graduates. Other states active in the junior college movement included Illinois, Iowa, Michigan, and Missouri.

THE BIOLOGICAL BASIS OF EDUCATION

The educational theories of the classical humanists were now faced with inroads by the new biological and sociological concept of man. Charles Darwin (1809–1882) had challenged the old concepts with his epoch-making *The Origin of Species* (1859) and *The Descent of Man* (1871).

The full impact of Darwin's theories, however, did not reach the consciousness of American educational leadership until the close of the nineteenth century. The new biological view of the nature of man led to the generalization that he was subject to the same scientific analysis as animals and plants; that his adaptation to his environment followed a natural biological and sociological process; that his mental and physical development proceeded from simple to complex forms; and, finally, that in his mental behavior he could be studied experimentally with the same technique as that applied to animals. The response of the classical humanists to this new approach was negative, and in desperation they formed a rear-guard action to maintain the *status quo.*

PSYCHOLOGY, A BIOLOGICAL SCIENCE

Previous to 1850 few attempts had been made to discover experimentally any connection between mind and body. Any scholar who dared investigate in this area was promptly ridiculed by faculty psychologists. In 1878 Wilhelm Max Wundt (1832–1920), a German physiologist, founded a psychological laboratory in Leipzig and through a series of experimental studies substantiated many facts stated by earlier investigators. The fame of his laboratory gained for Wundt an international reputation and attracted American students who returned to their native land imbued with the new scientific spirit. As a phase of his investigations, Wundt initiated a series of historical and analytical studies in the area of animal and human play interest (1900–1910) that had a far-reaching influence on the biological and sociological analysis of plays and games.

WILLIAM JAMES (1842–1910). The most celebrated follower of Wundt in the United States was William James, a graduate of the Harvard Medical School and an instructor of anatomy, physiology, and psychology there from 1872 to 1902. In his early career James was influenced by the pragmatic philosophy of Charles Sanders Peirce (1839–1914), who served as a part-time instructor of logic and mathematics at Johns Hopkins University and was a regular employee of the United States Coast and Geodetic Survey at Baltimore. Peirce first developed his pragmatic concept in an essay entitled *How to Make Our Ideas Clear* (1878). According to him, ". . . inquiry was initiated by a puzzling situation. The puzzle is resolved by the construction of a hypothesis, which by enabling us to anticipate the course of our experience, removed the element of surprise which would otherwise be present." The best method to test an idea was to examine the consequence which it produced in action. Peirce, however, pointed out that certain beliefs existed in which "there would not be any course of inquiry possible except in the sense that it would be . . . easier to interpret the phenomenon."[1]

James accepted the more tangible and practical aspects of Peirce's pragmatism, or experimentalism, and by-passed the more difficult abstractions. James advocated that all ideas in education should be critically examined and tested to learn their effects in practice. If an idea failed to live up to expectations, it should be revised and reconstructed until it produced the desired results. Armed with this measuring device, James dealt a crushing blow to the faculty psychologists and provided an objective approach to the scientific investigation of instincts, habit formation, imitation, mental discipline, transfer of training, and many other pet educational theories of the faculty psychologists.

E. L. THORNDIKE (1874–1949). A student of James's at Harvard and subsequently professor of educational psychology at Teachers College, Columbia University, Thorndike gave general and educational psychology a new point of view. After several years of careful psychological experimentation first with animals and then with children he published his book *Original Nature of Man,* which contained an impressive and lengthy list of what he called original tendencies, or what James identified as instincts. Thorndike's list aroused a host of eminent psychologists to scholarly combat, and their exchange of ideas attracted considerable public interest. Parents, teachers, and social workers came to the conclusion that human behavior was subject to modification through the process of education.

Thorndike made contributions in many areas, such as heredity, the learning process, child psychology, statistics, and mental testing. He destroyed forever the old theories of mental discipline and promoted a better understanding of the old concept of the transfer of training. He also introduced improvements in the classification of learners into homogeneous groups and in provisions for the exceptional child.

THE PSYCHOLOGY OF LEARNING

European research in the fields of physiology, neurology, genetics, and heredity provided the basis for experimental studies of the learning process. Wilhelm Wundt analyzed sense perception; Francis Galton made studies of heredity and suggested that human traits could be measured; Ivan Pavlov, as a result of his famous experiments with dogs, proposed the theory of the conditioned reflex in learning; Alfred Binet and Thomas Simon devised an intelligence test for children which utilized the established laws of association and memory, motor skill, and attention; and James Keen Cattell, Lewis M. Terman, Henry H. Goddard, E. L. Thorndike, and Charles Judd applied intelligence tests on a vast scale in the United States.

In 1913 Thorndike introduced his stimulus-response (S-R) theory of learning in his book *Educational Psychology*. Concluding from his experiments that animals learn by trial and error, he suggested that humans learn in the same manner. He interpreted learning as a result of the establishing of bonds in the reflex arc of the nervous system via the sensory and motor nerves. On the basis of this hypothesis, Thorndike proposed that man derived his ideas, concepts, and motor skills through interaction with his environment and subsequently formulated his famous Laws of Learning: Effect, Exercise, and Readiness. His stimulus-response theory, or connectionism, had considerable influence on educational methods and opened the school curriculum to technical subjects and natural activities.

THE SOCIOLOGICAL VIEW OF MAN

George Sylvester Morris (1840–1899), of the universities of Michigan and Johns Hopkins, late in his life as a professor of philosophy, worked out a concept of the social nature of man based on the idealistic philosophy of the German, George Wilhelm Hegel. The biological explanation of the social evolution of man, according to Morris, did not account for his nature as a social being. Man's theoretical problem was self-knowledge and his practical problem self-realization. In Morris' words:

> Man is thus first taught the lesson that his own spiritual substance, his thought and his will, or more technically expressed, the true self-consciousness in which is to stand his spiritual completeness, is not something that belongs to him in individual isolation and abstraction from all relations to nature, to God, and to his fellowmen, but is essentially dependent on them and only in them can become actual. Man is a spiritual being, was not made to be alone and in the strictest truth cannot be alone.[2]

GEORGE H. MEAD (1863–1931). A professor of philosophy at the University of Chicago, Mead expanded upon Morris' concept of man's social nature in a very logical and unique manner. He viewed man's self and mind as the product of his social interaction with his fellow men. As Herbart had maintained that the child's mind was a blank tablet at birth and his moral concepts the result of environment acting on it, Mead held that the child was born without a self, which did not become a reality until he distinguished between himself and others and learned by gestures, symbols, and signs what belonged to him and what to others. The word "tree," for example, was not a tree but for the purpose of communication a symbol that stood for tree. "The significant symbol is a social learning, and thus the mind is a social learning. An individual has to be a member of a social group that has symbols in common in order to become a self . . . it is thus the social activity of communication through significant symbols that distinguishes man from animals."[3]

JOHN DEWEY (1859–1952). A graduate of the University of Vermont and Johns Hopkins, Dewey was the foremost interpreter of the effect of industrial and social changes on American education. In his early career he was influenced by Morris, under whom he had studied at Johns Hopkins, but like Mead, he used his teacher's theories as a steppingstone.

Dewey was keenly aware of the biological concept of man as an organism in constant interaction with his environment, but he could not subscribe to the thesis that man's behavior was exclusively a matter of physiological stimulus-response. Instead, he favored Mead's concept of the self and mind as products of social interaction. He saw Froebel's educational theories as complementary to Mead's philosophy and applied Froebel's principles of learning by doing, or self-activity and self-expression.

Dewey's experimental school at the University of Chicago (1896–1903) reflected his belief that the child was inherently an active being with drives to communicate with others, construct, investigate, and create. In his opinion the school should provide outlets for these drives through activities in language, nature study, dramatics, art, music, and motor skills generic to the phylogenetic history of man. He maintained that the school cannot be a preparation for social life except as it reproduces the typical conditions of life. Thus the school should *be* life, not a preparation for it.[4]

In his characteristic manner, Dewey criticized Herbart's contention that interest was the sole motivating factor in learning, insisting that interest was not enough in itself but that the learner must also be engaged in an active situation. If the problem, or puzzling situation as Peirce called it, held genuine interest for the learner, he would exert the necessary effort and make the necessary observations that would lead to its solution.[5]

THE CHILD-STUDY MOVEMENT

Gymnastics, entrenched for more than half a century in the school program and educationally respectable because it contributed to the mental discipline of the learner, was in no immediate danger from the implications of the new biological and sociological concepts of man. A few elementary schools experimented with Dewey's proposed child-centered school, but the committee appointed by the NEA at the turn of the century to consider secondary school aims favored the continuation of the narrow objectives of the classical humanists. Nevertheless, evidence began to accumulate around the turn of the century which seemed to threaten for the first time the monopolistic position of gymnastics.

G. STANLEY HALL (1845–1924). A graduate of Williams College and a former student of Wundt in Germany, Dr. Hall began his teaching career as a professor of psychology at Antioch College in Ohio. In 1881 he was appointed professor of psychology at Johns Hopkins, where he remained until 1888, when he assumed the presidency of Clark University.

As the recognized leader of the child-study movement, Dr. Hall had much to say about the place of play, sports, and games in the education of the child. According to Hall, the qualities developed during preadolescence were, in the evolutionary history of the race, far older than the hereditary traits of body and mind which developed later and which could be compared to a newer and higher structure built upon primordial nature. He asserted that many of the tribal hunting, fighting, and playing proclivities of primitive man have outlived their usefulness, but that the child had to go through a series of stages which recapitulated those once serious pursuits.

In 1904 Hall published his voluminous book on the health and education of the adolescent, which he reprinted later in a condensed form entitled *Youth, Its Education, Regime and Hygiene* (1909). In this publication he reviewed the various gymnastic systems and bemoaned the fact that each was "too conscious of the others' shortcomings." In his opinion what was needed was a messiah who, "knowing the human body, gymnastic history and the athletic traditions of the past," could devise a suitable system of physical education.

Hall felt that games and sports filled the health needs of too few youths and for that reason gymnastics were still necessary. He pointed out that adolescence was the golden period for learning rhythms and dancing. Next in importance he placed the phylactic motivation of personal conflict, stating that no physical education program for boys was complete without boxing, fencing, and wrestling. For girls, Dr. Hall recommended that free play and games should always have precedence over indoor or uniform "commando" (Swedish) exercises. He also advocated boating and basketball, with their competitive features curtailed for girls.[6]

LUTHER H. GULICK (1865–1918). At Springfield College during the last decade of the nineteenth century, Dr. Gulick included in the YMCA program basketball, volleyball, track and field, and other sports that were practical. He also initiated the Athletic League of the YMCA in order to supervise athletic competition on a national scale. As director of physical education in the New York City public schools he founded the Public School Athletic League for boys and girls in 1903 and was instrumental in the introduction of folk dancing into the physical education program.

Gulick anticipated the trend toward natural activities in physical education by some thirty years.[7] In his work with children he noted that they found joy and satisfaction in plays and games and very little pleasure in artificially devised bodily movements. He found the same to be true of adolescents. He thought the explanation for this lay in the phylogenic background of man. The ability to throw, strike, run, dodge, jump, and climb were once necessary for survival, and those who lacked these abilities were eliminated. The neural and muscular systems of man were thus phylogenetically developed, with certain tendencies to action. As civilization progressed the activities vital to fighting, hunting, and fishing lost their utilitarian value, but the exercise of the tendencies toward neuromuscular movement was still important to the growth and development of the organism. Gulick suggested that they found expression in play and games and, as an example, cited baseball with its strong appeal for adolescent boys. This game contained the fundamental neuromuscular movements of running, jumping, throwing, catching, and striking.

JOHN MASON TYLER (1851–1929). A professor of biology at Amherst College, John Tyler wrote one of the most influential books of this period on the application of biological principles to the child's growth. *Growth and Education* (1907) had particular significance in the child-study movement because Tyler collected and interpreted the best available information on the biological, sociological, and educational aspects of child development. His extensive bibliography covered the period from 1870 to 1907.

Tyler held that it was necessary to discover the biological characteristics of every stage of childhood in order to plan intelligently the type of muscular activity most suitable for each age level. The muscular system was the key to the development of the brain as well as the lower organs, and the use of the hand was important in the development of the cortex. The fundamental nerve centers, like muscles, were older, tougher, and of greater endurance; the younger centers of the accessory muscles were weaker and more easily exhausted. The youth must be encouraged to use the older muscles of the trunk, shoulders, and legs. "He must run, jump, throw ball, and tussle with his mates. We shall find reason to believe that the most profitable period for this exercise is when the child is in the kindergarten or lower school grades."[8]

Like many of his contemporaries, Tyler saw a place for both gymnastics and natural activities. He included both under the heading of physical training. It was his belief that gymnastics were necessary to the harmonious development of the body, and he was partial to the German system. He thought play and games provided the best kind of physical education because they gave the most enjoyment. Like Froebel, he believed they had social value because "the conception of fair and unfair play is almost the first genuine and spontaneous moral distinction which the child makes."[8] Tyler recommended gymnastics as a counteragent to the cramped and strained sitting position of the schoolroom and suggested that a regular record should be kept of the child's growth by anthropometric measurements.

THOMAS DENISON WOOD (1865–1951). Born at Sycamore, Illinois, Dr. Wood received his A.B. and M.A. at Oberlin College and his M.D. at Columbia University in 1891. He served as professor of hygiene and organic training at Stanford University (1891–1901), professor of physical education at Columbia (1901–1927), and later assumed leadership in the health education movement. In 1910 he served as chairman of a committee of the National Society for the Study of Education assigned the task of studying the school health program and making recommendations.

The report defined the function of physical education as the supervision of fundamental motor activities expressed in play, games, dancing, swimming, gymnastics, and athletics. It stated that the great majority of physical educators had been ignorant of the general tendencies in education. "They have been trained narrowly, to think and to deal with physical education much as a detached problem and too largely on the materialistic physical plane." The physical education of the day was too occupied with seeking postural and corrective results, in training the body "too much within itself" without consideration for desirable social results, and in the development of abilities not identified with the needs and interests of the learner. In conclusion, "progress in physical education must be away from all formal, artificial kinds of movements" and toward natural exercise with due regard for ancestral habits and the future practical needs of the individual.[9]

CLARK W. HETHERINGTON (1870–1942). When C. W. Hetherington was four years old his family moved to California from his birthplace at Lanesboro, Minnesota. Typical of all early leaders in physical education, Hetherington was a finished performer in gymnastics and athletics, and his skill helped him defray the cost of his education at Stanford University, where he taught classes in physical education under the supervision of Thomas D. Wood. On graduation in 1895 he secured a position at the State Reformatory, Whittier, California. Here he made a study of 480 inmates and concluded that their social maladjustment was in part due to their lack of play as children. He organized one of the first gymnastic and athletic programs in a penal institution in the United States. After two years at Whittier, Hetherington attended Clark University and studied under G. Stanley Hall in the field of experimental psychology. His subsequent career included positions as director of physical education at the University of Missouri (1900–1910) and the University of Wisconsin (1913–1917), and California State Supervisor of Physical Education (1918–1921), followed by service on the faculties of the universities of Columbia and New York, finishing his career at Stanford.[10]

Hetherington was not only among the first to see the place of physical education as a necessary part of general education, but also contributed much of his energy and time establishing intercollegiate athletics as a supervised and controlled educational activity.[11] In addition to helping organize the National Collegiate Athletic Association and the National Amateur Athletic Federation, he was one of the founders of the Athletic Research Society in 1907, which in its early history made valuable studies of amateurism and athletic administration.[12]

Speaking at the National Education Association meeting in Boston in 1910, Hetherington interpreted the role of physical education in the light of prevailing biological and sociological theories. He pointed out that education was not directed exclusively to the mind or body but rather to the harmonious development of all human powers. Physical education, or "fundamental education," was an integral part of the educational process and involved four objectives: organic, neuromuscular, social, and intellectual development.

THE CHILD-STUDY MOVEMENT AND OUTDOOR ACTIVITIES

Discussions of man's biological nature in the early 1900s led to a consideration of the beneficial effects of outdoor life on his health. The idea of living in the great outdoors had a sentimental appeal for an imaginative public. Dr. Edward L. Trudeau had cured himself of tuberculosis by living out of doors near Lake Saranac, New York, and his experience initiated open-air schools for tubercular children in Germany and the United States between 1904 and 1908.

Probably the greatest single stimulant to public interest in outdoor life was President Theodore Roosevelt, whose broad experience included camping, ranching, and big-game hunting. His life and literary efforts no doubt contributed much to the international back-to-nature movement during the first decade of the twentieth century. Other factors which promoted interest in outdoor life included national and state park development, the community park idea, the outdoor pursuits made available by motor-driven vehicles, the phenomenal growth of the playground movement, and the increasing popularity of outdoor sports.

THE BEGINNING OF YOUTH SERVICE AGENCIES

Part of this movement were the youth service agencies, featuring organized camping, nature study, canoeing, boating, swimming, hiking, camp cookery, and woodcraft. Camping for boys began in the early 1880s and grew popular for both boys and girls after 1900. Ernest Thompson Seton conceived the idea of the Woodcraft Indians in 1902. Baden-Powell introduced scouting in England in 1907. Seton, Dan Beard, and William D. Boyce started it in the United States in 1910. In the same year Richard Schirrman initiated the youth hostel movement in Germany. Luther H. Gulick and his wife, long-time contributors to the camping movement, founded the Camp Fire Girls in 1911. Juliette Low introduced the English Girl Guides to America in 1912 and incorporated the organization as the Girl Scouts of America in 1913. Ever since 1860 Boys' Clubs had operated as loosely cooperative units, until 1906, when they were united as the Federated Boys' Clubs (Boys' Clubs of America, 1941). Dr. Marie Zakerzewska on her visit to Berlin was impressed by the recreational value of playgrounds for small children. In 1885 she was influential in establishing a children's playground on Parmenter Street, Boston, and the playground movement was well under way by the turn of the century. In 1906 the Playground and Recreation Association of America (National Recreation Association, 1930), a service agency, was founded to induce both municipal and rural communities to organize playgrounds and recreation centers.

PHYSICAL EDUCATION PRIOR TO WORLD WAR I

In 1909 Georges Hébert developed what he called a natural method of gymnastic instruction for the French marines at Joinville which received considerable publicity in the United States.[14] Edwin Fauver, of Princeton University, noted in 1914 that the majority of the colleges and universities required gymnastics and that very few students seemed to enjoy them and that even fewer kept them up after graduation. He suggested that in place of gymnastics undergraduates should be required "to gain a practical knowledge of handball, tennis, squash, and similar games," thus developing recreational interests that could be carried over into adult life.[15]

Nor was criticism in the early 1900s limited only to physical educators. William H. Burnham of Clark University stated in 1900 that gymnastics were based on the false premise that muscular development signified health, that symmetrical development was desirable, and that such exercise provided relaxation from study. It was his conviction that physical exercise should take into account the hygienic, social, and psychological needs of the individual, which gymnastics did not do.

Lewis M. Terman, in his book, *Hygiene of the School Child* (1914), claimed that educational leaders were out of step with advanced thinking in respect to physical education:

> Unfortunately modern education has been influenced in its attitude toward the body by medieval rather than Greek and Roman ideals. Physical Education has played an insignificant part in modern educational theory and still less in educational practice. . . . The latest textbooks on the principles of education all but ignore the subject, and no comprehensive philosophy of physical education has yet been attempted.[16]

GYMNASTICS IN THE PUBLIC SCHOOLS

Jessie H. Bancroft reported that previous to 1903 the elementary schools of New York City required twenty minutes of gymnastics daily, in addition to the recess period which called for an additional ten minutes. Under Dr. Gulick, who assumed his duties as a supervisor of physical education in the city schools in that year, the requirement was changed to fifteen minutes for gymnastic exercises and a similar period for games in the classroom or play yards.

A 1915 survey by the North American Gymnastic Union of the physical education program in 52 metropolitan cities disclosed that 352 teachers supervised gymnastics an average of fifteen minutes daily in the elementary and two periods weekly in the secondary schools. The 52 cities possessed 323 gymnasiums, and 41 reported additional gymnasiums and swimming pools under construction. One of the biggest steps forward was the recognition of the schoolyard as a playground area during school hours.

INTERSCHOLASTIC ATHLETICS FOR BOYS

In spite of the dominant position of gymnastics, many public schools conducted extensive interscholastic programs. In a survey of 225 secondary schools in 1907 Guy S. Lowman reported that of 34, 290 high school students, 28 percent were engaged in one or more sports.[17] A further breakdown showed that 23.5 percent participated in football, 23.5 percent in track and field athletics, 22.5 percent in rowing, 19.8 percent in baseball, 16.8 percent in basketball, 16.3 percent in ice hockey, 13.6 percent in tennis, and 8 percent in golf. Sixty-four of the high schools employed part-time coaches, while football required the largest staff. Eighty percent of the schools did not require a physical examination, 52 percent gave the athletic manager full authority to schedule games, and 64 percent required the keeping of books on gate receipts and an annual financial report. Dr. Lowman noted that academies conducted better athletic programs because physical examinations were required and interscholastic athletics were placed in more mature hands. Seventy percent of the high schools admitted that many abuses associated with interscholastic athletics needed to be corrected.

High schools and academies, particularly in the eastern and north-central sections of the United States, had tried to regulate interscholastic competition fairly early. In 1895 the Athletic Leagues in New Jersey and New York and the New England Interscholastic Association formed the National Interscholastic Association of the United

States, which operated for two years. Where competitive opportunities were limited, high school athletic leagues became affiliated with amateur athletic federations in their areas and played by their rules and regulations. An example of this was the affiliation of the Cook County High School Athletic League with the Cook County Amateur Athletic Federation in 1908. By 1916 the high school athletic associations of Illinois, Indiana, Iowa, Michigan, and Wisconsin organized the North Central Interscholastic Athletic Conference to regulate interscholastic meets sponsored by state universities.

INTERSCHOLASTIC ATHLETICS FOR GIRLS

High school girls engaged in interscholastic competition in basketball, field hockey, and track athletics. Of these, basketball was the most popular, and many physicians and physical education leaders were concerned about the harmful effects, emotional and physical, which might come from the excitement of competition. At a 1906 meeting of the Public School Physical Education Training Society of New York, George W. Ehler proposed a resolution disapproving of interscholastic athletics for girls and suggested that intramural competition be substituted. At the same meeting Jessie Bancroft proposed a resolution to bar the public from these contests and to play down their publicity. A few schools heeded Dr. Ehler's advice, among them Westtown High School, Pennsylvania, which sponsored a girls' athletic association in 1910 with a program of basketball, hockey, swimming, skating, and tennis.

By 1914 girls of the secondary schools of New England were playing basketball by Spaulding's rules for women, while those in the West and South played either by men's rules (AAU), with or without modification, or by Clara Baer's (Tulane) rules for girls and women. As public enthusiasm for girls' basketball increased, men coaches gradually supplanted women physical educators, girls adopted stricter training rules and heavier playing schedules, and increased their amount of travel with or without chaperones. Criticism was not long in coming; both Jessie Bancroft and Elizabeth Burchenal fought for intramural games as a substitute for interscholastic competition for girls.

The trend in higher institutions to adopt the plan of the women's athletic association in lieu of intercollegiate competition gradually paid off. Before World War I many women physical educators in public schools had introduced girls' athletic associations. In 1917 the state of Illinois established a new trend when it created the Illinois League of High School Girls' Athletic Association to control the programs of girls' athletic associations in the state.

MEN'S COLLEGES AND UNIVERSITIES

Gymnastics had so long formed the main part of physical education programs in colleges and universities that James A. Babbitt, in an address before the American Physical Education Association in 1903, optimistically predicted that it would not be long before "a definite American system of gymnastics will be established, uniform in course, apparatus and nomenclature—and associated with a simple, adequate and universally adopted plan of physical education."[18]

Babbitt's view was supported by facts disclosed by two interesting surveys made in 1907[19] and 1910.[20] Over 50 percent of the higher institutions had a department of physical education, and more than 90 percent offered a gymnastic course whether or not a department existed. Eight percent required gymnastics from two to four years, and half of that number gave credit. Approximately 40 percent required a physical examination of entering students, and of those examined a like percentage were assigned to corrective physical education classes. It is interesting to note that 60 percent of the institutions reported that they had gymnasiums and playing fields, but only 10 percent admitted having a swimming pool worthy of the name.

Over this peaceful scene, however, storm clouds were gathering, though the warning signs reached few gymnastic leaders. Many physical education administrators were conscious of increased student interest in sports and games, and some permitted both men and women students to elect sports activities after they had completed the prescribed years of gymnasium.[21] Some institutions even accepted participation on athletic teams in lieu of attendance at regular gym classes.

TRANSITIONS IN PHYSICAL EDUCATION

In 1908 Thomas D. Storey conducted a survey of the academic status and educational background of directors of physical education in colleges and universities. In a verbal report to the Society of Gymnasium Directors he stated that at the institutions surveyed, 41 percent of the directors had medical degrees, 3 percent doctor of philosophy degrees, 18 percent master's degrees, and 30 percent bachelor's degrees. His report showed that the medical degree continued to command respect as part of the qualifications for a directorship. Professional education was still struggling for recognition as an acceptable department or college in higher institutions, and a director trained in this area was employed with some hesitancy.

MEDICAL EDUCATION AND PHYSICAL EDUCATION

The qualifications of the administrator of physical education changed sharply after 1908, when Abraham Flexner conducted a study of medical education for the Carnegie Foundation. In this epoch-making survey, Flexner compared the standards for medical education in the United States with those in European countries and found that in comparison medical preparation in our higher institutions was extremely superficial. Flexner's study led to the upgrading of medical training in this country, and the tougher four-year curriculum plus internship and postgraduate work made the relatively unremunerative position of physical education director unattractive to medical men.

This critical study also had a salutary effect upon the preparation of candidates in other professional areas, among them teacher education. The reevaluation of curriculums in teacher-training institutions did much to improve the quality of personnel in general education and physical education. The improved status of teacher-training institutions and the gradual acceptance of education as a legitimate department of the college or university encouraged the employment of physical education directors with academic degrees, whether in law, history, engineering or whatever. This unfortunate development rested upon the increasing popularity of intercollegiate athletics; the physical education director's athletic record became more important than what he majored in during his college career.

With this change of emphasis the popularity of anthropometric measurements and the exclusive right of the medically trained director to provide health instruction suffered. Both men and women administrators had by now acknowledged the futility of the time-consuming anthropometric measurements administered during the physical examination. With increased student enrollment the medically trained administrator could no longer meet the demand for health instruction singlehanded. Colleges and universities began to draft men and women members from the department of physical education to teach the subject. The acceptance of nonmedically trained instructors was justified by requiring them to take biological science courses as part of their training.

INTERCOLLEGIATE ATHLETICS PRIOR TO WORLD WAR I

W. P. Bowen of Michigan State said in 1909: "It is surprising that the leaders of education in America should have for two decades failed to grasp the educational value of the work [intercollegiate athletics] . . . and have left it go off on a tangent."[22] Authorities tolerated what they considered a necessary evil and frequently left the management of intercollegiate athletics to undergraduates. Faculty members, graduates, and even undergraduate students with athletic experience served as coaches. Eventually the alumni moved in and took control of intercollegiate athletics. Unfair tactics, the employment of "ringers" for special games, and the use of the tramp athlete who enrolled in school for the football season were common under student management. The taking over of intercollegiate athletics by the alumni only multiplied these abuses and added new problems.[23]

Fortunately, a few institutions saw the need for the control of athletics. Between 1870 and 1890 Harvard University organized the Central Committee Plan of Athletic Administration. This body had faculty as well as student and alumni representation and bravely attempted to regulate intercollegiate practices. By 1900 three types of control were in effect: (1) centralized control by faculty, students, and alumni (New England); (2) faculty and student control (Southwest); and (3) exclusive student control. Since football caused the major headache, many higher institutions solved the problem by eliminating the game or, as on the West Coast and in the Southwest, by substituting soccer and rugby.

One of the forces which helped in the control of intercollegiate athletics was the conference.[24] The Western Conference was formed in 1895 in Chicago. The faculty delegates agreed that all future athletic boards should have faculty representation, that the number of football games per season should be limited, that only bona fide students in residence for one year should take part in intercollegiate athletics, that preliminary training for sports should not begin before September 20, and finally that institutions should assume the roles of "host" and "guest" to ease the tense atmosphere on contest days. From 1900 to World War I many intercollegiate conferences were established, a trend aided by the founding of the Intercollegiate Athletic Association (NCAA) in 1906.

The National Collegiate Athletic Association

The focal point of irritation among administrators in this period was the conduct of football. Coaches were employed solely because of their reputation for winning. Both athletes and spectators engaged in mob violence, sports officials were often biased, rules lacked uniformity, and drinking and betting were common among the spectators. Occupying the center of the intercollegiate athletic universe, football was at best a brutal affair. The great tactical plays included such power-packed formations as the V-trick, flying wedge, guards-back, tackles-back, turtle-back, revolving tandem, and the famous Minnesota shift. These called for brute force and body contact at a dangerous speed, as judged by the 68 deaths and 804 incapacitating injuries recorded between 1901 and 1904. The situation reached a climax in 1905 when Harold Moore, a sophomore back of Union College, was killed in a game with New York University. The Sunday *New York Times* gave the incident front-page billing, and news services spread the grim story across the nation.

Aroused public sentiment demanded immediate action. H. McCracken, chancellor of New York University, called a meeting of university representatives to discuss the problem. Most of the delegates arrived fully determined to ban football as an intercollegiate sport, but the persuasive Captain Palmer E. Pierce of West Point was just as determined to retain it. He argued for better regulation and a modification of the rules to eliminate power plays.

As a result of this meeting the Intercollegiate Athletic Association of the United States (National Collegiate Athletic Association, 1910), was founded in 1906.[25] A football rules committee was appointed to eliminate rough tactics, which among many important revisions introduced the forward pass to encourage open play. The NCAA favored the establishment of high ethical standards in intercollegiate athletics and the development of physical education in the schools, and supported intramural athletics at a time when physical educators were dedicated to the formal program.

The Organization of Intramural Athletics

Intramural athletics had been a part of American campus life from the beginning. In 1909 Princeton students organized the Intercollegiate Athletic Association and sponsored intramural contests in baseball and basketball. In the same year the students of Amherst organized the Intracollegiate Athletic Association, which sponsored interclass competition in baseball, freshman and sophomore rush, and basketball.[26] Students at Harvard organized dormitories into competitive rowing units and started interclass competition in rowing, football, basketball, and track and field athletics.[27] Between 1913 and 1914 the University of Michigan and Ohio State University formally organized departments of intramural athletics with the assistance of the intercollegiate department.

J. W. Wilce, chairman of the Committee on Intramural Sports of the Athletic Research Society, reported on a nationwide survey of intramural athletics in 124 colleges and universities made during 1917.[28] The study indicated that intramural athletics were favored by the intercollegiate associations out of the desire to promote an athletic program for all students or because of their value as a varsity feeder. Financial assistance was derived mainly from gate receipts and student tax, and less frequently from student organizations, the university budget, subscription, or special funds. The survey's respondees admitted that the war fever had added impetus to the intramural movement and that the faculties of 122 of the institutions were in sympathy with it.

WOMEN'S COLLEGES AND UNIVERSITIES

During the 1880's the common title for the women's department was the Department of Physical Culture; around the turn of the century the term "physical training" made its appearance. Early departments were generally limited to a single staff member, occasionally assisted by a part-time male member or a skilled performer from outside the institution. During the first decade of the century the increased enrollment of women students obliged many departments to add members, which in some cases totaled as many as six women instructors. Many had received their training at the Boston Normal School of Gymnastics or the privately sponsored gymnastic schools of Dudley A. Sargent, William G. Anderson, and Baron Nils Posse and his wife.

Gymnastics dominated the college program, and students performed free exercises; hoop, wand, dumbbell, and Indian club drills; marching; and exercises on the horse, buck, rings, stall bars, balance beams, and springboard. Corrective exercises for postural physical defects played a prominent part in the program. Occasionally a daring teacher introduced aesthetic or gymnastic dancing, which, in most cases, was a novel relief from the routine of classwork.

In answer to a growing demand from the student body, more and more women's departments began to offer sports and dancing on an optional basis after the completion of the gymnastic requirement. The latter generally included the freshman and sophomore years, extending in some institutions to all four years. Gradually women students were permitted to substitute tennis, basketball, hockey, fencing, or boating in partial fulfillment of the physical education requirement. Many women directors accepted the trend as a natural outcome of the improved status of women in an enlightened society and added baseball, swimming, golf, volleyball, fencing, soccer, track and field, cricket, hiking, and horseback riding. Some even organized women's athletic associations and sponsored intercollegiate competition in basketball, field hockey, track and field, and rowing.

An interesting feature in many programs was the annual spring celebration, which took the form of May Day festivals, athletic games, or exhibitions. In the East Barnard College sponsored the Greek games and Elmira College a May festival of which the old English maypole dance was a traditional part. In the Midwest the University of Illinois presented a spring program which consisted of scarf dancing, an Indian club drill, and a basketball game. The University of Wisconsin and Earlham College had a May Day festival, Marshall College organized an annual carnival exhibition, and the University of Cincinnati a Greek games festival.

The construction of gymnasiums at women's colleges was continuous from 1880 to 1900. These were small in size and designed for the drills and exercises of the gymnastic program. At the turn of the century with increased enrollment and expansion of the sports program, many were replaced by larger structures, and athletic fields, tennis courts, golf courses, boathouses, stables for riding, and hiking cabins were added. Very few coeducational institutions possessed gymnasiums for the exclusive use of women before 1900. Women either shared the men's facilities or utilized the wing or basement area of an old building on the campus. Thereafter gymnasiums appeared in increasing numbers, furnished with a variety of apparatus, indoor running tracks, and swimming pools. Outdoor sports areas became a necessity to accommodate archery, baseball, hockey, soccer, and track and field.[29]

PROFESSIONAL LEADERSHIP

One of the early promoters of sports for women in the East was Harriet Isabel Ballintine. She was a graduate of Sargent's school of Gymnastics and was appointed director of the gymnasium at Vassar College in 1891. Miss Ballintine incurred the criticism of press and gymnastic leaders in 1897 when she introduced her women students to track and field. Lucille Eaton Hill became a member of the faculty of Wellesley College in 1882 and was appointed director of the gymnasium in 1894. She had also studied under Dr. Sargent at Cambridge and was familiar with the German and Swedish systems of gymnastics. One of her major contributions was her 1903 book containing the techniques and rules of sports suitable for women.[30] Senda Berenson of Smith College, although trained in the Swedish system, was also a sports enthusiast.[31]

In the Midwest Delphine Hanna was another graduate of Dr. Sargent's gymnastic school. She introduced sports into the programs of both men and women at Oberlin at an early date. The women's program at the University of Wisconsin reflected the progressive leadership of Blanche Trilling and served as a guide in administrative practices for other institutions in the United States. She introduced archery, bowling, and social dancing into the women's program and applied the intramural idea to women's athletic associations.

ATHLETICS IN EDUCATION FOR WOMEN

The wave of enthusiasm for sports participation by women reached such heights that many feared for their physical well-being. Women were active participants in the cycling movement in the 1800s and made daring innovations in riding habits, one of which was the costume designed by Amelia Jenks Bloomer. In the year 1875, when the National Archery Association was founded, the first archery tournament for women was conducted in Chicago. The first ladies' tournament in golf was held in 1894 on the seven-hole course at Morristown and the first national tournament in 1895 at Meadowbrook.

One of the greatest spurs to the movement was the publicity given to the individual performance of women athletes. Margaret Custis of Boston won the Women's Golf Championship in 1907, 1911, and 1912. May Sutton at 13 won the Pacific Southwest tennis championship in 1900, the national championship in 1904, and was twice champion at Wimbleton. Eleanor Sears, a Boston society girl and a one-woman campaigner against the dominance of men in sports, was in the news consistently with her exceptional performances in tennis, golf, squash, rifle shooting, and swimming. In 1912 women were invited to compete in swimming and diving at the Stockholm Olympic Games.

According to Jacobs, women in higher institutions in 1901 engaged in basketball, tennis, baseball (indoor and outdoor), field hockey, track and field athletics, swimming, and rowing.[32] In 1901 Constance M. K. Applebee gave lectures and demonstrations on field hockey at Dr. Sargent's Harvard Summer School. Bryn Mawr organized the first women's college athletic association in 1891, and many other institutions followed suit in the next decade. These early associations devoted their energy to bicycle, hockey, tennis, and basketball clubs. In the early 1900s intramural sports changed to intercollegiate competition. This transition with its accompanying evils did not meet the approval of women directors of physical education, and attempts at regulation and control were in evidence as early as 1910.

Higher institutions recognized that sports participation and competition had become an inevitable part of college life for women. Women physical educators sought a saner and healthier approach to competition through the adoption of intramural athletics. Blanche Trilling, at the University of Wisconsin, led the way when in 1913 she organized the women's athletic association as a counterpart of men's intramural athletics. She developed a diversified program of activities and adopted a point system leading to awards.

In 1917 representatives of twenty colleges and universities met at Madison to exchange ideas on the promotion of women's athletic associations as a substitute for intercollegiate athletics.[33] The delegates voted to meet annually and invited the Women's Intercollegiate Athletic Council of New England (1914) to join forces in an organization to be called the National Athletic Conference of American College Women. In the same year the APEA created the Women's Committee on Athletics to safeguard the health and safety of women in athletics and to establish relevant standards and policies for sports competition.

The Association of Directors of Physical Education for Women, founded in 1910 by Amy Morris Homans, Wellesley College, also exerted an important influence in this transitional period. Its membership consisted of women physical education teachers and presidents of athletic associations in New England colleges for women. This group met with midwestern women directors of physical education at the University of Chicago in 1917 to form a similar organization. In 1924 the New England Association combined with the Midwest and Western Associations (1921) to form the National Association of Physical Education for College Women.[34]

TEACHER PREPARATION

Sixteen normal schools prepared teachers of physical education in 1902. The program was ten months in one school, two years in nine, three years in two, and four years in three. Professional leaders recognized that the quality of the program varied from institution to institution. They thought the answer to this rested in the enforcement of established standards by an accrediting agency.

The first attempt in this direction was made by Walter Truslow of the New York Physical Education Society at the national convention of the AAAPE in 1898. He recommended that a committee be appointed to set up standards and consider the issuance of diplomas of two grades, instructor and master physical educator, by the AAAPE. The resulting Committee of Nine reported in 1902,[35] and the ambitious two-year professional program then formulated would be a challenge even to the modern student attending a four-year training institution. The standards proposed by the Committee of Nine were approved by the general convention but voted down by the constitutional committee.

Another attempt to establish standards was initiated by Charles H. Judd, of the University of Chicago, at the second annual meeting of the Middle West Society of Physical Education in 1913. The report of its committee under a typically verbose title was published in the *January Review* in 1914. It recommended that the APEA appoint a committee that would accredit professional training institutions employing the standards it had developed.

By 1914 professional preparation was provided by twenty-four institutions in the United States with an enrollment of 2,800 students. As reported by W. P. Bowen, of Michigan State, in a survey of 22 of these, the quality of the professional program had not improved. The total hours of practice teaching varied from 36 to 320; of professional courses, 216 to 1572; of basic sciences, 35 to 1350; of liberal arts courses (English, mathematics, and languages) 0 to 264. Bowen noted that some programs placed too much emphasis on practical work with few theoretical courses. He also pointed out that the four-year teacher-training programs presented broader and higher-quality courses than two-year professional programs. He suggested that the APEA apply for assistance from the Carnegie Foundation to finance a more detailed survey such as the one this organization conducted on medical education in the United States.[36]

Professional training programs, particularly in universities, recognized the implications of the current sports movement to the preparation of physical educators. Courses in the fundamental skills and strategies of athletic sports gradually made their appearance. In 1911 the University of Wisconsin reorganized its professional program, and physical education majors were required to take fourteen different sports in addition to calisthenics, apparatus work, tumbling, and corrective exercises. The Department of Physical Education at Columbia University added preparation in athletic sports in 1915. The sports included were rowing, basketball, football, soccer, track and field athletics, handball, swimming, baseball, and boxing. In answer to the growing demand for the teacher-coach combination in public schools, Harvard University offered a six weeks' course in football and track and field athletics coaching in 1916. Shortly before the United States entered World War I, the University of Illinois formulated plans to introduce a four-year athletic coaching program within the College of Education leading to the bachelor degree.

The professional teacher program was also viewed in this period as the logical place to provide leadership training in recreation. C. W. Hetherington, chairman of the Committee on Normal Course in Play of the Playground and Recreation of America, suggested in 1908 that normal schools should include such a course. In Hetherington's opinion, it would be beneficial to all teachers regardless of their area of specialization. The following year Hetherington edited the *Normal Course in Play** as a guide to teachers and students in normal schools and to recreation supervisors training leaders on the job.

* Hetherington's book was revised in 1925 to include a more diversified program of arts and crafts, music and drama, and the new trend to establish community recreation centers and provide adult recreation.

NOTES

1. Philip P. Wiener and Frederic H. Young. *Studies in the Philosophies of Charles Sanders Peirce.* Cambridge: Harvard University Press, 1952, pp. 41–44.
2. Marc E. Jones. *George Sylvester Morris.* Philadelphia: David McKay Company, 1948, pp. 339–402.
3. Freeman R. Butts and Lawrence A. Cremins. *A History of Education in American Culture.* New York: Henry Holt and Company, 1953, pp. 340–341.
4. John Dewey. *The School and Society.* Chicago: University of Chicago Press, 1900, p. 67.
5. John Dewey. *Interest and Effort in Education.* Boston: Houghton Mifflin Company, 1913.
6. G. Stanley Hall. *Youth, Its Education, Regimen and Hygiene.* New York: D. Appleton and Company, 1904.
7. Luther H. Gulick. "Interest in Relation to Muscular Exercise." *American Physical Education Review,* 7:2 (June, 1902), 57–65. *Physical Education by Muscular Exercise.* Philadelphia: P. Blakiston's Sons and Company, 1904.
8. John M. Tyler. *Growth and Education.* Boston: Houghton Mifflin Company, 1907, pp. 41; 218–227.
9. Thomas Denison Wood. *The Ninth Yearbook of the National Society for the Study of Education.* (Part I) Chicago: University of Chicago Press, 1913, pp. 75–104.
10. Alice Oakes Bronson. "Clark W. Hetherington, Scientist and Philosopher." Salt Lake City: University of Utah Press, 1958.
11. Clark W. Hetherington. "Analysis of Problems in College Athletics." *American Physical Education Review,* 12:2 (June, 1907), 154–181. Arthur Weston. *The Making of American Physical Education.* New York: Appleton-Century-Crofts, 1962, 192–197. C. W. Hetherington. "Report of the Committee on Amateur Law to the Intercollegiate Athletic Association." *American Physical Education Review,* 15:3 (March, 1910), 165–181.
12. "The Athletic Research Society—Résumé of Organization, Work and Plans." *American Physical Education Review,* 17:8 (November, 1912), 585–598.
13. Arthur Weston. *The Making of American Physical Education.* New York: Appleton-Century-Crofts, 1962, pp. 159–165.

14. Georges Hébert. *Guide Pratique d'Éducation Physique.* Paris: Viuberts and Nony Editeurs, 1909.
15. Edwin Fauver. "A Suggestion for Making Required Physical Education Training of Greater Value to the College Students." *American Physical Education Review,* 13:3 (March, 1914), 200–203.
16. Lewis M. Terman. *Hygiene of the School Child.* Boston: Houghton Mifflin Company, 1914, p. 8.
17. Guy S. Lowman. "The Regulation and Control of Competitive Sports in Secondary Schools." *American Physical Education Review,* 12:3 (September, 1907), 241–255.
18. James A. Babbitt. "Present Conditions of Gymnastics and Athletics in American Colleges." *American Physical Education Review,* 8:4 (December, 1903), 280–283.
19. George L. Meylan. "The Place of Physical Education in the College Curriculum." *American Physical Education Review,* 12:2 (June, 1907), 101–108.
20. Luther H. Gulick. "Report of the Committee on the Status of Physical Education in Public Normal Schools and Public High Schools in the United States." *American Physical Education Review,* 15:6 (June, 1910), 446–454.
21. Alice Oakes Bronson. "Clark W. Hetherington, Scientist and Philosopher." Salt Lake City: University of Utah Press, 1958, 27–27. R. Tait McKenzie. *Exercise in Education and Medicine.* Philadelphia: W. B. Saunders Company, 1909, pp. 174–190.
22. W. P. Bowen. "The Evaluation of Athletic Evils." *American Physical Education Review,* 14:3 (March, 1909), 156.
23. Dudley A. Sargent. "History of the Administration of Intercollegiate Athletics in the United States." *American Physical Education Review,* 15:4 (April, 1910), 252–261.
24. George W. Woerlin. "Intercollegiate Athletic Conferences, Their History and Significance." (Thesis) Ohio State University, 1938.
25. Palmer E. Pierce. "The Intercollegiate Athletic Association of the United States." *American Physical Education Review,* 13:2 (February, 1908), 85. Harold M. Frindell "The Origin and Development of the National Collegiate Athletic Association—A Force for Good in Intercollegiate Athletics." (Thesis) New York University, 1938.
26. Paul C. Phillips. "The Extension of Athletic Sports to the Whole Student Body at Amherst." *American Physical Education Review,* 17:5 (May, 1912), 339–342. J. Edmund Welch. "The Influence of Sports on the Amherst Plan of Physical Education." *Proceedings,* The College Physical Education Association, 1962.

27. Dudley A. Sargent. "Competition in Athletics." *American Physical Education Review,* 15:2 (February, 1910), 106.
28. J. W. Wilce. "Report of the Committee on Intramural Sports, Athletic Research Society," *American Physical Education Review,* 23:4 (April, 1918), 199–212; 23:5 (May, 1918), 279–286.
29. Dorothy S. Ainsworth. *The History of Physical Education in Colleges for Women.* New York: A. S. Barnes and Company, 1930, pp. 28–31. Miriam Gray. "A Century of Growth—The Historical Development of Physical Education for Women in Selected Colleges of Six Midwestern States." Ann Arbor: Edwards Brothers, Inc., 1951.
30. Lucille Eaton Hill. *Athletics and Out-Door Sports for Women.* New York: The Macmillan Company, 1903.
31. Agnes R. Wayman. "Pioneers in Physical Education." *The Research Quarterly* (Supplement) 12:3 (October, 1941); "Lucille Eaton Hill." *Wellesley Magazine,* Wellesley College Library (August, 1925).
32. Edwin E. Jacobs. *Physical Vigor of American Women.* Boston: Marshall Jones Company, 1920, p. 49.
33. Mary S. Kissock. "The Function of the Women's Athletic Association." *Mind and Body,* 25:272 (October, 1918), 233–240.
34. Dorothy S. Ainsworth. "National Association of Physical Education for College Women." *Journal of Health and Physical Education,* 17:9 (November, 1946), 525.
35. "Preliminary Report of the Committee of Nine." *American Physical Education Review,* 6:1 (March, 1901), 81–83.
36. W. P. Bowen. "Preparation of Teachers in Physical Education." *American Physical Education Review,* 19:6 (June, 1914), 421–427.

Chapter 20

PHYSICAL EDUCATION IN THE UNITED STATES, 1918–1929

SOCIAL TRENDS IN THE 20s

BEFORE World War I women had served in the business world in capacities acceptable by the social standards of the time. During the war, however, they donned overalls and filled men's places in industrial plants and when the Armistice was signed were reluctant to relinquish their newly found role. In 1920 the Nineteenth Amendment gave women the right to vote, an event that was to affect all future social, health, and educational legislation. The Volstead Act, passed in 1919, encouraged illegal traffic in liquor and spawned gangsterism, with its accompanying evils. A new breed of reformers appeared who espoused everything from anarchism to Communism.

The release from war tension, the patterns of behavior projected by the motion picture industry, and the exhilaration that accompanied the economic boom, along with other factors, produced one of the most interesting social phenomena in the country's history, the Jazz Age. This era marked the decline of Puritanism in America, which found expression in a more liberal code of social ethics and a more permissive attitude toward the education of the young.

PROGRESSIVE EDUCATION

After 1920 the progressive education movement, based upon the educational philosophy of Dewey and Kilpatrick, attracted growing attention. Its advocates held that "vital personalities" could best be developed through participation in group activities and that respect for the individual was a basic aspiration of a democratic society. The school should provide the child with real social situations in which he could share in decisions of interest to all and thus cultivate his judgment, discernment, and tolerance. Critics of the movement, however, held that its method was neither progressive nor educational and that it allowed the schoolchild far too much freedom.

In retrospect it is apparent that the progressive education movement was a reaction against the old fundamental view that the school's function was to provide systematic training in foundation subjects, with informal learning supplementary rather than central. The progressive educator, on the other hand, placed little emphasis upon formal, systematic instruction but considered learning experiences acquired through group activity to be central. The teacher following this method functioned as a guide rather than a disciplinarian and merely encouraged rather than taught initiative, discipline, and responsibility.

PHYSICAL EDUCATORS DURING WORLD WAR I

Many physical educators, athletic coaches, and trainers served in the student voluntary physical conditioning classes in the prewar period and in the Student Army Training Corps organized later on the campuses. When the United States entered the war, the professional leadership responded immediately to the call for aid in conditioning soldiers. Among them were Dudley A. Sargent, Luther H. Gulick, J. H. McCurdy, George J. Fischer, George L. Meylan, Thomas A. Storey, and Joseph E. Raycroft. R. Tait McKenzie was active in both England and the United States. Dr. McKenzie joined the English Army as a recruit and after serving with the Physical Training Division at Aldershot, was assigned the responsibility in the Royal Medical Corps of routing disabled men to hospitals. In 1917 he returned to the University of Pennsylvania and was soon drafted as a consultant at Walter Reed Hospital, Washington, D.C., where he utilized his English experience in rehabilitative work.

The medical examiner's report on the physical condition of draftees between the ages of 21 and 35 emphasized the need for a physical training program in the country's more than fifty hastily established camps. Both the Army and Navy were forced to draw upon Army personnel who had training in physical education and athletic coaching. Major H. J. Koehler, director of physical education at West Point, was eventually assigned the duty of coordinating the physical training programs in the Army cantonments, and with a limited staff he shuttled back and forth across the nation.[1]

TRAINING PROGRAMS

Problems were met as they arose, and it was some time before thought was given to administration. The Commission on Training Camp Activities of the War Department was created, with Raymond B. Fosdick as administrative head. Under it the War Camp Community Service was set up, with Joseph E. Raycroft, of Princeton University, as chairman of the Athletic Division of the Army, and Walter Camp, of football fame and originator of the All-American football selections, as chairman of a similar division in the Navy. At the beginning the physical training program consisted of calisthenics drills, physical labor, and running. Dr. Raycroft eventually developed a more balanced program which included calisthenics, physical efficiency tests, mass instruction of athletic skills, obstacle course running, and competitive athletics. Later the work of physical educators of the YMCA and Jewish Welfare Board and city recreation leaders, called into service, convinced commanding officers in the United States and overseas that recreational sports should supplement the strenuous physical conditioning program.

Women physical educators emphasized conditioning programs for women who entered industry and for those who wanted to be fit because it was patriotic. Many of them entered newly created schools for occupational and physical therapy and saw service in hospitals at home and overseas as civilian Reconstruction Aides under the Division of Physical Reconstruction, Surgeon General's Office.

PHYSICAL EDUCATION IN THE POSTWAR PERIOD

In December, 1917, the Provost Marshal released the medical examiner's report, which indicated that of a total of three million men called to military duty under the Selective Service Draft over one-third were physically unfit for service. Of the men accepted, thousands were in poor physical condition and a great majority who reached the training camps had to be taught the simple rudiments of hygiene and diet as well as the fundamental skills of the simplest activities. In 1918 the committee on health problems of the National Council on Education, as the result of a survey of the health status of children in elementary and secondary schools, estimated that three-fourths of the 25 million schoolchildren were suffering from physical defects that handicapped their physical and mental development. In the same year a government study of the health conditions among a million industrial workers disclosed that the annual loss to the nation because of illness amounted to 270 million workdays. These reports seemed to indicate a loss of health and physical vigor in the United States through the lack of adequate provisions for health and physical education instruction in the schools.

LEGISLATION

The public, barraged by reports of the deplorable status of the nation's health in the daily newspapers and magazines, was moved to demand legislation for health and physical education instruction in the schools. A study of Table I indicates that twenty-eight states had legislation for health and physical education of the permissive or mandatory type by 1922. Fifty percent of the states listed laws enacted between 1917 and 1919. The Mississippi law contained a rider which made it inoperable until federal funds became available. The Virginia law carried an annual appropriation of $50,000, half of which was allotted to medical inspection in the schools under the state board of health and the other half to the supervision of physical education programs under personnel designated by the state department of education. The Virginia law also authorized local authorities to appropriate funds for medical inspection and physical education for schoolchildren, and the employment of school nurses, physicians, and physical education personnel.

Some states passed laws which made the provision for programs of health and physical education in the schools untenable. Some laws contained an incomplete statement of the aims of physical educa-

TABLE 1. STATES WHICH HAD LEGISLATION IN HEALTH AND PHYSICAL EDUCATION BY 1922

State	*Date*	*State*	*Date*
Alabama	1919	Missouri	1921
California	1866 1917	Nevada	1917
Connecticut	1921	New Jersey	1917
Delaware	1918	New York	1916
Georgia	1920	North Carolina	1921
Idaho	1913	North Dakota	1899
Illinois	1915	Ohio	1892 1904
Indiana	1919	Oregon	1919
Kentucky	1920	Pennsylvania	1919
Maine	1919	Rhode Island	1917
Maryland	1918	Utah	1919
Massachusetts	1921	Virginia	1920
Michigan	1919	Washington	1919
Mississippi	1920	West Virginia	1921

SOURCE: Abridged table from Paul E. Belting, "The Interest of the State in Physical Education as Exemplified in State Legislation," *The Athletic Journal,* 10:4 (December, 1929), 28–36.

tion, while others included no statement whatsoever. For instance, no direct reference to the purposes of physical education was made in the laws of Illinois, Mississippi, New York, Ohio, and Rhode Island. A brief statement of purpose was included in the laws of Nevada, New Jersey, North Dakota, and Oregon. More specific objectives were set forth in the laws of California, Indiana, and Missouri.

Superintendents of public instruction in state departments of education quickly realized how complex the task of state-wide supervision was going to be. As a result, administrative heads of state departments of education appointed state supervisors or directors of physical education to administer the law throughout the state. New York appointed the first state director in 1916 and by 1930 twenty-one states had regularly employed directors, with three or four additional ones providing directors on a provisional basis.

In 1926 the Society of State Directors of Physical and Health Education was organized.[2]

THE NATIONAL PHYSICAL EDUCATION SERVICE AND LEGISLATION

In 1918 P. P. Claxton, United States Commissioner of Education, called a meeting at Philadelphia of representatives from nineteen national organizations "to consider how in view of the proven lack of physical fitness on the part of our conscripted young men, an adequate, successful system of physical education may become universal." As the meeting progressed it became apparent that the objective was much too ambitious, and the committee suggested the organization of a national service with a field representative to promote physical education. The Playground and Recreation Association of America volunteered to support such a service with a special grant of $10,000. This new organization was called the National Physical Education Service, with Charles W. Savage of Oberlin College as field agent, and E. Dana Caulkins manager. In 1926 James E. Rogers, who had many years' experience in the field of recreation, replaced C. W. Savage. In the course of his duties "Jimmy" Rogers visited many schools and professional workers across the nation, and through his reports "Around the Country" in the *Review* and in the *Journal of Health and Physical Education* he became a valuable courier of news and a sounding board for trends in physical education.

FEDERAL LEGISLATION

As the movement for state legislation gathered momentum backed by public sentiment, professional organizations began agitating for federal legislation. Senator Arthur Capper (Kansas) and Representative Simon D. Fess (Ohio) in 1919 introduced bills into Congress which initiated legislation for health and physical education on a national basis. In 1920 the Fess-Capper Bill (S. 4787) was amended to extend its coverage and given a hearing before the Senate Committee on Education and Labor. Both the Democratic and Republican parties made health and physical education legislation a plank in their 1920 party platforms, although each was firmly committed to the belief that education should remain under state control. In spite of all this support, the Fess-Capper Bill was sent to the Committee on Education and Labor for study, where it expired.

In brief, the bill called for an appropriation of ten million dollars for the first year, to be distributed among the states on the basis of school population. Federal funds were to be matched by the states to provide a comprehensive program for all youths between the ages of 6 and 18. To be included were funds for the training and employment of teachers of health and physical education, nurses, and health supervisors. Granting of subsidies on the basis of effective plans for carrying out the work was to be in the hands of the United States Bureau of Education.

A REEVALUATION OF THE AIMS OF PHYSICAL EDUCATION

In 1919 the Society of Directors of Physical Education in Colleges (College Physical Education Association) appointed a special committee to formulate the aims of physical education in the light of current educational trends.[3] The report of the committee—consisting of Fred E. Leonard, Oberlin; R. Tait McKenzie, University of Pennsylvania; and Joseph E. Raycroft, Princeton—received wide publicity and appeared in the *Review* (June, 1920), and *School Life* (February, 1921). It stated that the improvement of the individual within the framework of his social relations was of greater importance than mere personal values. Games and athletics, it pointed out, produced many worthwhile social qualities. Contributing to these social aims were the conservation of health, and the development of strength, endurance, "self-respecting" posture, and neuromuscular control. The committee opposed past medical influences on the objectives of physical education and emphasized objectives other than health.

This bold stand, which implied that physical education had a greater purpose than simply that of building muscles and guaranteeing health, was met with a variety of reactions in educational and health circles. Franklin Bobbitt, an educator from the University of Chicago, commented that physical educators had overemphasized social aims to the neglect of the physical: "There appears to be a feeling among physical educationists that the physical side of man's nature is lower than the social or mental, and that . . . they, too, must aim primarily at those more exalted non-physical things of mental and social type."[4] William H. Burnham, of Clark University, less critically stated, "Physical education is not mechanized and standardized. It furnishes opportunity for the training of the whole individual. The aim of physical education today should be clear. It is an essential of education."[4] Educational sociologists, as a group, felt that it would serve no useful purpose for physical educators to urge as primary, or even as secondary, the objectives of social, civic, or moral education.

CLARK W. HETHERINGTON. In the welter of criticism which followed the publication of the committee's report, Clark W. Hetherington published his provocative *School Program in Physical Education* in 1922.[5] Hetherington announced that both the German and Swedish systems had contributed generously to the American program, but it was now clear that a program that was not indigenous to the soil could not long endure in American culture: "A system which has drawn its breath of life from a foreign culture radically different in its purpose from American life cannot be transplanted." What America demanded was a program of physical education activities which would help educate children for the free and self-directing responsibilities of a democratic society.

According to Hetherington the objectives of physical education should be stated in terms of general education: (1) the immediate objectives as expressed in the organization of child life in big muscle activities; (2) the remote objectives in adult adjustment and efficiency; (3) the objectives in development; (4) the objectives in social standards; and (5) the objectives in the control of health conditions. Under "remote objectives of adult adjustment and efficiency," Hetherington stated that though the physical activities of adolescence may contribute some protective and recreational skills with carry-over value, their main contribution is developmental. The objectives in development included those of the instinctive, intellectual, and neuromuscular mechanisms and organic power. Social standards were the idealized objectives; physical education should develop leadership and desirable moral habits, ideals, and attitudes. With respect to the control of health conditions, Hetherington observed that the physical educator no less than any other teacher must look after the health and safety of children.

JESSE FEIRING WILLIAMS (1886——). Born in Kenton, Ohio, Jesse F. Williams received his bachelor degree from Oberlin College, his M.D. from Columbia University, and his Sc.D. from Rollins College. He served as a physical education instructor for the blind in New York; assistant professor of physical education at Columbia University; professor of hygiene and physical education at the University of Cincinnati; and professor of physical education and chairman of the department at Columbia University until his retirement in 1941.

As an assistant professor (1911–1916) and professor of physical education (1919–1941) at Columbia University, Williams formulated his philosophy in a rich and vigorous educational environment peopled by such creative personalities as John Dewey, William H. Kilpatrick, Edward L. Thorndike, Thomas D. Wood, Clark W. Hetherington, and others.

Williams' book *The Organization and Administration of Physical Education* was published the same year as Hetherington's *School Program.*[6] In it Williams served notice "that formal calisthenics and gymnastics are a deformity in education," and that an immediate cure should be found. He stated that one system in vogue in a large metropolitan area represented "no particular achievement" and that many of its teachers lacked even a high school education. Williams deliberately smoked out the advocates of the formal systems and, via the *Review,* JOURNAL, and *Mind and Body,* precipitated one of the liveliest educational battles in the history of the profession. To the credit of all the combatants, however, a common ground of understanding was reached.

Like Hetherington, Williams emphasized that physical education was a phase of general education. It was his conviction that it should be taught not for the purpose of health or for the development of better soldiers, but "to provide an opportunity for the individual to act in situations that are physically wholesome, mentally stimulating and satisfying, and socially sound."[6] He suggested that physical education needed some scientific means of classifying motor ability, or Motor Quotient, which would be the analogue of the IQ, or Intelligence Quotient. In selecting activities, the physical educator should choose those which employed the fundamental muscle groups. They should be based on the growth needs of the child and have instinctive appeal. Classes should be organized by natural groups and conform in motive, performance, and physiological age.

Sports and games were good material because they had appeal and developed moral and social values. Williams felt that the time had arrived when school athletics should be conducted as an educational project and "not as a side show, extracurricular affair, or student amusement activity."

The qualifications of the coach should essentially be no different from those in any other branch of learning. Athletics was a legitimate part of the department of physical education. In athletic competition for girls he questioned the anatomical practicability of the broad jump, high jump, pole vault, running more than 100 yards, and weight throwing. He condemned competition by men's rules and did not favor coaching by men. He suggested that suitable standards should be developed for athletic competition among girls and women.

THE NEW PHYSICAL EDUCATION AND THE SCIENTIFIC APPROACH

In discussing the teacher's responsibility in 1926 Kilpatrick stated that civilization had outgrown the old school methods and curriculum. Modern civilization demanded new methods and a new curriculum. The spirit of the times was best expressed by Charles Judd, an educator at the University of Chicago, in a statement that there was too much physical training and too little physical education. The leaders of the natural or informal movement, as it now was called, launched an aggressive campaign under the Columbia contingent to acquaint professional workers with the new physical education. Thomas D. Wood and Rosalind F. Cassidy, a former student of Wood's and Williams', in 1927 published *The New Physical Education,* which virtually became a guidebook in the new method.[7] It dealt with the biological, psychological, sociological, and educational basis of the informal method, suggested programs of natural activities for elementary and secondary schools, and teacher qualifications. In 1927 Williams published the first of many editions of *Principles of Physical Education,* which enunciated principles based on scientific facts cited by Gulick, Hall, Tyler, Wood, and Hetherington to guide the organization and conduct of the new program.

FUNDAMENTALISTS AND THE INFORMAL METHOD

Among the informalists were educators who, though in accord with the new philosophy, suggested that the profession strive to achieve scientifically formulated objectives rather than depend upon empirically determined criteria which only partially met the demands of education in a changing social order.[8] To accomplish this emphasis should be placed on better teacher education, especially in philosophy, teaching techniques, and experimental research so that method would be based on scientifically determined facts rather than upon speculation and empiricism.

Although Williams had voiced this concept in the early 20s, Brace in 1925 was the first to outline a scientific approach for the profession itself. He pointed out that no educational program was complete which did not provide tests of intelligence, native motor ability, knowledge and techniques, rules, hygiene, performance, achievement, and attitudes.

VIEWS ON MEASUREMENT IN PHYSICAL EDUCATION

As the 20s progressed, growing interest in tests and measurements as scientific tools presaged an active era of research in the years ahead. David K. Brace pointed out in 1927 that the scientific work of Thorndike, Terman, Goddard, Judd, and others, and their vast scheme of measurement and quantitative investigations in the field formulated and executed before and after World War I, had had a profound influence upon the scientific application of measurement in physical education. He suggested that in measurement three objectives should be emphasized: (1) to classify pupils for the purpose of instruction, (2) to measure achievement, and (3) to further the learning process.[9] In the same year Frederick Rand Rogers, proposed the physical fitness index as a means of classification for pupils in the program. According to his reasoning, participation in large-muscle activities improved the fitness of the individual and resulted in an increase in strength. Logically then, a measurement of strength was also a measurement of physical fitness.[10]

Many physical educators were cognizant of the important role of tests and measurement in physical education, yet there was some concern about the possibility that the scientific interest might outweigh other objectives. As early as 1925 a few physical educators suggested that, in addition to determinating capacity for performance and measuring progress, the directors of the program should also consider student needs and interests. As Harry A. Scott, University of Texas, stated it: "Because there are individual differences in capacities and interests, departments must offer a wide and varied program of activities designed to meet the situation, and further provide adequate instruction and facilities to insure the greatest amount of participation."[11]

PHYSICAL EDUCATION IN PUBLIC SCHOOLS

ELEMENTARY SCHOOLS

Elementary schools were still strongly dominated by the formal system, particularly in large metropolitan areas, but, as in the high schools, natural activities were being made available in the higher grades under the 8–4 or 6–3–3 plans of organization. In states where legislation was given more than lip service, city supervisors of physical education were employed to organize a syllabus and assist classroom teachers in implementing it. As usual there were difficulties, such as the natural resentment of teachers to the idea of supervision and the quick turnover of grade teachers which often nullified hard-won gains. The city supervisor, however, was to play an important role in the future development of physical education on the elementary level.

In cities whose elementary schools had physical education, the subject was required in grades one to six for 150 minutes per week. The activities, whether formal or informal, were supervised by the classroom teacher, who was expected to follow the material outlined in the syllabus provided by the board of education. The 150 minutes per week were usually divided into ten periods of fifteen minutes each, coinciding with the accepted recess periods, one in the middle of the morning and one in the middle of the afternoon. Unfortunately some grade teachers looked upon this fifteen minutes as a drill period designed exclusively for formal activities. In progressive programs, however, two-thirds of the time was used in supervised play and one-third for free play, and in some schools an additional ninety minutes a week was provided. Several cities arranged annual field days or exhibitions in which all pupils participated.

SECONDARY SCHOOLS

In 1924 J. F. Landis made a study of the physical education program in 209 secondary schools in twenty-three states.[12] He found that a large number of high schools did not include physical education because they lacked gymnasiums. If they provided any exercise beyond the interscholastic athletic program, it was usually a daily period of five to fifteen minutes of the formal type. In schools with a physical education program class periods were held two to three times a week and averaged forty-five minutes in length. Some high schools looked upon the period as an occasion for military drill, and several devoted the entire period to it. Landis found that one-fourth of the time was devoted to calisthenics and marching tactics, one-half to games and "recreative" gymnastics, and one-fourth to talks on hygiene, bathing, and dressing. The growing popularity of interscholastic athletic programs was indicated by the fact that of 209 schools, 138 competed in baseball, 151 in basketball, 62 in soccer, 60 in football, 57 in swimming, 13 in track and field athletics, and 10 in tennis.

EXTRACURRICULAR ACTIVITIES

Kilpatrick's support of the project method lent respectability to extracurricular activities, which heretofore had been merely tolerated by secondary school administrators. Responsibility for supervising many of these fell to the department of physical education.

For example, club activities under the supervision of physical education in 1925 included hiking, dancing, swimming, seasonal sports, leadership, and first aid. Hunting and fishing clubs were organized in rural high schools. Surveys of club activities made in this period are difficult to interpret. In many cases the activities reported by school administrators as club activities were in reality part of the intramural athletic program. In any case, enthusiasm for extracurricular activities reached such proportions that it became a problem to fit all the club activities into the school program.

INTERSCHOLASTIC ATHLETICS

It was evident to school administrators and physical education leaders that some control of interscholastic athletics was necessary if they were to have any educational value. In 1923 the National Federation of High School Athletic Associations was established to (1) permit representatives of secondary schools to cooperate in developing sports rules, (2) standardize rules of eligibility for interstate and national competition, and (3) to encourage a working relationship with other amateur athletic organizations. In 1925 the National Association of Secondary School Principals endorsed the NFHSAA as the agency to represent high school athletics in their interstate and national aspects.

PHYSICAL EDUCATION FOR MEN IN COLLEGES AND UNIVERSITIES

As chairman of the Committee on the Status of Physical Education, Hygiene, and Athletics of the APEA, George L. Meylan reported in 1921 that of 230 institutions, 199 had a department of physical education with an administrative head commonly known as the director of physical education, who in many cases had the rank of professor and a seat on the faculty.[13] The average number of staff members per institution was four, over one-half of whom had the rank of assistant, associate, or full professor. Eighty-two percent of the staff was engaged in athletic coaching or had duties concerned in one way or another with intercollegiate athletics. One-third of the institutions provided instruction in hygiene, 50 percent supervised student health, and 23 percent checked the health aspects of the college community.

Better than three-fourths, or 180 departments in higher institutions, required courses in physical education and half of this number offered additional elective courses. The general tendency was to require physical education through the freshman and sophomore years, forty-four extended the requirement through the junior year, and twenty-nine through the senior years. Approximately three-fourths of the departments permitted students to substitute membership on the freshman or varsity athletic teams or participation in intramural athletics for the physical education requirement. Seventy percent granted credit for physical education courses, but this credit was an appendage to the requirements for graduation.

The departments surveyed had an impressive list of facilities for the period, including gymnasiums, playing fields, swimming pools, running tracks, boathouses, skating rinks, and tennis, handball, and squash courts.

As the boom of the 20s gained momentum, many new stadiums and gymnasiums graced the country's campuses. The Intramural Sports Building at the University of Michigan was one of the first buildings ever constructed for the exclusive use of intramural athletics. One of the most impressive buildings of the new field house type was that at the University of Minnesota. Other institutions to follow suit were Yale and the universities of Michigan, Pennsylvania and West Virginia.

Physical Education Administrators

In his 1921 report Dr. Meylan indicated that the director of physical education often had the rank of professor and a seat on the faculty and was as heavily involved in intercollegiate athletics as he was in the administration of his department. Harry A. Scott's survey of directors eight years later was more analytical and detailed than Meylan's study.[14] According to Dr. Scott, very few directors had been trained in their field, but were really employed because of their experience in athletics. Only 23 of 177 directors had majored in physical education during their undergraduate study, yet many of the directors were responsible for teacher preparation. Their areas of specialization included natural science (24), language (20), history (15), economics (11), and education (7). Forty directors had earned the master's degree, only four of whom received it in physical education and education; four the doctor of philosophy degree, and fifteen had medical degrees. In college the directors had played on one or more varsity teams, usually football, basketball, baseball, or track and field athletics, lettered in three sports, and acted as captain in one varsity sport.

In addition to his departmental obligations, the director spent an average of twelve hours a week on his coaching duties, six hours teaching theory courses in physical education, and three hours teaching theory in athletic coaching. Sixty-two directors did not belong to a professional organization of any type, while the remainder were affiliated with from one to six professional societies. Over 90 percent of the directors had not published a professional book and 75 percent had not published a magazine article in a professional jouranl. The favorite recreation of three-fourths of the directors was reading, but one-third participated in a wide variety of activities, including golf, handball, swimming, fishing, hunting, and gardening.

INTERCOLLEGIATE ATHLETICS IN THE POSTWAR YEARS

At its 1919 annual meeting the NCAA passed a resolution stating that physical education and athletics are an essential part of education and that the department responsible for them should be recognized as a legitimate department, answerable to the college or university administration. George L. Meylan's study indicated that 188 of 250 colleges and universities were in full accord with the resolution.[13] In actual practice institutional authorities administered athletics in 40 schools, faculty and students in 108, faculty, students, and alumni in 63, and students in only 6. The trend toward athletic conferences as another control measure continued in the New England, southern, midwestern, and Northwest Pacific regions in the early 1920s.

Prewar problems continued to plague the NCAA. Intercollegiate baseball players were constantly tempted by summer baseball, where prizes and rewards were often sold for cash. The NCAA defined an amateur sportsman as one who participated in sports solely for their physical, mental, or social values and to whom the sport is nothing more than an avocation. Policing intercollegiate baseball players became a frustrating duty for member institutions in NCAA's eight districts.

The AAU rule that basketball players must be certified as amateurs in games between colleges and noninstitutional teams had been a source of trouble before World War I. This situation had led the NCAA to publish its own basketball rules in 1905 and conduct competition independent of the AAU. After the war representation in the newly created American Olympic Association led to open conflict once again. Prior to the Paris Olympic Games in 1924 the International Olympic Federation ruled that the AAU should sanction all international competition. In 1923 the NCAA was requested by the University of Paris Athletic Club to send athletes to compete in the International University meet. Charles Paddock, a sprinter from the University of Southern California, competed in the meet and was suspended by the AAU for failure to register, which made him ineligible for the Paris Olympic Games. Other incidents in the 1920s widened the breach between the two organizations. The conflict springs from a difference of attitude toward amateur sports. The AAU believes in administrative control from the top, while the NCAA accepts local autonomy as the more democratic procedure.[15]

NATIONAL AMATEUR ATHLETIC FEDERATION

Early in the life of the Athletic Research Society (1907) C. W. Hetherington had called attention to the increasing number of amateur athletic organizations which, if combined, could be a power in the promotion and improvement of amateur sports in the United States. In 1911 the membership placed themselves on record as favoring a national conference or federation to regulate amateur sports somewhat as a college athletic conference did. In 1918 the NCAA authorized its executive committee to take steps to form a federation of athletic organizations. As a result, in 1922 Secretary of War John W. Weeks and Secretary of the Navy Curtis D. Wilbur called a meeting of representative athletic organizations in Washington, which led to the establishment of the National Amateur Athletic Federation. Its stated purpose was to promote physical education in educational institutions, encourage standardization of rules, facilitate the participation of U.S. athletes in the Olympic Games, and foster the highest ideals of amateur sport.

CARNEGIE FOUNDATION STUDIES OF COLLEGE ATHLETICS

Even before World War I trustees of the Carnegie Foundation, a philanthropic and impartial organization, had become disturbed over the athletic situation in American colleges and universities. In 1923 it gave a grant to a committee of the Association of Colleges and Secondary Schools of Southern States to study the place of intercollegiate athletics in twenty-three colleges and universities of the South.

As a result of this study, which disclosed many questionable practices in intercollegiate athletics, the Foundation was made a study of games and sports in British public schools and universities.*

At the request of the NCAA and its affiliated organizations, the Foundation also initiated a survey of athletic practices in American colleges and universities, which resulted in the famous Bulletin No. 23, *American College Athletics* (1929), among others.** The reaction of the lay public as well as professional leadership is ably summarized by D. A. Penick, president of the Southwestern Conference:

> The original standards of amateurism have disappeared. The days are gone when games were played for the game's sake. . . . Intercollegiate athletics is practically a profession. It furnishes the livelihood for coaches and trainees, and, in many cases, for the players. It furnishes public entertainment for money. It is commercialized by institutions. Its profits help in running the school financially. . . . In order to have these high powered

* Bulletin No. 18, *Games and Sports in British Schools and Universities,* 1927.

** Bulletin No. 24, *The Literature of American School and College Athletics,* and Bulletin No. 26, *Current Developments in American College Sports.* This last was an attempt to discover the reasons behind the undesirable practices revealed in Bulletin No. 23.

teams which will bring in gate receipts, there are the prevailing curses of recruiting and subsidizing athletes. Evils attended upon these practices include efforts on the part of smaller schools to maintain football teams o equal strength with those in schools many times as large, universal suspicio among institutions, insecure tenure of office of coaches, and the consequen determination of coaches to win games at any cost in order to hold posi tions—thus, the vicious cycle.[16]

INTRAMURAL ATHLETICS IN HIGHER INSTITUTIONS

At the time the United States entered World War I intramural athletics had become fairly well established in the East and Midwest. In the postwar years they experienced a rapid expansion in the far West, South, and Southwest. By 1930 approximately 170 colleges and universities had formally organized departments of intramural athletics. Leadership was furnished by Elmer D. Mitchell of the University of Michigan, who provided assistance to many neophyte intramural directors throughout the nation. In 1925 Dr. Mitchell published his *Intramural Athletics,* which for many years remained an invaluable guide to directors in both secondary schools and colleges. We should also mention Robert E. Lindwall's *Intramural Activities* and Edgar M. Draper's and George M. Smith's *Intramural Athletics and Play Days,* which furnished new high school intramural directors with important information on workable programs.

PHYSICAL EDUCATION FOR WOMEN IN COLLEGES AND UNIVERSITIES

Based upon the reports of twenty-seven colleges for women and universities, between 1927 and 1929, the women's departments of physical education had progressed from a staff of one and in some cases two instructors in 1910 to an average of 4.6 in 1929, with a high of eleven instructors in a single university. The total instructional staff for the twenty-seven institutions was 113, composed of 12 professors, 14 associate professors, 16 assistant professors, and 71 instructors. Of these, 4 held the medical degree, 2 the doctor of philosophy, 14 the master of arts, and 66 the bachelor of arts or science, and 26 had no degree. In four of the fifteen universities the women's department was organized as a separate division and the administrative officer held equal rank with the director of the men's department. In the remaining departments the women's division was included in the framework of the organization of the men's department, whose director regulated the women's budget and acted as a mediator between the university administration and the women's department. The average clock-hours of instruction per week for women physical instructors in universities in 1929 was 18.3 and in colleges was 19.9. The average total clock-hours per week which included teaching and supervision, conferences, clerical work, and committee meetings, was 24.8 for university and 26.2 for college women instructors. The average number of students per instructor in 1920 was approximately 200 and in 1930 was 166. Seventy percent of the colleges and universities assigned the women's department the responsibility of teaching hygiene for women. It was a common policy to excuse women from physical education classes during the menstrual period as long as she desired, which usually amounted to two or three class periods. A few allowed two class periods with makeups and several made no allowance for the menstrual period. In universities men continued to teach such physical activities as riflery, fencing, horseback riding, and swimming, although the consensus of the expert opinion of men and women directors of physical educators was against the practice.[17]

The activities of the required physical education program varied from institution to institution, but generally included gymnastics, individual and team sports, and dancing. Swimming was the most frequently required activity. The program was conducted two to four hours per week and, as a general rule, required in the freshman and sophomore years, with colleges for women particularly extending the requirement through the junior and senior years. Three-fourths of the women's departments offered elective activities, limited to the first quarter or semester by some schools but more frequently extended through the entire four years. Elective activities were divided into three categories: individual sports (apparatus stunts, archery, clogging, gymnastics, horseback riding, interpretative dancing, riflery, skating, swimming, track and field, and hiking), small-team games (bowling, fencing, quoits, and tennis), and large-team games (baseball, basketball, captain ball, folk dancing, hockey, soccer, and volleyball).

Toward the close of the 20s there was a remarkable growth in the number of well-equipped women's physical education buildings. Special mention should be made of those at Washington University, Seattle; the University of Oregon, Eugene; the University of California, Berkeley; the University of Texas, Austin; the University of Illinois, Urbana; and the University of Florida, Tallahassee.

Reform Movement in Athletic Competition for Women and Girls

The combined efforts of the Committee on Women's Athletics of the APEA, the National Athletic Conference of American College Women, and the National Association of Physical Education for College Women exerted marked influence on the attitude of physical educators toward intercollegiate athletics for women. In 1922 Mabel Lee, of the University of Nebraska, conducted a pilot study of fifty colleges and universities to determine the current status of intercollegiate athletics for women.[18] She disclosed that of the fifty institutions only eleven sponsored intercollegiate competition, in the following sports: basketball (11), tennis (9), field hockey (7), swimming (5), baseball (4), archery (2), rowing (2), and fencing (1). The largest number of intercollegiate sports sponsored by any one institution was seven and the least two. Varsity-type competition was more prevalent in eastern and southern institutions than elsewhere. Western institutions were substituting play or sports days for intercollegiate competition, and midwestern ones had adopted the telegraphic meet. She found that very few women directors of physical education favored the varsity type of intercollegiate competition.

Although women physical education leaders were successful in eliminating intercollegiate competition, they had lost touch with the amazing growth of athletic competition in elementary and secondary schools and industrial leagues. Girls fought intensely for district, regional, and state basketball championships which necessitated time away from school or job and frequent trips often unsatisfactorily chaperoned. Sporting interests were already commercializing on the tremendous public following drawn to these emotion-packed contests.

In the fall of 1922 the National Recreation Congress passed a resolution which voiced opposition to the status of athletic competition for girls. In the same year Clark W. Hetherington suggested to Blanche M. Trilling, chairman of the Committee on Women's Athletics of the APEA, that women physical educators take immediate steps to organize a national women's athletic association similar to the NAAF. Miss Trilling discussed the problem with Colonel Henry Breckinridge, President of the NAAF, and Mrs. Herbert Hoover was persuaded to call a conference in Washington in 1923. The meeting closed with the establishment of the Women's Division of the National Amateur Athletic Federation.[19] This body continued to work for high standards in athletic competition for girls and women until its amalgamation with the National Section on Women's Athletics of the American Association for Health, Physical Education, and Recreation in 1940. It operated through state committees, whose leaders interpreted its policies to professional workers and the general public via open forums, round-table discussions, and demonstrations. Through its efforts state basketball tournaments for high school girls were eventually eliminated, intramural programs widely adopted, commercialization of female athletics partially controlled, and the health supervision of participants improved.

Undergirding its activity was the Committee on Women's Athletics (NSWA) of the APEA. By 1925 this Committee had edited several handbooks on desirable practices and policies in women's athletics. Subcommittees on rules had published, through A. G. Spaulding Brothers, guides on basketball, field hockey, swimming, soccer, and track and field athletics. Ever since the formation of the Basketball Committee in 1905, the Committee had recognized the difficulty of securing satisfactorily trained officials. Local boards to approve basketball officials had been established in key cities, but increased interest in the game demanded an extension of this service. In 1928 Grace Jones, chairman of the Basketball Committee, called a meeting of representatives of local boards, which developed the Women's National Officials Rating Committee. This national body, working through local boards, provides examinations for candidates and rates officials according to their knowledge of the rules and ability to officiate. Its authority was soon extended to sports other than basketball.

DEVELOPMENTS IN PROFESSIONAL PREPARATION

State legislation for health and physical education in the postwar period increased the demand for teachers in these areas. In 1919 it was estimated that 40,000 additional teachers would be needed to meet the needs of public schools and higher institutions. The APEA considered distributing a pamphlet entitled *Physical Education and Profession* to graduating high school seniors and promoting professional courses in the 639 institutions of normal school or college caliber as yet uncommitted. It was also seriously concerned about the quality of professional programs already in operation in twenty-six normal schools in the United States. Of the some 200 men and 800 women physical educators graduated annually, it was the professional consensus that most of the men and at least half of the women were poorly equipped for their jobs. An accrediting agency with the power of enforcement was needed to insure satisfactory standards in teacher preparation.

By 1925 ninety-two normal schools, colleges, and universities offered four-year professional training programs, and twenty-six institutions offered three-year programs. The most frequent area of specialization other than health and physical education was recreation and athletic coaching. The University of Washington offered a major in recreation for both men and women. The universities of Illinois, Nebraska, Washington, and Wisconsin sponsored a four-year professional curriculum in athletic coaching leading to the bachelor's degree. Many institutions offered summer courses in athletic coaching, which by this time had become a fixed institutional practice. As the 1920s drew to a close the U. S. Department of the Interior reported that the number of institutions offering a professional program had increased to 210.

One of the guiding lights to professional teacher training of this era was Clark W. Hetherington.[20] He developed the concept that the training of physical education teachers logically belonged in the department, College, or school of education rather than the liberal arts college. He also maintained that the professional program should provide a broader cultural content than was prevalent. He cited his experience at the University of Wisconsin, where majors in physical education were required to take zoology, chemistry, anatomy, physiology, history, and English in addition to their professional courses and practice teaching. In his estimation a professional curriculum of this quality would increase the status and dignity of the profession in the eyes of other faculty members. Hetherington also believed that certification of physical education teachers properly enforced by state departments of education would improve the quality of professional training programs. In 1927 he played an important role in the Conference of Professional Training in Physical Education called by the United States Bureau of Education in Washington. This conference discussed the objectives of physical education, admission standards for prospective physical education teachers, curricula for three- and four-year professional training programs, and the place of the teacher-training curriculum in higher institutions.

Advance study in graduate education had been introduced during the first decade of the century at Columbia and New York universities and the North American Gymnastic Union. In the early 1920s a trend to increase the program of undergraduate professional education to a fifth year was shifted to advance work leading to the master's degree. By 1930 Springfield and Wellesley colleges and the universities of California, Cincinnati, Indiana, Iowa, Oregon, Utah, and Wisconsin, among others, offered graduate courses leading to the master's degree. Teachers College, Columbia University, and New York University offered work leading to the doctor of philosophy degree in 1924, and Stanford University and the University of Pennsylvania offered the doctor of education degree with a major in physical education in 1929.

NOTES

1. Charles Winfred Savage. "College Physical Education and the First World War." *Proceedings,* College Physical Education Association, 1940, pp. 33–40.

2. Paul E. Belting. "The Interest of the State in Physical Education as Exemplified in State Legislation." *The Athletic Journal,* 10:4 (1929), 28–36.
3. Harry Scott. "The Society of Directors of Physical Education in College." *Journal of Health and Physical Education,* 3:4 (April, 1932), 3–5. Glenn W. Howard. "The College Physical Education Association." *Journal of Health and Physical Education,* 17:7 (September, 1946), 410–411; 436.
4. Franklin Bobbitt. "Objectives of Physical Education." *American Physical Education Review,* 26:5 (May, 1921), 229–233. William H. Byrnham. "The Newer Aims of Physical Education and Its Psychological Significance." *American Physical Education Review,* 27:1 (January, 1922), 1–7.
5. Clark W. Hetherington. "School Program in Physical Education." New York: World Book Company, 1922, pp. 21–45.
6. Jesse F. Williams. *The Organization and Administration of Physical Education.* New York: The Macmillan Company, 1922, p. 18.
7. Thomas D. Wood and Rosalind P. Cassidy. *The New Physical Education.* New York: The Macmillan Company, 1927.
8. C. H. McCloy. "New Wines in New Bottles." *Physical Training,* 25 (1927–1928), 32–52.
9. David K. Brace. "Possibilities of Tests in Physical Education." *American Physical Education Review,* 32:6 (June, 1927), 506–514.
10. Frederick Rand Rogers. "The Measurement of Individual Needs in Physical Education." *American Physical Education Review,* 32:6 (June, 1927), 418–428.
11. Harry A. Scott. "What Should the Department of Physical Education Require of Its Students for Graduation?" *American Physical Education Review,* 33:3 (March, 1928), 142–151.
12. J. F. Landis. "A Study of Physical Education in the Junior High School and Intermediate School." *American Physical Education Review,* 29:5 (May, 1924), 260–264.
13. George L. Meylan. "Report of the Committee on the Status of Physical Education, Hygiene and Athletics in American Colleges." *American Physical Education Review,* 26:8 (November, 1921), 374.
14. Harry A. Scott. "Personnel Study of Directors of Physical Education for Men in Colleges and Universities." (Dissertation) Teachers College, Columbia University, 1929.
15. Paul Stagg. "The Development of the National Collegiate Athletic Association in Relationship to Intercollegiate Athletics in the United States." (Dissertation) New York University, 1946, p. 307.
16. D. A. Penick. "The Ideals of Intercollegiate Athletics—Are They

Attainable?" *Proceedings,* The College Physical Education Association, 1932, pp. 26–27.

17. Teresa Powdermaker. "Statistical Study of the Teaching Load of Women Physical Instructors." *American Physical Education Review,* 34:5 (May, 1929), 280–281.
18. Mabel Lee. "The Case for and Against Intercollegiate Athletics for Women and the Situation as It Stands Today." *Mind and Body,* 30:322 (November, 1923), 245–256.
19. Agnes Wayman. "Women's Division of the National Amateur Athletic Federation." *Journal of Health and Physical Education,* 3:3 (March, 1932), 3–7.
20. C. W. Hetherington. "Professional Training Course in Physical Education." *American Physical Education Review,* 25:5 (May, 1920), 186–194.

Chapter 21

PHYSICAL EDUCATION IN THE UNITED STATES, 1930–1940

THE PERIOD OF ECONOMIC CRISIS

THE stock market crash in October, 1929, signaled the end of the lush years of the 1920s, but the full brunt of the economic crisis was not to be felt for several years to come. President Herbert Hoover earnestly attempted to stem the downward trend of business, but the final collapse of the security and commodity markets and property values only increased public apprehension. Panic-stricken citizens hastily withdrew their financial assets from banks, further weakening the banking system. When Franklin D. Roosevelt assumed the presidency in 1932, the Seventy-third Congress immediately enacted legislation to strengthen the country's financial condition and restore public confidence.

A CHANGE IN SOCIAL PHILOSOPHY

When Congress adjourned in June, 1933, the United States had been introduced to a new social philosophy. The concept of rugged individualism which had marked the early years of this country's growth was now replaced by the concept of equal opportunity and "abundant living" for all. The Public Works Administration allocated more than three billion dollars for public construction, one-sixth of which was earmarked for the building of school facilities. The Federal Housing Cooperation was given funds for slum clearance and large-scale housing developments, which included nursery schools and playgrounds. The Civil Works Administration furnished employment for thousands of workers, teachers, and recreation leaders. The CWA also repaired and painted school buildings, improved schoolyards, and provided training for teachers and recreation workers. The Federal Emergency Relief Administration, among its many functions, utilized thousands of unemployed teachers in six different types of projects, one of which, adult education, included physical educators. The Works Project Administration allotted millions of dollars to the improvement and construction of sports and recreation facilities in educational institutions. The WPA also encouraged the introduction of public recreation programs by providing trained personnel.

The economic crisis brought the educational problems of youth into sharp focus. One-third of the employable citizens in the United States were between the ages of 16 and 24, and of this number 40 percent were unemployed. By 1933 their low morale had become a source of state and federal concern. Among many solutions suggested was that forecast by William James in his essay, *The Moral Equivalent of War* (1910). James had proposed that in times of emergency nations should take advantage of youth's proclivity for things military by organizing military-type units to combat the ravages of nature. Youth thus engaged would help promote the economy, develop a sense of loyalty and purpose, and improve their physical condition through labor. In 1933 President Roosevelt established the Civilian Conservation Corps under military supervision, and the first unit was organized at Luray, Virginia. In the CCC young men repaired and constructed facilities in state and national parks, reforested thousands of acres of denuded land and watersheds, and performed other services which later proved of value. In addition to his labor, the young enrollee was provided with an educational and recreational program.

EDUCATIONAL DEVELOPMENTS

At the beginning of the 1930s more than eleven million children went to rural schools, approximately one-half attending 165,500 one-room schools taught by a single teacher, many of whom were poorly trained. In 1931 the United States Office of Education reported that 50 percent of the youth of high school age were in school and that the influx of pupils of diverse mental, social, and economic backgrounds had created a tremendous educational challenge. Some of the more progressive high schools attempted to solve the problem through the homogeneous grouping of pupils according to test results, special classes for exceptional pupils, and use of the unit teaching method, in which pupils could pace themselves according to their intellectual ability. The 6-3-3 plan of organization had made rapid gains in urban areas. In rural areas under the traditional 8-4 plan the secondary school was limited as to variety and quality of courses; apparently the only salvation for these small high schools was consolidation. Pupils were spending less time on foreign languages, mathematics, English, home economics, and art, and more on commercial subjects. Physical education had made gains, along with the social sciences, music, industrial arts, and sciences.

In spite of attractive elective systems in higher institutions, the dropout rate of first-year students was mounting at an alarming pace. To counteract this, colleges and universities introduced new guidance techniques for beginning students. These took the form of freshmen week, orientation courses, special advisers, and survey courses in the humanities and social and natural sciences. Their effectiveness was handicapped, however, by lack of coordination with secondary schools. Admission practices of higher institution had altered to include new criteria, such as intelligence and aptitude tests and extracurricular and recreational interests.[1]

Among the interesting phenomena that reached fever pitch in the 1930s was preoccupation with curriculum construction. One institution, for instance, had 50,000 curriculum committee reports on file, representing years of work. Knight in his review of this situation states: "The interest in curriculum construction and reconstruction may have been a healthy sign but the general condition seems to reflect the absence in the United States of a consistent philosophy concerning the aim in life from which the educational aims of this country should be derived."[2]

EDUCATION AND THE DEPRESSION

Three million children between the ages of 7 and 17 were out of school, and in the early years of the depression many of those of working age were in job competition with eleven million adults. State and federal welfare and labor agencies had pursued an aggressive campaign to remove children from industrial employment,[3] but it was not until the National Recovery Act of 1933 that children were finally legislated out of industry. As a result thousands of children returned to school, 100,000 of whom were of high school age. This sudden influx of pupils taxed the teaching staff and facilities of the already overburdened public schools. As the full weight of the economic crisis began to be felt in late 1933, a survey of the school systems of 700 typical cities showed that they had of necessity eliminated instruction in art, music, home economics, industrial arts, and physical education, and reduced or discontinued health services.

Higher institutions were not only subjected to the same financial distress as the public schools but were the target of criticism by influential public figures and the press, in whose opinion higher education in the United States was positively degenerate. Entrance requirements were described as superficial, and coeducational colleges were called country clubs because they combined the unregulated use of the automobile with weekly dances and the indiscriminate use of liquor. Other critics pointed out that colleges were piling up elective courses with little intellectual content and downgrading the baccalaureate degree. Under this kind of criticism higher institutions began initiating reforms, which included restrictions of the use of automobiles on campus, more rigid control of the social calendar, and the strengthening or elimination of elective courses.

FEDERAL AID TO EDUCATION

The Federal Emergency Relief Administration in 1933 provided financial aid to college and university students under the title of

Federal Student Aid Programs.* The University of Minnesota was one of the first institutions to inaugurate the program and was followed by many others between 1933 and 1935. In 1935 President Roosevelt by executive order established the National Youth Administration as an independent division of the Works Project Administration to provide funds for the part-time employment of needy pupils in secondary schools and undergraduate and graduate students in colleges and universities.** The NYA made it possible for many deserving students to continue their education during the depression and expanded physical education, intramural athletics, and recreation.

In 1938 the President's Advisory Committee recommended that federal grants be given the various states for educational purposes. Appropriations were to start at $70 million for the fiscal year 1939–1940, and reach $190 million by 1944–1945. The Harrison-Thomas and Larabee bills, which were the outgrowth of this committee's recommendations, were received favorably by the Senate Committee on Education and Labor and were awaiting a hearing by the House Committee when the United States entered the war.

THE ECONOMIC CRISIS AND PHYSICAL EDUCATION

The introduction of physical education into the public schools had been proceeding at an accelerated rate up to the middle of 1932. During the next three years many of these gains were lost as educational institutions began to feel the pinch of reduced budgets. In the three crucial years 1932–1934 physical education personnel and budgets were reduced in 11 percent of the public schools, and approximately 40 percent dropped physical education along with other so-called "frill" subjects.

Cities with a population of 50,000 or more tended to retain

* A total of 1602 institutions of higher learning participated in the Program, and approximately 109,000 students received an average of 15 a month to help them through college.

** During 1940 and 1941 the National Education Association viewed the National Youth Administration and the Civilian Conservation Corps as federal agencies in competition with the public schools. In 1942 the matter came before Congress in considerating appropriations for the NYA and CCC and after a bitter debate Congress withdrew appropriations for both.

physical education, while those of lesser population not only eliminated it but were slow to reinstate the program when economic conditions improved. One of the tragedies of this period was the elimination of the supervisor of physical education from metropolitan elementary school systems. Professional leaders in the late 20s had slowly convinced school administrators of the importance of intelligent leadership in the planning and supervision of physical education programs, and now in times of economic stress these hard-won gains were lost.

ANTI-PHYSICAL EDUCATION MOVEMENTS

As in all periods of economic crisis, those opposed to physical education gave vent to their antipathy. They initiated legislation against the physical education requirement in public schools in Illinois, Indiana, Iowa, and California, but state physical education associations and other sympathetic organizations defeated these moves. The necessity to fight for survival was both a new and sobering experience for physical educators, who had assumed that the program had become a permanent part of the educational system. The implication was that the subject would be tolerated in times of luxury but eliminated when times were bad. As many professional leaders pointed out, physical education needed to do a much better public relations job in the future.

As a consequence of the reduction in staff, incumbent teachers had to assume additional assignments. Often the athletic coach assumed the physical education teacher's responsibilities. In the opinion of many professional leaders, physical education programs suffered since the coach continued to devote most of his energy to his athletic teams to the neglect of his added duties.[4] Physical education teachers qualified to teach any subject not on the non-essential list were usually retained. This situation had a marked influence on the thinking of administrators in teacher-training institutions.

THE DEVELOPMENT OF RECREATION DURING THE DEPRESSION

The depression accentuated the importance of recreation in the life of the American citizen. The public as a whole lacked the

TABLE 2. VALUE OF SPORTING AND ATHLETIC GOODS DURING THE BOOM AND DEPRESSION PERIODS

(Not Including Firearms or Ammunition)

Sporting and Athletic Goods[a]	*Total Value 1929*	*Total Value 1931*	*Total Value 1935*	*Total Value 1937*
Golf goods	21,067,216	23,338,654	10,492,198	13,797,080
Fishing tackle	9,760,370	6,761,170	7,581,662	10,883,490
Baseball goods	6,699,087	5,597,345	4,872,178	4,385,358
Tennis goods	4,650,543	4,296,378	3,230,219	4,628,897
Football, basketball, and boxing goods, inflated balls other than football and basketball	5,766,034	4,217,341	2,673,018	3,352,709
Skates and parts	4,872,593	2,689,365	3,435,597	4,631,851
Gymnasium equipment	1,073,082	1,296,881	371,811	594,436
Equipment for hunting and shooting	1,129,756	649,392	709,184	999,858
Skis and snowshoes	n. a.[b]	163,032	417,155	1,236,585
Toboggans and sleds	n. a.[b]	129,867	57,376	177,864
Other sporting and athletic goods including parts, not specified above	1,267,021	1,110,201	486,667	—
Sporting and athletic goods not reported by kind	—	—	2,132,267	3,479,136

[a] Clothing and footwear made especially for sporting and athletic purposes are assigned to the clothing industries, the knit-goods industry, the boot and shoe industry, etc.; and fishing line is classified in the cordage and twine industry.

[b] Not available.

SOURCE: Compiled from the Census of Manufacturers, U.S. Department of Commerce. (No data available for 1933.)

money to pay for the varied entertainments to which they had become accustomed during the boom period of the 1920s and as a result sought relaxation in less expensive community recreation programs. Attendance at recreation centers between 1932 and 1934 more than doubled. Financial assistance became available from various federal agencies for the repair, improvement, and construction of recreation facilities, as well as trained leadership in states wishing to inaugurate recreation programs. Recreation gave promise of making tremendous strides in the future.

THE PHYSICAL EDUCATOR LOOKS AT RECREATION

During the period of prosperity physical educators had maintained a keen and constant interest in the rapidly expanding public and school recreation program. The National Recreation Association was hard pressed to keep up with the demand for trained personnel. Physical educators and athletic coaches saw in this situation an opportunity to gain new experience as well as supplementary income. Many of them secured part-time employment in school, community, and municipal recreation programs, and some eventually left the field of physical education to become full-time recreation administrators and program directors.

In 1934 Eugene Lies of the National Recreation Association edited a provocative study entitled "The New Leisure Challenges the School."[5] He pointed out that with industry's reduction of the workday many workers were unprepared to make profitable use of their leisure time. He suggested that physical educators could make a worthwhile contribution here by including carryover activities in the physical education program.

In the same year Weaver Pangburn, also of the NRA, stated that recreation leaders at the Twentieth National Recreation Congress expressed the view that physical educators should take a more active part in preparing youth for leisure-time pursuits.[6] Other recreation leaders suggested that the physical education program should provide instruction in water safety, first aid and protective activities for the home and family.

In 1932 the American Association for Health and Physical Education appointed two committees to study ways and means whereby physical education could contribute to youth's leisure-time activities and at the same time combat the social evils of commercial recreation which had developed during the prosperous years.[7] The committees concluded that physical educators should place more emphasis on skills with recreational potentials.

In 1938 the Legislative Council of the AAHPE approved the change in its title to the American Association for Health, Physical Education and Recreation. Between 1932 and 1938 the school program in physical education had experienced certain modifications. Physical educators and teacher-training institutions placed more emphasis on sports which were recognized as having carryover value for leisure time. Progressive educators experimented with coeducational classes in swimming, folk and social dancing, mixed doubles in sports and mixed volleyball, bowling, and outing activities.[8] Not only did physical educators' interest in the recreation movement influence the educational program, but it also alerted them to the need for cooperation in the preparation of recreation leaders.

A Recreationist Looks at Physical Education

Jay Bryan Nash (1886——) was born in New Baltimore, Ohio, and received his bachelor's (1911) and master's (1927) degrees from Oberlin College, where he studied under Delphine Hanna. He secured his doctorate at New York University (1929), where his major professor was Clark W. Hetherington. Dr. Nash served as a high school instructor at Oakland, California (1911–1914); assistant supervisor of recreation at Oakland (1915–1918); assistant supervisor of physical education of the state of California under C. W. Hetherington (1918–1919); and superintendent of recreation and physical education at Oakland (1919–1926). In this last capacity Nash developed a city-school recreation system which attracted nationwide interest and emulation. In 1926 Dr. Nash was appointed professor of education at New York University and in 1930 became chairman of the department of physical education and health in the School of Education.

There is an interesting parallel between C. W. Hetherington and Dr. Nash in that both were active in recreation in their early careers and went on to make valuable and enduring contributions to physical education. Just as Dr. Williams adapted the educational philosophy of Drs. Dewey and Kilpatrick to the profession of physical education, Dr. Nash became an invaluable interpreter of Hetherington's philosophy of physical education in general education. The best example is Dr. Nash's publication *The Organization and Administration of Playgrounds and Recreation* (1928). The author is Nash, but the guiding principles are those of Hetherington, and one can sense the master's presence as the student expresses his partly formulated philosophy of recreation and physical education.

In the same year that Dr. Nash edited the first volumes of his popular *Interpretation of Physical Education* he published *The Administration of Physical Education* (1931). He was correct in stating in his preface that the book was a departure from standard works on the subject because the book was slanted heavily toward the problems of the recreation administrator. Dr. Nash's rethinking of the objectives of physical education, however, was impressive.

Dr. Nash stated that physical education had four objectives: the development of organic power, neuromuscular skills, interpretive-cortical power and emotional-impulsive "emergents." The first two objectives were generally accepted by the profession, but Nash approached them in a fresh and logical way. The emotional-impulsive goals represented the desirable social behavior which resulted when the interaction of the individual with the group was properly supervised. By "interpretive-cortical" power Dr. Nash meant certain "intellectual" consequences of physical education. The development of *organic power* was basic to the development of neuromuscular skills, interpretive-cortical power and emotional-impulsive outcomes, or "emergents."

INDIVIDUALIZED PHYSICAL EDUCATION

The introduction of recreational activities into school programs was only one of the many manifestations in physical education which can be traced to social, economic, and ideological changes. With the new emphasis on leisure-time preparation, a segment of the profession had discovered the forgotten student. These educators sought to reevaluate the objectives of physical education in terms of individual and social results rather than the number of skills learned. In their opinion, too much time had been spent on individuals who were blessed by heredity and a favorable environment, to the total neglect of those who were poorly coordinated and physically weak. It is from this era that such questionable terms as "physically illiterate" and "physical moron" date.

Drawing its inspiration from President Roosevelt's theme of the "forgotten man," the new program was to glorify the obscure or forgotten individual rather than fitting him into the program regardless of his capacity or ability. In the search to understand and equate individual differences, physical educators devised tests to measure athletic achievement according to age and sex, physical and organic efficiency, motor capacity, strength, physical fitness, motor skills in component parts of sports, athletic ability, cardiovascular efficiency, body mechanics, and many other attributes of the human organism. This particular group of educators introduced the profession to one of its greatest eras of scientific investigation, which developed an extensive literature and new tools of research.

PROFESSIONAL INTEREST IN FACILITIES

Aside from Dr. Hartwell's comprehensive report on gymnasium construction in 1885 and occasional articles in the *Review,* no concerted effort was made by the profession to consider facilities. In the early 1920s the Society of Directors of Physical Education in Colleges (College Physical Education Association) appointed a committee, of which George L. Meylan was chairman, to consider physical education facilities. Its work was published in booklet form in 1923, entitled *Physical Education Buildings for Education Institutions, Part I, Gymnasiums and Lockers.* The committee remained active, and following Dr. Meylan the chairmanship was held by Harry A. Scott until 1927, by A. R. Winters 1927–1928, and by Albert H. Prettyman 1928–1945.

The halt in the construction of facilities during the depression was only temporary, and as soon as the federal government entered the picture, building programs were resumed on a grander scale than before. In its early stages many obvious and absurd mistakes were made in architectural planning. This led to government provision of expert guidance in planning facilities. In addition, the National Recreation Association and the Recreation Division, Works Project Administration, issued many pamphlets as guides in planning recreation facilities. The College Physical Education Association also initiated the practice of collecting and filing architectural plans of college facilities which were made available to the profession on request.

By the end of the 1930s, the degree of interest in the planning and construction of facilities was demonstrated by many publications on the subject. Among them may be mentioned Herbert Blair's *Physical Education Facilities for the Modern Junior and Senior High School* (1938), Emil Lamar's *The Athletic Plant* (1938), George Butler's *The New Play Areas—Their Design and Equipment* (1938), Frederick W. Leuhring's *Swimming Pool Standards* (1939), and Ruth Eliott Houston's *Modern Trends in Physical Education Facilities for College Women* (1939).

EDUCATION AND NATIONAL DEFENSE

Unlike the wait-and-see attitude of the United States early in World War I, the aggressive diplomatic efforts and military expansion of European dictators in the late 1930s gradually developed a feeling of apprehension in the American public. In the summer of 1940, when the Nazi war machine swept past the supposedly impregnable Maginot Line on its way to Paris and the eventual subjugation of France, national defense became a matter of common public concern in the United States.

Early in September, 1940, the representatives of forty organizations associated with education met in Washington for the purpose of mobilizing the nation's educational resources in the interest of national defense. As an outcome of this meeting, a Committee on Education and Defense was appointed which was to play an important part in coordinating all educational resources useful to the nation's defense in the years ahead. In the same year the American Youth Commission recommended that provisions should be made for better health education and physical education programs in the schools and the extension of public recreation programs. In the Commission's opinion, there was a general lack of facilities for the development of healthy physiques among American youth, and what facilities did exist were least available to those who needed them most. The Commission also recommended that the nation-wide program should have the financial support of the federal government.

A RETURN TO FUNDAMENTALS

Leaders in physical education recognized early the purpose of the physical training and recreation programs of youth organizations and labor camps in the dictator states of Europe, and they hastened to remind the profession that the objectives of America's physical education had been subordinated during the depression period to recreation and social goals.

Arthur H. Steinhaus, George Williams College of Chicago, asserted that through the years the Germans had placed greater stress on physical development, while the American swing to education *through* the physical had made physical improvement a secondary aim.[9] C. H. McCloy pointed out that physical educators as a whole had failed to keep up with the trend of adult interest and participation in sports in this country and in Europe.[10] Adult participation was predicated on muscular development through judicious and regular exercise.

Jesse Fiering Williams warned:

> Certainly no society can ignore today the necessity for vigorous physique, strength, courage and endurance. . . . The criticism that we level at the college presidents, coaches and alumni for their successful big business methods to produce a good show on Saturday afternoon we ought to level at the student body of undersize, physically weak youth that allow sons of immigrants to take the game away from the boys. The inevitable necessity arises that education must not only provide vigorous rugged activities, but that it must also promote courageous spirit and attitudes or American civilization won't be worth saving.[11]

EFFORTS AT FEDERAL LEGISLATION

In 1939 the Legislative Council of the American Association for Health, Physical Education and Recreation passed a resolution for the establishment of a national committee to urge President Roosevelt and Congress to allocate federal funds in the pending National Health Bill to promote health, physical education, and recreation programs in the nation's schools. This resolution was prompted by the fact that in February, 1939, Robert F. Wagner, Senator from New York, introduced in the Senate a bill calling for the appropriation of $850 million to be pro-rated among the states and territories for a public health program. The AAHPER appointed a Committee on Legislation, with Jesse F. Williams as chairman. This committee attempted to secure an amendment to the National Health Bill which would give due consideration to adequate (1) health, physical education and recreation supervision in the schools through the state departments of education, (2) health service in land-grant institutions, and (3) health services for every state teachers' training institution.[12]

When the National Health Bill failed to muster Congressional support, Hiram A. Jones, president of the AAHPER, in July, 1940, appointed a committee to consider legislation for national preparedness through health, physical education, and recreation in schools and school camps. Consisting of Jesse F. Williams, chairman, Allen G. Ireland, Jay B. Nash, and himself, it recommended that an act of Congress provide: (1) a national director of health, physical education, and recreation with a staff including associate and assistant directors, research assistants and clerical and secretarial help; (2) a nationwide program planned by the director and his staff and carried out by the proper agency in the states; and (3) financial assistance to the states to provide for (a) teacher preparation, (b) improvements in facilities, (c) salaries for administration and instruction in the program, and (d) the construction, operation, and maintenance of school camps.

The funds were to be disbursed through the U.S. Office of Education to the various states and administered by the state departments of education and their local subdivisions. Each qualifying state would be granted a sum according to its proportion of the nation's children between 5 and 20 years of age.

The committee assured the profession that its plan was not designed to prepare American youth in the techniques of warfare as in European totalitarian states, but rather to instill in them the courage, stamina, and endurance prerequisite to military training.

In no instance did the committee condone school military drill as a substitute for physical education.

HOUSE OF REPRESENTATIVES BILL 10606

Subsequently the Committee on Legislation of the AAHPER, in cooperation with representatives of the U.S. Office of Education and the National Education Association, drafted a bill (H.R. 10606) introduced by Congressman P. L. Schwert of New York into the House of Representatives in October, 1940. It provided $100 million, one-half to be used for the improvement of the school health, physical education, and recreation program, and the other half to be employed in the establishment of public school camps. The funds would improve and extend personnel, teacher preparation, equipment, supplies and materials for school and camp programs and the development of programs in health, physical education, recreation, and camping.

Unfortunately, the bill drew the criticism of several powerful interest groups and minority groups associated with camping, recreation, and certain religious denominations. Their lobbyists were sufficiently effective to hamstring the bill, which died in the House Committee on Education and Labor at the close of the Seventy-sixth Congress. Undaunted the Legislative Committee of the AAHPER met at the Pennsylvania Hotel, New York City, to consider suggestions from individuals and professional organizations in the drafting of a new bill which it was hoped would eliminate many of the objectionable features of the original one.[13] In January, 1941, Congressman Schwert of New York introduced the revised bill (H.R. 1074), but it shared the same fate as its predecessor.

THE STATUS OF PHYSICAL EDUCATION IN PUBLIC SCHOOLS

By 1930 thirty-six states had enacted laws which required physical education in the public schools. Thirty-three states had mandatory laws which were effective in either or both the elementary and secondary schools. The states of Idaho, Mississippi, and North Carolina offered physical education on a permissive basis. Twenty states had appointed state directors of physical education, and a few others, with the assistance of state associations for health and physical education and the National Physical Education Service, were working in this direction.

Thirty-two states, representing approximately 80 percent of the total population in the United States, provided courses in physical education on the elementary level and a lesser number on both the elementary and secondary levels. Only a small percentage listed properly stated objectives of physical education. Twenty-seven states established standards for time allotment, twenty for the preparation of teachers and programs, eighteen for teacher certification, sixteen for equipment and facilities, and twelve for physical examination to determine classification in physical education classes and elegibility for participation in the athletic program. The twelve states which had not legislated physical education in the public schools appeared to have little interest in the area at this time.

In a 1932 survey of the status of health and physical education in 460 secondary schools, P. Roy Brammell noted that the trend in high school programs was definitely away from the formal type and in the direction of informal games and sports.[14] Interest in informal programs had increased the demand for more spacious indoor and outdoor areas, which were rapidly being met in the building of new junior and senior high schools. To meet the problem of larger classes, instructors had formed pupil leadership corps to assist in class instruction and management. The introduction of recreation after school hours, on Saturdays, and during summer months provided physical educators and coaches with experience in a new area as well as supplementary income.

Three-fourths of the secondary schools required physical education, and this requirement was generally met in the ninth grade. Junior high schools were doing a more effective job than senior high schools, and larger schools were conducting more efficient programs than smaller ones. The most outstanding trend in secondary schools was the organization of health, physical education, and interscholastic and intramural athletics under a single department head. The most frequently mentioned weaknesses in secondary schools included the absence of a corrective program, failure to follow up and correct physical defects, and total indifference to tests and measurements of pupil progress, teacher efficiency, and program effectiveness.

PLANNING AND EVALUATION OF PROGRAMS

In 1927 the College Physical Education Association appointed a Committee on Curriculum Research, with William R. La Porte of the University of Southern California as chairman. Its original purpose was to devise an acceptable program of physical activity for elementary and secondary schools that would eliminate duplication from year to year and encourage reasonable uniformity on a nationwide basis.

By 1935 the Curriculum Research Committee and its subcommittees had presented a program for the primary-level grades 1–3, elementary grades 4–6, junior high school grades 7–9, and senior high school grades 10–12, for both boys and girls. In the junior and senior high school grades the program was divided into core and elective activities on a time allotment basis and on a block arrangement by months and seasons. The results of this work were published in April, 1937, under the title *The Physical Education Curriculum—A Natural Program.*[15] Over 3000 copies were sold immediately, and it was used extensively on the elementary and secondary levels.

In the same year the committee presented score cards for the evaluation of school programs at the annual meeting of the College Physical Education Association: Health and Physical Education Score Card No. I for Elementary Schools, Grades 1–6, and Health and Physical Education Score Card No. II for Junior and Senior High Schools and Four Year High Schools.[16] These valuable score cards found immediate application. The work of this long-standing committee of the CPEA and its capable chairman, William R. La Porte, will always be viewed by the profession as one of the major achievements in its history.

INTERSCHOLASTIC ATHLETICS

P. Roy Brammell's survey of interscholastic and intramural athletics in 1932 included 327 secondary schools.[17] In most cases the director of physical education and the athletic coach were one and the same. Brammell noted that interscholastic athletic programs were confined to a few sports, which had developmental and social value but no carryover value for recreational purposes. A relatively small proportion of the total enrollment benefited from the program, and of those who actually entered only 60 percent played in a scheduled game.

Although interscholastic athletics were considered by school authorities part of the physical education program, they frequently dominated or just as often formed an independent part of it. In the majority of the high schools ticket sales and gate receipts provided the main source of financial support, and the board of education, department of physical education budget, and donations were mentioned less frequently. Brammell pointed out that it was not surprising that high schools devoted so much attention to the development of formidable teams to encourage attendance since they were so dependent upon gate receipts to finance the program. Interscholastic competition in the junior high school drew adverse criticism from educational leaders, medical authorities, and physical educators. Those who objected stated that the boy who concentrated on a few sports was deprived of the chance to develop broader sports interests, that boys of this age group were much too immature properly to evaluate the newspaper publicity and praise lavished on their athletic success, that in this crucial period of growth they were liable to physical damage and organic impairment from overexertion, and that if they started their athletic careers at so early an age they would lose their zest for varsity competition by the time they reached senior high school or college. Those who were sympathetic suggested that a well-organized and conducted intramural program should be substituted for interscholastic athletics. This would increase the versatility of the junior high school boy as well as the number of potential candidates for senior high school programs. Many junior high schools adopted this plan in spite of the protests of pressure groups, and intramural athletics became an important phase of the junior high school physical education program in the 1930s.

INTRAMURAL ATHLETICS IN THE SECONDARY SCHOOL

In Brammell's 1932 study 231 of 327 secondary schools stated that they had an organized intramural program. Basketball, baseball, and track and field athletics were mentioned most frequently. The girls' programs consisted of basketball, volleyball, and track and field athletics, with a tendency to replace the last with tennis in the senior high school. Most secondary schools attempted to correlate the activities of the physical education program with those of intramural athletics. The most popular competitive units were grades, physical education classes, and home rooms. The intramural athletic program was generally financed through interscholastic funds or the board of education and less frequently through ticket sales or pupil assessments. The majority of the secondary schools stated that intramural athletics was the responsibility of the department of physical education, and 96 of the 231 schools admitted that intramural and interscholastic athletics were combined for administrative reasons.

PHYSICAL EDUCATION IN COLLEGES AND UNIVERSITIES

As in the secondary schools, the physical education programs of colleges and universities were shifting from formal-type programs to informal activities. Some physical educators trained in the traditional formal method clung tenaciously to the old program, but the persistent infiltration of informal activities gradually undermined their position. According to James E. Rogers of the National Physical Education Service, higher institutions were meeting the demands of the expanded informal program with the construction of impressive gymnasiums for men and women equipped with swimming pools, additional space for a variety of activities, field houses, and spacious outdoor areas.

The early 30s were unique in the variety of activities introduced into colleges and universities. In many cases these were as novel to the instructor as to the student participant. Archery, badminton, lacrosse, paddleball, softball, speedball, squash, touch football, and miniature golf were introduced to many programs for the first time. Fieldball, lacrosse, and soccer were added to women's team sports. Students of both sexes pioneered in aviation, camping, camp craft, and outing clubs. Tap and clog dancing inherited from the theater in the 20s were under fire as a legitimate educational activity and had lost much of their appeal in the women's program. Folk and social dancing were gaining in popularity in sections of the country unhampered by a prejudice against mixed dancing, and both gave promise of becoming valuable additions to the physical education program. Women educators were just beginning to appreciate a new art form called modern dance but were at a loss as to how to convert it into a workable physical education activity.

ORIENTATION IN PHYSICAL EDUCATION

The introduction of orientation and survey courses into colleges and universities found immediate application in the required program of physical education. By 1934 two approaches in student orientation were evident.[18] In some institutions the orientation of students in physical education was just one phase of the general orientation course required of all freshmen. In others the department of physical education set aside several periods of the regular class to provide orientation.

In 1936 Seward C. Staley revamped the required physical education program at the University of Illinois, as described in a booklet entitled *A Sports Curriculum*.[19] He suggested that the old practice of limiting the teacher-learning of the physical education program to laboratory experiences alone should be expanded to include such types of learning activities as history, home economics, and English. Physical education should extend learning beyond the confines of the gymnasium and the boundaries of the playing field, to include an appreciation of the historical and cultural significances of sports, participation according to social and hygienic standards, appreciation of such technical aspects as rules, strategy performance and records, and recognition of the place and meaning of sports in one's own life.

INTERCOLLEGIATE ATHLETICS

The depression, following closely upon the heels of the famous Carnegie Foundation report on the status of American college athletics, left intercollegiate athletics open to much criticism. Some accused authorities in higher institutions of closing their eyes to such abuses as lowered admission standards for promising high school athletes, high-powered recruiting, proselyting, and subsidization. Other critics suggested that commercialization in intercollegiate athletics was only a reflection of the trend in every phase of American society. While critics were gaining most of the attention, professional leaders were devoting much constructive thought to the reevaluation of intercollegiate athletics as an educational force in American colleges and universities.[20]

With decreased gate receipts and growing public indifference to their plight, it became increasingly difficult for colleges and universities to maintain the elaborate intercollegiate programs of the prosperous 1920s. The athletic staff which had pyramided in numbers during the lush years was reduced, ambitious building plans curtailed, and athletic contests confined to rivals within easy traveling distance.

One of the casualties of the depression period was the intercollegiate football program of the small college. Gate receipts rarely paid expenses and emergency grants from the college budget were often necessary to keep the sport solvent. This willingness of the college administration to make up deficits, however, convinced the small colleges that they had a better chance of eventually achieving complete autonomy and financial control of intercollegiate athletics than did the larger institutions. At the same time their athletic representatives began to question the value of the NCAA in promoting and regulating intercollegiate affairs. They argued that the NCAA had been created in the first place by larger institutions and operated for their benefit. As proof of this, a review of previous years showed that the small college had never had proportionate representation on the committees of the NCAA. The small colleges were in a mood to strike out on their own, and all that was needed was some opportune situation to bring about the change.

ATHLETIC ORGANIZATIONS IN THE SMALL COLLEGE

In 1937 Emil S. Liston invited the basketball champions of the athletic conferences of small colleges to a national tournament in Kansas City. Sufficient unity of interest and purpose encouraged the establishment of the National Association of Intercollegiate Basketball in 1940. The membership was not aware that this body had a greater potential beyond the control and regulation of a single sport. By 1950 other sports interests in small colleges had requested representation, and in 1952 the organization changed its name to the National Association of Intercollegiate Athletics. The small colleges had now achieved what they had hoped for, a representative intercollegiate body composed of institutions of their own classification. The NAIA, in addition to its annual championship basketball tournament at Kansas City, conducts national meets in track and field athletics, golf, and tennis.

In 1937 a number of representatives from junior colleges in California met at Fresno to discuss the organization of a national athletic body to control and regulate competition among junior colleges. A committee was appointed to study the problem, with Oliver E. Byrd, of Stanford, as chairman. The committee report recommended that an organization be formed called the National Junior College Athletic Association, with a constitution and plan of organization similar to the NCAA. The NCAA is divided into sixteen regions to facilitate local autonomy and as a basis for the play-offs leading to national championships.

INTRAMURAL ATHLETICS IN COLLEGES AND UNIVERSITIES

During the decade 1930–1940 intramural athletics for men reached maturity. Guiding principles, standards, and policies were developed which gave the program stability and future direction. Intramural athletics began to appear more frequently within the department of physical education. In this association the intramural program benefited by a closer relationship with the service curriculum, use of facilities and equipment, and a more stable source of financial support. Intramural sports were more closely examined for their contributions to the physical welfare of the participant. With the decreased influence of the intercollegiate athletic department, regulation football appeared less frequently in the program; boxing, always considered hazardous, disappeared; and physical examinations and training periods were required for the more strenuous sports. To provide an opportunity for students to engage in a wider selection of recreational activities, many new sports were added to the intramural program. Among these were softball, badminton, fowl shooting, miniature golf, bait casting, archery, speedball, billiards, chess, croquet, horseshoe pitching, and ping-pong.

THE WAA IN COLLEGES AND UNIVERSITIES

Women's athletic associations continued to be guided by the principles established by the National Section on Women's Athletics and the Women's Division of the NAAF. The campaign to eliminate intercollegiate and interscholastic competition persisted, and in 1937 the National Section on Women's Athletics published the first of several manuals on standards in sports for women. With the rapid expansion of intramural programs and the addition of new features such as extramural competition and sports days, the need arose for interpretation of policies and standards as well as definition of terms. In 1938 a committee was appointed by the Midwest Association of College Teachers of Physical Education for Women to develop such policies and standards, which were endorsed by the National Section on Women's Athletics and by the National Association of Directors of Physical Education for College Women (NAPECW).[21]

By the middle of the 1930s the majority of women's athletic associations were sponsored by the department of physical education for women and the WAA. These two organizations maintained a cooperative control over rules and regulations and the general conduct of the intramural program. The most common source of financial support was the general student fee assigned to the WAA on a percentage basis and, where this arrangement did not exist, entry fees, charges for admission to intramural contests, and money obtained from special events. Approximately 75 percent of the WAAs in the colleges and universities sponsored extramural contests in the form of telegraphic meets and sports days. Factors cited by WAA representatives as a hindrance to intramural programs included late afternoon classes, inadequate staff and facilities, the wide variety of extracurricular activities on the campus, and lack of interest on the part of women students.[22]

PHYSICAL EDUCATION IN NEGRO INSTITUTIONS

Before and during the prosperous 20s Negro secondary schools and higher institutions tended to support interscholastic athletics, but placed little emphasis on general physical education programs. If such a program did exist, team sports dominated it. Hampton Institute, Howard University, Tuskegee, and Virginia State were able to construct new gymnasiums and stadiums in the 1920s, but other higher institutions were less fortunate. In view of the restriction in the use of public facilities by Negroes, one of the serious deficiencies in both secondary schools and colleges was the absence of swimming pools. Thomas J. Johnson in a survey of ninety Negro higher institutions disclosed that eight had swimming pools and only one offered instruction in swimming in the physical education program.[23]

In spite of much litigation in the courts over the right to equal educational opportunity, the years 1930–1940 witnessed a rapid improvement in Negro education in the United States, and physical education programs benefited accordingly. By 1935 thirty physical education teachers were employed in the Negro public school system of Washington, D.C. Many of these possessed bachelor's degrees and a lesser number the master's degree. Howard University boasted a staff of six full-time physical education teachers, three of whom had earned the master's degree. Fifty Negro leaders trained in physical education were serving in YMCAs, YWCAs, neighborhood houses, community centers, and playgrounds throughout the country. In such cities as Baltimore, Kansas City, St. Louis, and many other metropolitan areas qualified physical education teachers were serving in Negro public schools. In spite of this improvement, however, reports from the U.S. Office of Education indicated a continued overemphasis in Negro public schools on the interscholastic program, with apparently little interest in a general physical education program.[24]

In 1938 Oscar A. Moore conducted a personnel study of fifty-eight directors of health and physical education in Negro colleges and universities.[25] He found that 71 percent of the directors held master's degrees and that the remainder had earned the bachelor's degree. Of these directors 31 percent had completed their undergraduate work in health and physical education, while 60 percent of those who held the advanced degree had specialized in health and physical education.

Twenty-three percent of the Negro directors were members of the AAHPER and affiliated organizations, and 27 percent or over one-fourth had published one to five articles in professional journals. For supplementary income, they officiated in sports, taught summer school, played in professional sports, and worked in community centers, YMCAs, boys' clubs, and summer camps. Judged by prevailing standards, they were receiving salaries in the lower brackets, but those with advanced degrees and years of professional experience were paid salaries 30 percent higher than their fellow workers not so well qualified.

TEACHER TRAINING

In 1930 no professional preparation was required in Arkansas, Kentucky, Louisiana, Mississippi, North Dakota, Oregon, or Vermont to teach physical education and coach in the public schools, but four years of college were necessary to be certified. Fifteen state departments of education required a minimum of sixteen hours in physical education courses for certification. California, Kansas, Maryland, Michigan, Nevada, Pennsylvania, Oklahoma, Utah, and Wisconsin, however, had extensive requirements in physical education for teacher certification. In 1931 the State Division of Certification of Ohio required part-time teachers of physical education to have a minor of twelve semester hours and all full-time teachers forty semester hours. In 1933 New York State required teachers of physical education in secondary schools to have completed a four-year professional training course or its equivalent.[26]

THE NEILSON COMMITTEE ON TEACHER TRAINING

At a meeting of the Department of School Health and Physical Education of the NEA at Los Angeles in 1931, a Committee on Teacher-Training in Physical Education in the United States was appointed, with N. P. Neilson as chairman.[27] This committee was assigned the responsibility of formulating a set of standards to evaluate professional programs in teacher-training institutions. The committee revealed that 400 institutions in the United States provided professional training in physical education, but their catalogues showed such a wide variety of courses that they defied any effort at evaluation. After setting up standards for candidates, professional courses, teaching personnel, and facilities, the committee was faced with the problem of enforcement. A previous report by the Committee on State Certification Requirements of the AHPEA was used as a guide. It was decided that the right to train teachers of physical education should be granted institutions by the state department of education. Accreditation was to be according to school levels, elementary and secondary, and by subject matter. As each state department of education agreed to adopt the committee's standards, teacher-training institutions within the state were to be given a reasonable amount of time to make the necessary adjustments in their curriculums.

The Neilson Committee remained active and in the December, 1935, issue of the *Research Quarterly* published a final report under the title "National Study of Professional Education in Health and Physical Education." The report made recommendations as to specific standards and desirable professional courses, their content, and arrangement during the four years of training. As an outgrowth of the work of the committee, a subcommittee was established known as the National Rating Committee, whose members would evaluate the professional training program of any institution upon request. It was hoped that in this way an approved list of teacher-training institutions would eventually be compiled. The Neilson Committee also invited institutions to use its standards as a means of self-evaluation and improvement.

THE CPEA STUDY OF TEACHER TRAINING

As the nation advanced deeper into the depression, standards, however nobly conceived, meant little or nothing. By the middle of 1934 few teachers of physical education could secure positions, and those who retained theirs did so because they taught a subject not listed as nonessential. In the era of prosperity professional training institutions, pressed to meet the increasing demand for teachers, had paid little heed to the desires of school administrators. Surveys had indicated that as early as 1928 administrators wanted teachers and athletic coaches who could also give instruction in mathematics, business education, social sciences, and the sciences. It was not until 1931 that a double major was encouraged by New York University to meet the needs of schools in small communities.

As the economic situation gradually improved, the profession returned to the business of teacher-training resolved to provide a more useful program and a better product. Criticism of past training programs emphasized lack of cultural courses, poor selection of candidates, failure to keep up with graduates on the job, overspecialization in certain areas, too much time devoted to theory for those students interested in health, recreation, and athletic coaching, and tight schedules which provided little chance for electives. Such criticisms motivated the College Physical Education Association to appoint a committee in 1934 to study the effectiveness of teacher training by asking the opinion of the graduate on the job.[28]

Polling 2175 men teachers from every state in the union, the committee discovered that 55 percent were dissatisfied with their practice teaching experience, which they considered too theoretical and elaborate. The same percentage expressed general satisfaction with their courses, but 62 percent were dissatisfied with their coaching courses in football, basketball, and baseball, while instruction in track and field athletics was criticized by only 25 percent. Sixty-seven percent thought that training for future administrative responsibilities was poorly covered, and the same percentage felt that they lacked adequate preparation for advancement. The item "Relations with People" 62 percent marked as "not covered" or "insufficient," while "Preparation for Club Work" and "Training for Guidance" were marked by 74 percent as inadequately treated or completely ignored.

NOTES

1. P. Roy Brammell. *Articulation of High School and College.* Monograph No. 10, U.S. Office of Education, Washington, D.C., 1952.
2. Edgar W. Knight. *Education in the United States.* Chicago: Ginn and Company, 1951, p. 639.
3. *Physical Standards for Working Children.* Bureau of Publications, No.

70, Children's Bureau, U.S. Department of Labor, 1923. *The Health of the Working Child.* Special Bulletin No. 134, Bureau of Women in Industry, New York State Department of Labor, New York, 1928.

4. Edgar Fauver. "The Worth of Athletic Coaches as Instructors of Physical Education." *Proceedings,* The College Physical Education Association, 1932, pp. 44–50.
5. Eugene Lies. "The New Leisure Challenges the School." *Journal of Health and Physical Education,* 4:9 (November, 1934), 19.
6. Weaver Pangburn. "Toward Abundant Living: The Twentieth National Recreation Congress." *Journal of Health and Physical Education,* 4:4 (April, 1934), 19.
7. W. G. Moorehead. "Two Committee Reports on Leisure Time." *Journal of Health and Physical Education,* 4:10 (December, 1933), 34–36.
8. Gerald Richard Dalrymple. "A Survey of Coeducational Physical Education in Leading Universities and Colleges." (Thesis) Louisiana State University, 1937. V. Boynton. "Mixed Sport Days." *Journal of Health and Physical Education,* 8:9 (November, 1937), 560–561. Emory L. Cox. "Corecreation in Wichita." *Journal of Health and Physical Education,* 8:5 (May, 1937), 300–301. G. M. Gloss. "Corecreation in Physical Education Programs." *Journal of Health and Physical Education,* 11:1 (January, 1940), 31.
9. Arthur H. Steinhaus. "The Science of Educating the Body." *Journal of Health and Physical Education,* 8:6 (June, 1937), 345.
10. C. H. McCloy. "How About Some Muscles?" *Journal of Health and Physical Education,* 7:5 (May, 1936), 302–303.
11. Jesse F. Williams. "The Inevitable Necessity." *Proceedings,* The College Physical Education Association, 1939, p. 20.
12. Hiram A. Jones. "A Plan for National Preparedness Through Health, Physical Education and Recreation in Schools and School Camps." *Journal of Health and Physical Education,* 11:7 (September, 1940), 397. "Our Association's Program of Legislation for Preparedness and National Defense." *Journal of Health and Physical Education,* 11:9 (November, 1940), 523–527.
13. Hiram A. Jones. "The Revised Preparedness Bill." *Journal of Health and Physical Education,* 12:2 (February, 1941), 67–69; 117.
14. P. Roy Brammell. "Health and Physical Education." Monograph No. 10, U.S. Office of Education, Washington, D.C., 1932.
15. William R. La Porte. "Report of the Committee on Curriculum Research." *Proceedings,* The College Physical Education Association, 1935, pp. 8–35; 1936, pp. 5–21. "The Physical Education Curriculum—

A Natural Program." (Monograph) University of Southern California Press, 1937.

16. William R. La Porte. "Report of the Committee on Curriculum Research." *Proceedings,* The College Physical Education Association, 1937, pp. 78–101.
17. P. Roy Brammell. "Intramural and Interscholastic Athletics." Monograph No. 17, U.S. Office of Education, Washington, D.C., 1932.
18. William L. Hughes. "Orientation Courses in Physical Education for College Freshmen." *Journal of Health and Physical Education,* 5:10 (December, 1934), 22–24.
19. Seward C. Staley. *A Sports Curriculum.* Champaign: Bailey and Himes, Inc., 1936–1937. Seward C. Staley. *Sports Curriculum.* Philadelphia: W. B. Saunders Company, 1935.
20. Hugo Bezdek. "Modern Trends in Athletics." *Journal of Health and Physical Education,* 7:5 (May, 1936), 319. T. Nelson Metcalf. "Intercollegiate Athletic Policies." *Journal of Health and Physical Education,* 8:9 (November, 1937), 552. H. A. Scott, "The Position of the Coach in Institutions of Learning." *Proceedings,* The College Physical Education Association, 1937, p. 18.
21. "Policies for Sport Days and Intramural Athletics for College Women." *Journal of Health, Physical Education and Recreation,* 13:5 (May, 1942), 295.
22. Norma M. Leavitt and Margaret M. Duncan. "The Status of Intramural Programs for Women." *Research Quarterly,* 8:1 (March, 1937), 68–79.
23. Thomas J. Johnson. "Swimming in Negro Colleges and Universities." *Journal of Health and Physical Education,* 20:6 (June, 1940), 379.
24. Edwin B. Henderson. "Progress and Problems in Health and Physical Education Among Colored Americans." *Journal of Health and Physical Education,* 6:6 (June, 1935), 9.
25. Oscar A. Moore. "Personnel Study of Directors of Health and Physical Education in Negro Institutions of Higher Education." (Thesis) Springfield College, 1938.
26. Paul E. Belting. "The Certification of Teachers of Physical Education." *The Athletic Journal,* 10:8 (April, 1930), 22–30.
27. N. P. Neilson. "Report of Committee on Teacher Training in Physical Education in the United States." *Proceedings,* The College Physical Education Association, 1933, pp. 51–67.
28. J. W. Fredericks. "Final Report of the Committee on Professional Curriculum." *Proceedings,* The College Physical Education Association, 1938, pp. 123–130.

Chapter 22

PHYSICAL EDUCATION IN THE UNITED STATES, 1941–1949

THE WAR YEARS AND SOCIAL CHANGES

DURING the war years more than eleven million men were drained from war industries and essential peacetime occupations. Millions of women replaced men in industries, served in the armed services in order to release men for active duty, and engaged in many occupations which heretofore had been viewed as the exclusive province of men. At the end of hostilities a large percentage of these women continued as wage earners and salaried personnel, and the old social taboos against the working helpmate passed into oblivion. The desire for a more affluent existence revolutionized the food-packaging industry, introduced the two-car family, influenced the planning and construction of new homes, and increased the demand for numerous services and appliances that would free the modern housewife from the menial chores of yesteryear.

As early as 1920 the social structure of American society had begun to shift toward a new direction. The number of people engaged in agriculture as a livelihood was steadily declining and the number of industrial workers was growing. The greatest increase between 1920 and 1940 was in that segment of the population commonly called the middle class. This change in the social structure of American society has been explained by the tremendous technological advances in agriculture and industry which reduced the demand for unskilled workers and placed a premium on workers with technical competence and managerial ability.[1]

EDUCATION DURING AND AFTER THE WAR YEARS

In 1944 a total of 25,500 secondary schools had an enrollment of 5,750,000 pupils; 20 percent of these were enrolled in schools with less than 200 and 33 percent in schools with less than 300 pupils. Rural secondary schools were moving toward consolidation, though in certain regions strong resistance to this trend still persisted. The problem of the adolescent's economic security and recreational opportunities continued to concern educators. In 1944 the Educational Policies Commission[2] reaffirmed the stand of the American Youth Commission of 1938[3] for equal educational opportunity for all American youth regardless of economic status, geographic location, sex, or color.

The 1944 Commission proposed a secondary school curriculum called "Common Learnings," which included English, literature, history, science, citizenship, health, consumer economics, and housing. The Commission accepted health and physical education as "common studies," but believed that since they required specially trained teachers they should be conducted apart from the "common learning." The Commission further stated that physical education was not only indispensable to health but also contributed to the development of recreation skills and interests as well as desirable social experiences.

The knowledge gained by the federal government in cooperating with higher institutions in World War I proved most important in the development of an intelligent policy for military and scientific training during World War II. The research laboratories of universities were assigned problems in pure and practical research vital to the war program. One area, the study of electronics, was destined to open further possibilities for better living in the next decade.

Professional schools of medicine, dentistry, medical technology, physical and occupational therapy, and veterinary medicine were asked to accelerate their program in order to produce trained personnel. Hundreds of colleges and universities served as training centers for the Army, Army Service Forces, Navy Coast Guard, Marine Corps, and Maritime Corps, for the preparation of personnel in technical fields. In addition, colleges and universities continued the usual educational program for those men and women who remained at home.

VETERAN ENROLLMENT IN HIGHER INSTITUTIONS

As early as 1944 veterans were leaving the armed services at the rate of 100,000 per month and many of these resumed their educations under the provisions of the Veterans Rehabilitation Act (Public Law 16) and the Servicemen's Readjustment Act (Public Law 346), more familiarly known as the GI Bill of Rights. The American Council of Education reported in March, 1946, that the veteran enrollment in higher institutions had reached 417,324, or 30 percent of the total. The Council estimated that the capacity of higher institutions in 1947 would be 1,673,349 students, with the possibility that 45 percent of these would be veterans. Actual enrollment in 1947, as reported by the U.S. Bureau of Census, reached 2,354,000, of whom one million, or 42 percent, were veterans.

Higher institutions were bursting at the seams, and in an effort to meet the crucial situation negotiated with the War Production Board to secure A-type barracks, Quonset huts, and other surplus buildings as classrooms and housing accommodations for veterans and their families. Many playing fields, archery ranges, tennis and horseshoe courts on campuses throughout the nation were requisitioned as sites for these buildings. In addition, colleges and universities found it necessary to extend the recreation and intramural athletic programs to meet the needs of the veteran and his family.

PHYSICAL FITNESS AND WORLD WAR II

By December, 1941, approximately two million registrants between the ages of 21 and 35 years had been examined under the National Service Act of 1940, of whom 900,000 were rejected because of mental and physical defects and 100,000 for educational deficiencies. A cursory examination of World War II medical statistics would suggest a general deterioration in the health and physical status of the American male and female.[4] A closer study of the data shows that the principal reasons for rejections included dental defects, visual defects, cardiovascular conditions, musculoskeletal deficiencies, and defects of the feet. The last two items accounted for 10.8 percent of all causes for rejection. Among women, approximately one-third of the applicants were rejected because of psychiatric and neurological,* gynecological and genitourinary, cardiovascular, and visual causes, and less frequently because of overweight, ear, nose and throat conditions, tuberculosis, and dental defects.

THE NEED FOR A NATIONAL PROGRAM OF PHYSICAL FITNESS

It is apparent that most of the causes for rejection cannot be blamed directly upon physical education programs in the nation's schools, but rather upon differentials in standards of living and the inability or lack of desire to apply available knowledge and information made accessible by the school health and public health education programs. As the war went on, medical examiners became less discriminatory of those defects which were amenable to immediate correction and which would not handicap men or women in active service. Regardless of the interpretation of the medical examiner's statistics, the American public was made aware of the health and physical fitness implications of the large percentage of rejections through the press, radio, and lay periodicals.

The armed services devoted the first sixteen weeks to the physical conditioning of a soldier preparatory to technical training. They could have saved much precious time if these young men had been in better physical condition before entering military service. The circumstances which reduced the available manpower by 50 percent because of physical defects and educational deficiencies became a matter of national concern. The War Production Board knew that millions of man-hours were lost to war industries through sickness and disabilities that might have been avoided had the average citizen followed a sensible regime of health practices and physical

* The significance of neuropsychiatric problems in World War II was indicated by the fact that over 40 percent of the Army's medical discharges were from neuropsychiatric causes. Of the women applicants for enlistment in the Women's Army Corps between October, 1943, and September, 1944, over one-fifth of those rejected suffered from psychiatric and neurological conditions.

recreation. All signs indicated the need for a national effort to improve the health and physical fitness of the American citizen.

THE CIVILIAN DEFENSE PROGRAM AND PHYSICAL FITNESS

Prior to the 1940 elections President Roosevelt appointed John B. Kelley of Philadelphia National Director of Physical Training but did not provide him with a budget or staff, and as a consequence he made little progress.* After the election little interest was shown in national physical fitness until 1941, when President Roosevelt appointed Mayor Fiorella LaGuardia of New York City Director of Civilian Defense in Charge of Physical Fitness. A National Advisory Board was established with thirteen representatives from various interested national organizations and William L. Hughes of the AAHPER was appointed chairman.

The Advisory Board selected a team consisting of a man and woman assistant as national coordinators in each of the fields of health, physical education, and recreation in public schools, higher institutions, and communities. Their function was to develop specific programs of physical fitness in their areas and to correlate existing programs in schools, communities, and industries with the objectives of the Division of Physical Fitness, Office of Civilian Defense. Two regional representatives, a professionally qualified man and woman, were appointed in each of the nine Army Corps areas in the United States which were already operative under the Office of Civilian Defense. In a further breakdown in responsibility, state directors of health and physical education, where such positions existed, were appointed State Directors of Civilian Physical Fitness. In states that did not have such directors, a responsible and professionally trained individual was assigned the duty. In local

* The Philadelphia Board of Education through Alexander Stoddard, Superintendent of Schools, appropriated $100,000 for the organization of a city-wide physical fitness program. Eighty-five gymnasiums were opened and personnel provided from the schools' physical education staffs to condition potential draftees, men and women engaged in defense services such as air-raid wardens, and workers in war industries. Grover W. Mueller, City Supervisor of Physical Education, was in charge of the program. John B. Kelley used the Philadelphia plan for physical fitness as a pilot study and a guide for similar programs should budget and staff be eventually provided.

communities the Civilian Defense Committee selected a capable individual to take charge of the community's physical fitness program.

THE SPORTS BOARD

To promote nationwide interest in physical fitness, the National Advisory Board approved the organization of a Sports Board, whose members were sports celebrities and authorities in thirteen different activities. Mayor LaGuardia had already appointed Alice Marble, the tennis star, in 1941, to promote interest in physical fitness among women.

The appointment of the Sports Board was greeted with some deprecation by physical education leaders, who feared the key positions would fall into the hands of celebrities who had little appreciation of the conduct of a national program. As it turned out, the champion athletes reached the public in a way impossible for professionally trained teachers.

THE DIVISION OF PHYSICAL FITNESS

In February, 1942, President Roosevelt established in the Office of Defense, Health and Welfare Services, a Division of Physical Fitness to promote interest in health and physical fitness among all age groups. The Division was administered by the assistant director of the Office of Defense, Health and Welfare Services and consisted of two sections: School and College, and State and Community. The School and College Section, in cooperation with the United States Office of Education, was responsible for the establishment of policies and carrying out the program of physical fitness best suited to schools. The State and Community Section was to accomplish the same objectives in cooperation with local and state Defense Councils. The new plan simplified organization rather than drastically changed the format under which the former Office of Civilian Defense had functioned.

By executive order in April, 1943, a Committee of Physical Fitness was established in the office of the Administrator, Federal Security Agency, and John B. Kelley was appointed chairman. Its purpose was to (1) study problems in connection with the promotion of physical fitness with the assistance of the national organizations and agencies concerned; (2) serve as a central clearinghouse for information on physical fitness; (3) make available to states, local communities, organizations, and agencies the services of specialists in physical fitness; (4) promote regional institutes on physical fitness; and (5) prepare materials for the planning of programs in schools and communities.[5]

PHYSICAL TRAINING IN THE ARMED FORCES

During World War I Secretary of War Newton Baker had recommended that the administration of all physical training, athletic, and recreation programs within the United States Army should be the responsibility of Army personnel. At the opening of hostilities in 1941 this plan of organization was immediately implemented and General Frederick Osborn was appointed Chief of the Morale Branch. He placed a full-time recreation officer in each regiment to assist the commanding officer. The responsibility for the general program was assigned to Major Theodore P. Banks. Each subdivision of the Army was assigned a full-time morale and athletic officer. The personnel concerned were directly responsible to the Recreation Officer in each of the nine Army Corps areas.[6]

The Bureau of Navigation, United States Navy, entrusted the Morale and Recreation Section with the responsibility of advising the Chief of the Bureau on the morale and recreation of the enlisted men, including the coordination of activities provided by civilian organizations. Commander John L. Reynolds was in charge of the Morale and Recreation Section, and Lieutenant Commander Gene Tunney directed the general program of physical training in this section. The shore program was placed temporarily in charge of Lieutenant Commander George Hjelte and later assigned to Lieutenant Commander A. T. North. In the Army Air Force the physical training program was in charge of Major James E. Pixlee, who organized and directed it at thirty bases in the Gulf Air Corps Training Centers and twenty-five bases on the East and West coasts. In the Marine Corps physical training and athletic officers were trained in the Basic Officers' School, and men of ability and leadership, many of whom were former college athletes and All-Americans, were distributed throughout the units of the Corps. The United States Coast Guard and Merchant Marines provided physical training and athletic officers at their coastal training stations.

The Women's Army Corps (WACS), Women's Marine Corps, Women's Reserve, Women's Reserve of the Naval Reserve (WAVES), Women's Reserve of the Coast Guard (SPARS) and Women's Air Force Service Pilots and Women's Auxiliary Ferrying Squadron (WAFS), which were later combined into a unit designated as the WASP, all provided directors of physical training and athletics.[7] The women's branch of the armed services adopted the standards and practices of the National Section on Women's Athletics of the AAHPER in the conduct of sports competition and accepted the official rules of the NSWA in the regulation of sports.

The Army, Army Service Forces, Coast Guard, Marines, Merchant Marine, and Navy utilized hundreds of colleges and universities as training centers for specialists in technical areas and for basic training in certain branches such as the Army Air Force. The Navy initiated the V-5, V-7, and V-12 programs and established preflight schools at the University of North Carolina, State University of Iowa, University of Georgia, and St. Mary's College.[8]

The Army Air Force and the Army Specialized Training Program, Army Service Forces, as well as other branches used civilian personnel trained in physical education and athletics and the facilities of physical education and athletic departments in higher institutions in the program to train selected service men in technical fields. Many physical educators and coaches profited since they were maintained on the staff when physical education and intercollegiate athletic programs were at a standstill. Departments of physical education also benefited through the improvement of facilities and the inheritance of valuable sports equipment and supplies at the close of the war.

PHYSICAL FITNESS AND MORALE

A new type of program in 1941 concerned the health, welfare, and recreation of service men in communities adjacent to camps and military posts and in combat zones. A Division of Physical

Fitness and Morale was established in the Federal Security Agency, with Mark McCloskey, Director of Recreation of the City of New York, as chairman and coordinator. McCloskey drafted the help of many experienced recreation leaders. One of his important responsibilities was the direction of the United States Organizations (USO) which represented the services provided through the YMCA, YWCA, National Catholic Community Service, Salvation Army, Jewish Welfare Board, and National Traveler's Aid. The USO expanded its services to include many combat areas and secured the cooperation of Hollywood stars and other talented artists whose entertainment contributed much to the morale of the men in the armed forces.

Physical Training Programs

Naturally, emphasis in the service was upon physical conditioning exercises. These usually consisted of calisthenics, standing and ground drills, guerrilla exercises, grass drills, cross-country, steeplechase, or obstacle course running, relay races and combative contests.[8] In swimming emphasis was placed on strokes which had practical value in rough waters and skills which gave protection against underwater explosions and burning oil on the surface of the water. Instruction was given in lifesaving, use of the clothing as a buoy to stay afloat, and jumping into water from high places.

Service men were given repeated tests to determine the degree of the program's effectiveness and to measure individual progress. These tests were devised in consultation with such physical education specialists as C. H. McCloy, D. K. Brace, and others. Although they varied in the different services, they included push-ups to measure arm and shoulder extension strength; squat jumps or thrusts: leg strength and coordination; sit-ups: abdominal strength; pull-ups: arm flexor and shoulder strength; 100-yard pickaback: muscular endurance; Burpee (20 seconds): agility and coordination; and 300-yard runs: cardiorespiratory endurance.[9] In the administration of these tests, the "buddy" system was used under the supervision of the director of physical training and his assistants. Many test results furnished material for graduate study, but thousands of records still remain filed away, or are in the possession of the wartime directors of physical training programs.

Athletic Competition

All programs included intramural sports competition, and in certain branches such as the Marine Corps, where athletic competition was traditional, divisional baseball and football teams competed with service and intercollegiate teams. The Army featured intersquad or platoon competition to determine company and regimental champions. The Army Air Force encouraged off-duty sports competition through leagues composed of squadron teams, whose winners decided the unit or base championship. In the Navy training centers enlisted men were required to participate, as individuals or as team members, in a minimum of two sports per season. The Marine Corps provided interpost competitions to determine championships. Toward the close of the war more emphasis was placed on sports competition than on a program made up entirely of rugged conditioning exercises.

Results of the Physical Training Program

The testing program revealed many facts about the general physical condition of the average American male. Arm, shoulder girdle, and abdominal strength were woefully weak in comparison to leg strength. This fact suggested that school programs emphasized the use of the legs to the neglect of the trunk, shoulder girdle, and arm muscles. For many, the pull-up and push-up were difficult to perform, and the average performance fell far below that expected of men in the prime of their lives. In far too many cases posture was poor as it related to efficient bodily movement.

Only 72 percent of the white and 8 percent of the Negro men in the Navy could swim 50 yards. Many who could showed very little knowledge of swimming strokes and were not really at home in the water. The Great Lakes and coastal states had a higher percentage of better swimmers than did the Midwest and South.

The various branches of the services could have saved much

valuable time had enlisted men had some previous knowledge of the simple fundamentals of outdoor living. Those with experience in the Boy Scouts or hunting and fishing were best fitted for survival instruction in the out-of-doors.

Officers at training centers were impressed by the large number of men who stood around aimlessly during recreation periods because they were at a loss as to what to do. Charles E. Forsythe suggested that school programs had spent too much time, particularly on the secondary level, on the exceptionally skilled individual, and too little on those who really needed instruction in recreation skills.[10] Too many men were uninformed or uninterested in ways to maintain physical fitness, and far too many expressed a distinct dislike for the kind of physical education they had received in their schooldays. The exceptions were those who had participated in interscholastic athletic programs, however poorly organized and supervised.[10]

PHYSICAL EDUCATION IN PUBLIC SCHOOLS DURING THE WAR YEARS

ELEMENTARY SCHOOLS

In larger metropolitan areas physical education in the elementary school was scheduled daily while in smaller systems classes met two or three times per week. Periods varied from twenty to thirty minutes in length, with the majority requiring the longer period. In general, physical education classes were conducted apart from recess periods, and the trend was toward a daily one-hour period for free play. Where gymnasiums were not available, classrooms, hallways, auditoriums, and unoccupied rooms served for indoor programs.

The activities common to most programs included games, folk dancing, fundamental skills that lead to sports activities, marching, story plays, singing games, and stunts and tumbling. Many schools provided health instruction and postural work. As indicated in an excellent survey by Catharine A. Schmidt, in 1944 the tendency was to combine the fifth- and sixth-grade boys and girls, and the third and fourth, and first and second grades. Some schools, however, continued to teach physical education by separate grades.[11]

Very few elementary schools sponsored intramural athletics for girls, and in those that did the program included basketball, softball, ring tennis, volleyball, ping-pong, marbles, touch football, swimming, batball, and disks. Intramural athletics appeared more frequently in boys' programs, with team sports predominant. Grading systems in the elementary schools showed a wide variation in basic elements. The grade of "satisfactory" or "unsatisfactory" seemed to be growing in popularity. Tests in body mechanics, achievement tests, Brace's test of motor ability, physical efficiency, general achievement, and locally constructed tests were included in grading in some schools.[11]

SECONDARY SCHOOLS

In 1941 the Wartime Commission of the U.S. Office of Education studied the possibility of utilizing secondary school pupils in the war effort. A national policy committee worked out a plan which included the organization of a High School Victory Corps. The Victory Corps, which was to be voluntary, was designed to provide the high school pupil with preinduction training, guidance in critical wartime occupations and services, instruction in wartime citizenship, physical fitness and military drill, competence in mathematics and science, and preflight training in the basics of aeronautics.

The program for physical fitness recommended that boys and girls should have periodic health examinations followed up with the correction of physical defects, instruction in nutrition, safety education, first aid and a knowledge of personal, community, and military hygiene.[12]

The high schools as a whole responded with enthusiasm and, in cooperation with local and state civilian defense councils, organized Victory Corps which followed the recommended program within the limits of their personnel and facilities. A few high schools tended to emphasize military drill as a substitute for physical education. The profession, concerned about this practice, requested John W. Studebaker, Commissioner of Education, to determine the attitude of the War Department. Henry L. Stimson, Secretary of War, replied that in the opinion of the department it was more important for youth to be in good physical condition before induction than to have a knowledge of military drill.[12]

THE PHYSICAL EDUCATION PROGRAM IN SECONDARY SCHOOLS

A survey of forty-four of the forty-eight state superintendents of public instruction by Rosalind Cassidy and Hilda Kozman in 1943, indicated that secondary schools were actively concerned with the reorganization and improvement of the physical education program to meet wartime needs.[13] A majority of the high schools had adopted the Victory Corps as a means of motivating pupils to participate in the physical fitness program. Superintendents reported that local communities were keenly aware of the importance of the physical fitness program to national defense. Although programs leaned in the direction of conditioning activities, games, sports, and rhythmics were not discarded. Many recreation and coeducational activities, however, were crowded out by the demand for more rigorous exercise.

In 1944 the U.S. Office of Education reported that in 992 school systems 50 percent of the boys and 46.7 percent of the girls were enrolled in physiccal education classes. These figures indicated an increase of 6.3 percent for boys and 4.5 percent for girls over the school year 1942–1943 compared with increases in the school population of 15.2 and 5.2 percent respectively. The loss in pupil enrollment in physical education could be explained in part by the fact that many qualified physical educators had entered the armed services and no one could be found to replace them. Many secondary schools lacked the necessary funds to employ qualified persons and purchase equipment and supplies to conduct the national physical fitness program. Finally, many small schools had never provided a physical education program and did not intend to start one at this time.

In general the boys' program was geared to the recommendation of the Victory Corps manual. Programs were established of the commando and ranger type, which featured running, jumping, climbing, calisthenics, and combative contests. Obstacle courses were arranged with apparatus and other equipment in the gymnasiums and constructed out of doors of any materials at hand. A few high schools formed a Civil Air Patrol unit which provided training in military courtesy and discipline, infantry drill, Morse code, first aid, meteorology, and navigation. Certificates of achievement in physical fitness tests were awarded by the Victory Corps and the AAU. Approximately 80 percent of the secondary schools maintained their interscholastic athletic programs on a prewar basis through the economical use of playing equipment and regrouping schools to reduce traveling distances.

The programs of physical fitness for girls differed from the boys' in technique but were identical in spirit. Girls' programs continued to emphasize the major sports of speedball, tennis, basketball, volleyball, and baseball; the minor sports of deck tennis, badminton, shuffleboard, and table tennis; and dancing (square, folk, and social). In addition, many programs provided instruction in running, jumping, and leaping, proper ways of lifting weights, and general body mechanics.[13]

The Victory Corps did not provide physical fitness tests for girls because, as the manual pointed out, no acceptable ones had been established. The AAHPER appointed Eleanor Metheny of the Research Committee to determine norms for girls, which were completed with the cooperation of the NSWA and published in 1943.[14]

PHYSICAL EDUCATION IN COLLEGES AND UNIVERSITIES

As the war progressed colleges and universities emphasized programs of physical education which had value for national defense. The trend was toward fundamental activities such as running, jumping, climbing, throwing, weight-lifting, and tumbling. Interest in combative exercises was revived, and boxing, wrestling, fencing, jujitsu, and other activities that taught self-defense became prominent in many programs. Activities important to survival such as swimming and lifesaving and competition in vigorous team sports were featured.

Equipment and supplies were difficult to secure because of priorities established by the War Production Board, but the lessons learned in the repair and maintenance of equipment during the depression years paid off now. The construction of new facilities practically came to a standstill.

Women physical educators were busily occupied in the conditioning of young women for duty in the home, war industries, and armed services. The University of Kansas in 1942 required all full-time women students under 21 to take physical education, and the University of Oregon extended the physical education requirement through four years and specified that every woman student must take one term each of swimming, conditioning exercises, and modern dance. The Student War Council at the University of Wisconsin organized physical conditioning classes for all women in two optional periods each morning. The general physical fitness program featured conditioning exercises, instruction in body mechanics, and participation in games and sports.

PHYSICAL TRAINING *vs.* PHYSICAL EDUCATION

A matter of deep concern to the professional leadership was the manner in which those responsible for programs in public schools and higher institutions interpreted physical fitness. They were aware that many physical fitness programs were actually physical training programs copied after the physical conditioning programs of the armed forces. Glenn W. Howard pointed out that physical training programs were contrary to the purpose of physical education, and that the natural program of games, sports, and recreation activities, if properly supervised and conducted, would provide the desirable qualities of physical fitness so in demand by the armed forces.[15]

The fundamentalists, however, questioned whether physical education programs as currently conducted actually contributed to the physical fitness of American youth.[16] In their opinion the profession continued to place too much emphasis on social and psychological results, with a desultory attitude toward the physical objectives. Jesse F. Williams in an editorial in the *Journal* once more emphasized the basic concept he felt should guide the profession: "In an education through the physical, the principle requires that physical and physiological objectives be as prominent as social and psychological ones . . . either we take, support and defend a position of educating the whole man, or we join the 'muscle-builders, physical culturists, weight-lifters, gymnasts and formalists' . . . and devote ourselves to any education of the physical."[17]

STATE AND FEDERAL LEGISLATION

As in every war, public opinion favored legislative action to improve the physical fitness of the nation's youth. Since many laws inherited from the World War I era were of the permissive type, or if mandatory were generally ignored, state legislatures passed laws to eliminate misinterpretations of intent. By 1946 a total of thirty-four states had mandatory laws governing health and physical education, which were a definite improvement over past laws.

The social and political climate encouraged numerous attempts at federal legislation of the various bills introduced into Congress the School Health and Physical Education Act of 1946 (Revised) is of particular interest. This bill was designed by representatives of the AAHPER and provided grants-in-aid of twenty million dollars annually to the states, apportioned according to their total population between the ages of 5 and 19 years multiplied by the percentage of economic need.

In this bill physical education was defined as including all interscholastic athletics since some states held that it was illegal to appropriate tax monies for activities in which a gate receipt was collected. Recreation was not mentioned in the bill because it was felt that its inclusion would handicap its passage, and besides disagreement existed among recreation leaders as to the need for federal legislation in this area. In spite of an active campaign by the AAHPER, the bill never reached the voting stage in Congress. The persistent bugaboo of states' rights, fear of federal control and the activity of lobby groups representing special interests defeated practically every move to subsidize education in any form during the 1940s.

THE POSTWAR SITUATION IN PHYSICAL EDUCATION

At the close of the war professional leadership prepared for readjustment to new trends in the interpretation of the purpose of physical education. In the spring of 1946 a meeting of representatives from Harvard, New York University, Pennsylvania, Penn State, Princeton, and Rutgers agreed that the physical training programs in the armed forces demonstrated the need for a more vigorous program in the schools. The membership divided into four committees to consider the program.

The committee on the required program recommended the extension of the requirement of two years to four. It suggested that the first two years should be devoted to the development of general musculature, functional posture, and skills in sports and recreation activities, while in the last two years the student should be permitted to elect from a variety of activities. The committee on veterans' status felt that the returning veteran should be held to the same requirement as other undergraduates. The committee on measurement and evaluation suggested that a battery of tests be devised to screen, classify, and motivate the student. The committee on varsity sports and intramural athletics accepted the view that the intercollegiate program should attract the student of exceptional skill and a high degree of physical fitness, and that participation in the intramural program should follow the basic two-year course in physical education.[18]

The keen interest in the required program of physical education produced a series of studies which indicated that approximately 60 percent of the colleges and universities in the United States required from one to two years of physical education.[19] Approximately 70 percent granted full academic credit, and 50 percent computed the grade in physical education in the determination of honors by semesters. Only a small percentage of the institutions required the veteran to fulfill the physical education requirement, but the majority encouraged him to participate in the intramural and recreation program.

Credit in Physical Education for Veterans

In 1942 the American Council on Education established a committee to develop policies and procedures for the evaluation of the educational experience of men and women in the armed forces. The following year the Council recommended that full credit be given in first-year chemistry, first-semester mathematics and English to the veteran and "to allow him, if the college grants credit in ROTC, physical training, hygiene, or free electives, credit in these terms for his military training; not to exceed one-half semester."[20] Representatives of the AAHPER protested to the Council, requesting a review of the situation. It was the profession's belief that military experience in physical education and hygiene was not the equivalent in value to similar courses given in colleges or universities.[21]

The College Physical Education Association passed a resolution in 1949 stating that "no blanket credit be given in college physical education indiscriminately for physical training experienced in the armed services, but on the contrary that the College Physical Education Association recommends that colleges and universities grant credit with discrimination only where equivalence in content and instructional outcomes are established."[22] The Council, however, refused to alter its stand, and institutions were prone to grant blanket credit.

PHYSICAL EDUCATION FACILITIES

When the War Production Board placed on the priority list all materials vital to national defense, building construction of all types classified as nonessential to the war effort came to a halt. As the war situation improved, the War Production Board gradually lifted the ban on many building materials as well as sports equipment. By the end of 1945 many new gymnasiums, field houses, war memorial coliseums, community centers, and other facilities were on the drawing boards.

The CPEA appointed a Committee on Standards for Facilities, with Karl W. Bookwalter, Indiana University, as chairman, to develop guides for their construction in both higher institutions and elementary and secondary schools. Delbert Oberteuffer of Ohio State University, president at the time, invited the cooperation of the AAHPER and the NCAA in the development of standards. The committee's study was published in 1947 under the title, *College Facilities for Physical Education and Recreation.*

Caswell Miles, of the New York State Department of Education, at a meeting of the Executive Board of the AAHPER in Washington, suggested that a grant be obtained to finance a national conference on facilities. Theodore P. Banks, president of the Athletic Institute,* secured the approval of his board of directors to underwrite the conference, which was held at Jackson Mills, West Virginia, in December, 1946. With the aid of architects, engineers, and city-planners, the joint committee worked out the principles for functionally designed facilities. The results were published in 1947 in *A Guide for Planning Facilities for Athletics, Recreation, Physical and Health Education.*

Public interest in the construction of living war memorials to honor the men and women who had served or sacrificed their lives in the service of their country was initiated by the Athletic Institute in 1945. It published attractive and informative brochures and provided general and technical advice to educational institutions and communities interested in the construction of gymnasiums, coliseums, field houses, civic auditoriums, and community recreation centers as war memorials.

PROFESSIONAL PREPARATION

The Commission on Teacher Education and Professional Standards of the NEA survey on teacher supply and demand reported that in 1941 a total of 1705 men received a bachelor's degree in physical education. In its opinion too many physical education graduates had no larger appreciation of the challenge before them than the desire to promote a successful interscholastic athletic program. It was evident that the past struggle of the profession to raise standards in professional training programs had not been

* During World War I the federal government requested sporting goods companies to organize and pool their commercial interests to provide athletic goods for the armed services at a reasonable profit and of the best available quality. This spirit of cooperation eventually led in 1929 to the establishment of the Athletic Institute by the Chamber of Commerce of Sporting Goods Manufacturers for the purpose of promoting physical education, sports, and recreation in the United States. Since its creation the Athletic Institute has been influential in the establishment of the American Baseball Congress, Amateur Softball Association, National Industrial Recreation Association, National Commission on Living War Memorials, and the sports program of the U.S. Junior Chamber of Commerce, among others. After World War II the Institute has concentrated on the financial support of important national professional conferences in physical education and recreation and the publication of reports of these conferences.

fruitful. The National Rating Committee, which had developed from the work of the Neilson Committee, became inactive in 1937. Some claimed that the administration of the evaluative standards was too complex and others that a negative reaction had developed against their use.

The profession, however, did not give up; in 1939 Dr. Margaret Bell, President of the AAHPER, appointed a committee on professional education of which Elwood C. Davis was chairman. In 1941 the AAHPER gave this committee the status of a standing committee, known as the Cooperative Study of Professional Education in Health, Physical Education and Recreation.[23] Under the chairmanship of Dr. Davis it decided not to establish standards as in the past, but instead of review the more desirable practices in professional teacher education. This committee had just succeeded in developing a working philosophy when the United States entered World War II.

Many veterans returned to complete their interrupted professional education under the GI Bill. As a consequence the supply of male physical education teachers increased from a low of 495 in 1945 to a high of 7548 by 1950. This situation was of deep concern to the profession because many institutions were poorly equipped and the quality of their product left much to be desired. It was not until 1948, however, that time was found to improve the standards in teacher-training institutions.[24]

PROFESSIONAL PREPARATION IN HEALTH EDUCATION

School health education had benefited considerably from the renewed interest in the health of the schoolchild even before the end of the war. In 1944 the W. K. Kellogg Foundation of Battle Creek, Michigan, made it possible through financial grants for many state departments of education and health to conduct experimental programs in the improvement of school health. In the postwar years many states took advantage of these grants. In 1946 fifteen national organizations cooperated in the development of a guide which was published under the title *Suggested School Health Policies.* Official and voluntary health agencies financed workshops for the in-service teacher of health education and public health workers. In 1948 the Joint Committee on Health Problems of the NEA and the AMA published the third revision of *Health Education* as a guide for school health workers. The interest in school health education was phenomenal, and the demand for health teachers, health educators, and counselors kept pace.

The National Conference for Cooperation of Health Education in 1946 ranked teacher preparation next in importance to the need for standardization of the health examination in the school program. In 1947 Ruth E. Grout reviewed current suggestions for the improvement of professional education.[25] As summarized by Earl E. Kleinschmidt, M.D., these suggestions included (1) the cooperation of health education students with the health service division in the institution they attended; and (2) the need for instruction in the basic sciences, including anatomy, physiology and bacteriology, personal and community health, school health problems and child hygiene, methods and materials of health instruction, and observation in health service and practice teaching in the health programs of public schools. In 1948 the Third National Conference on Health in the College discussed the needs of teacher preparation and the publication *Health Education,* issued in the same year, devoted a chapter to the training of health educators.

PROFESSIONAL PREPARATION IN SAFETY EDUCATION

In 1944 the American Association of Teacher Colleges pooled resources with the National Safety Council in an effort to find out just what teacher preparation institutions should do to better equip the teacher in public schools for safety education. In 1947 the NEA, AAHPER, National Association of Secondary School Principals, and the National Commission on Safety Education in a joint meeting discussed the role of the physical education teacher in safety education.

The campaign of the National Safety Council and other agencies to eliminate the hazards of driving on the nation's highways before World War II gained momentum in the postwar years. Preparation of teachers in driver education developed in the postwar years with the financial assistance of automobile dealers and associations. Before the end of the decade Herbert J. Stack of the Safety Center,

New York University, stated that approximately 200 teacher-training institutions offered preparatory courses in safety and driver education.[26]

Preparation in Recreation Leadership

As a result of the tremendous advances made in public and industrial recreation during the 1930s an urgent need arose for personnel with a broader professional training and some means of certification and registration. The first move to upgrade the recreation profession was taken at a college conference held at the University of Minnesota in 1937, at which the needs of a broader education and certification were discussed. Other profitable meetings followed at the University of North Carolina in 1939 and at New York University in 1941.

The postwar years saw another surge of interest in school, public, industrial, and commercial recreation. This movement was assisted by the formation of state commissions on recreation and the increasing awareness of federal agencies of the need for recreational opportunities through the use of government facilities and public lands. The need for qualified recreation personnel pyramided. Representatives of the National Recreation Association, American Recreation Society, College Recreation Associations, National Industrial Recreation Association, and other interested organizations met at New York University in 1948 to consider the problems of professional preparation.

The Jackson's Mill Conference in 1948. At the meeting of the Teacher Education Section of the CPEA in 1948, Carl L. Nordly, president of the AAHPER, announced that the Athletic Institute had agreed to sponsor and finance a national workshop on professional education in health, physical education, and recreation. The two-week conference met at Jackson's Mill, West Virginia, in May, 1948, at a 4H-Club camp owned by the University of West Virginia. Nineteen national organizations cooperated in the conference, which was a landmark in the history of the profession's effort to improve its standards. The report of the meeting was published by the Athletic Institute in 1948 and entitled *The National Conference on Undergraduate Professional Preparation in*

Physical Education, Health Education and Recreation.[27] The common areas treated by the conference included accreditation of teacher-training institutions, faculty, facilities, professional program, recruitment, selection and guidance, placement and follow-up, laboratory and field experience, in-service education, graduate study, resources, and evaluation through cooperative student-faculty relationships.

THE GRADUATE CONFERENCE AT PERE MARQUETTE STATE PARK. Surveys in 1939 had indicated that a major program in graduate physical education was offered by fifty-six institutions in the United States, and by 1948 this number had grown to ninety-two. As indicated by the studies of Jack E. Hewitt during the school year 1942–1943, the regulatory power of the American Association of Teacher Colleges, Association of American Universities, and other national and regional accrediting agencies had done much to standardize and improve graduate study with a major in physical education.[28] Hewitt's survey gave the impression that graduate education had fared better than undergraduate physical education, but the professional leadership was aware that many problems still existed that needed attention. Some institutions had entered the field of graduate education with substandard programs, poorly qualified faculty, and inadequate library facilities for both undergraduate and graduate study.[29]

In recognition of these problems, Seward C. Staley of the University of Illinois called a conference of directors of graduate study in midwestern universities in 1946. This meeting proved informative and profitable, and additional conferences were held in 1947 and 1948.

The principals of the previous graduate education conferences felt that a wider representation was needed and that definite criteria should be formulated for those who guided graduate physical education. The services of the Athletic Institute were secured to sponsor and finance a graduate conference at Pere Marquette State Park, Grafton, Illinois, in January, 1950. The work of this conference was reported in *Graduate Study in Health Education, Physical Education and Recreation.*[30] The conference discussed graduate education in all three areas from the standpoint of admission requirements, counseling and faculty-student relationships, placement and follow-up, programs of graduate studies, qualification and experience of graduate faculty, and needed facilities and resources.

NOTES

1. R. Freeman Butts and Lawrence A. Cremins. *A History of Education in American Culture.* New York: Henry Holt and Company, 1953, pp. 483–484.
2. *Education for All American Youth.* Education Policies Commission, National Education Association and American Association of School Administrators, Washington, D.C., 1944, pp. 234–258; 103–110; 277–278.
3. Howard M. Bell. *Youth Tells Its Story.* American Youth Commission of the American Council on Education, National Education Association, Washington, D.C., 1938.
4. Harry A. Scott. "Implications of Recent Army Medical Examinations Statistics." *Proceedings,* The College Physical Education Association, 1941, 1954, 1958.
5. *Community Organization for Physical Fitness.* Committee on Physical Fitness, Federal Security Agency. Chicago: The Athletic Institute, 1944. *Physical Fitness for Production.* Committee on Physical Fitness, Federal Security Agency. South Carolina: Jacobs Press, 1944. *Physical Fitness in Industry.* Committee on Physical Fitness, Federal Security Agency. Chicago: The Athletic Institute, 1944.
6. Theodore P. Banks. "Army Athletics." *Proceedings,* The College Physical Education Association, 1941, pp. 95–98.
7. Jenny E. Turnbull. "The Physical Training Program of the WAVES." Journal of Health and Physical Education, 19:9 (November, 1943), 420. Donna L. Miles. "Physical Fitness and the W.A.C." *Journal of Health and Physical Education,* 14:8 (October, 1943), 408.
8. Theodore P. Banks. "Army Physical Conditioning." *The Athletic Journal,* 23:1 (September, 1942), 8. Joseph J. Verducci. "A Bird's-eye View of Physical Conditioning at the Alameda Coast Guard Training Station." *The Athletic Journal,* 23:10 (June, 1943), 7. Ernest B. Smith. "College Fort Worth, Texas." *Proceedings,* The College Physical Education Association, 1942, pp. 40–43. T. Nelson Metcalf. "The Physical Fitness Program for the Navy College Training Program." *Proceedings,* The College Physical Education Association, 1942, pp. 48–52.

9. E. E. Wieman. "The Physical Training Program of the Army Specialized Training Division Army Service Forces." *Proceedings,* The College Physical Education Association, 1942, pp. 37–38.
10. Charles E. Forsythe. "Some Things We Have Learned About Physical Fitness." *The Athletic Journal,* 25:10 (June, 1945), 18–26.
11. Catharine A. Schmidt. "Elementary School Physical Education." *Journal of Health and Physical Education,* 15:13 (March, 1944), 130.
12. *Guidance Manual for the High School Victory Corps.* Victory Corps Series, Pamphlet No. 4, Federal Security Agency, U.S. Office of Education, 1943.
13. Rosalind Cassidy and Hilda Clute Kozman. "Trends in State Wartime Physical Fitness Programs." *Journal of Health and Physical Education,* 14:7 (September, 1943), 357.
14. Eleanor Metheny. "Physical Performance for Girls." *Journal of Health and Physical Education,* 14:8 (October, 1943), 424.
15. Glenn W. Howard. "The Part of Physical Fitness in the Natural Program of Physical Education." *Proceedings,* The College Physical Education Association, 1941, pp. 59–61.
16. C. H. McCloy. "A Return to Fundamentals." *Proceedings,* The College Physical Education Association, 1941, pp. 73–77.
17. Jesse F. Williams. "Education Through the Physical." (Editorial) *Journal of Health and Physical Education,* 13:9 (November, 1942), 524.
18. Carl P. Schott. "The Post-War Required Problem." *Proceedings,* The College Physical Education Association, 1947, pp. 26–29.
19. John H. Shaw and Millard R. Rogers. "The Status of Required Physical Education in Colleges and Universities of the United States." *Proceedings,* The College Physical Education Association, 1947, p. 34. "National Association News." *Journal of Health and Physical Education,* 17:10 (December, 1946), 602–603.
20. George F. Cook. *Sound Educational Credit for Military Experience,* American Council on Education, National Education Association, Washington, D.C., 1943, p. 17.
21. "Credit for Military Training in Physical Education and Hygiene." (Editorial) *Journal of Health and Physical Education,* 19:9 (November, 1948), 607.
22. "Report of the Resolution Committee." *Proceedings,* The College Physical Education Association, 1949, p. 140.
23. Harry A. Scott. "Report of the Committee on Teacher Education." *Proceedings,* The College Physical Education Association, 1947, pp. 98–99.

24. H. L. Berridge. "Accreditation of Professional Education in Physical Education." *Proceedings,* The College Physical Education Association, 1948, pp. 44–52. H. Harrison Clarke. "Justification for Establishing Minimum Standards for the Preparation of Physical Education Personnel." *Proceedings,* The College Physical Education Association, 1948, pp. 53–60.
25. Ruth E. Grout. "Postwar Problems in Teacher Education in Health Education." *Journal of Health and Physical Education,* 18:3 (March, 1947), 138–139; 188.
26. Herbert J. Stack. "Progress in Safety Education." *Journal of Health and Physical Education,* 20:9 (November, 1949), 579.
27. *The National Conference on Undergraduate Professional Preparation in Physical Education, Health Education and Recreation.* Chicago: The Athletic Institute, 1948.
28. Jack E. Hewitt. "An Analysis of Graduate Offerings and Practices Leading to the Master's and Doctor's Degree in Physical Education in Institutions of Higher Learning in the United States." (Dissertation) University of Oregon, 1943. Jack E. Hewitt. "Requirements for the Master Degree in Physical Education." *Journal of Health and Physical Education,* 16:7 (September, 1945) 369–373; 406.
29. Allen Eric Weatherford, II. "Professional Health Education, Physical Education and Recreation in Negro Colleges in the United States." (Dissertation) Pennsylvania State College, 1948.
30. *Graduate Study in Health Education, Physical Education and Recreation.* A Report of the National Conference on Graduate Study in Health Education, Physical Education and Recreation. Chicago: The Athletic Institute, 1950.

Chapter 23

PHYSICAL EDUCATION IN THE UNITED STATES, 1950–

THE WORLD SITUATION

From 1949 to 1950 the Communist armed forces of North Korea made repeated attacks upon the Republic of Korea south of the 38th Parallel which marked the boundary of former military occupation by the Soviet Union and the United States. In 1950 the South Koreans appealed to the United Nations, and while the appeal was pending the Communists initiated a major military offensive backed by the Soviets. The UN member nations, with the exception of the Soviet Bloc, immediately boycotted the Communist government of North Korea, and President Harry S Truman informed a nervous world community that the United States would furnish the Republic of Korea naval and air support. By the end of 1952 the United States, the Republic of Korea, and fifteen member nations of the United Nations were engaged in one of the strangest wars in history.

In 1953 Joseph Stalin died and the U.S.S.R., under the leadership of Nikita S. Khrushchev, inaugurated a campaign of economic competition with the Western democracies as part of what was known as the "cold war." The remarkable economic recovery of West Germany, Japan, and Italy strengthened the movement toward European unification as a buttress against the Soviet bloc. At the same time, the democratic nations viewed with alarm the revolutionary movements in Latin America and Africa, which, in many cases, were Communist-encouraged. The U-2 spy-plane incident, the Cuban situation, and rising tensions throughout Southeast Asia served to aggravate the cold war.

NEW FRONTIERS IN SPACE

The development of the V-2 rocket by the Germans during World War II and the research of R. H. Goddard in the postwar years provided the technological basis for the development of the space satellite in the early 1950s. By the close of the International Geophysical Years of 1957 and 1958 man had advanced to the threshold of space exploration. During this pioneering stage the U.S.S.R. and the United States had successfully launched seven satellites. For several years space engineers had considered the possibilities of launching space vehicles powered by nuclear energy, and in 1955 the United States initiated a program called Rover to study the feasibility of solid-core reactors. The success of this program led to the development of the nuclear rocket engine and the substitution of nuclear power for chemical liquid in the third stage of satellite flight. Between November, 1961, and October, 1962, three United States astronauts suborbited and orbited the earth in 3,000-pound Mercury satellites and two Soviet astronauts orbited the earth eighteen and sixty times in the 10,000-pound Vostok satellites. During 1962 both the U.S.S.R. and the United States fired probes as part of their lunar and planetary exploration programs, and the United States developed Rangers III, IV, and V, designed for hard landing on the moon. At the end of 1961 the United States inaugurated the Gemini program, designed for a crew of two men, to remain in flight for two weeks. By the middle of 1962 the National Aeronautics and Space Administration (NASA) also announced the three-man-crew Apollo spaceship, to be sent to the moon, hopefully before the end of the 60s.

Space exploration also led to scientific and technological breakthroughs which could make valuable contributions to a world at peace. In 1958 the nuclear submarine *Nautilus* made a trip from the Pacific to the Atlantic under the Arctic ice pack. The *Nautilus* was powered by a uranium fuel, which could propel the submarine for 130,000 miles without refueling. In 1960 the Navy announced that the U.S. Polaris, an intermediate-range missile with a range of 1300 miles, had been fired from one of the tubes of the nuclear submarine *George Washington.* Since early 1960 space engineers have explored the uses of satellites in weather prediction and in communication via radio and television. The development of the rocket vehicle has also presented problems in space medicine, including oxygen–carbon dioxide exchange in a cabin surrounded by a vacuum, the effect of cosmic rays and high-intensity radiation on the human body, and mental and physical adjustment to weightlessness in space flight. Space exploration, like the first trips of Columbus to the New World in the fifteenth century, has provided man with new insights into the nature of the universe and the relationship of the earth to the cosmos.

SOCIOLOGICAL TRENDS

According to the Twentieth Century Fund, a nonprofit scientific research foundation, the average output of work per hour and consumer spending have tripled since 1900. A survey of consumer finance conducted by the Federal Reserve Board in the late 1950s indicated that the number of families with yearly incomes of $5,000 or better had increased by eleven million, while those with incomes less than this figure had decreased by seven million. The trend in the United States toward a middle-class society repudiates the Marxist theory that capitalist society will eventually divide itself into proletariat and capitalistic classes, the "haves" and "have-nots."

Reports of the United States Census Bureau indicate that during the last decade there has been a decided shift of population from metropolitan to suburban areas. Business, education, professional, and recreational services joined the exodus. Suburban life has popularized a new way of life, epitomized by comfortable and efficient homes, private swimming pools, and many other materialistic advantages that are highly valued by the average American citizen.

Prior to the 1960 census report, Robert W. Burgess, Director of the U.S. Census Bureau, predicted that at the current rate of increase the United States would have a population of 200 millions by 1970. Increase in population is not characteristic of the United States alone. The population of the world in the past fifty years has increased by more than three billions, or at an approximate rate of 130,000 human beings per day. Should this rate of increase persist for the next fifty years, the population will reach an explosion point where the world food supply will be totally inadequate to meet human needs.[1]

EDUCATIONAL DEVELOPMENTS

The crucial problem of education in the 1950s was the steady increase of the school population, with an accompanying inability to meet the demand for adequate financial support, facilities, and competent teachers. Ever since 1900 the American public had contributed a diminishing percentage of its national income to the support of education, and this situation was especially discouraging since more money was being spent on luxuries, recreation, and entertainment than upon the education of American youth. The School Facilities Survey in the mid-50s revealed that the school systems of the nation were short more than 340,000 classrooms, a situation which it was estimated would require $10–12 billion to correct. This estimate, however, covered only current needs, for future needs would require the construction of some 117,000 new classrooms annually.

Moreover, school systems in wealthier states were in competition with those of low-income states for teaching talent. Also, business and industry competed for personnel and removed many qualified teachers from the field. Problems such as these goaded educational leaders to seek federal legislation to assist the schools and underwrite inequities in teachers' salaries and facilities, but Congress was not in a mood to listen.

Sputniks I and II in the Educational Orbit

The success of the Soviet Union in the launching of Sputniks I and II in 1957 raised a storm of controversy among influential figures in the United States over the efficacy of scientific education in the schools. The United States Office of Education announced that the U.S.S.R. was turning out 60,000 scientists and engineers annually while the United States produced only 34,000. The Soviet Union spent 6 percent of its annual income for educational purposes while the United States spent only 4.5 percent.

I. L. Kandel,[1] Rear Admiral Rickover,[2] and other public figures suggested that some arrangement should be made to give attention to specially gifted high school students. President James Bryant Conant of Harvard University advocated a generous supply of scholarships for promising pupils in mathematics and science. Educators reacted to these proposals to provide gifted pupils with special considerations by declaring that they were undemocratic, discriminatory, and divisive.

On August 23, 1958, Congress enacted the first general law on education since the Morrill Act of 1862: the National Defense Education Act. This law authorized the expenditure of three billion dollars over a period of four years in loans and fellowships to college students of academic ability to undergird the teaching of mathematics, science, and modern languages, counseling and guidance programs in these areas, and the dissemination of scientific information and materials. Since Congress anticipated opposition from states'-rightists, it left the allocation of the funds and administration of the program up to the various states and their local communities.

NATIONAL INTEREST IN PHYSICAL FITNESS

In the wake of the "police action" in Korea the AAHPER, in conjunction with the United States Office of Education, called a meeting in Washington of the National Conference for Mobilization of Health, Physical Education and Recreation.[3] All organizations interested in the mobilization of education for national defense were invited to send representatives. The members of the Conference agreed that every effort should be made to improve the physical fitness of youth through such basic activities as running, jumping, climbing, throwing, lifting, dodging, and basic swimming skills for survival in the water, including submerging, underwater swimming, useful strokes, and distance swimming. One of the positive outcomes of the Conference was the preparation of physical fitness standards for youth of high school age, worked out by representatives of the AAHPER Armed Forces Committee in cooperation with personnel from the armed services.[4]

Following the Conference, the AAHPER appointed a Committee on Education for National Defense. A subcommittee on health recommended a thorough medical and dental examination for all children, with follow-up and health instruction based upon scientific information. A subcommittee on physical education recommended that the program in the public schools be centered around activities which developed physical fitness and provided self-protective and survival skills. This committee recommended a program of games, sports, and self-testing activities and discouraged the use of boxing, judo, and obstacle course running so prominent in the programs of the World War II period. A subcommittee on recreation recommended a balanced recreation program in schools, with additional opportunities for camping and other outdoor experiences.

THE KRAUS-WEBER TEST OF MUSCULAR FITNESS

On the hypothesis that some relationship must exist between the prevalence of orthopedic disabilities and muscular fitness, Drs. Hans Kraus and Sonya Weber, of the Posture and Therapeutic Exercise Clinic of Columbia University Vanderbilt Clinics, experimented for many years with some twenty tests and measurements to find a suitable diagnostic test of muscular fitness. The research team finally decided upon six functional tests, which they called the "Minimum Muscular Fitness Test."[5]

Because low back pain was a common disability in the armed forces and entailed the loss of many valuable man-hours, clinics were established at the New York University Bellevue Medical Center and Columbia University Presbyterian Hospital, with Drs. Kraus and Weber in charge, to conduct research in this area. A study of some 4,000 cases disclosed that 20 percent of the patients had true pathological conditions, while the remainder showed negative findings. The larger group was prescribed exercises to develop muscular strength and flexibility. It was quickly discovered that as soon as the patients permitted themselves to fall below the minimum level, pain symptoms recurred. On diagnosis, the findings were negative as before, but in all cases the patients failed in one or more of the tests of minimum muscular fitness.[6]

The next step in the research was to determine at what stage in the growth of the individual muscular conditions favored the occurrence of low back pain. Bonnie Prudden, Director of the Physical Fitness Institute of White Plains, New York, trained a team which, in association with Dr. Kraus, tested 4,000 schoolchildren in states along the Atlantic seaboard. The results showed that 56.6 percent of the children between the ages of 6 and 16 failed one or more of the tests of minimum muscular fitness.

To determine whether or not this performance was generic to all children, regardless of geographical location, Dr. Kraus, Dr. Weber, and Miss Prudden administered the test to 2,000 urban, suburban, and rural children in Austria, Italy, and Switzerland and found that these European children averaged only 8.2 percent failures. According to Dr. Kraus and his associates, American children, though they had the best food and medical care in the world, lacked sufficient exercise to keep them at a minimum level of muscular fitness.[7] The comparative test results of American and European children had tremendous news value, and Dr. Kraus and his associates were besieged by school personnel and parents for a description of their six simple and easily administered tests.[7]

PRESIDENT EISENHOWER'S COUNCIL ON YOUTH FITNESS

Hans Kraus appeared before many professional and civic groups, and his message appealed to John Kelley, former National Director of Physical Fitness during World War II, and Senator Duff of Pennsylvania. These two public figures approached President Dwight D. Eisenhower to discuss the significance of Dr. Kraus's disclosures. A luncheon meeting was called by the President on July 11, 1955, to consider the situation, to which he invited sports champions, prominent sports authorities, and sports writers. As a result of the discussion, Vice President Richard M. Nixon was appointed chairman of a committee to develop a national fitness program.

Almost a year later, on September 8, 1956, representatives of the

NEA, AAHPER and the U.S. Office of Education, among other organizations, were invited to the first national conference on fitness at Annapolis, which resulted in the establishment of the President's Council on Youth Fitness and the President's Citizens Advisory Committee on Fitness. Shane McCarthy was appointed executive director of the Council, and his office served as a clearinghouse for information on the national program for youth fitness.

The executive director traveled the length and breadth of the nation as adviser to educational, local, and state officials and community organizations in the promotion of fitness programs for youth. The Council released a series of publications, among which *Plan for Action* was described by *Sports Illustrated* as typical of most publications of the Council in being "primarily one of vaguely worded publicity and promotion releases for the fitness cause."[6] The President's Citizens Advisory Committee promoted fitness at the local level through the leadership of state councils of education and civic officials appointed by state governors. Some of these state councils never got beyond the talking and publicity stage, but others, organized and conducted excellent programs.

THE YOUTH FITNESS PROJECT OF THE AAHPER

Within a week after the establishment of the President's Council on Youth Fitness, the AAHPER held a Conference on Fitness in Washington and recommended that the Research Council of the Association conduct a national survey of the fitness of American schoolchildren. At a subsequent meeting in Chicago, Paul A. Hunsicker of the University of Michigan, was appointed director of the Youth Fitness Project of the AAHPER, and the Council agreed upon the test items to be employed in a pilot study of the fitness of schoolchildren on a nationwide basis.

Six tests in the battery, which included pull-ups for boys and modified pull-ups for girls, sit-ups, shuttle run, standing broad jump, 50-yard dash, and softball throw for distance, were contributed by Anna Espenschade, who had used these events over the years in her California testing program. The Council added the 600-yard walk-run as the seventh event. Aquatic tests were also added after consultation with Richard Brown of the American Red Cross, but this test was difficult to administer because of the general lack of swimming facilities in elementary and secondary schools.[8]

To assure a representative sample of schools for the pilot study, Dr. Hunsicker secured the services of the Survey Research Center of the University of Michigan. School officials were contacted, and arrangements were made with competent physical education personnel to administer the battery of tests. By June, 1958, Dr. Hunsicker and his co-workers administered the AAHPER National Fitness Test to 8,500 boys and girls in grades 5 through 12. When the data of the field workers were returned, Dr. Hunsicker's assistants punched the information onto IBM cards for statistical treatment. Percentile tables of the events based on the Neilson-Cozen Classification Index were formulated and the results published in the AAHPER *Youth Fitness Manual.*[9]

As a result of his statistical compilations, Dr. Hunsicker made several interesting observations. Children throughout the nation on the average made a very low score in the pull-ups, which substantiated the armed services observation that Americans, in general, were deficient in arm and shoulder girdle strength. School people who arranged for the testing equipment were hard pressed to find bars in gymnasiums for the pull-ups since most of this kind of equipment had passed out with the old formal system. The performance of girls did not improve with the increase in age level, as it did with boys, and Dr. Hunsicker suggested that this was due to the American attitude that girls were fragile and should not therefore be exposed to demanding types of physical activity. In the range of scores, however, some girls actually exceeded the performance of boys.[9, 10]

PRESIDENT KENNEDY'S COUNCIL ON YOUTH FITNESS

Even before John F. Kennedy assumed the presidency he wrote several articles expressing his concern for the physical fitness of American youth. One of President Kennedy's first conferences on the subject was called in February, 1961. As a result of this conference, the AAHPER was asked to assist in the preparation of materials to promote an effective national physical fitness program in the elementary and secondary schools. In March, 1961, President Kennedy appointed Charles "Bud" Wilkinson, head football coach at the University of Oklahoma, as consultant to his Council on Youth Fitness, and on the executive staff appointed Theodore Forbes, supervisor of health and physical education of the Sacramento Public City Schools, as director of health, physical, education and recreation; Richard Snider, managing editor of the Topeka *Capital-Journal,* as director of public relations; and Simon A. McNeely, a consultant in health, physical education, and recreation in the U.S. Office of Education, as an intermediary.

In the development of a plan of action the executive staff of the President's Council on Youth Fitness held conferences with the leadership of the AAHPER, representatives of the NEA, and other professional organizations. One of the first steps decided upon was the publication of the pamphlet entitled *Youth Fitness; Suggested Elements of a School-Centered Program,* which has become known to the profession as the PCYF "Blue Book." Part I is entitled "Concepts and Foundations," of which representatives of the AAHPER shared in the editorship. Part II, "Test Activities and References for a School-Centered Youth Fitness Program," is the slightly revised AAHPER Youth Fitness Test.

This booklet, which received wide distribution, recommended that schools should provide a daily period of fifteen minutes of vigorous exercise for developmental purposes. Although this represents the barest minimum, the profession was fully aware of the fact that 75 percent of the nation's schools had no daily period of physical education. A thirty-minute period was recommended five days a week, exclusive of the recess period for grades 1–6. The PCYF Blue Book also recommended that in junior and senior high schools a regular class period of physical education should be offered five days a week. Statistically, only 80 percent of the junior high school and 60 percent of the senior high school students are enrolled in physcial education classes. These classes of instruction are dovetailed with health education classes on a 2–2 or 3–2 weekly cycle. Actual physical education instruction in the nation's schools, therefore, is most inadequate as measured against the recommendations of the President's Council on Youth Fitness.

OPERATION FITNESS–U.S.A.

When in December, 1958, Vice President Nixon relinquished his chairmanship of the President's Council on Youth Fitness, it was assigned to the Secretary of Interior, Fred Seaton. Interviewed about his new responsibility, he replied that in his opinion the best way to become physically fit was to become a bird watcher.[6] Regardless of this remark, it was apparent to professional workers that the promotion of nationwide physical fitness by the federal government was never to progress beyond the appointive and publicity stage. Any gains to be made in the future would have to be achieved by professional, civic, and industrial organizations.

In 1958 the AAHPER inaugurated a positive plan for action called Operation Fitness–U.S.A., the promotion of which was assigned to Louis E. Means, Director of Special Projects. Between January and October, 1959, Dr. Means reported that Operation Fitness–U.S.A. had encouraged the administration of the National Fitness Test to over ten million children and youths. A total of 35,000 fitness kits had been distributed to educational authorities and emblems and certificates had been awarded to elementary and secondary pupils who had achieved the 50th and 80th percentile scores in the Youth Fitness Test. Dr. Means announced in the same report that a tentative program of projects had been outlined for Operation Fitness–U.S.A., which would require one to five years to complete.

CONTRIBUTIONS OF NONPROFESSIONAL ORGANIZATIONS

Local Junior Chamber of Commerce, in cooperation with Wheaties Sports Federation, also initiated a national fitness campaign. Bob Richards, Olympic pole vaulting champion, was appointed director and became a worthy missionary in the cause of fitness for American youth. The Wheaties company provided copies of the fitness test and a fitness slide-rule in the container of their product. The Jaycees furnished kits on the testing program and advice on the organization of a fitness program in the community.

After World War II many civic, fraternal, and industrial organizations sponsored sports leagues and athletic events for boys and girls of elementary and junior high school age. They kept millions of youngsters occupied during out-of-school time in sports and events and fulfilled a felt need which the school program would not or could not meet. Baseball had a tremendous following, and among its sponsors are the Veterans of Foreign Wars, American Legion, U.S. Junior Chamber of Commerce, YMCAs, Catholic Youth Organization, and county and municipal recreation systems. The Little League baseball teams include boys under 12 years of age, and the number who wish to play each year exceeds the supply of coaches and facilities. Boys in the 13–16-year age bracket participate in the Babe Ruth, Pony, and Colt Leagues. In 1953 the U.S. Junior Chamber of Commerce and the National Baseball Congress (Wichita, Kansas) organized a nationwide baseball program for boys 18–21 years of age called the Rookie League.

Sports participation, however, is not limited to baseball. Football is represented by Small-Fry and Pop-Warner Football Leagues and basketball by Iddy Biddy, Biddy, and Kiddy Leagues. The U.S. Chamber of Commerce sponsors annual junior golf and tennis championship tournaments, four leagues in baseball and one in basketball, Better Fishing League, Inc., Jaycee Leagues of the American Junior Bowling Congress, Jaycee Junior Hockey Leagues, Golden Gloves Tournament, Junior Rose Bowl Game (Pasadena), World Champion Rodeo (Phoenix) and among others, the National AAU Swimming and Diving Meet (Newark).

PROBLEMS IN COMPETITIVE ATHLETICS FOR CHILDREN

The sponsorship of these leagues and events by civic, fraternal, and industrial organizations are still subject to the criticism of medical and other professional groups, who claim with some justification that improperly supervised competition can be injurious to the normal development of the adolescent. Local publicity, the adulation of fans, and doting parents and relatives present a serious problem of psychological adjustment to the immature boy. Regardless of these admonitions, the sports league movement continues to gain momentum. It has the approval of the middle-class parent, who, in turn, is bringing pressure to bear on school administrators for a better representation of interschool sports in the physical education program. Parents reason that if their youngsters find joy and satisfaction in sports competition outside of school, why not conduct it in school under proper supervision and according to acceptable standards? Many schoolmen have become very susceptible to this kind of reasoning and no longer hesitate to take a positive stand in favor of interschool sports competition.

In connection with this problem, Theodore Bank, director of the Athletic Institute, stated in 1957, "I think we should accept the fact that competitive athletic programs for elementary school age children do exist, and that they will continue to grow in national popularity. I think we [physical educators] should aid in the development of these programs by furnishing our much-needed professional leadership, supervision, and instruction.* By doing so, we will insure the health and safety of every participant."[11]

INTEREST IN FACILITIES, EQUIPMENT, AND SUPPLIES

In 1947 fourteen professional organizations sponsored a National Conference on Facilities for Athletics, Recreation, Physical and Health Education. As a result of this conference the *Guide for Planning Facilities for Athletics, Recreation, Physical and Health Education* was published that same year. In the ensuing years it was felt that the *Guide* should be revised, and Caswell M. Miles, chairman of the Executive Committee of the National Conference, secured the assistance of the American Association of School Administrators to sponsor a second conference in 1955. The National Conference on State Parks, National Recreation Association, and the American Institute of Architects were invited to sit in on the conference.

In the same vein the AAHPER established a Council on Equipment and Supplies in 1955, with Thomas E. McDonough, Emory University, Georgia, as chairman and Charles Heilman, Drake University, Iowa, as secretary. The purpose of this Council was to assist physical educators, athletic coaches, and recreation leaders in the selection, purchase, and care of equipment and supplies. Since its organization the Council has secured the cooperation of manu-

* See *Physical Education for Children of Elementary School Age* (1951) and *Interscholastics in Junior High Schools—A Survey* (1959), AAHPER.

facturing companies and stimulated professional interest through exhibits of equipment and supplies at conferences and conventions. In 1959 the AAHPER and the Athletic Institute cosponsored a National Workshop on Equipment and Supplies for Athletics, Physical and Recreation at Michigan State, whose report was made available in 1960.

PHYSICAL EDUCATION AND INTERNATIONAL RELATIONS

Since the close of World War II the United States as a member of the United Nations, has cooperated with other member nations in the activities of the United Nations' Educational, Scientific and Cultural Organizations (UNESCO). Individuals and organizations in the profession of physical education have also done much to further the cause of international understanding and goodwill. Physical educators have participated as Fulbright lecturers and consultants in faraway places with strange-sounding names, and others have served as exchange scholars. In 1949 Anna Hess, University of Texas, and Dorothy Ainsworth, Smith College, conceived the idea of an International Association of Physical Education and Sports for Girls and Women and arranged the first meeting at Copenhagen, Denmark, the same year. Since then the International Association has met in Paris (1953), London (1957), and Washington (1961). The attendance grew from a membership of 225 and 15 nations in 1949 to more than 400 representing 60 nations. In 1943 the first Pan-American Congress of Physical Education was held in Rio de Janeiro to bring the physical education leaders in the Americas together for a discussion of common problems. The second meeting was held in Mexico City three years later, with little action. At the third meeting in Montevideo, Uruguay, in 1950, the Congress was overhauled and became more active in physical education affairs of the Western Hemisphere.

UNIFICATION OF PROFESSIONAL EFFORTS

Frank Stafford of the U.S. Office of Education in an examination of the international activities of the AAHPER was impressed by the amount of duplication and overlapping of effort. In 1949 he called a meeting at Washington of representatives of the AAHPER, the chairman of international affairs of the NEA, and representatives of the Pan-American Institute of Physical Education, American School Health Association, Continuing Committee of the International Association of Physical Education and Sports for Girls and Women, and the Committee on Aid to Foreign Physical Education. As a result of this meeting, the Joint Council on International Affairs in Health, Physical Education and Recreation was formed.

The Joint Council encourages the exchange of students and faculty members through scholarships, the exchange of books and letters among professional workers, and the assignment of recently returned American physical educators from foreign service as hosts to visiting foreign students and guests. The Council stands ready to help in all projects concerned with international affairs and to encourage a better understanding of the philosophy and objectives among countries.[12] In 1953 the Joint Council selected the University of Maryland as a depository for the periodical literature of such nations as England, France, Germany, India, Japan, and South Africa. The Council has also entered into cooperative projects with the Committee on International Relations of the American Academy of Physical Education, of which Dorothy S. Ainsworth is chairman.[13]

THE PEACE CORPS

In 1961 Congress passed the Peace Corps Act after President Kennedy had activated this body by executive order. Sargent Shriver, President of the Chicago Board of Education, was placed in charge. The purpose of the Peace Corps is to promote world peace and friendship by providing interested foreign countries with the services of Americans to help them meet their needs for trained manpower.

The policies of the Peace Corps may be summarized as follows: (1) the Peace Corps goes only where it is invited; (2) volunteers serve as co-workers and are "doers" rather than "advisers"; (3) volunteers serve two years without salary or draft exemption, but have the right to resign at any time; (4) volunteers receive an allowance sufficient to live in a modest manner; (5) volunteers receive a termination allowance of $75 for each month of satisfactory service; and (6) the Corps is open to all qualified single Americans above 18 and married couples with no dependents under 18.

Candidates undergo a two-to-three-month training program in a selected college or university in the United States. The Corps is guided in the selection of candidates by two important criteria. The volunteer must have the personality traits necessary to get along with people and the technical skills required for the job.[14]

Ghana, Nigeria, Tanganyika, India, Pakistan, Malaya, Thailand, Colombia, Chile, St. Lucia, and the Philippines were among the first countries to request the services of the Peace Corps. These early requests called for teachers, home economists, medical assistants, nurses, agriculturalists, engineers, journalists, mechanics, bricklayers, carpenters, and a wide variety of artisans. Early in 1962 Tunisia, Ceylon, Iran, Thailand, Bolivia, Venezuela, and the Ivory Coast applied for volunteers trained as physical educators, athletic coaches, and health educationists. By the middle of 1963 additional projects had been committed in Morocco, Colombia, Ecuador, and Venezuela, and it was estimated that approximately 150 volunteers trained in health and physical education, athletic coaching, and recreation would be needed to fulfill requests.

As the Peace Corps became increasingly involved in the recruitment of personnel in health, physical education, athletic coaching, and recreation and in the selection of suitable training centers, the assistance of the AAHPER staff at Washington headquarters was freely called upon. At the close of 1962 the AAHPER established the Peace Corps Project and appointed Raymond A. Ciszek, Western Washington State College, as director. The Project distributes information on Peace Corps needs to key professional personnel in colleges and universities, contacts uncommitted physical education graduates, and assists in the selection of institutions suitable for training programs.[15]

LEGISLATION FOR HEALTH, SAFETY, AND PHYSICAL EDUCATION

The Korean War presented an opportunity for the profession to seek assistance from the federal government in extending health and physical education instruction to the children of the nation. In 1951 the members of the AAHPER Legislative Committee authored a bill entitled School Health, Safety and Physical Education Instruction (H.R. 5853), which had the official approval of the Legislative Commission of the NEA. The bill was introduced in the House of Representatives on October 20, 1951. In substance, it authorized the appropriation of fifteen million dollars a year over a five-year period to assist the states and territories in extending and improving instructional programs of health, safety, and physical education. In 1952 H.R. 5853 was referred to the House Education and Labor Committee, from which it never emerged.

In 1958 the Division of Legislation and Federal Relations of the AAHPER formulated the School Health and Safety Education, Physical Education, and Recreation Instruction Bill (S. 4145), whose purpose was to assist the states and territories in improving their programs of physical fitness for schoolchildren to help meet the future manpower requirements of national defense. The 1958 bill was introduced without success in the Eighty-fifth Congress and again in 1959. As the decade closed, it was apparent that legislators were still reluctant to commit the federal government to a grants-in-aid program for physical education and recreation.

PHYSICAL EDUCATION IN THE PUBLIC SCHOOLS

THE ELEMENTARY SCHOOLS

One of the first National Conferences on Physical Education for Children of Elementary School Age was held in Washington in January, 1951. James H. Humphrey stated in 1953 that educational representatives of thirty-three states reported that urban areas were gradually regaining the services of supervisors of physical education in elementary schools after the lean years of the depression and the drainage of personnel during World War II.[16] Six states reported urban elementary schools with supervisors of physical education. Seventy-five percent of the states, at one time or currently, provided a course of study, and in the same percentage of states the classroom teacher assumed the responsibility of teaching physical education. Thus the burden of teaching physical education in the elementary school still fell upon the classroom teacher, a situation which made in-service training vitally important. Many states provided in-service training through the workshop technique made so popular during the 1940s. Other methods included institutes, extension courses, and summer courses in teacher-training institutions.

THE SCHNEIDER SURVEY

Elsa Schneider, specialist in health, physical education, recreation, and safety, U.S. Office of Education, conducted a survey of the status of physical education in elementary schools in the United States during the 1955–1956 school year.[17] Her survey revealed that in-service training was provided in 52 percent of the 177 school systems in which the classroom teacher taught physical education in grades 1–6 and in 170 school systems in which physical education was taught in the same grades by the classroom teacher with the assistance of a specialist. The number of specialists, special teachers, and consultants employed by the school systems in the survey totaled 5225, of whom 57 percent were men and 43 percent women. Elementary schools, as a rule, provided a daily instructional period of thirty minutes although recommendations called for two periods of fifteen to twenty minutes each. The programs featured a wide variety of activities, and those guided by teachers with in-service training were comparatively richer. Fifty-eight percent of the elementary school programs in urban areas conducted intramural programs, play days, and sports days, and 47 percent sponsored summer recreation as part of the school program or through the assistance of outside agencies. Gymnasiums and playrooms were included in the facilities of 54 percent of the 12,217 school buildings reported, and all-weather outside play areas were available in 48 percent.

THE SECOND NATIONAL CONFERENCE ON CHILDREN OF ELEMENTARY AGE

Two hundred representatives from thirty-five states and the District of Columbia attended the National Conference on Fitness of Children of Elementary Age* in 1959, in Washington, to consider ways whereby elementary school physical education might con-

* A similar meeting was held for secondary schools. See George H. Grover, "Professional Report from the National Conference on Fitness of Secondary School Youth," *Journal of Health, Physical Education and Recreation,* 30:4 (April, 1959), 47.

tribute to the fitness of children. The conference agreed that the school, in cooperation with agencies in the community, was responsible for the formulation of health policies and the provision of meaningful instruction in health and safety. Physical education should emphasize creativity, vigorous activities, and exploratory experiences in bodily movements through games, sport skills, and rhythmics.

The Conference recommended that teacher education institutions should cooperate with state departments of education in an effort to require elementary school teachers to take specific courses in health and physical education. It also recommended that pertinent research data and evaluative techniques that would assist in a better understanding of the child should be made available to agencies concerned with the elementary school child.

THE SECONDARY SCHOOLS

Dr. Karl W. Bookwalter, Bureau of School Services and Research, Indiana University, conducted a national survey of secondary schools between 1950 and 1954 by means of the La Porte Score Card No. II.*[18] This survey was one of the first to use this means of evaluating the secondary school health and physical education programs on a nationwide basis. It involved a total of 2748 secondary schools in 27 states, and the data represented the work of 31 independent studies of graduate students, most of whom were doctoral candidates. To assure reliability, the surveyor was supervised on several trial runs by a qualified professional worker before he was permitted to initiate the actual survey.

Dr. Bookwalter revealed that the boys' programs in health and physical education were 28 percent effective, while the girls' programs were anywhere from 4 to 9 percent more effective in some

* The La Porte Score Card No. II is composed of ten major areas of evaluation such as Organization and Administration, Activity Program, Athletics and Intramurals, etc. In each major area, depending on the degree that recognized practices are followed, a perfect score of 30 points is possible. The point values of all areas are totaled and divided by 3 to determine the percentage of compliance with accepted standards. Thus, a school which complied with all the standards in the ten major areas would have a total score of 300 and a percentage of compliance of $^{300}/_{3}$ or 100.

states. Negro school programs were, in the majority of cases, inferior to the whites'. The movement toward consolidated secondary schools appeared to be an important factor in the improvement of the rural high school health and physical education program. The programs of accredited high schools were of better quality than those of nonaccredited schools.

Dr. Bookwalter estimated that when the time consumed in role-taking, moving the class, lecture and demonstration, and other factors was excluded, the average secondary school pupil in the United States received approximately twenty hours of annual instruction in physical education. He found the adapted physical education programs 4 percent effective and, compared with the total program, the weakest phase. The gap between knowledge and practice in health and physical education in the nation's secondary schools appears to be still very wide.[18]

PHYSICAL EDUCATION IN COLLEGES AND UNIVERSITIES

Since 1954 the number of team sports offered in programs of physical education in higher institutions has tended to level off. The trend in most institutions has been toward individual sports, aquatic activities, and body mechanics (women's programs). The program for the atypical student is now generally designated "adapted physical education." By 1958 the average enrollment in adapted physical education was thirty-three students. Approximately 50 percent of the higher institutions that required physical education offered a planned program in team and individual sports, aquatics and rhythmics.[19]

At the close of World War II interest was resumed in coeducational instruction in such activities as archery, badminton, bowling, fencing, golf, tennis, swimming, and folk, social and square dancing. Variations in the level of skill made dual instruction in some activities impossible without modification or adjustment. Other activities were found too vigorous, or were recognized as more suitable to one sex. On the other hand, modern dance, which had been traditionally the exclusive province of women students, began to attract more and more men students in the 1950s. Women students also explored the possibilities of weight-lifting, with certain modifications. Corecreation, purely experimental in the 1930s, provided a more varied and better organized program, and became the responsibility of the men's intramural division and/or the women's recreation association. In some institutions the corecreation program was conducted by a student committee, with a faculty adviser.

Colleges and universities found themselves inadequately supplied with archery ranges, fencing, wrestling, and gymnastic rooms, handball courts, and playing fields. Expensive facilities such as golf courses, bowling lanes, riding stables, and dance studios remained for most institutions in the realm of long-range planning, and private, public, and commercial facilities had to be used instead. Approximately 75 percent of the higher institutions require students to purchase the entire gymnasium costume, while 10 percent furnish everything except tennis shoes. Sixty-two percent provide all the equipment necessary to participate in classwork, and of this number two-thirds requires no fee or deposit, while the remaining third charge a nominal fee.[19]

PROBLEMS IN PHYSICAL EDUCATION

In 1951 and 1961 the basketball scandals in several colleges and universities received considerable publicity, shocking the public and leading them to believe that intercollegiate athletics were permeated with unethical practices. In the search for other questionable procedures, critics noted that athletes who had chosen physical education as their major subject had a predominant schedule of courses in this area. They immediately accused academic advisers of "featherbedding" athletics' schedules to keep them eligible. Such publicity damaged the status of physical education in the eyes of the general public and in academic circles.

The pressure to secure operational funds and urgently needed facilities for a rapidly mounting student population created problems for the administrative heads of departments of physical education. For the first time they experienced direct attacks upon physical education as a requirement. As student enrollment increased, advisers were hard pressed to fit the physical education requirement into schedules filled with lectures, laboratory, and recitation periods. This situation became even more acute where physical education departments were limited by insufficient personnel and a fixed number of teaching stations.

Postponement of the physical education requirement was inevitable where restricted budgets and limited facilities did not permit the expansion of the program. In some cases it amounted to as much as 8–10 percent of those students obligated to meet the requirement. Instead of postponement, some departments employed proficiency tests to relieve the pressure.[20] By passing such tests a student could satisfy his physical education requirement, in part or in its entirety.

Administrators of physical education also had to be on the alert to the encroachment of the university administration upon playing fields and other outdoor facilities, which were urgently needed as building sites and parking lots. In some cases lost facilities were replaced by more desirable ones on newly acquired institutionsl property. The administrative head was also faced with the need to secure capital outlay for necessary buildings and swimming pools, which have a higher unit cost than most physical facilities on the campus.

THE REQUIRED PROGRAM IN JEOPARDY

The problems associated with the increase in enrollment became increasingly acute as the 1950s progressed. In many instances the attack on the physical education program was initiated by faculty members who still subscribed to the dichotomous philosophy of mind and body and autonomists who wished to control the physical education requirement.[21] Probably just as influential was the view of many faculty members that the modern physical education program was a social and recreational enterprise completely devoid of the vigorous activity essential to physical fitness.[22] They reasoned that if the program's objective was social and recreational, why not drop it and place all emphasis on intramural athletics or expand recreational facilities to encourage voluntary participation?

As pointed out by Raymond A. Snyder[23] of UCLA and Seward C. Staley[21] of the University of Illinois, these attacks are evidence that public relations is one of the most neglected phases in the promotion of physical education. A definite need exists in all educational gradients for an interpretation of the purpose of physical education to administrators, faculty members, and student body. Snyder also warned that with growing enrollment and increased emphasis on such favored subjects as mathematics, science, and foreign languages, all instructional areas will be carefully scrutinized and judged according to their utilitarian value.

PROFESSIONAL PREPARATION IN THE 1950s

The professional education program faced new problems in the 1950s which could not be anticipated at the time of the Jackson's Mill Conference. In 1955 the AAHPER established the Outdoor Education Project as a cooperative venture with the Associated Fishing Tackle Manufacturers and the Sporting Arms and Ammunition Manufacturer's Institute. Directed by Julian W. Smith, Indiana University, the Project emphasizes the training of leadership, the interpretation of its objectives to public schools and higher institutions, and the preparation and distribution of materials on the subject of outdoor education.[24]

In 1955 the National Conference on Undergraduate Health Education recommended that the essential prerequisites of the health education minor should include biological, physical, and social sciences. The conference suggested that the minor program should consist of fifteen to twenty semester hours in health and health education areas. The health area included personal and community health, vital statistics, epidemiology, nutrition, and other subjects. The health education area included methods and materials, health service, healthful school living, safety education and organization, and administration of the school health program. The conference urged that teacher-training institutions should be mindful of the possibilities of the minor in health education.[25]

In 1954 the school and college conference of the National Safety Council conducted a survey of safety education with the assistance of 155 supervisors and teachers in forty-one states. The response indicated that more safety instruction in public transportation and related areas was needed in out-of-school organizations and rural and senior high schools. Those polled felt that certain practices in safety education had little value, including courses on a national basis, safety materials with prominent advertising displays, and awards based on false values. The National Conference on Driver Education in 1953 recommended that driver education should be an integrated part of the high school program with the same status as other subjects, and that teacher-training institutions should provide qualified personnel to teach the course. The increased popularity of driver education instruction is indicated by the fact that by 1958 1200 high schools conducted such courses.

The National Recreation Association in 1952 created the National Advisory Committee on Recruitment, Training and Placement of Recreation Personnel. The American Recreation Society undertook a study of certification of recreation personnel which had an important influence on professional education. With the assistance of the University of Minnesota, the Society inaugurated the practice of collecting data on the supply and job placement of each year's recreation graduates. Recreation organizations, in a joint meeting with the Association for Higher Education, the National Commission on Teacher Education and Professional Standards, and the AAHPER in 1954, discussed professional preparation which led to the improvement of standards.[26] In 1953 the National Recreation Association, in cooperation with the Southern Regional Education Board, conducted a two-year study on problems related to the status and professional preparation of recreational personnel in the South.[27]

PROGRESS IN PROFESSIONAL PREPARATION

At the close of the Jackson's Mill Conference the profession recognized, as had leaders in the past, that some means of accreditation was essential. In 1949 a working relationship was effected with the American Association of Colleges for Teacher Education, and a Coordinating Committee on Problems of Teacher Education was formed to advise with the profession on selected problems. Through the combined efforts of the Committee for Improvement of Professional Education in Health, Physical Education and Recreation of the AAHPER and the Coordinating Committee of the AACTE, criteria for evaluation of professional education in the three areas were developed under the leadership of Carl L. Nordly, University of Minnesota, and used on an experimental basis in professional teacher-training institutions in his state during 1952 and 1953. After the period of experimentation, specialists in the three areas offered their services on a voluntary basis to professional training institutions in the evaluation of their programs.[28]

In 1954 the accrediting function of the American Association of Colleges of Teacher Education was transferred to the National Council of Accreditation of Teacher Education. The AAHPER decided at the Seventy-fifth Anniversary Convention in Miami Beach in 1960 to accept the NCATE as the accrediting agent for professional training institutions in health, physical education, and recreation. Under this arrangement, the state departments of education granted certification only to graduates of professional training institutions which had been accredited by the NCATE.

With accreditation of teacher-training institutions a reality, and in view of the progress which had been made in the past decade, it was inevitable that the profession should review its evaluative criteria established as a result of the Jackson's Mill Conference. In 1960 at the Miami Beach Convention the AAHPER scheduled the Professional Preparation Conference to meet in Washington in January, 1962. The Conference, under the chairmanship of Arthur A. Esslinger, University of Oregon, was organized into the professional areas represented by health and safety education, physical education and athletics, recreation and outdoor education, and the first phase of graduate education. The representatives of each of the areas were subdivided into five subcommittees who discussed criteria for student personnel, faculty, professional courses, laboratory experiences, and facilities and instructional materials. The report of the Conference led to definite commitments on acceptable criteria in all areas of professional preparation.[29]

NOTES

1. I. L. Kandel. *American Education in the Twentieth Century.* Cambridge: Harvard University Press, 1959.
2. H. G. Rickover. "Let's Stop Wasting Our Greatest Resources." *Saturday Evening Post,* March 2, 1957, pp. 19; 108–111.

3. "Mobilization Highlights." *Journal of Health, Physical Education and Recreation,* 22:2 (February, 1951), 9.
4. "Physical Fitness Achievement Standards for Youth." *Journal of Health, Physical Education and Recreation,* 22:5 (May, 1951), 13.
5. Hans Kraus and Ruth P. Hirschland. "Muscular Fitness and Health." *Journal of Health, Physical Education and Recreation,* 24:10 (December, 1953), 17–18.
6. "A Fit Week for a Second Look." *Sports Illustrated,* May 26, 1958, pp. 37; 38–39; 38.
7. Sonya Weber. "Kraus-Weber Tests." *Pennsylvania Journal of Health, Physical Education and Recreation,* September, 1956, pp. 14–15.
8. Paul Hunsicker. "Physical Fitness Tests." *Journal of Health, Physical Education and Recreation,* 28:7 (September, 1957), 21.
9. Paul A. Hunsicker. *A.A.H.P.E.R. Youth Fitness Manual.* Youth Fitness Project, A.A.H.P.E.R., Washington, D.C., 1958, pp. 1–3; 15.
10. Marjorie Phillips. "How Fit Are Our American School Children?" *Journal of Health, Physical Education and Recreation,* 26:6 (September, 1955), 14.
11. Don Boydston and Ross Merrick. "Basic Issues." *Journal of Health, Physical Education and Recreation,* 28:3 (March, 1957), 58.
12. Leonard A. Larson, Morey R. Fields, and Milton Gabrielson. *Problems in Health, Physical and Recreation Education.* New York: Prentice-Hall, Inc., 1953, pp. 13–16.
13. Dorothy S. Ainsworth. "Broadening Our Horizons. International Relations in Health, Physical Education and Recreation." *The Physical Educator,* 8:3 (October, 1951), 65.
14. *1st Annual Peace Corps Report.* Peace Corps, Washington, D.C., pp. 4–5.
15. Raymond A. Ciszek. "A New Dimension in International Relations for the Profession." *Journal of Health–Physical Education–Recreation,* 33:9 (December, 1962), 17–19.
16. James H. Humphrey. "The Status of Elementary School Physical Education." *The Physical Educator,* 10:2 (May, 1953), 43.
17. Elsa Schneider. "Highlights from the Study of the Status of Physical Education for Children of Elementary School Age in City School Systems." *Journal of Health, Physical Education and Recreation,* 31:2 (February, 1960), 21.
18. Karl W. Bookwalter. "National Survey of Health and Physical Education in High Schools, 1950–1954." Bureau of School Services and Research, School of Health, Physical Education and Recreation, Indiana University, 1955. (Mimeo., 32 pages)

19. Harold J. Cordts. "Status of the Physical Education Required or Instructional Programs for Men and Women in the Four-Year Colleges and Universities of the United States." *Proceedings,* The College Physical Education Association, 1959, pp. 43–49.
20. Ramon W. Kireielis. "Meeting Problems Created by Increased Enrollments Through the Use of Proficiency Examinations." *Proceedings,* The College Physical Education Association, 1958, p. 33.
21. S. C. Staley. "The Illinois Story." *Journal of Health, Physical Education and Recreation,* 28:7 (October, 1957), 15.
22. C. H. McCloy. "A Planned Physical Education Program? Or What Would You Like Today?" *The Physical Educator,* 10:2 (May, 1953), 41. Thomas K. Cureton. "How to Get the Physical Fitness Ingredient into Sport Education—To Improve in Sports Fitness." *Proceedings,* The College Physical Education Association, 1957, pp. 286–287. Ray O. Duncan. "The Great Debate of 1953." *The Physical Educator,* 11:1 (March, 1954), 7–8.
23. Raymond A. Snyder. "Interpreting Physical Education to the Several Faculties." *Proceedings,* The College Physical Education Association, 1958, p. 238.
24. N. H. Rogers. "The Meaning of Outdoor Education." *The Physical Educator,* 13:3 (October, 1956), 94–96.
25. Elizabeth S. Avery. "Health Education Steps Forward." *Journal of Health, Physical Education and Recreation,* 26:5, 6 (May–June, 1955), 25.
26. Harold D. Meyer and Charles K. Brightbill. *Recreation Administration—A Guide to its Practice.* Englewood Cliffs, N.J.: Prentice-Hall, Inc., 1956, pp. 218–219.
27. *Recreation as a Profession in the Southern Region.* (A Joint Publication of the National Recreation Association and the Southern Regional Education Board, 1952–1954.) New York: National Recreation Association, Inc., 1955.
28. Carl Nordly. "The Evaluation and Accreditation of Institutions Engaged in Professional Preparation in Health Education, Physical Education and Recreation." *Proceedings,* The College Physical Education Association, 1952, pp. 42–48.
29. *Professional Preparation in Health Education, Physical Education and Recreation.* American Association for Health, Physical Education and Recreation, Washington, D.C., 1962. Arthur A. Esslinger. "Professional Preparation Conference." *Journal of Health–Physical Education–Recreation,* 33:5 (May–June, 1962), 20–21.

APPENDIX: PROFESSIONAL ORGANIZATIONS

AMERICAN ASSOCIATION FOR HEALTH, PHYSICAL EDUCATION, AND RECREATION

William G. Anderson, director of physical education at both Yale University and Adelphi Academy, Brooklyn, conceived the idea of a national association to represent professional workers interested in physical education.[1] In 1885 Dr. Anderson invited his colleagues and friends of the profession to meet at Adelphi Academy, and Dr. Edward Hitchock was appointed chairman of a steering committee to consider the feasibility of such an organization. The committee recommended the formation of the American Association for the Advancement of Physical Education and Dr. Hitchcock was elected the first president.

At the second meeting of the Association in 1886 a constitution was adopted which stated that the purpose of the organization was "to disseminate knowledge concerning physical education, to improve methods, and . . . to bring those interested in the subject into closer relation with each other." The first constitution left the Association dependent upon its annual meeting for existence, and the leadership felt that a better relationship should be fostered between the Association and the various physical education societies organized in municipalities. Drs. Hitchcock, Sargent, and Gulick, who had been invited to attend the festivities of the North American Gymnastic Union in 1893, were impressed with the basic structure of this organization. Its strength and operation rested upon the activity of its local societies. A second constitution was adopted by the Association in 1895 which established ten regional sections, such as the New England, Mississippi Valley, and Southern sections with headquarters respectively in Boston, St. Louis, and New Orleans. Each of these regional sections was to be organized according to the plan of the Association, except that the National Council retained legislative power. In 1896 the Association had a total of 661 professional and affiliated members.

At the turn of the century Dr. Gulick and other professional leaders felt that the NAGU plan of organization did not provide adequate representation for the smaller societies. Dr. Sargent suggested that the Association copy the organization of the American Association for the Advancement of Science, which had been in successful operation for some fifty years. A new constitution was adopted at the Detroit convention in 1903 and the name changed to the American Physical Education Association. Although the new constitution provided for better representation, the problem of assigning voting power to local societies* and the necessity of a mail vote to choose officers led to many difficulties. A new constitution adopted in 1907 transferred legislative power to the National Council. This official body consisted of one representative from each society with ten active members in the Association, presidents of the sections (districts), past presidents of the National Council, the editor of the professional magazine, three members-at-large, and five members elected by the National Council. The new constitution made provisions for special interest groups and local and affiliated societies. Some of these were the Society of College Gymnasium Directors (1897), Secondary School Society (1902), Public School Physical Training Society (1904), and Therapeutic Section (1905).[2]

The Growth of a Profession

The interest in health and physical education at the close of World War I, the expansion of professional preparation, and the general prosperity stimulated the growth of the Association. Con-

* Some of the early local societies included the Bridgeport and Providence Societies of Physical Education (1895), Providence (1895), Boston, Springfield, New York City, and Philadelphia (1896), and Hartford (1897).

stitutional revisions in 1930 established the pattern of organization for the districts and favored the formation of state associations. By 1935 the districts consisted of the Eastern (New England, 1899, and Eastern, 1919), Central and Midwest (formed from the Middle West [1912] in 1934), Southern (1928), Northwest (1931), and Southwest (1935). The state and district associations followed the general organization as outlined in the constitution of the Association. This era witnessed the publication of many state and district newsletters and bulletins, and the professional magazine added state news reported by districts.

The membership of the National Council as well as the Legislative Council had often discussed the desirability of an affiliation with the National Education Association. In 1936 Agnes Wayman, president of the APEA, and Agnes Samuelson, president of the NEA, held several conferences on the subject of affiliation, and the details were worked out at the St. Louis convention of the APEA. In 1937 the Association was officially merged with the Department of School Health and Physical Education of the NEA. The APEA changed its name to the American Association for Health and Physical Education and a year later added "Recreation" to the title. In keeping with the change of title the AAHPER created the divisions of Health, Physical Education, and Recreation, each with its own head called a vice president. The twenty-three sections of the AAHPER were assembled, as far as possible, under the three divisions, and where various interest groups defied classification were placed in a General Division with the president-elect as chairman.[3]

In 1941 the Association moved to simplify its structural organization and reorganize its executive and legislative branch to conform with that of the NEA. The Executive Committee and the Legislative Council became the Board of Directors and the Representative Assembly respectively. Membership on the Representative Assembly was reorganized on an equitable basis for executive officers, sections, affiliated organizations, and states. In 1949 a reorganization plan was adopted which reduced the twenty-nine sections to twenty-four and combined some of them in the General Division. In 1952 divisions were made more functional by delegating more responsibility to the chairman and vice presidents, and in 1953 the stated aims of the association were revised to meet social and professional changes. The Men's Athletic Division was established on a tentative basis in 1954–1955 and the Division of Girls and Women's Sports in 1956, and both were granted permanent status in 1958. The Division of Safety and Driver Education received approval in 1959 by the Representative Assembly, and the Research Council became a section in the General Division.

The growing complexity of the Association and the increased demand upon executive officers and for additional services resulted in the appointment to the national staff of two associate and one assistant executive secretaries and special consultants in health education and international relations. At the close of the last decade the Puerto Rican Association of Health, Physical Education and Recreation made a bid for affiliation and was included in the organization of the Eastern District, and the Hawaiian AAHPER was placed in the Southwest District.[4]

PROFESSIONAL PUBLICATIONS

Prior to 1896 reports from the Association were issued from year to year. In 1896 the *American Physical Education Review* was edited in two issues by Edward Hitchock and his editorial committee, consisting of George W. Fitz and Ray Greene Huling. The next year the *Review* was printed quarterly and continued on this basis until 1908, when it was published in nine issues. George Fitz served as editor during 1900, 1904, and 1905, and Dr. Gulick in 1901, 1902, and 1903. James H. McCurdy, Springfield College, served as editor of the *Review* and secretary of the APEA from 1906 to 1929. As Dr. McCurdy stated in 1909, he intended the *Review* to present, first, the latest information on physical education and, second, as much material on related areas as was practical.

In 1929 Dr. McCurdy resigned as editor and secretary after twenty-four years of faithful service. The Association had just negotiated a merger between the *Review* and the *Pentathlon,* a publication of the Middle West District. The capable editor of the district publication, E. D. Mitchell, assumed the editorship of the new *Journal of Health and Physical Education* in 1930. Under Dr. Mitchell the *Journal* carried advertising on a larger scale, included many theoretical and practical articles, and featured news items on the state and national level. The growth of graduate education and the interest in tests and measurements in the 1920s produced far more articles than Dr. McCurdy could hope to accommodate in the *Review*. The Association in 1930 felt that the interest in research should be encouraged and initiated the *Research Quarterly*.[5]

In 1949 the *Journal* changed its title to the *Journal of the American Association for Health, Physical Education and Recreation*. This title was found to be somewhat cumbersome and in 1955 was changed to the *Journal of Health–Physical Education–Recreation* (JOHPER). The problem of meeting the current interest in the fields of health, physical education, and recreation continued to plague the editors of the *Journal*. Reports from the national and district conventions alone produced enough copy for nine issues of the *Journal* and the four publications of the *Research Quarterly*. Selection of material for publication, therefore, becomes increasingly difficult for both editorial boards.

As a department of the NEA, sharing its resources, the AAHPER not only extended its opportunity to work with other educational organizations but also expanded the Association's field of publications. Through the assistance of the NEA, the Association published its first convention proceedings in 1940, and the cooperation of the NEA made possible the printing of 10,000 guides for the National Section for Girls and Women's Sports (DGWS). The AAHPER published its first book, *Research Methods Applied to Health, Physical Education and Recreation*, in 1949 and its first yearbook, *Developing Democratic Human Relations Through Health Education, Physical Education and Recreation*, in 1951. The Association has ventured into many new areas of publication, such as *Physical Education for High School Students* (1955), reports of many joint committee meetings and lists of printed materials for sale by the AAHPER. In addition, valuable assistance has been rendered to the profession by the Athletic Institute, which has provided financial support for important conferences and the publication of conference reports.

THE GULICK AWARD

At the fall meeting of New York Physical Education Society in 1904 Luther H. Gulick proposed that a cash prize be given the author of the best article published each year on physical education.

After Dr. Gulick's death in 1918 George J. Fisher proposed that the New York Society award annually the Gulick Medallion for Distinguished Service to a worthy professional leader. R. Tait McKenzie was asked to execute the die for the medallion, and the design agreed upon depicted the bust of a young man bearing an olive branch in one hand and wearing a victory wreath on his head.

The first award was presented posthumously to Luther H. Gulick, and accepted by his widow at a special meeting at the Waldorf-Astoria Hotel in 1923. The Gulick Award was given to Jessie H. Bancroft (1924), Thomas D. Wood (1925), Thomas A. Storey (1926), Clark W. Hetherington (1928), and George J. Fisher (1929). The Award Committee became inoperative for a number of years, and in 1938 the Health Teachers Association took over the presentation, and the Award was given to Jesse F. Williams in 1939 and Jay B. Nash in 1940.

In 1943 Jay B. Nash, Secretary of the New York Society of Physical Education, informed the AAHPER that the members of the Society by unanimous consent granted the Association the privilege of presenting the annual Gulick Award. An interest-bearing fund started originally by Dr. Gulick was transferred and the right to use the die designed by R. Tait McKenzie granted the AAHPER. The Association established a standing committee to draw up a code of operation for the selection of potential candidates. The newly organized committee granted its first award to Charles H. McCloy (1944). To be eligible for the Gulick Award a candidate must be at least thirty-five years of age, and his contributions should be in the fields of health, physical education, and recreation.[6]

HONOR AWARD FELLOWS

The Association inaugurated the Honor Award Fellows in 1931. Honor Award Fellows are elected annually by the Award Committee and recognized with a Certificate of Honor. Candidates for this honor are selected by the members of the AAHPER and their names and qualifications forwarded to the committee in their particular district for screening.

A candidate to be eligible must be a member of the AAHPER and at least forty years of age, have a master's degree or its equivalent in study, have ten years of experience in some phase of health, physical education, and recreation, and be of good character. A candidate must show evidence of leadership in five of a list of fourteen different categories, such as office-holder in the AAHPER, section chairmanship in the District or National Association, presidency in the state, district, national associations, or the CPEA, committee work, addresses on health, physical education and recreation, publications, and other accomplishments.

WILLIAM G. ANDERSON SERVICE AWARD

The Anderson Award is presented annually to the person or persons who best exemplify William G. Anderson's philosophy of service to his profession and to mankind. The Award was initiated in 1948.

Any member of the AAHPER may nominate a candidate and send his selection to the district committee. A candidate must be at least forty years of age, and his contributions should have been made within the fields of health, physical education, or recreation or to the advancement of the profession through allied fields such as education, science, and others. Above all, the candidate must be of high moral character, and his contributions or service must express the spirit of professional devotion represented by the founder of the AAHPER. Miss Mazie V. Scanlan, supervisor of physical education in the elementary and junior high schools of Atlantic City, was granted the first William G. Anderson Service Award in 1948–1949.

FELLOW MEMBER OF THE AAHPER

The classification of Fellow Member is available to all members of the AAHPER who maintain five years' continuous membership, show evidence of professional status and service, and who secure three endorsements as specified by the AAHPER. The data on the application form are filed in the National Office to assist in the determination of eligibility for conferences, committee membership, and special responsibilities. These data are also useful in furnishing committees on awards and recognition, honorary degrees, and overseas assignments with additional information on the candidate's qualifications. The Fellow Member is a membership classification and is not to be confused with the Honor Award Fellow, who is selected by the AAHPER Honor Awards Committee.

AFFILIATED ORGANIZATIONS OF THE AAHPER

According to the constitution the term "organization" refers to the type of official service rendered by that body. In most instances these organizations originate outside the Association, yet their purpose is very closely allied to that of the AAHPER. An organization originally connected with the Association may have through aggressive leadership and expansion of service attained independent status, only to return to the AAHPER as an affiliated organization. This was the pattern of the National Intramural Association. In some cases an organization may seek affiliation with the AAHPER, be approved, and then withdraw. This occurred in the case of the American Physical Therapy Association, which is affiliated with the American Medical Association. In any case an organization may petition the Representative Assembly for affiliation thirty days prior to its meeting. The petition should include title, purpose, and officers, a copy of the minutes of its last regular meeting, and a list of its members who are also members of the AAHPER.

AMERICAN ACADEMY OF PHYSICAL EDUCATION

As early as 1904 F. Tait McKenzie, Luther H. Gulick, C. W. Hetherington, Wilbur P. Bowen, Ward H. Crampton, Fred E. Leonard, George L. Meylan, Paul C. Phillips, Dudley A. Sargent, and Thomas A. Storey participated in the founding of a professional society. This organization, representing some of the profession's great leaders, was called the Academy of Physical Education Society, but had no constitution, officers, dues, or election to membership. The members met annually the day after Labor Day for a week at Drs. Meylan's and Gulick's camp at Lake Sebago, Maine. The "Academy" ceased to function when the United States entered World War I.

In 1926 C. W. Hetherington, R. Tait McKenzie, William Burdick, Thomas A. Storey, and Jay B. Nash formed the more permanent American Academy of Physical Education, which had a definite operational plan. The first five charter members elected five more distinguished professional leaders, and this process continued with the exception of one year, until 1930, at which time the membership had reached twenty-nine. These members became known as the "Charter Fellows" and as a group adopted a constitution and by-laws. The constitution states that the purpose of the Academy is to advance knowledge in the field of physical education and to maintain and uphold its honor. The types of membership include Fellows, the active members who constitute the governing body; Fellows in Memoriam, deceased members who rendered exceptional service; Corresponding Fellows, members in foreign countries who have made outstanding contributions; and Associate Fellows, members from related fields who have rendered meritorious service.[7]

In 1937 the Academy broke precedent when it established the Committee on Awards, which presented the Award of the Academy at its annual meeting to the physical educator who had distinguished himself in the field. The 1937 Award was presented to R. Tait McKenzie for his contribution to American art and athletic sculpture and his creation of the Column of Youth which served as the model for the seal of the AAHPER. Nominations for the Award are solicited from the membership of the Association, and anyone is free to recommend an individual or group of individuals doing exceptional work in health, physical education, and recreation.

The Academy does most of its work through committees and commissions. The committees perform the Academy's necessary functions, and the commissions represent it in its relationships with other agencies or professional groups. For instance, the Committee on International Relationship maintains contact with professional leadership in foreign countries, while the Commissions on Definition, Plans, and Procedure cooperates with other professional groups to attain the Academy's objectives.[8]

AMERICAN COLLEGE OF SPORTS MEDICINE

The basis of the American College of Sports Medicine was laid fifty years ago by foreign physicians who turned their attention to the medical aspects of exercise and sports competition (see Chapter 11, under "Germany"). Informal meetings of physicians interested in sports medicine were held in the United States in the early 1950s. By 1954 sufficient interest warranted the organization of the American Federation of Sports Medicine. That same year the Federation participated in the fifty-eighth Annual Convention of the AAHPER, and Drs. Ernst Jokl and Jacob B. Wolfe of the Valley Forge Heart Institute and Hospital conducted the meeting. In 1955 the organization was incorporated as the American College of Sports Medicine.

Its purpose is to promote the scientific study of the effect of sports and other motor activities upon the health of human beings, cooperate with other organizations and agencies interested in physical fitness, sponsor meetings with professional men whose work and research have a relationship to the organization's objectives, encourage graduate study in the field, and correlate and publish research. The American College of Sports Medicine is interested in more than health for its own sake, including the prevention and treatment of sports injuries, physical conditioning, rehabilitation, body mechanics, and other related areas.

AMERICAN SCHOOL HEALTH ASSOCIATION

At the annual meeting of the American Public Health Association (1872) held in Cincinnati, Ohio, in 1927, Dr. William A. Howe, a tireless worker in the cause of the health of schoolchildren, organized the American Association of School Physicians. The Association's official publication was the *School Physicians Bulletin* (1930), which was mailed to some 325 school physicians in the United States. Dr. Howe served as the first president and Dr. L. W. Childs of the Cleveland Public Schools as secretary. During the next decade Dr. Howe served as secretary-treasurer and editor of the *Bulletin*.

As the status of school health service improved, school dentists and nurses and representatives of nonmedical organizations became regular participants in the annual meetings. During the presidency of Dr. John Sundwall, of the University of Michigan, in 1936, the constitution was changed to encompass not only medical personnel but also school health workers whose professional preparation included premedical sciences. The name was changed to the American

School Health Association, and its official publication was called the *Journal of School Health.* The purpose of the Association as stated in the constitution is "to promote comprehensive and constructive school health programs, including health instruction, health service and healthful school living." In 1938 the Association reached an agreement with the Child Hygiene Section of the American Public Health Association as to the division of program content and that same year applied to become affiliated with the APHA. Since then the American School Health Association has held its annual meetings in conjunction with the parent body. Through the years an excellent working relationship has existed between the ASHA, AAHPER, and APHA.

William A. Howe passed away on September 10, 1940, and in recognition of his services the American School Health Association established the William A. Howe Award. A committee selects a recipient each year who has rendered distinguished service in school health for the children and youth of America. The first Award was given to Dr. Howe posthumously and accepted by his widow. Since then the Howe Award has been received mainly by physicians, with a few doctors of public health and school nurses.[9]

AMERICAN YOUTH HOSTELS, INCORPORATED

Since the restoration of the twelfth-century castle as the first youth hostel in 1910 by Richard Schirrman at Altena, Germany, the youth hostel movement has touched practically every European country. The first youth hostel was established in the United States by Isabel and Monroe Smith at Northfield, Massachusetts, in 1934. The following year the Smiths were influential in the organization of the American Youth Hostel Association. The Association immediately joined the International Youth Hostel Federation, which then had a membership of seventeen foreign countries. The movement was assisted by the National Park Service, which helped to establish thirty-six hostels about fifteen miles apart over 400 miles of trails through the White and Green Mountains in New England. An official ceremony celebrating the founding of the Association was held on the campus of Mt. Holyoke College in 1935.

Approximately ten years after its founding the AYHA, with the assistance of local individuals and state and federal agencies, had established 250 youth hostels in the United States. The handbook provided the membership during this era contained information regarding hostel accommodations, names of house parents, facilities available, and points of interest along the way. Attached maps showed the approximate locations of hostels and routes to be followed through the Great Smoky and Ozark Mountains, around the Great Lakes, over picturesque Pennsylvania's Horseshoe Trails, along California's West Coast and New England's countryside.[10]

In 1947 the American Youth Hostels, Inc., moved its headquarters from Northfield to New York, and in 1948 Ben W. Miller resigned his position as executive secretary of the AAHPER to become director of the New York organization. A new program was inaugurated in which the AYHA sought to work in closer cooperation with schools and recreation and youth service agencies. The purpose of the present organization is to help young people develop an appreciation for the beauty and vastness of their native land and a better understanding of the peoples of the world through outdoor education and recreational travel. In 1950 the AYH sponsored twenty-seven different itineraries which included hosteling in nineteen European countries. In 1957 it sponsored twenty-two trips in North and Central America, Europe and the Far East.[11] The official publication is *Hosteling,* a quarterly magazine first published in 1950.

ASSOCIATION FOR PHYSICAL AND MENTAL REHABILITATION

The Associiation for Physical and Mental Rehabilitation was formally organized in October, 1946, by a group of corrective therapists attending a special course of instruction at the Veterans Administration Hospital, Topeka, Kansas. This organization was a natural outgrowth of the corrective physical rehabilitation developed and organized during and after World War II. The majority of the corrective therapists pursue their profession in Veterans Administration Hospitals. Their principles and methods, however, have application to the physical education program in public and private schools, colleges and universities, special schools and camps for the handicapped and atypical child, public and private rehabilitation centers, clinics and hospitals and nursing homes, recreational programs for the handicapped, and members of research teams.

The purpose of the Association is to promote medically prescribed exercise therapy, advance professional standards, sponsor programs of a scientific and professional nature, encourage research and publication of articles concerned with medical rehabilitation, and participate in those activities which will prove advantageous to medical rehabilitation and/or the Association.

The Association provides scholarships for graduate training in adapted physical education, sponsors scientific and clinical conferences, and has developed an extensive literature in the field. The Association cooperates with colleges and universities in the organization of a curriculum for the corrective therapist and assists in the organization of institutes and seminars on a local, state or national basis. The American Board for the Certification of Corrective Therapists was established in 1953. Each year the Association presents awards, including the John E. Davis Award, Annual Corrective Therapy Award, Rehabilitation Achievement Award, Life Membership Award, Honorary Membership Award, and Fellow Award.[12]

BOYS' CLUBS OF AMERICA

The first boys' club was founded in 1860 at Hartford, Connecticut, by Mary and Alice Goodwin and Elizabeth Hammersley. The original club was operated under voluntary leadership, and its program consisted of recreational games, reading, dramatics, music, and gymnastics done to music. The activities came to a halt during the Civil War and were resumed in 1868 as the Sixth Ward Temperance Society. In the same year the Union of Christian Work of Providence, Rhode Island, provided a room where boys could meet and took the name of the Providence Boys' Club. From these initial starts other boys' clubs were organized in Salem (1869) and New Bedford (1870), New Haven (1872), and New York (1876). Between 1880 and 1890 the movement spread to the West and boys' clubs were founded in Milwaukee (1887) and San Francisco (1891).

For years the boys' clubs operated on a loosely cooperative basis, and it was not until 1906 that the independent groups were drawn together in the Federated Boys' Club. In 1915 the name was changed to the Boys' Club Federation, to include similar oganizations in Australia, Canada, Holland, and the United Kingdom. Canada and England established a separate federation in 1929, and the United States members were consolidated into the Boys' Clubs of America in 1941.

Ever since their beginning the boys clubs have been interested in boys of low-income families, and the clubs are located mainly in urban areas where poverty, broken homes, truancy, and other social problems are greatest. Boys' Clubs of America has as its purpose the development of the social, physical, moral, educational, and vocational attributes of the adolescent. The affairs of the Boys' Club are administered by a board of directors composed of citizens in the community who serve without compensation. The organization is nonpolitical and nonsectarian, and draws its financial support from public contributions, endowments, and membership fees. The typical Boys' Club has a membership of 1000 ranging from 8 to 21 years of age. In 1946 the Boys' Clubs of America had a membership of 268 clubs with 250,000 boys, and ten years later had grown to 500 clubs representing forty-eight states.

Their program is based on the natural desires and interests of the growing boy, available facilities, and type of community. Common activities include games, sports and recreation, health education instruction, cultural projects, handicrafts and vocational classes, group clubs, leadership groups, parties and entertainment, and camping. The Boys' Clubs of America has recently inaugurated a $50,000 youth research project to determine the basic needs and interests of 14–18-year-old boys, since boys in this age bracket are the most difficult to attract and to work with in a sustained program.[13]

CANADIAN PHYSICAL EDUCATION ASSOCIATION

Physical educators in Canada formerly maintained membership in the AAHPER, and in 1930 the Association extended the privilege of provincial representation to the Quebec Physical Education Association. In 1933 Dr. A. S. Lamb, with the financial assistance of McGill University and the moral and professional support of the

Toronto Physical Education Association, established the Canadian Physical Education Association.

From the time of its founding the Canadian Association conducted biannual conventions and in 1944 held the first national convention at Winnipeg with all nine provinces represented. The constitution states that the purpose of the organization is to stimulate an active interest in health, physical education, and recreation, acquire and disseminate knowledge in these fields, establish programs under adequately trained personnel, establish professional standards, and cooperate with kindred organizations to further the objectives of the Association. The official publication is the *Canadian Physical Education Assocciation Bulletin.* The first issues appeared in mimeographed form in 1933, and it was edited as a magazine in 1937. As in the state associations of the AAHPER, the various provinces publish newsletters and bulletins.

During its brief existence the Canadian Association has accomplished much. The national and provincial organizations assisted in the establishment of local fitness programs in cooperation with the National Fitness Council. As an official body the Canadian Association urged the granting of certification to graduates of schools of physical education and convinced the provinces that scholarships should be granted to train personnel. The women's section has been active in establishing standards and policies in sports for girls and women and has been in close cooperation with the DGWS of the AAHPER. At the request of the National Fitness Council, a research Committee was appointed to formulate a scientific program of tests and measurement, investigate the problems of teacher and leadership training, prepare national standards for evaluating swimming and lifesaving skills, and review the data secured from the Youth Commission's Survey on Recreation.[14]

COLLEGE PHYSICAL EDUCATION ASSOCIATION

William G. Anderson, Dudley A. Sargent, J. W. Seaver, C. P. Linhart, W. L. Savage, George Goldie, F. W. Marvel, F. H. Cann, and a Mr. Sharp (or Shay) of Yale, met on November 6, 1897, in New York City to discuss an organization to further the cause of physical education in higher institutions. The meeting resulted in the founding of the Society of College Gymnasium Directors. In 1909 the title was changed to the Society of Directors of Physical Education, and in 1933 the present name was adopted. The purpose of the organization is the advancement of all phases of health and physical education in higher institutions. These areas include the required program, volunteer recreational activities, intramural athletics, intercollegiate athletics, teacher preparation in health and physical education, administration of health and physical education and health service, supervision and instruction. From its organization until 1930 the CPEA depended upon the *American Physical Education Review* to publish its addresses and committee reports. Thereafter the CPEA published its annual proceedings, which include the traditional president's address, minutes of the business meeting, committee reports, papers delivered, and membership roll.

From the very beginning the CPEA has conducted important studies through standing committees on many phases of physical education. The first major committee report was on the standardization of strength tests in colleges and universities. As an outgrowth of this study, R. Tait McKenzie was asked to develop a statuette of a strong man in characteristic pose. Other early projects included the Committee on Terminology, to clarify terms used in the profession, and the Committee on Construction and Material Equipment, which gathered plans and detailed description of college and university gymnasiums to be later deposited at Hamilton College, Clinton, New York.

One of the important committees from the standpoint of its contributions to the profession as a whole and its longevity was the Committee on Curriculum Research. The Committee on the Relation of College Physical Education to National Preparedness in 1940 recommended the organization of a Committee on Physical Education and Athletics to foster closer professional relationships with athletic interests. This step was not possible until the close of World War II, when a committee was formed with representatives from the AAHPER, the National Collegiate Athletic Association, and CPEA. Since then CPEA has participated in many joint committee projects which have had important professional significance.[15]

DELTA PSI KAPPA

The Delta Psi Kappa is a professional fraternity for women in health, physical education, and recreation. The organization was founded in 1916 at the Normal College of the North American Gymnastic Union (later affiliated with Indiana University) in Indianapolis. Its purpose is to recognize worthy women majors in physical education and develop greater fellowship among women in health, physical education, and recreation. The fraternity currently has thirty-one chapters in colleges and universities in the United States. Alumni associations are located in Chicago, Dallas, Indianapolis, Los Angeles, Newark, and Philadelphia. The official publication is the *Foil,* which is issued semiannually.

Delta Psi Kappa sponsors national projects to which all members contribute. Local chapters also carry out projects on their own, such as institutes in health, physical education and recreation in schools, radio and television programs, recreational nights, and play or sports days. Delta Psi Kappa is a member of the Professional Panhellenic Association, which has as its objective the promotion of high professional standards, mutual service and cooperation among professional women, and the extension of professional opportunities for women. The fraternity provides an Educational Loan Fund and established a Research Fellowship Fund in 1940 from which grants are given each year to professional women who are conducting studies of merit.[16]

NATIONAL ASSOCIATION FOR PHYSICAL EDUCATION OF COLLEGE WOMEN

The Association of Directors of Physical Education for Women was founded in March, 1910, when Miss Amy Morris Homans, of the department of hygiene, Wellesley College, invited women teachers and presidents of athletic associations in the New England colleges for women to convene at her institution. After the initial meeting the group met informally for the next four years. Since the membership had grown considerably during the interim, the Association decided to set up a more permanent organization with the members limited to administrative heads of departments of physical education.

A committee was appointed in 1914 to draft a constitution and a secretary was appointed. The first constitution was approved in 1916 at the Association meeting at Pratt Institute, Brooklyn. The purpose of the organization as stated in the constitution is "to discuss the problems of the organization and administration of departments of physical education in colleges and by definite cooperation, study, experimental and research work, broaden and increase the usefulness of such departments." Its title became the Society of Directors of Physical Education in Colleges for Women.

Impressed by the Society's activities in the New England colleges, the women directors of physical education in the Midwest convened at the University of Chicago in 1917 for the purpose of organizing a similar group. A constitution was drawn up which was patterned after the New England Society. A western society was established in Oakland, California, in 1921 and a constitution adopted at the next meeting, held in Eugene, Oregon. At the APEA convention at Kansas City in 1924, the three regional societies joined to form the National Association of Physical Education for College Women. In 1935 the women directors of physical education in colleges and universities of the Southern District formed the Southern Association of Directors of Physical Education for College Women and were immediately affiliated with the National Association.

In 1937 the Society developed a comprehensive plan of organization. Long-range planning committees were established in research, finance, public relations, and publications. At the close of World War II it changed its title to the present one, created a placement service for women graduates in health, physical education, and recreation, and furthered inter-American goodwill by offering scholarships to girls in Central and South America for study in professional schools in the United States. Since 1947 the National Association has conducted workshops to improve the status of physical education for women in colleges and universities and participated in many joint committee projects in health, physical education, and recreation.[17]

NATIONAL BOARD OF THE YWCA OF THE UNITED STATES

Prior to World War I the YWCA placed considerable emphasis upon the physical education program and was influential in the introduction of physical education for girls and women in foreign countries. At the sixth convention of the National Young Women's Christian Association, held in 1920, the organization endorsed the health program of the Bureau of Social Education of the National Board. The Bureau recommended that a Department of Health Education be formed, that medical examinations be required of all girls and women before they participate in athletic activities, and that part-time or full-time physicians be employed on local YWCA staffs.

The emphasis on health education originated in the work of the Bureau of Social Education War Work Council in promoting the Girls' Health League. Membership in the League entitled a girl to a physical examination by a woman physician, advice about nutrition and exercise, and instruction in games and sports. The interest in health education led the YWCA to pioneer in health examinations and in the establishment of minimum standards in this area. In recent years the National Board has concentrated on follow-up work.

The YWCA has promoted the concept of democracy within the Association, the social environment, and the world community. Its objectives include helping a girl maintain health and physical vigor in order to meet her responsibilities in the home, office, or factory. In each association the health director, with an advisory committee, is responsible for discovering the health needs of the young women in their community and for setting up a program to meet them.

In 1947 the YWCA employed 400 health education leaders, some of whom were sent to foreign countries to assist in the establishment of programs. The minimum requirements of YWCA workers is a bachelor's degree in health, physical education, and recreation, and an advanced degree is desirable. The National Board provides annual orientation courses, which are generally given during the summer months, and local staff members are encouraged to further their educations if facilities are available. The National Board publishes *The Women's Press* and *The Bookshelf,* as well as four issues of *Program Package* each year, which serve as an aid in program planning for the staff and volunteer workers.[18]

NATIONAL COMMITTEE FOR HEALTH AND PHYSICAL EDUCATION OF THE NATIONAL ASSOCIATION OF JEWISH CENTER WORKERS

The early Jewish neighborhood centers had their origin in agencies founded to provide religious education. These Hebrew mission schools were philanthropies and tended to be included among those dependent upon charity. The fact that they also tended to Americanize Jewish immigrants by submerging Jewish cultural activities, traditions, and interests was offensive to a large segment of the race. In reaction to this, in 1890, the Russian Jews founded the Jewish Alliance, with branches in the principal cities of the United States. This organization helped locate the Jewish immigrant in American cities and established Hebrew Literary Societies which not only helped assimilate the immigrant but also operated democratically under a positive Jewish policy. These Societies later formed the nucleus of the Young Men's and Young Women's Hebrew Associations (See Chapter 17).

At about the same time the Russian Jews formed the Jewish Alliance, interested Jews established the Federations of Jewish Charities, which devoted their energy to the promotion of Jewish activities. By 1915 a total of forty-seven Federations existed in the United States, which moved to consolidate functions and construct buildings to accommodate such organizations as the YMHA, YWHA, the B'nai B'rith, and other lodges. These buildings soon became recognized as "Jewish Educational Centers," "Jewish Social Centers," and community and communal centers. In practice, however, these institutions were very remote from community centers and more nearly resembled the Jewish settlement type of organization. The Council of Men's Hebrew and Kindred Associations, established in 1913, was the first modern American Jewish Community Center.[19]

In April, 1917, the Jewish Welfare Board was created to meet the needs of 250,000 young Jewish men who had served in World War

I. At the close of the war the Board assisted veterans to secure employment and make the necessary adjustments to civilian life. Since 1921 it has been a national agency for the YMHA, YWHA, and Jewish Community Centers in the United States. The National Board integrates these organizations into one nationwide enterprise.

The YMHA and YWHA generally serve as the focus of the activities of the Jewish Community Centers. Since their inception both the associations and community centers have employed physical educators. In their early history both were strongly influenced by the German system and its method of organization. They have kept pace with changing trends, and modern leadership is recruited from graduates of professional teacher-training institutions in the United States. The National Jewish Welfare Board reported in 1948 an affiliation of 321 Jewish Community Centers, which had 140 gymnasiums, 58 swimming pools, and 40 Health Clubs. The number of full-time professional personnel employed in the health and physical education departments of one hundred centers was 125.

In 1948 the National Board created and staffed a Department of Health and Physical Education which coordinates the national programs in the community centers. At the same time the National Health and Physical Education Committee was established to act as an advisory body to the Department. The National Committee has been active in the development of national programs and minimal standards for program planning, publication of manuals as guides, and the promotion of national athletic events.[20]

NATIONAL INTRAMURAL ASSOCIATION

Through the years intramural directors in secondary schools and colleges and universities have participated as a section within the state, district, and national organizations of the AAHPER. In addition, intramural directors of higher institutions have been active at the annual meetings of the CPEA and NCAA. At these meetings intramural directors formulated the philosophy and principles which have helped to guide the organization and administration of intramural athletics in educational institutions in the United States and Canada.

During the school year of 1948–1949 William Wasson, a teacher at Dillard University at New Orleans, received a Carnegie grant to study intramural athletic programs in Negro colleges. Wasson visited twenty-five colleges, whose intramural directors pointed out the need for a separate organization to permit the exchange of ideas and information on intramural athletics. With his colleagues, Wasson held the first organizational meeting at Dillard University in February, 1950, and founded the National Intramural Association.[21]

The purpose of the NIA is to encourage the exchange of ideas and to stimulate professional growth among its membership, promote the organization of intramural and recreational programs in educational institutions, publish general materials and research papers on intramural athletics, and foster cooperation with the AAHPER, CPEA, National Recreation Association, Educational Policy Committee, and other professional agencies. One of the first cooperative studies in which the NIA shared was the Conference on Intramural Sports for College Men and Women jointly sponsored in 1955 by the AAHPER, National Association of Physical Education for College Women, and CPEA.[22]

Phi Delta Pi

A national professional fraternity for women, Phi Delta Pi was founded in 1916 at the North American Gymnastic Union, Indianapolis. The fraternity provides a professional organization for women majors in health, physical education, and recreation, promotes the progressive development of physical education, and places emphasis on effective leadership. A group of women major students may organize a temporary chapter and elect officers and after due time apply for active status. The chapter must have a charter membership of not less than six and not more than eighteen members. The Phi Delta Pi has alumni chapters in Chicago, Indianapolis, Ithaca, New York, St. Louis, northern New Jersey, Philadelphia, Pittsburgh, Salt Lake City, and Los Angeles.

In 1934 the Phi Delta Pi sponsored a vacation camp for underprivileged girls at Camp Brosius, the summer camp of the North American Gymnastic Union at Elkhart Lake, Wisconsin. Since this time it has organized and financed similar camps at Whitcomb,

Wisconsin; Fulton County, New York; Salt Lake City, Utah; Medford, New Jersey; and conducted day camps in various cities. A Scholastic Loan Fund is available to needy professional students of high caliber. The fraternity also operates a magazine agency, whose income helps to finance camp projects. The Phi Delta Pi publishes the *Progressive Physical Educator,* which is issued semiannually, a triennial newsletter, and various booklets and pamphlets of professional interest.[23]

PHI EPSILON KAPPA

The Phi Epsilon Kappa, a fraternity, was founded on April 12, 1913, at the Normal College of the American Gymnastic Union for major students in physical education. The Alpha Chapter moved to Indiana University when the AGU became affiliated with the School of Health, Physical Education and Recreation of that institution. The purpose of the fraternity is to improve the general quality of professional work, provide a means through which students, faculty, and alumni can accomplish together the objectives of health, physical education, and recreation, raise the ideals, standards, and ethics of professional workers, insure life-long professional association of the members, and provide a fraternity for professional workers.

Prior to 1920 the Alpha Chapter confined its activity to the school environment at Indianapolis and after this date started a program of expansion which has established forty-one chapters in colleges and universities and seventeen alumni chapters in the major cities in the United States.

Chapters may be installed in colleges and universities which have a four-year major curriculum in physical education. An institution may organize a group with a minimum of fifteen major students, hold regular meetings for a year, and then petition for active status. Active affiliation is determined upon the basis of the professional and scholarly attainment of the membership. Phi Epsilon Kappa publishes the *Black and Gold, Pledge Manual,* and *Song Book and Ritual* for the use of the membership. The publication *The Physical Educator* is issued quarterly and has attained considerable professional stature through the years.[24]

PHYSICAL EDUCATION SOCIETY OF THE YMCA'S OF NORTH AMERICA

The Physical Education Society of the YMCA was established at Lakewood, New Jersey, in 1903. Its purpose, known as the "basic five," includes unification of professional workers in physical education, promotion of a fraternal spirit and fellowship, encouragement of original research, study of technical and professional problems, and cooperation with constituent or related agencies. The Physical Education Society holds separate triannual conventions, and between conventions business is carried on by an executive committee elected every three years by members in the state and area chapters. The professional organization is a part of the Association of Secretaries of the YMCA, which is a composite of all organizations represented in the YMCA. Although the Physical Education Society conducts its business separately, all physical directors must belong to the Association of Secretaries.

The Physical Education Society has made many valuable and lasting contributions to physical education, sports, and recreation not only in the United States but in some sixty foreign countries. An impressive list of members inaugurated camping in the United States and foreign countries, developed standards in anthropometric measurement, provided health service to businessmen's clubs, introduced playgrounds around the world, experimented with popular health and sex education instruction, organized the prototype of the Olympic Games in Asiatic countries, directed physical training programs in the armed forces, prepared trained leadership in the United States and foreign countries, trained aquatic leadership, organized programs in every phase of aquatics, and introduced the world to basketball, volleyball, and squash rackets.

The first conference of the YMCA physical directors leading to a permanent organization was held in 1902 at Jamestown, New York, and in the same year the magazine *Physical Training* was published. This magazine was later replaced by the bimonthly *Journal of Physical Education*. The Physical Education Society elects distinguished physical education directors annually to the Fellows of Physical Education, and the Roberts-Gulick Award (1925) is also presented yearly to the professional worker who has made outstanding contributions to physical education in the YMCA.[25]

SOCIETY OF STATE DIRECTORS OF HEALTH, PHYSICAL EDUCATION AND RECREATION

Informal meetings of state directors of health and physical education had been called in the early 1920s by Dana Cauklins of the National Recreation Association and Dr. James F. Rogers of the U.S. Office of Education. In December, 1926, James E. Rogers, of the National Physical Education Service, and Carl L. Schrader, Director of Health and Physical Education of the State of Massachusetts, invited state directors to meet in New York City to consider the organization of a society representing the interests of state directors. As a consequence, the Society of State Directors of Health and Physical Education was founded, with Dr. Schrader as president and James E. Rogers as secretary, in which capacity he served until 1940. In keeping with changes in the title of the national organization, the Society of State Directors added "Recreation" to its title.

The purpose of the Society of State Directors is to promote general appreciation and understanding of health, physical education, and recreation; establish programs in each state and keep active those which have been inaugurated; encourage a more cooperative relationship among professional personnel in health, physical education, and recreation; adopt wiser policies and procedures in state, interstate, and intersectional athletic contests; and foster professional and official efficiency among the members of the organization.

The Society has a record of noteworthy achievements. It has published timely studies and reports on its own or in conjunction with the American Association of School Administrators and the AAHPER. In 1924 the Society opposed interscholastic competition in football for elementary and junior high school boys and favored soccer as a substitute. In 1928 the organization went on record as opposed to Junior Olympic contests for boys and girls as well as national interscholastic competition in basketball for girls. In 1938 the Society led the way in eliminating boxing as an interscholastic sport, and the resultant publicity had a strong influence in decreasing the popularity of boxing as an intercollegiate and intramural sport in higher institutions. The Society has contributed many valuable studies to the profession through committee projects, including *The National Physical Achievement Standards for Boys, The National Physical Achievement Standards for Girls, Safety in Physical Education, The Scoring of Physical Education, Measuring the Program, Credit for Physical Education, Rural Physical Education, Physical Education and Athletics,* and *National Study of Professional Education in Health and Physical Education.*[26]

FÉDÉRATION INTERNATIONALE D'ÉDUCATION PHYSIQUE

European followers of the Ling system met in 1911 in Odense, Denmark, and formed the International Institute of Physical Education. The early organization included N. Sellen (Sweden) as president and Tissie (France), Meyers (the Netherlands), DeGenst (Belgium), and Knudsen (Denmark) as members. Through the years it became a sounding board for the theories and practice of the Ling system of gymnastics and a clearinghouse for research conducted independently of or in association with universities. At Brussels in 1923 the International Institute was absorbed by the newly established International Federation of Ling Gymnastics, which moved its headquarters to Sweden. Shortly thereafter, the title was changed to the International Federation of Physical Education (FIEP, from the French). In 1930 the FIEP published the *Bulletin de la Fédération Internationale D'Éducation Physique,* which contains specialized articles and news items of interest from professional leaders and organizations over the world. The *Bulletin* is published quarterly in six languages and has a distribution which includes sixty countries.

The purpose of the FIEP is to unite in common cause all those physical educators who consider that physical exercise is a means of physical education and that healthy recreation leads to the betterment of mankind. The organization also believes in the unification of international efforts to improve teacher preparation. It believes that this preparation, in general, should be implemented at the university level, hoping eventually to raise the status of physical education technicians to the same level as other pedagogical areas.

In 1959 the tenth session of the General Conference of UNESCO passed a resolution which suggested that the FIEP do all in its power to facilitate the coordination of the efforts of various international organizations related to physical education and sports. In the same year the FIEP collaborated with the newly organized International Council of Health, Physical Education and Recreation, a subdivision of the World Confederation of Organizations of the Teaching Profession (WCOTP). In the same spirit the FIEP has cooperated with the International Council of Physical Education and Sports of UNESCO. In 1960 the FIEP patronized the World Congress on Physical Education and Sports in Rome, which attracted specialists from fifty different countries. In the same year the FIEP supported the Luso-Brazilian Congress in Spain, to which Spain, Portugal, and the Latin-American countries sent representatives. The FIEP is a strong force in the promotion of international understanding among professional workers in physical education.[27]

THE PAN-AMERICAN INSTITUTE OF PHYSICAL EDUCATION

The foundations of the South American Conference of Physical Education Teachers Association were laid prior to World War I in what was then known as the Continental Convention of South American Associations. The charter members of the Conference held a second meeting in Buenos Aires in 1919 and decided to establish an amateur athletic union to regulate sports competition, publish sports rules and technical books, and promote a national interest in the folk dances of each member country.

The first Pan-American Congress of Physical Education was held in 1943 at Rio de Janeiro, its aim the general improvement and scientific orientation of physical education. The second conference was held in Mexico City in 1946, to discuss the problems of physical education and sports in Pan-American countries. Considering physical education a vital force for social justice and liberty, the members discussed ways and means whereby the bonds of friendship could be strengthened among the nations of the Western Hemisphere.

The Third Pan-American Congress of Physical Education was sponsored in 1950 by the Physical Education Commission of Uruguay. At this meeting, held in Montevideo, the title of the organization was changed to the Pan-American Institute of Physical Education. The South American professional leaders represented included Paul A. Previtalli and Carlos M. Barragan of Uruguay; Luis Bisquert, University of Chile; Major Jão Barbosa Leite, Brazil; and E. R. Brest of Argentina and president of the South American Conference of Physical Education Teachers Association. Dorothy Ainsworth, Hiawatha Crosslin, Norma Young, and C. H. McCloy represented the United States and the AAHPER and Felicio M. Torregrosa, of the University of Puerto Rico, the West Indies.

At the Montevideo meeting representatives interested in sports medicine organized their own group. Leaders in the field included Julio A. Mondria, Argentina; Guillerme de Souza Gomez, Luis H. Maluf, and Waldemar Areño, Brazil; Luis Bisquert, Chile; and José Faravelli Musante and Francisco Devincenzi, Uruguay. The main business of the conference was a consideration of the program of physical education in the elementary school and a discussion of the relationship between health and physical education. The next Pan-American Congress of Physical Education was held at Bogotá, Colombia, in 1953.[28]

NOTES

1. Harold L. Ray. "The Life and Professional Contributions of William Gilbert Anderson, M.D." (Dissertation) The Ohio State University, 1959.
2. Elmer D. Mitchell. "The American Physical Education Association." *Journal of Health and Physical Education,* 3:1 (January, 1932), 3–7; 46. William G. Anderson. "The Early History of the American Association for Health, Physical Education and Recreation." *Journal of Health and Physical Education,* 12:1 (January, 1941), 3–4.
3. Paul R. Washke. "The Development of the American Association for Health, Physical Education and Recreation and Its Relationship to

Physical Education in the United States." (Dissertation) New York University, 1943.

4. B. Bennett and Mabel Lee. "A Time of Conferences and Fitness (Part V: 1945 to 1960)." *Journal of Health–Physical Education–Recreation,* 31:4 (April, 1960), 78–85.
5. E. D. Mitchell. "Our Official Publication." *Journal of Health–Physical Education–Recreation,* 31:4 (April, 1960), 74–75.
6. "The Gulick Award, 1947." *Journal of Health and Physical Education,* 17:10 (December, 1946), 594. George J. Fisher and Jay B. Nash. "The Luther Halsey Gulick Award for Distinguished Service in Physical Education." *Journal of Health and Physical Education,* 16:6 (June, 1945), 302–303; 362.
7. R. Tait McKenzie. "The American Academy of Physical Education." *Journal of Health and Physical Education,* 3:6 (June, 1932), 14.
8. J. B. Nash. "The American Academy of Physical Education." *Journal of Health and Physical Education,* 17:1 (January, 1946), 8. Arthur H. Steinhaus. "From the Archives of American Academy of Physical Education." (R. Tait McKenzie Memorial Issue) *Journal of Health and Physical Education,* 15:2 (February, 1944), 64; 89.
9. Charles H. Keene. "The American School Health Association." *Journal of Health and Physical Education,* 17:3 (March, 1946), 147; 186.
10. Peggy Watts. "The American Youth Hostel Organization." *Journal of Health and Physical Education,* 14:6 (June, 1943), 316.
11. Ben W. Miller. "Hosteling–New Roads for Youth." *Journal of Health–Physical Education–Recreation,* 22:1 (January, 1951), 20–21.
12. *Association for Physical and Mental Rehabilitation, Inc.,* 1472 Broadway, New York 36, New York, N. D., pp. 1–6.
13. Walter M. Hall. "The Boys' Clubs of America." *Journal of Health and Physical Education,* 17:6 (June, 1946), 343–344; 387.
14. Doris Willard Plewes. "The Canadian Physical Education Association." *Journal of Health and Physical Education,* 17:5 (May, 1946), 273–274; 313.
15. Glenn W. Howard. "The College Physical Education Association." *Journal of Health and Physical Education,* 17:7 (September, 1946), 410–411; 436.
16. Estelle Gilman. "Delta Psi Kappa." *Journal of Health and Physical Education,* 17:8 (October, 1946), 482.
17. Dorothy S. Ainsworth. "The National Association of Physical Education for College Women." *Journal of Health and Physical Education,* 17:9 (November, 1946), 525–566; 575.

18. Grace M. Palmer. "The Young Women's Christian Association." *Journal of Health and Physical Education,* 18:3 (March, 1947), 150; 194.
19. Benjamin Rabinowitz. *The Young Men's Hebrew Associations (1854–1913).* New York: National Jewish Welfare Board, 1948, pp. 76–87.
20. Robert Morrison. *Health and Physical Education Activities in the Jewish Community Centers.* Jewish Center Division, National Jewish Welfare Board, 145 East Thirty-second Street, New York 16, New York, 1948, pp. 1; 108–109.
21. Edward F. Vermillion and Ellis Mendelsohn. *A Historical Sketch of the National Intramural Association.* Louisville: University of Louisville, 1958.
22. *Intramural Sports for College Men and Women.* American Association for Health, Physical Education and Recreation. 1201 Sixteenth St., N.W., Washington 6, D.C., 1955.
23. Martha A. Gable and Josephine Christaldi. "Phi Delta Pi." *Journal of Health and Physical Education,* 17:10 (December, 1946), 598–599; 638.
24. Wilbur C. De Turk and Fred E. Foertsch. "Phi Epsilon Kappa Fraternity." *Journal of Health and Physical Education,* 18:1 (January 1947), 11–12; 42.
25. M. L. Walters. "The Physical Education Society of the Y.M.C.A.'s of North America." *Journal of Health and Physical Education,* 18:5 (May, 1947), 311–312; 357.
26. George W. Ayars. "The Society of State Directors of Health and Physical Education." *Journal of Health and Physical Education,* 17:2 (February, 1946), 68–69.
27. "The Thirty-eight Years of the F.I.E.P." (Editorial) *Bulletin de la Fédération Internationale D'Éducation Physique,* No. 4, 1961, pp. 3–7.
28. Felicio M. Torregrosa. "The Third Pan-American Physical Education Congress." *The Physical Educator,* 8:1 (March, 1951), 16–17.

INDEX